THE ANATOMY OF MISREMEMBERING

To David

in

friendship & admiration

Cyril

A two-volume series

THE ANATOMY OF MISREMEMBERING

Vol. I. *Hegel*

Vol. II. *Heidegger*

THE ANATOMY OF MISREMEMBERING: VON BALTHASAR'S RESPONSE TO PHILOSOPHICAL MODERNITY VOLUME 1

Hegel

Cyril O'Regan

A Herder & Herder Book

The Crossroad Publishing Company www.crossroadpublishing.com
Printed in 2014

Library of Congress Cataloging-in-Publication Data

O'Regan, Cyril, 1952-
The anatomy of misremebering/Cyril J. O'Regan.
v. cm.
"A Herder & Herder book."
Includes bibliographical references and index.
Contents: v.1. Balthasar and the specter of Hegel.
ISBN 978-0-8245-2562-0 (v. 1)
1. Balthasar, Hans Urs von, 1905–1988. 2. Hegel, Georg Wilhelm Friedrich, 1770–1831. I. Title.
BX4705.B163O74 2013
193—dc23

2012031174

Dedication

Requiem

For Tommy O'Regan (1953-2007)

Early morning repeats itself.
The bridge stiffens in the wet
Wind that fluffs the water near

The weir. Leaden white silvered by the lamps
reluctant to give way to the grey morning
taking what's left of you.

Half-way across he slows to cough up
night on night, and hardly stopping
he rolls his own.

The hills rising mystically from the left
are theatrical, backdrop to the urge
to forget what night conjugates.

He looks for another night,
which records and resists, scuts
And scurries, and scathes of pressed

Wind in the door outside
the airless room, the screen
lighting up like a hallucination.

He will sleep a fitful sleep in the afternoon
through the noise of the street, doors opening,
and closing and the phone's siren sound.

Only two things give unease: the breeze
luffing in his afternoon dreams reminding him of promises
roaming under the Clare hills

and the words of love that tunnel
through the heart' s spectacular silence
towards a morning of fierce light.

Cyril O'Regan

Contents

Acknowledgements

I begin with an expression of thanks to John Norman Jones, who passed away October 2012, interrupting a twenty year relationship, which took the form of a protracted conversation which involved his own reflections on negative theology, scripture, and existence and his reflection on the work of others which decidedly included my own. John, who was not a Catholic, was a lover of all things Catholic, a connoisseur of all things mystical, and a promoter of all forms of theology that had intellectual substance. He understood the sometime partisan nature of theology, and was willing to permit it provided it passed intellectual muster. Needless to say, sometimes partisanship was quite simply, in his view, unredeemable. John did yeoman service at Crossroad, seeing to publication both popular and academic books in Spirituality, Mysticism, Historical and Systematic Theology. Many a prominent academic is in his debt. I think that Gwendolin Herder is in a better position to speak to this aspect of John's contribution than myself, even if I count some of these published authors among my friends. John was especially proud of his initiative regarding younger Catholic theologians. He networked, encouraged them to submit manuscripts, help them to clarify the basic conception of their book, to refine it in the writing stage, and to edit and proof-read. I have nothing like a full list of these younger theologians, all of whom are prominent in their own right, but I can recall the names of Kevin Mongrain, Anthony Sciglitano, Brian Robinette, Warren Smith, Grant Kaplan, Michael Lee, Dominic Doyle, and Michael Foat. Of course, John was the major enthusiast about my own two-volume project on Balthasar's deep conversation and argument with modern philosophical thought. And it was John who encouraged me to persist when the volumes were becoming larger than anticipated and taking longer than I ever envisaged. John did not insist that I publish with Crossroad, but he persisted so long and so consistently with setting me free on that score that it felt like I had no alternative. And in any event where else could I find such an editor, and where else could I find a person with whom I had such a long and truly enriching relationship? John and I were at Yale together, John as Ph. D student in the Department of Religious Studies, I as professor in the same Department. I knew John rather well from courses and exams and, of course, extra-curricular discussions which was the dimension in which John lived. Officially, I was even the director of John's wonderful dissertation on the language of negativity in Pseudo-Dionysius. Truth be told, however, I did the only thing that I could do with John and his projects: I stepped out of the way. The dissertation happened, and I think no one was as surprised as John that he had being mainstreamed in some way. John was not in the least contrary, and rather approved of authority rather than the opposite, and yet this extraordinarily intelligent, perceptive, and ascetic person was totally immune to the logic of utility. John did not pursue an academic career. In a matter of a few years he joined Crossroad. Years of inspired and inspiring leadership followed. The grace and courage he displayed in his dying were remarkable, but entirely fitting given a sense of who John was, or I should say speaking Christianly who John is. John had a habit of troubling hierarchies and an even greater capacity for avoiding reinscribing them to his own advantage. This was true of his relationship to Gwendolin Herder whom he regarded as friend and confidante, and who took John into her home in his final days.

Besides John there are a number of other people to thank. There are first the distinguished scholars who have endorsed this very long book. I want to express my thanks to David Tracy, John Thiel, Peter Casarella, Matthew Levering, Stephen Long, Rodney Howsare, David C. Schindler, Jr., and Graham Ward. Each has been generous in his praise, even as, or especially as, each revealed different and sometimes unexpected aspects of the text. I also want to express my gratitude to my friends for reading drafts of the book over the years. It behooves me to thank all of you for your forbearance with respect to a manuscript that must have tried your patience and took up more time in your intellectual life than was deserved. A special thanks goes to Kevin Mongrain and Tony Sciglitano, two outstanding Balthasar scholars whom I have known since they were undergraduates, and whom I have watched with pleasure grow into the compelling theologians that they are. My dear friend, Larry Cunningham read selected chapters with a particular eye to their readability. If he did not succeed entirely, it is not for want of trying. And, although John Cavadini did not read the chapters in this volume or the next, as chair and as the closest of friends, his unfailing friendship and generous support has been immeasurable. A special word of thanks goes to former graduate students who have read the manuscript with far more care than I wrote it. By this time over half have finished their dissertation and are launched on promising careers. If I forget someone here I will be sure to remember them in the second volume. My thanks to Peter Fritz, who has just written the best book on Rahner in years, to Todd Ohara, whose dissertation on negative theology is matched only by that produced by John Jones, to Todd Walatka who is breaking new ground in Balthasar's political theology, to Jennifer Martin, who is accomplished in all things, not the least of which is understanding the relation between Balthasar and Russian thought, to Andrew Prevot whose work on prayer sets a new standard for theological sophistication and synthesis, to Damon McGraw for all his belief in the project and for taking Newman as seriously as Balthasar, to Chris Hackett for turning a critical but entirely merciful eye not only to the first, but also to the second volume and for being able to see through and beyond both, to the incredibly talented Jay Martin and Patrick Gardner who, not yet at the dissertation stage, show signs of extraordinary intellectual an theological maturity. These immensely talented young theologians encourage one to believe not only that theology is going to be in good hands for years to come, but really in better hands than my generation which might justify the Plotinian adage that they give what they do not have. I owe to the intellectually omnivorous Troy Stefano a particular debt. It was he who in early Fall 2012 helped me bring the manuscript all the way home. He was tireless in cleansing it from gross infelicities, promethean in tracking down recalcitrant references, and his computer savy was not only to be admired, but made me secure with regard to the final product. His was truly a work of supererogation. Having had a manuscript in one's possession for what seems forever, there comes a time to recognize that this is the best you can do and just let it go. I have very much arrived at that point. Someone else perhaps, but not I, can do a better job at articulating the comprehensive, deep, and complex relationship between the theology of Hans Urs von Balthasar and the philosophical and religious thought of Hegel, which I take to be one of the major cruxes of modern theology, and one that theology must pass through to gain the possibility of a future Still, I would be no scholar at all if I did not entertain the prospect that I both can and will do more in the next volume which continues my exploration of the relationship between Balthasar and modern philosophy and in other books to come on the way Christianity is forgotten and misremembered.

This volume has as its companion a volume on the relationship between Balthasar and Heidegger. I intend to dedicate this volume to my dear friend John Norman Jones or simply to John. This first volume, however, is dedicated to my brother Tommy, who also died too soon. Silently included in this dedication is a homage to his wife Aggie, and their children, David, Thomas, Shirley, Deirdre, and Gillian. I have learned from my brother's loved ones that one can praise and mourn a person in the round, who in their faults as well as their irreplaceable gifts, illustrate that love alone is credible.

Abbreviations

Hans Urs von Balthasar

Apok	*Apokalypse der deutschen Seele*
B	*The Theology of Karl Barth*
Exp	*Expositions*
GL	*Glory of the Lord*
LA	*Love Alone is Credible*
MP	*Mysterium Paschale*
P	*Prayer*
SI	*Scandal of the Incarnation*
TD	*Theo-Drama*
TL	*Theo-Logic*

Hegel

Enc	*Encyclopedia of the Philosophical Sciences*
LA	*Lectures on Aesthetics*
LHP	*Lectures on the History of Philosophy*
LPR	*Lectures on the Philosophy of Religion*
PS	*Phenomenology of Spirit*

Other

Adv. Haer.	*Against Heresies – Irenaeus*
AE	*Analogia Entis – Przywara*
BI	*Beauty of the Infinite – David Bentley Hart*
BL	*The Bride and the Lamb – Sergei Bulgakov*
CD	*Church Dogmatics – Karl Barth*
FHS	*Faith in History and Society – Johann Baptist Metz*
GG	*Genesis and God – Thomas Altizer*
HH	*Hope against Hope – Johann Baptist Metz*
ID	*Idol and Distance – Jean-Luc Marion*
IL	*Illuminations – Walter Benjamin*
O	*Origin of German Tragic Drama (Trauerspiel) – Walter Benjamin*
PC	*Presentation and Critique – Franz Anton Staudenmaier*
PChr	*Philosophy of Christianity – Franz Anton Staudenmaier*
PG	*Passion for God – Johann Baptist Metz*
PH	*The Principle of Hope – Ernst Bloch*
Summa /ST	*Summa Theologiae – Thomas Aquinas*
TK	*Trinity and Kingdom – Jürgen Moltmann*

Endorsements

"O'Regan casts a new light on Balthasar's work by interpreting it as an attempt to construct a truly post-modern theology in response to the crisis presented by 'modernity's amnesia.' As O'Regan explains, this project involves not only a recollection of the living Christian tradition, but at the same time a constant resistance to the paradigmatic instances of 'misremembering' found in Hegel and (as he promises to show in the subsequent volume) in Heidegger. While he exhibits a real sympathy with Hegel's own critique of the Enlightenment, O'Regan convincingly demonstrates that Hegel's philosophy is in fact a Gnostic *Doppelgänger* of Christianity, and shows how Balthasar's practice of the specifically Christian *ars memoria* differs not only from Hegel's thought but also from that of many of his important heirs and critics. O'Regan's brilliant study is by far the most in-depth and sophisticated exploration of the complex role that Hegel plays in Balthasar's thought yet to appear."

—D.C. Schindler, author of *Hans Urs von Balthasar and the Dramatic Structure of Truth*

"The Anatomy of Misremembering offers the Church a new kind of genealogy. Focussing on the work of Balthasar's understanding of memory, the tradition and the narrative of mourning he invokes in the twilight of modernity, O'Regan examines here Hegel's complex but triumphalist recollection. With breath-taking ambition, matched with both erudition and a forensic incisiveness, O'Regan gathers together the premodern tradition and the fragments of it that modernity can never shake off, to prescribe a new basis for a genuinely post-modern theology. What is promised in a future volume on Balthasar and Heidegger, and what is already delivered in this book, is nothing short of amazing. The scholarly commitment it demonstrates provides the Church with a new way of proceeding that is as important as it is significant."

—Graham Ward, Regius Professor of Divinity, Oxford

In this projected two-volume study of von Balthasar's theology, Cyril O'Regan advances his reputation as one of our most insightful interpreters of modernity. Here, in the first volume of *Anatomy of*

Misremembering, he constructs a genealogical plot in which the main storyline is Balthasar's defense of Christianity against the assaults of Hegel's revisionist philosophy, particularly in what O'Regan describes as Hegel's intentional efforts to "misremember" Christian tradition according to what proves to be a Gnostic template. O'Regan is a most erudite narrator of Balthsar's project of Christian remembering, guiding the reader persuasively through the voluminous writings of Hegel and von Balthasar. And like von Balthasar, with whom he tacitly takes sides, O'Regan's narrative enlists a host of minor characters – Valentinus, Irenaeus, Augustine, Joachim, Hamann, Bulgakov, Moltmann, Metz, Bloch, and Benjamin – who are lined up on either side of the agon in order to display the nuance and complexity of this battle for authentic tradition. O'Regan's telling of this theological story is nothing less than a tour de force!

—John E. Thiel, Fairfield University

PREFACE:

FORGETTING, REMEMBERING, MISREMEMBERING

The Anatomy of Misremembering

'Modernity' is a word of crisis. This is so in two different but related ways. It is so first in the revealingly vague sense of disquiet felt with respect to an ongoing event in which new modes of thought, feeling, and life are prescribed which bear negatively on more traditional patterns of thought, feeling, and customary modes of life with their particular practices. This disquiet in turn fuels the urgency to conceptually pin down the shift by articulating its governing concepts and symbols, by unearthing its presuppositions, laying bare its hopes, and expostulating on its social, political, and religious ramifications. This sense of seismic shift in culture and society, of the need for analysis and conjugation, as well as the sense of the intrinsic and extrinsic difficulties such analysis involves, is perhaps best captured by G. W. F. Hegel in a text which, among other things, promises to go definitively beyond the Enlightenment as the quintessence of the modern. Struck by the universal sway of the Enlightenment, Hegel, writing in the *Phenomenology,* has recourse to metaphor:

> *. . . the communication of pure insight is comparable to a silent expansion or the diffusions, say, of a perfume in the unresisting atmosphere. It is a penetrating infection which does not make itself noticeable beforehand as something opposed to the indifferent element in which it insinuates itself, and therefore cannot be warded off. (#544)*[1]

The metaphor itself does not resist interpretation. Hegel suggests that the defining aspects of the Enlightenment are its omnipresence and its invisibility. If the Enlightenment is a perfume, it is not the exotic kind one notices: it is the perfume of the mundane, indeed mundanity itself. As it diffuses throughout the whole space, until it is essentially coincident with it, the Enlightenment becomes nothing less than the air that people breath in the modern world. Hegel underscores the importance of the analytic pair of omnipresence and invisibility two paragraphs later, noting as well the Enlightenment's power of 'infiltration' – the latter term capturing well the aggressive nature of the Enlightenment's omnipresence (#546).

The singular importance of this particular reading of the Enlightenment is that the Enlightenment cannot be exclusively defined by its battle against error, although critique, Hegel grants, is the Enlightenment's most conspicuous operation. While the apparent clash of principles with the forces of reaction and superstition might lead the disinterested observer to suppose that the outcome is uncertain, and that there are independent criteria whereby one might adjudicate the dispute, the truth is that the outcome is determined beforehand, since the universality of the Enlightenment guarantees that it is and will always remain in possession of the criteria of adjudication. The secret of the Enlightenment is that even as it provides the language of critique, it effectively immunizes itself from criticism. Although the promise of the Enlightenment may be that of total communication and transparency with respect to argument, nonetheless, it successfully positions all objection as merely partial and interested, subverting the process of submitting all presuppositions and principles to scrutiny by determining from the beginning which questions are valid or not. Anti-Enlightenment counter-proposals are excluded from the arena of argument on the formal grounds of anachronism: belonging essentially to a previous (and now definitively superseded) period, they can have no purchase in another, later, and more developed period. And it adduces this rule without taking intellectual responsibility for its historicism, or raising the question of the prospect of performative contradiction, the possibility that it cannot put its principles into practice without necessarily failing to live up to them. The Enlightenment successfully arrogates to itself all the rights of the *humanum*, for if the light does not shine everywhere, if there are nooks and crannies of shadows and darkness where traditional belief and forms of life are still to be found, these must constitute an underworld populated less by human beings than by gnomes and monsters. The Enlightenment frustrates opposition precisely because its determinacy is indeterminate, and induces sputter, since the only game in which it is willing to participate is one in which it is player, referee, and rules committee.

As the *Phenomenology* discloses, however, it is the business of thought to have a nose for the perfume of the Enlightenment, howsoever subtle its bouquet, and to be able to extract its essence. And, to change the metaphor, it is also the business of thought to make the invisible visible and by so doing raise the issue of adequacy and truth. This is precisely what the Enlightenment does not do, and cannot do: for the moment there is genuine argument, the outcome is uncertain. Moreover, for all its combativeness and abjuration of faith, the Enlightenment itself remains theologically inflected or reflected. It is theologically reflected in a substantive manner in its inalienable commitment to particular beliefs such as autonomy and equality, and the practices that promote them. But the Enlightenment is also operationally or procedurally theological in that the ubiquity of the Enlightenment mimes the ubiquity of the divine, parlayed in Christian views about divine providence and eucharistic theology. As a diffusive or disseminating power the Enlightenment satisfies the Hermetic description of God, found so inspiring by Hegel, which was brought into Christian theology by Nicholas of Cusa: God is the reality whose center is everywhere and circumference nowhere.[2]

A second sense of the word 'crisis' more explicitly reflects on the etymological sense of the term *krisis* which denotes a rupture or decisive break with previous forms of thinking, feeling, and life. This, of course, mirrors the way the exponents of the Enlightenment themselves interpret the nature of modernity, whether one is speaking of the primarily prescriptive sense it has in Bacon or the more nearly descriptive sense it has in *philosophes* such as Diderot and D'Alembert. Modernity is based on the refusal of what has gone before; the quarrel between the 'modern' and the 'ancient,' which marks if it does not quite define transition, is definitively settled in the exclusion, or at least the successful internment, of the old. The latest valorization of the ruptural model is provided by Hans Blumenberg in his monumental *The Legitimacy of the Modern Age*,[3] but Foucault can also be regarded as subscribing to this view, even as he, like Blumenberg, is forced to deal with the evidence of pre-modern discursive survivals.[4] The phenomenon of survival indicates that it is possible to interpret rupture in a less radical way. In this more moderate view, while the break constituted by the Enlightenment is deep and extensive in scope, it does not absolutely erase traditional Christian beliefs, practices, and forms of life. A significant part of the reason for this is that the Enlightenment is more nearly a procedural than substantive rationality. The implication here is that the hegemony of the modern rests not altogether in the fact that its mode of rationality is the most powerful available intellectual and practical regime, but rather in the fact that it behaves as the keeper of the metalinguistic rules with respect to the plural beliefs, assumptions, forms of life, and practices as they circulate through and structure a modern society. These rules are almost never referred to, and if referred to, only obliquely and sparingly so, yet they are the rules of adjusting and adjudicating between rival forms of belief, practices, and forms of life. Although they articulate very different views on historical reality, philosophers as different as Alasdair MacIntyre, Richard Rorty, and Charles Taylor, and theologians as different as Hans Frei, Jeffrey Stout, Michael Buckley, and John Milbank subscribe in effect to the latter more moderate interpretation.[5] Within this latter group, there is a smaller group who ascribe to a secularization view, that is, that important aspects of modernity's counter-tradition discourse operate in terms of the concepts and images of the tradition while disguising it.

Although in some analytic sense the *krisis* constituted by modernity is a catastrophe (*katastrophe*), since it involves a fundamental 'turning' away from one kind of ideological and social universe to another, it is important to point out that turning does not prescribe mourning. As Bacon showed in the sixteenth century, the French *philosophes* showed in the eighteenth century, and as Jürgen Habermas has shown in our own time,[6] celebration of the turning of catastrophe is a real and not simply logical possibility. Moreover, many thinkers critical of the Enlightenment would not welcome a 'roll-back' to the premodern universe of assumption left behind or seriously compromised in the *novum* that is modernity. Such radically different conceptualities as the Nietzschean line in philosophy and the liberal tradition in political thought and policy are of this persuasion. However, as the standard use of the word 'catastrophe' is loaded with negative affect, it is not surprising that accounts of the crisis of modernity often effectively amount to jeremiads concerning the eclipse of the premodern, whether the premodern is focused in philosophy (e.g. Eric Voegelin, Michel Buckley), in religious thought (e.g. Hans Frei, William Placher, John Milbank), or in literature (e.g. T.S. Eliot). Needless to say, the determination of the constitutive features of modernity has not been the same in all cases, and the genealogies of modernity have not cohered with each other. Even allowing for differences in focus, there is wide disagreement with respect to origins, huge variation in the names of the main culprits, and significant differences with respect to modernity's most prominent features.

In this crudely drawn map of reflective response to modernity perceived as a crisis it is not difficult to locate Hans Urs von Balthasar. As a thinker in line with 20th-century Catholic intellectuals such as Romano Guardini and Erich Przywara who are open to culture, Balthasar is persuaded that our innate sense of disturbance is right-headed, and that the discursive rationality of the Enlightenment is not simply one intellectual contender among others, but essentially sets the basic terms for what is thinkable, what constitutes the tissue of our feelings, and what is perceivable as a possible form of life. In this context it is intellectually irresponsible to proceed as if nothing has happened. Such unfortunately is the case, he believes, with Neo-Scholasticism, although the aptitude for 'as if' may in fact betray terrible anxiety with respect to a reality experienced as dominant and overwhelming. Balthasar is also persuaded that modernity represents a crisis in the etymological sense of the term, specifically that a profoundly negative shift has taken place with respect to the currency and authority of more traditional forms of thought and belief, practices, and forms of life. Balthasar, however, does not adopt the strongest possible version of the crisis view, namely that modernity absolutely erases traditional forms of thought, feeling, and life. Such a view does not correspond to the complex facts of the case in which these traditional forms share social and cultural space with other religious and non-religious ways of thinking, feeling, and being in the world. Balthasar prefers then the more moderate position that, in the modern world, the Enlightenment functions hegemonically rather than exclusively. That is, the argument between the Enlightenment and more traditional ways of thought and action continues to be played out.

On a first level the Enlightenment has to contend with the fact, sometimes disconcerting to its advocates, that premodern discourses, practices, and forms of life continue to survive. The hegemony of the Enlightenment is more nearly second level, in that the Enlightenment seems to possess the criteria of adjudication, which effectively displaces the burden of proof onto those who would argue for more traditional forms of life. Balthasar's key issues are the cultural and more specifically Christian costs to this hegemony which, Balthasar takes it, are enormous indeed. Christian beliefs in God, Christ, and the nature of human being are submitted to logical critique aimed at their destruction or attenuation; Christian practices are dissolved into the ways they perpetuate determinate power structures of a particular clerical class, and Christian forms of life are shown to be pathological in that they represent attacks on human integrity, autonomy, and legitimate self-regard. But even more enervating for Christianity is the complacency with which the Enlightenment assumes that certain Christian presuppositions can be taken to be refuted, and that distinctive practices such as prayer, and forms of life centered on worship are not only wrongheaded but truly incomprehensible. If both tactics set Balthasar's teeth on edge, it is not because of anger regarding the loss of home that provides security and consolation, or the frustration that as individuals we are cut adrift, although Balthasar sees no reason why we should not admit to the havoc this wrecks on selves and community. What is more important is that the Christian worldview, practices, and forms of life that are displaced have beauty, drama, and a genuine claim to truth on their side. Because of the dual nature of its attack, the battle against the Enlightenment constitution of modernity has to proceed then on two distinct tracks, the first of argument in the strict sense, the second on the level of rhetoric. In the latter case, the task is not so much to defend the truth of Christian belief, practices, and forms of life as to render them intelligible and meaningful. Of course, how to do this remains an issue for Balthasar, and his solution involves differences between his approach and that of the dominant mode of Christian apologetics and more specifically Catholic apologetics in the twentieth century, which attempted to adduce some non-theological rules of adjudicating Christian truthfulness.

In any event, Balthasar's reflection on modernity certainly issues in a narrative of mourning. His lamentation particularly concerns cultural amnesia and the loss of Christian tradition, defined for him by the history of the memory of the glory of God in Jesus Christ expressed in scripture, in doctrine, expounded in theological treatises, encoded in liturgy, and embodied in the practices of prayer, devotions, and works of charity. This forgetting of God, he believes, is tied to the forgetting of human being. Formally, then, Balthasar subscribes to Foucault's propositions that the death of God implies the death of human being.[7] In making this linkage Balthasar effectively joins hands with the post-liberal theology of George Lindbeck, the movement of radical orthodoxy, and such luminaries of the French Communio group as Jean-Luc Marion and students such as Jean-Yves Lacoste and Jean-Louis Chrétien, while serving as an inspiration to all three postmodern forms of thought. Arguably, in putting the issue of memory at the center, Balthasar comes particularly close to T. S. Eliot and Hans-Georg Gadamer, who if they point to memory as the problem also point to it as the solution. It is, however, a constitutive feature of Balthasar's thought that the eclipse of memory is not entirely due to the power of an alien discourse, practices, and form of life. As Balthasar points out throughout his oeuvre, and most tellingly in his great trilogy, Western culture and Western Christianity must take a significant portion of blame for its own enervation and exhaustion.

As already indicated, for Balthasar, at its most basic level tradition consists of the articulate memories provoked by the glory of God disclosed in the cross and resurrection of Christ. These memories will be various as they reflect the unique perspectives and performances of individuals, communities, and historical periods. Moreover, they will be various as a matter of fundamental theological principle and not simply as a matter of fact. As the phenomenon of phenomena, Christ is exhausted neither by any single perspective, nor their sum.[8] Still, it is the case that the multiplicity and variety of perspectives provide a more adequate response to a reality than individual perspectives however singular. But tradition also has a more reflexive aspect. Tradition is not simply a cornucopia of memories held by the church to be faithful to the primal mystery, but a memory of memories that critically sifts through individual memories for their aptness, their particular qualities, their relation to other perspectives, and their relevance for the moment. Arguably, a significant element of the genius of Balthasar is that he operates on this second level as well as the first. While admitting that such reflection is a function of the church as a whole, and by no means despising the role of the magisterium in the process,[9] Balthasar thinks that reflection is fundamental to the theological enterprise as such. Thus, however significant we judge to be Balthasar's own perspective on Christ and also the triune God, who is the ultimate horizon for divine glory, the participation in which constitutes the destiny of human being, Balthasar does not simply add one more perspective to those already in circulation in the dynamic, open-ended field of the production of memory. In the light of the christological criterion, which is at the same time trinitarian, since it is the Spirit that is the condition of the possibility of seeing Christ, Balthasar articulates the fundamental contours of the field of memory, makes concrete judgments as to the adequacy of particular memories, and shows persuasively how different perspectives, variously adequate or inadequate, group.

This reflexive and intentional grasp of the tradition is illustrated in the patristic retrieval which he shares with other exponents of *nouvelle théologie.* Balthasar makes a significant contribution to our understanding of the tradition in his luminous studies of patristic theologians such as Origen, Irenaeus, Maximus, Pseudo-Dionysius.[10] Yet, clearly Balthasar's sense of tradition is too dynamic, and too expansive to stop here. There are singular theologians in other periods that add indispensable notes to a tradition that is truly symphonic.[11] Anselm and Bonaventure are two medieval theological giants whose perspectives are perennially valuable, as are the perspectives of Ignatius and Pascal, and Barth in the modern period. Yet ultimately it is not simply Balthasar's greater catholicity that distinguishes him from all other theologies of ressourcement vintage. It is rather his deep conviction, sharpened in conversation with his mentor Erich Przywara and in critical dialogue with Karl Barth, that both non-theological Christian discourses as well as artistic and philosophical discourses are an indelible part of the Christian tradition. Literary and dramatic discourses in particular are given an uncommon seal of approval, since the beauty – terrible or otherwise – they intend bears a relation to the glory of Christ that is their transcendent intent.

As a dynamic field of memory, the Christian tradition – as with any tradition of discourse – is constantly threatened by forgetfulness. In a certain sense forgetfulness is coincident with the

Christian tradition itself. There was never a time in Christianity in which we do not find either straightforward forgetting of the mystery of Christ, or memories which themselves are sophisticated modes of forgetting the essential. Modes of thought before the modern age that exemplify this second form of forgetfulness include, for Balthasar, Origenism, Scotism, Nominalism, and *devotio moderna* among others.[12] Balthasar does not deny, however, that the Christian tradition also fails when memory functions as a form of hoarding. Hoarding is the other side of the modern aporia of remembering nothing or remembering everything. Balthasar espies in the 19th century French Romantic reconstructionist Chateaubriand,[13] for example, precisely such a failure, but he understands that the temptation for omnivorous retention is widespread in a period when the value of memory has been contested, and there exist social and individual imperatives to forget, and to forge identities independent of the beliefs, practices, and forms of life of the past. Balthasar sees that the relish for the antiquarian declares more a temperament than a religious disposition, a passion for security at all cost in a world experienced as the breakup of order and a brazen valorization of the new. Chateaubriand illustrates the phenomenon of the Enlightenment's other to which Hegel drew attention in the *Phenomenology*. When the Enlightenment becomes dominant, 'memory alone then preserves the dead form of the Spirit's previous shape as a vanished history . . .' (#546).[14] The Enlightenment infection is such that even as premodern forms remain, they are hollowed out. Even if Christianity casts a critical eye on the new, and inquires whether its newness is shadow or substance, Christianity is not the classicist dream of the contained past and its limited forms. For Christianity never affirms the old as the old, but only the old as the new, the ever new, as Augustine intimated with such unsurpassed eloquence in the *Confessions* (Bk. 10). Whatever Christianity is, it is not then a museum, which is an image by which Romanticism betrays itself as a bad form of Enlightenment. Nor are matters automatically helped if the image of the cathedral replaces that of the museum whose Enlightenment pedigree is, perhaps, too palpable. The image of tradition as a cathedral is profoundly misleading if it is taken to imply that it itself provides the foundation for life and thought, and if it is taken to mean that it is open to either the synoptic or panoptic gaze. This is to fetishize tradition, and mistake the subject-object of veneration. The cathedral is not itself an object of worship; it points to God as the exclusive object of worship, and reflexively points to the triune God as worship's very condition. Moreover, the kinesis of the cathedral and its freedom may get undersold if the focus is on size, proportion, and the repletion of artifacts and *objets d'art.* A counter to this aesthetic deformation, a more adequate grasp of the cathedral as the image of tradition, is to think of the cathedral as defined by multiple heterogenous spaces through which the worshiper moves. This kinesis, which excites freedom, subverts monumentality to reveal precisely the unfixed, the dynamic flow of religious life and the livingness of tradition.

Balthasar, however, remains more preoccupied with amnesia than with the largely reactionary frailty of over-stuffed memory. He senses with Eliot that modernity is bedeviled by a pervasive, deep, and aggressive form of forgetfulness, which not only makes it difficult for human beings to believe in Christian symbols and obey Christian precepts, but alters in a fundamental way the persuasiveness of Christian practices and forms of life, and the imaginative landscape of what is worthy of admiration and emulation. Although the concept of the heroic is relentlessly questioned and hollowed out, it does not cease to be part of the ideational furniture of modernity. One can be labeled a hero for all kinds of reasons, including the sheer accident of one's position in life, or for even highly unheroic behavior where winning against the odds is indistinguishable from winning at all costs. But if the concept of hero continues to have currency – if not necessarily its traditional meaning – Balthasar is acutely aware that the concept of the saint does not. Thus Balthasar's deep interest in hagiography, his view that theology is not simply about the saints but constituted by them, and his affinity to such important 20th century Catholic thinkers as Georges Bernanos and Charles Péguy for whom the thinkability, indeed the representability, of the saint is the crux of modernity.[15] In addition, Balthasar judges that this forgetfulness finds a seal of protection in and through the legitimation procedures of the Enlightenment, which stipulates that part of the price of being modern and rational, and thus truly human, is that one leaves behind the presumption, belief, and custom which constituted one's legacy.

It is not an accident then that the Enlightenment spawns a culture of deracination; for prescribing the move beyond roots is essential to the Enlightenment ethos. On behalf of modernity the Enlightenment presents the license to forget as essentially a matter of being human. The roots to be forgotten are endless and include nation, ethnic group, community, physical place, social and gender roles. The Christian tradition is, of course, an object of such forgetting, indeed historically the prime one, since it represents an obstacle to the Enlightenment ethos in general and the imperative to forget in particular in the memory enacted in liturgy, in its customs and cults which bring the past to bear on the present, and its commitment to particular beliefs and values that appear to have timeless sanction. In a variety of Enlightenment rhetorics and disparate chronicling of deviance, church tradition is blamed for obscurantism, authoritarianism, fanaticism, and its ultimate conclusion, that is, war. Balthasar understands that his task is to outbid modernity's amnesia of the Christian tradition, and to persuade us of the value and validity of Christian memory in and through what constitutes a vast – although non-demonstrative – presentation. This provides an explanation as to why the articulation of Balthasar's position on Christ, Trinity, human being, church, and the eschaton are invariably accompanied by discussion of numerous particular perspectives in the tradition. As he presents what amounts to a singularity, Balthasar cannot avoid being something of a choreographer or orchestrator of the Christian tradition which is a tradition of prayer, performance, and of first and second-order language with regard to the mystery of God in Christ. For access to Christ is given in the field of the plural memories of the glory of God in Christ, which are braided together, since their center is Christ and the triune God their circumference.

This colossal enactment of memory shows us more than what to remember and how; it shows us who we are or who we become in consequence. This is by way of offset to the terrible 'lightness of being' that is the result of forgetting.[16] Moreover, this lightness, which involves the reduction of human being to the three-dimensionalities of calculative rationality, hedonism, or heroic virtue, is, for Balthasar, non-ironically 'unbearable.'[17] While it is understood by most commentators and critics of Balthasar that this is an important plot-line for him, it is at best a story intimated or told merely in part. The full story would outline the substance and scope of memory that is ecclesial both in its interior disposition and in its range of reference. This would take in the entire historical church, would highlight Balthasar's decision to demonstrate the possibility of memory by enacting it, would call attention to the underlying conviction that Christianity can make its case by rendering an account of itself in forms of speech, practice and life that are intrinsically persuasive, because intrinsically beautiful, and would attend to the ultimate ground of its persuasiveness which is the glory of Christ dramatically rendered on the cross. In addition, such a story would involve placing Balthasar in a tradition of Catholic views of tradition, and critically assess the capaciousness and openness of tradition viewed from the perspective of postmodern thought. This is a story that needs to be told. And I intend to tell it, although it will have to be reserved for another occasion.

The story I wish to tell here concerns a more narrow, less visible, yet complementary aspect of Balthasar's dealing with tradition that bears on the possibility of a theology after modernity. It involves not so much the demonstration of memory against the actual 'bleeding out' of memory in the Enlightenment and its principled sanction, so much as a critical response to important post-Enlightenment responses to this exsanguination that emphasize memory as a solution. What I am offering then is what I call an 'anatomy of misremembering,' which presupposes forgetting and the will to resist it. In speaking of individual perceptions and memories, it is difficult in practice to distinguish misremembering from forgetting's failure to present *die Sache selbst*. Nonetheless, the semantic distinction is real. The locutions 'I forget' and 'I misremember' have different ranges. To say 'I forget' is to imply that a would-be recall of reality is put out of action, whereas to say that 'I misremember' is to imply a recall – often a very confident recall – that turns out to miss the mark. Moreover, misremembering has a tendency to be reflexive in a way forgetting is not. That is, misremembering is a response to forgetting which affirms the need and value of remembering as overcoming the disposition of forgetting.

Its failure, therefore, is different in kind than that of forgetting and, accordingly, must be dealt with quite differently. Balthasar's target then is a form of cultural and historical memory that omits critically to assess the truth conditions of its own history of countermemory, and fails properly to distinguish between apparent and real remembering. It is a failure that occurs when a form of thought self-consciously attempts to overcome what it takes to be a history of forgetting. For Balthasar to engage in the kind of resistance to misremembering displayed throughout his entire oeuvre, but especially in his trilogy, misremembering's scope must be expansive and necessarily have the discourse, practices, and forms of life of the Christian tradition as a crucial element of its concern. With respect to the trilogy in particular, I suggest that the complementary to Balthasar's massive articulation of the specifically Christian *ars memoria* is his meeting the challenge of two powerful acts of remembering wrongly, or misremembering, which he associates with the names of Heidegger and Hegel.

We have seen already that on Hegel's own account – with which Balthasar agrees – Enlightenment discourse demands the erasure of the traditionary and the customary, as it requires that faith based on traditions of belief, practice, and forms of life essentially recuse themselves from public life should they have the bad manners to perdure. But Hegel offers more than an illuminating diagnosis of the Enlightenment as constituted by a particularly aggressive form of amnesia, which can elicit consensus from very different intellectual constituencies with very different inclinations regarding the Western intellectual tradition and the Christian tradition in particular. Hegel proposes an alternative form of thought which is a singularly powerful system of 'recollection' (*Erinnerung*) in which much that is dismissed by the Enlightenment is retrieved as worthwhile and is rationally justified. On the formal level Balthasar has no quarrel with Hegel, and prefers him to the Enlightenment. Yet for him there are problems with Hegel's system of memory. Moreover, the problems are multifold. Significant portions of the Western intellectual and cultural traditions are omitted or reduced to schema. Looked at more carefully, Hegel's attitude towards the institutions, practices, and many of the beliefs of historical Christianity seem much closer to the Enlightenment than to Christian interpretation in that massive reinterpretation of Christian beliefs is called for and significant alterations in Christian life and practice is recommended. And there is the question of who precisely is the subject of the memory: God, human being, or some kind of equivocal in-between. All of this makes Hegel, for Balthasar, more an exacerbation than a solution to the problem of forgetting that constitutes modernity.

Heidegger's dissatisfaction with modernity is well documented,[18] and concerns in particular the lack of ethos, and the absence of consensus in evaluating discourse, action, and forms of life. For Heidegger, a structural feature of modernity is amnesia, which eschewing the categories of sociology and cultural history, Heidegger refers to as the 'forgetfulness of Being' (*Seinsvergessenheit*). Modernity is properly characterized by a turn to the subject which issues in the objectification of the world. Correlatively, modernity authorizes only discourses characterized by clarity, simplicity, and by the possibility of receiving determinate answers to the determinate questions posed by the legislating subject. The upshot is the marginalization of the non-univocal discourses of art and also the discourses of religion and even Christianity to the extent to which it does not fall prey to the cognitivist bias that seems to affect all discursive traditions in the West. Importantly, however, while modernity is, for Heidegger, an event, it is not without anticipation in the Western tradition. Indeed, for Heidegger the entire philosophical tradition is amnesiac with respect to *Sein*, *Dasein*, and their relation. In addition, when Heidegger does speak about the tradition of Christian discourse, he thinks of it as representing a history of forgetfulness of its kerygmatic roots,[19] which reinforces as well as being reinforced by the forgetfulness that constitutes philosophy. While Heidegger does point to exceptions, whether the pre-Socratics, Meister Eckhart, or Friedrich Hölderlin, these exceptions in effect prove the rule. In Heidegger's case the reinstallation of memory is paradoxical: memory is an event that has as its content a forgetfulness that goes beyond modernity and is coextensive with the history of occidental thought. Remembering the history of metaphysics is precisely remembering an ordinance of forgetting which takes on different shapes throughout Western history. There is also, as a supplement, a remembering of the very exceptional remembering of what is immemorial. Exceptional remembering constitutes for Heidegger a kind of school of memory to help in the construction of a post-metaphysical discourse that will at once lack the purity of philosophical discourse and be oriented to a future that has not and will never be given. While, undoubtedly, impressed with many aspects of Heidegger's analysis, Balthasar believes that Heideggerian memory is reductive, lacks the discrimination that separates memory in the full and proper sense from its spurious forms, and deprives thought of resources to overcome forgetfulness that leads to the nihilism that characterizes modern life.[20] Like Hegelian 'recollection,' Heidegger's memory then is a powerful form of misremembering that in addition to forgetting must also be overcome. Only thus is thought able to go forward to its real object, which is the memory of the incalculable triune God that cannot be made present, the God who is absolute future. Only thus can memories constitute a community with other memories in history. Only thus are we able to sketch an idea as to what a memory of memories might look like from the point of view of the theologian, who understands precisely that the memory of memories as such is the activity of the Spirit and by implication of the triune God who gives the Spirit as the gift of interpretation.

Resistance to these two powerful forms of misremembering is necessary, since powerful misrememberings look so much like memory proper. Misrememberings of the order of a Heidegger or a Hegel issue in discourses difficult to distinguish from Balthasar's own proposal which, like theirs, both substantively and genealogically, attempts to overcome modernity. It is precisely in his attempt to overcome modernity by means of a constructive theological position that refuses both the method and results of modernity, and his laying bare the foundations of modernity as in significant part self-induced amnesia with respect to the past, that Balthasar gives the appearance of closeness to Heidegger and Hegel. Specifically, Balthasar's theological aesthetics plausibly might be considered as a species of Heidegger's view of the 'lighting of Being' with the correlative of a receptive comportment to the mystery of reality's issuance, just as Balthasar's genealogy of modernity might be regarded as a variant of Heidegger's narrative of mourning in which modernity represents the obscuring of the possibility of manifestation, of what is of plenary value, in short an eclipse of the holy. Similarly, Balthasar's cross-focused dramatic theology, in which the concepts of kenosis and love function so prominently, and his view of the interpenetration of the discourses of art, philosophy, and Christianity might well be considered to repeat Hegel's modulation of Christianity as a religion of revelation (*Offenbarung*), which cannot in principle be surpassed, and also to repeat Hegel's generous view of what discourses count, since, unlike the Enlightenment, for Hegel, art and religion, as well as philosophy, are deemed to be disclosive of the real.

It should be granted then that a reading of Balthasar, which would insist that his thought represents ultimately a constitutive resistance to both of these thinkers is not obvious and cannot be simply read off of Balthasar's texts. It is one of my main burdens then to excavate mainly from the trilogy – but with reference to his entire oeuvre and especially *Apokalypse der deutschen Seele*[21]– this pervasive and structural resistance as the complementary of Balthasar's non-demonstrative defense of the validity of the Christian tradition as a milieu of compelling memory. Leaving it to the body of the two volumes to present the case, it is still necessary to provide some notice as to why these two thinkers loom so large. Without going into detail there seem to be a variety of factors, which operate at very different levels of provocation, that makes dealing with these figures exigent. Let me simply itemize. First, and most superficially, there is the authority of the discourses of these thinkers in European high culture, which is reflected not only in theological and philosophical discourse, but in the discourses of aesthetics, literary criticism, and political theory. Second, these discourses not only offer examples of constructive philosophy which intend to overcome the Enlightenment legacy that wounds culture and deforms human being, they articulate views of the history of philosophical discourse both in detail and with respect to overall orientation that put out of action much of what Balthasar would want in play. Third, precisely as philosophical discourses that are religiously inflected, these discourses question the value of traditional Christian discourses and its associated practices and forms of life. Fourth, the discourses of Heidegger and Hegel cast a jaundiced eye on the history of Christianity's relation to metaphysical discourse, determining in the case of one (Heidegger) that all such relations are bad for Christianity as they are for philosophy and in the other (Hegel) that Christianity has unfortunately subscribed to the wrong metaphysics, just as metaphysics has been too influenced by the 'commonsense' assumptions of religion when it comes to articulate its view of the divine and the divine-world and the divine-human relation. Fifth, these discourses take a critical view of the relation between Christianity and the various discourses of art, especially the linguistic arts of poetry and drama, and determine that the authority and validity of one displaces or replaces the other, art in the case of Heidegger, religion in the case of Hegel. Sixth, although not apparent on first view, both in their diagnostic and constructive sides the discourses of Hegel and Heidegger seem to show apocalyptic inclination.

A brief word about each of these six aspects, starting with the first which more nearly pertains to motive than substance. As a theologian, Balthasar understands himself necessarily to be a theologian of culture, since he is convinced that Christian discourse cannot be extracted fully from its social and cultural setting and escape the gravitational pull of secular discourses, which limit and condition Christian discourse, even as they are reflexively informed and altered by it. This assumption is fundamental, and accounts for a major point of separation between Balthasar and Karl Barth. Balthasar feels obliged on grounds of theological principle to take seriously those discourses, which have cultural cachet, inform artistic and literary criticism, political and social thought, and philosophy and theories of religion in general, and Christianity in particular. Given their highly influential views on the history of discourses, actions, and forms of life in the modern world as well as throughout history, and their views on the relation of Christianity with its ambiguous history and uncertain prospects to these discourse, Heidegger and Hegel, then, need to be engaged, not ignored.

The second aspect of the engagement-separation of Balthasar from Hegel and Heidegger is genealogical. Both Heidegger and Hegel provide master-narratives of the history of philosophy, indeed the history of discourse is an essential feature of their anti-modern enactment of the value of memory. For Balthasar, the authority of these master-narratives is such that they need to be engaged and their spell broken. It is true that these master-narratives are of very different types. On the one hand, Heidegger offers a narrative of mourning predicated on a primal fall of discourse, attended by massive change in practices and forms of life, which reaches its nadir in modernity; on the other, Hegel presents a triumphalistic teleological narrative in which modernity itself represents a kind of self-overcoming of its own inherent deficiencies. Throughout the trilogy Balthasar responds to both schemes as being illusory monoliths. The history of philosophy is neither a history of forgetting (Heidegger) nor recollection pure and simple (Hegel), but rather a history of forgetting and memory, or better a history of memory against a general backdrop of forgetfulness and sharing space with forms of thought that miss the essential and thus can themselves be characterized as species of misremembering. The history of philosophy then represents neither a form of 'sickness unto death' nor a sequence of dialectically related shapes safely housed in the museum of absolute thought. Rather it represents a record of desire, of response to the mystery of reality that is forever challenging, forever encouraging of question, forever discouraging of stock answers and amnesia.

A third aspect of Heidegger's and Hegel's projects of remembering that needs to be engaged is their respective recall of the role of Christianity in the discourse of the West and the genuineness or spuriousness of its sources. As Heidegger and Hegel critique constitutive aspects of the Enlightenment, they nonetheless rehearse numerous Enlightenment criticisms of Christianity. Christianity is alternately accused of being obscurantist and over-rationalistic, of being intellectually complacent while indicating huge anxiety with respect to alternate construals, of contributing to a debilitating form of individualism while insisting on the rights of community, of being committed to otherworldliness while playing the role of a political power-broker. Their respective forms of counter-memory neither issue in reinvesting the Christian tradition with authority, nor making persuasive its discourses, forms of life, and self-understanding. Indeed, precisely the opposite. Yet this is precisely what motivates Balthasar in the trilogy and defines his complex task. Hegel and Heidegger have arrived before him and have made difficult innocence not only with respect to the magnitude of the task, its possible redundancy, but also with respect to the difficulties Christianity faces in getting a hearing as an ingredient in the solution rather than the disease.

A fourth aspect of Hegelian and Heideggerian remembering is the way in which the relation between philosophy and theological thought is viewed. Balthasar concedes that the history of relation is somewhat checkered, but questions whether it is necessary to suppose, as Hegel does, that the relation throughout history has typically been invidious in that either bad forms of philosophy compromised faith or uncritical faith compromised philosophy. His questioning of Heidegger is no less sharp, since Heidegger thinks that a 'Christian philosophy' is nothing less than a 'round square,'[22] with the implication not only that philosophy is better off when open inquiry suffers no interference from faith, but that Christianity is itself when it is untrammeled by thought. At issue is whether this segregation of discourses is the best way, or even a possible way, of reading the relations between discourses. At issue also is whether the segregation of discourses is not an Enlightenment fiction that neither Hegel nor Heidegger have successfully overcome.

The fifth aspect of Heideggerian and Hegelian remembering of concern to Balthasar is their view that the relation between Christian discourse and the discourses of art and philosophy involve contradiction and not simply tension. In the case of Heidegger this understanding takes the form of suggesting that while great poetry and post-metaphysical philosophy – Heidegger's own philosophy is exemplary in this respect – can relate positively, such poetry can no more relate positively to historical forms of Christianity than post-metaphysical philosophy. Although Hegel seems to promote positive relation between discourses by arguing that art, religion, and philosophy all represent articulations of absolute spirit and truth, Balthasar worries about Hegel's claims that Christianity surpasses art and his claim that philosophy overcomes religion in general and Christianity in particular. This double overcoming reneges on the equality promised by giving each of these discourses 'absolute' status, and rules out the conversation that Balthasar feels is necessary for the health of theology.

A sixth, final, and hugely important, aspect of Hegelian and Heideggerian (mis)remembering in Balthasar's judgment concerns the apocalyptic horizon of both species of thought. This judgment, which Balthasar makes as early as *Apokalypse der deutschen Seele*, continues to be at the forefront of his analysis of Hegel in the trilogy. In contrast, it is somewhat more in the background when it comes to Heidegger, yet, nonetheless, remains an important part of his analysis. Throughout the trilogy Balthasar is clear that Hegel's form of apocalyptic bears a close relation to the modes of apocalyptic in the Christian tradition, at least insofar as biblical apocalyptic was assimilated in the theological tradition by figures such as Joachim de Fiore. Balthasar recognizes that Heidegger's form is more nearly Nietzschean than Christian, although he suggests that the Heideggerian modality may also connect with those modes of biblical apocalyptic which, unlike the book of Revelation, are extraordinarily epistemically reserved.[23] Another difference between the Hegelian modality of apocalypse and that of Heidegger bears directly on the intentionality, depth, and comprehensiveness of the engagement with the Christian traditions of discourse, practice, and forms of life. Especially when it comes to the former, Hegelian thought demonstrates a capacity to disfigure and refigure Christian symbols and narrative so as to present a plausible facsimile of the sort offered by historical Gnosticism. This would make Hegelianism a form of Gnostic or Valentinian apocalypse. Although disfiguring and refiguring of Christian symbols and narrative occur within Heideggerian apocalypse, it is less obvious, less systematic, and not as easily labeled simply as theological error. I will determine in the second volume that Heidegger's mode of apocalyptic belongs more to the horizon of Marcion than Valentinus.

Whatever the differences between the genres of apocalypse Balthasar seems persuaded that the commitment to apocalypse is not only an identifying feature of both Hegelian and Heideggerian thought, but in a way constitutes their horizon. This means that in both cases apocalyptic is not simply the remainder that follows on the critical sifting of the tradition of Western philosophy and the discourses, practices, and forms of life of Christianity, and on judgments about relations between Christian discourse and those of art and philosophy. Rather all retrieval and all criticism is made possible by a seeing from 'somewhere' (Heidegger) or from 'nowhere' (Hegel). Even if Balthasar makes clear in the trilogy that formally he prefers Heidegger's finitism, nonetheless, he commends both for understanding that reconstruction and deconstruction of traditions of discourse, action, and life flow from a perspective of 'seeing' of great urgency and authority. Indeed, as we will see in both volumes, Balthasar so fully accepts this point that his theology constitutes itself as an apocalyptic refutation of the different forms of apocalyptic thought of Hegel and Heidegger in which remembering amounts in the end to a misremembering.

As I argue, then, throughout these two volumes resisting misremembering is the complement to Balthasar's symphonic rehearsal of the tradition of discourse, action, and form of life of the 'catholic tradition' and also the way in which they involve conversation with other discourses and negotiations with non-Christian practices and forms of life. Understandably, it has been the latter that has received most attention, since Balthasar has justified and given courage to those who hope that the amnesia of modernity can find redress in and through a memory that can put the Christian tradition to reparative work. He is rightly seen to have proven the possibility of memory by richly exhibiting its discourses, by calling to mind its practices, and by expostulating on its ecstatic forms of life. It is time, however, in studies of Balthasar to attend to the way in which he deals with discourses with whose agenda he shows considerable sympathy and whose terms he often recalls. If there is any naïvité in Balthasar, it is of the second-order rather than first-order kind. Balthasar grasps fully the complexity of the contemporary situation of theology: on the one hand, the evacuative pull of amnesia, on the other, the self-presentation of forms of memory which, while recognizing amnesia, offer ways beyond that imply nothing less than the death of Christianity. Hegel and Heidegger make promises they cannot keep, seeming to make a genuinely postmodern theology possible, but in fact making it impossible.

In prosecuting this case the two volumes of *The Anatomy of Misremembering* come into proximity with David Bentley Hart's *The Beauty of the Infinite*.[24] While the lack of appeal to Balthasar's texts and the extensive encounter with postmodern thinkers such as Levinas, Derrida, and Deleuze among others might suggest that we are dealing with something other than the exercise in a Balthasarian-style theological aesthetics, which is the way Hart styles the book, on closer view Hart's description can be vindicated. Hart's book is divided into two parts, the first genealogical, the second systematic. The systematic part explicitly justifies the label of 'theological aesthetic,' since it features the triune God considered in the mode of the transcendental of beauty. Balthasar clearly provides the theological template for what amounts to nothing less than a paradigm shift in theology. In addition, there is no disguising the memorial character of Hart's rendition of theological aesthetics. While it is true that in terms of retrieval there is also significant substantive overlap between Hart and Balthasar: all the Eastern figures (e.g. Gregory of Nyssa, Maximus, Pseudo-Dionysius) approved of by Hart are approved of by Balthasar also. Even more importantly the substantive agreement specifies the formal agreement: theology is an act of recollection of the memories of the Christian tradition in which the phenomenon of God's self-gift to humanity is what makes possible Christian speech, action and form of life. This correspondence is not in the slightest undermined by the fact that Balthasar puts into play a much wider (West and East, modern and medieval as well as patristic) and more heterogenous band of discourses (literary and hagiographical as well as theological), and is more emphatic in bringing Christian practices and forms of life to mind. Moreover, despite apparent differences in the thinkers who are the object of critical scrutiny, it is evident in *The Beauty and the Infinite* that Hart considers Hegel and Heidegger to be the root of postmodern thought which at best runs interference on Christian discourse and at worse puts into question its very possibility. *The Anatomy of Misremembering* distinguishes itself from Hart's text in being essentially a double reduction: a reduction, on the one hand, to a textually specific Balthasar and, on the other, a reduction to more focused consideration of the capacity of Hegel and Heidegger to subvert as well as influence the theological enterprise. This reduction is, however, by no means a contraction. As Balthasar's take on the work of these two seminal thinkers is granted a measure of independence from the work of their epigones in theology, one gets a clearer idea of what is at stake from a theological point of view. Such a more focused treatment in turn also allows greater nuance in treating later thinkers who, though influenced by them, are not reducible to them.

The distinction between misremembering and forgetting does not mean that Balthasar understands misremembering to be an univocal concept. Indeed, it is best to think of misremembering as more or less analogical. Precisely because of his recollective response to Enlightenment amnesia, Hegel's appropriation of Christian symbol and narrative is highly focused and deliberately comprehensive. Since it quite self-evidently bears upon theological construction, religiously shaped practices and religiously constructed forms of life, Balthasar thinks it has the capacity to constitute a simulacrum of genuine Christianity, and thereby become a candidate for Gnostic ascription. Balthasar concedes that Hegel can and should be appreciated for elevating Christianity not only above other religions, but also above just about all cultural discourses, for putting Christ and the cross at the center of an adequate account of reality and for suggesting that the Trinity should be regarded as an encompassing horizon. But the trilogy shows – with some significant help from *Apokalypse der deutschen Seele* – that Hegel's thought should be submitted to a diagnostic in order to assess the degree of positive correlation between it and the mainline theological tradition. The results Balthasar believes are not Christianly bearable. Hegel revises the entire set of doctrines that articulate salvation history, that is, creation, incarnation, redemption, sanctification, and eschaton, as he also revises the relation between the divine milieu and the milieu of salvation, essentially making the former depend on the latter. Balthasar is as persuaded as Heidegger that Hegel's thought is an exercise in apocalypse, but differs from Heidegger in thinking that Hegelian apocalypse neither sums up the blighted history of metaphysics nor represents a repetition of biblical apocalyptic (either indirectly or directly), but rather represents a mode of 'Valentinian apocalypse' in which not only the biblical narrative, but authoritative Christian practices and forms of life (e.g., the saints) are subverted and replaced. Although Balthasar's position on Hegel rhymes with the position I advanced under my own name in *The Heterodox Hegel*, there is nothing here of a foregone conclusion.[25] Indeed, my own interests are served better by a significant degree of separation on the level both of result and analysis. For better or worse, Balthasar anticipates that Hegel-book, although he is as much if not more interested in the 'effective history' of Hegel in theology than in Hegel the theologian.

Balthasar's take on Heidegger is more complicated, since Heidegger at once both less self-consciously engages Christianity and comes much closer to it in terms of his recommendations concerning practices and forms of life. Throughout the trilogy Balthasar displays considerable ambivalence towards Heidegger. Balthasar accepts significant aspects of Heidegger's critique of the Western discursive traditions and shows himself favorably disposed towards Heidegger's counter-history of exception, acknowledges the fertility of Heidegger's disclosure model of truth that provides an adequate basis for a non-objectivistic form of knowing hospitable to Christianity and conducive to the elaboration of a theological aesthetics. In addition, Balthasar is fairly tolerant of Heidegger's separation of philosophy and theology, since he is convinced that there are some things a philosophy does that cannot be done by theology and vice versa, even if he never concedes that theology and philosophy are two hermetically sealed discourses. At the same time, subjected to closer scrutiny, Heidegger proves as much a competitor as an ally to the construction of a post-Enlightenment and post-modern Christianity. Heidegger's philosophy, on Balthasar's view, is corrosively critical – maybe even nihilistic – when it comes to the Western discursive traditions, is often parasitic on Christian discourse, and advocates practices (prayer and liturgy) and forms of life (worship and festival) that have their foundation broadly in specific Christian traditions that usually go under the banner of Christian mysticism or mystical theology. Heidegger, then, neither remembers scrupulously nor fairly, and tends to offer an alternative to Christian discourse, practice, and forms of life which involve a considerable amount of garbling. Since the garbling of Christian discourse in particular is neither truly focused nor comprehensive, we are not speaking of the construction of a simulacrum in the strict sense, but rather of a liminal religious discourse that appears to be inside and outside Christianity at once. Against the backdrop of his presentation of Heidegger in *Apokalypse der deutschen Seele* it is possible to read Balthasar in the trilogy as resisting a form of apocalyptic, which while very different from the form of apocalypse illustrated by Hegel, even showing some features that correspond to biblical apocalyptic, is finally at odds with the biblical apocalyptic that Balthasar wishes to retrieve and put in circulation.

For Balthasar, both Hegelian and Heideggerian forms of misremembering need to be policed precisely as theology refuses to constitute itself as merely critical and procedural, but pursues the thing itself (*die Sache selbst*) and reminds itself of the community of Christian discourse, its practices of worship, and its ecstatic forms of life both from and to the world. In trying to speak to both, I had two decisions to make: the first concerned order; the second whether it was possible to include Balthasar's treatment of both forms of misremembering between two covers. With respect to the first I went back and forth. I was convinced in turn by the aesthetic merits of moving from Balthasar's resistance to Heidegger's weaker form of misremembering and more epistemically reserved form of apocalypse to what we might call the metaleptic form of Hegel's misremembering of Christianity and his full-to-capacity form of apocalypse,[26] and by the advantage of starting with Balthasar's resistance to Hegel's stronger form of misremembering with its manifestly more immediate theological pertinence. I decided finally that while the latter ordering lacked the novelistic panache of the former, it was superior both from a pedagogic and pragmatic point of view. The issue of one volume or two also proved something of a trial. A one-volume *The Anatomy of Misremembering* was a real possibility. Importantly, however, it had conditions. In the case of Balthasar's resistance to both religious thinkers, it would involve prescinding from exploring the ancestry and history of effects of both Hegelian and Heideggerian discourse, from charting Balthasar's own ancestry of resistance as well as its effective history in postmodern thought, from following Balthasar's diagnostic clues about the apocalyptic complexion of Hegelian and Heideggerian discourses, and finally from describing Balthasar's resistance to misremembering in the apocalyptic mode as itself taking an apocalyptic form. Although again, these four major losses seemed too heavy to bear. With the first, one risked reducing Balthasar by taking out of play both the Balthasarian constant of genealogically linking modern with ancient discourses and much of the pertinence of Balthasar's intervention which is to counter the thought of Hegel's and Heidegger's epigones as well as theirs. With the second, one risked constructing Balthasar as a theological original and fail to give due weight to his understanding of the theological enterprise as necessarily communal. With the third, we also risked failing to acknowledge appropriately what Balthasar sees so clearly, that is, the seductive attractions of Hegelian and Heideggerian forms of misremembering as they are apocalyptically coded. With the last, we ran the risk of wrongly drawing the conclusion that an anatomy of misremembering requires a form of theology that is rigorously anti-apocalyptic rather than a different kind of apocalyptic theology. Thereby we misunderstand both our situation and Balthasar, and put out of play the potentially huge contribution that Balthasar can make both critically and constructively to theology as it groans towards taking full account of its apocalyptic dimensions.

INTRODUCTION

Although it is true that in the strict sense the trilogy neither provides a theory of modernity of the sort illustrated by the work of Hans Blumenberg,[1] or a relatively comprehensive description of the type provided by Charles Taylor and on a different scale by Louis Dupré;[2] and although it is true again that Balthasar refuses to see modernity as completely separate from its premodern origins and thinks of it as being as much constituted by responses to Enlightenment rationality as by it,[3] this is not to say that Balthasar does not provide plenty of evidence of modernity as a problem. Since I will have much more to say both about the complexity of modernity and its dialectical nature in a future volume on Balthasar and memory, I will only be schematic here. While much more than the trilogy is relevant with respect to Balthasar's understanding,[4] in the trilogy perhaps the texts that have illuminating things to say with regard to the phenomenon include *Glory of the Lord 1* and *Glory of the Lord 5*, *Theo-Logic 1*, and perhaps even *Theo-Drama 1*. Just as often indirectly through Heidegger as directly, in the two volumes of *Glory of the Lord* referred to above Balthasar suggests that the central mark of modernity is the eclipse of glory consequent on the turn to the representational subject who objectifies all of reality.[5] This is a point that Balthasar does not fail to make also in *Theo-Logic 1*, which if it succeeds *Glory of the Lord* in the trilogy, in reality precedes the earliest of its volumes by about twenty years, since this volume represents in effect the recycling of *Wahrheit der Welt* (1947). In excess of what these texts have in common, *Theo-Logic 1* also intimates that method and procedural rationality represent a truncation of reason that creates a hostile environment for Christianity and essentially severs the long-standing harmonious relation between philosophy and theology.[6] Balthasar does not understand that he is being novel either in his recommendation, which is totally classical, or even in his diagnosis. With respect to the latter, he would likely give Catholic thinkers like Erich Przywara and Romano Guardini much of the credit.[7] At the same time, he himself anticipates both of these points in *Apokalypse der deutschen Seele*, which represents his most extensive treatment of modernity. This is true even if the focus of *Apokalypse* is not on the Enlightenment, but rather on the various responses – themselves excessive – to the ontological depletion of reality that goes hand in hand with a depletion of the human person who becomes the instrument of his own instruments. On the basis of *Apokalypse*, and also the continuing influence of Heidegger when it comes to constructing modernity in the trilogy,[8] one can say that Idealist and vitalist reactions deepen rather than alleviate the objectification, which is at the same time the subjectification, of reality. Still, modernity is not defined solely by a particular set of stances towards reality, both those illustrated and occasioned by the Enlightenment, which are different in kind from those that prevailed in the premodern period. In Balthasar's view modernity also generates an ethos radically different in terms of expression and supposition from that current in the premodern period. As determined within the horizon of the modern, the relation between the modern and the premodern is largely polemical: no set of premodern practices can be normatively legitimated, just as no premodern forms of life can be judged to be inherently valuable. Brought before the bar of reason – whether interpreted narrowly or broadly – to find their sanction, they are judged to be lacking in warrant, and usually found to illustrate ignorance, superstition, fanatical excess, and for sure a lack of appropriate autonomy. This is why *Theo-Drama 1* can be regarded as contributing significantly to Balthasar's view of modernity in that ethos is its central concern. Balthasar is animated by the question of the possibilities for Christian ethos in a modern world which at best does not support it, and at worst represents the condition of its impossibility.

Balthasar, however, refuses the role of prophet of doom who fulminates against the wasteland. He can approach the position of T. S. Eliot, but is more hopeful, if not necessarily more optimistic. Modernity can only seem to make Christian belief, practice and form of life impossible. On pain of contradicting the belief that the laws of history are not immanent, it is denied to the Christian theologian to assert more than that the individual Christian and the church face extraordinary difficulties in an unpropitious time in which they are assigned the role of being judged rather than being the judge. Nonetheless, there is a way beyond the cul-de-sac of modernity. This necessarily involves a critical retrieval of the discourses, practices, and forms of life of the Christian tradition in all their amplitude and diversity. In various combinations and permutations the tradition holds to a view of reason as correspondence to reality in the mode of listening and attunement, to a view of human being as *imago dei* that finds only a risible correlate in the recommendation of truly 'modern man,' and to an ecstatic discourse that does not pretend to operate exclusively in clear and distinct ideas, but whose vocation is a kind of transparence to the mysterious depth of a triune reality best characterized as infinitely deep and inexhaustible giving. The way forward beyond modernity, whose tendency to pronounce on the historicity of all discourse is only matched by the tendency to deny it in its own case, involves then a going back not simply in order to find an orientation, but also to impress and express the energy that comes only from excess. '*Traditio*' means 'handing on': as such it is a giving of forms of language, life, and practice that strictly speaking are not our possession. Traditions of discourse and practice both envelop and invest us, and by so doing empower us in providing an overall orientation. Such a provision is both less and more than a roadmap: less in that it lacks the roadmap's degree of determinacy; more in that it provides what is truly requisite in that it does not bring us to the illusory place in which we forget the specifics of our situation and the unrepeatability of our questions. Of course, Gadamer has said as much.[9] Balthasar, ever the theologian, even as he endorses the traditioning process in general, is always focused on the horizon of the handing on of the Christian tradition as he takes stock of this tradition in its broadest compass. If the proximate agent of the giving is the church, the ultimate agent, as *The Glory of the Lord* and *Theo-Logic* make clear,[10] is the Spirit, who both enables and shapes our response to the mystery of Christ on the cross. Ultimately, of course, tradition is nothing less than the gift of the triune God, who grants the milieu and forms the medium in which response to the divine is shaped and articulated. This medium shows significant plasticity. Response is both plural and highly differentiated; the tradition is genuinely multivoiced and polyphonic.[11]

In a way, however, not seen since the middle of the nineteenth century Balthasar finds the way forward blocked by the authoritative figure of Hegel. The problem of Hegel is different in kind than the Enlightenment. Hegel is the unmasker of the pretensions of the Enlightenment. As texts such as the *Phenomenology* and *Lectures on the Philosophy of Religion* make particularly clear, Hegel sees through the Enlightenment critique of faith which involves not only an attack on the Christian belief system and style of discourse, but also a fundamental questioning of the value of its practices and forms of life.[12] At the same time the German philosopher is sensitive to the cost the Enlightenment exacts from human being whose autonomy is left without orientation, and whose knowing is contracted into an instrumental reason.[13] Hegel's whole project then is an attempt to move beyond what he regards as a social and discursive, maybe even ontological crisis, to restore order to discourse and historical existence, and to contribute towards a substantive ethos that combines what is best of the classical theory of virtue with a Christianity that provides vision and direction to practice.[14] Far from siding with the Enlightenment's slide toward amnesia, which is confirmed rather than counteracted in the appeal to the encyclopedia of knowledge, since what constitutes knowledge is more or less instrumentally defined, Hegel advocates memory, or in his terms, 'recollection' (*Erinnerung*). 'Recollection' is the cover term for a summing up of all the partial perspectives on reality, expressed in discourses that intend the truth,[15] and especially the discourses of art, religion, and philosophy that have the capacity to disclose it.

The problem for Balthasar, as it was for Hegel's 19th-century critics, is that memory is not only totally comprehensive, but also systematic: there are no logical or discursive gaps in the explication of reality, discourse, and their relation that do not submit to the mediating power of dialectic. While apparently offering an alternative and a solution to the endemic amnesia that singularly defines modernity, Balthasar raises questions as to whether Hegel's thought can be construed as memory in the full and proper sense. For while Hegel's thought formally satisfies the definition of being *memoria dei*,[16] there are problems concerning the nature and limits of memory, which centrally involve a profound confusion of the objective with the subjective genitive. Interpreted as a subjective genitive, the memory of God in Hegel's thought, especially insofar as it is conceived as a system, points to the overcoming of specifically Christian memory which, intending a reality with respect to which it is systemically inadequate, is indelibly inscribed in the economy of gift. Put most generally, Balthasar's concern is whether

Hegelian thought does not constitute a deeper danger than the Enlightenment, since it more surreptitiously liquefies and ultimately liquidates Christianity,[17] while seeming to enact a kind of memory that is difficult to distinguish from the memory that constitutes Christianity. At issue, then, is how we can diagnose and expose a colossal act of misremembering that puts us out of touch with the intellectual, moral and practical gifts of the tradition, and the gift of creation, redemption, and sanctification, which renders the triune reality of God, on which they depend. Although Balthasar's suspicions concerning Hegel are encouraged if not prompted by Barth's reservations,[18] it is quite clear that Balthasar's anxiety index is distinctly higher than Barth's. For Barth, it is the liberal Protestant tradition that must be resisted at all costs, and it is Schleiermacher who must be exposed as the Christian simulacrum. Balthasar inverts Barth's order of fear. As *The Glory of the Lord* makes clear, Balthasar does think of Schleiermacher as giving religious authority to the subjective turn in theology and putting it on the wrong path (*GL1*, 49-50). But it is unclear whether he would consider Schleiermacher, and the Pietist turn in general, more than a post-Enlightenment form of forgetfulness. Even in an explicitly theological text with systematic ambitions such as the *Glaubenslehre*, which creates the opportunity not only for a massive alternation of the Christian narrative, but also for disguising this fact, Schleiermacher does not enact the kind of powerful 'doubling' of the Christian narrative perpetrated in Hegel's almost contemporary *Lectures on the Philosophy of Religion*, which self-consciously represents a choice against a Schleiermachian method that marginalizes the notion of the Trinity and segregates theology from philosophy.[19] For Balthasar, it is this kind of doubling that brings the difficult to the brink of the impossible: in such an environment in the very exposé of forgetfulness, forgetfulness is deepened by the false memory that announces itself to have named and overcome it. This mutation of forgetting, which at the same time immunizes itself against the charge of forgetting by appearing to be memory, is what must be diagnosed and defeated. This makes struggle with Hegel a requirement for any viable post-modern theology, and makes Balthasar the precursor of David Bentley Hart who has influentially forwarded this thesis. Relatedly, it makes the diagnosis and defeat of Hegelian misremembering more exigent than the diagnosis and defeat of Heidegger's act of misremembering, without in any way suggesting that the latter is inessential. If Jean-Luc Marion and radical orthodoxy find a theological precursor in Balthasar's agapic surpassing of Heidegger,[20] arguably, it is only belatedly that they have come to appreciate that the critical encounter with Hegel is at least as important, precisely because Hegel's thought mirrors much more finely Christian theological discourse, and more nearly creates the illusion that at its center is the 'unforgettable' which resists being remembered adequately.[21]

More specifically, Balthasar finds the way obscured by the giant shadow Hegel casts on specifically contemporary theological reflection. Hegel's understanding of the historicity of the disclosure of truth and his view of the self-revealing God have been assimilated in significant part in contemporary theological thought. The theological appropriation of Hegel then stands in contrast to the theological appropriation of the religiously inflected thought of Heidegger. While such appropriation has been equally episodic in both cases, in the case of Heidegger it has been at once more horizonal and local, affecting mainly – although not exclusively – theological foundations. This has been so whether the Heidegger who is appropriated is more nearly identified with the phenomenological saving of appearances effected through the analysis of *Dasein*, the Holy as the site in which human being finds its true measure, language as the event of disclosure of Being, or the historical nature of interpretation and its determining force. By contrast, contemporary theological appropriation of Hegel has been more direct, more substantive, and more comprehensive. For the same reason it has also been more challenging. Hegel's rendering of a self-revealing divine, which adopts and corrects the cross-focused trinitarian God of Christianity by insisting on development and suffering and by abjuring any trace of mystery, has been felt strongly in contemporary theology in general, and acutely in contemporary German theology. Here two giant figures of Protestant theology stand out: Moltmann and Jüngel.[22] But the challenge presented by Hegel to the catholic view of tradition advocated by Balthasar, which eschews unilinear development, and which calls for dialogue between the discourses of art, philosophy, and religion at all times, is equally important. How a religious thinker construes the process of tradition, and evaluates and relates its sources and resources, is bound to have an effect on how that religious thinker understands revelation, the God of revelation, and the other than God that revelation intends. In addition, Hegel's evolutionist account of art, religion, and philosophy in which ultimate authority is denied to art and religion compromises the irrevocable validity that Hegel consistently asserts of these discourses. Openly admitting that the authority of art belongs to the past, effectively Hegel also consigns Christian discourse, forms of life, and practices to the 'museum' of the irrevocable past,[23] and thus ultimately to the mausoleum that inters the dead and keeps us safe from them. Balthasar would likely have found the designation of 'necrophilia,' brought into currency by the movement of radical orthodoxy, rhetorically excessive,[24] still with respect to Hegel it would have a peculiar aptness. For an economy which allows past voices merely to echo in the 'present' voice of philosophy is an economy of the dead rather than the living, since for Balthasar livingness in biblical witness is defined by memory and hope in the tensile conversation of a tradition. Resistance to Hegel finds its dramatic pattern and figure in the paschal mystery and Christ's descent to the dead – the giving of life, the giving of presence that is a future. Since on Balthasar's interpretation, the giving of life is the giving of voice coincident with the giving of sight, the harrowing of Hades on Holy Saturday is among other things a releasing of the voices and visionings of tradition.[25]

Given the duration of Balthasar's engagement with Hegel, which begins with *Apokalypse der deutschen Seele* in the late thirties and closes with the last two volumes of *Theologik*, written in the late eighties,[26] it is necessary to restrict the textual focus. As intimated already, I will rely largely on the trilogy. Reference to the *Apokalypse* will be inescapable. Numerous other texts of Balthasar, historical and topical, literary and devotional, will be referred to when appropriate, and sometimes will come in for explicit discussion. Concentrating on the trilogy helps us to see how resistance to Hegel on both the formal and material fronts is constitutive of Balthasar's magnum opus and helps to make sense of elements in the text that otherwise would go unexplained.

It is important, however, at the outset to appreciate that all resistance to Hegel is a function of Balthasar's respect for, even affinity with, Hegel. The affinity is contextual, substantive, and formal. It is contextual in the sense that both Balthasar and Hegel represent responses to the imperialism of the discursive rationality of the Enlightenment, and lay bare its epistemic, anthropological, religious, and social costs. More, as I have already indicated, Balthasar and Hegel represent critical responses both to the Enlightenment's performance and principled defense of cultural and religious amnesia. The affinity is theologically substantive in that Balthasar valorizes Hegel's dramatically colored view of the divine, his Johannine rendering of Christ as defined by the glory of the cross, and his determination that the Trinity is the encompassing as well as synoptic symbol of Christianity. The affinity is formal in that Balthasar affirms Hegel's understanding of the disclosive power of artistic, philosophical and religious discourse and his triangulation of these discourses, and thinks that any relevant theology will have to work within a horizon of understanding that acknowledges the necessity of the intermediation of Christian and theological discourses with other kinds of discourse.

Still, affinity notwithstanding, the impress of the great trilogy on all three fronts is finally vehement and systematic resistance. The main task of this book is to outline the substantive and formal disagreements between Balthasar and Hegel. I address the contextual differences between Balthasar and Hegel largely as a function of the differences on the substantive theological and formal levels. On the substantive theological axis, I elucidate Balthasar's structural resistance to Hegel's theological-philosophical commitments which fundamentally revise the grammar of Christian belief, and relatedly the practices and forms of life that deserve 'Christian' and philosophical sanction. On the more formal front I treat in some detail Balthasar's taking issue with Hegel's univocal developmental view of the tradition of artistic, religious, and philosophical discourses which achieve their realization in Hegelian philosophy as an articulation of the self-mediating structure of concepts. Needless to say, Balthasar's substantive theological resistance has priority and this asymmetry will be reflected by the fact that Part 2, which carries the main burden of the substantive considerations – but definitely not all – is of considerably greater bulk than my sketch of the agreements and disagreements between Balthasar and Hegel of a more formal kind.

I open in Part 1 with Balthasar's opposition to Hegel's construction of the Western discursive tradition or traditions. The rationale for beginning here, rather than with the more important substantive contretemps between these two encyclopedic religious thinkers, is, on the one hand, to highlight an aspect of the rapprochement and struggle between Balthasar and Hegel that might go unnoticed and, on the other, to suggest that the more formal struggle represents a rehearsal of the more crucial substantive struggle, as well as provides a frame of reference for the theologically unacceptable results produced in and by Hegel's system. Balthasar's critique of Hegel's trope of the 'death of art' provides nothing less than the *raison d'être* of the rehearsal of the relation between Christianity and drama throughout Western history, and serves as the reply to Hegel's view of the factual and principled separation of discourses of art, philosophy, and Christianity. While on the surface the casualty of Hegel's developmental scheme is art in general and drama in particular, the real victim, on Balthasar's view, is Christianity which, sundered from art, is not able to find sufficient resources to prevent the illusion of the resolution of history and the elevation of the finite subject to the divine point of view. Perhaps even more importantly, Part 1 considers not only how Balthasar questions Hegel's reading of the history of the so-called 'absolute' discourses of art, religion, and philosophy, as well as their relation, but also how Balthasar goes on the genealogical offensive. More specifically Part 1 outlines Balthasar's tactical counter-strikes in which Hegel's discourse is plotted as a development of lines of discourse whose relation to mainline Christianity is questionable to say the least. While these lines are multiple and include apocalyptic, various forms of Neoplatonism, and Gnosticism, I argue that Balthasar hints that the Gnostic line may be privileged. Acknowledging that Balthasar himself does not as such offer a genealogical theory that would account for apocalyptic and Neoplatonic as well as Gnostic strands in complex modern discourses, nor explain how these discourses both modulate and are modulated by post-Enlightenment modernity, I sketch what a more theoretically inflected Balthasarian Gnostic counter-genealogy would look like. Here I self-consciously supplement Balthasar.

Part 2 contains two substantial chapters that treat Balthasar's exposé of the epistemological, narrative, christological, and trinitarian deviations of Hegel's speculation from the common Christian tradition. The first of these chapters (chapter 2) deals with the first two of these interrelated deficiencies. It argues that Balthasar resists as illicit Hegel's pretensions to absolute knowledge, but does not do so in the name of those kinds of 'negative theology' that Hegel finds easy to dismiss as incompatible with Christianity as 'Revealed Religion.'[27] Rather what gives Balthasar critical leverage on Hegel's claim to a fully comprehensive and adequate account of divine being is also what prevents apophatic free-fall, that is, divine glory revealed in Christ as constituted by the absolutely excessive and ecstatic triune God. This triune God, Balthasar maintains, can never become an object of knowledge, even eschatologically. In many ways the second theme of the chapter is the pivot of Balthasar's argument against Hegel, since not only does Hegel's presentation of the Christian narrative fund absolute knowing by providing its essential content, but it also intrinsically affects Hegel's understanding of every theological topic from creation to eschaton, and even the immanent Trinity itself. More so even than on the formal level, Balthasar turns the tables on Hegel by availing of Hegel's own categories to hoist him on the petard. Aware that Hegel's *Aesthetics* privileges 'drama' above all forms of art, whether linguistic or not,[28] Balthasar argues that the sublation (*Aufhebung*) of the Christian narrative in Hegelian speculation ironically involves a generic regression. In Hegel's case the regression effectively validates a mythological kind of epic in which the triune divine is involved in a movement of self-development and self-actualization, one of the central conditions of which is suffering. I attend to four of the main features of this mythological program to which Balthasar non-systematically refers throughout the trilogy, mainly in *Theo-Drama*, but from time to time also in *Glory of the Lord* or *Theo-Logic*. These are, in order, monism, eros, a particular view of kenosis, and necessitarianism.

The second of the two chapters of Part 2 (chapter 3) focuses on Balthasar's objections to Hegel's distortions of what might be called the christological core and the trinitarian circumference of the Christian narrative. On both fronts, Hegel gives rise to great expectations that in the end, Balthasar judges, are disappointed. Hegel's rendering of the Christian narrative seems more christologically based than most post-Enlightenment theologies, and appears faithfully to represent the Johannine view of the glory of the cross to which creation, and resurrection, as well as the eschaton refer. Under scrutiny, however, Hegel's Christology disappoints: the unique singularity of Christ is less important than Christ as illustrative of a general principle of reality; the folding of resurrection into cross suggests resurrection's eclipse rather than it being a feature of a christological paradox; and finally the cross itself is reduced to its capacity for its meaning being made transparent to human beings, and appropriated by them, especially human beings in *Endzeit*. Arguably, even more important are the trinitarian distortions, for Hegel's trinitarianism both comprehends and represents a synopsis of the epical narration of the divine in and through which the divine develops and actualizes itself. Even with the hermeneutic of charity working at full tilt, it is evident that the level of distortion of traditional views on the Trinity is such that Hegel has to be seen to be romancing the tradition instead of taking it seriously. Crucially, on Balthasar's account, Hegel abolishes the immanent Trinity-economic Trinity distinction by making the immanent Trinity a function of the economy, and eternity a function of temporality. The confounding of the immanent and economic dimensions of the Trinity is, according to Balthasar, in turn part cause and in part symptom of a fully comprehensive theodicy that cannot brook the inexplicable, and in which the history of suffering is instrumental in the constitution of the divine. The excision of the inexplicable is also in place when Hegel not only avows divine passibility, but demonstrates its necessity. At the very least all talk of 'suffering' with respect to God is analogical for Balthasar, and the form that the attribution takes has to avoid the language of necessity.

Parts 1 and 2 provide, however, only the broad lines of Balthasarian resistance to Hegel. Part 3 fleshes out Balthasar's resistance along both the genealogical and substantive fronts by focusing on paternity and filiation as this concerns both Hegel and Balthasar. It now asks explicitly, who are Hegel's sons?, just as implicitly in Parts 1 and 2 it has been asking with Balthasar who are his true 'theological' fathers? Contrariwise, it now asks explicitly, who are Balthasar's fathers, just as it asked implicitly in Parts 1 and 2 who Balthasar's contemporary 'theological' sons were when it came to resisting Hegel's peculiarly grained trinitarian metanarrative that represents a doubling of the Christian narrative. Needless to say, some clarification is in order with respect to the choice of the language of 'filiation' and 'paternity.' There seem to be two invidious choices here: either Balthasar ignores female voices in the tradition, or I am ignoring the fact that he deploys them. I want to suggest that neither is the case. First, Balthasar is more rather than less inclusive of female voices in the tradition than most major 20th-century Catholic theologians. This is so even if a theologian were to object to the kinds of female voices that are prioritized, for example, Catherine of Siena, Catherine of Genoa, Julian of Norwich, Thérèse of Lisieux, and, of course, Adrienne von Speyr.[29] The point is that there is no exclusion of female voices in principle. Second, and even more importantly, attention should be paid to the two different tasks undertaken by Balthasar throughout his career, which are compacted in, yet also clearly illustrated by, the trilogy. As indicated in the Preface, these tasks are those of remembering, on the one hand, and providing an anatomy of misremembering, on the other. In the first case, the provocation is modernity's amnesia with respect to the gift of Christianity, and Balthasar's response is to be the choreographer of memory who puts into play as many Christian voices as possible, which if they are together symphonic, nonetheless individually strike very different notes.[30] With respect to the task of memory, which is also the task of the memory of memory, female perspectives have an important role to play. And it bears reminding that no matter how important an anatomy of misremembering is, it plays second fiddle to the choreography of memory of the Christian tradition in all of its aspects, its practices and forms of life, as well as its symbols, narratives, and doctrines. The simple fact is that Balthasar calls on a much more restricted set of thinkers when it comes to dealing with the anatomy of misremembering. With the possible exception of Adrienne von Speyr, none of his female representatives play a major role. But the same is true of many of male voices in the tradition; they too are not put into play in the anatomy of misremembering, whether the target is Hegel or Heidegger.

More specifically, in chapter 4 I raise the issue of the proximate and ultimate traditions of Balthasar's resistance to speculative Idealist discourse. I adduce the 19th-century Catholic Tübingen theologian, Franz von Staudenmaier (1800-56), as providing the proximate model of resistance to Hegel, while I suggest that Irenaeus is Balthasar's ultimate model to the degree to which Hegelian thought can plausibly be viewed as the return of Gnosticism in a post-Enlightenment situation and under post-Enlightenment conditions. Repeating Irenaeus is as central to diagnosing and refuting Hegelian misremembering, as repeating Augustine is central to the diagnosing and refuting of Heidegger's quite different form.[31] In addition, I discuss the credentials for paternity of Sergei Bulgakov (1871-1944) and Johann George Hamann (1730-1788) and enter a complex verdict in both cases. On the one hand, it can be shown that substantively Balthasar borrows much more from Bulgakov than from Staudenmaier. On the other, even if Bulgakov's speculative theology can be proven to be anti-Hegelian – which is something that Balthasar is anxious to demonstrate – it lacks the vehemence of Staudenmaier and his conviction that in Hegel's thought one witnesses the return of ancient forms of discourse (e.g. Neoplatonism, Gnosticism, apocalyptic) that refuse to die. Although confessedly Franz von Staudenmaier is not a household name in theology, and while it might seem somewhat recherche to give him the kind of attention I give him, I think it is important not only to point to the patristic and medieval periods as providing the main lines of influence on Balthasar's thought, but also to the specific influence of 19th-century thought, specifically 19th-century Catholic thought. I submit that when it comes to the art of memory, Johann Möhler, the founder of the Tübingen School,[32] and Matthias Scheeben,[33] are the two crucial figures; but when it comes to refutation of German Idealism, it is the much less creative Staudenmaier who is central. The other figure whom I regard as playing a vital – if not constitutive – role in diagnosing Hegelian misremembering is Hamann. Although unlike Staudenmaier and Bulgakov, Hamann comes before rather than after Hegel, and is an object of Hegel's own critical evaluation. The fact that Hamann's thought can be used to expose Christian lacks in Hegel should not be taken to imply that Hamann plays no role in remembering fundamental aspects of the Christian tradition fatefully lost in Enlightenment conjurations of Christianity which failed to think the one thing necessary, that is, Christianity is first and foremost a matter of vision that envelops as well as inspires all understanding; neutered the biblical text; marginalized doctrine; and made faith either a matter of belief that would have to come before the bar of rational justification or a matter of blind trust. It is no accident that Balthasar thinks of Hamann and Hegel in the form of an antithesis: it is not simply that Hegel fails to carry through on Hamann's promise of a visionary, even apocalyptic form of Christianity that defeats Enlightenment amnesia, but he represents a different kind of alternative to forgetting – a speculative alternative which, Balthasar shows, Hamann abjures in the way that Irenaeus abjures what he takes to be the Gnostic simulacrum of Christianity.

Chapter 5 considers Balthasar's general worries about the dissemination of Hegelian thought in contemporary theology in general, and in Moltmann in particular, which disable the discourses of the mainline theological traditions, while providing the opportunity for the return of both Joachimite apocalyptic and forms of speculative thought that resemble the Gnostic forms of thought critiqued by Irenaeus. This is not to suggest that there is no measure of orthodox reserve in Moltmann, but simply that the Hegelianism he would overcome is not successfully transcended, and in consequence the Joachimite and Valentinian ghosts that haunt Hegel's speculative discourse also haunt Moltmann's edifying trinitarian proposal. Focusing on Hegelian paternity in contemporary theology represents a reversal of the order of emphasis in chapter 4, where we focused on the lines of paternity active in Balthasar's *Auseinandersetzung* with Hegel. The shift of focus to Hegel's influencing rather than being influenced, which was the subject of Parts 1 and 2, underscores that the interpreter of Balthasar is obliged to answer the question: what pertinence does Balthasar's anatomy of Hegel's misremembering have for contemporary theology?

I consider Part 3 then to complement rather than repeat Parts 1 and 2. A surprising facet of Balthasar's combating of Hegel to which we draw attention in an *ad hoc* way in Parts 2 and 3 is that

Balthasar frames the rebuttal in terms of a contrast between inauthentic and authentic forms of apocalyptic. This is not a totally unsurprising result for a theologian whom, on the basis of *Apokalypse* and his repeated criticisms of various forms of apocalyptic throughout the trilogy, the interpreter might have concluded was constitutively anti-apocalyptic. Part 4 concerns itself with the paradox of Balthasar's construction of himself as essentially an apocalyptic theologian insofar as this construction bears significantly on the enterprise of providing an anatomy of misremembering in general, and an anatomy of Hegelian misremembering in particular. Crucial to any apocalyptic interpretation of Balthasar's own work is the producing of the evidence on its behalf. I argue in chapter 6 that Balthasar's rebuttal of Hegel's particular form of *apokalypsis* eventually assumes, especially in *Theo-Drama*, the shape of an apocalyptic form of theology which features the vision of the Lamb at the center of reality, as well as the parenthesis within which history happens. The vision of the Lamb is precisely the opposite of a victorious Christ who routes the enemy and avenges his persecuted; the Lamb is the symbol of the self-offer of God who in love takes on sin and goes all the way down to death to save human beings. And this vision is just the opposite of spectacle: in Revelation, as much as the Gospel of John, the Lamb calls forth a response in human beings to pattern their existence on the self-giving illustrated by the Lamb in all their actions, practices, and forms of life. In Balthasar's articulation of a paschal theology, the Trinity provides the ultimate horizon, the ultimate 'stage,' for all human action, and is the subject as well as object of worship. Indeed, I argue that Balthasar suggests more than that the triune God, and especially the Spirit, is the enabler as well as referent of worship, but that one can think of the self-surrender of the divine persons towards each other in the immanent Trinity as a form of doxology. In taking this radical stand, Balthasar wishes to cut off entirely all escape clauses in Hegel's articulation of the economic and immanent Trinity and their relation. Another fundamental element of Balthasar's specifically apocalyptic resistance to Hegelian apocalyptic, which illustrates elements of Joachimite apocalyptic and Valentinian apocalypse – although we hope to have shown already not in equal parts – is Balthasar's elevation of the agon between

Christ and the Anti-Christ. Balthasar is here not engaging in a jejune mythologization, but under the influence of modern thinkers such as Soloviev and Claudel, but perhaps ultimately Irenaeus, he thinks that a crucial element of the 'Anti-Christ' figure is dissimulation, which compels vigilance with respect to the glory of Christ and what this glory sanctions, and invites discrimination between the Johannine Lamb and the simulacrum that has been in play throughout the ages, and is found to be present in the authoritative discourse of Hegel's speculative philosophy.

If chapter 6 is largely descriptive and outlines the kind of Christian apocalyptic that can function as a redress to Hegelian apocalypse, chapters 7 and 8 are both more comparative and evaluative. Balthasar is put in conversation with other 20th-century religious thinkers, Catholic and non-Catholic, who enact an apocalyptic refutation of Hegelianism. For the purposes of this volume, the main figures are Johann Baptist Metz, who is Balthasar's main contemporary rival as the apocalyptic theologian in Catholic thought,[34] and two figures who serve as presuppositions of Metz's apocalyptic, and of much of contemporary apocalyptic discourse, that is, Ernst Bloch and Walter Benjamin.

In chapter 7 I focus on the main lineaments of Metz's apocalyptic proposal, while getting at its basic presuppositions and motives, on the one hand, and unearthing its apocalyptic precursors, on the other. Nothing of the analysis is free-standing; it takes place in an environment of comparison in which Metz evinces a complex view on Balthasar as a theologian of significant opportunity who like him offers a formally similar answer both to the Enlightenment and its overcoming in speculative philosophy. And Metz suggests a number of substantive agreements also, most conspicuously a commitment to the paschal mystery, and even a version of Holy Saturday. Yet Metz worries whether Balthasar's trinitarian commitments, as well as his continuing Johannine bias, prevent him from being the kind of theologian required for the modern age, if theology is to overcome its collusion with all in the modern age that conspires to ignore the victims of history, who are almost always invisible. The encounter – albeit one way – is the condition of an extrapolation of a conversation in which the issue is not the contrast between an apocalyptic (Metz) and a non-apocalyptic theology

(Balthasar), but between two styles of apocalyptic theology, one relatively minimalist in terms of epistemic claim (Metz), the other relatively maximalist (Balthasar), the one scrupulously avoiding the book of Revelation (Metz), the other according it foundational status (Balthasar). The actual encounter is a condition also of the meaningfulness of looking at the differences between Balthasar and Metz both in terms of motives and of precursors in the apocalyptic tradition. While both challenge the forgetting of the Enlightenment and the misremembering of speculative thought, the content of 'forgetting' is parsed differently by each, and the anatomy of misremembering is variously dominant or recessive. Worthy of sustained attention is the very different calibration of apocalyptic in both Catholic theologians, who inhabit very different traditions of apocalyptic discourse: the one (Balthasar) harkens back through Bulgakov, Staudenmaier, Hamann, and ultimately Irenaeus to a theological appropriation of Revelation, the other (Metz) has before him the 20th-century examples of Benjamin and Bloch, and comfortably accepts Bloch's historiography in which Joachim is a central figure.

Chapter 8 discovers as well as constructs an engagement of Balthasar and Walter Benjamin. There are very different warrants – one might even say kinds of warrants – for engaging these thinkers. The two most obvious warrants are first, prevailing assumptions notwithstanding, that Balthasar is a *bone fide* apocalyptic theologian and, second, that the apocalyptic thought of Benjamin, which continues to enjoy considerable currency in contemporary philosophical thought, is religiously inflected. Whereas the two most pertinent warrants, however, are first that Benjamin's apocalyptic is at the core of Metz's apocalyptic stance, and second that Balthasar engages both directly and indirectly Benjamin's apocalyptic thought, understanding it to be an answer to Hegelian style apocalypse, yet an answer that a Catholic theologian cannot fully embrace. Given that chapter 7 established the former, the main burden of chapter 8 is to establish the *bone fides* of Balthasar's engagement with Benjamin, while presenting the agon between two very different kinds of apocalyptic, one maximally visionary or eidetic, the one either non-eidetic or moving towards it. As indicated, neither this chapter, nor the one that precedes it, is purely descriptive. The crucial issue is what level of content is required in order for apocalyptic to hold on to the name of apocalyptic. Obviously, Metz makes very different choices than Balthasar both with respect to biblical texts and the level of vision, and presents a mode of apocalyptic which, while it does have a measure of content – specifically the narrative content of the passion, death, and resurrection of Christ – also shows significant signs of heading in Benjamin's direction, where content is almost entirely eclipsed, and where one is dealing not with a content that reformats history, but with the interruption of the rule of history and the laws of its discourses.

Balthasar's disagreements with Metz bear on his disagreements with Benjamin and vice versa. Elements of disagreement between apocalyptic modalities get sharpened in the case of Balthasar and Benjamin. Crucial here is the notion of 'fragment.' If Balthasar and Benjamin each oppose the 'fragment' to the Hegelian 'whole' and if each hark back to German Romanticism as a kind of precedent, they have a very different interpretation of 'fragment' which issues in different artistic preferences, indeed, different senses of what constitutes the possibilities and obligations of discourse after Hegel as after the Enlightenment. I will attempt to show that although Balthasar could be more sensitive to these issues, he can be developed to meet some of the more telling objections of Benjamin. With regard to what authentic discourse is, Benjamin, and even more so Adorno, offers complacent judgments that not only fundamentally question classical art, but also the very possibility of religion, understood as having a history constituted by symbols, narratives, doctrines, practices, and forms of life.

The subtitle of this book, which accounts for Balthasar's resistance to a constitutive act of misremembering of the Christian tradition and what grounds it, is provided by the French structuralist, Louis Althusser. No more a friend of a theological Hegel than a humanist Marx, Althusser rightly senses that the 'death' of Hegel's thought is not a genuine death: in *The Specter of Hegel*, Hegel's thought continues to enjoy at least a 'half-life' and refuses to be totally impertinent.[35] Through Althusser the notion of 'specter' has made its way into postmodern discourse, especially the discourse of Derrida.[36] For on Derrida's analysis, the overcoming of the philosophical or ontotheological Hegel does not kill Hegel off entirely.

Hegel continues to have currency in modern French thought as this thought is theologically flavored.[37] In the end, however, the very use of the language of 'specter' in postmodern thought is made possible by Hegel himself. In his general reflections on death as the disappearance of the particular, and in his expostulations on the death of Christ, Hegel's linkage of death and the arrival of Spirit exhibits an ambiguity: it is not clear whether the emphasis falls on the paradox or on the interval between death and real life.[38] The in-between of death and life is the space of haunting. It is perfectly clear that Balthasar's reading of Hegel constitutes nothing less than the most developed hauntology of Hegel undertaken from a specifically theological point of view. This hauntology consists in more than diagnosing and resisting the implicit and explicit influence of Hegel in contemporary thought in general and theological thought in particular, even those forms of theological or a/theological thought that maintain they have overcome Hegel. Balthasar's hauntology speaks not only to Hegel's haunting of contemporary discourse, but also to his discourse itself being haunted. It is haunted because in its post-Enlightenment discursive mansion it houses the ghosts of Christianity's premodern others, among whom one finds apocalyptic, Neoplatonism, and Gnosticism. Hegelian discourse is a specter, because its discourse is already spectral. And when it becomes an issue as to how hostile the ghosts are to Christianity, attention falls on Gnosticism as the ghost that is truly a *Doppelgänger*, and equally on the responsibility of the theologian to detect and to refute it.[39] Only such a refutation will make theology possible again, make it possible after modernity, make it legitimately postmodern, and for the same reason make it legitimately Christian.

PART 1

THE SPECTER OF HEGEL AND THE HAUNTING OF ANCIENT DISCOURSES

Substantive arguments in and about philosophy and theology may be complex enough. But when these arguments are framed by procedural and supporting arguments, the former setting the rules of the discursive game but often tipping the balance in a certain direction, the latter situating and thus neutralizing either potential or actual discursive challengers, then argument becomes extraordinarily complex and indefinitely frustrating. As a particular kind of supporting argument, genealogy is narrative construction that plots discourses, forms of life, and practices in a historical line that makes them at best anticipations of their full realization in the discourse, form of life, and set of practices that the genealogist wishes to defend, and at worse toxic discourses whose false glamour is removed once we see their benighted origins. In a sense, genealogy is as old as philosophy and theology. Aristotle provides a good example of this in the *Metaphysics* when he recounts the halting steps made by the Presocratic philosophers towards determining origin (*arché*) and cause (*aitia*), the adequate articulation of which is provided by his 'first philosophy.' Origen and Clement of Alexandria are exemplars as they determine the value of Greek philosophies by reference to Christianity that completes and surpasses them. In one of its more influential forms, genealogy maps rival discourses, forms of life, and practices not onto a line of succession that is completed in the discourse, form of life, and set of practices that one recommends, but rather onto a line of succession considered as other or foreign to one's own. The construction of 'otherness' is commonly associated with a pathological description, since as 'alien' a discourse cannot be introduced into one's own line without distortion and disturbance. As belonging to alien lines, such discourses are to be disowned, rooted out, or be the recipients of discursive scouring and performative scourging. An unsurpassable form of this practice is provided by Irenaeus in *Against Heresies* in which he suggests that the Valentinians are not only inadequately Christian in terms of belief, form of life, and practice, but looked at with the proper eyes Gnostics are not Christian at all, but in fact the extension of the pre-Christian or extra-Christian Gnosticism that disseminates wildly in the *oecumene*.[1]

Genealogy then is a discursive operation which puts manifolds of discourse, forms of life, and distinct types of practices on trial, and not untypically finds them to be lacking or deeply pathological. Now, while genealogy is almost coincident with the Western tradition of discourse and their correlative forms of life and practice, I want to suggest that it gets greatly exacerbated in the modern period, such that just about no philosopher or theologian can avoid it: either plot a rival discourse on a line, or experience one's own discourses being plotted. As the introduction indicated, one can see this genealogical tumescence already in the Enlightenment's positive construction of its ancestry. Yet one can more clearly see it in its negative construction of the ancient that it leaves behind. One can equally see it in Hegel's critical response to the Enlightenment in which the Enlightenment itself is inscribed in a master narrative that also plots in detail premodern Western discourses, including those that are explicitly Christian, which came under Enlightenment sanction. The *Phenomenology* provides the most influential example of this plotting in Hegel's oeuvre, but by no means the only one.[2] Subsequently, of course, both the genealogical narratives of the Enlightenment and of speculative Idealism are questioned and genealogically outnarrated. Nietzsche, and postmodern successors such as Lyotard and Derrida, provide good examples within the area of philosophy, as does also the critical theory of Horkheimer and Adorno.

Submitting the Enlightenment and Hegel to genealogical trial and thereby getting added leverage for a critique that has a broad substantive base, is also a feature of 19th-century theological thought, and Catholic thought in particular. The authority of Hegelianism is keenly felt in a situation in which Catholic theology is looking for models of philosophy that might be of assistance in helping it to deepen its understanding of its own commitments and to communicate more adequately in an idiom that is more comprehensible than that of medieval scholastic theology and likely to have greater cultural prestige. However attractive Hegel is in the effort to re-envision Catholic Christianity, the perception is that he has fatally departed from the Christian tradition on the level of ideas, practices, and forms of life. Hegelian thought requires massive rethinking of received Christian views on revelation, creation, the nature of the Trinity, and an acceptance of a very different relation between faith and philosophy than that sanctioned by magisterial thinkers such as Augustine and Aquinas, and for that matter also Luther and Calvin. Hegelian thought also requires a fundamental reorientation of religious practices such as worship and the practices that make for holiness in favor of the social and political. Finally Hegelian thought requires that the form of life to be lived involves no segregation from the world no matter what the purpose or final meaning. At the same time, however, there is the suspicion that the attractiveness of Hegel's position for Christians and especially for Christian thinkers rests in the more ancient and problematic discourses which Hegel is seen to continue by other means. Hegel is not simply the heir of the highly problematic Spinoza – although he can be viewed thus – he is the heir to much earlier discourses which early Christianity at the very least problematized, if it did not outright reject. In this genealogy, Hegel is a repository of ancient ghosts which wreak havoc with the possibility of an acceptable form of Christian thought. Hegel's thought troubles Christian discourse, twists it, even twists it inside out, and does so in significant part because of the ghosts that represent the reminder and remainder of those positions which Christianity either rejected, repressed, or at the very least marginalized.

Balthasar continues this 19th-century tradition and provides a classic 20th-century example of trial by genealogy. Given his interest in rescuing the traditions of Christian discourse and forms of life from their genealogical internment in the Hegelian system, which goes hand in hand with the correction of the meaning of major Christian doctrines and symbols, Balthasar acts as if there is no choice but to submit Hegel's thought, and that of his successors, to genealogical trial. Even if this is an operation that is ancillary to that of articulating substantive theological disagreement, nonetheless, it is a significant feature of Balthasar's challenge to Hegel's philosophical and theological authority and it is prosecuted in his work, and especially in the trilogy, with a comprehensiveness that few modern religious thinkers have matched.

Chapter 1

Genealogical Torment

Genealogical Torment

For Balthasar, putting Hegel's thought on genealogical trial involves accusing it among other things of imprisoning the tradition within a panoptic system, wherein all non-philosophical discourses become victims of the 'constriction of the concept' (*die Anstrengung des Begriffs*), which Hegel, of course, claims to abhor: such discourses are squeezed and cut down to size, and are made to serve conceptual articulation, wherein the particularity of discourses are muffled, and the practices and forms of life that they invest and in turn support negated. With only the slightest trace of exaggeration, one can say that Balthasar constructs Hegel's genealogy as a form of tormenting or torturing of the Christian tradition that requires rescue. The background trope of the rescue is Christ's liberation of the dead in Hades, his giving them voice and sight. This defensive aspect of Balthasar's submitting Hegel to genealogical trial is the subject of the first section. It focuses specifically on how Hegel covers over the proper history of art, religion, and philosophy, and thus is destined to misunderstand their proper relation. In something of the manner of a Trojan horse, Balthasar enters the Hegelian sanctuary, tells the story otherwise, and by doing so achieves a result considerably more hospitable to Christianity and more in line with the best thinking of the Christian tradition. Reflection on the offensive aspect of genealogical trial is the subject of the second section. Here Balthasar effects the incarceration of Hegel in showing how his speculative discourse can be plotted in lines of thought such as apocalyptic, Neoplatonism, and Gnosticism, which mainline Christianity has viewed as 'other,' and whose function inside Christianity has raised the issue of their potential or actual pathological character. Balthasar is engaging then in counter-genealogy in which Hegel's right to speak on behalf of Christianity is taken away, his 'view from nowhere' is discovered to be a very partial view to the margins of the Christian tradition, and his non-voice (or voice-over) is revealed to mimic voices alien to the Christian tradition. Hoisting Hegel on the genealogical petard is neither the fruit nor origin of disinterested interpretation. The interest in the integrity of Christian thought, practices, and forms of life, and the interest in their perdurance, is obvious as Balthasar engages a real intellectual force with what he takes to be a Christian counterforce of which he is only the executor. Inscribing Hegelian religious philosophy in apocalyptic, Neoplatonic, and Gnostic lines of thought represents so many tactical and opportunistic genealogical strikes intended to weaken Hegelian claims in general, and his genealogical claims in particular. If the main responsibility of the second section is to detail these strikes, questions concerning the compatibility of these ascriptions, and whether Balthasar in fact, or in principle, can move beyond genealogical tactics to a genealogical theory, come in for treatment in the closing pages.

Resisting Hegel the Genealogist: Defensive Postures

As the language of 'untimely' (*unzeitliche*) on the opening page of *Glory of the Lord* (17) hints at Heidegger as a possible philosophical interlocutor,[1] the very opening lines focusing on the problem of theological beginning seems to make a nod in Hegel's direction, specifically his famous discussion in *The Science of Logic* of the question 'With what do we begin?'[2]

> *Beginning is a problem not only for the thinking person, the philosopher, a problem that remains with him and determines all his subsequent steps; the beginning is also a primal decision which includes all later ones for the person whose life is based on response and decision. (GL1, 17)*

In themselves these hints can have no more status than that of literary references. But just as the Heidegger evocation turns out to be much more than that, and expands, as I have shown elsewhere, into a genealogical as well as substantive conversation that runs throughout the whole of *Glory of the Lord*, and indeed beyond, it is worth raising the question whether anything like such an extensive conversation is present with Hegel in *Glory of the Lord* or any other part of Balthasar's great trilogy.

Certainly, it has to be granted that strictly within the ordinance of *Glory of the Lord*, the genealogical engagement with Heidegger is more to the surface. That Hegel is the other genealogist to be engaged, however, becomes clear in *Theo-Drama 1*, where Balthasar feels it necessary to engage Hegel's famous death of art thesis. Balthasar writes:

> *Hegel, as a philosopher, announces the end of art and allots it to its relative place in the "system" as being on the whole a pre-Christian phenomenon that was bound to lead to the prosaic seriousness of real history. (70)*

Balthasar's discussion of Hegel's 'death of art thesis' (*TD1*, 57-70), in which he shows familiarity with *The Phenomenology of Spirit*, *Lectures on Aesthetics*, and *Lectures on the Philosophy of Religion*, throws both retrospective and prospective light on his constructive enterprise. Light is thrown on *Glory of the Lord*, the first part of Balthasar's trilogy, because one comes to see more clearly that for Balthasar, despite the shift from a disclosure to a productive model of art, with the corresponding emphasis on human creativity and mastery, even in modernity art continues to be a viable site for beauty, as the examples of Hopkins (*GL3*, 353-99), Péguy (*GL3*, 400-517), and Hölderlin (*GL5*, 298-334), among others show. And for Balthasar, the continuing viability, and thus the continuing validity of art, is a sine qua non if Christian discourse in general, and Christian theology in particular, is to avoid impoverishment by being deprived of a discursive other that nourishes it and helps bring it to itself (*TD1*, 267). For even if Balthasar celebrates Barth's achievement in which theology demonstrates its power by articulating itself in terms of its own rather than other discursive resources,[3] nevertheless, Balthasar's Catholic 'and' encourages him to think of theology as being dialogical through and through, requiring conversation with all aspects of experience and their symbolic rendering. This is the thrust of his argument in *Glory of the Lord* against Kierkegaard in particular (*GL1*, 49-53) and the post-Reformation dispensation in theology in general (*GL 1*, 48-9).

As Balthasar points out in *Theo-Drama 1*, however, Hegel has not one but two theories about the death of art, one generated from within aesthetic reflection, the other focused on the historical relation between art and religion, and specifically between art and

Christianity (*TD1*, 60-63). The first we have already gestured at, that is, the devolution of art into Romanticism, its thoroughgoing dissolution through subjectivization (*TD1*, 64). This makes productive dialogue between art and religion, or specifically between art and Christianity, difficult in the modern period, at least as long as Christianity insists on a disclosive reality to which it is responsive and by which it is governed. And for Balthasar this is precisely what Christianity has insisted on when it has been healthy, and which it must continue to insist on in order to avoid inconsistency and incoherence. Hegel's second theory involves a much larger genealogical claim. It states that the emergence of Christianity brings an end to art in general (*TD1*, 59-62, 70), and specifically an end to tragedy, which Hegel in the *Aesthetics* and elsewhere (e.g. *Phenomenology*) regards as the highest form of linguistic art, and thus, from Hegel's point of view, the highest form of art (*TD1*, 73-4). Of course, as Hegel asserts in his *Aesthetics*, art, and particularly drama, continues, but its validity has been thoroughly relativized by the appearance of Christianity on the world-stage. From Balthasar's perspective, however, the compliment paid to Christianity by Hegel is insidious (*TD1*, 59-62), because Christianity's overcoming of art, drama in particular (*TD1*, 59-60), sets the stage for its own overcoming by philosophy in which Christianity is speculatively redescribed and sublated (*TD1*, 61). Shadowing all of Hegel's 'death of art' discussion, and especially the second theory, is the view that philosophy is a master discourse that replaces religion in general, and Christianity in particular.

Balthasar's treatment of Hegel's 'death of art' thesis in *Theo-Drama 1*, however, does much more than retrospectively illuminate Balthasar's contesting of Hegel's genealogical thesis in *Glory of the Lord*. Its placement at the start of his construction of a dramatic theory shows that a critical engagement with Hegel is central to the constructive theological enterprise of *Theo-Drama*. And, indeed, already at this early stage in the Prolegomenon Balthasar does more than engage Hegel on the genealogical plane, he also raises important questions about Hegel's christological commitments and expresses preliminary reservations about the viability of Hegel's construal of the Trinity (*TD1*, 67, 69). I will discuss these reservations *in extenso* when I consider the more substantive side of Balthasar's critical engagement with Hegel in Part 2.

Importantly, Balthasar resists both sides of Hegel's genealogical thesis. I have already touched on Balthasar's resistance to Hegel's theory of the immanent dissolution of art in *Glory of the Lord*. *Theo-Drama 1* makes it evident that there is much more to say. In taking up what the Italian idealist philosopher, Croce, eloquently referred to as Hegel's 'funeral oration' (*un elogio fúnebre*) for art (69), Balthasar makes clear that not only is it necessary to engage Hegel's view about the principled impossibility of drama in the modern world, it is even more important to challenge Hegel's reading of the history of drama in the Christian period as a kind of postscript or postlude to the period in which drama played the central role of representing human being to herself in all the complexity of her finitude, givenness, sociality, and aspiration.

In an engagement that shows extraordinary comprehensiveness by keeping in mind Hegel's judgments in the *Aesthetics* on a wide variety of literary figures and styles as well as his theory of the genres of literary art and their development, Balthasar contests both the general and more particular aspects of Hegel's lugubrious announcement. Importantly, however, Balthasar's resistance to Hegel occurs in the context of some quite basic agreements. He agrees with Hegel that Romanticism offers the quintessential expression of modern drama; that modern forms of drama are inflected by high levels of self-consciousness and potential for irony; and that such high levels of self-consciousness and irony are damaging to aesthetic wholeness normatively realized in the Greek drama (*GL4*, 101-154). Again, he agrees with Hegel that Schiller is an emblematic figure of Romanticism (*GL4*, 156; *GL5*, 513-546; *TD1*, 215). Most importantly, he concedes that the post-Romantic trajectory verifies to a significant extent Hegel's diagnosis of the loss of proper objectivity in drama and thus its loss of authority. This is not refuted by the fact that some of the dramatic forms represent respectively objectivistic (e.g. Brecht) (*TD1*, 83-86) and voluntaristic (e.g. Artaud and the theater of the absurd) (*TD1*, 300 n.) alternatives to Romantic and post-Romantic self-consciousness. On the one hand, these forms of drama represent reactions to drama ruled by irony and self-consciousness and, on the other, the exceptions tend to prove the rule and, perhaps, suggest a more consistent Hegelianism in which everything, including self-consciousness, gives way to its opposite.

Nevertheless, for Balthasar, both Hegel's historical assessment of Romanticism and his judgment about its defining modernity are open to question. The questioning proceeds in and through a critical judgement of a dramatist who seems perfectly to fit Hegelian criteria. Agreeing that in many respects Herder looks like, and to some extent in fact is, an arch Romantic (*GL5*, 575, 603), nonetheless, the German man of letters produces in his extemporizing plays a form of drama in principle irreducible to the paradigm of self-consciousness (*TD1*, 179). This form of drama, arguably, points forward to a dramatic modality that realizes a more complex form of aesthetic wholeness than anything found in the classical Greek context, something that Hegel claimed for speculative philosophy rather than drama. In addition, though the general trajectory of drama in the post-Romantic period supports Hegel's judgment about the loss of objectivity, with Beckett's comic minimalism (*TD1*, 312, 322) and Pirandello's self-consciousness (*TD1*, 167, 232, 244-248) representing terminal points, clearly there are exceptions, as Balthasar's expostulations in *Theo-Drama 1* on the merits of the less well-known German language writers, Hugo Hofmannsthal (*TD1*, 215-32), Friedrich Hebbel (*TD1*, 198-203, 436, 442, 448), and Franz Grillparzer (*TD1*, 190-198), show well. All three dramatists transcend in important respects the modern paradigm of self-consciousness and instantiate an aesthetic wholeness that Hegel himself exclusively associates with Greek drama – a judgment which we shall show shortly is itself energetically resisted by Balthasar. While for English speakers Balthasar's reference to dramatists who write in German may appear recondite, it is not Balthasar's point that there are only German-language exceptions. His approving remarks on Arthur Miller in *Theo-Drama 1* (372, 385), and his remarks elsewhere on the exemplary dramatic importance of Claudel's *The Satin Slipper* (*Le Soulier de satin*) suggest otherwise.[4] Since Balthasar's stance is forensic, it is understandable why he proceeds as he does: he gains the greatest critical traction against Hegel's genealogy of aesthetic discourse by considering the unfolding of drama within the German speaking world which Hegel himself largely privileges. Hegel was not fully right about the modern drama that preceded him, and clearly did not anticipate the directions that drama was still able to take even in a context that was, indeed, marked generically by self-consciousness and irony.

The challenges regarding the descriptive accuracy of Hegel's judgments about modern drama, and its presumed trajectory, are supported by challenges to two basic principles of Hegelian interpretation. First, for Balthasar, the artistic, literary, and specifically dramatic discourses of modernity do not admit of the kind of univocal determination that defines Hegel's reading. Only empirical generalizations, themselves subject to qualification, are possible. Thus, at best, a Hegelian reading can attain only relative adequacy.[5] A second, and related, principle of interpretation in Hegel should also be resisted. Throughout Hegel's work 'self-consciousness' is condemned only to be dialectically affirmed. Although it proves vitiating in the realm of modern art, for Hegel, self-consciousness is not vitiating as such. Indeed, it finds appropriate expressions in social life, in Christianity, and philosophy, at least philosophy of the Idealist type. At the very least this makes Hegel's preference for the ancient drama somewhat equivocal, since the Greek drama that is preferred is in no way marked by self-consciousness. For Balthasar, the dialectical move of condemning self-consciousness in one discourse, only to elevate it in others, should be resisted in favor of a more consistent, if more nuanced, understanding of the rule of self-consciousness in modernity. Although self-consciousness may not be as absolutely hegemonic as Hegel construes it to be, what reasons can be provided that self-consciousness will not prove as destructive to religious and philosophical wholeness as it does with respect to aesthetic wholeness? Balthasar suggests that whatever discourse self-consciousness rules, it inevitably hollows out. In modernity, the hollowing out occurs right across the discursive board: philosophy, religion, and art are damaged by it. Yet at the same time no particular genre of discourse is vitiated as such. There are exceptions within each genre, though it is precisely the exception that proves the rule.

As with resistance to the first aspect of Hegel's dissolution thesis, Balthasar's resistance to the second aspect, namely the view that Christian drama is a contradiction in terms, has more particular and general dimensions. More particular aspects of resistance include the offering of counterfactuals, and hinting at possible incoherence in Hegel's reading of particular figures. With respect to the first point, Balthasar offers Baroque drama in general as refuting Hegel's contention that Christianity and drama cannot be successfully synthesized. The Spanish dramatist, Calderón (1600-81), whose influence through works such as *La vida es sueño* extended beyond Spanish drama to inflect even the drama of Shakespeare, is an especially exemplary artist, whose Christianity supports rather than undermines his art (*TD1*, 163-168, 252-255, 361-369). In addition, Hegelian figuration of Shakespeare is problematic, and not simply for the reason that it short-circuits the thorny question of the relation of Shakespeare to Christianity by stipulating that Shakespeare is 'post-Christian' (*TD1*, 118). It is so due to the ambiguity of Hegel's judgment in which from the point of view of dramatic paradigm, Shakespeare is less than the Greeks, yet more in terms of the representation of freedom supposedly central to drama.[6]

Balthasar's encyclopedic rehearsal of drama in the Christian period suggests that Hegel's history of drama in the Christian period is 'thin,' illustrative rather than demonstrative, more a metahistory than a history proper. Refutation of Hegel takes place not by means of an alternative metahistory, for this would leave the case undecidable, but in and through a 'thickly' rendered history of drama. Not the display of erudition, therefore, but methodological and conceptual needs dictate the tome-like quality of the Prolegomenon. In addition, in *Theo-Drama 1*, Balthasar is especially anxious to overcome Hegel's deafening silence on Roman drama which, arguably, reflects the philhellenic prejudice rampant in German Romanticism, and which extends all the way into the twentieth century to Heidegger via Nietzsche. For Balthasar, the omission is critically damaging to Hegel's account, for the Roman drama of Terrence (*TD1*, 109-11) and Seneca (*TD1*, 110, 136) is neither a Greek caricature, nor an ephemeral phenomenon: rather, this form of drama, with its Stoic ideological underpinnings, is both *sui generis* and a real force in the history of drama in the Christian period. If the Baroque dramatist Calderón is an exemplary Christian dramatist, he is so by negotiating with classic Roman styles and Stoic ideology. And, at the very least (*TD1*, 249-250), it is an implication of Balthasar's reading of Shakespeare, that without appeal to Stoicism in both its ideological and dramatic forms as a background, Shakespeare remains incomprehensible. Moreover, it is the very exclusion from consideration of Stoicism that has a deleterious effect on the question of Shakespeare's Christianity. This question can only be tried – if at all – by considering the relation between Christianity and Stoicism, a relation that Balthasar understands in *Theo-Drama 1* to be one of mutuality.

Another important aspect of Hegel's genealogical thesis also contested vigorously throughout *Glory of the Lord* and *Theo-Drama* is the view that the plurality of discursive forms is reducible directly or indirectly to the master discourse of philosophy. Like Balthasar's challenge to Hegel's history of drama, this too has both particular and general features. On the particular front, two Hegelian judgments on Greek tragedy are effectively submitted to critique. The first is Hegel's view that the Greek tragic world view is summed up in *Antigone*[7] with its unresolvable clash between the values of home and city, the tellurian and uranian dimensions of existence (*TD1*, 54-8). If Balthasar's treatment of Greek tragedy in *GL4* (101-54) does nothing to support Hegel's judgment of its pivotal and normative importance, in *Theo-Drama 2* the emblematic status of Antigone is expressly contested. Balthasar makes the point that the principle guiding Hegel's elevation of this drama is anthropological through and through, and that this principle, fully rendered in and justified by philosophical discourse, functions as an *a priori* (*TD2*, 384-85).

A second Hegelian judgment on Greek tragedy is also submitted to questioning. This is the judgment that Greek tragedy is in decline after Sophocles, and that Euripides is a tragedian manqué, an ironist playing the role of way-station to tragedy's eventual displacement by comedy, which represents a contraction of the tensional universe of the relation between the divine and the human and between competing interests in society. This judgment, merely implied in the *Phenomenology*,[8] made explicit in the *Aesthetics*,[9] and ironically made memorable in Nietzsche's very anti-Hegelian *The Birth of Tragedy*,[10] is vigorously contested. In an extraordinary rehabilitation of Euripides conducted in *GL4* (132-154),[11] the belated Greek dramatist does not signify the introduction of a self-consciousness that explodes the Greek religious universe. Rather, Euripides is a consummate Greek tragedian who does justice to the complex relations between the divine and the human, and who has a particular genius for painting the vulnerability and fragility of human being against the backdrop of the mystery of death, systematically evaded by Idealist philosophy, but unhappily also by a great deal of art and not a little theology in the modern period. For Euripides, Balthasar writes, 'death is the question, and human being must discover the answer which is always in his possession' (*GL4*, 133). The rehabilitation of Euripides, like Simone Weil's retrieval of Sophocles,[12] serves a theological purpose: even before Christ, and as an adumbration of the Gospels, Greek tragedy offers a superb representation of finitude and its hope for divine meaning that directly anticipates the christological kenosis that Hegel refuses any Greek tragedian. We will see in the next volume how Euripides can be thought to discipline Heidegger's reflections on death, which Balthasar considers to obviate its neglect in the philosophical tradition: Hegel's sage may dismiss as canard the immortality of the soul as he reflects on the elevation to the absolute idea, but the voice of the philosopher is in a real sense posthumous.

Acts of particular resistance in *Theo-Drama* are in the service, however, of broader issues. What is at stake in the debate about *Antigone* is not simply the correctness or incorrectness of a literary-historical judgment. Balthasar sees that the pattern of conflict in *Antigone* serves a model of, and is in fact redeemed by, the dialectic of philosophy.[13] By this means dramatic discourse is resolvable *directly* into philosophical discourse. Of course, the preferred pattern of resolvability of artistic discourse into the master discourse of philosophy in Hegelian texts is *indirect.* If Greek drama achieves its apotheosis in Christian representation, Christian representation *in turn* is sublated by philosophical discourse. Artistic discourse, then, for Balthasar, has an integrity that ought not to be compromised by its sublation in another discourse, whether religious or philosophical. The artistic discourses of Goethe (*GL5*, 339-407) and Shakespeare (*TD1*, 118) are not philosophical in even the most inchoate sense. And neither of them bears the kind of close relationship to the religious dimension of existence even after the fashion, for instance, of

Homer (*GL4*, 43-77) and Hölderlin (*GL5*, 298-338), nor to Christianity after the fashion of Calderón. Nevertheless, one can say that their discourses have intrinsic value. Moreover, the autonomy of each of the genres of discourses is essential for the health of the others. Not only Christianity's own autonomy vis-à-vis philosophy, but the autonomy of art vis-à-vis both philosophy and Christianity is an abiding interest of Christianity, or at least ought to be so, since the integrity of Christianity can only be maintained through dialogue with other discourses characterized by a similar level of integrity.

It is important to point out, however, that the issue between Balthasar and Hegel is not the principle of ordering. Balthasar allows with Hegel that the discourses of art, religion, and philosophy can be ordered. He disagrees with Hegel, however, about what constitutes the right ordering. Clearly, for Balthasar, philosophy cannot enjoy the hegemony it enjoys in Hegel. This is not to say, however, that philosophy does not enjoy considerable status in Balthasar. The level of engagement with philosophy is high throughout the trilogy. In *Glory of the Lord 4-5* a multitude of philosophies are considered, and Balthasar's response is by no means universally critical. In *GL4* Plato (*GL4*, 166-215) and Plotinus (*GL4*, 280-313) fare especially well, essentially because of the ecstatic and participatory dimension of their thought which rests on the trans-objective foundation of the transcendentals. And at the end of the *GL4* Aquinas is praised as a philosopher who, for all his Aristotelianism, is continuous with the great Platonic and Neoplatonic tradition of inquiry and thoroughly invested in giving a comprehensive account of the participation of all in *esse* (*GL4*, 280-313). Here Balthasar continues a support for Aquinas the philosopher which received a high point in *Wahrheit* in which *De Veritate* played the role of lead-text in an important investigation in truth (*TL1*, 23-7).[14] In *GL5* modern philosophers such as Kant and Heidegger fare quite well, although the mode of interpretation used to arrive at a positive assessment differs markedly. In *GL5* Balthasar tips his hands by speaking of dealing with an 'uncritical' Kant (*GL5*, 481-89). While the adjective obviously signals that Balthasar is going to road against the contemporary current by elevating the pre-Critical writings, what happens in fact is that the pre-Critical writings are invested with the power to interpret some of the writings of the Critical period, most especially the *Critique of Judgment* (1790) and Kant's famous text on the philosophical interpretation of the Christian narrative, *Religion within the Bounds of Reason Alone* (1793). If Balthasar is also anxious to show that his appropriation of Heidegger is critical, he leaves the reader in no doubt regarding the philosophical importance of Heidegger. In this respect, he remains faithful to the high estimation of Heidegger transparent in *Apokalypse 3* and in *Wahrheit*.[15] Neither is engagement with philosophy lacking in *Theo-Drama*. In *Theo-Drama 1*, for instance, Stoicism, Neoplatonism, dialogical and existentialist philosophy, and transcendental philosophy are all appreciatively – if only very passingly – engaged.

Still, the crucial point here is that at best philosophy occupies the same level as artistic discourse. Balthasar is at once being pragmatic and engaging in something of a straightforward rebuttal of philosophy's place in the hierarchy of discourses. On the pragmatic level, Balthasar is making the point that artistic discourse and especially the discourse of drama (also poetry) has the capacity to help Christians to understand themselves better and to push their faith to a deeper level, and has done so – if it has not been fully appreciated – throughout history. On the level of principle, Balthasar is challenging Hegel on his own ground. He accepts the preliminary feature of Hegel's analysis, namely, that like religion and philosophy, art is disclosing of the real as such, but rejects Hegel's view that the inadequacy of art in general, drama in particular, rests in its incapacity to move beyond symbol and narrative and achieve a kind of discursive univocity that alone brings about transparency. And operationally, at least, in the modern period philosophical discourse has liabilities that artistic discourse does not have: on the one hand, artistic discourse has a less checkered history than philosophy, which consistently has attempted to imprison the mystery of reality, and on the other, as a first-order discourse, putatively responsive to reality's deliverances, artistic discourse in general has principled advantages in terms of responsiveness and level of engagement. Making explicit a complaint implied in the retrieval of Hopkins, Péguy, and Hölderlin in *Glory of the Lord*, in *Theo-Drama* Balthasar complains of a constitutive lacuna in theology: 'No theological textbook has found it worthwhile to refer to the names of Shakespeare or Calderón' (*TD1*, 125). Clearly, he is suggesting that theological textbooks ought to. As he does so, Balthasar does not consider himself to be especially isolated, but rather making fully explicit a view that he sees represented in different ways in the work of both Romano Guardini and Erich Przywara. No more than in the case of these precursors is Balthasar leaving an opening for fideism. Philosophy continues to have dignity and pertinence for this theologian who thinks that one consequence of the analogy of being properly understood is the analogy of discourses in which philosophy continues to have an important role to play.

Despite, or perhaps even because of, the assistance accorded theology by art (*TD1*, 267), one might think that Balthasar is repeating without qualification the medieval hierarchy with theology as queen of the sciences. Although Balthasar does not deny that theology is first among equals, its relative primacy, based ultimately on faith's primal exposure to glory that shines through scripture, is only sustainable, first, by keeping in mind the irreducibility of these discourses, and second, only under the condition of theology's dialogical relation to these other discourses in which it submits itself to the prospect of amplification and correction. Balthasar's point, while essentially one of principle, also bears upon fact. It is certainly his view that in modernity the further theological discourses have moved from the aesthetic the more impoverished they have become. For the further the distance, the more risk there is that theology capitulates to the temptation of a univocal mastering discourse in which the mysterious givens of Christianity are explained. But beyond the threat of a univocist reduction, there is the more subtle danger of fostering the pretense of a dialogue between discourses that never truly occurs.

I have been arguing that Balthasar's trilogy, and especially *Theo-Drama*, evinces explicit resistance to Hegel's view of the career of art and its relation to the discourses of Christianity and philosophy. Resistance, indeed, is a matter of urgency, since, according to Balthasar, the upshot of Hegelian genealogy is a fatal compromise of the integrity of Christian discourse. Interestingly, in *Theo-Drama 1* Balthasar does not challenge Hegel's evolutionist view of philosophy in the same explicit manner. Given the specifically theological agenda of this part of the trilogy, perhaps this is not surprising. What is surprising, however, is that Balthasar does not make this point in *Glory of the Lord 5*, which with *Glory of the Lord 4* has the nature and status of philosophy as one of its major foci. Balthasar does make a reference to Hegel's evolutionary understanding (*GL5*, 586). The reference is especially worthy of note, since it is embedded in a discussion of Hegel's *Aufhebung* of both art and religion. But overall the reference seems to have something of the status of a casual remark. Nevertheless, lack of explicit resistance should not be regarded as determinative. One can, and indeed should, read Balthasar's implicit resistence of Hegel's dialectical view of the philosophical tradition as the other side of Balthasar's resistance to Heidegger's narrative of mourning in which the philosophical tradition represents from its very inception a fall, with Descartes marking a change of grade in the incline or decline.[16]

Many of Balthasar's criticisms of Heidegger's genealogy of philosophy apply also to Hegel's triumphalist version. Two criticisms are especially important. Balthasar's own reading of the philosophical tradition shows Hegel's model of the trajectory of philosophical thought to be as univocal and monolithic as Heidegger's. Hegel's reading of the philosophical tradition betrays an apriorist mentality that cuts every bit as deep as Heidegger's, however different their views of progress and regress, and however different their understanding of what grounds the movement of discourse, whether the 'play of Being' (Heidegger), on the one hand, or the 'cunning of reason' (*List der Vernunft*) (Hegel), on the other.[17] Second, not only Heidegger's reading of classical philosophy, but also Hegel's reading is implicitly challenged. If unlike Heidegger, Hegel does not think of classical philosophy as representing a fall, he does contend that classical philosophy labors under the handicap of an objectivistic orientation towards reality, and is correspondingly handicapped by an inadequate sense of subjectivity, freedom, and sense of history that is made possible only in modernity.[18] Different texts in the Hegelian corpus point to the advantage of the modern dispensation over the ancient. To take simply one example: to lovers of ancient wisdom who can only think of Descartes' turn to the cogito as a philosophical calamity, Hegel judges that in the best possible sense Descartes represents a revolution in philosophical thought that is both the opening up of an entirely different continent of thought and a kind of homecoming in which the inspiration of philosophy realizes itself.[19] In addition, Hegel criticizes classical philosophy on the thoroughly non-Heideggerian ground that philosophy ought not to be defined as the love of wisdom, an eros towards transcendence that cannot in principle be completed, as defined by wisdom which represents the culmination of a historical and cultural search for a transcendence of error and the realization of an inerrant vantage point.[20] As with a number of modern and contemporary thinkers, who are self-consciously anti-Hegelian, for example, Eric Voegelin, William Desmond, and John Milbank,[21] Balthasar's appreciation for Plato and the Platonic traditions in particular is considerable. In Plato and Neoplatonism, he finds a form of philosophical thought that is responsive to excess, mystery and giftedness, and that underscores the humility that makes responsiveness possible. If this judgment is made explicitly in *Glory of the Lord 4*, one can see it enacted more than twenty years before in *Wahrheit* in which the Neoplatonic understanding of the fecundity and mystery of the 'really real' provides the context for the articulation of the dynamic self-transcendence of human being defined as spirit.[22] That the embrace of Platonism and Neoplatonism is made with certain caveats, as we shall see shortly, does not mean in the slightest that it is not made with significant enthusiasm.

The importance of Balthasar's resistance, however implicit, to Hegel's schematization of the tradition of philosophy is twofold. Resistance is provoked in part at least because of Balthasar's own stake in philosophy precisely as an articulation of responsiveness to the plenitude and richness of reality. Although Balthasar's view of the nature of philosophy comes through clearly in the vetting of the philosophical tradition throughout *Glory of the Lord 4-5*, obviously *Wahrheit* must be taken as Balthasar's most concentrated statement. In addition, implicit resistance here reinforces Balthasar's more explicit resistance to Hegel's evolutionist model of the relation between discourses. For the trumping of art and religion by philosophy is finally focused in their trumping not just by any philosophy, but that form of philosophy which represents the realization of the aim of philosophical discourse, that is, the aim of an exhaustive explanation that banishes mystery from the precincts of discourse. Leaving until Part 2 detailed consideration of Balthasar's argument against Hegel's erasure of apophaticism from both Christianity and philosophy, one can say Balthasar's denial of the unsurpassed and unsurpassable status of Hegelian discourse, precisely as philosophy, helps further to undermine the prerogatives granted by Hegel to philosophy over the discourses of art and religion.

Light can be shed on Balthasar's resistance to Hegelian schematization by referring to the tack taken by postmodern thinkers, whose identity is determined in significant part by critique of Hegelian discourse as the acme of totalization. Of course, the primary objection to Hegelian thought in texts such as Adorno's *Negative Dialectic*, Lyotard's *The Postmodern Condition*, Levinas' *Totality and Infinity*, and Derrida's *Glas* is that it represents the claim to an absolute discourse that is explanatory of all reality without reserve.[23] This is found to be objectionable on epistemological, narrative, linguistic, and ethical grounds, or all of the above. Importantly, however, for purposes of comparison, various species of postmodernism object not only to the claim made on behalf of Hegelian discourse, but also to the hierarchical arrangement of discourses. Adorno, Lyotard, and Derrida in particular challenge Hegel on this point. With the possible exception of Derrida, the specific interest lies in the valorizing of art, since art in its various literary and non-literary genres can be understood to recognize the perspectivalism of all knowledge – without reduction to relativism – and to validate the irreducibility of the particular. Indeed, great art can teach philosophy what its authentic vocation ought to be. For Adorno,[24] the disjunctive and paratactic poetry of the later Hölderlin represents the cure for the false consolation of synthesis suggested not only in philosophy but in poetry of a more conventional cast. For similar reasons, the linguistic minimalism of Beckett and the atonal musical economy of Schoenberg effect a critique on the pretensions to closure that secrete themselves into all forms of discourse, but which are especially characteristic of philosophy and religion.[25] For Lyotard the reason why modernist painting is so singular is that it at once announces that it represents a particular perspective on reality, while refusing in its composition to permit aesthetic integration in the perceiver. Modernist art in general and not simply painting consists then in figurations of the sublime to which no subject is adequate.[26] According to Derrida, while one might be tempted to understand the French symbolist Mallarmé and Joyce as the literary equivalents of Hegel, in fact they represent the subversive opposite: by illustrating the priority of the semiotic over the semantic, they rupture the semantic closure that both the *Phenomenology* and the Hegelian 'system' in their different ways enact and justify.[27]

It should be noted that the exemplars of art that have leverage over against philosophy are different in the case of Balthasar and postmoderns such as Adorno, Lyotard, and Derrida. All privilege the artistic avant-garde in a way that Balthasar does not. Indeed, the avant-garde comes to enjoy a practical incontestability as it functions to undo the synthetic ambitions not only of philosophy (and by implication religion), but also of the artistic canon as such. For Balthasar, however, the avant-garde is itself contestable to the degree that it denies semantic and ontological potential. The literary and musical canon as a whole has critical leverage against philosophy, but also against belated and experimental forms of art. For Balthasar, Mozart's *The Magic Flute*,[28] Goethe's *Iphigenie* (*GL5*, 342-44) and *Faustus* (*GL5*, 348-51, 359), just about all of Shakespeare's plays,[29] and Hölderlin's *Bread and Wine* (*GL5*, 313, 315) and *Patmos* (*GL5*, 333-34)[30] contest philosophy's claim to render pellucid reality and the responsive subject. The main source of the difference between Balthasar and these representative postmoderns lies in the former's commitment to the semantic and ontological urgency of the work of art by contrast with the latter's commitment to the forms of language and the circulation of signs. In omitting the specifically modernist or the avant-garde from consideration, Balthasar effectively concedes the propriety of its post-Nietzschean reading, and does not raise the question of whether there is ontological intent in modernist art (e.g., the paintings of Kandinsky) that is simply not accounted for if the ironic, reflexive, and formalist nature of modern art is reified. Balthasar's resistance here is reactive rather than reflective: ironically it supposes just that kind of univocal determination of the modern prosecuted in Hegel's *Aesthetics*.

Balthasar's implicit criticism of Hegel's metahistory of philosophy, and his performance of an alternative, helps to indicate just how divided philosophical postmodernism is with regard to resistance. A brief review of this division serves to place Balthasar in a particular hemisphere. While a general distaste for Hegel's evolutionist schematization of the history of philosophy is evident everywhere, not a few anti-Hegelian postmoderns fail to avoid reinscribing important features of Hegel's epochal account. Adorno,[31] for example, tends to think of Hegel's thought as the realization of the rationalist and metaphysical bias of the Western tradition that begins in Plato. Thus, he agrees with Hegel in substance, but, as with Heidegger, for whom he expresses a particular distaste,[32] he turns what in Hegel is a compliment into an insult. In his seminal book, *Erring*, Mark C. Taylor,[33] the first important North American translator of Derrida, understands Hegel's discourse to realize completely the aspirations of Western philosophical and theological discourse. Thus the way beyond Hegel can only be in and through an aesthetic Nietzscheanism that follows the disenchantment of the Hegelian spell rather than in or through the philosophical tradition itself. In ways much more similar to Balthasar, postmoderns such as Levinas, Marion, Caputo, and Milbank challenge the dialectical reading of the philosophical tradition that would neutralize the critical potential of a pre-Hegelian philosophical discourse. For Levinas, not only do Plato and Neoplatonism have critical purchase, but to a limited extent so also does Descartes,[34] who represents for Heidegger, as well as for Hegel, the fateful modern turn to the subject as the ground of the coincidence of certainty and truth. For Marion,[35] Neoplatonism in its symbolism as well as its apophatic mechanisms can theoretically override the brazen claims of Hegelian philosophy. Caputo, after Derrida, believes with Marion that the texts of Plato and Neoplatonism have genuine critical potential, even if he cavils with Marion regarding the degree.[36] And finally, Milbank thinks that Neoplatonism with its emphasis on plentitude and dynamis, and also Aquinas – if he is interpreted aright – cannot be graphed on a line showing univocally development or decline. Indeed, with respect to both, Milbank is much less reserved in his enthusiasm than Balthasar. For him, it is not necessary to distinguish between Proclus and Plotinus or to worry about whether a distinction should be drawn between Maximus and Pseudo-Dionysius, on the one hand, and Maximus and Johannes Scotus Eriugena, Cusanus and Eckhart,[37] on the other. And as his reflections on Aquinas make perfectly clear,[38] he is made much less uncertain than Balthasar that the *Summa* does not make theology ancillary to philosophy. As with Balthasar, Milbank understands the tradition of Western philosophical and theological discourse to be wholesomely plural. And despite a tone that is apocalyptic, Milbank thinks of these traditions as illustrating flows as well as ebbs. In the modern period, there are always discourses that not only light up the general gloom, but genuinely push forward the frontiers of religious, philosophical, and needless to say, artistic discourse.

Counter-Genealogical Construction

THAT HEGEL IS AN IMPORTANT argumentative partner in *Glory of the Lord* is indicated by Balthasar's going beyond a genealogical defense to actually mounting a genealogical counterattack. In fact, Balthasar's genealogical counterattack is complex and involves quite a number of different ways of naming Hegelian thought. Specifically, Balthasar graphs Hegel into a number of genealogies of discursive deformation in which his own thought serves as the final and most toxic example. These various emplotments construct different Hegels, Hegels as different as an aesthetic Hegel continuous with Romanticism, a Hegel that continues various lines of Neoplatonism inimical to philosophy that emphasizes excess and the astonishment and rapture of the self, an apocalyptic Hegel who continues the heterodox form of apocalypticism discernible in Joachim of Fiore, and finally a Gnostic or Valentinian Hegel. With respect to these emplotments of Hegelian discourse, one can neither assume that they enjoy the same genealogical force, nor even the same kind of force. While the issue of the amount of force is ultimately paramount, the issue of kind of force is significant, since it may very well mark off the first emplotment from the other three which differ from it in having a more wide-angle lens with respect to the specific line of discourse Hegel is thought to complete, and being somewhat less dependent on the structural, more nearly typological contrast between 'theological aesthetic' and 'aesthetic theology,' which is an essential binary pair in *Glory of the Lord*.

(1) Post-Romantic Aestheticization: As the organization of *Glory of the Lord 5* shows clearly, the default genealogical or

counter-genealogical strategy is to plot Hegelian discourse in the tradition of Romantic reaction to the Protestant elimination of the aesthetic (*GL5*, 513-546; see also *GL1*, 48-9, 79-80). Although Balthasar believes that the reaction is both necessary and justified, he is convinced that neither Romanticism nor Idealism reinstate the aesthetic dimension at the heart of the best patristic and medieval theological and mystical discourses, which in quite different ways demonstrates a responsiveness and humility before the disclosure of divine glory that suggests their relative adequacy. Nor do Romanticism and Idealism respect the distinction between artistic and religious discourses, nor their integrity. Romanticism and German Idealism represent, for Balthasar, less the reprise of the genuinely aesthetic dimension of Christianity than the illicit operation of including Christianity in an aesthetic program that transcends and transforms it (*GL1*, 79-80). German Romantics such as Herder and Schiller are both examples of a process of aestheticization in which Christianity loses its integrating power (*GL1*, 81; *GL5*, 527; 548-549), and becomes thoroughly eviscerated (*GL5*, 528). This process achieves its apex in Hegel. Both Hegel and the Romantics manage to drown out the voice of Hamann (*GL1*, 49, 80-83), who preserves the proper distinction between religious and aesthetic discourse, and on this basis elaborates their intimate relation. Hamann endures the pathos of exceptionality long before Kierkegaard and for Balthasar with more purpose, because he possessed considerably greater balance in his articulation of both the relation of nature and grace and the relation between discourses. In picking out this figure as a kind of leaven in the German cultural wash of Romanticism and Idealism, Balthasar suggests a line of development that is more interrupted by Kierkegaard than completed by him, a line that awaits its postmodern completion. I will have considerably more to say about the importance of Hamann in Balthasar's articulation of a counter-tradition in Part 3, but for the moment it suffices to suggest that Balthasar by no means thinks that Romanticism, which was emerging in the last decade of Hamann's life, and German Idealism, which was over two decades in the future, need to be considered as monoliths.

Needless to say Balthasar does not confound Romanticism and Idealism. There are important differences. The main difference is that for Hegel philosophy is the discourse into which all other discourses resolve, whereas the Romantics recognized the superior claims of art, since artistic discourse not only declares a freedom lacking in confessional Christianity, it also exceeds the reach of conceptualization which, as Kant had shown, was limited to the world of sense. At an essential level, however, Balthasar perceives a kind of discursive monism uniting both Romantic and Idealist visions, even as they are underwritten by a general aesthetic commitment that emphasizes the union of differences, the integration of plurality, and the concordance of discordance. *Apokalypse*, arguably, makes more clear than *Glory of the Lord 5* that one of the most conspicuous aspects of the phenomenon of Romanticism and Idealism is the issue of discursive authority: what discourse is more apt to account for the complex human and social world of modernity? Of course, the question itself occurs against the backdrop of competing certitudes, for example, the language and culture of traditional Christianity or the language of science or a philosophical language that takes science seriously (Enlightenment and Kant in very different modes). As indicated already, grossly speaking Romanticism and Idealism answer the question differently, the former suggesting that art is the discourse that integrates all the others, the latter that philosophy is the only such discourse. Accommodations are made, of course, by both discourses to the other: Schiller, who in the *Aesthetic Letters* provides the matchless expression of why art should be regarded as the best candidate for discourse authority, makes more than a few concessions to philosophy, at least as philosophy can be made aesthetic.[39] And being as proud, as Schelling is, of the achievements of a post-critical philosophy, does not stop him from suggesting in his *System of Transcendental Idealism* that art may very well have more integrating power than religion and philosophy.[40] Not incidentally, however, art is beholden to the beneficence of philosophy for its status.

Hegel's thought, then, is a supreme instance of the dispensation of an 'aesthetic theology,' which is both structurally the contrary of 'theological aesthetics' and its historical competitor. As Balthasar makes clear in *Glory of the Lord 1*, the constitutive aspects of theological aesthetics, submitted to attack by the simulacrum of aesthetic theology, are supplied by scripture. As proposed in the foundational volume of *Glory of the Lord* (*GL1*), but as rendered in the volumes on scripture (*GL6* and *GL7*), central to a theological aesthetics is the view of the divine as a free self-communicating personal 'I,' the perception of the self as constituted in the free response of faith and praise, and the vision of creation as graced, at once radically mysterious in terms of origin and suffused by divine presence. Such features are biblical in the general sense. In the context of the New Testament, these elements are configured in the light of the *mysterium Christi* in such a way that Christ is understood to be the unsurpassable rendering of the free personal God, to provide the archetype for faith in its basic disposition and way of life, and to illuminate and complete the order of creation without compromising its integrity.[41]

In *Glory of the Lord* Balthasar does not show in any systematic fashion how Hegel's aesthetically disposed thought subverts or distorts a theological aesthetic defined by these constitutive features. At one level, the subversion is simply an implication of Hegel's status as a prime example of 'aesthetic theology,' the contrary to the theological aesthetics Balthasar regards as normative. But throughout *Glory of the Lord* there are places where Balthasar brings up specific infractions. It is clear that Hegel is understood to support an impersonal rather than personal divine (*GL1*, 235), indeed, a divine that is a process of self-constitution in which otherness is a necessary moment (*GL1*, 49). At the same time, Balthasar is no less insistent than in *Apokalypse* that Hegelian thought represents one of the supreme instances of modern titanism (*Apok 1*; 615; *GL5*, 420, 423) in which the authentic disposition of openness of the self is overcome. In addition, Balthasar challenges the Hegelian form of necessity that naturalizes the grace that underwrites and elevates nature. We will have much more to say about Balthasar's resistance to necessity as an ineluctable feature of Hegelian dialectic in Part 2. Here it suffices to point out that one of the ways in which Balthasar argues the point is to suggest a distinction between an aesthetic and a logical 'must.' Whereas an aesthetic 'must' of rightness and verisimilitude is consonant with freedom, logical necessity is not (*GL5*, 347; *GL6*, 406-407). In confusing one with the other Hegel trespasses both against the biblical *dei* and the theological 'must.' The latter, he argues, receives exemplary expression in the works of Anselm (*GL2*, 211), perhaps nowhere more saliently than *Cur Deus Homo*, whose distinction between 'necessary reasons' and 'reasons of appropriateness' has often been thought wrongly to legitimate a fundamentally rationalistic orientation to divine reality. Lastly, of course, Hegel's thought is not focused on the unsurpassability of Jesus of Nazareth (*GL5*, 423), such that this optics essentially informs all perspectives on the divine, creation and humanity.

This critique of Hegel as an 'aesthetic theologian' only seems to be left behind in *Theo-Drama*'s examination of Hegel's christological and trinitarian thought, which offers highly plausible alternatives to the standard ecclesial renditions. Hegelian substitution becomes possible in part when the aesthetic key to the classical tradition has been forgotten, and in part when the tradition unnecessarily narrowed itself in the course of its elaboration. Indeed, genre categories such as drama and epic, which are central to Hegel's own aesthetics, can themselves be used to undermine Hegel's alternative post-Christian christological and trinitarian sophistications. This will be thematized in the next chapter which deals in a more focused way with Balthasar's opposition to Hegel's substantive theological proposal and the narrative genre within which it articulates itself and the narrative operators that constitute it.

Before proceeding to discuss the other emplotments of Hegel, it is important to characterize the present one more broadly. Obviously, a significant feature of this emplotment is a cultural history assessment in which Hegel's discourse is seen to depend on, or at least presuppose, the discourse of Romanticism,[42] and thus repeat in some modified way its stressed relation to Christianity. Balthasar does not attempt to prove this dependence, or argue in detail how this dependence shows itself in Hegel's texts, nor go into detail about the ways in which Hegelian discourse differs from Romanticism, indeed is often critical of it. Dealing only with the essentials, Balthasar leaves this work for others. For Balthasar the basic difference between Romanticism and Idealism is captured in their fundamental option for the discourses of art and philosophy respectively. But, for him, with respect to the place of Christianity, and the integrity of its content – which is his exclusive interest – this is in an important respect a difference without a difference, for

Christian discourse gets relativized by both. The functional and structural continuities between Romanticism and Idealism are, he is convinced, much more important than the discontinuities. Functionally, philosophy displaces and replaces Christianity in Hegelian speculation, as art does within the horizon of Romanticism, and structurally the organicism that is hallowed by Idealism represents the characteristic of Romanticism that is truly defining, and which marks it off from an anti-aesthetic Enlightenment, which is hostile in a straightforward way to the deliverances of Christianity. Both Romanticism and Idealism exhibit a friendliness to Christianity that turns out to be counterfeit as they hollow out the actual substance of Christian belief and encourage practices and forms of life more consonant with the specifically modern emphases on autonomy and knowledge, interpersonal relations, and sociality. In this horizon of thought, obedience becomes anachronistic, ignorance culpable, and interpersonal relations, scenes of eros or its stymying, and sociality something to be managed rather than the gift of connectedness predicated on community subtended by the communion of divine persons.

As already suggested, the genealogical emplotment of aesthetic theology is different in kind from the other three in which Hegel is plotted in trajectories as various as Neoplatonism, Gnosticism, and apocalyptic. On the one hand, as a category 'aesthetic theology' is less determinate and more broad-ranging than any of them, since in principle we can say that what is wrong with Neoplatonism, Gnosticism, and apocalyptic among other things is that they tend to inscribe and alter the biblical narrative, and recommend changes in standard Christian practices and forms of life, or at the very least call for a radically different interpretation. Considered thus, the category is not of significant use in undermining the credibility of Hegel. Considered, however, through its major historical instance in Romanticism – which is what links *Glory of the Lord 5* with *Apokalypse* – Balthasar's genealogical point is extraordinarily useful, even if its range is much more historically narrow than the other attributions, whose original discourses are traceable back to the earliest centuries. We start with Balthasar's inscribing Hegel in a Neoplatonic trajectory, in which the distinction in kind is, arguably, less obvious than is the case with respect to Gnosticism and apocalyptic. The fact that we deal with the inscription of Hegel in turn in Gnostic and apocalyptic trajectories ought not be taken as suggesting a ranking in which as last in the order of treatment, apocalyptic is given pride of place. No ranking is intended at this stage; and as I point out, such ranking may well go beyond Balthasar's explicit intent. This does not mean that the issue of ranking does not arise. To raise and answer this question is to supplement Balthasar. In anticipation, I wish to suggest that in the final analysis it is Gnosticism rather than apocalyptic that has the best credentials as a precursor discourse and the greatest capacity to include these other discourses as it deranges the biblical narrative, changes the meaning of crucially important Christian doctrines, and proposes different practices and forms of life in addition to esoteric interpretations of standard Christian practices and forms of life.

(2) *Neoplatonic Trajectories*: In *Glory of the Lord* Balthasar appeals to two Neoplatonic lines of filiation to place Hegelian discourse, and thereby displace its authority. The first is the line of philosophy of spirit (*Geistesphilosophie*) that Balthasar takes to run from Eckhart through Cusanus and on to Hegel (*GL5*, 50, 208). The second is an erotic line of Neoplatonism that runs from Bruno through Romanticism to Hegel (*GL5*, 260-64; 578). In the former case, Balthasar focuses on the claim to noetic adequacy not only with respect to worldly beauty, but also with respect to divine glory. In the latter he concentrates on the Promethean drive at the heart of the modern anthropological frame of reference. Not uninterestingly, he sees that the domination of eros in the Romantic and Idealist periods, which he covers so extensively in *Apokalypse 1*, has origins in the late Renaissance and not simply in the Enlightenment.[43] For him, it is only in reaching their completion in Hegel that both Neoplatonic lines become transparent and reveal their inner relation. In the context of Hegel's work one discovers the *libido dominandi* at the heart of a Neoplatonism of a philosophy of spirit, and finds the noetic ambition at the core of the urge for reality conceived as a totality. For the ambition to penetrate reality thoroughly compromises the *analogia entis* and collapses the creator-created distinction. Even when the conceptual apparatus of negative theology is in full display – or paradoxically especially when it is full display – the tendency of both

of these lines is towards the abolition of all mystery, whose excess dictates its transcendence of the metaphysical horizon.

As the work of Eckhart shows with particular clarity,[44] when Neoplatonism operates within the horizon of an identity-metaphysics, Christ comes more and more to be interpreted symbolically rather than as the 'concrete universal' which offers at once a definition of both God and human being, without in the slightest confusing them. From the side of Bruno, the dynamically modified emanationism, which deletes transcendence from the divine-world picture,[45] culminates in the claim to a form of knowledge that surpasses ratiocination. This knowledge, while it in principle makes transcendence accessible, is factually speaking a secret. While Balthasar's reservations with respect to the secret more nearly correlate with the reservations of Marion than Derrida,[46] he finds this aspect of Neoplatonism particularly objectionable. Despite Hegel's suspicion with respect to the secret, and principled objection against apophasis in discourse, it admits of being inscribed in his discourse of reason (*Vernunft*), which precisely exceeds what is possible for ratiocination or the understanding (*Verstand*). For Balthasar the normative view of the relation of faith and knowledge is given in the Alexandrian theology of Clement and Origen. Granting their Platonism, Balthasar underscores the sobriety with which they articulate the relations between faith (*pistis*) and knowledge (*gnōsis*). Knowledge is an expression and extension of faith, and faith is not ignorance but inchoate knowledge (*GL1*, 138-41). Moreover, the context of all knowing, notwithstanding its level of development, is the ordering of the self toward the triune God (*GL1*, 131, 141). This means that all believing and knowing is tied to praxis, and it is because this is so that the saint can be thought of as the exemplary instantiation of the specifically Christian form of knowing that is always illustrated in action, in Christian practices and forms of life.[47] The 'correspondence' achieved by the saint is not simply intellectual. It is the bestowal of all affect and intellect, all sense and motion, the entire time of the embodied self to Christ and through Christ to the triune community. Thus, the nuptial image is never impertinent. Correspondence is attunement, and beyond attunement ecstasy. If this ecstasy is Marian, the amen is what shapes the core of a life rendering the self transparent to the divine other. More, it is this amen that grants the joy that surpasses all happiness. But as Balthasar insists time and time again, what is important about the saint is not individual genius or idiosyncrasy.[48] To think this is fatally to succumb to the subjectivist modern paradigm. The saint is an ecclesial person whose aim is to excavate the unrepeatable call or mission that defines them and to which he or she bears witness. In this sense the less idiosyncrasy the better; for idiosyncrasy is what darkens the self that would be mirror of Christ.

Whatever the difficulties with respect to validating either of these Neoplatonic emplotments of Hegel's discourse, and their relationship to each other, it is obvious that in making his judgments Balthasar is far from eccentric, and indeed is relying on received traditions of interpretation. While charting Hegelian discourse as the end-point in a trajectory that begins with Eckhart's assimilation of Neoplatonic philosophy has hardly functioned as a hermeneutic default for the interpretation of Hegel, nonetheless, it has had a fairly honored career. In the shape of Franz von Baader, a 19th-century Catholic thinker who acquainted Hegel with Meister Eckhart, and other speculative western mystical thinkers, this emplotment enjoyed favor in Hegel's own day.[49] Moreover, it has been revised with a significant degree of persuasion and conviction by interpreters of Hegel dissatisfied with the reductionist rationalistic and/or transcendental profiling of Hegel in which much of what is truly exciting about Hegelian thought, not least of which is its religious and mystical bent, is lost.[50] Arguably, Balthasar's connection of Bruno's Neoplatonism with Hegel's thought represents a less well-traveled interpretive path. Yet here again, Balthasar's position is hardly eccentric, given the favorable mentions Bruno receives in Hegel's *Lectures on the History of Philosophy*,[51] and the status the Nolan enjoys in German Idealism in general,[52] where Neoplatonic views of the divine and the divine-world relation function critically with respect to standard Christian and theistic understandings of a divine-world relation in which the world comes into being by divine fiat and signals, but in no way fundamentally expresses, the divine. In summing up Bruno's form of Neoplatonism as erotic, Balthasar features the anthropological displacement-replacement of the divine that is fully realized in Hegelian discourse. Here there is more than a merely formal or structural overlap between Balthasar's

Glory of the Lord and Blumenberg's *The Legitimacy of the Modern Age*: while Balthasar privileges *Heroic Fury* (*GL5*, 260-64) in the way the more cosmologically focused Blumenberg does not, nonetheless, the elevation of the world complements the elevation of the human being and vice versa. As manifestations of the expressivity of the divine, both human being and world are constitutive of divine self-identity that cannot any longer be summed up by the categories of aseity, unnecessitated creative activity, and excess of creative potential over creative fiat.

Needless to say, removing some of the strangeness of Balthasar's Neoplatonic emplottings does not make them valid. Plausible as either emplotment is in itself, serious difficulties beset both and their relation. When Balthasar advocates the *Geistesphilosophie* Neoplatonic option, he leaves us in the dark as to who the couriers of Eckhart and Cusanus might be between the 15th and 18th centuries. In not filling in the connections Balthasar risks providing not so much a genealogy as a typology, which has considerably less explanatory force precisely because it can work without any appeal to direct or indirect mediation of previous positions. Again, when Balthasar enjoins reading Hegelian discourse as a realization of the discourses of Bruno, he leaves unexplored how Hegel's metaphysically erotic view of the divine-world and the divine-human relation both squares with Bruno's sometime agapaic view of these relations and repeats Bruno's non-dialectical and non-agonistic view of the relation between superabundant first principle and the world. Just as importantly, Balthasar seems to avoid explicitly raising the questions whether and in what way these two Neoplatonic trajectories are related. Do they, for example, overlap in the modern period, such that Bruno can be construed to represent both a continuation and emendation of Cusanus and derivatively of Eckhart? And finally, what have these two trajectories got to do with another Neoplatonic suggestion which, if made somewhat in passing in *Glory of the Lord* (*GL5*, 228), is a commonplace in Balthasar's work as a whole? This is the suggestion, first launched in Hegel's day, that Hegel's thought represents the recrudescence of Proclus.[53] In Balthasar's hands this is not a compliment: Proclus' thought represents a philosophy of identity in a way the thought of Plotinus, plausibly, does not (*GL5*, 214, 234-35). The mystical 'suddenly' (*exaiphnes*) wins out in the *Enneads* in a way it does not in the speculatively overdetermined *Elements of Theology*. Balthasar's point is that if Christian Neoplatonists such as Pseudo-Dionysius, Maximus, and Bonaventure are to be judged as theologically sound, then two conditions must be satisfied. First, however obvious the presence of Proclus, both from an architectonic and symbolic point of view, the mode of Neoplatonism in all the above figures is in principle more nearly Plotinian than Proclean, since these discourses do not as a matter of fact validate the emanationist dynamic that leads to a collapse of the divine into world, and the elevation of world into the divine. Second, in the final analysis any tendency towards identity in these Christian Neoplatonic discourses is resisted by recalling the biblical view of divine freedom and goodness that grounds the analogy between God and world. To the degree to which Hegel articulates an identity-philosophy, forgetful of the *analogia entis*, he is Proclean, Eckhartian, and Brunan all at once. As a matter of fact, however, in the trilogy Balthasar does not trace the two more modern Neoplatonic trajectories back to Proclus, even though he has the example of a 19th-century German theologian such as Franz Anton Staudenmaier (1800-1856) who did so. In this lies the excess, at least from a genealogical point of view, of 19th-century genealogy, which Balthasar seems to be recalling, but not fully appropriating. I will have much more to say about the relation between Balthasar and Staudenmaier in parts 2 and 3.

(3) *Gnostic Genealogy*: Yet another, even less self-evident judgment, is consistently made throughout the trilogy and other texts: Hegel is deemed to repeat, though not without mediation, the transformation exerted on Christianity by Gnosticism (e.g., *TD1*, 131; *SI*, 5). In an important sense, the trilogy recycles a proposal made as early as *Apokalypse* (1937-9) in which Romantic and post-Romantic titanism justified 'Gnostic' ascription. What is different in the trilogy is that Balthasar is somewhat clearer about the criteria of ascription: any modern repetition of ancient Gnosticism involves recapitulating and justifying an essentially mythological model of the divine. This mythological model is dramatic, even tragic in its depiction of the becoming of the divine which others itself (*SI*, 2; *GL2*, 38-9), and undergoes alienation, only to overcome it and achieve integration. If postulated as an origin, divine integration

is posited as a result, a victory over what would deny it perfection of the really real and fully comprehensive consciousness and self-consciousness. Within this mythological framework, the event of the cross is absorbed into the structure or structuration of the divine (*TD2*, 79, 83-88), discarding thereby the historicity, unsurpassability, and saving significance of Christ (*TD1*, 423). The accusation that Hegelian thought represents a repetition of Gnosticism is also made outside the trilogy. It finds a particularly eloquent expression in *Mysterium Paschale.* Explicitly addressing Hegelian thought, Balthasar issues the following judgment:

> *At a level incomparably higher than that of Valentinian Gnosis, we find repeated here the same process of turning the mystery of the Cross into a piece of philosophy, and in both cases the God-man (the primordial Man), by his self-revelation coincides in the last analysis with the self-understanding of man himself. (MP, 62; see also 63-5)*

The emphasis falls heavily here on the continuity between Hegel and Valentinianism, despite Balthasar's marking the higher level of Hegelian thought, which necessarily involves greater reflective distance from the governing 'mythological' narrative. Crucially, for Balthasar, the entire myth is an object of knowledge rather than faith (*TD2*, 89, 115; *SI*, 5, 30). And, of course, it is faith that is constitutive for Christianity, as exemplars of Christian theology such as Origen and Augustine – and not simply Irenaeus – show.

From Balthasar's perspective, this mythological point of view represents a complex threat to Christianity. It represents a systematic threat insofar as it bears the likeness of the biblical view, while really being a total transformation of it. In *Glory of the Lord* Balthasar agrees with Irenaeus that the specific threat of Gnosticism lies in the comprehensive nature of its falsification (*GL2*, 39). This suggests also that the specific threat of Hegelianism is the comprehensive scale of an alteration that disguises itself, and can plausibly pass as a discourse with a genuine Christian content (*GL2*, 42). With respect to Gnosticism in general, and not simply its classical instances, Balthasar is prepared to use the truculent language of 'vampire' and 'parasite' (*SI*, 1). The evaluative intention could not be more clear. Balthasar's language draws attention to the declamatory heresiological tradition to the point of giving it a gothic twist. In doing so, Balthasar reveals his debt once again to 19th-century Catholic thought. Linguistically, Balthasar's choice in language evokes Möhler, whose views on tradition are so important to him,[54] even if substantively he is closer to Staudenmaier's form of critique which depends less on the diagnosis of an existential malady than on an uncovering of a complete distortion of the Christian narrative.[55] In any event, in the modern context of an either-or between rationalism and fideism, an either-or to which Christianity itself has contributed in theological styles that are either overly conceptual or simply pietistic reaction-formations, Balthasar believes that Gnosticism represents a deep theological threat. A mythologized or remythologized biblical discourse represents an exciting and powerfully attractive, because fundamentally aesthetic, third option that satisfies imagination as well as emotion and intellect. However esoteric the discourse it is not private: it is intended to have community reference, although it may well be the agent of intercalating the community to which it refers.

There can be no doubt that Balthasar's depiction of Gnosticism owes much to Irenaeus, who is regarded by Balthasar as one of the theologians most in need of retrieval in contemporary theology. But Irenaeus' 'theological aesthetic,' which is lauded in *GL2*, is an act of resistance to Gnosticism conceived as a simulacrum of truly Catholic Christianity. This resistance is considered to be of sufficient importance to be brought forward by Balthasar in an anthologization of *Against Heresies* in which the Irenaean rebuttal to Gnostic disfiguration of the biblical narrative, with its concomitant defocusing from Christ and tradition, is laid bare. If the core failure, according to Balthasar in *The Scandal of the Incarnation* (10), lies in Gnosticism's inability to understand the reality of Christ as the God-man (see also *GL2*, 60-2, 66, 67, 71-2), this failure is accompanied by an arrogant presumption of knowing that can safely by-pass the straightforward deliverances of scripture and tradition. Indeed, the presumption authorizes tendentious interpretations of the biblical narrative that run in just the opposite direction to the community interpretation and the community's rules for interpretation. Balthasar records with approval Irenaeus' objections to the

Gnostic separation of the demiurge from the unknowable transcendent divine and the separation of Christ from the law-giver of Genesis, and affirms Irenaeus' energetic defense of the biblical God as being both mysterious and creative, at once a God of justice and love (*SI*, 17). Balthasar takes note too of Irenaeus' positing of the goodness of creation and the creative act against Gnostic provocation that creation is the abortive offscouring of a being that is less than divine (*SI*, 24). Here Balthasar implies that in belated religious-philosophical modes of thought, identifying creation with fall will be one of the constitutive marks of the return of Gnostic modes of thought (*SI*, 2).

Crucial to any defense against historical Gnosticism, or its return in modernity, is a dramatic Christology of the kind elaborated by Irenaeus. As the divine-human who suffers and dies on our behalf, and who expresses God's love, Christ is the center of the drama of salvation history. Indeed, Christ represents the 'summing up' (*SI*, 53-8) or *anakephalaiosis* of all of history, of Adam and everything granted in the dispensation of the Old Testament. Christ effects salvation on our behalf, but the mediation of grace and truth occurs through the Church that abides between Christ and the eschaton. The Church is an embodiment of Spirit, not of individuals, who become, as *Theo-Drama 3* makes clear, persons in the full and proper sense only in the context of their unique mission in the Church and for the world.[56] The Church is fundamentally eucharistic (*SI*, 90-2), that is, it is the instrument for the communication of God's saving presence through the sacrifice of Christ. In Christ's sacrifice we have our hope for the last days and the resurrection of the body (*SI*, 94 ff.). We will have much more to say about Balthasar's diagnosis of the modern avoidance of the eucharistic understanding of church, and especially Hegel's disguise of this forgetfulness, in Part 2.

More important than linguistic resonance between Balthasar and other 19th-century ascriptions of 'Gnosticism' and 'Valentinianism' are the relations between Balthasar and 19th-century Protestant and Catholic thinkers concerning criteria of 'Gnostic' attribution. Here even though Balthasar is more familiar with Catholic sources such as Möhler and Staudenmaier, it is Hegel's student, Ferdinand Christian Baur, who is truly seminal. In 1835 Baur proposed in his great text, *Die christliche Gnosis*, that Hegel's dynamic presentation of a divine, which becomes through its relation to the world, represents a development of ancient gnosis, and has its proximate starting point in a form of post-Reformation thought focused in speculative fashion on the living God.[57] Essentially agreeing with Baur's view of the haunting of modern thought by Gnosis, Staudenmaier adopts the Irenaean stance that it is incumbent on the theologian to name the ghost that haunts philosophical Christianity or Christian philosophy, as the preliminary to excising or exorcising Christianity's false double. It is Staudenmaier, therefore, who offers the specific 19th-century precedent for Balthasar's analytic rather than evaluative 'Gnostic' labeling of Hegel's discourse.

I will have more to say about Staudenmaier's substantive critique as well as genealogical plotting of Hegel in Parts 2 and 3. What I want to emphasize now is that no more here than in his other genealogical counter-strokes does Balthasar produce warrants for his placing Hegel in this invidious thought-trajectory. For example, Balthasar does not attempt a critical assessment of Irenaeus' view of Gnosticism as representing a tendentious reading of scripture that disfigures the biblical narrative as it makes an illegitimate claim to adequate knowledge which has this narrative as its specular or spectacular content. Nor does Balthasar bring Irenaeus' view into conversation with the analyses of scholars of Nag Hammadi texts, for whom the interpretive default tends to be that of dualism, both metaphysical and anthropological. Nor again does Balthasar inquire into Baur's criteria of becoming, relationality, and agon in the divine as identifying 'Gnostic' modes of thought in modernity. Nonetheless, however unforthcoming Balthasar is on all these issues, criteriologically, he does enjoy an advantage over Eric Voegelin, who is the thinker who has most popularized a 'Gnostic' ascription of Hegel.[58] For it is much easier to bring in a 'Gnostic' or 'Valentinian' verdict on the basis of the textual evidence for an integrated narrative of divine fall and recollection than make inferences, as Voegelin does, from an ancient or even modern text to a peculiarly Gnostic state of soul defined pathologically as determined by arrogance and alienation.[59] Indeed, Balthasar's Gnostic reading of Hegel may be eminently redeemable, even if it is not redeemed as a matter of fact by Balthasar.

Balthasar himself provides at least hints as to how to enact conceptually such a redemption. One such hint is Balthasar's endorsement of Irenaeus' diagnosis of a gap between the surface and depth semantics of Gnostic, and especially Valentinian myth (*GL2*, 59): while the surface narrative meaning of Valentinian myth seems (i) to suggest a distinction between a divine not subject to the trauma of fall and development, and an aspect of divinity that is so subject, and (ii) to suggest an equilibrating movement of loss and recovery of divine perfection in which the integrated divine is once again the equal of the aboriginal unfallen divine, the depth narrative meaning suggests a more dynamic view in which the perfection of the recovered divine exceeds the fracturable perfection of origin (*GL2*, 41, 58-9), and in consequence suggests serious compromise to the axiom of divine impassibility. This is so because the non-divine of which pathos can be predicated is not a different ontological reality than the divine perfection of origin, but the divine in the form of antithesis. Counterintuitively then, for Balthasar, as for Irenaeus, classical Valentinianism commits itself at least inchoately to a developmental and agonic view of the divine. This says more about the true nature of Valentinianism than a dualistic anthropology which whatever its particular features, fits fairly well into the governing dualistic assumptions of the Hellenistic world when it comes to an understanding of human being. It is possible, as the eminent scholar of Gnosticism, Hans Jonas, suggests, that Valentinianism may better be described as a form of dialectical monism than as a species of dualism.[60]

This reading of Valentinianism which, as both the *Lectures on the History of Philosophy 2* and the *Lectures on the Philosophy of Religion* evinces,[61] and as Hegel himself shares, helps the case for positing continuity between classical Valentinianism and Hegel. For at least some of the more obvious differences between narrative ontotheologies of the Hegelian stripe and classical Valentinian narratives can be accounted for by pointing to Hegelian thought as the fully explicit and fully appropriated commitment to a dramatic and developmental view of the divine that is inchoate in classical Valentinianism, and which is stoutly resisted by Irenaeus. Balthasar succeeds, then, in removing an important objection about material continuity between Valentinian and Hegelian narrative renditions, and suggests that continuity is envisagable, even if difficult to track. But, of course, there lies the rub. How are we to track continuity? What kind of continuity is consistent with pointing to significant material differences in narrative that reflect the different fields of Hellenistic and modern discourse? Answering these questions involves going beyond Balthasar, although not in a way that is unfaithful to him. In particular, such supplementation awaits notice of what Balthasar takes to be defining of Hegelianism, and more specifically in what way it distorts the biblical narrative. It also awaits treating the challenge to 'Valentinian repetition' supplied by historicists in general, and Blumenberg in particular,[62] who would claim that Hegel's specifically modern commitment to kinesis and history separates him from classical Valentinianism, just as it separates him from Aquinas. The questions that remain unresolved, or untried, in Balthasar's own texts point to a central conundrum: the question of the status of Balthasar's genealogical or counter-genealogical proposals, and not simply his 'Gnostic' hypothesis. I will deal with some of these issues at the conclusion to Part 1 and briefly revisit them in Part 2 after I have completed treatment of Balthasar's material resistance to the substance of Hegelian ontotheology. I turn now, however to the fourth, and final counter-genealogical stroke operative in Balthasar's complex account of Hegel's ancestral discourses.

(4) Apocalyptic Genealogy: For Balthasar, authentic, that is, biblically saturated, Christianity is defined by '*Apokalypsis*,' a disclosure to a contemplator who is precisely not a spectator, who rather is radically involved in a seeing that finally is more an acceptance of being seen than a seeing which commands reality as it commends itself. In this sense, for Balthasar, as perhaps also for Marion somewhat later in his expostulations on the notion of icon,[63] John and Paul are regulative.[64] Of course, this view of Christianity as the definitive form of apocalypse, because regulated by Christ as the definitive form of divine disclosure, is not the issue of a single statement of scripture, but the fruit of a proper exegesis of the Gospels as they find their center of gravity and integration in the Gospel of John (*GL1*, 10; *GL6*, 19). Interestingly, given the reservations expressed in *Glory of the Lord* about apocalyptic as a genre of biblical literature (*GL6*, 321-4, 342-3), Balthasar begins the substantive

theological investigation of *Theo-Drama* (*TD4*, 15-61) with a reading of Revelation that understands it to depict the stage of divine and human interaction precisely as action, as well as the script within which the drama of salvation unfolds. History is a drama between infinite freedom and finite freedom, a drama of refusal as well as acceptance, in which God remains faithful and sends the Lamb who is crucified on our behalf. The paschal lamb is at the center of a liturgy that is historical and cosmic, but which has a trans-historical and trans-cosmic reference. Read in this way, Revelation is not fully continuous with modalities of inter-testamental forms of apocalyptic literature which suffer from an excess of curiosity precisely in proportion to the experienced loss of divine presence. Rather it is authentically Johannine, and constitutes a genuinely biblical and ultimately genuinely Christian apocalypse.

Balthasar's defense and rehabilitation of biblical apocalyptic is one of the most surprising features of his thought, and we will comment on it voluminously in Part 4. Notwithstanding this, in general Balthasar shows significant distrust for apocalyptic as a biblical genre, and even greater suspicion of post-biblical modes of apocalyptic thought. In *Apokalypse*, for example, if brands of thought as different as Nietzsche's and Schiller's are lumped together as forms of apocalyptic, there is a special emphasis on the radical eschatological thrust of Hegel's thought and that of his successors. In its discussions of Hegel and his non-theological and theological successors alike, *Theo-Drama* appears genealogically to annotate this judgment by pointing to the 13th-century heterodox apocalyptic thinker, Joachim de Fiore (*TD3*, 45, 400; *TD4*, 446, 458-9; *SI*, 4-5). Balthasar finds the template for the basic lines of his analysis of the Joachimite inspiration of Hegel's thought, and thus derivatively of various important modes of contemporary thought, in Henri de Lubac's *La postérité spirituelle de Joachim de Flore*.[65] Without reproducing, or even attempting, anything like the comprehensive account of the filtering of Joachimism from the Reformation offered by de Lubac,[66] Balthasar points to some of the basic marks of Joachimite repetition in Hegelian discourse. Most obviously, Hegelian discourse recalls the horizontalization of salvation history, in which the immanent Trinity tends to be reduced to the conditions of the economy that in classical Trinitarianism exhibits rather than defines it (*TD3*, 400, 512; *TD4*, 428, 446). Of course, Hegelian discourse also recalls Joachim in making the Christ event penultimate rather than ultimate, and relativizing the New Testament, indeed the canon as a whole. Effectively, Hegel's Joachimite predilections dictate that Christ comes to be considered a symbol of a generic divine-human union rather than the sacrament of salvation. Moreover, Balthasar sees in a particularly acute way the evacuation of the specifically Catholic substance. Casualties of Hegel's pneumatic displacement from Christ include the Church as the Church founded on Christ, the Church as institution, and the sense and validity of the sacraments (*TD3*, 400; *TD4*, 458). The price, for Balthasar, is exorbitantly high, and Christianity, and especially Catholicism, should be loath to pay it. Balthasar is totally aware that the pneumatic shift is not only a characteristic of Hegelian thought. In a way that Möhler grasped with exceptional acuity, and to which Balthasar avers more than once in *The Office of Peter*,[67] this does little more than explicate the Protestant principle which insinuates itself in modernity in its incomprehension regarding the claims made on behalf of the church. Pneumatic shift is a widespread and continuing cultural and social phenomenon that does not require an account of its Joachimite and/or Hegelian provenance. Even granting this, however, it is important not to ignore the Joachimite and Hegelian factor. It is Hegelian thought that not only avers the Protestant principle, but accounts for it in terms redolent of Joachim de Fiore and argues for its validity, indeed, on its own terms demonstrates its validity.

Contemporary theological validation of Joachim in thinkers such as Moltmann confirm, for Balthasar, their deep ties to the Hegelian tradition, and justify questioning the ecclesial usefulness of their theology. Here, as with de Lubac, substantively Balthasar takes his stand with Aquinas and Bonaventure against Joachim,[68] who are similarly exercised by Joachim's perceived displacement of the authority of Christ and church as institution. Much more can and will be said about Balthasar's Thomistic and Franciscan patrimony in Part 4. From a genealogical point of view, however, it is Staudenmaier who provides the genealogical paradigm for both de Lubac and Balthasar. Although Staudenmaier implicates Hegel in the Gnostic and Neoplatonic traditions, he also views Hegelianism as a recrudescence of Joachimism that should be combated.[69] Balthasar, after de Lubac, is aware that the issue does not lie solely in the basic commitments to an unrealized eschatology and the relativity of the Old and New Testament dispensations.

For Balthasar, as for Hegel, but increasingly since the nineteenth century, these hugely important commitments involve exegetical issues. Nowhere is this more evident in Balthasar's oeuvre than in *Theo-Drama 5*. Although the precise nature of the exegetical issues, and how they are to be adjudicated, have shifted in the period between Hegel and late 20th-century theologians, something like an anagogic-futural hermeneutic gets legitimated in which the Spirit is honored subjectively as well as objectively over Christ. Now while this most directly affects the status of the New Testament as the *point d'aperçu* for the biblical text, it also affects the Old Testament. And it does so, not simply since surpassing the former implies surpassing the latter, but also because the *raison d'être* for surpassing the New Testament is that it has not sufficiently surpassed the Old Testament depiction of God and specifically of God's relation to humanity in the modes of creation, covenant, law, and concomitantly createdness, fidelity/infidelity, and obedience. In this way, Balthasar sees that if Joachimism is not Marcionite in a straightforward way, it shares common anxieties regarding the Old Testament (*TD4*, 457). Of course, the Marcionite complexion of Joachimism might in the end function as a discrimen between Hegel and Joachim, for Hegel seems to be involved in much more than a derogation of the Jewish aspect of the Christian tradition and an advancing of the more spiritual aspects of the New Testament. Hegel, of course, in his post-Enlightenment situation seems to inhabit such a Marcionite stance, as does much of German and English Romanticism.

But more than this seems to be afoot. Hegel wants not only to downplay the biblical God who is creator and lawgiver, but to reinterpret such a God according to an economy in which evil is necessary, even if in the end it turns out to be more or less a *felix culpa*. This suggests that something more may be afoot in Hegel than in the Enlightenment and the Romantic appropriation of Christianity interested in constructing a form of religion without the sediments of institution, dogmas, or presumptions of a transcendent deity demanding obedience and often sacrifice. Relative to this, Hegelian thought seems to operate on quite a different explanatory level. By and large, rationalist and Romantic appropriations of Christianity were pragmatic: if Christianity as a whole cannot be set aside for reasons of cultural coherence, the perduring value of its symbols and the force of its basic narrative, and the possibilities of transformative effect on the individual and communal plane, much of it can be set aside. What neither offers is a repackaging of Christianity, which involves a retelling of the entire biblical narrative, a considered reinterpretation of its basic symbols, a reinterpretation of Christian practices that involve a change of fundamental priorities. Granted the difficulties of thinking of some Enlightenment forms and Romantic forms of Christianity as 'Marcionite,' it is quite clear that if there is an ancient model for Hegelian-style apocalyptic, it is neither genuine biblical apocalyptic, nor the Marcionism that Irenaeus tendentiously outed as 'gnōsis.'

The Supplement of Theory

Obviously, the multiplicity of Balthasarian counter-genealogical schemes in which Hegelian discourse is plotted raises questions about redundancy and overkill. More importantly, however, the multiplicity raises the question of the status of these counter-genealogical schemes: whatever Balthasar's intention, do these schemes function rhetorically or conceptually? Put more specifically, do these counter-genealogical schemes mainly function to dissuade us against accepting Hegelian thought as a legitimate Christian specimen by persuading us that it drinks from a variety of poisoned wells? Or do these counter-genealogical schemes together explain the genesis of Hegelian discourse which would judge Christian discourse to be superannuated (See *TD4*, 457)?

It is not difficult to bring in the verdict that as deployed by Balthasar the counter-genealogical schemes function rhetorically. In a game of essentially outbidding Hegel on his own geneaological ground, they opportunistically serve to undo the authority of Hegel's philosophical-theological discourse by pointing to sources to which his discourse is reducible. Moreover, all four of these lines of thought are either metaphysically suspect because they compromise the *analogia entis* and represent a Promethean escalation of selfhood with a consequent immanentization of reality, religiously suspect in that they offer deformed versions of biblical Christianity as this has been plurally – yet coherently – rendered throughout the mainline Christian tradition. Most likely they are both. An important feature of Balthasar's style of counter-genealogy lies in the appeal, implicit and explicit, to the history of Hegel interpretation and critique in which genealogical and counter-genealogical construction is prominent. As I have already indicated, Balthasar has ready at hand 19th-century genealogical (e.g. Baur) and counter-genealogical (e.g. Staudenmaier) discourses that depict Hegel variously as the completion of Neoplatonic or Gnostic modes of thought, as well as accounts that construe Hegel even more narrowly as the realization of Eckhartian thought (e.g. von Baader, Baur). In addition, available from the nineteenth century also are a variety of counter-genealogies that plot Hegel in the pneumatic eschatological tradition of Joachim de Fiore, a plotting that is articulated in the twentieth century by Henri de Lubac in much greater detail and with considerably greater depth of analysis.

While the number of counter-genealogical schemes deployed is not absolutely decisive in judging that Balthasar's counter-genealogies are rhetorical rather than conceptual, without strong evidence that Balthasar is sensitive to the issues of the conceptual boundaries of 'Gnostic,' 'Neoplatonic,' or 'apocalyptic,' and how these together are supposed to determine Hegelian discourse, the plurality of counter-genealogical schemes points in this direction. I will address the issue of sensitivity to conceptual boundaries in due course. At this juncture, however, I want to put on record that even considered as functioning merely rhetorically, the plurality of counter-genealogical schemes is subject to constraints. (i) Typically, in Balthasar's texts the counter-genealogical schemes are not laid side by side for examination. Given the opportunistic nature of counter-genealogy, in different texts of Balthasar Hegelian discourse is plotted onto a particular blighted line of discourse on the basis of metaphysical or theological deficiencies that are of specific concern to the Swiss theologian. The reader does not take in the plurality and variety of these counter-genealogical schemes at a glance.

(ii) For the sake of rhetorical effectiveness the number of counter-genealogical schemes is in any event small. Should the plurality be brought together in and through interpretation, the number cannot be so large as to discourage taking any counter-genealogical scheme seriously. (iii) While counter-genealogical schemes can be in tension with each other, they cannot be incompatible. For example, neither 'Neoplatonic' nor 'Gnostic' genealogical attribution is incompatible with 'post-Romantic aesthetic' attribution. On the one hand, 'post-Romantic aestheticization' is at least in part a culture-history label, whereas the others are more nearly taxonomic in that they are concerned with the basic structure (narrative) of Hegel's discourse. On the other, without contradiction Hegel's discourse could give evidence of all three, indeed equally of all three. Similarly, 'apocalyptic' attribution is not incompatible with any or all of the above attributions, since Hegel's discourse could plausibly show evidence of 'apocalyptic' inflection as well as evidence of the three other inflections. Since genealogically inflection amounts to infection, one is talking, then, of a singularly sick discursive specimen to avoid culturally and theologically resist.

Again it should be reminded that Balthasar does not go where ideally a genealogist of the haunting of modern discourse would go. He is satisfied continually to test Hegel's discourse against the discourse or discourses of the theological tradition; he is content to make particular judgments about what ancient discourse is responsible for the eccentricity of Hegel's theological orbit. Admitting then that as it stands the status of Balthasar's counter-genealogies is rhetorical and not conceptual, is there any way in which Balthasar's counter-genealogies can be conceptually validated or redeemed? I enter two caveats, however, even as I raise the question. First, it is not my intent to address this question fully in this chapter. What I say is quite provisional, and requires the two chapters of Part 2 for its full context. Second, and more importantly, there are advantages as well as disadvantages to genealogical and counter-genealogical constructions that do not rise to the level of theory. Needless to say, the advantages of a rhetorical genealogy in part at least reflect the generic disabilities of theory. While theories demand much greater consistency and possess considerably greater alethic potential, their very virtues expose them to the temptation to sacrifice richness and unruly detail to the attractive clarity of reductionistic explanation. Thus, if it is important not to underestimate the value of theory, it is equally important not to overestimate it as well. The danger is that what is from a theological point of view very much secondary will usurp the place of what is primary.

In the large scheme of things, theology is more nearly the exercise of judgment regarding what sets of beliefs, what narratives, and practices can safely be embraced by the community as 'Christian' and what cannot. Only exceptionally does theology engage in the business of providing criteria as to what is or is not legitimately Christian, and present a theory whereby we can map different forms of deformation alongside the chart of the emergence and preservation of ideas, practices, and forms of life that are taken to constitute the Christian tradition. This is not to say that either the criteriological or genealogical enterprise lies outside the domain of a theologian in principle, and especially of the modern theologian. As a modern Europeanly situated theologian, Balthasar feels that he has to engage in both enterprises. At the same time, no more than Barth does he think that this is the primary task of the theologian. What is primary is the celebration of the trinitarian God who has saved us through his overwhelming love made present in Christ, a celebration that has practical as well as contemplative dimensions, and expresses itself in a splendid variety of forms of life all of which are in the last instance modes of worship, even those that involve care of bodies and souls of Christians and non-Christians. For Balthasar, the specifically genealogical or counter-genealogical task, while not an *adiaphora*, belongs decidedly to the second-place. The more pressing matter of reminding the Church of the multitude of cultural and discursive temptations practically speaking makes theory something of a luxury. Theory as such is not prohibited, but its exercise presupposes concrete acts of diagnosis of would-be Christian discourses, or discourses supposedly sympathetic to Christianity.[70]

Another advantage of a more nearly rhetorical form of genealogy or counter-genealogy is its relative expansiveness and flexibility by comparison with a more conceptual model governed by more explicit or more stringent criteria of inclusion. For instance, operating within a more nearly rhetorical mode of genealogy it is possible to include under the rubric of 'Joachimite apocalyptic' not only Hegel but also his left-wing successors such as Feuerbach, Marx, and Ernst Bloch. And though Balthasar does not speak very precisely to the issue, perhaps it is worth raising the question whether 'Joachimite apocalyptic' includes the apocalyptic of Walter Benjamin and the negative dialectics of Adorno, which Balthasar sees as anti-Hegelian discourses. Of course, at the very minimum, one would have to pay attention both to the fact that these thinkers articulate a much less utopian form of apocalyptic that is extraordinarily ascetic in its epistemic claims. Of course, one might have to do considerably more. While I address the issue in some detail in Part 4, my only point here is that any genealogical attribution can be fairly loose, and usefully repress distinctions that can be made. In certain circumstances it might not be ecclesially important to distinguish modes of apocalyptic from the discourses of the church, apocalyptic or otherwise, since both are in the business of offering alternatives to the biblical narrative, the meaning of its basic symbols and practices, and both are preoccupied with suggesting either new forms of life or revising the interpretation of old ones. Again, operating within a rhetorical style genealogy, it is open to the genealogist to suggest that wherever in contemporary theology nature and human being are posited not so much as images of God but as constitutive of the divine, then this theology finds its ultimate ancestry in strands of Neoplatonism that can variously be identified as Eckhartian, Brunan, and Proclean. An obvious case for such inclusion would be Hartshornian and Whiteheadian forms of process theology. But Moltmann, who pledges some fealty to such a position, and a feminist such as Sallie McFague might be included. Finally, of course, given the general intuition of comprehensive and intensive deformation of biblical narrative, it is possible to include under 'Valentinianism' not only Hegelianism and its immediate German and North American offshoots, but possibly forms of Christianity overdetermined by Jungian psychology, a transgressive style of literary criticism (e.g. Harold Bloom),[71] and examples of postmodern thought such as that of Mark C. Taylor that are self-consciously anti-Hegelian,[72] but which promote a simplification and reinterpretation of the Christian narrative.

Confessing then the luxury of theory, my question is whether Balthasar's genealogical or counter-genealogical rhetoric provides the bases for a modification that would qualify it as theory. Now while this more theoretical or conceptual model could not go under the banner of Balthasar's name, it can be called 'Balthasarian' in that it extrapolates from, as well as offers a supplement to, Balthasar's more rhetorically aspirated genealogical discourse. Addressing this question even in a provisional way demands an inventory of the factors that inhibit and/or promote the move from rhetoric to concept. I begin with the former, which underscore the very obvious gap. Most of the inhibiting factors have been laid down already, since what makes Balthasar's actual model rhetorical is what leaves it conceptually underdetermined. Although, as I have implied, conceptual determinacy is not automatically ruled out in a situation of multiple counter-genealogical attribution, the risk of categorial fuzziness is significant when one suggests that a discourse is simultaneously 'Neoplatonic,' 'Gnostic,' and 'apocalyptic.' What I would add to this is the observation that the risk is magnified when in the manner of a Staudenmaier and an Eric Voegelin, Balthasar suggests that Joachimite eschatology and Valentinian speculation are both species of 'gnosis' (*SI*, 4-5). For now differences between Valentinian speculation which represents, according to Balthasar, a total mimicking of the biblical narrative,[73] and second-order forms of biblical apocalyptic such as Joachim's radically eschatological theology of history, are ignored and different 'apocalypse' forms collapsed. As I will underscore shortly, Balthasar can be read as intimating a relation between apocalypse discourses that only becomes apparent in thinkers like Hegel, yet in conflating distinct genres of narrative discourse Balthasar risks compromising both his genealogical claims about Hegelian discourse and a taxonomic reading that recognizes signs that betray very distinct brands of apocalypse discourse present in post-Enlightenment discourses of a speculative vintage.

If categorial fuzziness functions to inhibit the possibility of conceptual rendering of Balthasar's complex counter-genealogical construction, there are, however, offsets that more than compensate for it. I wish to underscore in particular an implied hierarchy between Balthasar's counter-genealogies, with the advantage going in the last instance to Gnosticism or Valentinianism. The priority of 'Gnostic' over 'Romantic aesthetization' lies in large part in the advantage of a genealogical category over a category of cultural history. Categories of cultural history are completely time-bound in a way the categories of genealogy are not. The point of genealogy after all is to disrupt the idea of dividing history into distinct periods that follow each other sequentially and which, from an analytic point of view, forms a self-enclosed whole. Genealogy suggests that history does not permit self-contained epochs which are explicable largely in terms of themselves, but which suppose what has gone before as an efficient cause. As I have indicated more than once already, genealogy is a discourse of haunting, thus essentially a hauntology. The genealogical battle as such, then, is between 'Gnosticism,' 'Neoplatonism,' and 'apocalyptic.' The relative priority of Valentinianism over Neoplatonism of an Eckhartian, Brunan, and Proclean stripe and Joachimite apocalyptic rests on two factors: first, the perceived level of threat with respect to biblically normed Christianity and, second, the ability of a genealogical category to account for the scope and level of integration or deviation from mainline Christianity evident in Hegel's dramatic narrative of a divine that gains itself only through trauma and loss.

For Balthasar, the seriousness of the Neoplatonic threat to biblically normed Christianity cannot be overstated. A consistent theme in Balthasar's patristic recovery is the issue of whether, and if so where and when, Christianity is compromised in its negotiation with Neoplatonic thought.[74] In continuity with major patristic writers both East and West, Balthasar does not abjure the risk of negotiation. Indeed, against any and all advocates of the 'Hellenization of Christianity' hypothesis, Balthasar validates negotiation when the aim is to adopt non-Christian culture to Christian principles. Balthasar is also aware that negotiation is a practice as old as the New Testament itself, but that it is reflectively warranted in the ancient Christian tradition. Christian principles, ultimately grounded in Christ as Word, are replete, and show their plenitude in their ability to assimilate and transform non-Christian culture to which they do not bear an antithetical relation given the internal link between creation and redemption. Balthasar understands that it is Augustine who most forthrightly points to Christianity's demonstration of power in making all would-be alien cultures a *spolatio Aegyptorum*. Balthasar, however, recognizes well that there are failures as well as successes in negotiation, and that even in the case of the latter, success is rarely absolute. Still, Balthasar does not believe that Neoplatonism is constitutively a problem for Christianity. From the very outset of his career Balthasar recognized that all forms of Platonism and Neoplatonism present challenges as well as opportunities for Christian assimilation. Origen, for example, is caricatured if he is regarded reductively as a Platonist, but there are Platonist elements that are not sufficiently transformed in a theology which if speculative at some points is fundamentally biblical and ecclesial.[75] In addition, Gregory of Nyssa in Balthasar's early judgment is at crucial moments not as critical of the implications of the borrowed 'Platonic' discourse as he might be, especially when it comes to the doctrine of God and the view of human being as a knower.[76] With this general reservation attending real appreciation of the gift to Christianity provided by Platonism and Neoplatonism, in the trilogy it is notable that Balthasar confines his reservations to the Proclean, Eckhartian, and Brunan varieties. Even here in the most glaring instances of compromise of the would-be regulative Christian host, Balthasar suggests the specifically Christian element is not totally vitiated. Balthasar's treatment of Pseudo-Dionysius and Meister Eckhart shows this with particular eloquence.[77] While it goes beyond Balthasar's explicit statements, it is possible to infer that the transgressive and metamorphic capability of even the most Christianly corrosive brands of Neoplatonism is not absolute. Particular varieties of Neoplatonism can and do affect negatively the biblically normed Christianity that engenders and shapes specifically Christian forms of life, but clearly not to the extent demonstrated by Valentinianism which, in line with Irenaeus, Balthasar takes to represent the intentional and comprehensive deformation of the biblical narrative of God who reveals who he is in salvation history.[78] This difference is important. As we will see in the next two chapters, Balthasar judges, and in significant part demonstrates, that Hegel's discourse represents not a partial but a total transformation of Christianity, indeed nothing short of the generation of a Christian simulacrum, which bears more than a family resemblance to the Valentinian constructions critiqued by Irenaeus in *Against Heresies*.

The dominance-recessiveness relation between Gnosticism and apocalyptic is considerably more difficult to adjudicate, and not simply for the reason that, as stated earlier, Balthasar tends to blur the boundaries of related but distinct genres of apocalypse discourse. With de Lubac, Balthasar thinks of radically eschatological forms of Christianity as posing a widespread threat to Christianity in the modern period. In a hyperbole intended to awaken us to the dimensions of the threat, he avers at one point that the followers of Joachim are as numerous as the sands on the seashore (*TD4*, 446; *SI*, 5). Following de Lubac in exposing the Joachimite infiltration in Hegel, Balthasar exceeds him in problematizing its effects in Hegel's theological successors, and especially in Jürgen Moltmann. In the final analysis, however, for Balthasar, neither in the case of Hegel nor his successors does the eschatological torquing of Christianity define their respective discourses. Radical eschatological versions of Christianity such as Joachimism distort key structural elements of the biblical narrative, but not all of them (nor any of them absolutely radically). The christological and the pneumatological dimensions of the biblical narrative, and their relation, are read contrary to the received tradition in which Christ continues to be normative and the Spirit is always the Spirit of Christ. In addition, the definition of the institutional Church as the sacramental locus of Christ as well as the authentic teaching authority is emended and pushed in a more charismatic direction. It matters little whether the charismatic is mystic, monk, the Hegelian sage who deals in retrospect rather than prospect, or the critic of the body political and church structures. Nevertheless, in principle, and sometimes in fact, this apocalyptic form of Christianity can leave intact the specifically trinitarian and protological dimensions of the biblical narrative. Although I will have much more to say on this matter in Part 4, forms of apocalyptic such as that of Joachim, in continuity with the book of Revelation, which is the biblical text that commands his attention, and in continuity with Augustine who makes Revelation an object of reflection in Books 20-22 of *De Civitate dei*, do not necessarily question the standard view of the incommensurability between the creator and the created, nor deny that the triune God is the sovereign Lord of history. Given Balthasar's assessment that the disturbance of both the trinitarian and protological dimensions of the biblical narrative is especially marked in Hegel, as we will see shortly (Part 2), and conspicuous enough in a successor such as Moltmann to justify critique (Part 3), ultimately one can say that there exists in the trilogy a general tendency towards prioritizing the Valentinian genealogy or counter-genealogy over apocalyptic.

I would argue, therefore, that in the final analysis significant elements in Balthasar's counter-genealogical discourse promote, maybe even provoke, theory. I have provided an outline of this theory in *Gnostic Return in Modernity*. This theory consists of an explanatory model which has more general and more specific facets. On the more general side, the explanatory model offers a grammatical rather than invariant content account of continuity between ancient examples of Gnosticism or more specifically Valentinianism, which respects the specific contexts of the Hellenistic and the post-Enlightenment fields with their different assumptive sets. Part of the assumptive background of ancient Gnosticism, which it shares with other Hellenistic discourses, is a pessimism with respect to the world in which change for the good is impossible and a default dualism both with respect to world and what transcends it and with respect to the self in its bodiliness, in its desires, in its institutional and ecclesial embodiments. By 'world' is meant not simply the physical stuff of the cosmos, but all that constitutes the domain of the livable and the affirmable space, whether human relations in which selves love and are loved and comprehend each other, whether the social institutions provide meaning and deliver peace, and whether the religions are transparent with respect to truth. By contrast, the assumptive backdrop of post-Enlightenment and also post-critical Hegelianism is a general optimism with respect to the world in spite of the manifest recalcitrance to freedom, a conviction that genuine reciprocity is evident in the world despite the more than occasional horrors of war and persecution enacted on religious as well as non-religious grounds. Not only can progress be made in this world, but progress and development mark the world, indeed, mark it all the more loudly when one pays more than passing attention to what hinders it. In addition, in the kind of narrative we find in a post-Enlightenment discourse – but also post-Romantic discourse – such as that of Hegel, one should not expect to find the kind of dualism that characterizes ancient Gnosticism. Certainly, one should not expect to find the same level of yearning for the 'beyond' as the cure for the 'here' or the 'whither' or 'whence' as the cure for the now. The self is physically, psychically, and socially embodied, and if the institutions of religion can hinder, they can also help, and if the practices and forms of life of Christianity are not obviously transparent of meaning and truth, what is required is a hermeneutic that can extract what is valuable from what is not.

This represents only the most cursory acknowledgment of one of the major differences in context. In fact, it is at once a kind of shorthand and substitute for what would likely be a non-determinate description of what makes the ancient world ancient and the modern world modern. This can hardly be the burden of this book, perhaps even of any single book. Its purpose here is to flag that at a bare minimum any genealogy with the kind of *longue durée* type with which we are dealing will have to acknowledge that differences between ancient and modern discourses are inevitable. The point that I am emphasizing is that while this chastens expectations with respect to continuity, it does not rule them out altogether, especially if one adopts a grammatical rather than content-invariant model. What metamorphic narratives in the ancient and modern periods have in common is that they equally instantiate a 'Valentinian narrative grammar' that encourages great variety in narrative formation both within the Hellenistic field and between the Hellenistic and the modern field.[79] Thus, as a condition of the application of 'Valentinianism' to determinate bands of Hellenistic and Hegelian and post-Hegelian bands of narrative discourse, it is understood that discourses from both eras enact a radical transformation of key features of the biblical narrative such as the vision of the transcendent God, this God's relation to the creator, the nature of creation, Christ, church, and eschatology. Now if post-Enlightenment Valentinian discourses exist, we would expect them to be much more dynamically and monistically aspirated than is the case in Valentinian narratives of the Hellenistic period. But the 'more' here would underscore the point that we are not dealing with an absolute contrast. It would suggest that the modern Hegelian versions of Valentinianism radicalize features such as development and constitutive agon that are more nearly repressed than absent in the classical genres of Valentinianism, such as *Ptolemy's System*, *The Gospel of Truth*, and *The Tripartite Tractate*.[80]

But this is to make a point made at least implicitly by Balthasar himself when he points in *Glory of the Lord* (*GL2,* 39, 42-3) to the doubleness of Gnostic narratives, and Valentinian narratives in particular. As I have indicated already, this doubleness consists essentially in the tension between the apparently circular narrative of the surface of the text, whose ontological implications are both static and dualistic, and the non-circular narrative that functions on the depth level, which is dynamic and basically monistic in that even the throes of matter are expressive of spirit. Although this insight is partly obscured by Balthasar's conventional emphasis upon Valentinian dualism, and by reference to spiritual ill-health summed up in curiosity, his marking of this insight as an enduring contribution of Irenaeus effectively makes Irenaeus more our contemporary than the current guild of scholars who, for all their philological and evaluative scruple, regularly recycle received pieties about ontological dualism and stasis.[81] For in reprising an Irenaean point on the level of hermeneutics and narrative analysis, Balthasar's reading proves much more sophisticated than the careful, microscopic analyses of the texts of Nag Hammadi prosecuted in the name of a science. Unburdened by the demands of theory these practitioners enact a theory about the object of their concern that is positivistic in the extreme.

More specific facets of the theory sketched in *Gnostic Return in Modernity* reflect on: (i) the increased porosity of Valentinian style narrative to non-Valentinian forms of narrative such as Neoplatonism and apocalyptic in the post-Enlightenment field, which, nonetheless, Valentinian narrative regulates; (ii) how these regulated or enlisted Neoplatonic and apocalyptic narratives in turn affect the dominant Valentinian narrative structure and modify such classical Valentinian commitments as a negative view of the order of creation and history, and a negative view of sacrifice and suffering.

With regard to the phenomenon of 'enlisting,' particular attention is paid as to how the Neoplatonic *exitus-reditus* pattern, founded on divine agape, comes to serve a narrative program dominated by the divine's erotic drive towards perfection or self-perfection. Attention is also paid to how apocalyptic emphasis on salvation history and on the Lamb as sacrificed from the foundation of the world is co-opted or 'inscribed' into a dramatics of divine self-development in which sacrifice ceases to be, as in Revelation and the Gospel of John, the expression of a gratuitous love, but becomes an essential element of a narrative economy in which loss pays ontological, epistemic, and existential dividends.[82] In this respect Hegelian and post-Hegelian Valentinianism is not only counter-biblical, but more specifically counter-Augustinian. One way of looking at modern Valentinian forms of thought is to construe them as inverted forms of classic texts of Augustine. Whereas, for example, the *Confessions* describes a movement of the creature's fall and conversion in relation to an absolutely full reality, whose grace abounds, and towards whom the only proper attitude is prayer, Hegelian and post-Hegelian mythological thought is focused on the journey, fall and *conversio* of a God whose movement of development is funded by lack and whose self-referential activity of sundering and integration require the Holocaust of the creature and the world. One can (re)mark a similar inversion of *De civitate dei*. Modern Valentinianism overrides the dialogue of infinite and finite freedom, which in that text is axiomatic, makes creation itself evil, and makes the aporia of evil its own answer since evil becomes the ground of good. One can also see the systemic inversion of *De trinitate*. The more salient elements of this inversion include the immanent Trinity becoming a function of the economic, the notion of person being disqualified, thus leading to a divine that is not triune but rather a triadically-structured divine self-consciousness,[83] and the doxological self being erased as the self is elevated into being a condition of the divine both in terms of its actuality and its self-consciousness.

With regard to the reflexive affect and effect of enlisted narratives, I reflect specifically on how in its enlisting of Neoplatonic narrative, Hegelian developmental erotics acquires the appearance of agape, sufficient to give the illusion that Hegel belongs in the same company as a philosopher-theologian such as Bonaventure. Again, attention is paid to how apocalyptic discourse circulates within the enframing Valentinian discourse, and especially on how its validation of history as the history of salvation effects a massive horizontalization or 'distention' of the metamorphic Valentinian narrative.[84] Here once again, the point is not purely analytical. Reflection on how apocalyptic discourse distends the dominating Valentinian narrative helps us to understand how the presence of these discourses and their more hospitable relation to biblically normed Christianity functions to disguise the truly radical metamorphosis of Christianity prosecuted by Hegel and his successors, but perhaps also by precursors such as Jacob Boehme.[85]

This intense and interested counterfeiting of biblically normed Christianity makes Hegel look much more of an ally to Christianity in modernity than the Enlightenment which subjects Christianity to withering critique when it is not enjoining forgetfulness. This makes Hegel and Hegelianism all the more dangerous. A truly adequate postmodern form of Christian thought and Christian life sees through a simulacrum that is 'post-Christian.'[86] If the epochal suggestion here is basic, Balthasar's label of 'post-Christian' is not focused exclusively on a genetic account. As his texts make clear, 'post-Christian' applies to classical varieties of Gnosticism. Here Balthasar may very well take Irenaeus at his word concerning the *gnostikoi*'s importation of a pre-Christian form of thought which then sets to rework the biblical narrative. In this sense, Gnosticism is constitutively 'after,' because it presupposes a discourse and a faith that serves as material for its act of usurpation

In his counter-genealogical strikes against Hegel, Balthasar draws attention to, but leaves uncommented on, a number of significant difficulties regarding his counter-genealogical deployment of the notions of 'Neoplatonism,' 'Gnosticism,' and 'apocalyptic.' While in his defense this is hardly unusual, nonetheless, the question naturally emerges when one talks about the repetition of these discourses in Hegel, or particular versions of them, whether one is talking about content-invariant continuity or something much weaker, something like family resemblance. It is difficult also to repress the question whether Hegel repeats these discourses equally or whether one is dominant and how this dominance gets enacted. To handle these questions and others like them demands what I have referred to as the supplement of theory. The most important concept in a theory of the repetition of ancient discourses in German Idealism, or for that matter in any post-Enlightenment discourse, is that of 'narrative grammar,' which represents a third option that lies between the extremes of positing a content-invariant continuity of narrative and suggesting nothing more than family resemblance. While the concept can be used to talk about the perdurance of Neoplatonic and apocalyptic narratives in post-Enlightenment discourses, and especially in German Idealism, my focus has been on 'Valentinian narrative grammar,' since Balthasar provides significant evidence that the problem with Hegelianism is that it represents a comprehensive and distorting mimicking of the entire biblical narrative. As for the issue of whether this dominance should be assessed in quantitative or qualitative terms, we resolutely chose the latter. We do so based both on hints provided by the way in which in the Hellenistic environment Valentinian narratives can include these other narrative discourses, as well as the post-structuralist concept of 'overdetermination,' which proposes to think of the dominant as that which regulates the other elements within a field, each of which supplies partial explanations. In extending Balthasar, I speak of the Valentinian element in Hegel's discourse 'enlisting' or 'inscribing' the two others. This 'enlisting' or 'inscribing' helps to fashion a mode of Valentinianism which at once looks more like standard Christianity, while also being less modernly objectionable, in that it is more history and time friendly, and more developmentally inflected. Hegelian speculation seems neither to be out of joint with traditional Christianity, nor fighting against the fundamental assumptions of the post-Enlightenment age.

The benefits of providing a genealogical supplement to Balthasar here are enormous. One obvious benefit is to move Balthasar beyond the limits of 19th-century counter-genealogy in which if all of Balthasar's basic insights are circulating, the fundamental questions are not getting asked. Coming from just the opposite side, there is also the benefit that Balthasar represents a real alternative to the theory of Hans Blumenberg, which forbids talking about a post-Enlightenment discourse as if it were a metamorphic form of an ancient discourse, and logically therefore should rule out 'Neoplatonism' and 'Gnosticism' as being continued in any way in German Idealism. In fact, this is, indeed, Blumenberg's official position, and is put forward in *The Legitimacy of the Modern Age*. This embargo, however, seems to be contravened by Blumenberg himself in *Work on Myth* in which he tends to think of the *theopoiesis* of Hegel's and Schelling's divine as 'Gnostic' in a fundamental way.[87] Blumenberg gives an example of a thinker who does not seem to be able to do without the ghosts of things past that he has already insisted cannot appear. And perhaps this failure points to the value of the kind of counter-genealogy of Balthasar, who presupposes continuity, but cannot explain the mechanism.

Concluding Remarks

THIS CHAPTER SHOWED THAT AN IMPORTANT SUBTEXT of Balthasar's trilogy is his engaging Hegel on the level of genealogy. For Balthasar, it is necessary that the discourses of the Christian West be rescued from a genealogical scheme that ablates and depotentiates them, and refuses to think of the interdependence of art, religion, and philosophy as a condition of their independence. But it is equally, or even more important, that the Christian appeal of Hegel's own thought be damaged by looking closely at its pedigree and tracing it back to its origins. As we saw, these origins are plural: and either are intrinsically hostile to the biblical narrative or in certain intellectual environments will prove to be so. Counter-genealogy is a form of strong reading in which Hegelian thought is defined in terms other than its own discourse and its account of the conditions of its genesis. A strong reading of Hegel is necessary, however, for a number of reasons. First, Balthasar understands with Kierkegaard and Catholic theologians of the nineteenth century that Hegel will either explain or be explained. Moreover, this kind of reading is strategic and limited, that is, it is engaged in only to the extent to which Hegelian thought pretends to be a continuation by other and better means of the theological and not simply the philosophical tradition. Were Hegel not thought to bring faith and reason together rather than separate them, and were he not thought to indemnify the symbols of the Trinity and the incarnation, then Hegel would not be the theological threat that he is, although by the same token neither would he be a philosopher from whom theology can get much assistance. Second, this strong reading, strictly speaking, represents in the first place a redirection of the violence enacted in Hegelian interpretation against scripture, which is deprived not only of normative status but ultimately of its role of source for all that is Christianly avowed and justified, and in the second place a redirection of the violence expressed against the theological tradition, which is affirmable precisely to the degree to which it allows itself to be revamped *in toto*. Third, Balthasar can be understood to turn the energy of repression enacted in Hegelian thought against itself in a sort of cathexis. In his *Lectures on the History of Philosophy* and in *Lectures on the Philosophy of Religion* Hegel surprisingly recalls Neoplatonism and Valentinianism. Undoubtedly, the purpose is the critical one of showing that there is another way of doing philosophical and theological business than has been envisaged by the Enlightenment, by fideism, and Kant in his demands that Christianity be practically translated. Still, given Hegel's dialectical-historical account of both the emergence and development of religious and philosophical thought in which his own thought is conceived as the apex of both, Neoplatonism and Gnosticism are necessarily buried in the past and thus cannot be regarded as warping Hegelian thought. In short, the developmental dialectic in which numerous species of religious and philosophical thought are both links in the chain and various ascending stairs toward absolute knowledge rule out the prospects of them being ghosts. On Balthasar's account, however, Neoplatonism and Gnosticism, and also apocalyptic, can be ghosts, because they cannot be quarantined in the past. Apocalyptic, Neoplatonism and Valentinianism shadow a would-be master discourse that cannot master them. Each haunt it, wound and cut it, especially Valentinianism.

As a genealogist, Balthasar functions, as we have seen, in the rhetorical mode. This means first that Balthasar is more reactive than active. It is Hegel who chooses the genealogical weapon in plotting the developmental line between art, religion, and philosophy, as well as the development within the expression of all three discourses: in the case of drama, specifically a development that sees the gradual replacement of plot by character and a gradual deepening of the self-consciousness and irony with respect to dramatic production; in the case of Christianity a development of the message of Christianity through and beyond its cultural instantiations that achieves its realization, in one aspect, in the Reformation, and in another in the Enlightenment; and the case of philosophy, a development from its magisterial Greek beginnings in which all of reality and its differentiations are articulated, but within an objectivistic framework, which it takes two millennia to replace, and put in place a framework that sanctions the prerogatives of subjectivity. Balthasar's response is to argue against the hierarchical view of the relation between discourses, and to contest Hegel's historical descriptions of their relation as well as Hegel's developmental schema with respect to all three. With respect to Hegel's hierarchy he insists on the space of conversation and dialogue as normative for Christianity and conducive to its integrity and well-being, and, as we drew out in some detail, he offers counterfactuals with respect to Hegel's claim that in terms of discursive authority Christianity so definitely replaces art that Christian art would necessarily be a contradiction in terms. When dealing with the issue of the relation between art and Christianity Balthasar also manages to contest Hegel's normative judgments concerning various species of drama. Relatively speaking, only sketches of the opposition to Hegel's developmental schematics for Christianity are provided. In the case of the former, one could afford to be ascetic, since much of what is said in Parts 2, 3, and 4 by way of what are Christian resources is grist for the mill in terms of a refutation. And with respect to philosophy, it is already evident from the little that we have said about the topic that Balthasar by no means thinks that the turn to subjectivity enhanced philosophy, or that philosophers such as Plato and Aquinas (who is hardly mentioned in Hegel) are mere ingredients in the master-discourse that is the Hegelian system.

Crucially, Balthasar also launches a series of genealogical counter-strikes in which Hegel's discourse is plotted in lines of discourse which, from the vantage point of the mainline Christian tradition, are either problematic or insidious. These emplotments are intended to reveal the true face of Hegelian discourse and remove its Christian mask, which is in the end a '*masque funèbre*.' Of course, the apocalypticism, Neoplatonism, and Gnosticism that interrogation of Hegel's speculative discourse makes visible are not pure repetitions of their pre-modern modes. This is not simply due to the complexity of Hegel's speculative narrative in which at least three discourses make an appearance. More importantly, there is the post-Enlightenment context of Hegel. This means that one understands Hegel's project to be an effort to overcome the Enlightenment's amnesia with respect to the discourses, forms of life, and practices of Christianity, and the non-Christian discourses, forms of life and practice that fructify it, even as one is mindful of the way that Hegel backslides into an Enlightenment world-view, and sanctions its forms of life, and practices. Balthasar's counter-genealogy is prosecuted against Hegel on the basis of this recognition. For Hegel does not and cannot retrieve a pristine form of Neoplatonism, apocalyptic, or Gnosticism. He repeats them, where repetition involves novelty and emendation. Novelty and emendation must be kept particularly in mind when one suggests that Gnosticism may very well be both the integral narrative discourse, as well as one discourse among others, in the complex weave of Hegel's discourse. Admitting that in his genealogy or counter-genealogy Balthasar never adopts a fully consistent stance concerning the priority of the three ascriptions, not to mention actually arguing for the priority; but on the basis of hints, I extrapolated that the basic tendency of Balthasar is towards asserting Gnosticism as the integrating narrative discourse that enlists Neoplatonism and apocalyptic as agents of a transgressive program vis-à-vis the Christian narrative. This can be presented as a result, however, only by moving beyond the level of rhetoric onto the level of theory that can offer an explanation both for the possibility of continuity that does not violate historical specificity and for the overdetermination in the complex narrative manifold of Valentinianism. The explanatory discourse, the outline of which is provided in *Gnostic Return in Modernity*, is necessarily a supplementary discourse, although one faithful to the basic drift of Balthasar's genealogical discourse. Now whatever the merits of a theoretical or conceptual development of Balthasar's genealogy, it should be remembered that justification of both the rhetorical and theoretical models depends on whether apocalyptic, Neoplatonic, and Valentinian discourse can actually be read off Hegel's speculative discourse and the discourses of his theological successors. Without an examination of the substance of Hegel's discourse and that of his followers, we have only touched on the possibility of ascription. Thus Part 1 necessarily points to Part 2, which reviews Balthasar's examination of the substance of Hegelian discourse, as a condition of any genealogical ascription.

It should be clear by now that Balthasar conceives of the enterprise of genealogy as both continuous with heresiological discourse while at the same time being discontinuous with it in being specifically modern. I have spoken already to Balthasar's understanding of Hegel's historical location. He possesses a similar understanding of his own situation in the wake of Hegel and its inescapable complexity. However much a heresiologist like Irenaeus is the pattern for Balthasar's own discourse, the contexts of the operation of genealogical discourses are radically dissimilar. Time is the interval that rules out duplication. Moreover, the non-duplication can be justified on both Irenaean and Balthasarian grounds that the circle is broken, and that the unilinearity of history is of theological significance. In addition, in the modern environment (i) appeals to scripture are necessarily less transparent because of rival interpretive schemes, although not necessarily less assured; (ii) appeals to tradition are less apodictic, since there exists a sense of the plurality and variety of tradition unimaginable to the heresiologists; (iii) while genealogical discourse continues to have ecclesial location, when compared not only with the early heresiologists, but also with a 19th-century figure such as Möhler, who to an extent articulates a mixed discourse, part heresiological, part genealogical, it is not ecclesiastically-focused. Specifically, such a discourse is not invested with institutional authority: it proceeds by persuasion, which if it does not eschew argument, is more nearly characterized as a discourse of unveiling the real narrative face or faces behind the Christian narrative mask.

For Balthasar, challenging misremembering is essential to the contemporary theological task. Challenging Hegelian thought is absolutely crucial, since this discourse represents the most powerful act of misremembering that Christianity encounters in the modern world. Hegelian thought generates nothing less than a simulacrum. This counterfeit is a discourse that houses ghosts and especially the ghost of Gnosticism, which at the same time is a *Doppelgänger.* Still, important as the enterprise is, it is not on a par with the real vocation of the theologian, which is remembering the live voices of the tradition as they witness to the mystery of the triune God revealed in Christ, and as they attest to the logic of love. Balthasar understands this memory of memory and of the primary phenomenon to be creative, to involve a going on that is part of the traditioning process itself. Memory is as such a spiritual practice in Pierre Hadot's sense. Countering misremembering represents a supplement to the primary *ratio* of theological activity. Yet, as a supplement, it is not necessarily a contingent feature of such activity. Genealogy has its own role to play in theology as a spiritual practice.

PART 2

GLORIOUSLY AWRY:

HEGEL'S EPIC DEVIATION

As I have used the term, as enacted by a discourse, 'misremembering' is a false memory: the discourse is at once mindful of a forgetfulness that is both socially and culturally endemic and historically deep, and proposes itself as the overcoming of this forgetfulness on both fronts. The result, however, is a deepening of the forgetfulness that leaves the Enlightenment and its consequences – which are broadly nihilistic – intact. In a quite obvious sense, 'misremembering' deepens forgetfulness by putting out of action the memory of tradition, unraveling its rich tapestry, and by ignoring the polyphony of its voices which admit of no reduction to a unitary vision. By doing so, it raises the challenge of whether and how a postmodern theology is possible. In Balthasar's view it is Hegelian discourse which constitutes the most blatant act of misremembering in modernity, and by doing so refigures and reconstitutes modernity itself. It is precisely his mode of memory or recollection (*Erinnerung*) of Western discourses and his articulation of the relations between art, religion, and philosophy that domesticates Christianity by removing what identifies it objectively and subjectively: on the one hand, the God of incomprehensible and unanticipatable love disclosed in the incarnation, passion, death and resurrection of Christ, and on the other, a defining responsiveness that articulates itself in an attitude of gratitude and praise, in prayer, in discipleship, and in the enacted memory of the eucharist.

Resistance to Hegel then must go all the way down and not simply all the way across; that is, it must expose not only Hegel's squandering of the resources of the tradition, but also his misdescription of the phenomenon that makes memory and misremembering possible. In principle, the exercise of countergenealogy is a discursive practice that touches directly only on the secondary manifestation of the Hegelian system, the way in which it erects a defense of the authority of its discourse, which is putatively self-certifying, by specifying the obsolescence – more or less 'planned' – of the discourses of art and religion and all other versions of philosophy. In the last chapter I detailed the genealogical counterstrikes Balthasar makes against Hegelian genealogy and how these undercut Hegel's procedure of discursive legitimation. It is time, however, to speak to Balthasar's direct confrontation with the substance of Hegelian thought, which constitutes the core act of misremembering of (the phenomenon of) Christianity in its objective and subjective poles. Unavoidably I have touched on elements of this substantive confrontation already. That it is difficult to do more than analytically separate genealogical from substantive discussion is evident in our depiction of Balthasar's countergenealogy. For in plotting Hegel's discourse as the terminal point of various lines of philosophical and/or theological discourses, which from the point of view of mainline Christianity are regarded as thoroughly compromised, Balthasar provides the basic contours of the agon between a discourse, whose pledge of fidelity to the Christian tradition cannot be redeemed, and another, whose pledge can. Nevertheless, Balthasar's attack on the philosophical and theological commitments of Hegel and his contemporary children – particularly his theological children – can be understood outside the context of counter-genealogy, although each of these two different aspects of critique are mutually reinforcing. Both are aspects of misremembering on the other side of the forgetting that provides modernity's very basis. But misremembering is both reaction and superstructure and cannot be dismissed as being merely an accidental feature of modernity. Modernity cannot be named, at least cannot be named properly, outside a misremembering that involves appeal to more ancient discourses that similarly propose their own sacred line of discourse inside or outside the main line of Christian discourse and similarly bend Christian discourse to a narrative program at odds with the 'plain sense' of scripture.[1]

In Part 2 I present the first steps in an extended argument to the effect that in the trilogy Balthasar's encounter with Hegel essentially belongs to the order of confrontation, even if *Auseinandersetzung* with Hegel supposes that the discourses of Balthasar and Hegel share important sympathies and display a number of common features. The qualifier is important in two different but related respects. It grants that there is some basis for readings of Balthasar that consider Hegel's thought to be constitutive of Balthasar's trilogy, while at the same time suggesting that the underlying agreements in fact intensify the opposition and make the disagreements all the more motivated. At the outset, however, I want to underscore the total and constitutive rather than partial and contingent character of this confrontation. This is necessary, since on the basis of overlaps between Balthasar's and Hegel's thought an interpreter might be inclined to ameliorate and to judge the confrontation to be 'more or less' rather than absolute. The problem with the 'more or less' model is double: it suggests that disagreements between Balthasar and Hegel are on the same level as agreements, and that disagreements and agreements sum to a fixed quantity. By contrast, the model of total confrontation, which is endorsed here, supposes that disagreement lies deeper than the agreements, and that these disagreements represent the dynamic organizing forces of both discourses.

It is important to understand that Balthasar's thought belongs to the line of confrontation with Hegel illustrated in modern theology by Barth, and in the nineteenth-century by Kierkegaard.[2] And it is equally, and perhaps even more important to understand that Balthasar's thought links up with a specifically Catholic refutation of Hegel which, if it has contemporary manifestations in the work of Claude Bruaire, Emilio Brito, André Léonard, and Xavier Tillette,[3] also has deep roots in the nineteenth century, with its focal figure being the Tübingen theologian, Franz Anton Staudenmaier (1800-1856). In the second of the two chapters that follow I touch on the theological confrontation between Balthasar and Hegel over a range of theological topics as diverse as Christ, Trinity, theodicy, liturgy and sacrament, the view of human being, and Church. The first of the two chapters, however, organizes its reflections on difference around the issue of the relation of faith and knowledge and the relation of philosophical and theological discourse to the biblical narrative. The depth and range of Balthasar's departures from Hegel on these issues suggest nothing less than that Balthasar can be regarded as the most expressly anti-Hegelian of all contemporary theologians. This is only confirmed when we examine in detail in chapter 3 Balthasar's disciplining of Hegel's christological and trinitarian thought. Of special interest in chapter 2 is the way Balthasar avails himself of the categories of Hegelian aesthetics, especially those of drama and epic, to expose Hegelian thought as a misremembering of the glory of the God revealed in Christ and the doxological subject that is the correlative of this glory, *Kabod* in Hebrew, *doxa* in Greek.

Chapter 2

Toward Substantive Confrontation

Toward Substantive Confrontation

If Balthasar's breaking the spell of Hegel is predicated on a confrontation, which is as intense as it is total, confrontation itself presupposes both points of genuine overlap with Hegel and real influence by Hegel on Balthasar regarding his understanding of the post-Enlightenment situation and his use of aesthetic categories, especially those of literary genre. While it is not only these elements that make Hegel's thought attractive – its Neoplatonic, apocalyptic, and finally Valentinian elements contribute mightily to this – the overlaps between Hegel and Balthasar and the actual influences of Hegel on Balthasar force the question of whether the glamor of Hegel's thought is not in some way deserved. There are a number of features of Hegel's parsing of the nature of philosophy and the relation between philosophy and Christianity that suggest that following Hegel is more nearly positive than negative, his influence more nearly healthy than toxic.

First, there is Hegel's understanding that as with the discourses of art and religion the discourse of philosophy is fundamentally disclosive or epiphanic.[1] This is to take issue with dominant strains in Enlightenment thought which would reduce philosophy to method or procedural rationality. Philosophy delivers on the promise to name what is. Moreover, philosophy is not simply a composite of punctual moments of disclosure and insight, but the movement which intends to articulate the entire domain of the real including the self. At its best, Hegel's holism corresponds to the eros of classical philosophy whose urge for illumination does not stop short of elucidating the entire network of the real and its dynamic processes. Second, although Hegel's own metaphysical articulation proves problematic for Balthasar,[2] Hegel's critique both of the abstraction of the classical metaphysical tradition and its commitment to a static ontology are not entirely misplaced. Hegel's commitment to concreteness in general, history in particular, and his unfolding of the dynamic of Being bear hints of the kind of take on Being as *dynamis* and *energeia* that Heidegger would wish to recover, and that Balthasar in his own way, as illustrated by *Theo-Logic 1*, is prepared to celebrate and not simply second and recommend.[3]

There are two further features of overlap between Hegel and Balthasar with respect to their understanding of philosophy. One of these, and thus the third overall, is Hegel's consistent avowal of the hospitality of philosophy towards Christian discourse. This provides welcome relief from both the hostility of the *philosophes*, as well as the more pervasive implicit accord of separation whose purpose is to protect the integrity of both discourses by suggesting that each is imperial within its own proper domain. A fourth, and final, point of overlap is that Balthasar and Hegel share common ground with respect to the claim that the discourses of religion and philosophy have the same object – broadly identifiable with the true[4] – but render it in different but not necessarily incompatible idioms. Once again, formally speaking Hegel's position is fairly classical. It may very well turn out that materially speaking Hegel's concept of philosophy is fatally flawed – and we will speak to this at the start of the next section – but this identification of the fundamental isomorphism of discourse, predicated on the intimate connection between the discourse of Being and the discourse of God, is not one of them. Unlike Heidegger,[5] then, as Balthasar suggests in *Glory of the Lord* (*GL5*, 572-90) and makes abundantly clear in *Theo-Logic* (*TL1*, 51-2, 57, 101-02; also 230, 237-39), a deep interconnection between *to on* and *to theion* does not necessarily vitiate Hegel's enterprise.[6] If a responsible species of postmodern thought must pronounce on what separates these emphases, it can neither take for granted that these discourses signify different realities, nor summarily call for the abolition of one at the expense of the other.

While the last prohibition is edged against Heidegger's own order of priorities, the prohibition also applies to species of postmodern thought that suggest theology completely trumps or 'evacuates' philosophy.[7] Within a Balthasarian frame of reference to adopt the latter position still would be to move within an essentially Heideggerian economy which, on the basis of the separation of philosophy and Christianity, fundamentally elevates philosophy at the expense of Christian discourse, and arguably elevates specifically 'philosophical' and perhaps also 'aesthetic' practices at the expense of specifically religious practices and forms of life that are doxological in both shape and substance.

At the same time, features of Hegel's understanding of Christianity, and the way this construal of Christianity influences the articulation of Hegelian philosophy, mark Hegel off positively from even the best of Enlightenment thought. Hegel's texts have a visionary – even mystical – quality lacking in most forms of modern Protestant and Catholic thought with their different propensities toward fideism and rationalism. And this vision is truly comprehensive in scope, having in view the entire dynamic enactment of the divine with the cosmos and humanity. While 'speculation' functions usually in Balthasar as a pejorative, especially when used in connection with Hegel, it is not always so. To 'speculate,' to see as in a mirror, need not imply self–referential subjectivity.[8] It can suggest – after Cusanus who for all his difficulties preserving the *analogia entis* is Balthasar's model here[9] – a unique view taken on the whole, not the non-perspectival view that is ultimately licensed by German Idealism. Just as important as the dynamism of the object of vision is its dramatic character. The divine depicted by Hegel is just the opposite of the *deus otiosus*, the idle God who may or may not act in generating an other, but in the event of such an act remains blissfully disengaged. This divine is a divine that relates intimately and essentially to the physical world and the world of human spirit, a divine unsparing in its releasing itself into its other,[10] and sacrificial in losing itself in its other, defined by what is non-spirit and non-life. Indeed, the constitutional relationality of Hegel's divine in fact involves a vulnerability more in line with biblical depiction than with metaphysically oriented renditions of the apathetic God that have been conspicuous both in confessional forms of Christianity and its rationalist alternative (e.g. *TD2*, 9, 49, 62, 72, 105, 120-1, 294-5, 302).

In addition, on the surface at least, Hegel's rendition of Christian thought is profoundly Johannine in its figuration of Christ as the expression of divine love and the cross as the center not only from which this love shines forth, but also the point at which the relation of the divine to world and humanity turns and points towards their divinization. A final commonality, and thus a feature of Hegelian thought that not only is, but also ought to be, appropriated by Christianity, is Hegel's reclamation of the symbol of the Trinity from the desuetude it fell into in the modern period either through intentional marginalization in Protestantism or through the obfuscation in Catholicism resulting from rote repetition of the taxonomic abstractions of Neo-Scholasticism. Balthasar agrees then with a Hegel supporter such as Moltmann in *The Crucified God* and *The Trinity and the Kingdom* and elsewhere that Hegel not only showed that the Trinity functions as the necessary horizon for the redemption enacted through Christ, but also as a necessary horizon for the doctrine of creation and for a perspective on last things. He also agrees with Moltmann that in contradistinction from the main thrust of Protestant thought in the modern period, Hegel presumed that the Trinity provided the horizon for a view of the Church that has experiential and practical as well as theoretical force, and consequently represents a reply to Kant and Schleiermacher that Christian thought should take seriously.[11]

Over and beyond this web of commonalities, which in part makes sense of Hegel's philosophical and theological attractiveness to a Christian theologian in the struggle with the Enlightenment, Balthasar self-consciously continues Hegel's project of steering between the Scylla and Charybdis of the two great defaults in modern Christianity: the one a vacuous fideism consequent to the great divorce between faith and reason which, if completed in the eighteenth century, plausibly has antecedents within 14th- and 15th-century Christian thought and practice;[12] the other, the construction of a rationalist surrogate for religion which empties Christianity of the meaning of its constitutive symbols, especially but not exclusively the incarnation and the cross.[13] Moreover, Balthasar shows no compunction about borrowing categories from Hegel to articulate the whys and wherefores of a vision of the relational divine. Ironically, the critique of both metaphysical and mythological thought prosecuted in the body of *Theo-Drama* is done so under the aegis of the categories of 'epic,' 'drama,' and 'lyric' famously articulated in Hegel's *Lectures on Aesthetics*.[14]

The commonalities between Balthasar and Hegel are sufficiently broad and the borrowings sufficiently nontrivial that they have tempted some commentators on Balthasar, who are interested in the prospects of a specifically postmodern theology, to imagine that Hegel and Balthasar are saved or damned together.[15] As I have indicated already, however, commonalities and borrowings function simply as presuppositions; moreover, presuppositions that ground the argument between Balthasar and Hegel and account for its intensity. Here I focus on the ways in which Balthasar exploits commonalities and even in some cases borrowings from Hegel to specify the fundamental rupture between his avowals on the nature of philosophy, its relation to Christian discourse and practice and those of Hegel. Discussion of rupture on this front, however, functions as a preliminary to the more important theological rupture specified by widely different understandings of the nature of the divine, its relation to world, self, and history, and the nature and meaning of Christ. These are the topics of the next chapter.

All four elements of overlap between Balthasar's and Hegel's view of philosophy and its relation to Christian discourse conceal much more serious disagreements. With respect to the first of the overlaps, while Balthasar agrees wholeheartedly with the epiphanic status of philosophy, for him the Hegelian conception lacks entirely the quality of interruption, the suddenness (*exaiphnes*), that characterizes the best of classical philosophy.[16] If epiphany is defined by interruption, then Hegelian thought belongs more nearly to the order of the steady-state of inexorable progress than the order of 'suddenly.' Moreover, in Hegel epiphany does not merely intend the whole, as is the case in the classical philosophical tradition that is normative for Balthasar, but instead insight is expanded by increments until all of reality is brought into the domain of the concept which forms a circle (*TL1*, 50; also *TL3*, 45; *GL5*, 585). Reaching its ultimate form in the categorial dynamics of the Hegelian system, conceptual discourse is a discourse as recollection and mediation. From Balthasar's point of view Hegel's form of holism respects neither the limits of knowledge, which are ineliminably finite, nor what Heidegger would refer to as the ontological difference between Being and beings. Balthasar advocates in *Theo-Logic* not only that a more appropriate image of truth precisely as unstinting search is the spiral, but also suggests against Hegel that truth does not require infinite articulation in order to be truth, and that Hegel's view of *Erscheinung* offers the outline of a disclosure model of truth that is apt for a finite subject (*TL1*, 65, 88, 138-39, 146, 216-17). Emended under the aegis of the axiom of finitude, Hegel's view is serviceable, but now truth becomes available in the fragment (*TL1*, 127), which becomes a catchcry for the later Balthasar and the title of a small but not uninfluential book.[17] And, of course, the finitude is responsible for the perspectival characterization of truth that contrasts with the view that Hegel elaborates in the *Phenomenology* which demonstrates the sublation of all perspectives in the absolute view (*TL1*, 185-87), which is precisely 'the view from nowhere,' to avail of Thomas Nagel's well-worn locution.

For, as Balthasar elaborates it in both *Glory of the Lord* and *Theo-Logic*, Hegel is not wrong in his critique of pietistic fideism, nor is he wrong in his critique of the kind of negative theology represented by Kant's Romantic successors. For here the area that is confined to 'unknowability' is privative, and thereby fails to articulate anything like a positive sense of mystery as the excess of Being (*TL1*, 9, 37, 40 *inter alia*).[18] For Balthasar, the proper reply to Jacobi and Schleiermacher is not, as Hegel suggests, as early as *Faith and Knowledge* (1802) and as late as the *Encyclopedia of the Philosophical Sciences* (1827), the deletion of everything mysterious.[19] For Balthasar, the proper reply to any and all adoration of the 'Unknown God,' of which there are a variety of species in the Christian tradition,[20] is not self-justifying conceptualism, the articulation of a radical logocentrism, in which nothing is irreducible to meaning. The proper reply, which is at the same time the proper reply to Hegel, involves a redefinition of the really real as excessive, and as such the condition of all being as well as the condition of its discourse. It also involves a truly dialectical view of the relation between unword and word that cannot be conceptually mediated.[21] Balthasar repeats then in significant measure Heideggerian objections to Hegel's thought as enfolding the parousia in which reality is completely given to knowledge (*GL5*, 585, 587-88).[22]

At the same time, Balthasar's objection to Hegel recalls – although it does not exactly reproduce their commitment to apophasis – critiques of Hegelian totalization made familiar by Adorno and latterly by Derrida.[23] Unlike such critics, however, Balthasar sees Hegel as deforming rather than realizing the inclination of classical philosophy. Classical philosophy proposes with respect to reality; it does not dispose. Its most finely articulated conspectus always remains defeatable at the level of experience as well as explanatory coherence. For *pace* Heidegger, classical philosophy is, according to Balthasar, question rather than answer (*TL1*, 23-25, 110-11, 208), quest rather than arrival (*TL1*, 62, 67), exposure to the deliverances of reality rather than mastery (*TL1*, 40) The combatting of Heidegger's view on classical philosophy is carried on throughout *Glory of the Lord*, especially in volumes 1 and 4. I do not need to reproduce the details here, since I treat the matter at some length in the succeeding volume. It does bear mentioning here, however, just how influenced Balthasar is in *Theo-Logic 1* by Przywara's defense and recovery in *Analogia Entis* of a classical philosophical tradition against Hegel, who would retrieve it on terms other than its own, and Heidegger who would wave it away as the primary instance of *Seinsvergessenheit.*

Similarly, the second of the major overlaps functions merely as the foreground of a much more fundamental disagreement concerning the content of philosophical vision. Although Balthasar can affirm the dynamic, vitalist aspiration of Hegelian metaphysics, from the point of view of the classical and medieval traditions he sees that the ultimate inspiration of Hegel's thought is monistic and that it fatally compromises the *analogia entis* (*GL5*, 573-74). This after all was the point at issue especially in the various plottings of Hegel on the same axis as Eckhart, Bruno, or Proclus in *Glory of the Lord 5*. The objection is consistently lodged, and is made with particular force in *Theo-logic*, where continuing to talk of Hegel's compromising of the *analogia entis*, Balthasar complains loudly of the monological nature of Hegelian *Geist* (*TL1*, 229-31; also *TL2*, 48). Of central importance, of course, is the compromise of the distinction between Being as such and beings, which destroys the transcendence of the former and the inalienably gifted difference of the latter. But as the integrity of the latter is compromised, so is the concreteness to which – it turns out – Hegel ultimately is only verbally committed. Much more than Hegel, for Balthasar, a philosopher such as Aquinas is committed to the concrete multiplicity of the world. While Balthasar makes the positive point about Aquinas' essential commitment to concrete multiplicity in *Glory of the Lord 4* (393-412) and validates thereby his Aristotelianism, the contraposition of Hegel and Aquinas occurs in *Theo-Logic*. If the first volume of *Theo-Logic* constitutes essentially a re-reading of Aquinas on truth in line with the kind of reclamation projects of Maréchal, Rousselot, Lonergan, and even Rahner's *Spirit in the World*, which sees transcendence as given in the embracing of multiplicity, it also involves an essential contrast between Aquinas' real commitment to concreteness and multiplicity with the spurious version proposed by Hegel which is ruled by abstraction and effectively erases multiplicity. Given the proximity of the production of *Wahrheit* (1946) and Balthasar's creative retrieval of Maximus, whom early in his career he thought to offer an answer to Hegel,[24] it is safe to assume a close connection in Balthasar's mind between these figures on the responsiveness and responsibility of philosophy. In *Theo-Logic*, Maximus (invisibly) and Aquinas (visibly) function as something of a tag-team to represent a philosophical alternative to the bleeding of the concrete and the multiple that Balthasar thinks is an abiding characteristic of the discourses of modernity, and against which postmodern philosophies with varying degrees of ethical depth and meretriciousness have directed their howls of protest.

For all its sound and fury a 'non-philosophy' is not necessarily a liberating reply. Importantly, in *Theo-Logic 1*, the philosophical answer is but the preliminary to the real answer that must necessarily be theological. The theological answer is in the first instance christological. Etched in Maximus,[25] and developed in a theological figure such as Bonaventure,[26] the answer is that it is precisely in the person of Christ that concreteness and difference are provided their authority. The very unrepeatability of Christ whose person is a function of an irreducible mission grounds the unrepeatability of each human person. Repetition then of Christ is repetition of the unrepeatable, an enactment of receptivity to the who that is being only in becoming. Finally, of course, the theological answer is trinitarian. Given powerful, if different expressions, in Thomas and Bonaventure, as *Theo-Logic 2 & 3* articulate it,[27] it is trinitarian difference, that is, the distance and relation between the hypostases that grounds the concreteness and multiplicity of the world, which although without an immanent ground of synthesis (one way of interpreting Hegel) is not without such a ground in transcendence.

The third major overlap, namely Hegel's and Balthasar's shared view of the intrinsic hospitality of philosophical and religious discourse with respect to each other, again functions as a backdrop for the assertion of difference. As Hegel's discourse actually enacts or effects the intimacy of philosophical and religious discourse, it is evident that the relationship is thoroughly unequal, and that all power of judgment and adjudication is vested in philosophical discourse. In *Glory of the Lord 5* Balthasar remarks on the tyrannical nature of such a discourse that proceeds under the cover of the discourse of Spirit (*GL5*, 574, 579-80). The authority of Christian discourse is essentially undone, and both the form and substance of theological, even aesthetic, discourse get colonized. It is clear to Balthasar that for Hegel the Bible is not scripture, but a culturally important text that has shaped Western consciousness for evil as well as good, even if it remains possible in the modern age – albeit with some difficulty – to save the appearances. The problems with the biblical text are multiverse for Hegel: the texts of the Bible problematically include the texts Christians share with Jews (*GL5*, 579-81), and the so-called 'New Testament' shows the influence of these texts, as it also illustrates a tension between the basic message and life of Jesus and the claims made on his behalf (*GL5*, 583-84). In *Glory of the Lord 5*, Balthasar spends considerable time on the so-called *Early Theological Writings*, presumably with a view to underlining just how consistently aggressive – if not thoroughly transgressive – is Hegel's hermeneutic of the biblical text. Balthasar, obviously, finds the hermeneutic of the New Testament, with its resultant Christology, objectionable: about the former he will have much more to say in *Theo-Drama 2* and about the latter in *Theo-Drama 2 & 3*. But with a treatment of the Old Covenant looming in *Glory of the Lord*, he expresses particular horror regarding the display of vindictive anti-Judaism which sets a new low for German thought of the period.

Although Balthasar is familiar with *Lectures on the Philosophy of Religion* (*GL5*, 584-85), he seems disinclined to look for evidence that Hegel modified his position to any appreciable extent. Hegel's position is taken to be systemic, and Balthasar objects to it as much on grounds of justice as any Hegel critic of the twentieth century, not excluding Rosenzweig and Derrida.[28] But as his treatment of the Old and New Covenant in *Glory of the Lord 6 & 7*, with its Christian and specifically Irenaean view of the relation between Hebrew scriptures and New Testament, makes clear, a principled hospitality towards Judaism is a requirement for the very identity of Christianity that comes with the coherence of the biblical text.

Hegelian takeover of Christian substance is not exclusively invested in a peculiar and particularly unecclesial reading of the biblical text – avowal of fidelity to Lutheranism notwithstanding. Hegel allows, as the Reformers do not, that doctrines need not be distorting, although often they are, as is the case, for example, with the doctrines of sin and Christ, and especially with the Trinity. Doctrines are at the very least intimations of the reflection by the Christian community of the meaning of salvation in history, and are worth the trouble of extracting the intended and legitimate meaning from the all-too-propositional husk that smacks of a deficient view of reason, that is, of *Verstand*. But again, it is philosophy that grants the permission to interpret and is the executor of such interpretation.

Balthasar's critical stance with respect to Hegel's philosophical expropriation of Christianity, which is summed up in the above objections, has a long history in philosophy and theology. Balthasar is aware that in the philosophical arena, Schelling objected to it in Hegel's own day, and that even more famously Kierkegaard did in the immediately following generation. While Balthasar is prepared to grant something to Schelling's positive philosophy by way of rectifying the imbalance (*GL5*, 570-72), he is less persuaded than he was even in *Apokalypse* that Schelling succeeds, or is even capable of succeeding, given that a developmental ontology is dictating to Christian witness (*GL5*, 561). In *Apokalypse 1* Balthasar does not give the 'late Schelling' the kind of leeway typically accorded him in both Catholic and Protestant theological (e.g. Walter Kasper, Wolfhart Pannenberg) circles in the latter half of the twentieth century.[29] Paying more attention to the middle and later works of Schelling than he does in *Glory of the Lord*, Balthasar indicts Schelling for his developmental ontology that is based on the figure of eros as 'poverty.' Even in texts from the very latest period of production such as *Philosophie der Mythologie* and *Philosophie der Offenbarung* (1840-41) (*Apok 1*, 238), Balthasar espies the working of the developmental ontology. From his point of view, therefore, the authority of this ontology is not restricted to the early work, nor does it cease with the *Freedom Essay* (1809) or the *Ages of the World* (1815).

Balthasar essentially side-steps Kierkegaard's critique of Hegel. His familiarity with Kierkegaard is such that this is not because he does not get the point of Hegelian critique, or thinks in principle that Kierkegaard in *Philosophical Fragments* and *Concluding Unscientific Postscript* respectively has not made telling objections against dialectical mediation in the Hegelian system. It is rather that he is unpersuaded about the positives of Kierkegaard's position. Ostensibly, the issue has to do with the lack of a theological aesthetic in Kierkegaard (*GL1*, 40-50), who makes a too unilateral distinction between the aesthetic and religious spheres. But the real issues are either elsewhere, or corollaries of Kierkegaard's interesting but not sufficiently thought through differentiation of spheres. While it would be unfair to say that Balthasar has an allergy to irony, he is made nervous by it, and agrees with Hegel in thinking that irony is a mark of the modern. Thus, although Balthasar would undoubtedly concede the legitimacy of the category of 'Christian irony,' he would wonder whether in the last instance Kierkegaard is not infected by that which he would overcome. The corollaries of the lack of a theological aesthetic are also worrying: the experiential and subjective dimension will be given significant priority over the objective and revelatory dimensions of Christianity. In this situation the status of scripture will remain somewhat ambiguous and that of doctrine even more so. Finally, the very idea of an institutional-historical church will be compromised, and with it the sense of the practices and forms of life that witness and maintain it. It is obvious that these debits put Kierkegaard at a serious Christian disadvantage vis-à-vis Hamann, whom Kierkegaard on more than one occasion insists is his main precursor. Hamann is not plagued by a specifically modern form of irony which evaporates substance. As Balthasar makes clear in *Glory of the Lord 3*, Hamann is the sole Protestant survivor when it comes to a theological aesthetic (*GL3*, 49-53). His irony is non-modern because it is enlisted in the service of a religious form of thought that is aesthetic because deeply biblical (prophetic and apocalyptic), fulsomely doctrinal, and thoroughly ecclesial.

In the arena of theology more narrowly defined rather than that of Christian thought in general,[30] the objection to Hegelian *Aufhebung* of Christianity was a commonplace in Catholic readers of Hegel, who were his contemporaries. Balthasar's erudition means that he is aware of the reservations expressed by the Catholic speculative thinker, Franz von Baader (1765-1851), who senses a mystical thrust in Hegel's thought that is ultimately compromised by a logicizing impulse. Although Baader continues to worry about the relationship between Schelling's thought and that of Christianity,[31] he believes that the compatibility ratio is significantly higher here than it is in the case of Hegel. Balthasar's knowledge of the so-called 'Tübingen School' also provides him with important resources for his critique of Hegel. While Balthasar's knowledge and appreciation of Möhler, the founder of the School, is easy to establish,[32] it is also clear that Balthasar is familiar with the thought of Franz Anton Staudenmaier (1800-1856). Importantly, however, the constructive contributions that Staudenmaier makes to theology are dwarfed by Hegel-critique, which begins to accelerate in the middle of the 1830's and peaks in the late 1840's. This critique continues to be relevant within the Communio circles within which Balthasar moves, and crops up in works by Xavier Tillette and Emilio Brito among others.[33] There may or may not be a direct line of influence from Staudenmaier, and the Tübingen theologian may well play simply a confirming role. But there can be no denying that in terms of scope and concentration of Hegel-critique that Staudenmaier is Balthasar's major Catholic precursor. Crucially, the critique focuses on the relation between the doctrine of the Trinity and the Hegelian concept, which in Hegel's scheme is the privileged site of the mediation of representation and thought.

I will return to the Staudenmaier-Balthasar relation in Part 3. But before I leave off discussing Balthasar's precursors with respect to this particular point, from the perspective of actual influence on Balthasar's critique of Hegel it is necessary to point to Barth and Przywara, who were unable to come to terms on the issue of analogy. By contrast with his polemics against Liberal Theology in the Kantian and Schleiermachian tradition, Barth's rejection of Hegel is judicious and finely calibrated as it separates out the promising and the well-intentioned from that which was inimical to Christian form and substance.[34] Observing the intimate relations in Hegel's system between Hegelian philosophy and Christianity, on the one hand, and Hegelian philosophy and theology, on the other, Barth objects to the way in which Christianity is valued only as recollected by philosophy and theology valued only to the extent to which it is validated by a discourse that has the capacity for justification. In *Analogia Entis* Przywara also shows himself aware of the problems Hegel provides both philosophy and theology, given his sense of their profound intimacy (*AE*, 71). The two main problems are Hegel's essentialism (*AE*, 215) and his excision of the mystery that is proper to theology and even the best philosophy (*AE*, 89-95). As both *Wahrheit* (1946) and his Maximus book show, from Balthasar's point of view, as with Przywara, Hegel's essentialism requires redress. Arguably, it is Przywara who sets the terms for Balthasar's assessment of the critical capacity of Kierkegaard vis-à-vis Hegel by suggesting that Kierkegaard's existentialism is dialectically related to Hegel's essentialism (*AE*, 215). The second of the two objections is arguably even more powerful, and speaks to Balthasar's view of the analogical nature of all language of God. It is not surprising that in *Analogia Entis* Przywara arrays Augustine and Aquinas against Hegel on this point (*AE*, 86-7). This is not an unfamiliar pattern for a Catholic philosophical theologian, and it is, moreover, a pattern he will follow throughout his entire career. Yet, however unsurprising, it is not uninteresting that in pointing to the magisterial tradition as resources to combat Hegel, Balthasar will tend to privilege figures such as Irenaeus, Nyssa, and Maximus rather than the more conventional Catholic pair.

The fourth and last point of overlap, that is, the agreement between Hegel and Balthasar concerning the unity of philosophy and Christianity in their aspiration for truth must be seriously qualified when submitted to critical scrutiny. Balthasar denies one of the basic premises for Hegelian sublation of Christianity by philosophy, namely the separability of form and content. The mode of articulation of truth in Christianity is not incidental to its content: difference in form implies at least some measure of difference in content. While Christian witness and philosophical thought can say similar things, they cannot say the very same thing. Hegel cannot preserve the content of Christianity to the extent to which he is willing to confound 'revelation' and 'manifestation' and do away with its expressly symbolic character, which hints at inadequation in the very act of apprehending reality. In protesting the former, Balthasar joins ranks with Hegel's Protestant and Catholic critics of the nineteenth century. Even for a theologian as speculative as Franz von Baader, the excision of unanticipatable revelation and its doctoring into 'manifestation,' which is conceptually amenable in the way the giftedness of revelation is not, crucially separates Hegelian thought not only from all actual but also all possible Christian thought.[35] Interestingly, in *Theo-Logic 2*, Balthasar recalls Franz Rosenzweig's account of this distinction that marks nothing less than the difference between the religious and non-religious point of view (*TL2*, 51).

In arguing for the latter, Balthasar has in mind Hegel's discussion of the symbol in the *Encyclopedia*, *Phenomenology*, and *Lectures on the Philosophy of Religion* in which symbol is reduced to mere sign, and primed for conceptual takeover. After the manner of, but without the help of, Ricoeur,[36] Balthasar believes that symbol is irreducible to thought, just as the referential function cannot be reduced to a univocal pattern. Balthasar's attack against Hegelian semiotics is just the opposite of that conducted by Derrida, who wishes to disabuse philosophy and discourse in general not only of its alethic ambitions, but also its semantic pretensions.[37] For Balthasar, the symbolic discourse of religion, and especially of Christianity, is neither semantically destitute nor devoid of referential function. It is simply the case that, as Augustine recognized so well in *De doctrina christiana* (1.6), given the reality intended, reference cannot be fully secured from the side of language itself. Accordingly, Balthasar judges, Hegelian thought cannot endorse a use of language whose primary function is doxological, that is, defined by its responsiveness to an overwhelming reality that is impossibly given and must be marked, praised, and celebrated. To say that Hegel cannot think of discourse as liturgy, or as liturgical, is to say the same thing. It follows, that any use of the language of 'worship' (*Gottesdienst*) in Hegel has to be regarded as idiosyncratic at best, and misleading at worst. Importantly, Hegel's thought is rife with discussion of worship while denying, as he does in the *Encyclopedia* (#62-3) and the *Lectures on the Philosophy of Religion* (1821 MS E 84, G 4; 1827 E153, G 63-4), conditions such as unreciprocal ontological dependence and gratitude that make it possible.[38] But 'worship' is not only a particular signified in the system, but a designation of philosophy itself precisely as the mode of knowledge that realizes its precise contribution to what it corresponds to (*Enc* #62-63).[39]

Indeed, in the specific context of articulating the relationship between Christian and philosophical discourse, Hegelian worship has to be regarded as counterfeit. These differences in turn imply that Hegelian discourse cannot preserve the meaning of prayer, and the practice it underwrites. As Balthasar makes clear in his magisterial book on prayer,[40] the language of prayer makes sense if and only if prayer expresses a situation of interlocution, if prayer both implies and performs an inadequation between the one who prays and the one prayed, and where the praying self or community cannot supply the conditions of the possibility of address. It is the latter which makes prayer impossible, indeed, which makes it the discourse of the impossible. It is this aspect of prayer that gets taken up and developed by Jean-Louis Chrétien under the felicitous rubric of 'wounded speech.'[41] But all of this is covered over by Hegelian dialectic. Dialectic rules out dialogue, and it trades all possibility into actuality. Nothing is impossible to thought; and the impossible is nothing to it. If there are wounds in thought, they can only be temporary. As Hegel pronounces famously in *Lectures on the Philosophy of Religion*, 'Knowledge is the wound that heals itself' (*LPR 3* 1824 E 206 G 138-39).[42] This means precisely the *coup de grâce* of prayer. In the end, Balthasar subscribes to the view of many Hegel critics before and after him: in the Hegelian system one cannot pray. More, Hegel justifies prayerlessness, the forgetting of prayer, which Balthasar's French literary trio of Péguy, Bernanos, and Claudel, thinks indelibly marks modernity. By making the speculative concept and worship coextensive, Hegel contributes to forgetting and in effect sets in motion the deeper forgetting which is the forgetting of forgetting. This deeper forgetting is the proximate condition of misremembering.

Sensitive to the attractions of Hegel, and mindful that he encourages reexamination of ways of theologically expressing faith that lack self-evidence, Balthasar thinks that in the end Hegel is a seducer. Hegel seduces because Christian thinkers in the post-Enlightenment period long for cultural and philosophical blessing, and fail to attend carefully to the content and cost of the blessing. Should they do so, they might well discern that the blessing is a curse. Hegel is a seducer in that he has persuaded Christian intellectuals that only as elevated into the holy of holies constituted by conceptual articulation is Christianity protected from the savage attacks of the Enlightenment, and possibly safe also from the ravages of time. Hegel's discourse constitutes an absolution of Christian discourse: Christian discourse is treated tenderly in being forgiven for the systemic faults of its discourse and its practices that cut against the Enlightenment axiom of autonomy, and released to become its true self in philosophy. The price is repentance of the nature, function and reference of its language and the meaning of its practices. But such repentance is, on Hegelian grounds, eminently sensible. The reward is nothing less than the gaining of discursive integrity that Christianity failed to illustrate throughout its entire history. The 'absolution' is also absolution in the technical sense that Heidegger provides the term in his critique of Hegel in *Hegel's Concept of Experience*:[43] the finitude of language is dissolved as through an anticipatory vision, or *skepsis* in the original sense, as language is pruned of genuine dialogue, specifically of the speaker and the one spoken to. Abolished also is the ecstasy of language that participates in the reality that it elucidates. Hegelian thought defeats not only the silence that would defeat discourse, either before or after making it impossible; it also defeats the discourse that performs its abjection, that even in its eloquence amounts to little more than stutter and stammer. If the resources and courage for resistance are provided primarily by the Christian thinker's immersion in the Christian tradition and by recall of the revelation that is given testimony to in scripture, the resistance is focused in asking hard questions regarding the *Aufhebung* of Christianity by philosophy, such questions as, 'If *Aufhebung* both cancels and preserves, is cancellation regulative?' and 'If preservation is a reality, what precisely is preserved?' These are questions about forgetting and misremembering, provoking the insight that after all Christianity is not quite itself when it has been remembered in and by the concept, that it looks most definitely out of sorts, in fact looks wraithlike and ghastly.

Confrontation Theologically Specified

GIVEN BALTHASAR'S FOCUS ON PHILOSOPHY in volumes four and five of *The Glory of the Lord*, it makes sense that he would discuss the basic constitution of Hegelian philosophical discourse and its happy or unhappy disposition towards the discourse and practice of Christianity. By contrast, in *Theo-Drama* and in volumes two and three of *Theo-Logic* the emphasis tends in the main to fall on Hegel's thought as itself a mode of theological discourse that has to be resisted at all costs. As I have indicated already, if Balthasar approves of the vast conspectus of Hegel's thought and especially its apparently dramatic profile, its functional christocentrism, its refocusing of modern theology on the Trinity, the reservations spread wider as they cut deeper. Paralleling what I did in the previous section, I will speak initially to those reservations that are a function of theological overlap, and then turn to other reservations which are more implicit although just as important. I conclude with some reflections on how all these elements of confrontation hold together simultaneously to name Hegelian apocalypse discourse as representing something like Gnostic return.

Illicit Elevation of Knowledge

BALTHASAR AFFIRMS THE CHRISTIAN AMBITION to see the life of faith in the widest possible perspective. Yet in line with his rejection of completeness with regard to the articulation of philosophical insight, he believes that neither faith or its language, nor its second-order translation, amounts to anything like all-encompassing, self-certifying knowledge. It is precisely to this apotheosis of knowledge that Hegelian ontotheology or theology pretends. This is 'gnosis' in the negative rather than the positive sense specified in and by the Alexandrian fathers (*GL1*, 137-9), formally just the kind of gnosis illustrated by the Gnosticism of the first centuries of the common era and rejected by Christians, even those who did not subscribe to Tertullian's fideistic council of *credo quia absurdum*. The properly Christian form of knowledge of God is always knowledge of the divine understood precisely as mystery. Speaking of the mystery of God, which is the mystery of salvation – although not totally reducible to it – the following passage from *Theo-Drama* is typical:

> *. . . this mystery , even when it has been revealed (apocalypsis), is not some configuration that can be grasped in its totality by earthly understanding. It remains a mystery of faith. The deeper our knowledge of it, the more unfathomable (Eph 3:8) the divine love becomes . . . And for this knowledge, as we showed at the beginning of the Aesthetics, we need the "eyes of faith." Lest the object of our beholding should turn into an "absolute knowledge," however, it was necessary to distinguish our endeavor from that of Hegel in particular. This we did at the start of the present work (Theo-Drama 1, 54-70). "Absolute knowledge" is the death of all theo-drama, but God's "love which surpasses all gnosis" is the death of "absolute knowledge." (TD2, 89)*

But this affirmation of mystery with its intra-textual reference to the inaugural volume of dramatic theory is not only typical of *Theo-Drama*, but of the trilogy as a whole. Speaking broadly one can say that in both *Glory of the Lord 1 & 5* and *Theo-Logic 1* Balthasar inveighs against Heideggerian stereotypes of Christian thought both as fundamentally propositional and as demanding a sacrifice of intellect, and argues that Christianity is intrinsically oriented towards reality as mystery. What can be affirmed in the strictly philosophical sphere is deepened rather than negated when philosophy reaches out towards theology, as Balthasar thinks it must do, in order to become itself. This finds its most programmatic statement in the introduction to *Theo-Logic 1* (9), even if the main agenda of that text is to insist on the necessity of philosophy for the realization of theology. The formal correspondence between the Introduction and the encyclical, *Fides et Ratio*, need not detain us.[44] Suffice it to say, dealing with only one thrust of what is mutual belonging, Balthasar wishes to underscore the paradox that philosophy is most itself when it surpasses itself in a discourse that, strictly speaking, depends on revelation. In any event, he is convinced that what is true in the ontological order is true also with discourse: *sum* is defined by *sursum.*

Consistently denying that he is a negative theologian in the strict sense, that is, a theologian whose abiding commitments are to apophasis and to silence considered as both the beginning and end of a mystic quest, Balthasar understands that God is comprehended as the incomprehensible one. This formulation, whose ultimate source, as Balthasar makes explicit on more than a few occasions throughout *Glory of the Lord*, is the fourth Lateran Council (1215), also recalls Barth, who plays a special role as a prompt and prod in the post-Hegelian environment for a position that has impeccable traditional credentials. Of course, here one should not ignore Przywara who critically engages both Barth and Heidegger and insists on the fundamental compatibility in the Catholic tradition of the dual commitments to analogy and to mystery (*AE*, 86-95, 334-35, 419, 423, 428, 439). The axiom of the incomprehensibility of God is a position that Balthasar finds articulated consistently throughout the patristic and medieval periods, and which finds classic representatives in Maximus and Bonaventure. Here Augustine is also especially important: although he is following Przywara, Balthasar makes his own the Augustinian formula, *si comprehendis, non est Deus* (*GL1*, 180, 450, 461-2; *GL7*, 16).[45] For Balthasar the lack of epistemic humility, which is an essential feature of Hegel's speculative discourse, precisely as adopting the divine point of view, is indicative of a form of theological vision that lacks ecclesial grounding. For all its ambition of self-certification, Hegel's discourse lacks the authority that can only come from speakers and hearers of Christianity who function as the conscience of Christian discourse and reliable interpreters of its normative symbols. These interpreters do not simply pass on (*traditio*), but in and through interpretation reveal new facets of the phenomenon of Christ and thus 'give back' (*redditio*). This giving back is what makes the tradition ever new. The tradition is an open-ended process of continual excavation, perpetual quarrying of what has not been said, what has not been said adequately about the exigent reality of love and forgiveness which governs all Christian response and makes it possible.

For Balthasar, Hegel does not so much forgo as redeem the Enlightenment promise of mapping all of reality, natural and cultural. He articulates a method that is only approximately set down by thinkers such as Bacon, Descartes, and the *philosophes* (*TL1*, 71, 93, 103-04), for the new method answers to the classical sense of *met-hodos*, which construes method as a 'way,' a narrative of the becoming of reality and of the discourses that would grasp it.[46] A crucial aspect of this mapping is the assigning of a place to religion in general and Christianity in particular, in history, in society, and in discourse. The upshot is the eclipse of the horizon of transcendence that makes the very search for knowledge, not to mention its acquisition, possible. Although Balthasar already underwrites both Platonic *zetesis* and Aristotelian *thaumazein* in his reflections on metaphysics in *Glory of the Lord 4 & 5*, his definitive statement is contained in *Theo-Logic 1* in which (under the influence of Przywara) he articulates Aquinas' view of human being's self-transcendence towards the truth. This text, which recycles the much earlier *Wahrheit*, figures Thomas as summing up the metaphysical tradition, precisely as *philo-sophos*, the love of wisdom, not wisdom itself: the attainment of the latter is precisely the ambition of Hegel's thought and announced as such in the Preface of the *Phenomenology*. In any event, even the best of metaphysical discourses, even those that feature prominently the knowing subject's orientation towards the truth, point to their completion in theological discourse proper. A properly Christian discourse, from Balthasar's point of view, is a thoroughly christologically regulated discourse which has the Triune God as its ultimate horizon. This constitutes the crux of Balthasar's understanding of his own theological enterprise. As such it is otiose to proof-text. With different emphases and modulations it is the position advocated throughout each of the three parts of the trilogy. But this vision is upheld by faith, is embodied in the biblical text, and is not the prerogative of theologians. At the same time, knowledge (*gnosis*), and not simply faith (*pistis*), is a real possibility, since, properly understood, gnosis defines deeper penetration of Christian mystery that is the substance of Christian faith. Taking the Alexandrian fathers as his standard (*GL1*, 137-40), Balthasar understands authentic Christian *gnosis* not only as faith-based but faith-shaped, since Christian knowledge cannot master the excess of Being which shines through the crucified one. Precisely in its commitment to contemplation or *theoria,* Christianity renounces the optical illusion of God coming within a field of vision and presenting a content to be exposited.

Thus, while Balthasar does nothing to correct or rescind Hegel's critique of post-Kantian negative theology that insinuates agnosticism, apophasis is a necessity of theology. Hegel could be right about Jacobi and Schleiermacher. Indeed, plausibly he might help us to understand what is wrong with Gregory of Nyssa (*GL1*, 170), Eckhart (*GL1*, 196; *GL5*, 196; *TD2*, 155) and even John of the Cross (*GL3*, 109, 114-15).[47] But Hegel's criticism does not touch Maximus, Pseudo-Dionysius (*GL1*, 174, 185, 205), or Bonaventure (*GL1*, 267-72), precisely because it applies only to unrestricted and not christologically regulated apophasis. It is the latter that Balthasar takes not only to be normative, but also standard in the Christian tradition. In unrestricted or radical apophasis, the linguistic net is torn to expose a transcendence that does not admit of attribution, and plausibly does not admit of relation. One is reduced to silence in corresponding to the deafening silence that greets intentionality, a silence moreover, on which one has no purchase as to whether it is fuller or emptier than word. By contrast, although an absolute necessity of Christian discourse, apophasis is constrained. Within the canonic perspective this is illustrated already in the discourse of Hebrew scripture both in the prohibition against idolatry and in the appearance of the sovereign God who strictly speaking cannot appear (*TL2*, 67). And, of course, the constrained nature of apophasis finds its definitive exhibition in the New Testament, in which apophasis becomes a function of the revelation of God in Jesus Christ. If this is true in general, it is grasped profoundly by Paul (*GL6*, 72-3).[48] Without a doubt, however, it finds its definitive expression in the Gospel of John, precisely the text Hegel views as underscoring the univocally kataphatic commitment of Christian discourse. For Balthasar, although Christ represents above all, to use the terms of *Theo-Logic*, the 'exposition' (*Auslegen*) or interpretation of the Father (*TL2*, 11), who is invisible (*TL2*, 67-8), his iconic status does not remove mystery so much as focus it (*TL2*, 66). This, after all, is one of the central axioms of a theological aesthetic, which as it refuses kataphatic reduction into history, proposition or sign, also obliges the Christian to take a stand against a mystery without portfolio.

While not completely evident that Balthasar's clarification of contemplation in *Glory of the Lord 1* is undertaken with Hegel explicitly in mind, clearly if contemplation is precisely non-spectator-like in that the other, or totally other (*das Ganz Andere*), is not made the object of a gaze, the clarification is of consequence regarding the Christian credentials of any form of thought that would deny reality exceeding the reach of the concept (*Begriff*). This view of contemplation, expressed with such force in *Glory of the Lord 1*, is grounded biblically in *Glory of the Lord 6-7*, where human seeing and cognition is never the match of the divine glory that inspires ecstasy and eros. As responsive to a glory (*doxa*) that exceeds it, contemplation is irreducibly doxological. The view offered in *Glory of the Lord* is not gainsaid when Balthasar in *Theo-Logic* comes at the problem in the register of truth rather than beauty. Truth is the superabundant reality intended by an ecstatic subject, which at the same time supplies the very conditions of a co-respondence that goes to the root of the self and does not stop at cognition in the narrow sense (*TL1,* 138, 142, 216-19). What is merely suggested in *Theo-Logic 1*, given its putting in parenthesis of specifically theological considerations, is brought out more clearly by the other two volumes of *Theo-Logic*. It is Christ who supplies these conditions, since emphatically Christ is the way, as the Gospel of John announces *(TL2*, 11-16; *TL3*, 17), and the Spirit who definitively interprets the way. In any event, this is precisely not the kind of worship authorized by Hegel, for whom, following Epictetus and Spinoza, precisely as true worship (*Gottesdienst*), self-reflective conceptual knowledge represents the abolition of difference, ontological and epistemological, between selves and the divine.

Balthasar's resistance to Hegel-like raids on the inarticulate differs substantially from that prosecuted by post-Nietzscheans such as Bataille and Blanchot, who insist against the inclusive ambitions of Hegelian knowledge on excess and non-knowledge.[49] In interdependent ways, both support an unrestricted apophasis, even as this apophasis is focused enough to proscribe any form of transcendence that suggests a real Other to whom the speaker bears a relation. Here whatever its critical ratio against the Hegelian absolute, this particular form of postmodern apophasis continues Hegelian immanence when it inscribes the prohibition against

Jenseits that fundamentally marks Hegel's texts almost from the beginning and which received a classical expression in the section on the 'Unhappy Consciousness' (*das unglückliche Bewusstsein*) in the *Phenomenology*.[50] It is not a little interesting that at least in the case of Bataille, Balthasar's concerns expressed in *Glory of the Lord 5* about the internal relation between apophasis, absolute immanence, and human self-elevation come home to roost. It is also ironic, since just as Bataille disconnects negative theology and Hegel, Balthasar connects them and shows that the denial of negative theology may prove consistent with other features negative theology sometimes supports. More hospitable to Balthasar's resistance is the view proposed by Jean-Luc Marion in *The Idol and Distance* and *God Without Being* in which the ontological difference finds its correlative in the experience of the icon and thus in being seen rather than seeing.[51] Here Marion deepens what already is a Balthasarian condensation of what is at once a Johannine and a Pauline trope. It is only in being seen that the seer avoids idolatry. For this is to be constituted by the icon, definitively identified as the expropriating gaze of Christ. While Pseudo-Dionysius, Maximus the Confessor, and even Hölderlin are put into play explicitly against Heidegger, whose apophasis is judged to be problematic, implicitly they are also put into play against Hegel's proscription against apophasis. Whatever might be the intended range of application of Hegel's proscription, it would not apply to modes of apophasis that are christologically – and thus kataphatically – grounded and trinitarianly sustained. More hospitable also to Balthasar's thought than that of an atheology and Derridian deconstruction is the position of those theologians who come under the umbrella of 'Radical Orthodoxy.' Whatever their ambiguity, even ambivalence,[52] regarding the theological viability of Hegel, thinkers in this manifold appear to be united in their affirmation of the centrality of the doxological both in the order of discourse and in the order of existence, which, of course, finally says something about the true order of things.

Not simply the discourse of praise, but discourse as praise is proper to Christianity, which celebrates almost operatically what the Enlightenment condemns: human beings in community in the radically heteronomous posture of praise and celebration of that which infinitely surpasses, that which radically upsets closure, and that which is 'nearer' than near in which we participate and are sustained. Here Balthasar and Radical Orthodoxy are of one voice against the Enlightenment's double displacement: the displacement of the interest in participation with a more narrow interest in salvation, and the general displacement of the latter (Kant continues to hold out) by knowledge, which at a limit can come to be understood *as* salvation. More consistently than Radical Orthodoxy, Balthasar sees that Hegel's own thought ratifies the *as*, which, of course, is at the same time to erase it. Knowledge *is* salvation. However, it is so only under certain conditions. It cannot be merely instrumental knowledge; it cannot be merely procedural, the iteration of a method which opens up reality, but which in principle can never come to an end; it cannot leave any aspect of the individual subject, society or the state unexplored. Knowledge must be total and describes an all-embracing circle of meaning and truth in which no area of reality is left conceptually underdetermined (cf. *TL3*, 45). Hegel provides the post-Enlightenment figure of gnosis. The figure is brazen in two senses: it is both presented in the open, and on biblical grounds it represents an idolatrous substitution. The irony is that its brazenness succeeds, where subtle disguises have failed.

Although Balthasar does not make the point totally explicit, it does seem to be his view that Hegel's panopticism is insufficiently resisted when the inadequacy of perspectives is laid squarely on the fallen self. Balthasar is Augustinian enough to allow that sin has epistemic as well as moral and spiritual effect. But he is also Augustinian enough to understand that prohibition against the divine point of view is built into the Christian vision of reality in which knowing is correlative to the knower's finitude, and especially finitude as enfleshed. The first Augustinian tendency is clearly seen, for example, in *De civitate dei*, which with its interests in overcoming sin and its turbulent contexts and consequences, emphasizes the distinction between the pre-eschatological and eschatological orders of knowing. Here we see 'through a glass darkly, there face to face,' which gets translated as the distinction between not-seeing and seeing. Although I am not positing direct textual influence here, I do intend the connection to be more than formal, despite the palpable lack of reference to this great text of the 'late' Augustine in Balthasar's portrait of Augustine in *Glory of the Lord 2*

(95-143). For given Balthasar's anthologization of this text, as well as his reference to it in *Theo-Drama 4* in his discussion of authentic Christian apocalypse (*TD4*, 15-67), it would be unwise to presume that the thought of Augustine does not inform in any appreciable way Balthasar's theological reflection and experimentation. The second tendency, arguably, more in evidence in *Ennarrationes in Psalmos*, suggests a relativization of the distinction between the pre-eschatological and eschatological orders of knowing. It is of no little interest that it is Augustine, defined by the second strand, who is enlisted as the authority for a view not of static beatific vision, but of the 'dynamic becoming' of ecstatic knowing apparently indifferent to the distinction between the pre-eschatological and eschatological state. Balthasar insists that even the beatific vision does not remove God's incomprehensibility (*GL2*, 186). What surprises is not simply that in entertaining 'eternal becoming' Balthasar is appealing to a notion that lacks canonic status, but that it is Augustine rather than Nyssa who is the vehicle. Balthasar defined himself early on as a serious student of Gregory of Nyssa, and is familiar with his divagations on *epektasis* in *The Life of Moses* and other texts.[53] Apophasis, then, is more than an impediment that the finite knower must suffer, an obstacle that postmortem existence itself overcomes. Rather

> *. . . the Word of God is never something settled for good and all that can be surveyed like a clearly defined landscape, but something that comes forth ever anew, like waters from a spring or rays from a light. And so it is not enough to have received "insight" and to "know the testimonies of God," if we do not continually receive and become inebriated by the fountain of eternal life (Enarrationes in Psalmos, 118, 26.6).*

Balthasar goes on to add a gloss to this loose Augustine quotation:

> *The lover already knows this; the beloved's face and voice are every moment as new as if he had never seen them before. But the being of God, which is revealed to us in his word, is not only for the eyes of the lover. In itself, in all objectivity, it is the unique marvel, ever new. No seraph,*

> *no saint in all eternity could "get used" to it; in fact, the longer one gazes into this mystery, the more one longs to go on gazing, glimpsing the fulfillment of that to which our entire creaturely nature aspires. (P, 25)*

The avowal of 'eternal becoming,' as a constituent element of apophasis properly understood, does not marginalize Nyssa. In fact by availing of Augustine to make the point, Balthasar not only reveals as canard the contrast frequently made between the iconography of the afterlife of the Eastern and Western churches, but succeeds in bringing Nyssa within the theological pale. True one can see the trace of a subtle correction in a christological direction; this after all was the thrust of his concern with Nyssa in his book on the Cappadocian in the early 1940's, and supplied at least part of the *raison d'être* of trying to find a kind of apophatic theology that did not jeopardize either the christological center or trinitarian horizon of Christian thought.

Balthasar's support of 'eternal becoming' in *Theo-Logic 3* – the last volume of the trilogy – represents something of an exclamation point for an idea that he has long maintained. It is anticipated in *Theo-Logic 1*, which determines the human subject as constitutively erotic and ecstatic, as well as in other parts of the trilogy. A careful read of the section on 'Subjective Evidence' in *Glory of the Lord 1*, in which a properly 'theological aesthetic' is contrasted with an 'aesthetic theology' of a Hegelian sort, provides evidence that the rapture of human response to divine glory (*doxa* or *Kabod*) is not limited to the pre-eschatological state. Rather with Bonaventure and Hamann as related measures, Balthasar seems to be making a statement about the self qua finite. Its openness and responsiveness to the Word is what defines it as such. There is no translation of state, no elevation (*Erhebung*) in the Hegelian sense, that would deplete mystery not to mention wipe it out. If anything the eschatological state deepens mystery as it makes more exorbitant the knowing love that intends it. Balthasar is more emphatic in the second and third volumes of *Glory of the Lord*, specifically in his essays on Pseudo-Dionysius and John of the Cross. Although in *Glory of the Lord 1* Balthasar laid it down that these two thinkers were two supreme exemplars of theological aesthetic in the Christian tradition (124-5), he is not without anxiety concerning the level of apophasis – thus the asseveration that in advance puts them both above such figures as Irenaeus, Augustine, Anselm, and Bonaventure and below them. But whatever the problems on this front with either, it is clear that the idea of an eschatological plumbing the depths of God is not one of them. In the case of Pseudo-Dionysius, although at his best the incomprehensible is found in the comprehensible Word (*GL2*, 174, 185), what is exposed is so inexhaustibly rich that 'infinite approximation' is in order (172). Balthasar clearly recognizes the close relation between Pseudo-Dionysius and Nyssa on this point (170), and aside from suggesting that Nyssa's eros might be more aesthetically, that is, christologically configured (170), he is no more embarrassed by the idea than theologians such as Rahner and Kasper.[54]

Balthasar concludes a line of thought that he thinks can and should be released from the shackles of too imperious a form of apophasis by reminding that what is true of human beings is also true of the angels (207). Undoubtedly, however, from Balthasar's perspective in *Glory of the Lord*, it is John of the Cross who is the theologian most insistent on this point in the Western tradition. In the opening pages of his essay, Balthasar lovingly records John of the Cross' emphasis on the mystery of the triune God being irremediable (*GL3*, 113-16). Incomprehensibly near, God does not admit of ever being named; the soul enters the 'thicket' (*espesura*) of God and can always enter further. Importantly, however, this is not to be lost in the markless way of Eckhart's desert. God is the triune God, not the Godhead beyond God, the God beyond ebullience and fecundity. Balthasar seems even to have grasped the underground revolution enacted in John of the Cross' thought concerning the theological virtues, that, arguably finds its true echo in the thought of Péguy: faith hopes as well as loves, just as love believes and hopes (134-5).[55]

Theo-Logic 1 is a foundational text for Balthasar's view that 'eternal becoming' evolves as an implicate of the radical nature of apophasis. Even without christologically contextualizing divine mystery, which essentially remains *hors de texte*, this 1946 production insists on this point (*TL1*, 3, 37, 206 *inter alia*). The concept of 'eternal becoming' or its cognate 'eternal futurity' enters discussion two-thirds of the way through the text (*TL1*, 203). Parsed as 'ever intensifying promise,' Balthasar makes it clear that this eros towards the not-yet as the never-to-be-realized correspondence defines the ecstasis of the self. What is disclosed – here Being as such – should be defined as 'that which comes' (*der Zukommen*) (*TL1*, 197), specifically that which comes from outside the matrix of time present, past, and future and thus grounds the possibility of transcendence. Keeping the theological destination of this appraisal of reality in mind, and especially Balthasar's lack of embarrassment even in this early text, to identify Being and Love (*TL1*, 112, 123-25, 209) and relatedly Being and God (*TL1*, 51-3, 57, 101-02 *inter alia*), it is possible to say that long before Moltmann and Pannenberg, Balthasar had identified God and the absolute future. Undoubtedly, Balthasar's language is here redolent of Schelling's *The Ages of the World* (1815), but Balthasar can hardly be committing himself to Schelling's speculative view of the ontological or meontological becoming of God, a view that *Apokalypse 1* regards in all its Romantic and Idealist variations as a thorough dead-end. If the Schellingian echo is accidental,[56] Balthasar is extraordinarily aware of another Romantic-Idealist echo, that is, the attraction of the asymptotic approximation to knowing (as participation) as something like an anthropological universal. After speaking of eternal futurity as an 'ever-intensifying promise,' which means that the human subject forever seeks even that which it has found (*TL1*, 203), Balthasar goes on to add a rider:

> *. . . the aspect of infinity in truth is due not so much to the subject's insatiable, Faustian urge to know as to the ever-transcending breadth and plenitude of existing things in themselves. (TL1, 203)*

The substantive point is important, easy to grasp, and does not require historical annotation: in the sphere of a metaphysics of finitude the eternal becoming of a knowing that fully engages a finite self is due to the inexhaustible richness of reality. Still historical annotation can be supplied, and reflect worries that go to discourses that are inside the Christian tradition as outside. While it is true that Balthasar is able to validate Nyssa's view of *epektasis*, it is also the case that in his early work on the Cappadocian thinker, he worried about the radical apophaticism in which in the knowing that is 'stretched forth' (lexical root) there is a hint that this has as much to do with the constitution of the subject as with the mysterious nature of God, indeed, God as triune. Nonetheless, there is equally considerable evidence that over his career Balthasar's concerns about Nyssa on this point were very much assuaged. Indeed, it is possible to say that they were assuaged to the extent that when David Bentley Hart makes Nyssa's *epektasis* the corner-stone of his theological aesthetics in *The Beauty of the Infinite*,[57] he is perfectly justified in thinking that his project continues and develops that of Balthasar. Still for the record Balthasar shows himself anxious in *Theo-Logic 1*, written within a few years of his major Nyssa text, to resist an emphasis which, in his view, is a perennial possibility within the apophatic tradition that shows reluctance to submit itself to christological and trinitarian regulation.

The most obvious referent of Balthasar's rejection of a deficient interpretation of the infinite progress is to the view adopted by both the German Enlightenment and Romanticism. The 'Faust' reference veils as well as unveils; it veils in that it might give the impression that Goethe is either the sole or main target of the reference. It is antecedently unlikely that this is the case, even if Goethe's Faust is convicted of a false *Hingabe* in *Apokalypse 1*. There are a number of reasons. First, it is clear that already in *Theo-Logic 1* Balthasar is being influenced by Goethean ideas of form and measure in what amounts not only to a book on truth, but also a book on the relationship between truth and beauty. This will only deepen over the decades and receive its consummate expression in the aesthetic architectonics of *Glory of the Lord 1*.[58]

Second, there are any number of other suspects. Fichte certainly stands out, since his exemplary *Wissenschaftslehre* pronounces more vehemently on the future than any of the German Idealists,[59] and more rigorously than any Romantic, even Hölderlin at his apocalyptically most excessive. Third, and perhaps most importantly, Balthasar seems to refer not so much to the Faustian figure as such, as an epistemic aporia to which the figure of Faust represents one of the possible answers. Balthasar is sensitive (*TL1*, 203),[60] as Hans Blumenberg will be later,[61] to Lessing's generative question of whether it is better to be forever in pursuit of knowledge or actually come to term in knowledge and risk satiation and the puerility with which it is accompanied. Lessing, of course, gives a very different answer to the one provided by Balthasar, and opts for the dynamic of knowing that is the favored side of a binary opposition. For Balthasar, however, if 'eternal' and 'infinite' refer to what aims to be known, then there is a genuine third option not noted by Lessing, and not allowed into Hegel's system. In *Theo-Logic 1* Balthasar keeps faith with his thinking in *Apokalypse* that unrealized as well as realized eschatology are two sides of the same coin. The difference is that now he thinks that they are theologically and not merely culturally questionable. To pay attention to the continuity is to pay attention also to another and, arguably, more encompassing figuration. In *Apokalypse*, although Lessing and Fichte, and even Kant (*Apok 1*, 91-3) articulate a mode of 'unrealized eschatology' that Hegel submits to a fundamental critique, they represent one side of a Promethean dispensation, the other side of which is represented by Hegel's more confident rendition. Balthasar seems to grasp inchoately what becomes transparent in Blumenberg: the figure of Prometheus is plastic enough to include the kind of episteme represented by the figure of Faust.

Now, as inflected by doxology and by unrestricted desire, specifically as an answer to Hegel, Balthasar's rendition of apophasis puts him in conversation with postmodern critics of Hegel, some who do and some who do not share his enthusiasm for the theological tradition. As has been illustrated well in French postmodern thought, the insistence that dialectic is a form of work – the 'labor of the negative' (*Arbeit des Negativen*) as Hegel famously refers to it in the Preface to the *Phenomenology* (#19) – has proved provocative. For as thinkers as different as Bataille, Foucault, and Derrida have realized, this is essentially to make conceptual formation an economy that annuls non-sense, what cannot be translated into the regime of knowing that provides its own certificates of warrant. Thus, the interest in the anatomy of 'excluded' discourses and especially how they might bear on the totalizing regimes of knowing typical of modernity. Foucault suggests the an-economic regime of 'madness' as a critical lever against domesticating reason; Bataille fashions a negative theology or a/theology whose sovereignty exceeds the mastery of the system; and most famously Derrida's discourse decenters, disseminates, prevents an ultimate meaning taking hold.[62] Balthasar never addresses these kinds of radical solutions, and it is likely that he would have problems with all. I have mentioned his difference with Derrida already; his separation from the other two would be equally profound. In the case of the counter-regime defined by madness – indeed that is madness – it is not clear that Foucault has escaped the dialectical logic that he fears embraces all: madness is also a logic, indeed a logic that is incessive rather than excessive, because it is a logic of obsession.[63] This is a logic for which Hegel has the key: understanding (*Verstand*) by the nature of the case tends towards analysis, particularity, and reification. Madness defines understanding in its form of the strangulation of the concept (*die Anstrengung des Begriffs*), and confirms its failure to rise to the level of the Reason (*Vernunft*). Perhaps this rules out Hölderlin's madness as being a trope of what exceeds Hegelian logic;[64] rather, precisely as madness, it is interned, for the logic has the formula. Nor can Bataille's a/theology serve as an exit; for as it embraces and interprets the negative theology tradition, it does so only with a view to unraveling commitment and intentionality. There is no truth larger than the experience or non-experience of the self; certainly not the truth of the community or a tradition, or the truth of its witness which is a central preoccupation of Balthasar's entire trilogy, and which also suffuses his hagiographical work.[65]

There is, however, one point at which the postmodern discourse opens out onto Balthasar's discourse and vice versa, and this is the idea of laughter in one, humor in the other. Now it is true that Kierkegaard provided the basic contours for this in the nineteenth century. Hegel's discourse, he divined, cannot be defeated straight up; the philosophical and religious task is to inflict damage, without falling into the system's gravitational pull which digests all critique. Tactics rather than positions; strategies rather than syllogisms are required to refute. Central is irony. In quite different ways, Bataille and Balthasar follow Kierkegaard, Bataille very closely with his 'laughter' that exceeds the system, Balthasar very much at a distance in his 'holy fools' and 'humor of the saints.' It is no accident that in *Glory of the Lord 5* the sizable sections on 'Holy Fools' (141-204) and 'metaphysics of saints' (48–140) are found together. This suggests that these sections are intended to interpret each other, a view that seems to be confirmed in *The Office of Peter* wherein speaking of the humor of the saint Balthasar seems to bring out the foolish or ludic element of sainthood. The kind of doubling in *Glory of the Lord* can be taken to suggest, on the one hand, that as depicted in Western literature from Cervantes to Dostoyevski, 'holy fools' are ordered towards the ex-istence of the saint, defined by ecstasy that draws a parabola with regard to the form of Christ, and, on the other, that saints are excessive with respect to any and all forms of logic, whether instrumental or speculative. The concluding volume of *Glory of the Lord* is a paean to the christoform and cruciform love that exceeds metaphysics in which it is impossible not to recall Bonaventure, and difficult not to recur to *Glory of the Lord 1* in which Balthasar elaborates his maximalist view of Christian existence within the Bonaventuran brackets of rapture. But where Bonaventure is in play, Francis cannot be far behind. Francis is the ludic saint par excellence. And, it is important to remember, the saint is simply the Christian who has let go, who has accepted his or her mission that involves the evolution of a unique unrepeatable form of life, a *Gestalt* in the Goethean sense of the term.

Indeed, the ludic excess of good form Balthasar suggests is what is typical of the saint and constitutes the saint not only as a theological resource, but an actual source. The saint enacts the wildness of scripture, which is the wildness of love, and as she does, she defeats the all-knowingness of any and all systems. In his elucidations of Péguy, Claudel, and Bernanos, this is a point to which Balthasar constantly recurs. The point is made with special clarity in *The Office of Peter*, where Balthasar finds room to praise the English along with his French canon. He appropriates for the Catholic G. K. Chesterton's attack on seriousness as a true virtue and his praise of 'frivolity' (*P*, 305) and a certain 'airiness' in the fiction of C. S. Lewis, which is powerful in its innocence and childlikeness (*P*, 305). It is in this text too that one finds another portrait of Kierkegaard than that provided in *Glory of the Lord 1*, where the portrait is the humorless Lutheran critic of the aesthetic (47-53), who for this reason proves no match for Romanticism's and Idealism's aesthetic high-jacking of Christianity. Kierkegaard is, indeed, a kind of poet, one who brings it to bear on the critique of all kind of seriousness and especially Christian and philosophical seriousness. Since Hegel is the most serious of the serious, Kierkegaard is being re-read as a thinker who might after all provide a critical measure, as did his 'wild' predecessor Hamann. Balthasar sees that humor everywhere witnesses to humility and evinces the Christian confidence that the mystery to which her existence is pledged is abyssal. But the abyssal is not abysmal; it is marked by generosity and love, because marked by the one who is in solidarity with us. Which is to say that the cross and humor are not contraries; indeed, that in a mysterious way humor becomes humor only in seeing and being obedient to the cross. Humor is not just any kind of laughter. Humor is neither debilitating irony nor sneer; it is compassion.

Deviant Epicality and Its Notes

GIVEN THE SUGGESTIONS ABOUT GNOSTICISM made in the last chapter, I cannot argue that the substitution of salvation for knowledge in Hegel's work, which not only excises the ethical but rules out of count dialogue between a transcendent divine and human being, is sufficient for the ascription of Gnosticism or Valentinianism. A mere nod in the direction of the Hellenistic discourses suggests that the identification of knowledge and salvation was also a tendency in certain forms of Neoplatonism.[66] At best, the identification of salvation with a form of encompassing knowledge is a necessary but not sufficient condition for the return of Gnosticism. As I have indicated already, Balthasar is distinguished for having adopted the narrative aspect of Irenaeus' diagnostics, that is, in his seeing that the truly crucial feature of Valentinianism is how it plays fast and loose with the biblical narrative, how it systemically alters the biblical narrative and disguises this alteration. Put simply, the most revealing mark of Valentinianism, and thus what indicates its return, is the way in which in and through a form of transgressive interpretation, the biblical narrative is made a function of another narrative with a rival set of meanings, especially as this pertains to envisaging the relations between divine, world, and human being defined as spirit. From Balthasar's point of view, more than any other modern thinker, the great 'rationalist' Hegel compels one to think the relation between Christianity and myth. More, Hegel forces one to think of the nature of myth as it consorts with the highest ambitions of reason. What is myth in the wake of the emergence of science? What is myth after the division into disciplines? What is that form of myth that has as one of its attributes an entire program of demythologization? Why is it so attractive? Why does it remain so attractive when it has so often been exposed? Why does it take so long to die? Above all, the question: 'Why is it not dead?'

It is essential to see how the trilogy negotiates these questions and especially the early volumes of *Theo-Drama.* But it is equally important to point out that these questions go back to *Apokalypse*, where Balthasar essentially puzzles over why the Romantic, Idealist and nihilistic brew after the Enlightenment had seemed to cement the claims of procedural rationality. Why apocalypse in a modernity that is non-apocalyptic? Why the felt need for a vision of the whole in which neither the divine, cosmos, or human are privileged, nor are equally privileged? The simple answer is that reason had a dynamic towards vision that could not be restrained, a need for a view of the whole that could not be bought off. The trilogy assumes this essentially cultural answer, as it introduces two interrelated questions: in what way is the holism of Romanticism and Idealism a function of its relation to Christian discourse in general and the biblical narrative in particular? In what way and how seriously is Christianity damaged by an association in which mythological narratives come to function as simulacra of the biblical or Christian narrative, and what criteria or notes can we adduce to find them out? These questions, obviously, imply a much broader range of critical concern than Hegel, but *Theo-Drama* in particular makes it clear that Hegel should be considered as first among equals on any list of suspects, given his theological as well as philosophical authority in modern thought. By comparison with much of modern theology, and even a considerable portion of pre-modern theology, Hegel's depiction of the divine and its relations to both world and humanity proposes a relationality that is truly dramatic and finds its focus in the cross. In *Theo-Drama* Balthasar critically explores the issue as to whether Hegel's theological thought truly has a dramatic character. What is at stake in this inquiry is nothing less than the measure of its fidelity to Christian tradition. Scripture and the theological tradition equally give witness to the dramatic character of God's engagement with the world and human beings, where this implies that God is intimately involved in the fate of humanity and the world while not being ontologically dependent on it. Operating in terms of the categories of 'lyric,' 'drama,' and 'epic,' which he draws from Hegel's aesthetics,[67] Balthasar uses them to critique Hegel's fundamental theological orientation (*TD1*, 42-57; 77-8). Balthasar brings in the verdict that the thought of Hegel and his theological successors is epical rather than dramatic in the strict sense.

Summing up the basic drift of *Theo-Drama 1*, one can say that on the most general and formal level drama supposes the negotiation between distinct centers of freedom and intentionality with outcomes that are prospectively open. Given that one of these agents is divine complicates matters, for infinite freedom cannot simply be imagined as the binary opposite of finite freedom, but rather the reality that subtends it and thus is constitutive of negotiation (*TD2*, 189 ff).[68] This is a case where the material specification necessarily rings a change on the category itself. Still, the definition of 'drama' operative in *Theo-Drama 1* can serve as a criterion whereby to determine whether a theological system is dramatic in the full sense, or merely 'pseudo-dramatic' (*TD3*, 137), having in fact regressed to epic which, according to Hegel's own elaboration in *Lectures on Aesthetics* as elsewhere, belongs to a lower level of linguistic performance than drama. This is the nub of the complaint in *Theo-Drama 2* against the Hegelian propensity to envision all event as structure, as illustrating a pre-given pattern of meaning that never allows 'happening' simply to happen, that outbids the *hapax legomenon* from the beginning. A mark of the epic viewpoint is the incorrigibly retrospective vantage point of Hegelian thought in which

> *. . . the history that involves God and man is eviscerated, absorbed into a "system" that can be viewed and grasped as a whole, and in particular the dramatic climax of the biblical end-time is obliterated in a "noon-time," a twilight in which Minerva can fly. (TD2, 125)*

Moreover, in this history it is clear that the conditions of drama are not met, since the conditions of dialogue or dialogical relation are not met.[69] There are not two subjects in what Hölderlin, more genuinely biblical than Hegel, spoke of as a 'conversation,' but one (*GL5*, 302, 310, 320-21), which equivocates between the infinite and finite, the divine and the human. Any activity from and to the divine in the Hegelian system must be referred to the divine as grammatical subject in the throes of becoming the fully actualized (*wirklich*) subject of reality.[70] An obvious reflection of Hegel's distance from the dramatic structure of biblical depiction is his refusal to sanction personal language with respect to God, and his disinclination to apply such language to individual grammatical subjects whose reality is constituted proximally by community and ultimately by the relationality of the divine as subject.[71]

As epical, Hegel's articulation of the divine can be characterized as mythological, and even more specifically as theogonic in that the divine becomes or develops only in and through the world and human being. For Balthasar this is to move theological discourse in the most eccentric possible orbit vis-à-vis the theological tradition, for in his view the Bible, which the tradition is obliged to interpret, must be considered as constitutively and not simply as accidentally anti-mythological. The point is axial in Balthasar's treatment of the Old Covenant in *Glory of the Lord 6*. Whatever the remnants of Sumerian and Akkadian mythology recalled in Genesis and the Psalms, the Old Testament represents a rupture with the mythological programs of the Ancient Near East. Balthasar refuses to even entertain a *Religionsgeschichte* approach to the passion, death, and resurrection of Jesus that would lump Jesus with Osiris and Dumuzi and make the New Testament another instance of trafficking in the 'dying God' motif. Moreover, however plausible the characterization of the Bible as the 'biography of God,'[72] as narrated, God's development belongs to the order of human appropriation rather than to God as such. When writers in the first centuries defended immutability,[73] it could be argued that the term functioned as much as a rejection of mythological optics as a decided metaphysical preference of which the Church fathers are now commonly accused. Balthasar observes that in Hegel's discourse, as well as the discourse of his successors, divine development or self-development has pathos as one of its conditions. From this he generalizes that in the Hegelian and post-Hegelian field of narrative agonism and theogony are internally related (e.g. *TD2*, 9, 302). Again, however, this point is a long-standing one, and can be tracked as far back as *Apokalypse* in which Balthasar reflects on what he determines to be the shared Idealist view of 'mystical potentiality,' which continues to enjoy at least a half-life in the twentieth century.[74] While not particular to Hegel – Fichte (*Apok 1*, 176) and Schelling (*Apok 1*, 208 ff.) also provide examples – Hegel illustrates the commitment in an unequivocal fashion (*Apok 1*, 597 ff). Over the course of a life-time, Balthasar shows himself as committed to the theogonic construal of Hegel as any religious thinker in the twentieth century.

Balthasar's only serious rival in this respect is the Russian orthodox thinker, Iwan Iljin, whose great 1918, *Filosofiia Gegelia kak uchenie o konkretnosti Boga i cheloveka* (*The Philosophy of Hegel as a Doctrine of the Concreteness of God and Man*), received a partial German translation in 1946, thus some years after the appearance of Balthasar's *Apokalypse*. Appearing as *Die Philosophie Hegels als Kontemplative Gotteslehre*,[75] this text translated only with the first twelve of twenty one chapters that treat Hegel's thought as the quintessential form of onto-logical speculation, and did not reproduce in German the last nine chapters which touch on the more explicitly social but also theological aspects of Hegel's thought. The basic thesis of *Die Philosophie Hegels* is that as Hegel's thought sums up Western thought, it sums up its swerve from the concrete. Taking Hegel's *Science of Logic* to be his pivotal text, Iljin believes that the only verdict to be rendered concerning Hegel's thought is that it presents an ontotheology in which the Christian divine – indeed triune divine – is interpreted by or replaced by a panlogistic version of a mythological God defined by 'theogenetic process' and tragedy.[76] Iljin presents this as simply a scholarly judgment, denying that it is based on his profound Eastern orthodox convictions about the fullness of the triune God and the impassibility of God.[77] Maybe one way to think of an essential thrust of David Bentley Hart's *The Beauty of the Infinite* is that it completes the refutation of Hegel from within orthodox thought by refusing to separate as neatly as Iljin theological from philosophical objection.

In construing Hegel's ontotheological vision as mythological, Balthasar does not forget Hegel's post-Enlightenment situation. Specifically, he does not claim that Hegel merely repeats ancient theogonies, whether of Babylonian, Hesiodian, or Orphic variety, which at different levels of self-consciousness offer an account of the becoming of divine forces or personae marked by knowledge and will. But Balthasar does believe with the philosopher of culture, Hans Blumenberg, that there exists in Idealist as well as Romantic thought a program of remythologization that complements Enlightenment demythologization; in fact it is nothing less than a program of 'total myth' in which the story incorporates precisely those elements of recalcitrance and evil that tend to deny the possibility of story.[78] In addition, it is evident that by pointing to Gnosticism as an analogue for Hegel's mythological view, Balthasar in effect commits himself to the view that Idealist mythos is of a second-order rather than first-order kind. Here Balthasar might usefully be read as deploying a distinction that finds different expressions in Blumenberg's distinction between organic and artificial or literary myth and Ricoeur's distinction between unreflective and logicized myth.[79] It is precisely as articulating a second-order myth that Hegel's thought so successfully masquerades as authentically Christian and masks its anti-Christian bias and ethos.

Balthasar mostly contents himself with the two surface features of myth – the developmental narrative and suffering (e.g. *TD2*, 9, 62) – and does not attempt anything like a systematic analysis of its depth features. Nonetheless, by means of scattered remarks and specific criticisms throughout the trilogy he provides hints regarding its structural properties. The first property of Hegel's mythological depiction is *monism* (*TD2*, 261). For Balthasar, not only in Hegel, but also in successors such as the Catholic philosopher, Anton Günther (19th-century) and Jürgen Moltmann (20th-century) who try to correct him, there is insufficient independence of God from the world. On the one hand, the world and human being are reduced to being occasions and instruments of divine becoming and development. This represents the derogation of the finite. On the other, the coming to be of the world and the becoming of human being is hallowed as nothing less than the development of the divine. This represents the exaltation of the finite. Balthasar recognizes well that the derogation and exaltation of the finite and the correlative exaltation and derogation of the infinite are simply two sides of the same Hegelian coin defined by the formula so dear to Hölderlin, that is, the formula of the *Hen kai Pan* (*GL5*, 240, 572-77). The 'One and All' abolishes the space of dialogue, while reifying a non-dialogical space that is the result of a pincers-like operation on both terms of dialogue. It is dialogue that constitutes monotheism. Monotheism, especially biblical monotheism, is always the inveterate enemy of monism, since it implies the dialogue between incommensurables. This is a point, which Balthasar's reflection on 'dialogical' philosophy at the end of the introductory volume of *Theo-Drama* shows well, which is shared by the two Jewish religious thinkers, Martin Buber and Franz Rosenzweig (*TD1*, 626-43) who collaborated on the German translation of the Hebrew Bible. Relative to critical measure, however, it is Rosenzweig, one of the great 20th-century critics of the Hegelian system, who gets pride of place.[80] It is Rosenzweig who sees clearly the consequence of reneging on the alterity of the one who says 'I will be who I will be' both with respect to God, who is made a function of the world, and a self which finds itself always encouraged to regard itself as self-posited (*TL2*, 50-2). Although honorably mentioned in *Theo-Drama*, it is in *Theo-Logic* that Rosenzweig receives a fundamental affirmation. The context and content of Balthasar's affirmation is Rosenzweig's notion of 'revelation.' In contrast to much of classical philosophy that allows for direct continuity between the divine and the non-divine world and non-divine human being, and in contrast to Hegel who mediates the difference in his notion of 'manifestation,' revelation is breach and rupture (*TL3*, 51). Revelation establishes the irreducibility of transcendence, its unthinkability, as well as its place: it is what must be thought from the beginning, not as conclusion; the outcome of the exhaustion of explanation.

In his critical use of Jewish philosophy of dialogue against Hegel, Balthasar opens up the prospect of a productive conversation with Levinasian and post-Levinasian critique of Hegel, even if he does not actually pursue it. The overall contours of Rosenzweig's and Levinas' project are different, with Rosenzweig's dialogical thought supposing a dialogue between finite and infinite others in a way not supported by Levinas' major texts, and Levinas' thought being dominated by relations between human beings. With *Otherwise than Being*, however, Levinas introduces concepts such as 'revelation' and 'prophecy' that are part and parcel of a vocabulary of resistance to the speculative violence of Hegelian *Geist* with its assertion of totality and its making impossible of transcendence.[81] The link to Levinas is at the same time the link to Derrida, given their common opposition to Hegel and the influence of the former's articulation of the 'Other' on the latter. But there is also a particular link between Balthasar and Derrida that threads itself through Rosenzweig. While Rosenzweig was convinced that in the final analysis Hegelian dialectic proved hegemonic with respect to any notices of dialogue that might be provided in areas of subjective and especially objective Spirit, what he writes about Hegel before *The Star of Redemption* does not totally rule out the presence of such a tendency.[82] Interestingly, Balthasar proposes a similar complexification of the monism of Hegelian thought. Balthasar suggests in *Theo-Logic* that in Hegel's elaboration of the family in *Lectures on the Philosophy of Right* a dialogical correction of his dialectical mediation comes into view (*TL2*, 44-5, 59-62). Unfortunately, however, Hegel closes off an opening that would have been productive for the entire system. Here Balthasar is perhaps being at his most charitable and approximates contemporary readings of Hegel which would attempt to bring to the fore elements of Hegel's thought that provide critical leverage against his own worst instincts.[83] In *Glas* Derrida demonstrates that a reader of Hegel should not make even this concession, thinking rather that the dialogical notion of family is in fact primed for dialectical takeover, and confirms beforehand the monistic and tyrannical impulse of the Hegelian system that is as inveterately anti-Jewish as it is antidialogical.[84]

For Balthasar what is true of Jewish monotheism is even more true of Christian monotheism. For the God of Christian witness not only admits the world and human being into relation and dialogue, but grounds dialogue between God and God's other precisely as the differentiated reality of three persons. Not metaphysical dualism or pluralism then, but trinitarian monotheism represents the antithesis of any and all varieties of monism, whether static or dynamic, whether steady-state or developmental. Whatever form this trinitarian monotheism takes, whether that of Augustine, or Thomas, or Bonaventure, Hegel's dialectical monism, whose ambition is to 'reconcile' part with part and part with whole, is put at arm's length. Referring to a passage in Hegel's *Lectures on the Philosophy of Religion*, Balthasar sums up a whole line of reflection on Hegel:

> *. . . in Hegel's system, the "other," which is a "moment" in the fulness of the Divine-One, is ultimately swallowed up and devoured by this unity. Individual being must be ready to disappear in the engulfing absolute. (TL2, 120; see also TL2, 44)*

The 'summing up' represents a crystallization of Balthasar's own view of Hegel's dialectical mediation or self-mediation, but also it fairly literally sums up 19th-century criticism, reflected differently by Kierkegaard and by Hegel's German critics, above all Franz Anton Staudenmaier, whose critique of Hegel we will deal with in some detail in Part 3.

The second structural property of mythological thought is *eros.* In the epical or mythological ambit the movement of divine becoming is self-consciously understood as a teleological process. This view differs decisively from the biblical view, as well as the view of St. Thomas who in *De potentia* and in the *Summa Theologica* explicitly denies potentiality in God.[85] Indeed, in Hegelian thought the divine is erotic in the strict Platonic sense, since for the divine to achieve coincidence with the perfection at which it aims, it 'needs' the sublatable otherness of the world and human being. Having the *penia* or 'lack' of the *Symposium* explicitly in mind, in a number of texts Balthasar issues a demurral on behalf of what he takes to be the biblically normed view. *Theo-Drama* makes the point concisely:

> *Nor does the poverty come before wealth: it is not as if God must first go out, in the trinitarian processions in order to gain himself (as Idealism imagines) . . . (TD2, 257; see also TD2, 91).*

In a number of places *Theo-Logic* provides greater specificity to an Idealist position that almost gets reduced to code (*TL2*, 23-4; also *TL3*, 41-2). In *Theo-Logic 2* Balthasar finds it useful to supply a textual example of what he takes to be the stock Hegelian position:

> *If the concept [in its highest form as the absolute idea] is defined to be the truth of being and of essence, we must reckon with the question why we did not begin with this concept itself. The answer to this question is that, where the knowledge proper to thought is concerned, it is impossible to begin with truth, because the truth that constitutes the beginning rests upon sheer assertion, whereas truth must as such stand the test of thought. (Enc #159 zu; cited TL2, 23)*

Balthasar will insist upon truth being the 'beginning,' and will not abide the notion that thought is the measure of truth, rather than truth being the measure of thought. In different ways both *Theo-Logic 1* and *Glory of the Lord 1* are galvanized about the issues of beginning and measure and their relationship.

The mythological view represents the binary opposite to the metaphysical view of God that considers the divine in complete abstraction from its acts and elaborates the properties of the divine based on this abstraction. Precisely as such, however, the metaphysical view can also be regarded as epical, since it too pretends to articulate the disinterested divine point of view, what Balthasar refers to as 'philosophical sublimity' (*TD2*, 9). At the very least adopting the divine point of view, or the non-perspectival view, is a necessary condition for 'epical' ascription, and leaves it open as to whether it can serve also as the sufficient condition. In any event, both species of epic are unfaithful to biblical witness. Balthasar's considerably more detailed treatment of the mythological variety suggests an asymmetry that requires explanation. Part of this explanation is surely contextual: resistance to the mythological species appears to be more urgent, since, on the one hand, the metaphysical and/or degenerative neo-Scholastic view has lost ecclesial and theological currency and, on the other, the mythological view offers an attractive alternative to a view that appears to enjoy at best a half-life in contemporary thought and incapable of fundamentally challenging a modernity characterized by procedural rationality and an operative atheism. Plausibly, however, part of the explanation has to do with the sense of 'epic' deployed to cover very different species, neither of which is dramatic in the way that Christian discourse and existence is. In the case of Hegel's more or less mythological view, 'epic' refers not only to the relatively disinterested wide-angled lens view that refuses fully to identify with any of the players in a play that exceeds them – which Hegel in his *Aesthetics* insisted characterized Homer in general and especially the *Iliad* – but also refers more specifically to a divine, whose very development functions to resolve doubts about the extent and nature of this divine and the character of its interaction with the world and human being. By contrast, the metaphysical tradition, whether in objectivist or subjectivist mode, seems to instantiate the first and softer criterion, while violently rejecting the second.

For Balthasar, the erotic view has to be opposed by the properly Christian view of the divine as pure love and gift (e.g. *TD2*, 286; *TL2*, 23-4, 28, 48, 117-18 *inter alia*). As *Glory of the Lord 6-7* registers it, scripture renders a God of love who, for all that, is a God of exorbitant demand on individual and communities. From the perspective of the New Testament, righteousness and mercy are understood to interdefine each other, precisely because God is love. For Balthasar the biblical view finds its consummate expression as well as its center of gravity in the Gospel of John (e.g. *GL7*, 10; *TL2*, 11-24, 67 *inter alia*). The agapeic view of God rendered in scripture, and consummately in John, is also, according to Balthasar, faithfully reproduced or rearticulated in the theological tradition. This is the view of Augustine who turns out to be more than a merely aesthetic thinker as rendered in *Glory of the Lord* 2, but also a truly apocalyptic thinker (*TD2*, 88-9; *TD4*, 21). This is the view of Anselm, whose rehabilitation from the rationalist caricature is only insufficiently achieved by characterizing Anselm's thought as aesthetic (*GL2*, 211-57), that is, a form of thought grounded in a vision of Christ as mediating between God and human being. Anselm's thought is also dramatic (*TD4*, 255-61), in that sin opens an expanse of alienation that the mediator overcomes. In this respect, at the very least Gustaf Aulén's distinctions between the mythological and forensic views of atonement, and between

Anselm and Irenaeus, represent exaggerations.[86] And finally, Anselm is a thinker who hints at a 'logic' of divine action otherwise than the principle of sufficient reason *(TL2*, 22-4; also *LA*, 27, 32, 87). Superlatively, the Johannine view of love is the organizing insight and indeed concept of Bonaventure's thought which, as with Anselm's, is displayed in the three registers of aesthetics, dramatics and logic. Supplying nothing less than the basic coordinates of Balthasar's theological aesthetic in *Glory of the Lord*, Bonaventure does not make a major reappearance in Balthasar's oeuvre until the last volume of *Theo-Drama*, where his view of love and participation is used to chasten Hegelian construals of the relation between the triune God and the world. And, of course, in *Theo-Logic*, it is Bonaventure who once again gains pride of place in Balthasar's articulation of the triune God as indissolubly love (*TL2*, 89; also *LA*, 88, 105, 116). Defined, then, by scripture and the theological tradition as love, the divine does not give from lack but rather from superabundance (*TD2*, 258-9). The perfection of God is originary; it is the perfection of God precisely as origin (*TL2*, 22-3). God does not acquire perfection in and through a process of self-determination and mediation. God is from the beginning this perfection that gives endlessly. Reminding oneself of Oscar Wilde's well-known apothegm in the preface to *Dorian Gray* to the effect that all art is quite useless, one could say that 'God's art' is also useless in that it exceeds utility: indeed, 'God's art' is the prime analogate of such excess. No return can compensate for the gift of reality that the triune God gives without expectation of return. Nor is it conceivable that the giving of the triune God in creation, redemption, and eschaton can pay off for God as if it were an expression of 'the cunning of reason' (*List der Vernunft*). The triune God does not 'come to be all that God can be' on the back of his world and his creatures.

Against Hegel it is necessary to insist on agape over eros. But Balthasar does not presume that resisting Hegel on his thoroughgoing commitment to a heavily ontologized view of eros involves the exclusion of every and all modes of eros. The erotic objection or the objection to the erotic only applies to a view that would envision eros as a privative form of being dynamically oriented towards fulfillment. Balthasar is unwilling to subscribe to Nygren's binary opposition,[87] which he believes unhelpfully validates the polemical side of Luther. As Balthasar makes clear in *Glory of the Lord 1*, Luther's sundering of grace and nature represents a catastrophic break from the theological tradition which at its best held these in tension and balance (*GL1*, 44). The sundering opened up nature and grace as two incommensurable tracks, whose disunion both Romanticism and Idealism were tempted to resolve. While Balthasar does not insist that the sundering of eros from agape is a function of this split, or determine perspicuously in what ways it relates to it, it is not incidental that he provides eros with a generous space of enactment, while insisting that human desire for God represents a response to God's love and is enabled by it. There is nothing careless about divine love, nothing disinterested. In fact, the love of God is constituted by an interest that is infinite both extensively and intensively. God is superbly interested in everyone and everything, as well as infinitely more interested than any particular finite creature; indeed infinitely more and at a deeper level than the most self-serving eros of a particular being.

The problem with Hegel here is twofold. Formally and materially, he can influence a would-be Christian discourse by demonstrating the validity of his view, by persuading that the view thus demonstrated has at least minimal, if not in every case impeccable Christian credentials. But Hegel can also encourage, as he so often has – witness Kierkegaard – a reaction formation that puts the authentically Christian view out of action, and possibly sets the stage for absorption by Hegelian style logic which feasts on antitheses. Support then of the Johannine view of God as love, whether 1 John 4 or John 1:18, does not imply that it is legitimate to attribute eros to the triune God. What it does imply is that the discourse of eros must at every point be regulated by the view that God, specifically the triune God, is fullness from the beginning, and that one must think of Hegel's account of an indigent beginning not only as being unacceptable from a philosophical point of view, but as finding no motive in John or the tradition of Christian interpretation. The following passage deserves to be quoted in full:

Theo-Logic can afford to begin with the absolute fulness because it is as such already God's self-exposition for the world, which,

> *furthermore, the Holy Spirit (who is not the absolute Spirit of Hegel), in a never-to-be-concluded progression, simultaneously exposits and deposits in created spirits. It could, of course, be said that there is a certain neediness in the theo-logic that corresponds to the neediness of the Hegelian beginning: the poverty of the fleshy existence of God and World. Yet this poverty is not an abstraction, but of love, a "blessed poverty" (the first words of Jesus' preaching, Mt. 5:3), because it is poverty freely chosen to enrich us (2 Cor. 8:9). (TL2, 23-4).*

Balthasar's logic of love, a logic from above (*kata-logic*) rather than below (*ana-logic*), comes to serve as something like a theological rule in the French Communio group who, with different degrees of awareness and different degrees of intensity, sense in Hegel the obverse of the Johannine and the theological tradition for which John is regulative.

The third structural property of the mythological view is the tendency to assert that the process of becoming of the divine is *necessary* (e.g. *TD2*, 397). For Balthasar, necessity can be explicitly asserted, as it is in Hegel's own texts (*TD2*, 226; *TL3*, 42), or implicitly, as it is in the theological discourses of Moltmann (*TD2*, 227-9), which if it avails of the language of freedom, arguably, does not escape any more successfully than the later Schelling does the gravitational pull of necessitarianism (*GL5*, 570). In Moltmann, as in Schelling, freedom is restricted by the metaphysical rule that the divine would be imperfect if the divine did not go out into the world (*TD5*, 229). For Balthasar, divine freedom is compatible neither with logical, ontological, or physical necessity. Balthasar agrees with Barth's judgment that Hegel gerrymanders the notion of divine freedom,[88] but he finds it worthwhile to emphasize more the gratuity and whylessness of divine freedom than its power to dispose. Arguably two of the more powerful expressions of this emphasis in the trilogy are provided by *Glory of the Lord 5* and *Theo-Logic 1*. In the crucially important closing pages of both volumes, gratuity and whylessness take center stage. *Theo-Logic 1* is especially instructive since it engages Hegel's view of appearance as it is articulated in his logic of essence (*TL1*, 216-23; esp. 218-19; also *TL1*, 65, 88, 135, 146) in order to affirm Hegel's exclusion of arbitrary divine will, but also to deny Hegel's Spinozistic equation of divine freedom with divine necessity. Encouraged by what is most Christianly sober in the broad Christian Neoplatonic tradition, Balthasar insists on the groundlessness of divine communication (*TL1*, 222-23). The stress on whylessness is, however, compatible with narrative verisimilitude as this is elaborated in *Glory of the Lord*. This essentially involves the aesthetic rightness of the movement and direction of the drama of and between infinite and finite freedom. For Balthasar, this rightness finds expression in the very different biblical 'must' (*dei*) and more specifically 'must' as it is rendered in Luke's Gospel (Luke 9:22).[89] Aesthetic rightness receives its most subtle and reticulated theological reflection in Anselm (*GL2*, 211-13). By contrast with all other forms of 'must,' the 'must' of aesthetic rightness and narrative verisimilitude is compatible with multiple twists and turns in the divine plot, and even a denouement that does not exclude all surprise.[90] To favor narrative verisimilitude is to suggest both a relationship between beauty and goodness and beauty and truth, which are central to the trilogy, and whose central outline is prepared for in *Theo-Logic 1*, which rechristens *Wahrheit* (1946).

One can think of Balthasar's astonishing essay on Anselm in *Glory of the Lord* as an act of ecclesial generosity in which the aesthetic recontextualizing of Anselm's discourse serves to mainstream his theology and not make it solely an effect of apologetics whose success is suspect and whose interest is marginal (*GL2*, 211-59). But one can also think of this essay as liberating Anselm as a critical proxy to chastise rationalisms of Scholastic and Nominalist vintage, but even more of speculative vintage, of which none greater can be thought than that of Hegel. Anselm is especially apt for this purpose, given both his rationalist reputation, and because together with Eckhart, he is one of the few medieval thinkers Hegel thinks worth enlisting as a precursor in his speculative program which centrally involves the transfiguration of Christianity.[91] Thus, however Christ's expenditure or sacrifice on our behalf is to be thought, Anselm's account in *Cur Deus Homo* suggests that it cannot be thought in Hegelian terms as necessary for the divine to be truly infinite in that nothing remains outside its ordinance (*TD4*, 255-61).[92] Similarly, whatever the value of the ontological argument precisely as religious, that is, precisely as it bears upon the adhesion of the Christian and the incommensurable God, the religious believer neither enacts nor participates in a process of self-legitimating thought in which the divine effectively actualizes itself. The divine is fully actual as origin. This is precisely the provocation for thinking its perfection. The argument does no more than follow a pattern of thought that is as genuinely ecstatic as it is finite. As Balthasar insists: in Anselm reason is systemically prayerful. The Hegelian rendition suspends both the ecstasy and the finitude of thought. Any and all necessary reasons in Anselm give the lie to Hegelian necessity: they are images or tropes of the logic of love, which is otherwise than Hegel's spurious theologic. Structurally, however, the release of Anselm from the clutches of the kind of interpretation enacted in Hegel's *Lectures on the Philosophy of Religion* also represents the release of John. 'Precisely,' Balthasar avers, 'in John, where the world has already been created in the Logos and fashioned in conformity with him, this immanencing is reserved as pure grace' (Jn 1:14, 16-17) (*TL2*, 67; *TL3*, 42). But freedom and grace are precisely what Hegelian logic disallows, as the 'going forth' is regarded as necessary, and the mystery of divine love disclosed in Christ becomes a 'universal law' (*GL7*, 214).

It is precisely this sense of grace, however residual it is, that makes Hölderlin more than an apostle of the 'One in All,' and makes it possible to see his poetry as offering leverage against the explanatory thirst of the metaphysical tradition and the eclipse of specifically Christian ecstasis. In *Glory of the Lord 5* Hölderlin is figured as a poet of 'grace,' even as the specifically Christian content of 'grace' or *charis* remains open. Balthasar makes a nod to its Greek (Homeric and Pindaric) and Christian facets without choosing between them, or feeling the need to choose between them. What makes it unnecessary to decide is what also makes it unnecessary for Przywara, who writes an influential book on the great German poet,[93] namely, the analogy of being. For the analogy of being expresses itself in the analogy of discourse: non-biblical discourse provides an analogy for scriptural discourse which remains incommensurable just as God remains *semper maior.* Marion develops this line of interpretation in his great essay on Hölderlin in *The*

Idol and Distance (80-138) when he reduces Hölderlin to his Johannine presuppositions, and shows how together with the very best of apophatic theologians such as Pseudo-Dionysius, he exceeds the totalizing regime of metaphysics that Heidegger has justly censured. Of course, it follows logically, therefore, that as Balthasar exceeds Heidegger he exceeds Hegel, who is regarded by Heidegger as the apotheosis of the metaphysical tradition. But not simply 'logically': Marion has to be fully aware of how Hölderlin, as a supporter of the 'One in All,' can himself be read as eclipsing grace. If Balthasar and Przywara sense a tension in Hölderlin that involves at least an occasional declension away from the essentially Johannine matrix of his inspiration, Marion offers a radical Johannine reading in which Hölderlin is the poet of the double exposure centered in Christ: God's self-exposure to the world and human beings responsive exposure to divine humility.

The fourth and final structural property of Hegel's mythological construal is a particular and idiosyncratic rendition of the trope of kenosis. Simply put, Balthasar understands that the biblical, that is, christological meaning of kenosis, as registered in Philippians 2:5-11 and 2 Corinthians 8:9,[94] undergoes a fundamental alteration within the mythological horizon of thought in which the accent falls on divine development (*TD2*, 182-3). For Balthasar, there are three elements to Hegelian deviance.

(i) First and most basically, within the Hegelian mythological context kenosis refers to the substance of the divine rather than its form (*TD3*, 136-7; *TD5*, 223-4). Hegel substitutes, therefore, for a properly morphological interpretation of kenosis an essentialist view that plays out unreflectively in his theological appropriators, but which also gets endorsed in theological frameworks that are not univocally Hegelian such as that of the radical kenoticists of the late nineteenth century (*TD2*, 183-84).[95] However this is understood in terms of its possibility, however imagined with respect to whether emptying ultimately involves ontological decrease or increase, the essentialist interpretation of kenosis at the very least radically undercuts divine sovereignty and transcendence. In its specifically Hegelian form, as Balthasar understands well, it also tends to undermine the tri-personal view of the divine and possibly even the very notion of person itself. As we will see in the next chapter, Balthasar controversially understands Hegelianism to instantiate a novel repetition of modalism (*TL3*, 46-7). Granting the validity of Hegel's plotting a trinitarian backdrop to christological kenosis, Balthasar is anxious to obviate Hegel's modalistic extrapolation:

> *For with the kenosis of Christ, eternity has put itself in motion and has passed through time with all of its darkness. There is no alienating hiatus between the Father's remaining at home and the Son's going forth on his pilgrimage, for the "distance" of the kenosis is a mode of intratrinitarian nearness and the circumcession of the divine hypostases. In the kenosis of the Son, it is true that "his innate form of God" stays back with the Father, is "left behind" with him, both as a pledge of his faithfulness to the will of God and a "reminder" to the Father of how much he himself is committed to the world adventure . . . In this kind of tension between eternity and time, God is not split apart, but more than ever is with himself, for he perfects the free commitment that he began with creation. (Exp 4, 138)*

(ii) Second, in mythological schemes of a Hegelian type kenosis is understood as an operation of iteration. The intra-trinitarian relations and even creation, and not simply the saving reality of Christ, can be understood kenotically, and plotted on the narrative side as an invariant application of the same operation. As Balthasar's own work and that of theologians he admires, such as Sergei Bulgakov, show clearly, imagining kenosis as a plural event need not imply that a theologian has stepped outside the tradition. Indeed this kind of experiment in imagination might be necessary if a contemporary theological expression is to avoid the anodyne. Still, Balthasar points to some ever present dangers. The generalizing of kenosis can and does serve in the case of Hegel and his epigones to deflect attention from Christ and redemption (*TL2*, 23-4), and blur the boundaries between incarnation and creation (*TL2*, 85), on the one hand, and Christ and the Church (*TL2*, 78), on the other. For Balthasar, the problem does not so much lie in extending the trope beyond its application to Christ, but in forgetting that we are dealing with an extension that ought not to compromise the event of Christ, nor compromise the integrity of the domains of creation and Church. Balthasar understands his own fairly radical position on kenosis to be informed by Bulgakov. This is to say also that therein Balthasar finds his model of resistance. *Glory of the Lord 7* could not make the point more eloquently:

> *It is therefore preferable to be guided by some of Bulgakov's fundamental ideas . . . and to take the "selflessness" of the divine persons, as of pure relations in the love within the Godhead, as the basis of everything: this selflessness is the basis of the first form of kenosis, that lies in creation (especially in the creation of man who is free), for the creator has given up a part of his freedom to the creature, in the act of creating; but this he can dare to do only in virtue of his foreseeing and taking into account the second and truest kenosis, that of the Cross, in which he makes good the uttermost consequences of creation's freedom, and goes beyond them. In this kenosis – as the surrender of the "form of God" – becomes the decisive act of the Son, who translates his being begotten by the Father (and in this, his dependence on Him) into the expressive form of creaturely obedience; but the whole Trinity remains involved in this act, the Father by sending out the Son and abandoning him on the Cross, and the Spirit by uniting them now only in the expressive form of the separation. (GL7, 213-4)* [96]

Referencing the *The Incarnate Word* Balthasar shows himself thoroughly indebted to Bulgakov's taxis of kenosis. The taxis is necessary in order that the drama of the triune God's relation to the world mirrors Hegel's speculative chain of kenosis. However, Balthasar contests Hegelian interpretation of every link in the chain, as well as the meaning of the chain. Balthasar underwrites the personal matrix of relation at the level of the Trinity; underscores the sacrifice enacted by the Son on the Cross without prejudice to the sovereignty of the Father; and insists that the order of creation is the generation of a genuine other and not a divine self-othering that compromises finite freedom and removes the possibility of dialogue.

(iii) In the mythological context kenosis turns out to behave ironically. For in fact, divine emptying is a form of divine filling, thus kenosis is a form of *plerosis* (*TL2*, 22-4). Here without explicitly saying so, Balthasar seems to agree with a reading of Hegel that Thomas Altizer unfurled in his 'death of God' theology (*TD5*, 244) and to which Altizer continues to remain faithful even as he attempts to outline the lineaments of an apocalyptic, post-Christian theology: procedurally a discourse of emptying, even nihilation, the discourse of kenosis is finally another way of talking about divine self-realization.[97] This is a diagnosis of Hegel that Balthasar shares with contemporary Catholic commentary on Hegel of a Communio stripe (e.g. Tillette, Brito, and Marchesi),[98] with the influence going both ways. The theological effects are disastrous: God is exposed as risking and sacrificing nothing. At a level beyond the circulation of concept, such a God is a trickster who feigns giving; at a level nearer the circulation of concept that intercallates mind as divine, this God is a sublime narcissist, or better the narcissism of sublimity in search of a subject. In any event, such a God is not a God of love, the Christian God of sheer gift.

Surprisingly, as I intimated earlier, Radical Orthodoxy, otherwise so relatively friendly towards Balthasar's enterprise, represents something of a break in consensus. For some the prominence of the trope of kenosis in Balthasarian and Hegelian discourses bespeaks genuine affinity in theological position. The question to be decided is not, as in the case of Communio philosophers and theologians, what precisely is the degree of separation between Hegel and Balthasar, but rather whether given this basic agreement with respect to the trope Hegel drags Balthasar down into the epical quagmire, or whether Balthasar manages to elevate Hegel and take him beyond his recessive tendency towards a 'restricted economy.' At the same time it should be mentioned that in line with both postmodern and Communio Catholic critique of Hegel, Milbank, and a number of other thinkers in the Radical Orthodoxy movement, construct a Hegel whose developmental narrative eclipses gift and thus is an agent of the nihilism that marks modernity.[99]

As with his reservations about the ontotheological profile of eros, reservations about the developmental and teleological curve of kenosis in Hegel do not mean, for Balthasar, that kenosis and plerosis are contraries. Simply to protest that they are antithetical constructs is to be involved in a self-defeating reaction formation and fail to rise to the level of subtlety of the biblical and theological tradition. In *Theo-Logic 2* Balthasar makes it clear that John thinks that the event of the incarnation and the cross and resurrection, which exposes the divine to the human condition and its vicissitudes, portends a fullness. Having John 1:16 explicitly in mind (*TL2*, 22-3), Balthasar does not take the easy way out by suggesting that fulfillment is translatable without remainder into soteriology, although it may well be the case that the soteriological element is dominant. The submission to incarnation and suffering offers nothing less than an 'exposition' (*Auslegen*) of God. As the paradoxical coincidence of emptiness and fullness, or more adequately, of emptying and fulfilling, Christ is the icon of the divine. Christ displays a dynamic movement at the heart of the divine that is itself a generosity without reserve.

Needless to say, the properties of monism, eros, necessity, and a peculiar modulation of kenosis are neither neatly separated, nor easily separable in Hegel's discourse. When Hegel speaks to the 'fulfillment' of the divine as the 'really real' in the Neoplatonic sense of the term, both the iterative view of kenosis and an erotic interpretation of love are involved. This is especially the case in the *Phenomenology* and *Lectures on the Philosophy of Religion* which continue to sanction the language of 'love' in the way the *Encyclopedia* does not. In *Theo-Logic* in particular Balthasar follows this line of implication even if ironically he invokes the *Encyclopedia* as support (*TL2*, 22-3; *TL3*, 41). Similarly, Hegel's monistic bias is tied intrinsically to a commitment to necessity that is all the more inured by attempting to write freedom into its articulation. If Hegel's system is predicated on the overcoming of theological or ontotheological voluntarism and thus of nominalism, such an overcoming is hindered rather than helped by the exclusion of freedom from the divine being of beings, who proceeds in Hegel's texts as the substance that is subject,[100] or the substance whose goal is subject. Rather, Hegel adopts the Spinozist strategy of interdefining freedom and necessity, even as he attempts to recognize freedom more fully by loosening it from the axiomatic chains of book 1 of the *Ethics* (props. 33-36). Hegel tries to signal his transcendence of Spinoza in a number of ways: for example, by appeal to a Christian doctrine of creation, by speaking of the other of world as coming into being by 'free letting-go' (*frei Entlassung*) of the Idea,[101] and especially by having very much in mind, whenever he speaks of necessity, the aesthetic model of Schiller for whom necessity is rightness and appropriateness in free play.[102] All of this gives a different complexion to Hegel's system than Spinoza's which not only is monist but also static. Still, the distance between Spinoza and Hegel is a difference within the same. Hegel is every bit as much committed to unity, only unity is mediated in and through difference. Otherness and multiplicity find an endorsement that they do not find in Spinoza, at least the Spinoza who remains outside of the Deleuzian band of interpretation, which would make Spinoza one of the greatest pluralists in the philosophical tradition. Moreover, if there is more looseness and give in Hegel's system, for all that there is no less necessity. The world of nature and finite spirit is no less logically and ontologically necessary than in Spinoza. Balthasar sees clearly how logical and ontological necessity serves Hegel's dialectical monism. However the aesthetic reading of Schiller assists in Hegel's modification of Spinoza, necessity in Hegel is more than the 'serious play' of Schiller's *Aesthetic Letters.* Balthasar sees even more clearly how necessity outbids the kind of love endorsed by the Christian tradition, love as agape but not without the energy of a desire that is the expression of a fullness unimaginable to human being in history.[103]

The four epical properties that define the Hegelian mythos separate it entirely from the biblical narrative. As a second-order myth, which embodies and recommends the triumph of knowledge over faith, Hegel's thought recalls Valentinian metamorphosis of biblical Christianity, which also celebrates the movement beyond the exoteric into the celebration of the 'secret' open only to the initiate, who is the post-Enlightenment articulater of the absolute narrative. As suggested in the last chapter, recognizing with Blumenberg the difference represented by modernity, it is only to be expected that there would be some differences in the way in which the modern Valentinian metanarrative gets modulated. It is possible to read Hegelian-style mythos as an exacerbation of the merely inchoate developmental, erotic, and agonic tendencies of classical Valentinianism.[104]

I will return to the issue of Balthasar's discernment of the relation between Hegelian and Valentinian thought in the next chapter when I deal in some detail with Balthasar's and Hegel's rival interpretations of the Trinity. What I would like to do now is intimate briefly what Balthasar presumes to be the anthropological corollary of Hegel's epical narrative. Functioning variously as conviction and conclusion, Balthasar's settled view is that an indelible feature of Hegel's narrative ontotheology is its refusal to recognize and embrace difference. The business of Hegelian narrative, as with Hegelian logic, is to mediate, and thereby overcome difference: this is so whether the pair is Being and nothing, the Trinity and the world, infinite and finite knowledge, concept and history, nature and spirit, life and death, church and world. As I have already indicated, from the traditional Christian point of view that Balthasar is anxious to defend, this riddles the proper understanding of the reality of the divine, the world, and the human. While hardly an existential philosopher of a Kierkegaardian ilk, Balthasar by no means neglects the consequences with respect to a proper understanding of human being. The abolition of difference not only compromises the hoary theologoumenon of creation from nothing, thereby representing a challenge to divine sovereignty, it also excludes the experiential and phenomenological evidence of the sheer givenness and giftedness of beings that arrive with no self-certification.[105] And excluding this experience, Hegel's thought forecloses the prospects for a reflective affirmation of this being-given as good that is stated boldly in *Theo-Logic 1* (217-19). In *Glory of the Lord* the articulation of the interconnection of the transcendentals of beauty and goodness and truth mark a challenge to Hegel's deterministic view of appearance.[106] Needless to say, the very concept of 'theo-drama,' which *Theo-Drama 1* makes clear, is provoked by Hegel's view of drama and dialectic, supposes the transcendental of the good as providing the ultimate horizon of action without which nihilism prevails. The exclusion of the good also rules out beforehand a posture of gratitude to the other or totally other as origin. Epical narratives of the Hegelian sort – which may very well involve repetition of Valentinian epics – exclude therefore not only createdness but reflexive owning of createdness in creatureliness.

The abolition of difference in Hegelian epic also has effects on who is regarded as the human exemplar. In the Hegelian scheme exemplarity is illustrated, on the one hand, by the hero in history, who is availed of by the 'cunning of reason' to execute some non-obvious rational purpose and, on the other, by what the generative interpreter of Hegel, Alexandre Kojève,[107] calls the 'Hegelian sage.' For Balthasar by contrast, if we put Christ in brackets – and we are barely allowed to – the exemplary human is ultimately the saint,[108] although a holy theologian is also invested with a degree of exemplarity. All the theologians who provide examples of 'clerical theological style' are saints of the church.[109] The difference could not be more stark. In *Lectures on the Philosophy of History* Hegel can validate the non-moral Napoleon, because although he wreaks havoc in all of Europe and fails in his grand design, nonetheless, he shifts power in ways helpful to the increase in human knowledge and self-determination, and leaves behind him a legacy in law and politics. While Balthasar does not essay an ethical rebuttal, he is as much repelled by this form of consequentialism as most of Hegel's critics. In agreement with an opinion that dates from *Apokalypse* (*Apok 1*, 575, 602) and is threaded through his book on history,[110] in *Theo-Drama 1* Balthasar makes it plain that no Christian can accept Hegel's proposal of history as determined by immanent laws of historical development that essentially rules out eschatology, since it rules out judgment. At the same time, Hegel validates the speculative philosopher – who is precisely the opposite of the prophet – whose genius is entirely retrospective, but absolutely encompassing. If the image of the owl of Minerva is in one sense a submission of the humility of the philosopher,[111] it is at the same time the ultimate in hubris. For Balthasar, this 'twilight' knowledge is knowledge not from the finite but from the infinite point of view, and turns the philosopher into an operative of a theodicy machine calculated to justify history, humanity, and God, and their indifference (e.g. *TL3*, 47). The philosopher 'who surveys the whole' (*TD2*, 35) also seconds the judgment of history, confessing that no other can be thought even if it can be wished. The philosopher delegitimates complaint, and confirms the victims in their invisibility and voicelessness.

As with thinkers as various as Adorno and Ricoeur, Löwith and Metz, Balthasar raises his voice definitively against this aspect of Hegel's thought. Of course, Heidegger too mounted an objection but, as we shall see in the second volume, it is not clear that in the end he does not exhibit a non-theological correlative, a kind of ontodicy, which like Hegel's theodicy, denies the need for justification only to make the denial itself the justification. For Balthasar, it is not only Job who refutes this complacency of thought, but Christ who both represents us and is in solidarity with us. For Balthasar in the trilogy as without, although Christ represents the archetype, a more proximate exemplarity is illustrated by the saint, who fully takes on her unique mission as an unrepeatable reading of the life of Christ. The saint is indeed defined by excess, by a radical love that goes beyond the bounds of justice. As exemplary, the saint is transparent of and to the gift of Being which, at the same time, is the gift of the triune God. From Balthasar's reflections on prophecy in *Glory of the Lord 6*,[112] it is clear that all saints are animated by the prophetic, not in the deficient sense of making predictions, or even having intimations of judgment, but rather in the sense of being called, and constituting a challenge to the manifold forms of idolatry and injustice, individual and social satisfaction, and proving a scourge to the discourses of justification. The saint is not marked by the 'glamor' of the hero. She is marked rather by the *charis* that refers away from the self towards Christ as the referent. However much Balthasar affirms the Homeric hero as a figure of *charis* (*GL4*, 43-78), he is as aware, as is Simone Weil,[113] that the glamor of the hero is often a false glamor, precisely the opposite of the love illustrated by the saint which moves towards the condition of incognito.

Although Balthasar does not draw out the contrast between the saint and the Hegelian sage, on the one hand, and the Hegelian hero, on the other, with all the sharpness that one would like, it is clear that he has inspired others to do so. First among equals is Jean-Yves Lacoste. In his book *Experience and the Absolute* these contrasts assume a high profile.[114] As one might suspect, it is the refusal of the saint to be serious that challenges the portentousness of the negative, which can always supply reasons and present guarantees. Lacoste here essentially puts an exclamation point to the affirmation of the ludic, which we discussed earlier in the chapter, by focusing the battle between Christianity and secularity as a battle between Balthasar and Hegel. In contrast, because of the extraordinary influence of the great French trio of Péguy, Bernanos, and Claudel on his thought, in Balthasar's texts the opposition between saint and hero is more generic. There is a battle of images between the 'hero,' who is thought to represent the virtues of the community, and the saint, who tends to fall outside the social and cultural grid, and thus outside visibility. The saint then is a minimum to the hero's maximum, and suffers precisely from the difficulty of representation to which it has been the genius of Weil to call our attention.[115]

A further way in which Hegel's epical narrative compromises the dramatic Christian view is in his thoroughly dialectical view of life and death, in which death is the instrument of life, indeed greater life. This instrumental understanding effectively removes the tragic element from death and effaces its horror. In the Gospel narratives death still remains tragic in its posing itself as final – even if tragedy does not have the final word. By contrast, in the Hegelian system death is rendered in such general terms that it becomes a general principle of the cosmos rather than an event or catastrophe that has each individual as its subject and recipient. As Euripides (*GL4*, 141-54), so scorned by Hegel,[116] suggests, death is unique as it is universal. And it is Euripides who intimates that the ultimate may not be truly ultimate, that beyond this finality may lie an impossible finality. For the Gospel writers this finality is the finality of resurrected life that shouts out the unthinkable generosity of God as giver: through the love of Christ the giving is a giving back of a narratively embodied life, defined by relation, that reaches beyond the pagan redress into coordinates as wide as the infinite distance between divine persons. For Balthasar, Hegel cannot think the resurrection of the embodied self (*TL2*, 19). Thus creation, incarnation as a 'once only,' and the other Christian mysteries that make up the *mysterion* of Christianity are impossible to thought. Hegel can think illumination that overcomes the epistemic and ontological *chorismos* between the infinite and finite, and the divine and the human. Hegel can fold time into eternity to construct something other than the 'non-philosophical' everlastingness of the Christian tradition, which from Hegel's perspective Kant unfortunately repeated.[117] In doing so, however, Hegel articulates a Stoic and Spinozist line of thought, while at the same time showing more affinity with the Platonic view of the immortality of the soul than the view of the resurrection of the body. Hegel can also be seen to be involved in a repetition of the kind of view sponsored by the Gnostic *Gospel of Truth* in which eternity seems to be coextensive with the moment of vision, towards which Balthasar affects an Irenaean kind of distance.

On Hegel's own terms, drama is to be preferred to epic. Thus, to characterize Hegel's thought as epical is to hit Hegel at a vulnerable point. On the surface, however, to tar Hegel with the epic brush is more nearly to announce a falling short of the authentic Christian portrayal than an actual deviance. Most certainly, it does not announce anything like systemic deviance. Not just any epic construal implies deviance in the strict sense. 'Deviant epicality' does not amount to a pleonasm. Balthasar makes the stronger rather than the weaker argument concerning the epical nature of the Hegelian system. Hegelian epicality, constituted by monism, eros, a self-filling form of kenosis, and necessity, not only fails to translate the Christian narrative into terms that are faithful to Christianity's dramatic ethos, it effects a wholesale distortion of the Christian narrative which renders the drama of the triune God's relation to the world as founded and sustained by gratuitous love. Changed is the meaning of each episode of the biblical narrative, as well as the meaning of the narrative as a whole. 'Creation' means something other than the product of a gratuitous act: in effect the world coproduces the producer; evil is ontologized to coincide with the positing of a world; redemption is a built-in process dialectically carried out in and through history; history delivers the final judgment on society and human being that can and should be vindicated by the philosophical sage.

Above all, Hegelian thought supposes a catastrophic effect upon traditional views of Christ and the Trinity. More patently here than anywhere else, Balthasar sees the eclipse of the glory of God, a glory consisting of God's sublime sovereignty and holiness (which includes terribleness) and unsurpassable goodness and gratuity. In its sin of fundamentally distorting the Christian narrative, and thus, its sin of narrative deviance of epic proportions, Hegel's thought further eclipses the actuality and possibility of a doxological vision of Christianity. Both narrative deviance as well as the eclipse of the doxological are deepened when Hegel insists that symbol is void outside its recuperation in the Hegelian concept. The elevation of epical refiguration of the Christian narrative to the level of the concept indemnifies it, and specifically insures that all traces of what cannot be constrained by logic must be extruded from a Christianity that needed the adolescence of the Enlightenment in order to come of age.

Hoisted on the Epical Petard

NOW WE WILL HAVE MUCH MORE TO SAY about Hegel's epical alteration of traditional Christology and doctrine of Trinity in the next chapter, for while it is true that Balthasar contests Hegel at every point, for example his understanding of creation, his construal of sin, his view of the end, Hegel's understanding or rather misunderstanding of Christ and the triune God remain pivotal. For Balthasar agrees formally at least with the view that Hegel first articulated in the *Phenomenology* (Sect. 7) and which thereafter became Hegelian dogma: all Christian theologoumena must be threaded through the event of Christ or the event that is Christ (*PS* #748-770), and it is the Trinity that provides the horizon that embraces all theologoumena and integrates them (*PS* #771-87). But two questions at least deserve to be broached as this chapter accelerates towards conclusion: first, does Balthasar's own work, and especially the trilogy, escape epic pull?; second, does Balthasar spurn myth as such? Of these two questions, the second is by far the more important from a systematic point of view and, accordingly, will receive significantly greater attention.

The first question is hardly an artificial construction. The very expansiveness of the trilogy is both its most attractive and most repellent feature: the facility with which the entire gamut of Western culture, as well as the history of theology, is treated suggests a somewhat epic vantage point; more, while often Balthasar's readings of particular figures are superb (e.g. Pseudo-Dionysius, Maximus, Anselm, Barth, Homer, Bernanos), he is sometimes casual and schematic. Specialists could complain respecting just about anything, for example, his reading of Hopkins or Shakespeare, his treatment of Kant, Augustine, and even Hegel. The level of detail is not always high, and evaluation does not always follow from the analysis. Not only Balthasar's detractors, but also his supporters can have reservations about these aspects of his thought. This kind of objection is fairly low-flying; it would qualify Balthasar's thought as epical in the generic way he himself sometimes uses it with respect to any system of thought that affects a view of the whole, whether mythological or non-mythological. Balthasar would still be too systematic, too teutonic for his own good, or the good of his theological program that supports the view of the whole in the fragment. This objection, however, would by no means exclude the different and stronger claim, the kind of claim made by such as Rahner to the effect that Balthasar's own theology is 'mythological' and/ or 'gnostic' in that it attempts to see the connection between the triune life and passibility. Balthasar's testy response in the foreword to the *Theo-Drama 5* (13-14) is hardly sufficient. Nor, arguably, is the replete text which follows. It can rightly be said that Balthasar's reply rests in his entire work in which he enacts a distinction between what he takes to be a dramatic and an epical theology which, while they look similar, have completely different co-ordinates. The former is as gloriously orthodox as the latter is heterodox, as epistemically humble as the latter is self-vaunting, as respectful to scripture as the latter considers scripture at best to be extraordinarily malleable[118] – and at worst daimonic misinformation that disturbs autonomy and disrupts the possibility of individual and communal self-appropriation.

The fact that the meaning of Balthasar's theology is in significant part determined by negation of the kind of justificatory second-order metanarrative typical of Gnostic systems of the first centuries does not mean that Balthasar is hostile to myth as such. Arguably, it is this lack of hostility to myth that makes Balthasar a target for Rahner, whose epistemology discourages the kind of ontological claim with which myth is invested. Stipulating that the level of myth is of the first-order rather than second-order kind, there is positive as well as negative evidence for Balthasar's hospitality. Balthasar's critique of historical-critical method,[119] which arises out of a more Enlightenment paradigm, gives a negative indication of openness to myth. As one might expect, *Glory of the*

Lord 6 & 7 carry much of the load regarding why myth cannot and should not be excised. After the Prolegomenon all of the volumes of *Theo-Drama* share the burden, although *Theo-Drama 4 & 5* constitutes something of a crescendo. Arguably, Balthasar's most positive defense of myth occurs in *Glory of the Lord 4* in his discussion of Greek tragedy, which is conducted with the understanding that it operates within, while defining and refining, the mythic contours of Greek thought. An important motive for such an extended treatment is that Greek tragedy offers both an analogy to and an adumbration of Christ's suffering and redemption, which is archetypal and as such unsurpassable. Adumbration, however, consists only in part of the continuity of theme: suffering, death, and the impossible finality that exceeds both. In part also, continuity rests on the understanding of what narrative figuration – broadly understood – can and cannot achieve at the level of knowledge. Tragedy, like the Gospel, can and should effect insight concerning the space of action and reaction between human beings and the realities that exceed them. But no more than the Gospel – or any theology that devolves from it – can Greek tragedy provide a divine point of view: in fact, such a view is not only essentially, but self-consciously excluded; the non-identity of the human and the divine is axiomatic. Given that difference is inscribed into the order of things, should actors or spectators not proceed on this basis, then guilt is inevitable and disaster likely. Balthasar then would subscribe to Ricoeur's adage that 'the myth gives rise to thought,' while also assenting to Ricoeur's rider that thought never exhausts the narrative it intends.

In supporting myth, Balthasar can allow that a discourse admits of being called myth even when there is some reflective sense of the merely relative adequacy of the myth to the reality that it would render. This is surely the case with respect to both Greek tragedy and the biblical text. It is possibly – even probably – the case that a modicum of distance is required in order for a discourse to be dramatic. Balthasar's conditional validation of myth and unconditional recommendation of a dramatic point of view in the end sum to a strong affirmation of apocalyptic as essential to a discourse that would resist Hegelian panopticism. On the face of it, this asseveration seems exaggerated, even likely entirely wrong.

After all, 'apocalypse' is a pejorative in Balthasar's text of the same name, and right across the trilogy in his counter-genealogical movement Balthasar pursues Hegel as an apocalyptic as well as a Gnostic thinker. To be either, it seems, is to be lost as a Christian resource. And then there is Balthasar's detailed treatment of biblical apocalyptic in *Glory of the Lord 6* (321-42) in which apocalyptic is thought to be degeneratively speculative. Importantly, however, it is not evident in his ascription of 'apocalyptic' that Balthasar is decrying any and all versions of apocalyptic. The targets seem relatively restricted: on the one hand, Hegel's speculative discourse that rewrites the biblical narrative and elevates it into the concept, on the other, the messianic Joachimite code that lays buried in Hegel's discourse and is activated by epigones of Hegel such as Feuerbach, Marx, and Bloch. In the context of *Glory of the Lord 6* Balthasar simply does not explicitly raise the issue of whether there might not be apocalyptic species that avoid both metalepsis and radical historicization. It turns out also that the objection to apocalyptic as a genre is restricted in terms of its targets. The objection applies fundamentally only to the productions of apocalypses such as 2 Enoch and 4 Ezra in what Balthasar refers to as the 'long twilight' between the testaments. But, then it appears not necessarily to apply all such apocalypses: Daniel is vigorously exempted on the grounds that it has roots in the prophetic tradition that these other non-canonic apocalypses apparently circumvent.

Certainly Balthasar's reluctance to condemn all forms of apocalypse in Christianity is fueled by the anxiety concerning symbolic depletion in the modern world which manifests itself in our stunted practices of reading the biblical text. The kind of vision that marks apocalyptic may be a requirement in a world without vision or with multiple visions all of which compete and none of which hold our attention. But vision may also be required to answer the kind of vision enacted in Hegelian thought, which itself arises as a response to the eidetic erosion of Christianity. Balthasar is not persuaded that either Neo-Scholasticism or transcendental theology will prove a match for Hegelian-style epical theology. And it turns out the exemption of Daniel is the fruit of larger motivations than holding on to a canonic text. It is crucial to Balthasar's own strategy of preserving the central apocalyptic text in the canon, that is, Revelation

(*GL1*, 358-60; *GL6*, 324-42). The purpose is not conservation, but to have in play a symbolic-narrative text that reads the Fourth Gospel and is read by it. Together with the Fourth Gospel, which represents the 'vanishing point' (*GL7*, 10) of New Testament witness, Revelation provides the intimate contrary to Hegel's epical regime by presenting the dramatic blueprint of divine action (*TD4*, 45) and presenting the tableau of human response.

It is Balthasar's intention to highlight the fundamental opposition of paradigms that makes the opening of *Theo-Drama 4* (15-58) so important. There Balthasar provides an interpretation of Revelation not matched anywhere else in his wide-spread work. Although in part this extension is the effect of a homage to von Speyr's copious reflections on Revelation (esp. *TD4*, 181; *GL7*, 359), this is not the full story. The points are chiseled: simultaneously both the most visionary and dramatic text of the Christian tradition, Revelation is a book of the *agnus dei*, whose absolute significance in and for history is disclosed against a trinitarian backdrop. The figure of the Lamb is not only the axis upon which the world turns (*TD4*, 44), but the figure of crisis and judgment who separates out the elect from the non-elect (*TD4*, 48). But the crisis is also aesthetic and alethic. The Lamb represents a terrible kind of beauty, which would be easy to mistake for ugliness, and a mystifying form of truth. Around the figure of the Lamb polarization occurs (*TD4*, 51); and the Anti-Christ is the counter-figure. Balthasar, interestingly focuses not on the violence of the Anti-Christ, but rather on the Anti-Christ as the lie. The vehemence of no is attested then in the refusal of truth rather than in the refusal of peace.

Much more could be said about the apocalyptic landscaping of drama and the dramatic landscaping of apocalyptic. Since I will be treating the matter in detail in part 4 it suffices here to introduce a further line of reflection on apocalyptic, this time on the nature of its discourse. For Balthasar, it is essential to the meaning of Revelation that vision gets validated: this, after all, is the meaning of *apokalypsis* (*TD4*, 47; also *TD4*, 51-2). Importantly, however, apocalyptic seeing is just the opposite of gnosis in which in effect the self becomes the theme (*GL6*, 324). The resistance to gnosis is embedded in the symbolic surface and depth of Revelation; the cascade of symbols, their veritable 'bacchanalian revel,' suggest the object of vision is elusive; their sublimity suggests a revelation that does not yield its secrets (*TD4*, 20, 27). Without availing of Ricoeur's language, Balthasar does think of the symbols as overdetermined in meaning. They are neither reducible to determinate historical referents, nor can their meaning be exhausted by conceptual translation (*TD4*, 20, 27). This, necessarily, points to the more systematic issue of whether there can be a positive relation between apocalyptic and apophasis. *Glory of the Lord* is more helpful on this point than *Theo-Drama*. Laying the foundation for their compatibility in the first volume by figuring Christ as the icon of icons, thus visible precisely as the reality that is invisible, Balthasar puts a point on it later in the volume on the New Covenant when he argues that the figure of Christ provides the very conditions of the ungraspability of God (*GL7*, 15-6, 109, 287). This figure is, of course, through and through paschal, as the Johannine corpus triumphantly underscores (*GL1*, 438-9).

Chapter 3

Great Deflections

Great Deflections

To 'deflect' means to exert a counterforce to a force that would damage what someone holds precious, to push it wide of its mark, make it err. As I have said often enough, while Balthasar's thought has to be considered in the final analysis to be a creative retrieval of the entire *Catholica*, his theology is structurally marked by his deflections of would-be blows to Christianity, its discourses, practices, and forms of life. While Balthasar thinks that Christianity shows signs of dying from a thousand small wounds in the modern period – some of them self-inflicted – the ability to incapacitate is invested in very few forms of thought, since only the few dare to undertake the task of recoding Christian discourse entirely, suggesting new forms of practice, and even new forms of life. Hegel is one of the few; perhaps its leader. In the theological field, de-flection has something – if not everything – to do with re-flection, since successful deflection pushes the Hegelian proposal back into itself thereby revealing it to be a reflection of the real thing that it would incapacitate and replace. For Balthasar then, in essential respects Hegelian thought is a *Doppelgänger*, what the Irish philosopher, William Desmond, has felicitously called a 'counterfeit double.'[1] In the previous chapter, we produced a broad outline of what this means, in terms both of the conditions that make doubling possible and plausible, and how the double can be distinguished from the original. The two general features we focused on were the ambition in Hegel to adopt the divine point of view and the epic nature of dialectic. Considerable time was spent isolating the interlocking mechanisms of Hegel's epical construal as this refigures the biblical narrative, and in doing so aids and abets the commitment to comprehensive and self-justifying explanation. To understand how these mechanisms work individually and in concert is in significant part to be able to show how the copy differs from the original. I underscored that refiguration went all the way across, that is, no narrative episode and thus no theologoumenon, for example, creation, church, or eschaton was left unaffected. I also insisted that refiguration went all the way down, that is, the meaning of a particular narrative episode or theologoumenon was entirely changed. And lastly, I suggested that the epical character of Hegel's thought guarantees that the level of deviance of the whole exceeds that of its parts, since the developmental thrust of Hegel's narrative contributes significantly to the skews observable on the level of individual theologoumena.

Still chapter 2 remained largely schematic. More focus on particular theologoumena is required to see what is at stake in a specifically mythological take-over of Christian discourse. Here I make up for the lack by offering a detailed analysis of Balthasar's deflection of Hegelian distortions of the biblical and traditional views on Christ and the Trinity, although other theologoumena will make their way into discussion under the umbrella of our treatment of one or other of these theological topics. There is nothing arbitrary about this choice: Balthasar cannot be thought as other than a christological-trinitarian theologian, indeed one who repeats the kind of interpretive choices of Hegel who, from the *Phenomenology* (1807) on, articulates Christ as the center to the trinitarian circumference in an effort to outbid Enlightenment enervation of Christian doctrine, and to outmaneuver Kantian and post-Kantian avoidance. In the first main section I bring out what Balthasar takes to be the main features of Hegel's troubled relation to the biblical and traditional view of Christ. While Hegel's indebtedness to Luther's theology of the cross contributes to broad departures from the theological tradition, I argue that the nub of the issue seems to be Hegel's and Balthasar's respective understanding of the Johannine corpus, specifically, choice of texts, the principles of interpretation, and the default interpretive tendencies. Obviously, all that we learned about eros and kenosis in the last chapter is in play, as is the little we learned about Balthasar's apocalyptic figuration. For Balthasar thinks that in the post-Enlightenment situation the retrieval of the tradition demands a creative elaboration of an apocalyptic Christ.

The second main section deals with the conflict between Hegel's and Balthasar's views on the Trinity. The commitment to the doctrine is in both cases quite extraordinary; the architecture similar in that as the Trinity is the *arche* and *telos* of salvation history, it also supplies its energy and force. Not without some irony, it is nonetheless true that at least formally both appear to repeat the structure of Augustine's *De Trinitate*. Yet, the overlap is not simply formal. It is impossible to deny that there is a significant area of agreement regarding vision and substantive articulation. Both agree that a proper doctrine of the Trinity articulates the living God and not a philosophical abstraction. They agree also that no adequate rendition of the Trinity can avoid having the cruciform figure of Christ at the center, where the latter in turn makes confident and unilateral assertion of impassibility suspect. But disagreements there are. The dividing issue is the relation between the immanent and economic Trinity. Specifically Balthasar is concerned that in texts such as the *Phenomenology* and *Lectures on the Philosophy of Religion* Hegel confounds them, thereby compromising the integrity of the immanent Trinity, and the graciousness of all things in their referral to an origin that is replete. Of course, in Balthasar's case, as well as in Hegel's, the topics of Christ and Trinity are only analytically separable. It is not only that Christ is the *point d'aperçu* of the drama of the divine and world in both cases, and that the Trinity provides the horizon within which the christological concentration-point becomes transparent. Obviously, this is crucial: how Christ is figured rules in or out what is sayable about the Trinity and vice versa. Yet, the internal nature of the connection encourages carrying threads of discourse across from discussion of one topic to another. Two threads that weave in and out of our treatment of Balthasar's deflection of Hegel are eucharist and apocalyptic figuration. Each crosses over from one plane to another: the eucharist cannot be confined to Christology as it concerns a gift that not only refers to creation and eschaton, but also to the entire horizon of the Trinity; apocalyptic figuration of Christ cannot avoid saying something about the Trinity, which is the presupposition of sacrifice. Balthasar thinks, however, that theology very much hangs in the balance as to how eucharist refers to Trinity and whether or not trinitarian involvement is involvement of persons. Balthasar is equally concerned whether the crossover from the christological plane of apocalyptic to the trinitarian not only guarantees the divine status of the Son, but establishes a doxological matrix that begins and ends with the relations between divine persons.

Christological Derailment

Given the Christocentrism of Balthasar's theological program, it makes sense to go into some greater detail about

Balthasar's resistance to Hegel's delineation of Christ. On examination, for Balthasar, Hegel's delineation turns out to be inherently problematic. Once again, however, Hegel's reflection authenticates traditional features that make it appear to transcend the Enlightenment's dismissal and/or marginalization of revelation. First, Hegel's acknowledgment of Christ as the fullness of revelation gains depth in a context in which the divine is understood to be one continuous act of revelation. In particular, as creation refers to incarnation as to its completion (*TD2*, 281), incarnation refers to creation as its supposition. Hegel's Johannine focus on the cross as the fulcrum of dramatic divine initiative is the second christological positive. A third achievement of Hegel's Christology is its wedding of 'from above' and 'from below' approaches. Hegel is specifically recommended for his ability to see, if not necessarily expound, the narrative enactment of Jesus against the backdrop of Christ's relation to the Father of whom he represents the perfect expression. A fourth and final positive christological contribution, according to Balthasar, is Hegel's referring of Christ to the Church and his plotting of Christ's mission against the backdrop of the eschaton.

Yet all of these recalls represent a merely apparent rather than a real memory of the tradition which allows for huge variety and is always necessarily unfinished. Ultimately, all the constructive and positive features of Hegel's Christology are undermined by what Balthasar takes to be false steps. If Christ is the full manifestation of the divine, and thus formally the 'concrete universal,' neither in Hegel himself, nor his theological successors, is there anything concrete about the envisagement. Although influenced by Johannine theology, the 'claim of the individual man, Jesus Christ, cannot be ultimate in the Hegelian system, but only symbolic' (*TD2*, 423). The particularity of Christ being irrelevant, Hegel's Christ cannot satisfy Barth's material definition of the *concretum universale.*[2] Hegel's definition, Balthasar says on more than one occasion, provides nothing more than a general formula of the relationship between the divine and the world, and the divine and the human (e.g., *GL5*, 583-4; *TD3*, 64 ff.). A sign of the trespass against irreducible personhood (*TD2*, 415), which in turn undermines the claim that Christ is the fulness of revelation, is the observable conflation in Hegel of the orders of creation and incarnation (*TD3*, 64 n. 18; also

TL2, 15, 19-20). Without referring explicitly to the fact that in some of Hegel's texts, for example, the *Phenomenology* and *Lectures on the Philosophy of Religion*, both creation and incarnation are referred to the Son,[3] Balthasar is made anxious by what appears to be a difference in degree rather than of kind between creation and incarnation as modes of divine manifestation. The enduring, as well as systemic, nature of this confusion is shown by its recycling in a number of 19th-century Protestant and Catholic theologians in the Hegelian line such as Philipp Marheineke, Christian H. Weisse, and Anton Günther.

Balthasar well recognizes, of course, that the Hegelian confounding represents the strongest version of a much more widespread phenomenon in modern theology. No less than Barth does he object to the conflation of two distinct orders which effectively nullifies the absolute difference and otherness of Christ. Balthasar, however, spends considerably more time than Barth attacking a theological position in which the case for the confounding is less a reflection of cultural circumstance and more an expression of a systematic argument. For, on Balthasar's view, the 'weak' confounding, which is widespread in modern thought, points to the 'strong' Hegelian confounding as its logical destination and the site of its argumentative justification. He provides the rationale as to why it is Hegel rather than Schleiermacher who demands resistance, although Balthasar is aware that the choice is not an agonizing one, since he can depend on Barth's resistance to Schleiermacher and Liberal Theology. The distinction between the two orders and the elaboration of essentially a two-prong strategy of refutation is Balthasarian rather than Barthian. Whether the inflection is the emphatic *Nein* of his dialectical phase or the serene putting aside in the *Church Dogmatics* of that which is not included in and by the Word, it does not make sense in a Barthian scheme to negotiate differently. This is precisely what is legitimated in Balthasar. It only seems paradoxical that Balthasar, who is considerably more irenic than Barth, is more focusedly negative. The analogy of being, which underlies the analogy of discourse, allows a spectrum of approximations to the biblical rendition of the Word, without the incommensurability and unsurpassability of the disclosure of scripture being open to challenge. Yet the same commitment to analogy encourages distinguishing between nuisances and genuine threats, and going on a high state of alert only in the latter cases. With discernment comes the judgment that there do in fact exist concentrated pockets of discourse, apparently friendly to Christianity, that have to be relentlessly as well as ruthlessly exposed as counterfeit. If there is an irony at all, it is precisely the openness to non-Christian or not-yet Christian discourses that encourages the apocalyptic inflection of theology, and more precisely the apocalyptic theology of history and history of theology.

Deficiencies also betray themselves in Hegel's theology of the cross. Essentially, Hegel confuses a *cross-contracted* Christology with a *cross-focused* theology of the kind evident in such exemplary representatives of the Christian tradition as Irenaeus, Origen, Maximus, Anselm, and Bonaventure.[4] In a cross-contracted Christology, of which Luther's theology of the cross with its specific emphasis on the *sub contrario* represents the prototype (*MP*, 52-3, 62), resurrection is so much a function of the cross that it risks being eclipsed altogether. It is to obviate precisely such an eclipse that Balthasar advises:

> *. . . we cannot speak of the cross in isolation but must always see and express its other side, its inner meaning, which is made plain in resurrection. (TD3, 50-1; see also TD2, 19; TL2, 19-20)*

While such a correction of Hegel can also be found in Wolfhart Pannenberg,[5] what is unique to Balthasar is that the issue between Balthasar and Hegel on this point proceeds on the level of a hermeneutics of John. Balthasar can grant with Luther and Hegel the pivotal significance of Johannine optics in which resurrection is enfolded in or contracted into the cross. For Balthasar, however, while the Gospel of John provides the most ample as well as most perspicuous of christological horizons, John's perspective is neither exclusionary nor monolithic. As *Glory of the Lord* makes especially clear, while in a certain respect synthetic (*GL7*,12), its voice is single and singular. There are other voices in the New Testament canon which qualify and modulate it. It is not only the theological tradition that is polyphonic, but also scripture. Indeed, the polyphony of the theological tradition reflects the polyphony of witness illustrated in the New Testament, but also in the Bible as a whole. As such, the New Testament figures a cross-focused rather than cross-contracted Christology which, while it sees resurrection as embedded in the cross, also recognizes that it is a narratively separable element. It is precisely on the basis of a narrative difference between Good Friday and Easter Sunday, which Balthasar recognizes is expressed in different ways by Melito of Sardis, Origen, and Gregory of Nyssa, that he is able to elaborate his theology of Holy Saturday. The theology of Holy Saturday is, undoubtedly, a characteristic feature of Balthasar's Christology and also one of the most controversial. While this theology exploits the dramatic soteriology of the early Christian tradition, as well as calls on 2 Peter and hints in Revelation, arguably this theology represents a development of tradition of the same order as 'universal salvation' and 'eternal becoming.' We will examine this theology in a little more detail in Part 4. For the moment suffice it to say that the theology of Holy Saturday has a critical as well as constructive intent vis-à-vis Hegel's 'speculative Good Friday.' Denying the thinkability of Good Friday, Balthasar considers Holy Saturday to represent its hyperbolic echo while intimating the power of love in absolute separation. Holy Saturday is the break in the order of time and eternity in which Christ enters the condition of the dead: it is the narrative hiatus of which Hegel and his followers do not dare to speak.

I will further underscore the anti-Hegelian element of Balthasar's theology of Holy Saturday in my discussion later on the opposition between Balthasar and Hegel on the level of theodicy. What I wish to point to now is Balthasar's criticism of a second feature of Hegelian discourse, which is associated with its tendency towards a contraction of Christology into the cross, namely, the excessive level of abstraction in Hegel's depiction of Christ. Although Hegel's Christ, at least from the *Phenomenology* on, expresses a divine exposed to fragility and death,[6] yet somehow beyond it, transcendence is not unequivocally specified either in terms of who the subject of transcendence is, or the manner of transcendence. Is it Jesus Christ, for example, who transcends and overcomes death?, or is it the Church for whom Christ's message and life is paradigmatic? (See *TL2*, 44; *TL3*, 17, 22-3). Or is it the Hegelian State as the embodiment of community (*Gemeinde*)? And does the overcoming involve the resurrection of the body as taught by Paul, and which was insisted on by theologians such as Irenaeus and Tertullian as a *discrimen* between Christianity and the religions of the surrounding culture? Or is overcoming simply identifiable with the mind's elevation to the eternal world of thought? (e.g. *TD1*, 601; *TD2*, 125). Furthermore, abstraction haunts the reading of Christ's relation to the divine. Indeed, as *Theo-Drama 5* and *Theo-Logic 2* make particularly clear, Hegel's language is anything but Johannine in its refusal to speak to the personal relation between Christ and the Father. For Balthasar, this relation provides nothing less than the interpretive key for reading the identity of Jesus Christ. It is in and through an understanding of the Johannine figuration of the relationship between Christ and the Father, particularly with respect to Christ's openness and receptivity to the Father's will, that it becomes possible to elaborate not only a theology of mission (*TD2*), but through this to articulate a non-functionalist Christology from below (*TD3*) and even to provide the fundamental contours of a dynamic, non-metaphysical view of the Trinity (*TD5*; *TL 2-3*).

Beyond interpreting John aright – and this Hegel palpably fails to do – there is the theological need to figure Christ in light of the Pauline pair of 'sin' and 'wrath.' Neither symbol plays a major role in Hegel despite their prominence in Luther whose thought Hegel putatively embraces.[7] To reject, as Hegel does, the traditional Christian understanding of sin as the irrational and rebellious refusal of the good is, for Balthasar, both to fail to grasp the human situation and to put out of circulation an element that contributes mightily to the dramatic character of salvation. Moreover, to so totally marginalize God's wrath is to sentimentalize the terrible power of divine love and to sanitize a drama in which the imperative of love always exceeds the coexisting coefficient of justice which, however, is never reneged on. For Balthasar, Christ is the site of the 'wondrous exchange' on behalf of created beings who have opened up an abyss between themselves and God, an abyss that can only be bridged when sin in all its horror is confronted and judged and taken up in the boundless transforming love of the triune God.

Here Balthasar opposes to Hegel a theology of atonement that refuses to follow Gustaf Aulén in thinking that the Western tradition splits between the classical or mythical view and the juridical view represented by Anselm. The Irenaean view of a harrowing of hell is put in opposition to Hegel's view of atonement which excludes the devil and hell, and reinterprets the drama of atonement to be the at-one-ing of the divine in and through an antithetical condition for which at the same time it is wholly responsible. But, as *Theo-Drama 4* in particular makes clear (255-66), the atonement theology of Anselm also can be put into circulation not only as a venerable expression of the theological tradition, but as a buttress against modern simulacra. Although this species of atonement theology is considerably less mythopoetic than its classical ancestor – and both helped and hindered by its demythologized rendering – it too resists conceptual takeover. Balthasar is convinced that no genuinely Christian reflection on atonement can be made a function of reason. Insofar as the bases of any proper view of atonement necessarily remain biblical, it is evident for Balthasar that the various symbols of atonement operative in the Bible in general, and the New Testament in particular, constitute a constellation rather than a system. Each of these symbols, whether of representation, substitution, penal satisfaction, or solidarity with the sinner relates closely without being reducible to each other (*TD4*, 240). Nor are they capable of being synthesized in a larger whole (*TD4*, 240). Moreover, the various symbols of the New Testament, which often retrieve but refigure symbols of long duration in Hebrew scripture, provoke theological reflection without ever becoming reducible to it.

Now Hegel's willingness even to entertain a doctrine of atonement is to be held to his credit. It distinguishes him from the Enlightenment for which the doctrine was as much an ethical scandal as an intellectual challenge. It also distinguishes Hegel from much of Romanticism, which also found the doctrine to be repugnant, interfering as it did with the principle of personal responsibility, even if there was less assurance about the form that responsibility would take or the sensibility that it either presupposed or brought into being.[8] But in the end, Hegel is more dangerous than either, precisely because he embraces the symbol, and because his embrace is verbal rather than real. By comparison, the adoption of the symbol by Hölderlin is more genuine, even if in his major poems there are tendencies to contest the uniqueness of Christ's atonement, indeed to make it expressive of the law of reality – *Hen kai Pan* – and thus anticipate and certify Hegel's view.[9] Importantly, here we are dealing with a dissociation of Hegel from Luther who, although pointed to consistently as a source of mixed blessings, cannot be regarded univocally as a poisoned well. Certainly, Luther's view of the *sub contrario* shows negative capability towards being enlisted in a post-Christian program. *Mysterium Paschale* makes the point concisely:

> *If we rest content with the simple sub contrario, then we shall be forced to take the path that travels from Luther to Hegel. A purely dialectical Christology becomes transformed into a "sheerly" philosophical dialectic, into a "worldly" discourse. (52)*

Nevertheless, Luther articulates a view of substitution which, although marked by a certain onesidedness, is properly biblical and not a little traditional in its appeal to the two-natures and communication of properties (*TD4*, 284-90). Not a trace of this is to be found in Hegel's dialectically rinsed rendition of Christ.

As with Barth, a major constructive feature of Balthasar's remembering of the disclosure given in Jesus Christ is a remembering of atonement. Of course, Balthasar distinguishes himself from Barth by giving authority to the history of remembering that is the theological tradition. But an even deeper *discrimen* is to be found in the fact that once again Balthasar spends considerably more energy fighting post-Enlightenment renditions of Christian symbols and the Christian narrative that make it appear that Christianity has been protected against the ravages of disbelief and irrelevance. Balthasar sees with Kierkegaard that Hegelian views of atonement and reconciliation are little more than sleights of hand that remove the either-or that defines the dramatic situation of Christianity in the modern age. Faced with forgetfulness the Christian, and more especially the theologian, is incited to remember. The exercise of memory is that upon which we stake our hope for outbidding amnesia. The exercise is a practice. There are battles and skirmishes, but no Armageddons. It is otherwise when one is dealing with Hegel, the colossal creator of simulacra. For Balthasar there can only be all out battle against misremembering. It is difficult not to invoke Tolkien: Hegel is Sauron, the dis-embodied all-seeing-eye which will inevitably destroy unless all the resources of resistence – intelligence, perception, courage, and tradition – are marshaled against it. There is nothing of a night battle;[10] it is battle for keeps.

What is true with respect to Hegel's treatment of atonement is true also with respect to what might be called Hegel's 'christological method' or 'christological logic' (*TL2*, 49). Again, while from Balthasar's perspective Hegel is to be congratulated for refusing to sanction the contemporary binary opposition in theological method between 'from above' and 'from below' approaches in Christology, in Hegel, as well as his philosophical and theological successors, the emphasis falls improperly on autonomy rather than obedience. For Balthasar, however, the elevation, perhaps even reification, of autonomy does not find its measure in scripture. The Old and the New Testament suggest the primacy of obedience, with John 6:38 and Luke 22:42 being passages that essentially sum up the entire biblical dispensation. Obedience to his salvific mission identifies the person of Jesus Christ. As early as his book on Maximus (1942),[11] Balthasar understood his insistence on Jesus' receptivity to mark a distance from Hegelian style Christology. Maximus is explicitly invoked in *Theo-Drama*, as Balthasar resists the autonomy motif in Hegel and Hegelian-style theology. The emphasis on autonomy, Balthasar judges, can only issue in a titanic elevation of the self (*TD2*, 197, 201-02). In continuity with Maximus, underscoring receptivity involves, for Balthasar, positing two wills in Christ, the one finite, the other infinite, a view that is underwritten by the two-nature formula of Chalcedon (*TD2*, 215; also *B*, 115-6; *TL2*, 69-70).[12] The two-will view, however, is never asserted at the cost of the unity of the person of Christ, nor to secure the ineluctable autonomy of the divine will. As the discussion of the person of Christ necessarily points to the trinitarian horizon, Balthasar suggests that the obedience of Christ is grounded in the anterior infinite receptivity of the Son who receives the gift of Himself from the Father (*TD5*, 91-2; also *TL2*, 48-9; *LA*, 118).

In any event, at no point in principle or in fact does Hegel support a Chalcedonian view of Christ.[13] Rather his Christology is thoroughly monophysite (e. g. *TD2*, 184; *TD1*, 67) with the 'from above' aspect meshing seamlessly with the 'from below': Christ is the divine precisely *as* human, the human precisely *as* the divine. But this implies, as already suggested, the replacement of the properly morphological understanding of kenosis by an essentialist form (*TD2*, 182-4; *MP*, 25-6, 32-4; *TL2*, 85), and inscribes Christology in a completion dynamic in which Christ is reduced to being an instrument of divine self-realization. To accuse Hegel of monophysitism seems quite odd in a situation in which Balthasar also accuses Hegel of evacuating Christology altogether by reducing Christ to a function of 'otherness' equally served by the world of nature and finite spirit. Balthasar, however, believes that christological evacuation and monophysitism are two sides of the same coin. Given the dialectical nature of Hegel's thought, one can focus on either the compromise to the finite or the infinite effected in making the finite a function of the infinite. In pointing to the monophysite contour of Hegel's thought, Balthasar thinks that he exposes as a corollary not only the compromise to the independence of created being which, if it is ordered to Christ, is not determined by him, but also the entire space of cultural production. Balthasar hints that Chalcedon, or even more precisely Maximus' dythelite development of it,[14] guarantees the independence of culture that is necessary for Christianity's health, which depends to a considerable extent on dialogue. Balthasar, never having only one line of precedent when he can have many, is not shy about suggesting that Hamann plays a critical role in thinking of Christ as embracing all of cultural production, and also suggesting that his roots lie less in Maximus than in Irenaeus, particularly in the latter's view of recapitulation (*anakephalaiosis*) (*GL2*, 52).[15] Whatever the range of precedent adduced, Balthasar can on occasions be marvelously limpid, as is in the following passage from one of his more minor works: 'Christ does not force anything into the narrow confines of a christological theology, but from within itself gives room for a metaphysics of creation . . . as well as a philosophy of history and culture' (*Exp 4*, 109).[16] In going down this road, Balthasar in a more substantive theological register makes a point that had a more genealogical complexion in the Prolegomenon to *Theo-Drama*. The answer to Hegel's erasing of the *analogia entis* and the correlative analogy of discourses cannot in the end consist in stipulating that cultural discourses are not reducible to Christian revelation, nor in the appeal to the commonsense of the tradition as a brute fact that answers all questions beforehand. Rather, the answer is provided from within a Christology that Hegel beggars, but which Balthasar insists provides the key to all that is and can be said, where the latter is essentially inexhaustible.

Finally, for Balthasar, if any theological construction in modernity suggests the danger of a pneumatic displacement of Christ, it is Hegelianism (e.g. *TD3*, 45-8; *TL2*, 22; *TL3*, 17, 34, 46; *Exp 4*, 105-06). As *Glory of the Lord* points out, Hegel's later writings do little to alter this radical pneumatic tendency announced in his very earliest work (*GL5*, 584). There the Farewell Discourses of John's Gospel (16-17) are read to suggest the necessity of the disappearance of the concrete individual, Jesus of Nazareth, so that his meaning can be realized in the 'spiritual community' (*Gemeinde*), Hegel's translation and substitution for the institutional Church with its doctrines, liturgy, devotional practices, and forms of life. Returning to John 16:13-15 in *Theo-Drama*, Balthasar insists against the Hegelian reading: 'Nevertheless, the Spirit does not speak of his own accord but draws everything from the treasures of Christ which are those of the Father' (*TD5*, 31). The point is important enough to bear even more repetition than is usual for Balthasar. He advances the proposal throughout *Theo-Logic* (see *TL2*, 15-6, 32), and leaves the reader in no doubt that the instrumental role of the Spirit is not only a basic theological conviction, but one set explicitly against Hegel's rendition in which Christ is effectively the instrument of the Spirit (*TL3*, 17). Now while Löwith, Heidegger, Derrida, and a host of other critics of Hegel have noted that there is a strong tendency towards a 'realized eschatology' in Hegel,[17] Balthasar goes to considerable trouble to underscore as fundamental the 'not yet' character of the actualization of community, which was taken up and developed by the Hegelian left-wing in the nineteenth century, and in the twentieth century by negative dialectics and philosophies and theologies of hope.[18] Whatever the prospects for full appropriation of the meaning of Christ in history, the fact that there is appropriation signals for Hegel that the incarnation and the cross do not in the strict sense constitute the pleroma that Paul rightly, in Balthasar's view (*TL2*, 22-3), thinks they do. In fact, Hegel gives the Christian good reason to think that the incarnation and the cross are not fundamentally kairotic, if one adduces as a criterion for the use of the term that they inhere proleptically in eschatological fullness.

Despite his teleological language, for Balthasar, Hegel's viewpoint is incorrigibly retrospective rather than prospective. Here Pascal's conviction of the cruciform nature of all of history until the second coming represents an antidote to Hegel's view.[19] On Hegelian grounds, the incarnation and the cross enact a promise coincident with the order of finitude that the community in its historical elaboration fulfills. From Balthasar's perspective this reading of the incarnation and cross relativizes differences between Hegel and his contemporary theological successor, Jürgen Moltmann, which are generally couched in terms of the contrast between 'realized' and 'unrealized' eschatology. From the traditional baseline of the absolute unsurpassability of Christ and his intrinsically regulative character, Hegel and Moltmann can be seen to represent simply different accents of the 'not yet.' In both cases the finality of the incarnation and the cross are undermined. In particular, John's insistence on the irreducibility of a realized eschatology is either ignored or misread. It is ignored insofar as Jesus himself is read as the preacher of the kingdom rather than its message. And it is misread insofar the absoluteness of Christ, from which both swerve, is neither a *nunc stans* nor the absoluteness of the punctiliar past, but as Balthasar renders it so eloquently in *Theo-Drama 5*, the absoluteness of the one who refigures and reweaves time (*TD5*, 25, 30-2). Kairotic refiguration includes within it a dynamic towards the eschaton not defined in terms of the cessation of time, but rather in terms of the full disclosure of the glory of God, fully expressed in the incarnation, passion, death and resurrection of Christ, re-presented in the eucharist, but still partly veiled in history. Kairotic time is a parenthesis,[20] an already in which the 'not yet' continues to abide. Pondering this in the opening section of *Theo-Drama 5*, which calls on his analysis of Revelation in *Theo-Drama 4*, Balthasar writes:

> *The only remaining question is whether John's strong emphasis on the "already" of redemption and judgment does not actually mask the "not yet" that is stressed by the other writers, in such a way as to obscure man's situation, a situation in which he always has to decide. For it cannot be disputed that the standpoint of Johannine theology is primarily christological; it is anthropological only within the over-arching Christology. At the same time we must not forget the constant Johannine exhortation to "abide," which is parallel to the Synoptics' command to "watch." (TD5, 33)*

The paradox here is that the new configuration of time, in which meaning is realized, does nothing to lessen dramatic tension – as would be the case in a Hegelian scheme – it heightens it. For Balthasar, the realization of meaning is never a given for thought, but something more like a wager that despite the appearance of the destruction of meaning, meaning inheres.

In agreement with de Lubac,[21] in *Theo-Drama* and *Theo-Logic* Balthasar suggests that the model for this displacement is supplied in both cases by Joachim de Fiore (e.g., *TD2*, 128; *TD3*, 400, 512-3; *TD4*, 425, 446, 458; *TD5*, 144, 181-2).[22] In terms of content, the critical position Balthasar takes with respect to Joachim recalls rather faithfully the criticisms leveled at Joachim by St. Thomas in the *Summa* (*ST* I, Q39, art 5; also, I-II, Q106, art 4) (*TL2*, 208, esp. n. 79). Balthasar agrees with Thomas that a Joachimite-style pneumatology thoroughly compromises the finality of Christ, and has the disastrous consequence of downplaying the institutional church as the mediation of Christ's grace, and correlatively of entertaining too high an estimate of spiritual church which realizes the meaning of the christological event as an anagogic sign. This, of course, is nothing less than the full realization of freedom and knowledge in the human community. Balthasar has a heightened sense of how Joachimism functions in post-Enlightenment discourses to baptize Enlightenment progressivism in the name of a pneumatological or apocalyptic discourse that upsets the regulative christocentrism of Christian thought.

Ultimately, however, neither the motive nor form of Balthasar's resistance to Joachim is reducible to St. Thomas. As *Glory of the Lord* shows from the outset the standard by which any pneumatism is judged is Bonaventure's paradigmatic christocentrism which forestalls even the merest hint of relativization, by making Christ the subjective as well as objective condition of perception and knowledge, and by making the drama of the crucified Christ eternally relevant to our understanding of the triune God. The Spirit plays a role in unfolding this recognition, but does not become the object of regard. Perhaps doing justice to Bonaventure results, as Balthasar's critics have suggested, in an underdeveloped pneumatology,[23] but whether this is so or not, Balthasar's consistency across the trilogy is evident. What is laid down systematically in *Glory of the Lord 1* is historically contextualized in the essay on Bonaventure in volume 2. Moreover, for Balthasar, the mystery of the incarnation and the cross is, then, transhistorical and thus inclusive of all of history. If there is a 'not-yet' dimension to the redemptive event – and Balthasar could not make clearer in *Theo-Drama 5* that there is – then it is within christological parentheses. *Theo-Drama* and *Theo-Logic* deploy or re-deploy Bonaventuran christocentrism against Hegelianism, understood as a new outbreak of Joachimite apocalyptic. If *Theo-Logic* does so explicitly (*TL2*, 208; *TL3*, 416-18), *Theo-Drama 5*, which represents Balthasar's most sustained argument against every and any form of 'unrealized eschatology,' is hardly less urgent. Moreover, both texts display the very interesting doubling of Thomas and Bonaventure. Throughout *Glory of the Lord*, Bonaventure and Thomas tend to function as equally valid but exclusionary theological options. Were one to choose a philosophical theologian, then the choice of Thomas is to be recommended, given his superior grasp of cosmos. Were one interested, however, in a theologian's theologian, then Bonaventure is to be preferred, given his christocentric and trinitarian focus. In *Theo-Drama*, neither Bonaventure nor Thomas is a conspicuous presence. But interestingly, in Balthasar's expostulations on God's transcendence towards the world and the world's transcendence towards God in the latter stages of *Theo-Drama 5* both are called on to represent the Christian position. This doubling is even more conspicuous in *Theo-Logic 2 & 3*, (*TL2*, 28, 33; *TL3*, 120), in which Thomas enjoys a rehabilitation in which Christology and Trinity are no longer regarded as epiphenomenal with respect to his philosophical theology, a version of which – albeit a highly Neoplatonic version[24] – is supplied by *Theo-Logic 1.*

It is tempting to look at this internal rehabilitation of Thomas vis-à-vis Bonaventure in the context of a dispute with Hegelian forms of 'unrealized eschatology' as anticipating a similar rehabilitation in Marion,[25] given not only the general link between Marion's thought and that of Balthasar, but also their common understanding of the eucharist and their common resistance to an inauthentic sense of *anamnesis.* As is well-known in his various expostulations on the *cultus* in *Lectures on the Philosophy of Religion*, Hegel spends a considerable time assessing the relative validity of various theologies of the eucharist. He dismisses the Catholic rendition because of its view of transubstantiation, which he takes to express an objectivist metaphysics, and supports instead a view of real presence in which the presence is predicated on the appropriating community.[26] Real presence then quite literally is a construct of the community or church, which is identified with the Spirit.[27] The full realization of real presence depends on the community being in end-time, and its relative grasp that it, and not Christ, is the real object of its discourse. In chapters 5 and 7 of *God without Being* Marion attacks Hegel's specific view and its weaker derivatives, as well as more home-spun 'communitarian' or 'spiritual' views that proceed without Hegel's powerful systematic apparatus. One plausible way of looking at Balthasar's reflection on the eucharist, especially in *Theo-Drama 4*, is to think of it as articulated against Hegel. In the eucharist, Christ remains the indispensable actor who comes to us and forms the very community that would receive him (*TD4*, 394-7; also *TD4*, 362; *TD5*, 115). This is not to say that we are passive; but it is to say that our agency is paradoxically one of receptivity and malleability. Making selves receptive and encouraging malleability for the reception of the passion, death, and resurrection of Christ are actions of the Spirit (*TD4*, 405-6). The Spirit's reference to Christ is perhaps made most clear in the following passage:

For the community of faith, the offering of Christ's self-sacrifice to God the Father in the Holy Spirit is, first of all, a way of assimilating

> *the mind of Christ which is eucharistia, praise and thanksgiving of God. (TD4, 400)*

In his treatment of the eucharist, Hegel and his epigones have, from Balthasar's perspective, fundamentally reversed the order of reference, and made Christ refer to the Spirit rather than the Spirit to Christ. Arguably, this represents the fundamental thrust of *Theo-Logic*, negatively in *Theo-Logic 3* in which Hegel's inflation of the function of the Spirit is resisted (*TL3*, 17-23, 35), positively in *Theo-Logic 2* in which Balthasar could not make more clear that Christ is the kingdom in person (*autobasileia*) (*TL2*, 78), and as such the subject of the exposition of the Spirit (*TL2*, 18, 32). Importantly, in *Theo-Logic* Balthasar balances the insistence on this fact by pointing out that the Son is the exposition of the Father (*TL2*, 11). Christomonism is the Charybdis that must be avoided as much as Hegel's pneumatological Scylla (*TL3*, 35). Speaking back to Hegel in the terms of John 16, Balthasar speaks of the Son's 'handing over' of authority to the Spirit (*Exp 4*, 107-08). The Spirit, however, which can, indeed, act relatively independently, is always the Spirit of Christ.

Yet this is simply one item on a long chain of forgetting and its veiling. For Balthasar, it is crucial, however different its form of manifestation from the Son, that the Holy Spirit be understood as a divine actor with hypostatic density (*TL3*, 46) and not be a name whose referent is the appropriating community in which it is supposed to inhere.[28] In sum, it is Hegel's flattening reinterpretation of memory in which the community subject is elevated to the divine position that horrifies Balthasar. Hegelian *anamnesis* is a stratagem in which the community divests itself of the concrete particularity of Christ, and in its reference to Spirit concludes in abolishing transcendence altogether. Through pneumatic displacement, the community's memory of Christ becomes self-referential, as it more or less successfully hides the hubris that memory could possibly be powerful and integral enough to constitute real presence. For Balthasar, *anamnesis* becomes possible only to the extent that in the eucharist we are remembered by God in Christ. The eucharist is not only the enacted reconciliation of us with the triune God, but the enacted memory of God as God is turned towards us. And this memory of God is the answer to the community of Israel's longing to be remembered by God (Psalms), and Job's more individualistic reprise.

In the salvo he launches against Hegel at the very start of *Theo-Drama*, Balthasar draws a line in the sand: in the Paschal Mystery unrepeatable individual selves are saved by Christ the concrete particular (*TD1*, 65). The point is repeated at the end of *Theo-Drama* (*TD5*, 349), where Christ does not so much designate a sphere of beings to be saved as touches each of them individually. This 'touching' constitutes the resurrection, the repetition, the 'giving back' that so much embarrasses Hegel that he elides it in his work either into the cross or into Spirit interpreted as appropriating community (*TL2*, 19-20). But, for Balthasar, as with Paul, the cross without the resurrection remains a question mark. And to substitute Spirit for resurrection, whether directly or by way of Pentecost (*TL3*, 17), does not give the answer to the question that will not be stopped: Is death all that there is for me, especially when it is another name for society and community? This community demonstrates in Balthasar's view distinct tendencies towards evasion and delusion: it speaks of everything except the resurrection, and when it is not silent, it presents the simulacrum of 'infinite knowledge,' which is no one's knowledge in particular. In speaking to the elision of the resurrection and its discounting, Balthasar reprises one of the objections to Hegelianism that had most traction in Hegel's own day. But perhaps a portend of the disputed nature of resurrection in the modern world is provided as early as Robert Bellarmine in *De Controversiis*,[29] where he observes that refusal to take seriously the resurrection is the most lasting and intractable of all anti-Christian assumptions. Bellarmine makes the point with full awareness that the denial of resurrection was a lynchpin of ancient Gnostics. Balthasar can go a more direct route, and call on Irenaeus, the self-ascribed biblical theologian. Balthasar takes for granted Paul's expression of faith in the mystery of resurrection, and our participation in the resurrection of Christ. But in general he tends to favor Revelation, whose central vision is the Lamb's overcoming of death.[30]

It would, of course, be a mistake to think that either Hegel or Balthasar make the case that the eucharist can be understood outside a trinitarian horizon. What makes the refutation of Hegel's view of the eucharist so imperative then is that Hegel has properly assigned the site. It is clear already, however, that Balthasar controverts basic Hegelian understandings of Christ as Son, the meaning of the passion, its relation to resurrection, and especially the relation of Christ as Son to the Father. But the eucharist also involves the invocation of the Holy Spirit (*epiklesis*). Thus, the eucharist, which is enacted by the church and in a sense is constituted by it, has a trinitarian matrix. Balthasar thinks that this speaks to the way theology, which suitably fears Hegelian construction of the relation between memory and salvation, should respond. For Balthasar, while it is true that the foreground conditions of a refutation of Hegel's view of the erasure of personal immortality are to be found in Christology, nonetheless, the ultimate conditions of refutation are to be found in the personalism of the perichoretic Trinity. The *communio sanctorum* subsists ultimately in the *communio* of persons.

From the perspective of a properly theodramatic construal, Hegel's Christology represents the victory of structure over event, and of manifestation over revelation that answers to no logic, at least no logic that specifies or answers to human rationality.[31] Even if the complaint is a familiar one, and dominates Catholic and Protestant critique of Hegel, Balthasar's registering of it is unique in its grasp of how and why Hegel's view can look so attractive, in its teasing out of the relationship between christological deficiencies and deficiencies in construing human beings, the church, and the nature of the eschaton. Balthasar's approach distinguishes itself especially in its grasp of the fact that Hegel's Christology represents an eclipse of the glory of Christ, which provides the *raison d'être* for reflective Christian discourse and for Christian forms of life and worship. This eclipse is more dangerous than that effected and recommended by the Enlightenment and accepted and celebrated by Nietzsche; more dangerous, because disguised. In this eclipse Christ is merely a symbol for humanity, his glory our glory, and the process of his enactment in history human self-glorification. Christ is the Titan under the figure of humility who gives us ourselves, or gives us our task, which is to own our gigantic promise, to recollect ourselves in and through the detour of history which constitutes our pedagogy. As recollected, Christ is the sign of *our* arrival;

he is not the *hapax legomenon* that is arrival itself. Christ is a permanent exhibit in 'the museum of the shapes of Spirit' (*German*) – to recall the famous locution from the Preface to the *Phenomenology*. From this recollective and aesthetic vantage point Christ preforms our sufferings and struggles in the saeculum, and we give them substance, and see them serve our becoming divine, and the divine becoming actual. To which Balthasar does not – but might – reply in the words of the Irish poet, Patrick Kavanagh: 'sometimes Christ bleeds in the museum.'[32]

Yet again, however, Balthasar puts himself under the obligation to avoid a reaction-formation that would make him a hostage – however indirect – of the thinker whose system always seem to imprison, a systematic web that seems to extend almost infinitely to enwrap that which would escape its lines of implication. Balthasar has learned that aspect of Kierkegaard's lesson well, and would undoubtedly agree with Foucault that at the boundary and term of discourses which condemn Hegel's discourse, the discourse lies waiting.[33] Just as one does not oppose faith to reason, but properly maps their relation, and just as one does not simply decry the epicality of Hegel's so-called Christian thought, but thinks the comprehensiveness of the Christian vision otherwise than in the Hegelian register, so also here one does not replace Hegel's systemically flawed Christology by an equally problematic Christomonism. Although it is only in some moods that Balthasar would identify the *Church Dogmatics* as headed in this direction (*B*, 242), Barth is not the only answer, indeed not the answer. The theological answer is in the end the Catholic answer. This answer is in the first instance 'catholic' in the sense that it represents the testimony of the broad Christian tradition as expressed in such thinkers as Irenaeus, Origen, Augustine, Bonaventure, Aquinas, Pascal, and Hamann. In this view, Christ completes creation, as grace completes nature. Neither totally independent from Christ, nor reducible to Christ, the order of nature and its discourses are not simply not fallen, but embody a goodness, which while corruptible and corrupted, is yet not vitiated. This is the view that Balthasar shares with de Lubac (*B*, 295-302). This is also the view of Przywara (*B*, 255-57, 328-9), whose side Balthasar definitively takes in his argument with Barth over the status of the *analogia entis*.

To sum up Balthasar's critical relation to Hegel respecting the understanding of Christ, it can be said that he thinks that Hegel's Christology represents something of a débacle. Importantly, however, the débacle lies not solely in what Hegel gets wrong; rather, in significant part it is a function of the fundamental Johannine aspects of Christianity that Hegel recalls, for example, the centrality of love, its definition by the cross, and the trinitarian horizon of all history and suffering. In the end, however, Hegel betrays John and the Christian tradition by replacing the event of love by a 'logic' that is speculatively manipulable and self-authorizing (*TL2*, 22-3, 49). This logic, which sets up a restricted economy of suffering and sacrifice, is made possible by Hegel's folding of distinct narrative elements of the Christian tradition into each other, for example, creation into incarnation, incarnation into cross, resurrection into cross, and cross and resurrection into the community, particularly the community invested with eschatological pedigree. In Hegel's case John represents a wasted opportunity, or perhaps represents precisely the discursive opportunity to displace and replace a Christianity that can neither meet the demands of autonomy nor self-justifying reason that mark modernity as both achievement and project. As Balthasar brings down the curtains on his literary career in *Theo-Logic* it is remarkable to observe that this is a point that he made concerning German Idealism and Romanticism as early as *Apokalypse.* That John is availed of only to be displaced and reconfigured is no less true of Schelling and Fichte than it is of the author of the *Phenomenology*.[34] Again, from very early on in his career, arguably, it is only Hölderlin who preserves a sufficient commitment to the genuinely Johannine inflection of Christianity not to be wholly taken-over – although even here, unlike Marion, Balthasar consistently marks the regressive elements. For Hegel it is no impediment to speculative take-over that in John's Gospel meaning cannot be separated from fact. And, of course, 1 John 4:6, which supplies the famous proposition 'God is Love,' incites a cooption by reason that necessarily bleeds it of the mystery and gratuitousness that are crucial to its sense. *Apokalypse* puts epigrammatically what is belabored in *Theo-Logic*: The real issue of the Christian with Hegel concerns 'the curse of misused love' (*Apok 1*, 618).

Romancing the Trinity

A MAJOR, IF NOT THE MAJOR, REASON accounting for Hegel's attractiveness in contemporary theological circles, is Hegel's recovery of the symbol of the Trinity. This represents for Balthasar (*Apok 1*, 648) every bit as much as it does for Protestant thinkers such as Jüngel and Moltmann, the constitutive theological advantage of Hegel over Schleiermacher. Especially important are Hegel's integration of the discourse of the Trinity and the discourses of the cross, and his ability to persuade that it is the Trinity that provides the widest-angle lens possible of divine engagement with the world and finite spirit that cannot be incidental to God's personal identity. Balthasar understands Hegel's attractiveness here, and thinks it is for good reason that Hegel's trinitarian thought has had the kind of impact that it has had. Nevertheless, for Balthasar, it is with respect to the Trinity that all of Hegel's problems, including those of the nature and limit of knowledge, epic figuration, and Christology, come home to roost. It is precisely Hegel's trinitarian articulation that justifies the charge of gnosis, accusations of monism, eroticism, necessitarianism, and the operation in Hegelian discourses of an ironic and iterative form of kenosis, and that gives credence to the criticism of his monophysite christological commitment, and of the related tendency to blur incarnation with creation, on the one hand, and with the eschaton, on the other. Hegel's thought elicits this response quite simply because Hegel's epical elaboration is coextensive with his trinitarian thought. Essentially different sides of the same coin, Hegel's trinitarian thought expresses in synoptic mode his epical refiguration of the Christian narrative, and conversely his epical refiguration elaborates a mode of trinitarian thought in which not only is the biblical narrative of God affected, but so also is the entire network of primary doctrines that correspond to and elaborate different segments of the biblical narrative. For Balthasar, it is all but self-evident that Hegel's trinitarianism involves a devastating emendation of the classical construal of the Trinity. With the standard being set throughout the trilogy as much by Maximus and Bonaventure as Augustine and Thomas, Balthasar diagnoses Hegel's view, and that of his theological successors, to be totally unfaithful to the theological tradition. Infrastructurally the two main areas affected are the traditional understanding of the immanent and economic Trinity and their relation, and the way in which suffering can be predicated of God, although these areas include Balthasar's resistance to Hegel's excessive pneumatology and his related undermining of liturgy, and above all Hegel's defeat of the doxological.

Refiguring and Disfiguring the Immanent and Economic Trinity

I BEGIN WITH BALTHASAR'S ANALYSIS AND CORRECTION of Hegel's understanding of the immanent and economic Trinity and their relation with special reference to pneumatological exacerbation and the antipathy towards a liturgical mode of thinking. Balthasar grants that theological successors to Hegel such as Moltmann and Jüngel attempt to correct Hegel in ways that make him less eccentric vis-à-vis the theological tradition, while still having critical leverage on it. With regard to the immanent Trinity, the missions of the Trinity, and their relation, Balthasar believes that such correction is necessary, but at the same time extraordinarily difficult to effect in a way that is adequate theologically. The power of Hegel's depiction of the immanent Trinity derives in significant part from the way in which it emends the classical view in a radical and comprehensive fashion. The diversions from the traditional perspective are manifold. If the unilateral dynamism of the divine on the 'logical' or virtual dimension puts a hypostatic or personal interpretation of the divine as ground of the world under considerable pressure, its identity thrust effectively rules it out. In an insight that is original, even if not entirely unanticipated, as we shall see in the next chapter in 19th-century critique of Hegel, Balthasar suggests that Hegelian figuration of the Trinity represents a repetition of modalism or Sabellianism (*TD1*, 67; also *TL3*, 47). Repetition, however, is not recrudescence; the dynamic key of Hegel is very different from the static metaphysical key of classical Sabellianism.[35] Still, the result is the same: instead of unity being constituted in and through the divine persons in relation, 'Father,' 'Son,' and 'Spirit' are in Hegel's published and unpublished works alike simply 'moments,' indeed 'disappearing moments,' of a dynamically conceived teleological unity.[36] Again, the erotic and teleological tendency of Hegel's trinitarian articulation rules out the possibility of understanding intra-trinitarian relations as transcending the economy of exchange. A non-economic construal is possible, Balthasar thinks – and here he is followed by Milbank and Hart[37] – if and only if the immanent Trinity is defined as origin rather than end or origin-end (*TL3*, 227-8; also *TL2*, 22-24), and full rather than empty (*TL3*, 226; also *TL3*, 41-2).

Similarly, Hegelian forms of Trinitarianism are haunted by the specter of necessitarianism. This is so, even when, or especially when, there is some attempt to define necessity as freedom and freedom as necessity. For Balthasar, as with Barth, this Spinozistic kind of interdefinition effectively means freedom's eclipse (*B*, 275). A significant part of the problem is the over-concern in Hegel and his epigones with a nominalist or voluntarist God. This encourages the false opposition of a God whose relation to the world is defined by decree and a divine dependent on the world that it grounds, in and through which it actualizes itself. In what is very much more than an elegant aside, Balthasar avers that in Barth divine freedom does not dissolve nature into 'a pointillist series of dissimilar and discontinuous momentary events' (*B*, 191). Perhaps the thinker who has done most to justify the binary opposition of necessitarianism and voluntarism, which is operationally accepted in much of modern theology, is Hans Blumenberg. This historian of ideas, and particularly the ideas that express and even ground modernity, historicizes the either-or of necessitarianism and voluntarism by making the latter the dialectical result of the former.[38] That this is not pure description, however, is evident in Blumenberg's lauding the correction of theological voluntarism in the modern world by Renaissance Neoplatonism and German Idealism, which essentially does away with the transcendent God altogether and grants authority to the cosmos and human being in equivocal measure.[39] On the basis of the story of derailment he tells in *Glory of the Lord 5*, while Balthasar is prepared to acknowledge the dialectical relation between these two species of thought, he is less than sanguine about the consequences for philosophy, and appalled with respect to the consequences for theology. Admitting that a correction is in order, Balthasar considers Idealist thought to be precisely the wrong kind of correction, in fact the kind of overcorrection that makes matters worse. Hegelian dialectic proves in his view to be a very blunt instrument in thinking that the contrary to the voluntarist God is the God whose reciprocal dependence or co-dependence on the world admits of a rational justification.[40]

As *Theo-Logic* in particular makes clear, in the tradition, there are a host of more adequate anti-nominalist views, although those of Thomas and Bonaventure are especially worthy of note. Granted differences in vocabulary, style, and emphasis, both Thomas and Bonaventure articulate scrupulously restrained forms of Christian Neoplatonism that suggest that while God cannot be mastered by any human logic, neither is God defined by arbitrariness and caprice.[41] Barth's depiction of a trinitarian divine that 'loves in freedom' at the very least anticipates Balthasar's conjugation, even if because of its residual voluntarism or actualism it cannot provide the template.[42] Now while Balthasar shows sympathy for the trope of *Bonum diffusivum sui*, he is sufficiently critically aware to realize that in itself the trope cannot protect a trinitarian system from a necessitarian interpretation (*TL3*, 42). Not only Hegel,[43] but also Moltmann, as we shall see later, can put this trope to uses that are inimical to those of the mainline theological tradition. That the Trinity is being referred to an origin of infinite generosity is obviously a theological good, but this good can be compromised in subsequent interpretation if the emphasis falls on necessity in any of its registers, whether physical, logical, or ontological. Balthasar is sufficiently aware of the history of Neoplatonism to be concerned that such can happen. As we saw in chapter 1, it is his considered judgment that in Proclus one sees the tendency toward compromise. But the tendency is not altogether absent in Plotinus. Trinitarian theologians, who avail of Neoplatonism, have, therefore, to proceed with caution in order not to compromise on freedom, while not falling into the trap of thinking of freedom and necessity as a binary pair. For the Trinity, which defines agape, is essentially beyond freedom as well as necessity. Balthasar thinks that this is the consensus view of the Christian tradition, one shared by Pseudo-Dionysius and Augustine (*TL2*, 37), Aquinas (*TL2*, 28, 33), and Bonaventure (*TL2*, 28). And, it seems also shared by Anselm (*B*, 144). In his reference to Anselm in *Glory of the Lord* Balthasar translates 'necessary reasons' (*rationes necessariae*) by 'rightness' (*rectitudo*), by which he means aesthetic rightness or aesthetic aptness (*GL2*, 211-12). In *Love Alone* Anselm's view of the rightness of the Trinity's expression is explicitly enlisted against the necessity of manifestation in Hegel (*LA*, 87).

Finally, when an ironic form of kenosis is operative at both the level of the immanent Trinity as well as the economy, it is impossible to retrieve the sense of the Triune God as the *communio* of equally replete divine persons open to each other and involved in giving and receiving that defines their mode of relationality (*TL3*, 227-8; also *LA*, 115). Hegel's view at once supposes that kenosis operates on a single and linear axis, and that it always moves from emptiness to fulfillment across both the immanent and economic domains. By contrast, for Balthasar, kenosis both at the level of the immanent and economic Trinity cannot be reduced to one axis any more than the persons of the Trinity can be reduced to an undifferentiated divine unity. Moreover, as *Theo-Logic 2* makes clear with a force unmatched anywhere else in the trilogy, while ontologically speaking each of the divine persons has to be considered as unsurpassably full and fulfilled, the receptivity and openness at the core of each person suggests something like a *coincidentia oppositorum* of emptiness with fullness (*TL2*, 23-24; also *TL3*, 226). In this coincidence of wealth and poverty, which cannot be further unpacked, there is no overcoming of the particular emptiness that marks the constitutional receptivity and relationality of divine persons. Balthasar thinks that the *communio* view of the Trinity represents the very best that the tradition has to offer (*TL3*, 37 ff), although he suggests this without any prejudice to the contribution made to the elaboration of the Trinity by Augustine and Aquinas, who in many contemporary genealogies of trinitarian discourse function as fundamental points of derailment.[44] Augustine and Aquinas remain in his view as indispensable as Hugh of Saint Victor and Bonaventure. Indeed, as *Theo-Logic 2 & 3* express it, no one trinitarian paradigm is sufficient to encompass the richness of the mystery of the Trinity. While the Augustinian-Thomist model runs the danger of compromising on the differentiation of the persons, and of distorting the relation between human beings and the Trinity by recourse to analogies that have a conspicuously individual base, contrariwise the social model of the Trinity runs the risk of failing to reflect adequately the unity of the divine, as well as runs the danger of merely projecting into the divine desirable interpersonal and/or social relations.

Hegel's apologists notwithstanding, Balthasar considers Hegel's trinitarianism to represent a disastrous emendation of the understanding of the immanent Trinity within the Christian tradition. But, one religious thinker's disaster is another's windfall. Balthasar realizes that it is not sufficient to diagnose Hegel's view as untraditional, for this may very well be taken as a compliment. The theological tradition can be read as having come to a dead-end, as having inflicted on itself any number of debilitating injuries, as being chronically corrupt or essentially stillborn. In fact, the differences of these judgments has not prevented a number of trinitarian genealogists from attributing to the tradition all of the above. A condition that must be satisfied if Hegel is to be seen as 'distorting' the trinitarian tradition, is that this tradition is viewed at the very least in a favorable light. In modernity condemnation becomes well-neigh automatic if the tradition in the form of Nicaea and the regnant theological tradition is accorded the kind of authoritative status that makes it unnecessary further to reflect on the Trinity. Balthasar does not think that the tradition of trinitarian thought possesses this kind of status. Nothing in the tradition offers a perspective that is more than relatively adequate; this because of the illiminable mysteriousness of divine reality. Yet, this tradition, which is as much process as result, and which is ongoing even in his own work, possesses persuasive authority. For Balthasar the logical coherence of Hegel's triadically structured divine is the fruit of its being totally out of sync with the theological tradition. Whatever its merits – and these necessarily must be non-theological – Hegel's view is not an expression of the basic trinitarian grammar of the Christian tradition which is permissive of numerous emphases. However variant trinitarian talk is in the theological tradition, in no case does it authorize an impersonal account of the divine, a representation of the trinitarian divine as virtual rather than fully actual, and a bespoken trinitarian reality as being both quintessentially erotic and defined by logical and metaphysical necessity rather than by freedom and love. Other differences may count, such as differences between social and non-social views of the Trinity, without these differences counting as grammatically pertinent in the strict sense. In a sense the battle with Hegel enjoins a kind of hermeneutic of charity for theological disagreement within the broad Christian tradition.

Relatedly, Balthasar takes Hegel and his epigones effectively to have done away with the *oikonomia* by turning the history of salvation into the history of God, and conversely the dynamics of trinitarian life into the history of salvation (*TD2*, 42). If the economy is only the divine outside of itself, and as such in a mode of alienation, then, whatever the express intent of Hegel, neither the contingency nor openness of history are respected. Considered thus, human beings are instruments in the self-referential narrative of the divine in which the divine becomes the same through the hiatus of difference. In addition, if God is codependent on the dynamic processes of the world and on human history in order to become (*TL2*, 44-5, 67), then God's own agency is compromised, for without the world and human being God does not have sufficient actuality (*Wirklichkeit*) to be an agent. Moreover, for Balthasar, it is only against the backdrop of the real, and not simply the virtual, agency of the triune God that human agency comes to have shape and meaning. This agency is suffused and defined by gratuitousness and excess in rendering and tending to others.

Thus, for Balthasar, a properly Christian view of mission corrects a Hegelian view of human being as the image of God, which represents an exacerbation of the Enlightenment commitment to autonomous self-reflection to the point of a titanic elevation of the self against God. Balthasar had come to this conclusion as early as *Apokalypse*. Throughout the trilogy he makes the point emphatically. In doing so Balthasar explicitly recalls Hegel's hermeneutic of the creation and fall stories of Genesis in which the divine image is not only interpreted within a developmental horizon, as is the case with Irenaeus and Nyssa, but crucially human being as image displaces or supplants the biblical God who, as in Gnostic texts, is revealed as jealous. In a reference to Hegel which demonstrates a detailed knowledge of his texts, Balthasar writes: 'According to Idealist philosophy's interpretation of the legend, the serpent's interpretation obliges him to choose; he sins and thus gains access to self-consciousness' (*TD4*, 162). There are two sites for Hegel's transgressive hermeneutic, the one representing an elucidation of a fairly formal point of logic in *Encyclopedia* (#24 zu), the other a passage from *Lectures on the Philosophy of Religion* (1821 MS 104-5; 1824 207; 1827 302). In the case of both texts Hegel argues that alienation is indeed the result of the will to know, but his evaluation differs crucially from the traditional Christian view of this being a case of blameworthy pride. Even as Hegel agrees that there is something like Augustinian incurving in the self-assertion patent in Adam's choice, such a choice is as legitimate as it is intelligible. After all, the serpent told the truth, even if the emphasis should fall on realization rather than on what is given.[45]

As *Theo-Drama 2* makes particularly clear, mission provides the norm for agency, indeed the norm for personal identity. Personal identity is given in and through the embracing of a unique call to service, not in the exercise of *liberum arbitrium*, nor in Romantic becoming in which experiences are the fodder in one's self-making, nor finally in a Hegelian mode of renunciation in which the individual and the community appropriate themselves by allowing generous space to expropriation in the objective structures of family, civil society and the state, as well, of course, as the discourses of art, religion, and philosophy.[46] The false humilities of Romanticism and Idealism are the subject of explicit critique in *Apokalypse* and once again in *Glory of the Lord 1 & 5*: expropriation is not temporal but terminal. Neither the self, nor the community, can invest all happening with meaning and meaningfulness, and by so recollecting, gather itself into a harmonious whole. Balthasar is less sanguine about Romantic and Idealist forms of *Bildungsroman* than a Hegel commentator such as Ricoeur who shares many of his concerns with Hegel.[47] In a certain sense, here Balthasar has more in common with Derrida who rails against closure at all levels of the Hegelian system whether (onto)logical, theological, anthropological, or social-political, even as he sides with Hegel in suggesting that Christianity provides good reasons as to why philosophy should validate closure on all of these levels.[48]

In defining human being in terms of 'mission' Balthasar ensures at once that his anthropology is christologically grounded and that it admits, even demands, a trinitarian horizon for its full and adequate articulation. For in Christ and through the Spirit each human being participates in the mystery of the Trinity, which is a mystery of love and donation. If the christological and trinitarian backdrops are Johannine, so also then is the view of human being. Put on the path of personhood by 'call,' each human being imitates Christ whose response to 'call' is so complete that mission defines his 'I.' Of course, given the axiom of the incommensurability, as well as the phenomenology of religious life, in every other human being – the case of Mary is exceptional in this respect [49] – the response is less than complete, so that there exists a residuum of the I that escapes definition by mission. Reading John particularly through the eyes of Ignatius, there exists an infinite variety of calls and thus an infinite variety of personal identities. For Balthasar, a community is constituted by the interlacing and enhancing of the personal identity of each of the members. Only considered thus does the church mirror trinitarian *perichoresis* defined by giving and receiving of gift. Repeating a point made especially by Catholic critics of Hegel in the nineteenth century, for Balthasar it is important that it is the church and not the State that defines community. For even if, as Balthasar points out in *Theo-Drama 4*, the church can properly be regarded as 'person,' this supra-individual person does not, as is the case in Hegel's State, suspend and sublate the unique individual identities of its constituent members. Rather it is what makes possible these individual identities. Just as there is an irreducible core reality in Father, Son, and Spirit resistant to the logic of relations,[50] such also is the case in the community defined by church, which consequently provides the norm by which the State is judged rather than the other way around. Balthasar does not offer once again a liberal critique of Hegel's totalitarian view of the State. Instead he offers a communitarian alternative, which is ecclesially coded. He senses, as the Jewish religious thinker, Franz Rosenzweig, did (*TL2*, 51), that in Hegel the State is an *Ersatz* of the church that functions as the organon of imputed community in an alienating modern environment defined by individualism, utility, and merely contractual arrangements. Balthasar believes that Hegel provides us with no good reason to think that this idolatrous substitution is not only theologically but also humanly disastrous. Its blessing of the secular involves the evacuation of the holy, as its humanizing thrust represents a descent into the abyss. Only Hegel's linguistic restraint, then, disguises the secret that Nietzsche shouts from the rooftops, or at least on a busy street: 'God is dead.' Here it seems that *Apokalypse* is more percipient than the trilogy, which does little to elaborate the relation between Hegel and Nietzsche. In *Apokalypse* Balthasar sees, possibly with the eyes of Heidegger, that it might be style rather than substance that separates these two great German thinkers.[51] Self-consciously enacting Balthasar's program of theological aesthetics, this is a genealogical point that David Hart makes in his *The Beauty of the Infinite*.[52] Given the absence of reference to *Apokalypse*, it is necessarily a point that he makes on other than Balthasarian grounds.

Throughout the trilogy, and especially in *Theo-Drama* and *Theo-Logic*, Balthasar understands the substitution of the church by the State to be a function of the pneumatological twist Hegel, following the tradition of Joachim, applies to the economic Trinity. Liberated from its role as re-presenting Christ in the order of history, and becoming a function of Spirit, whose task is not so much to exposit the meaning of the person of Christ as clarify the message that is in principle separable from him, the 'church' becomes a free variable that can be filled with any content. As *Theo-Logic 3* has it, the content is at least as adequately supplied by Hegel's three forms of 'objective spirit': family, civil society, and the state. Of course, the church as the church, which for Hegel means the Lutheran church, continues with Hegel's blessing, in that it represents a site of memory of the message which, it turns out, was always a message to the future to instantiate a way of life that is free, democratic, and non-ascetic. Effectively then, the church does not stand to one side of modern culture and society, but in a sense provides its basis. Balthasar's objection is the one rendered by the Tübingen School in the nineteenth century: Hegel's view of the church represents both the apotheosis of the Protestant principle and its performative refutation. Much in the same way as Judaism, the Catholic church is diagnosed as an anachronism. Within history, it has no historical effect; it is impotent to create and justify secular institutions, which is the real business of church as this has been revealed in principle in the Reformation and in fact in the elaboration of institutions that generate autonomy and knowledge.

No longer admitting a sacramental interpretation, neither is the church fundamentally in control of the interpretation of its own cultic practices. When Hegel accepts the Lutheran interpretation of 'real presence' in *Lectures of Philosophy of Religion* (e.g. 1824, 236; 1827 337), this is not simply a matter of theological preference in which he is persuaded of its superiority over rival Catholic and Reformed views on biblical and traditional grounds. Without explicitly mentioning transubstantiation, Hegel does indeed object to what he takes to be the misalliance of epistemic naiveté and bad Aristotelian metaphysics. But his real point is that eucharistic anamnesis is less memory *of* Jesus Christ as the irreplaceable event of sacrifice and compassion disclosed in the narrative of his death and resurrection, than memory as communal self-awareness in the now, as this now anticipates the future of perfect actualization (*LPR3*, 1827, 337). Moreover, all suggestion of contemplation is ruled out. This memory, which is precisely not a memory, since the referent gets displaced onto the users of the signs, points to other social practices of self-affirmation and self-elevation that displace and replace eucharist as a practice.[53]

Balthasar thinks Hegel is to be congratulated on seeing what many more traditional theologians failed to see, namely, the trinitarian matrix of the church and the sacraments. Here, however, as just about everywhere else, the Christian realities are turned inside out to serve interests that are simply not theirs, and ingested into a program of the ontogenesis of the social world thought to be ingredient to – if not identical to – the ontogenesis of the divine itself. Although Hegel insists throughout his career that the Catholic church has no religious validity, and consistently recycles Reformation and Enlightenment stereotypes about Catholic otherworldliness and asceticism (e.g. *PS* #223-230; *LPR3* 1824, 286),[54] even more importantly he so qualifies the validity of the church in even its Protestant instantiation that it amounts to a disqualification. The validity of the church lies in its role as metaphor, its ability to point to a reality on the thither side of its language and practice. How it interprets what is going on is beside the point: first-order uses of religious language and first-order engagements in communal practice are not in a position to interpret meaning, or to distinguish real from notional intention. Insight is blurred, the message is garbled, and requires a dialectical filter to edit out the obscuring background noise. Read thus, the church can only be considered a sign, not a symbol of Christ. The erasure of its symbolic nature goes hand in hand with an erasure of its dramatic character, its being the site of intersection of infinite and finite initiatives and receptivities (*TD1*, 66-7). What in principle is the case, of course, becomes transparent when the church is understood to fall short of its vocation and forever be in need of the assistance of the Spirit to move it forward as it exposits and renders the mystery of Christ.

As Balthasar points out (*TD4*, 384), however, it is the eucharist, which constitutes the *raison d'être* of the church, that is the quintessence of dramatic action. Here the words spoken and the ritual actions performed by the priest and participated in by the community are at the same time conditioned by the one who is being remembered (*TD3*, 231; *TD4*, 405) and empowered by the Holy Spirit. The latter point is made emphatically in *Theo-Drama* : 'Since he is the Son, he can only give himself if he also enables [Christians] to participate in his proceeding from the Father. However, the grace of sonship is always identical with the bestowal of the Spirit of Christ' (*TD4*, 366; see also *GL1*, 573). This conjunction of divine and human action in performance is forgotten in the Hegelian scheme of things, as well as the interlocked roles of Christ and the Spirit. It is this interlocking that is, for Balthasar, crucial (*TD4*, 366, 400, 405-6; *TD5*, 384). It is possible, Balthasar concedes, to so emphasize the role of Christ that the Spirit can get forgotten. This is an unhappy byproduct of the tradition's justified insistence on the crucial role Christ plays in his own celebration. Hegel reminds theologians of what the theological tradition always knew; that is, the Spirit also plays an essential role in the eucharist in bringing us to Christ and in remaking us in his image (*TD4*, 406; also *TD1*, 67). Hegel, however, pushes too hard in the opposite direction, making Christ the obliging disappearing moment as the spiritual community (*Gemeinde*) comes to appreciate its divine status, an appreciation that grows into full cognitive appropriation in the move from *Vorstellung* to *Begriff.* This effectively pries apart rather than links the Son and the Spirit, and therefore forgets what the theological tradition so richly and so variously exhibits. Citing John 16, which is an important site for Hegel's pneumatology, Balthasar advises that the would-be Christian thinker would do well to remember that 'nonetheless, the Spirit does not speak of his own account but draws everything from the treasures of Christ, which are those of the Father' (*TD5*, 31).

Still, the problems of Hegel's depiction of the eucharist lie at a more profound level than the whiting out of its dramatic character. In a move, which is to some extent anticipated by Matthias Joseph Scheeben, to whom Balthasar refers in *Glory of the Lord* as the greatest German theologian after the Romantic period (*GL1*, 104),[55] and which in turn anticipates Marion's position,[56] Balthasar implies that Hegel's view of the eucharist demonstrates an even greater neglect of the role of the Father. Although Balthasar acknowledges that in his early texts Hegel, like his friend Hölderlin, can speak of the relation of the Son to the Father,[57] it is precisely this relation that gets suspended in Hegel's treatment. If the Son is not treated adequately in *Lectures on the Philosophy of Religion*, still the Son has sufficient reality to be submitted to interpretation. The Father is, however, essentially deleted, or put to the task of unfolding something like a process of self-depletion in a process of kenosis that renders him redundant (*TL3*, 41-2, 46). For Balthasar, the 'death of God' is not, as Hegel thinks, the birth of God. It is a death or erasure from which God cannot recover. Here Nietzsche, as usual more honest, gets it right. Specifically, without the Father the eucharist, which Hegel endorses as he submits it to revisionist interpretation, becomes incoherent. For the offering of the Son in the Spirit is the offering to the Father. Passages from *Glory of the Lord* and *Theo-Drama* echo and reinforce each other. The first passage reads, 'The eucharist is directed to God the Father. It is the Son who gives thanks in this self-surrender, and the church gives thanks with him and through him' (*GL1*, 573). The second is even more emphatic: 'As an act of thanksgiving to the Father . . . the eucharist also shows that the Father is the Lord of the eucharistic banquet, who, in the Holy Spirit, permits Christ, the Head, thus to give himself to his members' (*TD3*, 243).

Getting the eucharist wrong then is essentially to get the economic Trinity wrong and vice versa, and to get the latter wrong is *eo ipso* to get the immanent Trinity wrong. Directly invoking Hegel, in an especially rich passage, Balthasar underscores the point:

> *We cannot speak of a "process" in God . . . The triune love is always there in the perfect form of Eucharist; "behind the sacrifice of the Son stands the consubstantial loving surrender of the Father as the source of the Eucharist," and not only this, but the absolute self-surrender of every divine person to every other – and nothing in the "economic" sphere can intensify this surrender. (TD5, 265)*

What might be called Balthasar's trinitarian realism is expanded on throughout *Theo-Drama* and *Theo-Logic.* Balthasar also makes clear that he sees in Irenaeus' economic trinitarianism a fundamental theological orientation which, although it admits of deepening, cannot be surpassed. Crucially, this kind of trinitarianism ought to enjoy critical leverage over modern trinitarian thought and be of assistance in diagnosing deformation. In effect, the trinitarian battle is one between Irenaeus and Hegel. Hegel fails to see what Irenaeus so plainly sees in *Against Heresies*, the dramatic action of the persons of the Son and the Spirit who cannot be etiolated of their personal identity to become expressions of a realm of undifferentiated perfection. This means that Hegel cannot remember what Christian memory is like, or rather intentionally misremembers it, flattening to a uniform plane of meaning the dramatic curve given to it by the interaction of the community with the three persons of the Trinity and the distinctiveness and relatedness of their modes of action. In this interaction, the community and individuals in the community are remembered in their very act of remembering, for the eucharist effects the redeeming presence of a God who never forgets or gives up on us, who is for us at the very edge of nothingness and sin.[58] If the foreground of this event is christological, the backdrop is trinitarian (*TD4*, 344). Hegel's misremembering, which amounts to a reproducing of the basic vocabulary of the Christian view and a similitude of its grammar, goes deeper still when the question of how eucharist participates in the eternal event that is the triune God is asked. Here Balthasar introduces the split between the eternal and the temporal, and recurs to the symbolic operation of the eucharist and indeed the church as eucharist. Hegel beggars the vertical dimension of Christian Trinitarianism by failing to come to grips not simply with liturgy, but with the inescapable liturgical dimension of the church and by implication the entire cosmos.

If Balthasar had already made this point in the very title of his Maximus book, *Kosmische Liturgie*, the concept recurs in the trilogy in a much more heightened eschatological form. In fact it would be better to say that the point is apocalyptically indexed. And it is this genuinely apocalyptic index that is completely absent in Hegel. 'In Christ,' Balthasar writes,

> *the Spirit goes out into the world in union with the church, in order to make present the sacrifice of the "Lamb as if it were slain" and thus to enable the church to share – anew each time – in the Pasch of Christ, now that the Lamb's sacrifice has become heavenly and eternal. In this liturgy heaven continues to have effect on earth, but on the basis that what has been taken up into heaven, has been "consummated" (John 19:30). (TD4, 416)*

It is no accident that the above passage comes near the end of *Theo-Drama 4*, in which Balthasar argues that the framework for interpreting theo-drama is provided by the book of Revelation. But Revelation also provides the indispensable horizon for a liturgical view that is more nearly dramatic than aesthetic. In short, Revelation articulates an 'apocalyptic liturgy,' which does justice to the earthly and the heavenly and their intersection. One extraordinarily interesting corollary is that if Balthasar is prepared to label as 'apocalyptic' the thought of Hegel and his theological successors, it is only under the proviso that Hegel repeats Joachimite apocalyptic and/or Valentinian apocalypse against which he pits his own specifically Johannine version. Against the aggressive horizontalism of Joachimism in modernity, which in Joachim's case – although not in Hegel's – is produced through an interpretation of Revelation (*TL2*, 200), Balthasar insists on Christian apocalyptic's vertical dimension. Yet, as chapter 1 showed clearly, commitment to the vertical dimension of reality does not guarantee the adequacy of Christian vision. At the very least a non-hypostatic differentiation of the divine pleroma in Valentinianism, which historically speaking shuttles between monistic reticence and carnivalesque reproduction, is possible. The Valentinian view of perfection, which also involves conceiving the world as antithesis, is just the opposite of a Christian view of the triune God constituted by giving and receiving, which finds consummate expression in the cross that transforms rather than negates the world. Hypostatic density is underscored by what could be thought to be the introjection of a thanksgiving of Son that properly belongs to the economy were it not that thanksgiving itself is the fruit of the eternal conversation. In line with an interpretive practice that reaches a crescendo in *Theo-Drama 5*, in the following passage from *Theo-Logic*, Balthasar presents himself as annotating Adrienne von Speyr:

> *In receiving, therefore, the Son is not only thanksgiving (eucharistia); he is also gift in return, offering himself for all that the Father's self-giving may require; his willingness is absolute. Nor does this imply any subordination, as between "master and servant:" the Son shares the same, native, divine sovereignty, and freedom that the Father is . . . . (TL3, 226)*

Not incidentally, this quotation is taken from Speyr's commentary on John, and the Hegelian citation embedded in 'master and servant' is unmistakable. Whether Speyr intends it or not, Balthasar can only hear Hegel, and thus see that the crucial issue is separation of Christian from Hegelian eidetics. The Hegelian reconstruction of the immanent and economic Trinity fundamentally distorts both, and Hegelian articulation of their relation effectively involves their destruction. If within a traditional frame of reference – whether Western (e.g. Augustine) or Eastern (e.g. Cappadocian), Dominican (e.g. Aquinas) or Franciscan (e.g. Bonaventure) – mission (*missio*) depends on procession (*processio*) (*TD3*, 151), in Hegel and his theological successors mission and procession tend to be conflated. Depending on point of view, one can emphasize the absolving of the infinite or the finite, or the eternal or the temporal. Whichever is emphasized, Hegelian trinitarianism is just the opposite of the economic trinitarianism exhibited by Irenaeus (*TD1*, 69) which, as with Hegel, maps the entire Christian narrative. It is in light of the collapse of the immanent Trinity into the economic and vice versa in Hegel and his successors that Balthasar expresses his reservations about Rahner's famous axiom of identity:

> *The laws of the "economic" Trinity arise from the "immanent" Trinity, and they do so in astounding variations . . . But the economic Trinity cannot be regarded as simply identical with the immanent. (TD3, 157)*

Balthasar is not suggesting that the Rahnerian formula as such is mischievous. Nor is he suggesting that after the manner of Hegel and his theological successors that Rahner identifies the immanent with the economic Trinity. The real issue with Balthasar lies rather with what the formula might appear to license in trinitarian discourses less interested in the theological tradition than Rahner and more exercised in critiquing its immanent-economic Trinity distinction as wrongheaded. This is what happens, Balthasar believes, in the Hegelian and post-Hegelian theological traditions, which at best comport themselves in a cavalier and opportunistic manner, and at worst behave in a totally intolerant fashion towards the theological tradition taken to be constituted by sophisms.

Divine Passibility and the Symbolic Milieu

INFLUENTIALLY, AND INTENTIONALLY, the Hegelian tradition, which has yoked together the elaboration of the Trinity with the vision of a 'suffering God,' disturbs the classical tradition's picture of an uninvolved and essentially impassible divine. For Balthasar, the Hegelian tradition has to be regarded as right to the extent to which it diagnoses the mismatch between theological discourse and the deliverances of scripture and popular piety, which paint a picture of a God who is otherwise, who is with and for us, and who in the form of Christ goes into the abyss of the Godforsakenness of sin and death. Nevertheless, if the theological tradition is subject to deformation, Balthasar believes it presumptuous to think that the full meaning of 'impassibility' has been comprehended, and invidious to operate with the unexamined assumption that the entire classical theological tradition can be painted with the 'impassibility' brush. Here the subject of correction is more nearly Moltmann the theologian than Hegel the philosopher, since it is Moltmann rather than Hegel who is focally more interested in the way a deficient metaphysics affects theological discourse rather than in the adequacy of a metaphysics that supports the unchangeability and impassibility of the ground of being. In this respect, Balthasar's own detailing of the impassibility-passibility discussion in the theological tradition in *Theo-Drama 5* essentially indicts Moltmann's narrative of mourning concerning the theological tradition's exclusion of suffering in God. Too committed to the Hegelian overcoming of a metaphysical tradition that cannot think difference and contradiction, and too wedded to Luther's earliest estimation of the theological tradition which is condemned in its entirety, Moltmann's genealogy is simple-minded in its understanding of 'passibility' and 'impassibility' as they function in the tradition, and guilty of erasing differences within the polyphonic unity of the Christian tradition respecting both the figuration and the understanding of the divine.

Dealing with the second of these points first, in *Theo-Drama 5* Balthasar takes it that no more than Heidegger's thesis of the aboriginal fall of philosophy is Moltmann's thesis of the aboriginal corruption of Christian theology in and by metaphysics capable of surviving critical examination. Exemplary traditional theologians such as Maximus, Hilary of Poitiers, Anselm (*TD5*, 222), and latterly Barth (*TD5*, 236-9) present complex views about God's openness to the world of suffering and sin that cannot be summarily dismissed as showing signs of either general metaphysical or specifically Platonic infection. The compliment to these figures does not replace the affirmation of Bonaventure's cruciform trinitarianism that provides the fundamental heuristic of *Glory of the Lord.* And then there is Balthasar's extraordinary championing of the work of Speyr in this regard, so much so that throughout *Theo-Drama 5* their voices are essentially blended. This is not to claim that the entire theological tradition should be given a clean bill of health in this respect, nor to deny that the theological tradition has more than occasionally betrayed its faith heritage. Balthasar's point, however, is that diagnosis of deformation or betrayal is an evidentiary matter.

Deformation cannot simply be assumed; the argument for corruption has to be made on a case by case basis. Although Balthasar believes that the evidence will not support the view that metaphysical and rationalistic infection is total in the Christian theological tradition, he does admit that such infection is fairly widespread. Examples of it can be found throughout Christian history. Resisting the 'acute Hellenization of Christianity' hypothesis, for example, does not mean that one outright denies that early forms of Christian thought were overly influenced by Platonic and Greek views on the metaphysical constitution of the divine, construals which were assisted, and in turn were assisted by, an anthropology which emphasized *apatheia*. From the very beginnings of his forging of theological identity in his reflections on Origen (or rather his tradition) and even on Nyssa, Balthasar is concerned with the way Platonism runs interference with respect to the biblical *Gestalt* of faith. In addition, Balthasar agrees with modernity's detractors that it is shot through with rationalism at the level of assumption, practice, and self-legitimation. He is also of the view that theology, both Protestant and Catholic, has colluded with this rationalism, which cannot think of a God who suffers as other than a mystification. He is at least as vehement as Rahner is towards Manual Theology. And he shares the view of the Tübingen School that the dominant Catholic apologetic rationales of the eighteenth century, in which the justification of the authority of the church precedes the exposition of Christian mysteries and essentially warrants them, constitutes a theological dead-end.[59] And Balthasar repeats a common complaint of 20th-century revivers and/or revisioners of Thomas, namely, that Thomas' case is hindered rather than aided by the synthesis of Scholastic thought made in the Baroque period by Suarez (*GL5*, 21-9).[60]

The critique of some questionable strands of thought in the ancient world, and especially the critique of modernity, does not function, however, as a diversion in which the medieval period is happily excluded from criticism, thereby protecting what, arguably, is the most influential swathe of the tradition of Catholic thought. As Balthasar notes time and again, medieval thought had its share of rationalisms. If in *Glory of the Lord* Scotus is especially singled out (*GL5*, 16-21), it is interesting that although Aquinas is validated (*GL4*, 393-412), he does not appear to operate precisely as

Scotus' contrary. While the proximity of the praise for Aquinas' use of analogy and the correlative condemnation of Scotus' identity-philosophy might incline one to think that Balthasar intends an absolute contrareity, the opposition is restricted to metaphysics. When the theological as such comes into view, it seems to be Bonaventure who provides the ultimate contrast, at least within the horizon of theological aesthetics. Indeed, from *Glory of the Lord 1* it appears evident that it is Bonaventure who is regarded as the more regulative theological figure. It is Bonaventure rather than Aquinas whose thought is christologically saturated and whose horizon is constitutively trinitarian. And it is Bonaventure rather than Aquinas who introduces the transcendental of beauty into the very precincts of the trinitarian divine.[61] These considerations leave intact the logical possibility of a more qualified ascription of 'rationalist' to Aquinas, since the account of Aquinas could give the impression that a metaphysics of Being functions foundationally for the elaboration of *sacra doctrina.* While the potential damage inflicted on Aquinas' theological credentials would necessarily remain hypothetical, since any ascription of rationalism proceeds from an argument from silence, it is sufficient for Balthasar to involve himself later in the trilogy in a move of correction in which Aquinas is granted theological *bona fides.* This is true particularly of his trinitarian thought. As Balthasar comes to terms with Thomas in *Theo-Logic*, he makes it abundantly clear that Thomas' trinitarianism does not suffer by contrast with that of Bonaventure (*TL2*, 28-33). Thus even if Aquinas' view of God as *esse seipsum* is not sufficient to overcome the traditional, more or less Platonic, construal of immutability and impassibility, it is more than plausible that the trinitarian figuration of the *Summa* (1. Q 26-43) would achieve this task. Balthasar, then, would not be unsympathetic to the kind of position advanced by Gilles Emery,[62] which if it would press the prospects of a trinitarian refiguration of Thomistic metaphysics, is by no means skeptical regarding the dynamic and ecstatic character of *esse.*

Accepting, then, that the rationalist predilection of the theological tradition implies the necessity of some kind of repair, the question is whether the Hegelian counter-assertion of 'divine passibility' represents a legitimate correction. Balthasar thinks that it does not, both because it fails to recognize legitimate uses of 'impassibility' in the theological tradition, and applies 'passibility' univocally to both God and creatures. In trying to articulate a legitimate space for the attribution of 'impassibility,' Balthasar does not take the easy way out by determining that 'impassibility' translates the unchangeableness of divine promise vouchsafed in scripture. While Balthasar believes that theological thought has to remain faithful to scripture's depiction of a God who is in solidarity with his sinful creatures even to the point of death on their behalf on the cross, at the same time the biblical depiction of a God, as transcendently sovereign, also demands fidelity, as Barth showed, complaints of monarchicalism notwithstanding. Thus, although 'impassibility' need not be 'metaphysically' specified, and more particularly Platonically specified, Balthasar does not think that impassibility, and immutability which grounds and funds it, are without ontological implication. At the very least, impassibility suggests that as radically different than finite creatures God does not suffer in the way his creatures do, is not vulnerable to outside influence in the same way (*TD5*, 216), is not subject to any kind of metaphysical compulsion (*TD4*, 322-23; also *TD3*, 523), or that God avails of the opportunity in experiencing the world and its history to actualize potential that otherwise would not have become truly real. 'Impassibility' is a marker – perhaps even a necessary marker – of difference, of incommensurability. One could even go so far as to say that 'impassibility' is a required protocol for Christian speech about God.

This is bad news for all post-Hegelian theologians, who typically behave as if the attributions of passibility and impassibility are ingredients in a zero-sum game. At the same time, it should be admitted that what I am calling his protocol defense of impassibility has not overly impressed Thomists who desire a more sustained and rigorous defense of impassibility.[63] Stronger metaphysical sensibilities demand less concession to Hegelianism, and less complicity in the mythology of divine suffering that Balthasar would overcome. While it is true, for example, that Balthasar denies change (*TD3,* 523) and potentiality (*TD2*, 261; *TD5*, 394) to God, Balthasar's insistence on divine responsiveness to the world (*TD3*, 523; *TD5*, 214-15) and divine enrichment in an openness and vulnerability expressive of God's love (*TD5*, 339, 412, 514) can only seem as if Balthasar falls victim in the end to the Hegelian Trojan horse.[64] Arguably, Balthasar could have gone much deeper on the metaphysical front than he does in *Theo-Drama*, although it should be reminded that for him love is always event (*TD5*, 91-2), that love is always without need, and that on the basis of *Theo-Logic 1* event is event only as superabundant actuality as origin. Within his Thomistic frame Weinandy, for example, cuts deeper. But so always does Hart, who in *The Beauty of the Infinite* is more interested in supplementing Balthasar than replacing him. A Balthasarian view of impassibility can sustain correction and welcome supplement, but, as *Theo-Drama* makes particularly clear, how you defeat Hegel is as important as defeating him. Since Hegel was neither totally wrong in suggesting a more dynamic view of God nor in his critique of the metaphysical tradition, a total victory is not the way towards Christian truth. Balthasar fears that a fully successful defense of a more traditional view of impassibility could prove merely pyrrhic. As *Theo-Drama 2* (9, 53-4, 77) suggests, it risks leaving uncorrected its own tendencies towards an epical – even if non-mythological – point of view. More modest, certainly, than Hegelian speculation, it risks being too interested in demonstration. With respect to the issue of impassibility in Balthasar's view, there is a 'so far, no further' clause, or as Balthasar puts it, 'we can follow the idea for a certain distance, then it breaks off' (*TD5*, 264).

This is something that Hegel and post-Hegelians gloriously fail to understand. A conspicuous mark of Hegelian and post-Hegelian attribution of 'passibility' to the divine is the failure to understand the symbolic nature of discourse as well as the analogical predication of discourse. As indicated already, to the extent to which 'suffering' is applied to God, its predication should be tempered by the ontological difference between God and creatures. Balthasar's embracing of this point seems to have gone unacknowledged by Rahner, who accuses Balthasar of having Gnostic tendencies with respect to the attribution of 'suffering' (*TD5*, 13-4). Although Rahner is engaging in a genealogical operation of a rhetorical kind, which is second nature to Balthasar, the main point appears to be epistemological: Balthasar illicitly imports categories that apply in the sublunar and human sphere to the divine sphere where they have no competence. Balthasar insists on the analogical nature of predication and that all similarity between divine and human existence suggested in the use of the term 'suffering' is hedged in the recognition that a single term is being used to cover two ontologically different domains. If analogical predication is supported by the revelation of a God who, precisely as different, is with and for us, revelation also mandates exploration – which can only be probative – of what difference the difference of God makes with respect to the nature of the suffering so evident on the cross. Here concepts as such fail, and strictly speaking we are no longer dealing with analogy but with symbol. As an aesthetic theologian, pleading epistemic humility, Balthasar still demands the right to make suggestions as to who this God is who behaves towards us as creator, redeemer, and sanctifier. As creatures the eros to truth will not be stayed, even if what is asserted will not admit of justification. As creatures grounded in faith, the eros to praise cannot be stayed. Christian praise is at once copious and scrupulous, venturesome and restrained, baroque and desert-like, but importantly neither one without the other. Apophasis, for Balthasar, is ineluctable, precisely as an operation of restraint on a discourse that is an intense and copious response to the superabundance of the divine origin that is precisely a trinitarian origin. For Balthasar, scripture gives every bit as much evidence for such loquacity as silence. Yes, there is silence before the *Tetragrammaton*, astonished wondering before the glory of Christ which in the Gospels seems to exceed all pre-given formats, but there is also much speech, hyperbole, and articulation of divine glory in very different venues, divine glory caught in flashes and divine glory pondered and meditated. As negative theology is a gift of scripture that cannot be reneged on by the theological tradition, neither can scripture as aesthetic and dramatic be downplayed. Perhaps in the end, however, Balthasar is demanding more from the Christian than that she understand the complementarity of the apophatic and the kataphatic in the Christian tradition. He wants to suggest that as silence can be eloquent, there is a silence to the cascade of image, the torrent of speech respecting God that marks the Christian tradition: the non-desert silence, a joyous silence participating in trinitarian fecundity.

Balthasar wishes to steer between the univocal predication of Hegel and the tendency in Rahner to proscribe analogical predication when it comes to *sacra doctrina*. In this sense, Balthasar understands himself to be more continuous with the Augustinian and Thomistic traditions than Rahner's suggestion of equivocity, even as he insists on reserve and scruple in predication. Granting the need to go interpretively beyond what is expressly stated in scripture, precisely in order to be faithful to its basic intention, Balthasar thinks it legitimate to put in play terms such as 'super-kenosis' (*TL2*, 217-8), 'super-time' (*TD5*, 30-1, 250, 310), and 'super-space' (*TD5*, 93, 245, 263) as more disclosive of divine life than 'immutability,' 'eternity,' and 'non-extension.' Importantly, however, the terms that Balthasar proposes to complement the more traditional ones or inflect them, are symbols rather than categories in the strict sense. They aim at a trinitarian divine, but cannot guarantee success of their referential aim. Most certainly, they are not explanatory in the strict sense. Not only these terms, but no foreseeable set of such terms, are able to function in an explanatory capacity vis-à-vis the trinitarian divine characterized as mysterious and defined as constitutively excessive. At the same time, these terms are more nearly second-order than first-order, since they presuppose and interpret the biblical symbol of 'kenosis' and suggestions of altering of time and space hinted at in biblical apocalyptic. These terms, then, suggest something like an explanatory function, while denying it. For unlike concepts or categories proper, whether Aristotelian, Kantian, or Hegelian, explanation by means of second order symbols or ciphers is understood to be probative and incomplete, and inadequate to its referent. The appeal to, and use of, meta-symbols and/or conceptual ciphers represent nothing more nor less than relatively adequate attempts to name the triune life of the divine that is not other than the economy which it grounds. The cure for explanatory hubris, however, inheres in their very use. For such meta-symbols unname in the very act of naming, but importantly unname directionally rather than into the agnostic void.

In his most concerted elaboration of these meta-symbols in *Theo-Drama*, Balthasar does not strictly speaking argue for their legitimacy, after the manner, for example, of Karl Jaspers whose work offers extended reflection on 'ciphers' of transcendence, or what he refers to as the 'Encompassing.'[65] He limits himself to pointing to conceptual need, specifically the need for a responsive and responsible discourse to render the 'living God' of the Bible. This task is the task of all theology, and not simply Luther. Certainly, the task cannot be sub-contracted out to Hegelianism, which comes to be understood as compensating for what the mainline traditions forget, leaving for later adjudication whether the supplement is not in fact the reality. Since the 'living God', for Balthasar as well as Hegel, finds its definitive expression in John, the battle with Hegel becomes in *Theo-Drama* a hermeneutic of John. Christian apologetics, he believes, are not served by rote repetition of divine immutability and impassibility, since the issue is how to understand the application of these terms with respect to the ferociously loving and vehemently engaged God rendered by scripture. Still, it might fairly be suggested that the trilogy represents such a comprehensive re-landscaping of the theological terrain that fundamentally sets limits to the meaning of 'immutability' and 'impassibility.' A considerable amount of this landscaping is achieved in and by theological aesthetics. For what defines theological aesthetics is the form or 'superform' of Christ, which cannot be other than cruciform. It is important to Balthasar that before any theological analysis, whether an ontological analysis of Christ's nature and person or analysis of the properties of the Son precisely as a divine person, that the *Gestalt* of Christ represents a challenge to the linear nature of human logic. One could think of the three meta-symbols I refer to above as further reminders that however valid the symbols of 'immutability' and 'impassibility' are, it will be important to bring out their specifically Christian meaning which cannot be tied exclusively to Greek metaphysics and its regime of binary oppositions of an ontological sort. It is time, however, to discuss these meta-symbols in more detail.

'Ur-kenosis,' which refers to the trinitarian event in which the Father empties himself to give space to the Son, is understood as the ground of the radical kenosis of the incarnation and cross that is the subject of Philippians 2:5-11. Balthasar does not draw attention to Hegelian anticipations. Yet, given his knowledge of Hegel's texts, it is unlikely that he is unaware of Hegel's appeal to kenosis at the level of the Trinity either in the *Phenomenology* (#770), where the Word uttered by the Father represents his emptying, or in the *Lectures on the Philosophy of Religion* (1821 MS, 83), in which Hegel speaks with somewhat of a greater distance from Christianity about the 'self-emptying' (*Selbstablassen*) of the universal and abstract divine.

Yet, whatever the degree of anticipation, Hegel fails to grasp that intra-divine kenosis is a relation that is as much constituted by the paternity and filiality as explaining them. Paternity and filiality suggest that the operation of kenosis at the level of the immanent Trinity cannot function without terms that name irreducible realities, moreover realities that are at once full and defined by openness and receptivity, not exclusive of the grounding activity of the Father (*TL2*, 66).

It would not be going too far to say that Hegel's dynamic rendering of a Trinity consisting of 'transient moments' (*PS* #771) is tied in the closest possible way to the view that the immanent Trinity at best supports the view that there is one subject or one person.[66] Leaving in parentheses the fact that Hegel thinks of this subject or personality (*Persönlichkeit*) almost exclusively in terms of self-consciousness, another issue is that the kenotic dynamism at the level of immanence only allows Personality to be understood as goal rather than origin, result rather than pure givenness. The following statement from *Lectures on the Philosophy of Religion* is typical: 'It is precisely in the divine unity that Personality, just as much as it is posited (*gesetz*) is posited as resolved (*aufgelöst*); only in appearance ...' (*LPR3*, 1824 194). Hegel does not concede in the slightest that his view of intra-divine kenosis represents a fundamental departure from Christianity, at least Christianity properly understood. Rather, he thinks here, as on a number of other fronts, that the mainline Christian tradition proves inadequate to its fundamental inspiration. From his perspective, it is not clear that the minority or heterodox Christian traditions do any better – although Jacob Boehme may be an exception.[67] Since, however, in their case the one and only failure consists in the inability to commit fully to a dynamic kenotic view that is inchoately represented, they are primed in a way the mainline theological traditions are not for sublation – thus conceptual justification - in and by the Hegelian system. The following passage about Valentinianism is extraordinary by any measure:

> *In brief, the source of many so-called heresies lies purely in the turn to speculation, which, in the transition from the One, the universal, to the process of distinction, distinguishes this activity from the universal,*

> *hypostatizes it apart from the universal (sie hypostasiert getrennt von jenem), which [is supposed] to stand over against it as abstract. Considered more closely, however, this Logos has already itself the characteristic of return (der Rückkehr) within itself, since it contains a moment that must be distinguished in order to comprehend the distinction exactly. The resolution consists in the fact that Spirit is the Totality, and the first moment itself is grasped as first only because, to begin with, it has the determination of the third, of activity. (LPR3 1821 MS 86)*

Here Hegel mines narrative dynamism, moved by a form of iterative kenosis, from precisely the Valentinian tradition to which Balthasar often suggests that he belongs. Kenosis at the level of the immanent Trinity is not energy without direction. It is intrinsically teleological, having as its goal fully realized divine subjectivity or personality. Balthasar's entire reflection on the immanent Trinity is set squarely against this non-hypostatic view, its view of personality as result rather than origin, as well as the understanding of kenosis as an operation arising from poverty rather than wealth (*TD2*, 258; *TD5*, 84, 428). And, as we saw in chapter 2, Balthasar grasps as clearly as Altizer that in Hegel's system kenosis does not stop at the intra-divine level, and that personality does not complete itself at the level of intra-divine Spirit. Nature and especially historical human subjectivity are enlisted in the becoming of a subjectivity that is divine in the metaphysically fundamental respect that no contrast with it is thinkable. The objection here is the generic one that in flattering this metaphysical axiom, Hegel effectively reduces the economic and immanent Trinities to each other.

Fortunately for Balthasar, however, there exists not only a 19th-century negative anticipation, but a 20th-century positive anticipation of 'ur-kenosis.' This anticipation by Balthasar's own admission is provided by Sergei Bulgakov (*TL2*, 217-18). Although Bulgakov's esoteric and Idealist leanings are sometimes a cause for concern, Balthasar thinks that Bulgakov's theology represents just the kind of critical engagement with modern speculative thought required to move beyond theological stagnation in which neither the immanent Trinity nor its relation to the economy is thought. Formally

Hegelian in that ur-kenosis is linked to the kenoses of creation and eschaton as well as incarnation and cross (*TD4*, 323), Balthasar concludes in *Theo-Logic 2* that Bulgakov's thought is anti-Hegelian in its commitment to hypostases and the vision of the entire economy as gift. In the important trinitarian discussion, the build-up is slow. Arguing against Hegel's idea of a 'Father who generates the Son in order to come to know himself,' Balthasar first offers his own rebuttal, which involves a very different view of the Father.

> *. . . the immemorial priority of the self-surrender or self-expropriation thanks to which the Father is Father cannot be ascribed to knowledge but only to groundless love, which proves the identity of love as the "transcendental" par excellence. (TL2, 177)*

Glossing this avowal with a demurring from Marion's opposing of love and Being in *God without Being* (*TL2*, 177, n. 9), Balthasar goes on generously to acknowledge his intellectual debts. The passage is worth quoting in full:

> *We can understand this only if we dare to speak, with Bulgakov, of a first intratrinitarian kenosis, which is none other than God's positive "self-expropriation" in the act of handing over the entire divine being in the processions, or with Ferdinand Ulrich, of the unity of "poverty" and "wealth" in absolute being itself. Love can thus be considered the supreme mode, and therein the "truth" of being, without for all that, having to be transported beyond truth and being. By the same token, whether we think philosophically in terms of worldly being or theologically in terms of divine being, there is one thing we cannot do: ascribe the transcendentals simply to divine being devoid of distinction. On the contrary, we have no choice but to anchor them in the process of the hypostases. Indeed, if we abstract from this process, we cannot even speak of a divine being or essence in the first case. The identity of the divine essence is found in the positive self-expropriation of the divine persons, which in all three is one, true, and good. (TL2, 217-18)*

Whatever their differences with respect to Spirit on the level of both the immanent Trinity and economy, both Balthasar and

Bulgakov interpret the immanent Trinity as a matrix of giving and the entire economy as gift. This applies in an especially acute way to 'last things' that are the object of reflection in the second and third volumes of *Theo-Logic* as well as *Theo-Drama 5*. For neither can 'last things' be imagined in the manner of Enlightenment progressivism, Marxist dialectic, or the march of Hegelian *Geist* as teleological result; 'last things' can only be expressed apocalyptically, that is, as a kind of transformative ingression of the triune God who would be 'all in all.'

The analogy between the worldly and divine dimensions of reality is also in operation in Balthasar's proposal of 'supertime' as a meta-symbol to render the livingness of the divine. Balthasar grants to Hegel and his epigones their point that the essentially contrastive envisaging of the relation between time and eternity essentially bankrupts Christianity. In thinking of eternity as the *nunc stans*, the triune divine is deprived of the energy and exigency that mark time. The irony is not lost on either that the supposedly inferior dimension of time possesses unquestionable positive qualities denied to the supposedly superior dimension of eternity. While Balthasar shares with Hegel the problem about depicting time and eternity, he does not share his solution. In line with Przywara in *Analogia Entis*, in *Theo-Logic 1* Balthasar essentially accepts Heidegger's insight in *Sein und Zeit* that the hinge to the Hegelian system lay in Hegel's conception of the relation between the concept (*Begriff*) and time.[68] Taking Hegel's famous asseveration at the end of the *Phenomenology* about time being 'the empirically existing concept' (*die Zeit ist der daseinende Begriff selbst*)(#46) to be exemplary, Heidegger thinks that the compliment to time is no compliment, and that the saturation of time with non-temporal meaning inscribes a form of Platonism. Hegel's Platonism is focused in the erasure of the unanticipatable future (*der Zukommenden*) (*TL1*, 197), which alone makes time ecstatic. Obviously, Hegel's attempted synthesis generates more than one kind of concern. It is possible – maybe even necessary – to worry also about the status of the concept when time seems to be so essential to its definition. Thus, if from one point of view the problem is the depletion of the exigency of time, from another point of view the problem is the leakage of transcendence. In a sense, then, one could conceive of Hegel's own view as systemically doubly troubled. This doubleness casts a light on Feuerbach's 'transformational criticism' and Marx's turning Hegel on his head, by indicating that in Hegel's own conjugation of eternity and time there continues to be a quarrel between immanence and transcendence. Unlike Heidegger (*TL1*, 203; also 66, 88, 138), however, Balthasar is concerned with the prospects of the eternal pole of the relation touched on in the *Phenomenology*, and he agrees with Feuerbach and Marx about the essential doubleness of Hegel's view which, on the one hand, allows his thought to be read as radically immanentist and, on the other, suggests a commitment to a revisionist view of eternity in which, having overcome time, eternity is possessed of a non-temporal dynamic and defined in terms of divine-human self-knowing. This second aspect of doubleness is where the 'Gnostic' aspect of Hegel emerges with particular definition.

Balthasar's task then is to envisage 'eternal life' as more rather than less dynamic than time, and while doing so keep in mind the analogical nature of discourse regarding 'eternal life,' the personal or interpersonal nature of this life, and the absolute distinction between the triune God and creatures who participate in the triune life. As Balthasar provides the basic contours of his view of eternal life as 'supertime' in *Theo-Drama 5*, and supplements this account in *Theo-Logic 2 & 3*, he envisions eternal life as unthinkable event, absolute emergence, and unanticipatable surprise. Of course, in thinking of the triune God as event, no less than Jüngel, Balthasar has to be understood as reprising Barth. Nor is any guesswork involved. The point is suitably underscored in Balthasar's book on Barth, which validates the notion of event even as it defends against its actualist deformation. In considering the divine life under the aspect of emergence, Balthasar could be thought to appropriate and displace Heidegger's parsing of *energeia* onto the triune God. Supporting an interpretation of Being as *energeia* in both *Glory of the Lord 5* and *Theo-Logic 1*, Balthasar can be understood to accept under advisement the link between *energeia* and time. But, here as elsewhere, however, it is not as if Balthasar has a single interlocutor, nor that all conversations with previous thinkers are critical in nature. Balthasar has before him Nyssa's construal of the fulgurating triune God, and correlatively his construal of time marked by stasis.[69] While, undoubtedly, it is David Bentley Hart's achievement in *The Beauty of the Infinite* fully to have rendered the Nyssan alternative to modern and postmodern construal,[70] he is not mistaken in thinking that he enjoys a Balthasarian precedent. After Nyssa, Balthasar considers the emergent divine under the auspices of perpetual fecundity rather than as in Hegel – as knowledge or self-knowledge.[71] In addition, as we outlined in the last chapter, for Balthasar the infinity of the triune God permits participation in knowing and loving in the triune God. Yet participation specifies a gap between the finite knower and lover and the one who calls forth knowing and loving, the One whom Maximus refers to as 'unparticipatable.'[72]

This brings me to Balthasar's most hyperbolic parsing of 'supertime,' that is, eternity as everlasting surprise. From one angle, 'surprise' is simply a more concrete way of talking about the lack of closure in our affective and cognitive response either on the hither or thither side of the eschatological line to the ungraspable divine. Yet, there is an obvious sense in which 'surprise' understood in this way reflects the reality of the triune God as a dynamism that does not lend itself to anticipation. When this more objective perspective comes into view, as it does, for example, in *Theo-Logic 1* (197), the divine is ciphered under the aspect of the future, the unanticipatable future, rather than the future that is the aim or goal of the past and the present, what Ernst Bloch referred to in *The Principle of Hope* as the *futurum* rather than the *Zukunft*. In speaking of God in this way, Balthasar keeps company with Rahner, Kasper, and Pannenberg. And he does so for similar reasons, and plausibly with a similar precedent for the locution of 'absolute future' in mind. For similar reasons, given that he shares their interest in protecting the incomprehensibility of the triune God from non-speculative as well as speculative forms of rationalism. With a similar precedent, since all three German theologians – although this is more clear in the case of Kasper and Pannenberg[73] – can find in Schelling's articulation of an 'epochal' divine a specifically theological answer to Hegel's articulation of the philosophical concept. Appealing to Schelling against Hegel is a 19th-century story, and figures like Franz von Baader and Franz Anton Staudenmaier represent its different inflections. It is obvious, for Balthasar, that ultimately

Schelling's thought may be of very limited constructive use for Christianity. This is Balthasar's judgment in *Apokalypse 1* (205-46) and in *Glory of the Lord 5* (557-72), the two texts in which Schelling is treated extensively. Still, Schelling's work represents a more than frivolous engagement with Christianity, and there are ideas in Schelling which not only provide the theologian with critical leverage over Idealist speculation, but open out Christianity beyond petrified orthodoxy. Pointing to the texts of Schelling's post-Idealist middle period, which includes the *Freiheit* essay (1809), *The Stuttgart Lectures* 1810) and *The Ages of the World* (1815) in particular, while Balthasar judges that the 'theogonic' temporal mapping of the divine leaves much to be desired, he is of the view that 'epochality' emblazons dynamism without reducing God to time. It is within this framework that Schelling makes his most notable contribution, that is, his thinking of God as the 'absolute future.' If German theology of the twentieth century is anything to go by, this parsing mirrors in its theological fecundity the excess of a divine uncapturable in anticipation.

However, with respect to the image of 'super-time,' Schelling's *Die Weltalter* simply serves as background once again to a lexical foreground provided by Bulgakov. Although when Balthasar uses the meta-symbol he does not cite Bulgakov, the concept is gestured to in *The Lamb of God* and fully developed in *The Bride of the Lamb.* As the latter text suggests, for Bulgakov the appropriate location for the operation of the concept is eschatology, or eschatology as it is trinitarianly qualified. Bulgakov is not in the least shy in insisting that 'supertime' is time as it has undergone radical transfiguration, that is, time understood apocalyptically, as well as christologically (*BL*, 384-85; 376, 347). An aficionado of Revelation just like Bulgakov, Balthasar could not agree more, but, arguably, would want to make as much of a point as to how the concept of eternity is also transformed. Perhaps, it is here, laudable as Bulgakov's distance is from Schelling, that Schelling continues to make a significant contribution in the refiguration of the notion of eternity that is crucial for the health of contemporary theology.

As both our treatments of '*ur-kenosis*' and 'supertime' indicate, in his analyses Balthasar cleaves closely enough to the Hegelian view to get critical traction on the theological tradition become ossified, and far enough so that Hegel and his tradition of discourse are themselves the object of a critique. 'Super-space' does not, at least straightforwardly, have a critical correlative in Hegel. As his *Philosophy of Nature* (# 246) clearly shows, after Descartes Hegel cannot think of space outside pure extension. For Hegel, any extrapolation of the *partes ex partes* of extension into the divine would conflict with the demand that the divine exhibit the internal mediation of Spirit which only begins to show itself with time. At the same time, the notion of 'space' or 'spacing' cannot altogether be excluded from the divine, given Hegel's predilection to speak of the divine before the creation of the world in the spatial language of 'realm' or 'kingdom,'[74] and even more importantly to think of logical articulation of categories that maps the immanent Trinity to be the dialectically unfolded milieu of thought. Balthasar might best be viewed as at once challenging the impossibility of a view of spacing other than that adopted by Descartes and indeed modern science as a whole, and condemning Hegel's substitution of the space defined by intra-trinitarian relations by logic, indeed, by a logic of relation that proceeds at different intensities of satisfaction and distinct levels of internality.

For Balthasar, as used especially in *Theo-Drama 5*, the meta-symbol of 'super-space' at a penultimate level points to the eschatological horizon of action in which the referent is not the worldless spirit that has either not yet arrived at creation and incarnation or is about to let it go, but rather an apocalyptic heaven and earth that re-presents the world transformed and transfigured (*TD5*, 93, 245, 263). The ultimate horizon, the horizon of horizons, is defined by the love of the triune God, and more specifically defined by the distance or *diastasis* between the Father and the Son traversed by the Spirit (*TD5*, 94, 98, 245; also *TD4*, 323; *TD2*, 266). There is no beyond with respect to this distance. To modify a comment by Wittgenstein: one cannot fall outside it. But infinite distance is in the end an invitation, as *Theo-Drama 5* makes especially clear in its concluding section concerning the world's ecstatic movement towards God: genuine participation in the triune God is just the opposite of the Hegelian confusion, which thinks of all letting be of otherness as a means by which Spirit comes to itself. Distance truly lets otherness be, while being in a sense its embrace. For Balthasar, distance is what Heidegger thinks *Ereignis* is, the nearness of the far, the far of nearness, but, of course, with the proviso that *Ereignis* itself is modeled on the ecstasy of agape that is passionate and caring 'without why' (*ohne Warum*) (*TD5*, 405, 508; also *TL1*, 223).

It is perhaps Marion, who, more than any other contemporary religious thinker, has capitalized on Balthasar's meta-symbol of 'distance' to probe the possibility of a difference beyond ontological difference. Importantly, however, Marion also deploys 'distance' against Hegelian difference. *Idol and Distance* makes this perfectly clear:

> *This means that the distance does not separate us from the Ab-solute so much as it prepares for us, with all interiority, our identity. It denotes, therefore, the positive movement of the Ab-solute which, through it being set at a distance, ecstatically disappropriates itself from itself in order that man might receive himself ecstatically in difference. In receiving himself from distance, man comprehends not only that distance comprehends him, but that it makes him possible. (ID, 153)*

Here Marion follows closely Heidegger's critical commentary on Hegel, while submitting it to a theological critique which, nonetheless, does not outstrip the resources of phenomenology.[75] Crucially, this critique of Hegelian difference, whose precedents are found both in Hölderlin's and Pseudo-Dionysius' discourse of the relation between Father and Son, remains on the level of the economic. Effectively Marion trims Balthasar here, while his mentor Bruaire follows Balthasar at a more rarefied philosophical level in reconceiving how difference is produced and suffered at the level of the immanent Trinity beyond or beneath the Hegelian code of resolution.[76] No more in Balthasar's case than in Bruaire's does resisting Hegel's dialectical smoothing issue in the disintegration of the Trinity into divisible units. Balthasar would agree with the Cappadocians that the Trinity is characterized by indivisibility (*adiastematic*) rather than divisibility,[77] but that this too opens rather than closes reflection, and is not necessarily compromised by the *dia* of *diastasis*.[78]

I have tried to indicate some precedents for Balthasar's articulation of 'superspace' and how his reflection is edged against Hegelian thought in general and Hegelian difference in particular. It must be confessed, however, that I have somewhat skirted around its symbolic character. Here as throughout *Theo-Drama*, Revelation can be understood to provide both code and warrant. In its 'aeonian' view of time, which involves the transformation of time, by purging it of its redundancies, Revelation demands that we rethink together both time and eternity. Aeonic time is the time of glorification coincident with eternal life. Similarly, 'superspace' is space relieved of its indifference, transformed into an elastic matrix that serves as the condition of thanksgiving and the giving of glory. Certainly, Bulgakov assists Balthasar here, as he does with Balthasar's meta-symbols of '*ur-kenosis*' and 'supertime,' although, arguably the assistance is somewhat less decisive. Still, it is probably not an accident that the text which offers Bulgakov's most capacious account of 'supertime' also talks at some length about the radical transformation of space. Moreover, *The Bride and the Lamb* talks about both the transformation of time and space together (*BL*, 383-5) in the context of an elaboration of the meaning of 'new heaven and earth' of Revelation 21. Bulgakov suggests once again that Balthasar's probative discourse on refiguring the divine and what is heavenly proceeds by a hermeneutic of scripture, and proceeds in particular with an interpretation of the most symbolically dense text of the Bible. Once again, however, it would be a mistake to conclude that with Bulgakov one has found the 'missing link,' and that the other considerations to which we have attended are either less important or not important at all. However close Balthasar is to Bulgakov's apocalyptic understanding of the transformation of space, once again Balthasar presses for something more radical: that the imagined apocalyptic transformation of space lead to the thought of the distance or interval of the divine within which the entire world participates. Sticking rigorously to non-conceptual anticipations of 'supertime,' it is tempting to suggest that behind the meta-symbol lies the analogy of the musical interval. While necessarily speculative, Balthasar's competence in music performance and theory, his conviction that the triune God can be considered under the transcendental of beauty, his agreement with Barth about the eschatological status of some of Mozart's music,[79] and finally his readiness to apply musical analogies throughout his work (e.g. symphony or polyphony) at the very least suggest that Balthasar is open to this musical application to what the triune God is and not simply what the triune God does.

In any event, distance is the opposite of Hegel's view, or any warmed-over panentheism, intended to rid itself of the embarrassment of pantheism which suggests a one-to-one correspondence between the divine and the world. For Balthasar, the recourse to 'panentheism,' as representing the retreat position for those who would either continue or correct Hegel, is idle. Balthasar agrees with Jacobi, one of Hegel's *bêtes noires*, in thinking that the change of term is purely verbal. Almost all supporters of pantheism posit some kind of non-worldly reserve. They must do so first on grounds of logical coherence: for a reality to be within another (more material) reality is to be in excess of it. And they must do so in order to distinguish their position from that of naturalism with which pantheism has sometimes been confused. From Balthasar's perspective, every influential form of pantheism has in fact been a form of panentheism, which only goes to show that panentheism is a major enemy to be resisted in a post-Enlightenment situation in which in philosophical and theological quarters scientific naturalism functions as much as an embarrassment as theism, whether of the non-trinitarian or trinitarian variety. Importantly, Balthasar outs Hegel without falling into the trap of Jacobi's fideistic alternative. *Theo-Drama 5*, while remaining thoroughly faithful to his earlier articulation of 'cosmic liturgy,' represents as capacious a view of participation of the world and human being in God as found anywhere in modern theology. Were one to look in Hegel's immediate field of view, it would not be Jacobi who would figure the non-reductive alternative, but Hamann, who sees the cosmos and history as caught up in the adventure of Christ's being all-in-all.

We will have more to say about Hamann in part 3, but it is time to put a point to our elaboration of the interconnection between symbolization and genuine apophasis in Balthasar's reflection on the triune God. Expatiation on the meta-symbols or conceptual ciphers of '*ur-kenosis*,' 'supertime' and 'superspace' all serve the purpose of a creative re-landscaping of theological discourse that helps in the project of overcoming modern forgetfulness, but also in the diagnosis of speculative misremembering. It is possible, maybe even necessary, to read Balthasar as reconceiving 'impassibility' and 'passibility' as they apply to the ecstatic triune divine. That is, Balthasar believes that his meta-symbols help to tutor the language of 'impassibility' such that specifically Christian use involves an emphasis on dynamism and receptivity not there in the Greek metaphysical tradition. At the same time his meta-symbols constrain Christian usage of 'pathos' by reminding that 'suffering' can only be applied analogously to the triune God, indeed in such a way as not to impinge on divine sovereignty, or even more generally on God's agential power. But Balthasar does not seem to think that a *tertium quid* of a fully sufficient explanatory kind can be supplied. Instead, he offers what is best called a *protocol* for modifying the claims that come from the passibility and impassibility sides.

The general lack of explanatory interest displayed by Balthasar, or the suggestion that the demand for explanation cannot be satisfied with respect to the triune God, who grounds our knowledge rather than being grounded by it, is not likely to appeal to more explanatorily inclined theologians who believe that a much more determinate case – one way or the other – can be made than Balthasar provides. What Hegel's own response would look like is fairly obvious: Balthasar lacks the conceptual seriousness that evidences the genuine philosopher, indeed, the genuine Christian thinker. Explanation is not only possible but actual, given the very nature of Christianity as a revealed (*geoffenbart Religion*) or revelatory religion (*offenbare Religion*). In the *Phenomenology*, *Lectures on the Philosophy of Religion*, and the *Encyclopedia*, this has the meaning that the symbols, narratives, rituals, and practices of Christianity give themselves to thought, in fact give themselves exhaustively to thought. One is left with no other option than a developmental and agonistic construal of the divine that can be philosophically justified. For contemporary theologians who write in Hegel's wake, even if 'pathos' when applied to the divine does not rise to the level of explanation proper, its fit with the Gospels is such that the opposite is inconceivable. It is this very inconceivability that fuels the rage against traditional theological understandings of divine 'impassibility', and accounts for the vehemence of its denunciation in which traditional

God-talk comes to represent nothing less than the self-betrayal of Christianity.

As we pointed out earlier, dissatisfaction can also characterize the faction that supports the classical view in the current debate. Obviously, it would be unreasonable to expect that all supporters of divine 'impassibility' would be comforted by the distance Balthasar enjoins that theologians take from the tradition in which impassibility is understood to be without remainder the binary opposite of passibility, and where this opposition is thought to express and to support the ontological gap between God and world that is in danger of being compromised. For some, any quarrel with the dominant metaphysical forms of 'impassibility' is taken to compromise Christian truth. Renouncing conceptual tidiness, Balthasar thinks that Christian theology is required to refigure metaphysical concepts such as impassibility. It must do so, firstly, because the biblical evidence does not uniformly support it, and, secondly and crucially, because the cross is the central Christian mystery. If refiguration puts him in conversation with thinkers such as Bulgakov who think with as against Idealism, and even Schelling, Balthasar is persuaded that this is a small price to pay. Reservations with respect to Balthasar's proposal need not be doctrinaire. They can and in fact do reflect the demand for explanation, which Balthasar not only does not satisfy, but which he oftentimes impatiently – perhaps too impatiently – withdraws. Thus the more subtle criticism of Balthasar's reception in impassibility quarters that his insistence on protocol is peremptory in that it is invoked before any conceptual effort has been made to show positively what a notion of 'impassibility,' which is influenced by but not reducible to Platonism, conceptually might bear. This is a basic thrust of Thomas Weinandy's criticism of Balthasar expressed in his own trilogy that focuses on the topic of the Trinity and suffering.[80] Is Balthasar entitled to presume, for example, that Aquinas' concepts of *esse seipsum* and *actus purus* do not admit of a receptivity that go at least part of the way of correcting the unintended effects of the assertion in *Summa* I, Q13, art 7, namely that while the world has a real relation to God, God has not a real relation to the world? Could it not be the case that it is only what is absolutely not in 'need' that loves, and that we have all been seduced by the Platonic myth of love as satisfaction of the need for wholeness? Finally, could one not think that in Christ we have the greatest proximity to our condition and the greatest difference embodied in a person who unites without confusion a divine and a human nature?

Undoubtedly, it is unfair to reduce Weinandy's penetrating and wide-angled defense of the conceptual contours of 'impassibility' to a series of rhetorical questions. But my purpose here is not to render the details of Weinandy's position, or any other proponent of divine impassibility, but simply to understand Weinandy's frustration with that which falls short of explanation. Earlier when I focused on the conundrum of the impassibility or passibility of God, I suggested Balthasar is at least mindful of Weinandy's particular kinds of concerns, and not indulging in the kind of mindless exclusion of theological voices that is typical of post-Hegelian and Process-oriented theologians. In this regard it is more than a little interesting that in *Theo-Logic 2 & 3*, in which Balthasar's anti-Hegelianism is still in play, Balthasar offers his most sustained comments on Aquinas' trinitarian thought. The suggestion seems to be not simply that whatever the value of Hegel's diagnosis of the traditional construal of the Trinity, Aquinas represents much more nearly the solution than the problem. On his view, Thomas provides the positive way beyond Hegel's palpably deficient view of divine pathos. Specifically, as deployed by Aquinas, 'impassibility' is irreducible to Platonic metaphysics, irreducible, first, given Aquinas' view of creation and providence in which God bears a non-contrastive relation to the world,[81] and, second, given Aquinas' view of the Trinity, which is defined intrinsically by relation and by its eccentric thrust towards another.'[82]

One could read this as a confession by Balthasar that he had shown unseemly haste in proceeding beyond explanation to protocol. One might even read *Theo-Logic 2 & 3* as something of a recantation of the limited possibilities of a defense of 'impassibility.' Yet none of this would suggest that Balthasar would essentially repent of his avowal that in the end the theologian must forsake explanatory for protocol discourse. However tenaciously the theologian corrects from the passibility side in order to do justice the incommensurable difference of the triune God, and however hard the theologian tries to distend and open 'impassibility,' Balthasar does not believe that anything like definitive demonstration of the complexion of the divine is in the offing. *Theo-Logic* makes clear in a way *Theo-Drama* does not, that (a) conceptual articulation from either side is welcome, and (b) especially from the 'impassibility' side. Balthasar does not envisage, however, that elucidating Thomas will be sufficient. Thomas is strengthened when he is paired with Bonaventure, who more emphatically defines the entire Trinity as love, and whose cruciform credentials shout at us more loudly. But even together they are not sufficient. We can best know where explanation breaks off when we have truly attempted it. But explanations from both sides will, Balthasar insists, surely need to break off at some point. All explanations are referred to a height and a depth that is beyond them and into which they disappear. The trinitarian God is epistemically an asymptote.

Beyond Hegelian Theodicy

To contest Hegel's trinitarian thought as representing an epical deformation of a theologoumenon that is faithful to the drama of the triune God's relation to the world is necessarily to contest Hegel's theodicy. The objections are many. Hegel fails sufficiently to respect the mystery of suffering which Balthasar, with thinkers as diverse as Kant, Ricoeur, Wiesel, Burrell, and Gutiérrez, thinks is exposed in Job.[83] Hegel whitewashes the range and depth of human evil-doing and effectively deletes sin as an operative concept from Christian discourse.[84] Finally, and crucially, Hegel articulates a trinitarian divine that moves from potentiality to actuality through the intermediary of the evil doing, violence, and suffering that defines the history of humankind. Within the Hegelian ordinance the suffering of individuals and groups counts only to the extent to which it contributes to the pedagogy of history whereby human beings in the modern period come to maximal realization of freedom and self-awareness. For Balthasar, this is not so much to redeem suffering as to hallow it. It most certainly is not to pay homage to the particular that is the victim of the devastation of history: rather it confirms and justifies the particular as waste, as being without meaning, or as only having meaning outside itself.

Individuals, groups, even civilizations are so much detritus, flotsam and jetsam brought up and out on the historical tide, less sound and fury than immemorial loss. The secret of Hegelian recollection, or the secret of the secret, is that not only does it remember what it remembers badly, but the mass of the dead are forgotten and the forgetfulness is justified.

Balthasar and Derrida are ironically one in their assessment: the alchemy of the Hegelian system produces the *caput mortuum*, literally the 'dead remains,'[85] despite its assured dialectical method of sanitation. Reference to the trinitarianly articulated Spirit as essentially providing a justification for human being, God, and their indifference, unequivocally merits ethical condemnation. Balthasar's rejection of Hegelian eschatology in general and trinitarian eschatology in particular finds a philosophical template in Critical Theory's protest against the Moloch of history, whether justified by Hegelian dialectic or historical materialism (*Exp 4*, 97-9). The protest against Hegel is not purely theoretical; it aims for transformation of the world, while being aware of the imminent danger that transformation of the world will come be immanentized. Both of these points are to the fore in *Theo-Drama 5*. Balthasar will insist on the legitimate horizontal dimension to history and our responsibilities towards each other and the broader society (*TD5*, 175-80), while at the same time remaining aware that the 'kingdom of God' is forever in danger of being reduced to a purely worldly kingdom. *Theo-Drama 4* also has much to say about the necessity of the struggle for justice in the world and the church (*TD4*, 482-86), but with multi-dimensional provisos for interpreting the real demand for transformation of the social as identical with the mission of Christianity. Balthasar's essay, 'The Claim to Catholicity,' gives as good a digest as there is to be found in Balthasar. Balthasar writes approvingly of faith appearing as 'a world-transforming deed. The transformation of those social structures that directly prevent the message of Christ from being understood by the poor, oppressed and exploited is an essential element of the Christian mission' (*Exp 4*, 84). Here Balthasar's thought is in line with his positive reflection on the biblical prophetic in *Glory of the Lord*, where he grasps fully the constitutive importance of Yahweh's preferential option for the poor (*Anawim*) (*GL6*, 314 ff).

Of course, Hegel not only forbids hope in general, but especially hope in the particular person, Jesus of Nazareth. For Hegel, personal identity is shaped by the actualization of personal and social freedom and by the commitment to knowledge of self and others, not by participation in Christ. Indeed, such participation would represent an impediment to the complex task of forging individual and communal identity in a modern world committed to the value of the secular in general, and autonomy and knowledge in particular. For Balthasar, however, it is participation in Christ that permits us to dare to hope that history does not provide the final word, but rather that the final word to us is God's love for us, one of whose notices is our very desire for God. No more than Hegel in *Lectures on the Philosophy of Religion* does Balthasar deny the necessity to critique popular images of the 'afterlife,' whose basic logic is that of 'going on.'[86] The justice of Hegel's critique, notwithstanding, there is an eschatological promise of 'eternal life' in Paul and John that is betrayed by Hegel, and betrayed by every revisionist who insists that 'eternal life' is a metaphor for the full realization of an ethical or cognitive virtue in the here and now. 'Eternal life' is, for Balthasar, a symbol of unbroken participation with the triune God, in whom we live and have our being. And if death is the breach, the hiatus that would stamp itself as absolute, 'eternal life' is the promise of death's powerlessness, that the breach has itself been breached by love, overcome in the descent of Christ into Hades, in his giving of sight and voice to the ones forgotten in history.

'Eternal life,' for Balthasar, represents the limit to, but not the abolition of, the tragedy of history. Hope, however, is the modality and measure of its apprehension. As such, it suggests a divine comedy that is other than Hegel's. As with all comedies it has a finale in which reconciliation is dominant, but which, nonetheless, does not retrospectively purge history of its accidents or white-out its tragedies. What stands in the way of Hegelian laundering is the Paschal Mystery, especially as this features Holy Saturday as the lowest point of the arc between Good Friday and Easter Sunday. The abyss of Christ's being abandoned or given up (*pardonai*) by the Father leads to his solidarity with the dead. This solidarity with the dead suggests in turn a total revision in the figuration of power, since the identification with the powerlessness of the dead is not erased in Jesus being raised from the dead. Jesus is not simply the Lord of death and life, but a fellow of the dead. Thus, their inherence in Christ who reveals the invisible Father (*TL2*, 67-8), reveals him as love without ever suggesting that this can be grasped. In the Paschal mystery Balthasar finds expressed the triune God as hyperbolic goodness and gift. It is the primary expression of gift that is offered by the church (which Hegel evaporates) and in the eucharist (which he profoundly misinterprets).

Still, how are we finally to characterize this trinitarian theodicy? As we saw in chapter 1, Balthasar offers more than one ascription of Hegelianism. We are variously told that Hegelianism has a Neoplatonic, an apocalyptic, and a Valentinian identity. Now while Balthasar does not choose between these ascriptions in a principled way, I provided several indications as to why the Valentinian or Gnostic ascription is in general to be preferred. Special difficulties seem to be introduced, however, when Hegel's theodicy or his inclusive narrative of divine becoming is trinitarianly specified. For here apocalyptic and Neoplatonism seem to have significant advantages, since we can find trinitarian forms of apocalyptic (e.g. Joachim) and trinitarian forms of Neoplatonism throughout the Christian tradition (e.g. the Cappadocians, Augustine, Maximus, Bonaventure *inter alia*). The same cannot be said for classical Valentinianism which is essentially a pre-Nicene phenomenon. Nevertheless, this disadvantage is more than offset by the two following considerations. First, Valentinian articulations of the pleroma could be read à la Blumenberg as an anticipation of the critique of a hypostatic Trinity, which is self-consciously carried out in Hegel's system. Second, it is Valentinianism rather than apocalyptic and Neoplatonism that provides the model for truly radical and comprehensive deformation of the biblical narrative, or what I call elsewhere 'metalepsis.'[87] Of course, this still leaves us with another set of difficulties foremost among which are the apparent circular form of Valentinian narrative by contrast with the developmental curve of Hegelian theodicy and the static dualistic ontology of Valentinianism by contrast with the dialectical monism of Hegel. Neither of these difficulties, however, turns out to be decisive. For if the surface narrative of Valentinianism is circular, Balthasar sees with Irenaeus – but also with Hegel[88] – that there is a developmental undertow (*GL2*, 39). And again, for Balthasar, a static dualist ontology is a surface rather than a depth feature of Valentinianism, which seems to suppose a continuity of divine reality from perfection through alienation back to perfection again. I summed this up by suggesting in the Balthasarian supplement in chapter 1 that Hegelian narrative is a permissible lexical instance of Valentinian narrative grammar, even if it departs from the classic forms of Valentinianism of the first centuries of the common era.

The question must be asked: if Hegelian narrative theodicy represents an important modern instance of the return of Valentinianism, does this suggest that trinitarian thought itself shows a particular aptitude for this return? Balthasar does not explicitly cogitate on this issue, but it would seem that theological forms of thought that are trinitarian illustrate greater propensity for Valentinian repetition than other forms of theology that are not so centrally focused on the Trinity. This concern may very well be at the heart of Rahner's objection to Balthasar's form of theology, however imprecise his actual characterization of Balthasar's thought as 'gnostic.' While the modern renaissance in trinitarian thought has shown that there is no need for trinitarian theologies to be speculative in principle, the concern expressed by Kant and Schleiermacher about trinitarian articulations signaling a divorce from Christian experience and first-order language is not without warrant. Trinitarian reflection can become speculation in the void. Unlike Kant and Schleiermacher, and unlike Rahner, Balthasar does not wish to prohibit extrapolation from what is directly given in experience or the first results of scriptural reading. Extrapolation represents something of a crossroad in which there are prospects both for extrapolations that are christologically regulated and for extrapolations that are not. Christologically regulated extrapolations obviously imply that the figure of Christ remains the principle of interpretation and is neither replaced nor replaceable by the individual or communal interpreter. But more broadly it implies an understanding of the church as the privileged site of divine action of redemption and sanctification. The church is the reality that is constituted by Christ's self-gift and in the eucharist remembers and celebrates this gift that gives life. As living in Christ, and into

Christ, the church essentially remembers forward in its expressions and symbols, but also in its actions.

None of this characterizes Hegel's trinitarian thought. In Hegel's texts, as Balthasar complains so often, Christ functions as mere code: Christ is the historically dispensable particular, who provides the occasion for the belated modern appropriation of autonomy and our consciousness. Equally in Hegel's texts, if the church is not an encrustation, it is an accident that can be sloughed off in eschatological times as the mere preparation for its secular replacement and realization. And eucharist is not an event; specifically it is not the event of redemption enacted by the death and resurrection of Christ enabled by the Spirit. It is a memory of the meaning or application of Christ as this relates to the kingdom of God, which definitively is not invested in his very person. Although like Balthasar, Hegel seems to privilege the Gospel of John, he will have nothing to do with the Johannine compacting of kingdom in Christ. From Hegel's point of view, Balthasar's insistence on the validity of Christ as *autobasileia* (*TL2*, 78) can only signal Catholic regression. And finally there is nothing in Hegel's interpretation of the church or the world that would indicates that liturgy is actual or possible. No word or action evokes its transcendent correlative, or calls it down onto the earth. As an extrapolation, Hegelian trinitarian thought is not properly christologically regulated. As christologically regulated extrapolation joins Balthasar to the mainline trinitarian tradition, Hegel's christologically unregulated extrapolation links Hegel with Valentinus. Balthasar insinuates this link in *Theo-Logic 3* in which Irenaeus gets positioned as a major trinitarian thinker, despite the systematic handicaps of an inadequately articulated distinction between the immanent and economic Trinity by a theologian whose theology of the 'two hands' fully justifies the ascription of 'economic Trinitarianism.' Moreover, christologically regulated trinitarianism represents the cure for the speculative deformation of Hegel and Valentinus precisely because in it the richness of revelation defeats the poverty of Hegelian appearance and Valentinian showing, while paying due respect to the mystery of the triune God who is known finally as unknown.

Hegel's trinitarianism is epical in that the economy is not the expression of the love of the triune God, but the mode of satisfying the need of a virtual Trinity to become more real and more self-conscious in and through the media of the world, history, and humanity. Lost is the sense of the surpassing fullness of the biblical God, and the sense of the being of the world and humanity as gift. Lost also is the insight, captured magisterially in Irenaeus, that the Bible speaks of a drama of incommensurate freedoms in which tragedy can and does happen. And lost too is the intuition that there is no higher point of view than drama, that drama requires vigilance and listening but above all performance, that the truth is to a significant extent a making true. With respect to this 'making true,' *Theo-Drama* prefers the language of mission, *Glory of the Lord* prefers that of witness or testimony, while *Theo-Logic 1* prefers that of decision. Hegel's epical trinitarianism excludes all of these, and in doing so constitutes a monumental deviation from the mainline Christian tradition the only template of which is to be found in Gnosticism. In this deviation the glory of God in Christ, in creation, and in the eschaton is eclipsed. Paradoxically, were Hegel not an aesthetic thinker the eclipse would not be so total. Ironically, were Hegel not so apparently dramatic a thinker, the eclipse would not be so deep. It is from this night in which unfortunately not 'all cows are black' – to turn Hegel's *bon mot* against him[89] – but in which Christian discourse and its correlative forms of life and practice are effaced that Christianity needs to be rescued. Hegel and not the patristic and medieval traditions represents the true 'Babylonian captivity' of discourse.

Necromancy

WHILE HEGEL DOES NOT GLIDE OVER or glide past the Christian trinitarian tradition, as is the wont of even the benign side of the Enlightenment, on the bases of his anatomy of its deflection from this tradition, Balthasar judges that he very much gilds it. Again, while Hegel does not excuse himself from positively presenting the doctrine of the Trinity on the Kantian or Schleiermachian grounds that it is neither essential to ethics nor Christian piety, Balthasar thinks that he profoundly misrepresents it. The genius of Balthasar lies not in how loud he cries wolf in this regard, but in his outlining the mechanics of misrepresenting whereby something like a 'double' is generated. This implies, of course, that there is an absolutely intrinsic connection between Hegel's epic construction and his trinitarian expostulations: Hegel's trinitarian thought is through and through epical, and it is his trinitarian articulation that provides shape to the epical elaboration of the divine in which all the major Christian theologoumena are torqued and the mysteriousness and gratuity removed from discussion of God and God's relation to the world. It is his constant attempts to analyze the different aspects of this intersection in the trilogy that make Balthasar an anatomist of Hegelian thought. In this anatomy Hegelian thought is diagnosed as a profound act of misremembering, which involves at once gestures of recall and untoward distortion of trinitarian discourse as this has been rendered in and by the theological tradition. This is not to say that there is not something in Balthasar in excess of the cool anatomist. One can admit also the operation of a more existentially involved or prophetic naming of Hegel's declensions on the level of the Trinity, which amount to a single comprehensive declension, given that the Trinity maps the entire Christian narrative. A crucial aspect of prophetic naming is mourning, and Balthasar very much mourns what has been forgotten: for example, trinitarian persons, their hypostatic integrity and their personal relations, the fontality of the Father, the repleteness of all divine persons, their boundless graciousness toward a world that need not be and toward the world's desires which need not, but in fact matter, and matter utterly to Father, Son, and Spirit. And there is mourning also for what is foreclosed, and which needs to be brought forward as ongoing tradition that always outbids the 'already.' The foreclosed is structurally as well as epochally 'postmodern' in Lyotard's sense of 'future anterior.' Here Balthasar experimentally thinks of the Trinity as the utmost horizon of gift, a circle of giving and receiving, characterized by abandon and ecstasy which, reflected superbly in the cross, also casts a halo over all that is created. Foreclosed also is any reflection on the Trinity that would conceive it as a doxological matrix, a domain not only in which the proper relation of creatures to the glorious community of the Trinity is clarified, but where thanksgiving is grounded in the disposition of the trinitarian persons towards each other.

As Feuerbach extracts the humanist kernel from Hegel, and Marx the social-historical fundament, Hegel extracts from the tradition of Christian discourse its dynamic, non-hypostatic essence. Creedal formulations, major lines of Western and Eastern reflection: none of these have weight. Balthasar deploys all of these resources against Hegel, at one time Nicaea, at another Chalcedon, at one time Augustine, at another Nyssa, at one time Thomas, at another Bonaventure, and does so in the knowledge that these probings are never called on positively by Hegel. Indeed, they are simply not called on. Balthasar does not adduce as proof of Hegel's calculated misremembering that the only 'trinitarian' thinkers he cites are Valentinus, Proclus, and Jacob Boehme, the first a Gnostic, the second a Neoplatonist whose thought presents challenges to Christian trinitarian assimilation, the third a heterodox Lutheran. His counter-genealogy, however, suggests that he is not unaware of how these forms of thought inflect Hegelian dialectic. In any event, in Hegel's misremembering the mainline Christian trinitarian is squeezed into a few dogmatic formulae, and waved away as incomprehensible when not totally wrongheaded. The conversation and argument in and of the tradition is, for Hegel, 'inessential,' a remainder or leftover. Here Balthasar could only demur from Derrida's judgment in *Glas* that Hegelianism reveals that Christian trinitarianism is always in collusion with a mode of thought that excludes.[90] Rather Hegel's trinitarianism excludes the tradition of trinitarian reflection and has it as a remainder. For Balthasar the violence of this exclusion in turn facilitates the production of a system of thought which proceeds to justify other violent exclusions, and concludes in justifying violence in general. Although Balthasar makes this point less well than David Bentley Hart,[91] again Hart can find in Balthasar a precedent. Thought properly as the ultimate horizon of ecstatic love, the Trinity does not function to instantiate or underwrite *'tout comprendre est tout pardoner.'* More than knowledge *(TL2*, 106), love is a different kind of knowledge; in the Trinity an inexplicable compassion, in human beings a hope that despite appearances all will be well.

In *Apokalypse* Balthasar's assessment of Hegel is couched in the language of apocalyptic: Hegel is a burning fire, a judgment (*Apok 1*, 558). A plain reading of the passage involves paying attention to the depiction of Hegel as representing a crisis in thought that demands decision for or against. There is every reason to suppose that in the late thirties, as in the middle eighties, the judgment on Hegel crystallizes into brilliant No. In this apocalyptic reaction to a genre of thought which is itself apocalyptic, Balthasar is mindful that 'judgment' (*Urteil*) in Hegel requires separation, specifically separating out what is living from what is dead. If Hegel performs this with respect to the Christian tradition in general, and the trinitarian tradition in particular, the favor must be returned. To echo Croce, with whom Balthasar opens his reflection on Hegel's aesthetics in *Theo-Drama*,[92] there are living elements in Hegel, but there is much that is dead. Yet Hegel is such a magician that he is able to make what is Christianly dead in his thought appear to be the most alive: he re-presents a living reality and by so doing offers ghosts. Hegel is in effect the arch-necromancer. Maybe more.

The question of whether Hegel might even be more dangerous again depends in significant part on critical assessment of Hegel as a Johannine thinker, a thinker of the cross and divine love as they mutually define each other. Hegel's Johannine template will always make him an object worthy of Christian consideration. Yet it is precisely Hegel's teasing out of the implications of John, his extrapolation of its 'logic,' that makes him the religious thinker in modernity towards whom Christian should exercise extreme caution. The cross in Hegel's trinitarian narrative not only eclipses resurrection and ascension, but demands nothing less than a reversal of metaphysical priorities from immutability to mutability, from impassibility to passibility. Balthasar, as we have seen, refuses to legitimate any of this. The mystery of the Pasch is set off against the trinitarian background, but the sacrifice is ingredient in no economy, or ingredient only in the non-economy of love that gives beyond all measure. And here is where Revelation, which is effectively excluded from Hegel's Johannine canon, comes into play. From Balthasar's point of view, Revelation reinforces the Gospel of Love by further elaborating the cruciform mystery of love, and complements it by drawing greater attention to the trinitarian stage of the 'handing over' enacted on the cross (*TD4*, 53). It also supplements it, and does so in three fundamental ways concerning the cross: (a) the cross represents the fundamental hope of the dead (*Exp 4*, 402,

410-11), (b) the cross is judgment as well as reconciliation (*TD4*, 54-5); (c) the cross is the provocation of provocations and leads to an escalation of resistance to Christ as truth (*TD4*, 51-6, 437, 446, 468; also *TD5*, 50, 207, 271).[93]

Only the third supplement need engage us here. Since we reflected at some length on this topic at the end of the last chapter, we can be brief. The provocation of the Lamb lies in the rendering of an unthinkable love, of an unimaginable innocence, and an ungraspable truth. No particular response is compelled; the response can be hate as well as love, deliberate wickedness as well as innocence, articulating the lie as well as expositing the truth. In Balthasar's work as a whole all these responses are pondered including the negative ones. As *Theo-Drama 4* shows clearly, in the context of an application of Revelation Balthasar puts a particular emphasis on the lie (*TD4*, 51-6). The lie is, of course, an existential state, at once voluntary and involuntary, in which the self ensures its own economy against the challenge of the excess of truth which commands change. But, as Balthasar calibrates it through Claudel among others,[94] the lie, associated with the Anti-Christ, is the discourse of dissembling that fabricates a pleasing simulacrum of the truth in which the offer of life is the offer of death. In Balthasar's hands, then, necromancy is folded into the figure of the Anti-Christ who articulates the possibility of immanence and the impossibility of discipleship and adoration.

Balthasar is convinced that no more splendid a Christian simulacrum has been constructed in the modern period than that of Hegel. While Heideggerian phainesthetics too produces a simulacrum, as I will argue in detail in the next volume, it is both less expressly theological than Hegelianism and lacks its comprehensiveness. Heidegger's is an embarrassed form of misremembering when compared with the perpetual vigilance of the system which vacuums the theological tradition and airbrushes the entire Christian narrative to produce the matte-finish of the Idea to which the philosopher as the ambassador of humanity essentially elevates himself. Heidegger will recall the 'call' of and to the self; its receptive ecstasy towards truth, and correlatively the *es gibt* and the appropriation that is precisely expropriation. But Heidegger avoids Christ, and talks around rather than to Hölderlin's speaking of and to Christ. And he remains as convinced as the early Luther that the discourse of the Trinity reflects the pride of reason, its will to control mystery. With respect to Christianity, Heidegger's *modus operandi* is to contract its range of symbols that have philosophical pertinence and to submit the remainder to the cleansing agent of a deliberative hermeneutic that insists that all symbols that are savable must be interpreted otherwise than they have been throughout the Christian theological tradition. It is only Hegel, then, who is a proper candidate for 'Valentinian' ascription, for it is only Hegel who has the immodesty essentially to rewrite the biblical narrative and redescribe each and every theological construct that marks a node on the narrative chain. Hegel rewrites not some but all of the narrative episodes from creation to apocalypse, and does not exclude the trinitarian prologue or epilogue. Such rewriting, facilitated by the four features of epic narration we considered in the last chapter, in which Hegel generates a developmental ontology, makes him the great anti-Christian figure.

Balthasar wants to name both discourses as belonging to the land of unlikeness; they can neither prepare nor gloss traditional Christianity. This naming, no matter how much it is the work of an individual theologian, is not effected on his or her behalf, nor is it fundamentally prosecuted in the theologian's own name. Rather it is effected on behalf of the Church, and prosecuted in the name of Christ, whose person is disclosed in his relation to the Father and the Spirit. Polemic then is christologically, even trinitarianly indexed, for the 'ecclesial' nature of the theologian guarantees that naming is a response to the givenness of Christ and occurs within trinitarian brackets. This is even more true of constructive theology, which actually enacts the responsiveness, thanksgiving, and adoration that polemical theology diagnoses as missing in theology and other cultural discourses. Balthasar shows, however, that there need not be a division of labor, and that orchestrating the tradition, allowing its symphonic measure to be appreciated, is in his case polemic's other side. Besides, it is the more important side; indeed, so much more important that polemic might be regarded as its seam or crease. It is easy to forget that Balthasar advises from the opening volume of the trilogy that the Trinity is not simply the object of tradition, but its subject. If in *Glory of the Lord* the emphasis is on tradition as the gift of response to the glory of God in Christ enabled by the Spirit, in *Theo-Drama* it is obedient discipleship to the paschal mystery. These two parts of the trilogy differently inflect what might be called the forum of the economic Trinity. But never avoiding the risky, Balthasar feels that tradition can be traced back into the dynamics of the immanent Trinity itself, specifically the 'handing over' of the Son by the Father and the Son's acceptance of this handing over. Balthasar gives full expression to this view in an extraordinary passage in *Theo-Drama 4* in which he unfolds the theodramatic horizon of Revelation.

> *The motif of traditio, "handing on," beginning in God and extending to the creation through him who is "the beginning of God's creation" (3:14), will prove to be a fundamental theme of the theo-drama, constant through all acts. Traditio begins within God (as the doctrine of the Trinity formulates it), and this prevents God's self-giving to the world from being interpreted mythologically: God is not swallowed up by the world. It is not through this self-giving to the world that God becomes a lover – he already is a lover. And this same traditio, this same self-giving within the Godhead, also means that God does not merely hover above the world as the hen of philosophy, as the noesis noeseos: rather, the divine self-giving becomes the prototype and archetype of his self-giving to the world and all the traditio that follows from it. (TD4, 52-3)*

The lacing of negatives suggest Hegel as the other; the mythological construction in which God becomes dependent on the world; its justification in and by a false logic of love; and the *noesis noeseos* with whose self-celebration the *Encyclopedia* (#574) concludes. Apocalyptic justification of tradition must go out to meet its degeneratively apocalyptic refutation.

Retrospect and Prospect

IN A VERY OBVIOUS WAY Part 2 is the substantive complement to Part 1, in which we suggested that in one of Balthasar's more powerful genealogical strikes against Hegel he writes him into the history of Gnosticism or perhaps better into its return. Hegel's metanarrative will both repeat and deviate from ancient forms of Gnosticism. It will repeat it in that Gnostic, or more specifically Valentinian, return is recognized in and through a transgressive hermeneutic practice which leaves no aspect of the biblical narrative (as read in practicing Christian communities) intact, and which constructs an alternate metanarrative in which the acquisition of saving knowledge is pivotal in the story and serves to justify its validity and truth. Balthasar diagnoses Hegel's speculative philosophy as generating the most plausible of Christian *Doppelgängers* in the modern period, even if in his complex discourse there are elements that can be traced to other influences, for example, Neoplatonism and radically eschatological forms of apocalyptic. Hegel's metanarrative will deviate from the ancient forms of Gnosticism insofar as his metanarrative valorizes time and history, emphasizes the agonic features found recessed in classical Valentinian narratives, and unfolds the entire metanarrative as nothing less than the self-development of the divine. In this respect, we can say that a structural difference between ancient and modern forms of Valentinianism is that in an exemplary modern version such as that provided by Hegel the originary pleroma is not absolute and gives way to a superior perfection, a pluperfection, as it were, that comes into being in and through tragic fall and recovery. In his *Lectures on the History of Philosophy* Hegel makes the extraordinarily interesting suggestion – which in fact provides the basis for F. C. Baur's *Die christliche Gnosis* – that appearances to the contrary, the narratives of ancient Gnosticism admit of being read in this teleological way. Perfection is a finality, and as such the movement towards this perfection is always on the way, virtual perfection always surpassed. Balthasar corresponds to Hegel and Baur on this point, although he with the figure he is exegeting, namely Irenaeus, have come to bury Gnosticism rather than to praise it. In his essay on Irenaeus in *Glory of the Lord 2* this is expressed as an insight and not further developed. But Balthasar contributes mightily to easing the difficulty of how we can imagine continuity between dynamic teleological metanarratives in speculative thought and ancient forms of Gnosticism which are supposed to subscribe to a static ontology and whose basic form is that of pure circularity, a return to the beginning after an alienating misadventure. As I argued in Part 1, Balthasar simply does not have a meta-language in which to speak of the sameness and difference between modern and ancient forms of Valentinianism, thus the need for the kind of methodological supplement I provided in the closing pages, which, nonetheless, his own insight calls for.

In and through a series of probings throughout the trilogy of Hegel's understanding of the relation between speculative philosophy and Christianity, Balthasar determines that Hegel offers a 'double' of Christianity in which every episode of the Christian narrative and the associated doctrine is distorted in ways that either line up with those of ancient Gnosticism or are continuous with it in important respects. These distortions, or what I call 'deflections,'[95] are discussed in the second of our two chapters (ch. 3). The first of our two chapters (ch. 2) focused on the modulation of Hegel's metanarrative substitution, which Balthasar determines to be that of epic. Balthasar has no compunction about borrowing categories from Hegel – here categories of his aesthetic theory – and turning them against him. When it came to the linguistic arts, which in Hegel's view are the highest of all arts,[96] Balthasar endorses Hegel's preference for 'drama' over 'lyric' and 'epic,' while importantly having a different view of the nature of drama than Hegel, who conceives it in terms of the clash between ethos and the State. Crucially, however, Hegel's philosophy which, on the German philosopher's own account, represents a speculative transcription of Christianity, principally of its narrative, but also of some of its practices and forms of life, is a species of epic rather than drama. It looks at the life of God, which is constituted by history, from the disinterested divine point of view. This view is just the opposite of an actor making her way with a narrative that is no more than a searchlight, and practices and forms of life that both anticipate and confirm the commitment to a narrative that is a matter of faith rather than knowledge. Although Balthasar is hardly a proponent of the most extreme forms of apophasis, whether premodern (e.g. Eckhart) or postmodern (e.g. Derrida and Caputo), he regrets the total ejection of apophasis from the Hegelian rendition of Christianity in which revelation is not revelation of mystery, but revelation at the expense of mystery, the sign of its depletion and the demand for its erasure. As suggested – although nowhere presented systematically – Balthasar seems to have grasped that a particular set of narratological features complement the move made by Hegel towards epistemic competence without reserve. Hegel's rendition of the Christian narrative is monistic or monological and fails to preserve the irreducibly dialogical aspect of biblical Christianity in which there are two unequal centers of action and responsiveness, one finite, the other infinite. In Hegel's speculative enclosure (which is also a kind of foreclosure) the Christian metanarrative is interpreted as articulating a degeneratively erotic divine, that is, a divine in which the basic drive is towards a perfection that presupposes an initiating lack. Balthasar, as we saw, defined the triune God in terms of Johannine agape, while refusing to exclude all elements of eros from the triune God who wishes to be with us and save us despite the fact that we can add nothing to God's being or existence. Hegel's epical construction removes from the Christian narrative not only features of contingency, but anything that smacks of grace. Hegel fails to see that divine love, while not in any way arbitrary, cannot proceed under the figure of logical or ontological necessity. And finally, Hegel is a connoisseur of the figure of kenosis and boldly and appropriately thinks that it does not exclusively refer to the incarnation, but may be considered as an operation that is constitutive of the identity of the trinitarian divine itself. But in his epical romance, once again Hegel spoils this insight by thinking the figure under the auspices of his view of eros and necessity. Kenosis is not the figure of gift, but the figure of economic exchange in which the divine becomes more and more until it is fully actualized.

The concentration in this chapter, as also in the next, is on Hegel's disfiguration-refiguration of the biblical narrative, what under the influence of Irenaeus I called in *Gnostic Return in Modernity* 'metalepsis.' Still at strategic moments throughout this chapter I validated my principle that Hegel's *Aufhebung* of Christianity is not confined to the narrative, but also has profound effects on practices and forms of life. For example, the doxological practices of prayer and liturgy are submitted to such redescription that they are unrecognizable. If petition is *verboten*, thanksgiving is little more than a recognition of the necessity of the amoral logic of history.

If worship is endorsed, it is not a worship of another, but rather either the self-referring community that has appropriated its divine status or even the self-satisfaction or complacency of a discourse that transcends individual subjects. We noted with respect to forms of life that from Balthasar's Christian point of view, Hegel objectionably favored both the hero and the philosopher to the saint who performs the text of Christianity by conforming to Christ.

The second chapter of Part 2 specified further the way in which the epical deformation of the Christian narrative finds its fruit and source at the level of specific theological doctrines. Since we are talking about the construction of a *Doppelgänger* we can reasonably expect that all first-level Christian doctrines get deformed. Not only for reasons of economy, but also because Balthasar pursues Hegel into the areas that reflect Hegel's own priorities, chapter 3 concentrated on Hegel's christological and trinitarian deflections. This is not the contraction that it at first sight might appear to be. Balthasar understands with Hegel the close relation between reflection on Christ and reflection on creation, on the one hand, and the close relation between reflection on Christ and reflection on the church, on the other. To question Hegel with respect to Christ suggests problems with respect to Hegel's views of creation and church. In addition, to tackle Hegel's trinitarian thought is not simply to object to Hegel's treatment of a particular doctrine, but to contest them all, since the articulation of the relation between the immanent and economic Trinity is an articulation of the entire Christian narrative which provides the bases of all the major doctrines. With respect to Hegel's Christology Balthasar (1) judges that Hegel plays fast and loose regarding the singularity of Christ in his effort to extract a universal meaning to be appropriated by the Christian community; (2) notices that Hegel has exacerbated the monophysite thrust of Luther's Christology and twisted it in a more anthropological direction; and (3) senses how the passion and death of Christ are at the same time dislocated from resurrection and made to serve a dialectical logic in and through which God is made actual (*wirklich*).

With regard to the Trinity, Balthasar argues that Hegel has confounded the immanent and economic Trinity and by doing so effectively abolished both. Since for Hegel the Trinity effectively maps and gives a synopsis of Hegel's dynamic metanarrative, it is here that the features of epic narrative formation come most conspicuously into play: monism, eros, necessity, and a modality of kenosis that is without the gratuity and generosity that is acclaimed in the biblical text and honored in the mainline theological traditions. In this dismantling of the immanent-economic distinction, Hegel articulates a new dynamic form of Sabellianism. The first casualty is the tripersonal view of the Trinity, in that person or personhood has to be denied altogether of *Geist* or can only be attributed to Spirit or Idea at the term of the process of divine self-actualization. Needless to say, this form of Sabellianism differs in important ways from the various species of the third century, whether the more abstract form of an essence that lies deeper than all personal specification or a more monarchical form in which one of the persons essentially is coextensive with the essence (Father). Hegel's speculative thought may rightly be thought to correspond to either, largely depending on the role Logic plays in our assessment of Hegel. Given the status of *Lectures on the Philosophy of Religion* for Balthasar in interpreting Hegel, the second more monarchical type offers the more helpful template. It is with respect to this type that one sees clearly the inversion: whereas in the classical type of monarchical Sabellianism, one of the persons, that is, the Father, is from the beginning the deep ground of the Son and the Spirit, and thereby relativizes them ontologically, in the case of Hegel it is the Spirit who is the deep ground of the Father and the Son, since they point towards the Spirit as their ontological perfection.

Balthasar recognizes that an important aspect of Hegel's trinitarian thought – especially as it is informed by and intersects with his christological thought – is his view of divine passibility. Balthasar spends as much time throughout *Theo-Drama* arguing against this particular Hegelian construction as he does arguing against the epical nature of Hegel's rendering of the Christian narrative. This is hardly surprising, since Balthasar thinks that the death and rebirth of the divine is a fundamental feature in epical narratives of a 'mythological' sort, which is the way he characterizes Hegel's speculation in *Theo-Drama*. In an important sense, Balthasar welcomes Hegel's challenge, since he does find signs of thoughtlessness throughout the Christian tradition when it comes to squaring the biblical depiction of Christ and his relation to the Father in the Spirit with theological explanation. In this respect, Hegel promises a needed scouring of the Christian commitment to divine impassibility. Hegel, however, goes too far, in fact much too far, and this leads him over the Gnostic edge in which passibility is necessarily an attribute of a divine whose perfection is actual at the end rather than the beginning of a story. Hegel's problem is that he attributes suffering univocally to the divine. 'Passibility' can be ascribed to the divine only analogically. In his respect, the kind of post-Chaledonian Christology of Maximus, which speaks more loudly to the communication of idioms, is of more help than a purely Chalcedonian Christology in which the insistence on two natures in one person facilitates removing suffering from any possible description of God. The analogical predication of suffering is neither the only, nor the favored route suggested by Balthasar. He stands behind the basic intent of the ascription of 'impassibility' while dissociating himself from some of its more Platonic formulations. He advises a rethinking of 'impassibility' consistent with the authentic erotic profile of the God of agape, the divine self-giving that is the source of the world, and the sacrifice of the Son that is the meaning of history. Balthasar himself does not himself do this rethinking in a disciplined way, but points to resources, articulates the basic conceptual needs, and with the use of ciphers, variously conceptual and symbolic, makes probative gestures as to how we might dynamically figure the triune God in ways that are post-Hegelian.

Overall then Part 2 fills out in terms of content what it would be like, on Balthasarian grounds, to conceive of Hegel's would-be 'Christian philosophy' as Valentinian (Part 1), and to make a significant attempt to redeem its validity claims. Full redemption would not be easy even if Balthasar had a more sophisticated theoretical apparatus than in fact he has. One has to grant that the lack of such an apparatus makes it extremely difficult: the links made between Hegel and ancient Gnosticism are often made on intuitive rather than argumentative grounds, and Balthasar never adequately addresses how Hegel can be Valentinian in some respects and Neoplatonic and apocalyptic in others. Still the level of intuition is high, and one can trace the outline of the case that however many 'speculative' repetitions the reader of Hegel espies in his discourse, in the last instance the regulative discourse is that of Valentinianism. In very obvious ways then, Part 2 is the pivot of the entire book in that it gives substance to a great cry of alarm regarding Hegel, and a call to battle. Although he proceeds under the banner of the 'great modern rememberer,' from a properly Christian perspective Hegel is in fact the 'great modern misrememberer.'

This result could do with considerable deepening and amplification. Happily the seeds for such are sown in these two rather lengthy chapters. One comes to a deeper appreciation of Balthasar when one sees him in a line of a tradition of theological discourses that diagnose the generation of a 'double' of Christianity. Although only in passing, I mentioned Staudenmaier and Bulgakov as precursors of Balthasar's resistance to Hegel on either the christological or trinitarian level or both. Since I mentioned a number of others, it seems useful to decide the question whether and why among the many critiques of Hegel that include Kierkegaard, Kojève, Adorno, and Derrida these might be given pride of place. I argued that explicitly (Staudenmaier) and implicitly (Bulgakov) the theological thought of these two thinkers represents a comprehensive correction of Hegelian speculative theology. Hegel is deliberatively engaged, and is viewed as making a genuine contribution to Christian thought, even if much of what he says is problematic. Balthasar explicitly mentions Hamann as a kind of antidote to Hegel *avant la lettre*, and though an anachronism a Hamannian critique of Hegel can be teased out a bit more than Balthasar actually does. To these two post-Hegelian figures and a modern religious figure, who precedes the German philosophy, one has to add the figure of Irenaeus, who when it comes to diagnosing Valentinian 'doubles' and thus Valentinian 'misremembers,' has no equal. Indeed, it can be said that these three other figures and Balthasar himself can be plotted in the 'Irenaean' tradition. This is one of the central topics of Part 3.

More explicit attention to the other side of the coin is also required. Balthasar engages Hegel not for scholarly and historical reasons. His engagement with Hegel is motivated, because of the 'history of effects' of Hegel's discourse in Christian theology. Critical references to Hegel on this or that point are often attended by reference to one or other of his theological successors. Here Moltmann holds pride of place. It behooves us then to complement our discussion of Balthasar's lineage in the anatomy of misremembering with a discussion of how Balthasar senses and articulates the dissemination of this misremembering in modern and contemporary theology. Part 3 will give this complement its due. Now, perhaps one of the more surprising things in articulating Balthasar's resistance to Hegel's thought is how Balthasar compels us to recur to the language of biblical apocalyptic. Hegelian speculation is after all a form of *apokalypsis* – perhaps Joachimite on the surface but ultimately Valentinian – so it would be easy to conclude that Balthasar's theological counterweight is non-apocalyptic. But this is not the case. *Theo-Drama* elaborates a self-consciously apocalyptic form of theology. Much more can and should be said about this move that is made more questionable by featuring Revelation, a text with a troubled history, laid siege to in the modern period as it is constructed as the totalizing text extraordinaire. Moreover, this text is not implicitly but explicitly a text of violence, indeed, of a violent God. In this context, it would be interesting to compare and contrast Balthasar's specific apocalyptic resistance of Hegelian apocalypse with other modern and postmodern modes of apocalyptic resistance. Balthasar legitimates one comparison by speaking of Benjamin's apocalyptic negation of Hegel's totalitarian nightmare, and this connection suggests another, a comparison with Johann Baptist Metz, a Catholic reader and admirer of Balthasar's thought, but whose apocalyptic allegiance is in the end quite otherwise. Part 4 will discuss all of this in considerable detail.

PART 3

OF FATHERS AND SONS

As with Karl Barth the ascription of originality to his work would not be welcomed as a compliment by Balthasar. To be an ecclesial theologian – which in Balthasar's view is co-extensive with being a theologian – is to participate in the dynamic drift of tradition, which if it rings changes on the given discourses of the church, nevertheless does so in ways that are faithful to their basic intention to glorify the wholly Other who is the ground of all theological discourse. This is true even when the issue is less that of remembering well than resistance to powerful misremembering. Without fully adducing its history, Balthasar understands himself to be in a tradition of resistance to Hegel. Certainly, he understands that his resistance to Hegel is just one of the many ways in which he is continuous with Barth, and recognizes that many of the most pertinent theological criticisms of Hegelianism were lodged when it was in its heyday.[1] At the same time, as we saw in parts 1 and 2, Balthasar understands himself to be in a tradition of resistance to Valentinian narrative thought of which Hegel's system represents the supreme modern instance. Thus, in his resistance to misremembering, which involves a more or less willful distortion of the Christian narrative and basic Christian beliefs, which in turn affects the cogency of Christian forms of life and practice, Balthasar can be thought to have both post-Enlightenment precursors and ancient precursors such as Irenaeus.

Arguably, Balthasar's resistance to Hegel might have remained at the level of what is to be found in Barth[2] and much of 19th-century Catholic criticism where opposition is reactive and somewhat official, were it not for the fact that Hegel's specifically theological authority has been so powerfully resumed in contemporary theology in the shape of Jüngel and Moltmann.[3] Balthasar is especially concerned with Moltmann, whom he takes to endorse an essentially Hegelian program in evangelical dress. Whatever the number of Hegel's specifically theological 'children,' whether they speak English or German, French or Russian, their present-day existence essentially removes the option of simply rehearsing prior refutations. Hegel will need to be refuted again now that the specific consequences of his thought can be seen in forms of theology that have been privy to the essential objections against Hegel's thought, and thus have had time to emend the more offensive aspects of the Hegelian program. Balthasar sees Hegelianism as Hegel read through the 'history of theological effects.' Of particular concern to him are those forms of theology whose overall contours are shaped by an epical narrative and in which the theologoumenon of the Trinity plays a decisive role.

Part 3 then concerns ancestry: both Balthasar's ancestry, as he functions as a diagnoser and refuter of the monumental misremembering that is encoded in Hegel's trinitarian metanarrative, and the Hegelian ancestry of contemporary theologians who, wittingly or unwittingly, do not escape the gravitational pull of Hegel's epical narration. Figurally, it is about fathers and sons, and the different sides of paternity and filiation. For when the issue is not memory as such – for which there are mothers and daughters as well as sons – but rather misremembering and its memory, it looks as if Balthasar's world, however contingently consists of sons and fathers. As Turgenev and Dostoyevski have made more clear than most,[4] this world is fraught in that it articulates in essential ways fidelity and betrayal, often one under the sign of the other. What does it mean for Balthasar to constitute himself in his theology as a son of prior anatomizers of misremembering and the generation of simulacra? What degree of autonomy does the son enjoy, who continues or repeats his fathers? And can difference be granted or acquired without violence? These are questions that will come in for attention in addition to the obvious one of actually naming modern and premodern fathers for our two main contestants. Again, what does it mean for Hegel not simply to continue in his words, which are precisely much more than words, but for him to have progeny, not all of whom acknowledge him as a father? What is it to be a son, turning a deaf ear to the broader theological tradition, beginning again, or beginning again after Hegel, whose systematic ambitions have to be curtailed, while much of his diagnoses of the spiritual plight of modernity, key elements of his metaphysics, and his insights into Christianity are to be sustained? How original after the Hegelian original can a theology be; and will Hegel allow any to proceed beyond him, and thus in a proper sense succeed him? These are the questions that part 3 addresses.

Part 3 consists of two chapters. In chapter 5, the first of the two chapters, I search for premodern and modern fathers who tutor the son in what I have referred to as the anatomy of misremembering. Now while it is true that Balthasar can rightly be understood to be influenced by the entire history of the religious critique of Hegel and by the totality of the heresiological tradition, I suggest that constellations of influence find focus and form in particular figures. I explore first whether and in what way the Hegel critique of the Tübingen theologian, Franz Anton Staudenmaier (1800-56),[5] represents an anticipation of Balthasar's critique of Hegel not only with respect to theological substance, but also in its casting about for the ancient lineage of Hegel's discourse and commitments. If I bring in the verdict that Staudenmaier does indeed supply a precedent, especially given his sense that at its basis the disconnect between Hegel and the tradition can be defined in terms of narrative structure and its trinitarian articulation, I do so without prejudice to Balthasar's own theological integrity. Again while any number of pre-modern theologians can be called on in an ad hoc fashion to resist Hegel on particular points – Augustine, Nyssa, Anselm, Aquinas, Bonaventure, and Maximus represent some of the more important examples – given what I have written in the previous chapters, it should come as no surprise that the ultimate premodern father for Balthasar in his venture of resister of specifically speculative misremembering is the 'church father' Irenaeus who isolates, describes, and ecclesially resists Valentinian discourse.

No more than in the case of Staudenmaier is the integrity and individuality of Balthasar's refutation of systematically deformed Christian narrative put into question by Irenaean precursorship. If Irenaeus provides the template for Balthasar's diagnosis of narrative disfiguration and the offering of a christocentric and trinitarian alternative that is ecclesial,[6] the details of Balthasar's diagnosis and refutation necessarily diverge from that of Irenaeus, given their very different historical and cultural situations and the very different complexions of the mythological discourse they refute. It is worth exploring also whether Balthasar's views of church and tradition replicates exactly that illustrated in *Against Heresies*, and what accounts for differences with regard to authority and its operation. While the aim of this chapter is categorically to name Irenaeus and Staudenmaier as the premodern and modern father respectively, the case for what might be called the 'virtual' paternity of two other thinkers is also explored. These two thinkers are the Russian speculative theologian, Sergei Bulgakov (1870-1943) and the Lutheran thinker Johann Georg Hamann (1730-88) respectively.[7] They are placed in a different category to the first two, because particular difficulties attend either being included as staples in Balthasar's anti-Hegel line of authority. In the case of Bulgakov, the main difficulty is not that Balthasar refers sparingly to Bulgakov – he refers even more sparingly to the Catholic Staudenmaier – but rather the lack of consensus as to whether Bulgakov ever transcended the Idealist and Gnostic traditions which, plausibly, were secreted through Vladimir Soloviev (1853-1900), and receive their best exemplification in the thought of Nicholas Berdyaev (1874-1948).[8] Again, while one of the main difficulties with Hamann is that his work is a critique of the *Aufklärung* of Kant and his ilk rather than Hegel, who himself sought to overcome the existential, epistemic, linguistic, metaphysical, and theological shortfalls of a disastrous rationalistic contraction of religious thought, the real difficulty lies elsewhere. As a Lutheran thinker, Hamann does not connect as easily with the broad Catholic tradition as Staudenmaier, and even judged in terms of his own confession, he is singular and unique. The ascription of 'Magus of the North' (*Magus in Norden*) is thus something of a double-edged sword,[9] at once suggesting a kind of supereminent authority and effecting a marginalization. Difficulties, for Balthasar, are just that, and as with Newman, even a large sum of difficulties does not amount to a fundamental objection.[10] In the case of Bulgakov, the issue of paternity is worth exploring not only because Balthasar rejects the interpretation of Bulgakov as 'speculative' and thus determined by German Idealism, but also because of his significant borrowings from Bulgakov, for example, Bulgakov's dramatic soteriology, his emphasis on the cosmic dimension of salvation, his focus of the Johannine corpus which involves essentially a rehabilitation of Revelation, his symbolic construal of the dynamic milieu of the Trinity, and finally and crucially his construction of the history of theological thought as a battle between truth and the lie in which the most salient feature of the lie is how it disguises itself as the truth. The Balthasarian warrants for including Hamann are no less impressive. Balthasar not only thinks highly enough of Hamann to devote a major essay to him in *Glory of the Lord 3* (239-78), but in his genealogy of the decline of the aesthetic in the modern world in *Glory of the Lord 1*, which essentially involves its separation from the good and the true in and through a process of subjectivization, Hamann is perceived just as much as the contrary to Hegel's totalitarian form of aesthetic recollecting as a powerful response to Enlightenment amnesia and fragmentation. From Balthasar's perspective, Hamann and Hegel represent the emblematic attempts to overcome the forgetting of the Enlightenment. Only the former, however, represents the way forward. The way forward is through a non-identical repetition in which Hamann is seen as intrinsically connected to the broader theological tradition and not simply as a correction of an invidious trajectory of post-Reformation thought. Although Balthasar's discussion of Hamann in *Glory of the Lord* licenses in particular the 'theological aesthetic' dimension of Hamann's multivaried discourse, with its stress on divine glory in Christ as regulating the language of creation and cultural discourse as well as the inspired speech of the Bible, it is suggested, however, that the use to which this christocentrism is put points to a template that exceeds the aesthetic as such. As Balthasar points to the glory of God in Christ in Hamann's work, he underscores not only the prophetic impulse behind Hamann's intervention in a scene marked by forgetting and attenuation and not a little reinvention, but also outlining of an apocalyptic horizon for all of history, which is a history of witness and its failure. In sketching the apocalyptic horizon Balthasar does not draw back from a deep commitment to Revelation and the Johannine corpus more generally, something he has in common with both Irenaeus and Bulgakov especially. These thinkers – and I do not exclude Staudenmaier – with different intensities inhabit a biblical apocalyptic horizon which has as the converse of the positive eschatological vision of the Lamb, a keen eye for what dissimulates and betrays Christianity.

Chapter 5 concludes by reflecting on what unites the two fields of paternities, the categorical and the virtual, and what relativizes them. There are two major foci of inquiry. The first concerns whether it is legitimate to say that all four examples of Balthasarian paternity, whether virtual or categorical, are fundamentally

'Irenaean,' or better put 'Irenaean' in the last instance.[11] The second brings us back to the concluding chapter of part 2, and the apocalyptic figuration of theology, and asks whether all examples of paternity, which are candidates for 'Irenaean' ascription, are at the same time examples of Christian apocalyptic which address and redress deformed forms of Christian thought. Here, however, I will be no more than probative. It is the task of part 4 to provide a full and detailed account of the apocalyptic nature of Balthasar's thought, to determine its specific genre, and to bring it into critical conversation with other contemporary forms of apocalyptic theology that define themselves as much against the Hegelian overcoming of the Enlightenment as the Enlightenment itself.

By contrast with chapter 5, chapter 6 concentrates on Balthasar's unveiling of the identity of Hegel's theological children, which is at the same time the unveiling of Valentinus' children, since on Balthasar's account Valentinianism supplies the ultimate code for Hegel's narrative ontotheology of Spirit (*Geist*). Such unveiling would be unnecessary were paternity commonly admitted. But this is very much the exception rather than the rule. As with heresiological discourse, Balthasar distinguishes, in *Gestalt* terms, figure from ground. The ground or background of filiality is broad, and embraces theologians unhappy with metaphysical depictions of God that emphasize stasis, immutability, and impassibility, theologians enchanted with pneumatological renditions of Christianity, and perhaps those who in general stipulate that the divine, triune or otherwise, be conditioned by the world that it conditions. Balthasar would be loath to dismiss the kind of 'Hegelian' diagnostic of contemporary trinitarian thought undertaken by David Bentley Hart.[12] Hart's enterprise is continuous with what Balthasar attempts, and every bit as necessary. As a critical supplement in which the bar is lowered for 'Hegelian' ascription to include what Balthasar would regard as ground rather than figure, Hart's diagnosis presupposes first that the case be made with regard to trinitarian discourses that explicitly evoke Hegel and seem to be most saliently marked by his actual discourse and not simply by his unhappiness with the metaphysical burdens – such as they are – of the classical theological tradition. As with his own patrimony in the anatomy of misremembering, Balthasar thinks that the Hegelian lineage is focused and constituted quite literally as specific figures. Balthasar, however, finds the case for Hegelian filiality most compelling in the case of Jürgen Moltmann. But even here, Balthasar recognizes that the task of demonstrating Moltmann's essential fidelity to Hegel is made more difficult by the self-conscious way Moltmann distances himself from the 19th-century religious philosopher, as he corrects the theology of *The Crucified God* to take account of contemporary Protestant and Catholic criticisms. Balthasar judges, however, that none of the individual corrections, nor even their sum, is sufficient for Hegelian paternity to be denied. In the end – if only in the end – Moltmann's theology fails to escape the gravitational pull of Hegel's thought. This pull is exercised even in, or especially at, those points in which Moltmann seeks to correct Hegel, and at which he appeals to other traditions of discourse to displace Hegel. From a Balthasarian perspective, it is questionable whether the substitution of 'love' for 'Spirit,' which leaves intact such essential features of Hegel's narrative as necessity, eros, and kenosis that forms a developmental chain, is in itself sufficient to overcome Hegel. Nor is it evident that Moltmann's appeal to the traditions of Neoplatonism and Kabbalah help introduce the requisite degree of separation, since these discourses can be included within a Hegelian regime, and may very well actually be included within it.[13]

If the previous chapters have offered anything like an adequate reading of Balthasar's take on Hegel, it follows that to be named a 'son of Hegel' is ipso facto to be named a 'son of Valentinus.' Balthasar recognizes that this allocution is shocking and, as applied to a theologian influenced by Hegel, hardly self-evident. Yet for him, it follows as a matter of genealogical logic. Moltmann's thought, however trinitarian, however doxologically modulated, does not break the line of Valentinian paternity, the generation of simulacra, since it fails sufficiently to distance itself from Hegel's epical narrative which, Balthasar believes, represents the exemplary modern instance of Valentinian metalepsis. Balthasar understands himself to provide in *Theo-Drama 5* and *Theo-Logic 2* in particular both the light and mirror in which Moltmann can see his other face, his face as other, and especially the way this other face alters and reorganizes a Christian face that would be dazzled by Christ, and so dazzled find itself in the nowhere-everywhere of the trinitarian dance that provides the measure for all gazes and for all praise. That there is not a trace of vituperation in Balthasar's analysis, that the note struck is one of regret that a well-meaning and often edifying theologian has been unsuspectingly caught in the spider web of the narrative grammar that generates Christian simulacra, adds pathos and persuasiveness to Balthasar's argument about Moltmann's Hegelian and Valentinian sonship.

While I focus in the main on a very particular example of sonship, I remain interested not only in plural instances, but in instances that are quite differently calibrated. My brief reflection on Jüngel's candidacy helps in some measure to pluralize numerically, although necessarily only probatively, since it is not evident whether Balthasar renders a constitutive verdict as to whether Jüngel manages to produce a theology that remains, as Barth's did, uncorrupted by Hegelianism, or whether he succumbs to Hegel's trinitarianism, which is ruled by an alien narrative grammar. Balthasar is not being over-scrupulous; he simply wants to assess whether there are differences in level of culpability that call for explanation. These differences matter in his view, even if examination of a theologian such as Jüngel suggests extending a line of debit to other theologians, who more superficially engage Hegel. Thus Hart and Milbank also are genuine supplements in this respect.[14] Given the similarity of the way in which Moltmann and Jüngel exploit Hegel in order to render a narrative trinitarianism that overcomes the bad metaphysics of the classical theological tradition, questioning Jüngel does not help with regard to the possibility or actuality of more than one Hegelian line. To pluralize the Hegelian line, I will reflect briefly on the relation of Balthasarian diagnostics to the Hegel-riddled theology of Thomas Altizer. Beginning with Balthasar's comment on the 'death of God' theology in *Theo-Drama 5* (244), I will broaden Balthasarian diagnostics to his later apocalyptic divagations. I conclude that in terms of Balthasar's diagnostic, however revisionist Altizer's theology is with respect to Hegelian metanarrative, that in the end in radically compressed form it repeats it by other means and thus in the final instance provides an example of a Valentianian revision of biblical apocalyptic that Altizer intends to support.[15]

Chapter 4

Balthasarian Fathers: Modern and Premodern

When Balthasar deals with Hegel and his influence he understands himself to be broadening and deepening Barth's debate with Hegelianism. At the same time, he positions himself, at least in the trilogy, with the profound critical theological engagement with Hegel constituted in the contemporary field of scholarship by French Catholic thinkers such as Albert Chapelle, André Léonard, Xavier Tillette, and Emilio Brito.[1] Given what he understands of what it means to be an ecclesial theologian, one would expect a backward glance at least at 19th-century critique of Hegel. Balthasar dutifully obliges. 19th-century Catholic critics of Hegel such as Hermann Weisse (*TD1*, 589), Anton Günther (*TD1*, 589) and Franz Anton Staudenmaier (*GL1*, 73; *TD2*, 331-33) are invoked to provide signposts for where theology might go after Hegel. What surprises is that there is no mention of Kierkegaard. The omission is hardly incidental, in that ignoring Kierkegaard means ignoring Barth's historiography which makes resisting Hegel a function of the battle between Christendom and authentic Christianity. Why the silence? Although the question need not detain us here, Balthasar's general depiction of Kierkegaard provides something of a clue. In *Glory of the Lord 1* (49-53) Balthasar reads Kierkegaard as fulfilling the non-aesthetic, decisionistic tendency in theology that essentially defines the Reformation, although this tendency is also to be found in the period of late Nominalism. This constitutes an essential derailment that leads to the bleeding of Christian substance, whose objective center is provided by the glory of God revealed in Christ. This suggests that whatever the 'genius' of Kierkegaard, he does not offer much sustenance to Christian thinkers interested in faith being the subjective correlative of objective Christian mystery, rather than Christian mystery being the objective correlative of faith. Kierkegaard is simply too fideistic to represent the solution to the calamity constituted by the Enlightenment. Indeed, it is possible – and here Balthasar would likely agree with Hegel's account in the *Phenomenology* (# 527-555)[2] – faith itself is part of the dialectic of the Enlightenment in which the Enlightenment gets confirmed. And by innuendo, if not by express statement, Kierkegaard is simply too individualistic, too much an example of the Protestant principle, too little constituted by memory that defines a tradition. Of course, these general reservations are logically consistent with an embrace of Kierkegaard as a critic of Hegel. Balthasar, however, tends to view literary outputs wholecloth and estimate them relative to their capacity to encapsulate the substance of Christian truth. Tactical alliances are not second-nature for him. Nor does he show either much aptitude for or empathy with rhetorical and forensic strategies – however useful they might be – as these are divorced from the Christian position, which he wishes to defend. Finally – although here somewhat conjecturally – Balthasar is made nervous by the rhetorical strategies themselves, which feature irony. As we pointed out in chapter 1, in *Theo-Drama 1* Balthasar fears that irony is the quintessential mode of modernity. At the very least its enlisting in the Christian cause is an ambiguous good. One cannot be sure that irony will not ultimately hollow out what it was intended to defend.[3]

If Balthasar essentially deprives himself – in the way that Barth does not – of the precedent of Kierkegaard when it comes to critique of Hegel, this does not mean that he altogether deprives himself of the assistance of the nineteenth century. It is simply a matter of Balthasar's ecclesial way of doing things that he either evokes or invokes witnesses on behalf of the prosecution or defense. The references to Weisse and Staudenmaier are at least indicative of that. The real question is whether, implicitly or explicitly, Balthasar repeats in something like a systematic fashion another, non-Kierkegaardian, mode of Hegel critique. If the answer to this question is yes, and if in the end Balthasar conjugates his critique of Hegel along the lines of 19th-century Catholic critique, while reproducing its level of exigency, it should be admitted at the outset that he provides no explicit treatment of 19th-century Catholic critique, nor is there any express reflection on its nature and limits.

Staudenmaier Redux

THE REFERENCES IN PARTICULAR TO Staudenmaier throughout the trilogy, however, are instructive. For example, in *Theo-Drama* Balthasar praises Staudenmaier's anthropology and theology of history precisely in their difference from Hegel (*TD2*, 331-3). An earlier reference to Staudenmaier, however, suggests that

Staudenmaier's opposition to Hegel necessarily is global even as, or especially as, Staudenmaier looks for precedents in the tradition to bring to bear on a speculative discourse that threatens Christian discourse in an unprecedented way. Balthasar produces a surprising opening in the Introduction to *Cosmic Liturgy*. His first words:

> *When Staudenmaier, as a young man, recognized that the theological task before him was to uproot the pantheism of Hegel and looked around for a model who would not only be enlightening, but sufficiently grounded in history to be reliable, he came upon the figure of Scotus Erigena. It was a happy choice: there the relationship of God and the world, the emergence of all things from God and their return to him, were seen despite the pantheistic dress of Neoplatonism with an essentially Christian eye. (29)*[4]

The truly important point here is Balthasar's appreciation of the importance of Staudenmaier's task rather than his recommendation of Erigena as sufficient for the task. In the trilogy, and especially *Glory of the Lord*, Balthasar is not persuaded that Erigena is not apt for this task, although it should be pointed out that even on the opening page Balthasar is persuaded that Maximus would have been a better choice, for precisely here one would not be dealing even with a Neoplatonic dress. Given that Staudenmaier is also recalled in the French literature on Hegel,[5] it is worth raising the question whether Staudenmaier's vehement rejection of Hegel's epic narration serves as the template for Balthasar's argument. Although I argue strongly that Balthasar's anatomy of Hegelian misremembering recalls Staudenmaier on both substantive and genealogical axes that have been under consideration in the previous chapters, it should hardly be necessary to insist that repetition is not the same as reproduction. However unusable Kierkegaard's thought is, for Balthasar, from the point of view of Hegel-critique, as well as the vantage point of a constructive theology that can overcome modernity, his concept of 'repetition' does not fall into this category.[6] Repetition necessarily signals non-identity. Although it is possible to view Balthasar as attempting to do for the twentieth century what Staudenmaier did for the nineteenth, that is, to perceive him as taking on the influence of Hegel or his left-wing successors in the broader culture and resisting Hegel's influence within theology, the situations are quite different. The passage of time, and especially the ebb and flow of reputation, necessarily makes the contemporary authority of Hegel's discourse more complex and equivocal. Moreover, although the link with Marx is already made by Staudenmaier, the connection is now more adamantine, even if much of the more interesting cultural and philosophical discourse of the century, whether in German thought in the shape of Adorno and Critical Theory, or French thought from Kojève to Sartre, from Hyppolite to Derrida, and from Bataille and Blanchot to Foucault have successfully argued for a degree of separation denied in classical Marxism. Moreover, in the domain of aesthetic theory, Hegel has continued to be relevant. There are any number of reasons for this. Almost certainly, one such reason is the astonishingly rich conjugation of treatment of genre, historical periodization, particular artistic judgment, and sensitivity to art's social matrix and expressive role illustrated in his *Lectures on Aesthetics*.[7]Another is that Hegel's aesthetic theory represents an alternative to the Nietzschean and Marxist account of the production of art, both of which proceed primarily in terms of categories of power rather than truth. Balthasar's debate with Hegel is indelibly marked by this aesthetic contribution and its interpretation.

More specifically in the religious domain, contemporary interest in Hegel reflects an on-going crisis of Christianity, and the search for alternatives outside as well inside Occidental modes of thought. In our treatment of Heidegger in the succeeding volume, we suggest that in drawing a line in the sand between Christianity and other religions Balthasar is as much interested in outmaneuvering syncretism as he is in making determinate judgments with respect to relative value and truth. Syncretism is a patent expression of nihilism. But even when syncretism is not defining, the contemporary context in which Hegelianism recommends itself is marked by a plurality of options that could not have been imagined in the less complicated world of Staudenmaier. A constitutive attraction of Hegelianism is that while it is not syncretistic and thus does not overtly conspire with nihilism, it can be read to acknowledge and include plurality.[8] This serves as a background feature of speculative philosophy's adoption and adaptation of Christianity and of its contention that it is true to the real intent of the Christian tradition, while also redeeming what is best about modernity. In addition, compared with the nineteenth century, as the level of the demand for a theodicy discourse has over the twentieth century increased at the same exponential rate as the demand for its abolition, however problematic it turns out to be in the final instance, Hegelianism shows itself to be more in tune than standard renditions of Christianity with death and the evil-filled world.[9]

Although the broader cultural shift provides merely the background for Balthasar's reflection, it is indispensable for understanding him. Balthasar is forced to deal with it, either negatively or positively, as a function of his intervention in the religious conversation prompted by the Hegelian line in contemporary theology, and especially German theology. If contemporary theological recommendation of Hegelian refiguration of Christian symbols very much constitutes the foreground, it is important to remember just how important Balthasar takes Hegel's reflections on aesthetics. For, as *Theo-Drama 1* marks it, our understanding of aesthetic theory and history bears on specifically theological outcomes. Balthasar's Hegel-critique has then its own context that insures he does not reproduce Staudenmaier. Moreover, when it comes to theological 'style,' nothing like a reproduction occurs. Balthasar's commitment to tradition precisely as the rich orchestration of individual and communal memory irreducible to sameness indicates a more inclusive temperament than Staudenmaier, whose view of the tradition is much more monolithic. In addition, by contrast with Staudenmaier, whose language is as wooden as his tone is obsessive and vitriolic, Balthasar's style – even when he is involved in critique – is marked by poise, grace, and meditative finesse.

Still, notwithstanding huge differences in cultural and intellectual context, it is remarkable just how close Balthasar's critique of Hegel is to that prosecuted by Staudenmaier in his *Presentation and Critique of the Hegelian System* (1844) and other texts of the 1840's.[10] While the early Staudenmaier's estimate of Hegel was less harsh, with Hegel regarded as in equal part opportunity and danger,[11] Staudenmaier's reservations regarding the philosophical and cultural as well as theological viability of Hegel's discourse and that of his epigones gradually congealed into a sustained critique that matches that of any religious thinker in the nineteenth century.[12] Unlike the master 19th-century rhetorician and agent of disguise, Kierkegaard, however, there is nothing indirect, episodic, or tactical about this attack on Hegel. In his mammoth book, all of Hegel's published and unpublished work is examined with a view to ascertaining whether it evinces any continuity with traditional Christian takes on the Trinity, creation, anthropology, history, Christ, Church, and eschatology, and whether it subscribes to the ethical, devotional, and liturgical practices that are implied in traditional Christian beliefs as well as provide their context. While Staudenmaier gives particular attention to the doctrine of creation (142-64; also 496-505), he judges that Hegel's system compromises all Christian theologoumena, and that Hegel's elevation of discourse from *Vorstellung* to *Begriff* serves both to confirm and disguise this fact (16-24).[13]

In *Presentation and Critique* the summary concept for the systematic unity of departures from the theological tradition is 'pantheism.'[14] Staudenmaier's use of the concept contains the judgment that one of the main effects of Hegel's univocal application of the categories of becoming, process, development, and agon to the divine is to dissolve the distinction between the finite and the infinite and to make one the function of the other (496-505, 583). In an extraordinary anticipation of the Balthasar of *Theo-Drama*, Staudenmaier makes the point that Hegel's system abolishes the 'play' between infinite and finite freedom.[15] Perhaps the most interesting qualification of Staudenmaier's attack is his claim that Hegel's system, whose effect on the symbolism of Christianity is given full expression in *Lectures on the Philosophy of Religion*, represents a regression to 'theogony' (*PC,* 771).[16] Now, Staudenmaier's use of the category of 'theogony' is more typological than historical. There is, for example, no reference to the theogonic discourses of ancient culture, whether Hesiod's *Word and Days* or the theogonic speculations of the Orphics. Understanding that in some sense the category is being applied outside of its native environment of myth, and being utilized to account for particular tendencies in higher-order discourse, theogony, for Staudenmaier, is thought to specify pantheism. Conceived in general as an offshoot of pantheism, which is defined by the tendency to conflate the divine and the world, in

Hegel's case specifically 'theogony' both expresses and is expressed by a dynamic and generative dialectic which abolishes difference, real relationality, and dialogue between distinct orders of freedoms (*PC*, 499). The mutual dependence of the divine and the world and the divine and human being, in Staudenmaier's view, obliterates the integrity of each, reducing the divine to that which ontologically depends on it, while paradoxically divinizing the world and inducing the apotheosis of human being (*PC*, 653).[17]

For Staudenmaier in *Presentation and Critique*, Hegel's *Lectures on the Philosophy of Religion* show with particular clarity just how far he has moved beyond the classical Christian God-talk of divine aseity that proscribes the necessity to create (772). For Staudenmaier, aseity is neither a merely contingent theological option nor a dogmatic excrescence; rather it serves to protect the gratuity of divine acts of revelation (170-7), which is fatally compromised in and by the necessity characteristic of Hegel's system (433-61).[18] Dialectical necessity guarantees that the divine becomes all that the divine can become, and that nature and finite spirit – precisely as other than the divine – are the media of divine self-actualization. Human consciousness of God is particularly important in Hegel's scheme, for this consciousness is nothing less than divine self-consciousness (782).[19] Although he does not apply the term to Hegel's system, it is clear that before Balthasar, Staudenmaier is concerned with the 'erotic' modality of Hegel's narrative ontology just as much as he is concerned with its necessitarian character. This is so because dialectical necessity is fueled by lack, correlative to potentiality, in the divine that seeks satisfaction in the actualization of the divine. Staudenmaier wishes only to make the negative point that Hegel fails the test he thinks is set by the theological tradition, and which finds its consummate expression in Thomas: God is perfect actuality from the beginning, and that precisely as pure actuality nothing is lacking for his existence (*nulla rei indiget ad existandum*). One does not find here or elsewhere in Staudenmaier's oeuvre any balancing of this reflection by an equal insistence on the generosity and prodigality of divine origin, which also is not without eros for a world that comes to be in its 'let it be.' Here Balthasar is significantly in excess of Staudenmaier, mainly due to his Christian Neoplatonic commitment to the coextensivity of divine agape and the diffusive generosity of origin, this despite the interesting fact that one of the most salient features of Staudenmaier's thought is his opposing Christian Neoplatonism to Hegel.[20]

Had Staudenmaier stuck to this very general level of critique he would be worth remembering as a trenchant critic of a powerful and influential philosophical system which, in the name of elevating Christianity and granting it intelligibility and apologetic cache, had effectively eclipsed it. He would also be worth remembering as a critic who senses that Hegel's system outbids any and all Christian views of creation, and not simply its voluntarist and nominalist versions towards which Hegel affects a particular distaste. Still, it has to be said that the above criticisms of Hegel were not unusual in Hegel's day and essentially fueled the assault on his position as being pantheistic, even as their avowal has become relatively standard in contemporary commentary on Hegel.[21] At best then, the commonality of these important criticisms of Hegel satisfy a necessary but not sufficient condition for Staudenmaier being regarded as a genuine anticipator of Balthasar and conversely Balthasar being regarded as a genuine repeater of Staudenmaier. A feature of Staudenmaier's critique of Hegel that distinguishes him from his contemporary, Kierkegaard, even at his most theologically concentrated as in a text such as *Philosophical Fragments*,[22] is his concern for the effect of dialectic on the Trinity. And it is precisely this trinitarian concern that represents the sufficient condition for genuine anticipation and genuine repetition. Now while Staudenmaier's focusing of Hegelianism in the symbol of the Trinity is an identifying feature of his critique, trinitarian focus as such is not original to him. In this regard he follows the Tübingen theologian F. C. Baur, who edited Hegel's *Lectures on the Philosophy of Religion*, and in whose early work the symbol of the Trinity played a central role.[23] Staudenmaier differs markedly from Baur, however, in his judgment of Hegel's trinitarianism. Whereas in *Die Christliche Gnosis* (1835) and other texts, Baur recommends Hegel's dynamic trinitarianism as the authentic development of original Christian esotericism,[24] noting its developmental complexion, Staudenmaier decries the abolition of the immanent Trinity-economic Trinity distinction that goes hand in hand with the abolition of the real distinction between the divine and the world. As Staudenmaier diagnoses it, in Hegel's texts the missions do not express the superabundant reality of the Triune God; rather, they provide the means by which the initially abstract and thus imperfect divine becomes actual, fulfilled, and thus perfect. Staudenmaier underlines Hegel's rejection of the perfection of divine origin, and his insistence on perfection as a telos.

As with Balthasar later, Staudenmaier sees that Hegel's trinitarianism represents a seismic shift from the tradition. And as with Balthasar later, Staudenmaier also sees that the focus on mission issues in an economic trinitarianism that bears little resemblance to that instantiated in the mainline Christian tradition. For whereas in a traditional figure such as Irenaeus, the 'economic' qualifier points to perspective and interest and does not involve a deliberate ontological stance, in the case of Hegel it does express an ontological stance, which in effect gives ontological priority to the economy. For it is a constitutive feature of the Hegelian position that *arche* is truly *arche* only in teleological realization. Although Staudenmaier does not use the language, his conclusion is very much in line with many of Hegel's postmodern critics: within an archeoteleological economy the sheer giftedness of creation, its being 'without why,' is fatally compromised.[25] In his *Philosophy of Christianity* (1844),[26] Staudenmaier develops further the trinitarian objection broached in *Presentation and Critique*. He offers an ascription of Hegel's trinitarianism that anticipates Balthasar in the closest possible way: Hegel's developmental trinitarianism constitutes a specifically modern form of Sabellianism. Hegel fails to support the view of persons in relation on either the immanent or economic levels of the Trinity. Instead of persons, Hegel offers logical relations which have ontological implications. For Hegel, 'Father,' 'Son,' and 'Spirit' identify neither individual persons nor their coinherence, but rather operations of a self-differentiating and unitary divine (*PChr*, 38-44, 798-810, esp. 800-02, 809). Here Staudenmaier sees what many late 20th-century commentators on Hegel's appropriation of the Trinity have failed to see, and some have denied, that effectively Hegel presents in a fully articulate form[27] a new species of developmental modalism that situates itself critically against classical trinitarianism.[28]

For Staudenmaier, the nearest thing we get to a personal subject in Hegel's thought is the community (*Gemeinde*). It is in the community – the 'we' – that the personhood or individuality of God is realized. Of course, for him, in *Philosophy of Christianity* this identification not only degrades the divine, it also illegitimately divinizes human beings (*PChr*, 653, 741). But it is two other complaints about Spirit defining community, and in turn being defined by it, that more nearly mark Staudenmaier as an anticipator of Balthasar. Staudenmaier complains that Hegel's idea of community constitutes a displacement of focus and authority away from Christ onto a spiritual elite. Staudenmaier also complains that in the final analysis the milieu of community shifts away from the church onto the State (*PChr*, 634-35). Both of these complaints, as we saw in the last chapter, are lodged by Balthasar against Hegel. For Balthasar, as for Staudenmaier, the second infraction supposes the first. As spiritual community, as the *Ersatz* of the church, is cut loose from Christ, the prospect is opened up of community being interpreted outside the context of the church defined by the memory of the passion, death, and resurrection of Christ and by practices consonant to the mystery of his saving sacrifice. On the principle that interpretation abhors a vacuum, community (*Gemeinde*) will tend to get identified with such ready at hand reductions as the State, civil society, or, in Marx's revolutionary hands, the proletariat.[29] Balthasar is Staudenmaier's heir in all of these respects. From *Apokalypse* on, the general association of Hegelianism with Marxism is made, with Marxism being precisely what it claims to be, the dialectical translation of speculative thought into praxis.[30] Only gradually does the more 'real life' substitution of the church by the State assume a more prominent role in Balthasar's discourse. *Theo-Logic 2 & 3* are particularly important in this respect. For while Balthasar, as with Hegel, can stipulate the importance of structures to mediate the Spirit, the identification of the media not only signify the ultimate subject of discourse, but the fundamental attitude of human being as either titanic or open to the deliverance of a divine love that can be recalled only as unanticipated.

The power of Staudenmaier's analysis resides largely in his encyclopedic knowledge of Hegel's texts and his ability textually to document his judgments about Hegel's positions on creation, theological anthropology, and above all Trinity. Although the tone of Staudenmaier is sometimes vituperative, he is able to argue successfully that in texts such as the *Phenomenology*, *Lectures on the Philosophy of Religion*, and even *The Encyclopedia of the Philosophical Sciences*, Hegel has no truck with anything that resembles a traditional view of creation, and a traditional view of the heteronomy of human spirit. Again, an analysis of Hegel's texts supports Staudenmaier's opinion that Hegel's commitment to the church as a medium of salvation, thus as sacramental, is minimal, and this because, and not despite, Hegel's insistence that the memory of the passion and death of Christ effectively brings the community into participation with the divine. For, as we have already commented on at some length in chapter 3, Hegel tropes real presence such that the eucharist functions as a metaphor of what is effected in human personal and social life as a whole. Divine presence is enacted by elevating human beings to their rightful status as autonomous agents co-constituted as selves in the exchange of recognition with other selves. At the same time, texts such as the *Phenomenology*, the *Encyclopedia*, and *Lectures on the Philosophy of Religion* also make it clear that Hegel's rehabilitation of the symbol of the Trinity has less to do with his intention of retrieving a classical doctrine that has fallen into desuetude than with his view that the revisionist road taken by Schleiermacher's archeology of consciousness and Kant's practical philosophy represent various dead-ends with respect to religious knowledge that can be rationally certified. A trinitarian metanarrative is sufficient to function as the agent of true reason (*Vernunft*), since it is already in some real sense the story of historically specified reason. This trinitarian narrative of the realms of Father, Son, and Spirit, as *Lectures on the Philosophy of Religion* intimates and *Encyclopedia* elaborates, justifies itself by producing and satisfying internally generated criteria of what is to count as knowledge.[31] Balthasar, of course, sees this every bit as clearly as Staudenmaier, although, arguably neither possess the clarity of the Russian orthodox thinker, Iwan Iljin, whose work I have mentioned a few times already.[32] In any event, their common objection is best stated in the language of Lyotard: the problem with a metanarrative is not simply its comprehensive range, but rather that in addition it has built into it the metalinguistic function of the justification of its discourse and its rights to preside over all other narratives.[33] Hegel's ruse is to take himself out of what is essentially a contest between narratives with supporting arguments by maintaining that his discourse is the judging discourse and the discourse judged.

Staudenmaier's criticism of Hegel's trinitarianism is not one criticism among others, since in Hegel's texts the symbol of the Trinity provides nothing less than the theological form of his entire theogonic narrative. An encompassing trinitarian theology of a deviant sort requires an equally encompassing orthodox articulation. This Staudenmaier provides in *Die christliche Dogmatik*,[34] which is best regarded as the constructive correlative of the polemical *Die philosophie des Christenthums.* The second volume brings out clearly the economic starting point of Staudenmaier's trinitarian thought, its insistence on the reality of divine persons, and *perichoresis* as the dynamic figure of tripersonal relation. What makes Staudenmaier conclusively, however, the emblematic anticipator of Balthasar is that throughout his sprawling texts his substantive critique of Hegel focused on the Trinity goes hand in hand with genealogical critique. Following on F. C. Baur's *Die Christliche Gnosis*, Staudenmaier sees Hegelian discourse as completing trajectories of discourse that are in tension with more standard versions of Christian discourse. In his *Hegelsbuch*, he suggests that Hegelian pantheism instantiates Neoplatonism (149 ff).[35] While the list of exemplars of Neoplatonism is broad, interestingly two of the more prominent figures are Proclus and Bruno (3, 49), concerning whom, we have seen, Balthasar consistently has reservations he does not have with respect to other examples of the Neoplatonic tradition, whether non-Christian or Christian.[36] In other texts from the 1840's, Hegel is plotted in trajectories that have their origins in Joachim de Fiore and ancient Gnosticism respectively.[37] Even less than Balthasar does Staudenmaier attempts to make sense of how Hegel's discourse simultaneously realizes three different premodern discourses, or separate out the various strands of these discourses in Hegel's conceptuality, whose very abstraction makes it easy to disguise actual historical discursive debts. Nor does Staudenmaier pursue the question whether any of these strands of discourse exerts significantly greater influence than the others in Hegel's conceptuality to the point perhaps of dominating and regulating the other real discursive presences. A particular mark of Staudenmaier's genealogical program is its failure adequately to distinguish between

Joachimite apocalyptic and Gnosticism as sources, or better 'poisoned wells,' of Hegel's Christianly distorting discourse. This failure, repeated in different ways in the thought of Eric Voegelin and of Balthasar himself, is a failure to discern the intimacy in the modern period between discourses that are logically and historically separate. It is precisely this kind of failure in Balthasar that encouraged the kind of genealogical supplement I offered in chapter 1.

Although the various attempts by Staudenmaier to effect a link between Hegelian discourses and a band of premodern discourses, all marked by exorbitant claims to knowledge and by metanarrative structure is by far the more important contribution made by Staudenmaier from a genealogical point of view, Staudenmaier also anticipates a much narrower genealogical trope of Balthasar. This concerns what might be called the dialectic of the modern period. In *Philosophy of Christianity* and other later texts,[38] the Tübingen theologian speaks to the internal logic of the movement from the Reformation to German Idealism as the exposition of a deep-seated monism: in the one case God is everything, and creation is nothing; in the other, the world is everything, and God is effectively nothing. For Staudenmaier, this means that extremes meet. Staudenmaier's fairly formal point about the fearful symmetry of apparent opposites has its theological correlative, therefore, in the surprisingly deep relationship between radical voluntarism and metaphysical necessity. Balthasar touches on these counter-intuitive insights at least twice throughout the trilogy, but it is touched on also at a number of points in the Barth book. In the genealogy of the eclipse of beauty in modernity in *Glory of the Lord 1*, Balthasar basically draws a line between Luther and Hegel, although he acknowledges that in the case of Hegel one is dealing more with the discovery of the proper locus of beauty and refiguring its definition than with its excision and the refusal of determination. By contrast, in *Theo-Drama* Luther's sustained theological voluntarism and positivism are viewed as not only failing to stem the speculative tide, but as in effect positively encouraging it in a way that mainline Catholic thought, which avoids Luther's extreme purism, does not.[39] I am not suggesting that Staudenmaier functions as the actual source of Balthasar's view of the relation between the Reformation and Idealist thought. *Analogia Entis* is just as likely – if not more likely – to be the proximate source.[40] What I am saying is that the work of Staudenmaier provides if not the only, then the most developed instance in Catholic culture of a mode of genealogical analysis of Idealist speculation that traces the proximate as well as ultimate dynamics of development. Of course, Staudenmaier is to a considerable extent repeating Baur's *Die christliche Gnosis*, but in doing so essentially reversing the sign. Whereas Baur can celebrate the linkage between the movement from Luther to Idealism and the movement from the speculative discourse of Valentinus to Luther, and what amounts essentially to an infolding of the former narrative in the larger narrative that goes from ancient to modern speculation, Staudenmaier can only react in horror. Lighter on emotion, Balthasar's critical evaluation is not less severe: Gnosticism is a catastrophe as is speculative Idealism – if not only that – and the Reformation facilitates the move from one form of catastrophe to the other and by doing so essentially reveals a common thread.

While it is the substantive and genealogical critique of Hegel that defines Staudenmaier's work and constitutes him as the model for Balthasar's repetition, his figuration of himself as a Hegel critic is also worth brief comment. Here too it is possible to find a clue toward uniquely identifying the style of Balthasar's critique of Hegel. On the one hand, Staudenmaier's determining of Hegel's discourse as a terminus of Joachimite apocalyptic puts him in the position of such orthodox Joachim naysayers as Aquinas and Bonaventure, who see Joachimite apocalyptic as compromising the centrality of Christ and marking as questionable – because relative – the present constitution of the church with its determinate beliefs and practices. On the other hand, in claiming that Hegel's discourse is the realization of Gnosticism in the modern period, Staudenmaier figures himself as Irenaeus battling a specifically post-Reformation and post-Enlightenment form of Valentinianism. Irenaean figuration in particular, however, is betrayed by tone as well as by genealogical chutzpah. The tone is exigent, even vitriolic, and is theologically and ecclesially and not simply personally motivated. Staudenmaier judges Hegelian philosophy to be a pseudo-Christian language that mimes and subverts the entire complex of Christian language, undercuts the dispositions that embrace ritual and institution, and renders otiose any apprehension of the self as radically heteronomous and doxological. As such, Hegelian thought constitutes nothing short of a discursive crisis that must be met with a tone of exigency that matches that of Irenaeus doing battle with Valentinianism of the first centuries of the common era.

In substance, genealogical tendency, and finally figuration, Staudenmaier's Hegel-critique anticipates that of Balthasar, and, as with Johannes Möhler and to a lesser extent Johann Sebastian Drey, puts the ineluctably 19th-century character of Balthasar's thought in relief.[41] Without prejudice to his late modern context, and his aspiration for a theology that is postmodern, in his critique of speculative theology as with respect to his view of the church and the theological tradition, Balthasar takes a step back into the nineteenth century in order to complete their thought. He does so with the view that one step backward is more than one step forward. Again, I insist that the uniqueness of Balthasar's contribution is by no means compromised by his repetition of Staudenmaier. This is so not simply on the general grounds that one can expect differences in judgment regarding details, and differences in interests which become clear in the articulation of a positive vision. While Balthasar thinks that on the whole Hegel constitutes a real danger to Christian faith, and thus is definitely in line with the later Staudenmaier, he also thinks of him as an opportunity to be exploited both on the level of theological method and substance. In this sense he follows the earlier rather than the later Staudenmaier.[42] Specifically, he expands on the sense of opportunity by opening up theology to the language of art in general and drama in particular. In addition, not only does Balthasar, like Barth and Kierkegaard before him, focus much more than Staudenmaier does on Hegel's christological debits, he thinks that Hegel's christological debits are regulative in a way that Staudenmaier does not seem to see, and in any event does not address. And, finally, of course, there is the movement of history, and the generation of new contexts in which Hegel has authority. Unlike the 1840's, the authority exercised by Hegelian discourse in contemporary discourse is less obviously social-political than theological. Hegel's epigones are no longer Friedrich Strauss, Bruno Bauer, and Karl Marx, or even apostles of reconstructed Marxism such as Lukacs, Kojève, and Sartre, but the likes of Bloch and

Moltmann, whose particular kind of discourse is even more open to being summarily dismissed as 'theological' than was the Left-Wing Hegelianism of Marx's day. The battle is now more nearly *within* the church than *between* the church and the world, although the battle inside the church is the battle between the church viewed as church and the church viewed as world. This calls for even greater discernment, greater subtlety in diagnosis, and more finely calibrated instruments of removal. Ingredient in this finer calibration is granting some validity to Hegelian concerns with the Christian tradition which, as I indicated in chapter 3, sometimes too emphatically insisted on divine sovereignty, too unilaterally underscored divine aseity, and too uncompromisingly underscored human heteronomy without the corresponding emphasis on participation in Christ and through Christ and the Spirit participation in the trinitarian divine.

Repeating Irenaeus

To REPEAT STAUDENMAIER IS NECESSARILY to repeat Irenaeus, who is the first theologian of stature who detects and refutes what he takes to be the insidious and comprehensive disturbance of Christian thought represented by Valentinianism's systematic altering of the biblical narrative. In *The Scandal of the Incarnation*, Balthasar names Hegel's discourse as representing a peculiarly modern form of Valentinianism that should be refuted as the comprehensive deformation of Christian thought (*SI*, 1). While both detection and refutation are in play throughout Balthasar's trilogy, arguably, as the detection is most to the fore in the second two parts of the trilogy, and especially in *Theo-Drama*, the positive theological value of Irenaeus with his insistence on the centrality of Christ in the drama of salvation history is more to the fore in *Glory of the Lord 2*.

It turns out in fact that Irenaeus enjoys advantages over Staudenmaier both as a detector of discursive deformation and as systematic refuter. Irenaeus is much keener than Staudenmaier on the transgressive nature of Valentinian style hermeneutics, and specifically on how it differs *toto coelo* from an ecclesial hermeneutic (*TD2*, 91-136). The advantage of Irenaeus over Staudenmaier as a precursor stands out clearly on the christological front. Irenaeus' theology is not only underpinned by a christological optic, but is christologically saturated, and this precisely because of his trinitarian commitments. In rendering this judgment, Balthasar explicitly refers to Book 4 of *Against Heresies*, and especially emphasizes 4. 20 (*TD2*, 118). There is nothing in Staudenmaier to rival Irenaean figuration of Christ as recapitulation (*anakephalaiosis*), both as a positive doctrine and a hermeneutical tool to interpret scripture and salvation history. It is ultimately Irenaeus who provides the model for the agonistic figuration of true and false gnosis that is a structural feature of Balthasar's trilogy, introduced in the first volume of *Glory of the Lord*, underscored in connection with Irenaeus in *Glory of the Lord 2* (60-2, 66, 71-2), and deployed in *Theo-Drama* and *Theo-Logic* in the critique of Hegel and his theological and activist epigones. The following passage decisively expresses Balthasar's agonistic figuration and its link to Irenaeus:

> *The situation is somewhat similar to Irenaeus' campaign against Gnosticism, but is more acute as the gnostic sects that claim to have the correct interpretation are no longer outside the Church; they are inside her, claiming to have the proper scientific tools and to be in authentic communication with all religions and world views . . . A battle of the "Logos" with the Catholica herself is totally unavoidable. (TD4, 460)*

The present time, perhaps all Christian time, is a time of *Ja* or *Nein* (*TD2*, 145). But yes or no is not defined by Barth's *Epistle to the Romans.* Refusing to distinguish in the absolutely exclusive way between faith and knowledge and between faith and the religions, yes and no, for Balthasar, refers focally to the fundamental option for or against comprehensively distorted specimens of theology of the Hegelian sort. What Balthasar in his book on Barth would consider the discrimen between Barth's theology and Catholicism, precisely the Catholic 'and,' funds Balthasar's more focusedly negative, more nearly Irenaean approach to Hegel. But the fact is, arguably, based on principle. A polymorphously negative attitude towards culture and religion risks being amorphous, and thus the No risks losing its bite. By contrast, when the governing tendency towards the religions and culture is 'yes,' even if a halting one, 'no' is reserved for that which is seen not simply to be 'impure,' but a real other that threatens the substance of Christian faith. One way of formulating the difference – and one way in fact in which Balthasar himself expresses the difference – is that Barth's early text is apocalyptic more in tone than in substance, while Balthasar's trilogy and especially *Theo-Drama* is apocalyptic in substance while seriously ratcheting down the vehemence of apocalyptic tone.

It is no accident then that Balthasar recurs to Irenaeus in *Theo-Drama*, which is the main site of the apocalyptic determination of Balthasar's thought both in its constructive and polemical sides. Balthasar at best implies the apocalyptic constitution of Irenaeus' thought in his two main reflections on the theologian of Lyons outside of *Glory of the Lord 2*. But his characterization of the operations and motivations of Irenaeus' biblical hermeneutic, as well his vivid sense of the agon of truth with the lie in history suggest that the ascription would be unproblematic. And, of course, a superficial examination of *Against Heresies* and especially Books 4 and 5 would tend to bear this out. Important throughout, the Johannine tradition increasingly asserts itself in both of these books.[43] The Gospel of John gives color and content to the Pauline image of recapitulation by underscoring Christ's obedience (5.13), his eucharistic sacrifice that constitutes the identity of the church (4.18) and is the ground of the salvation of the world (5.2), and the doxological relation between the Son and the Father (4.27) that is the model for human existence as witness. The Gospel of John then is both understood and deployed as an inherently anti-Gnostic text, and most certainly anti-Valentinian text. It is not only the Gospel of John that gets deployed; Irenaeus also deploys Revelation, even as Irenaeus recurs to other apocalyptic texts (Daniel, 5.25) and other apocalyptic pericopes such as the temptation narratives (Luke 4, Matthew 4)(*Adv. Haer.,* 5.21) and the separation of the chaff from the wheat (Matthew 25). Revelation serves both constructive and polemical purposes. A visionary text, Revelation suggests an indissoluble connection between vision and doxology, and between doxology and incorruptibility of the flesh (4.20). Interestingly, given both our broaching of apocalyptic in chapter 4 and the fact that *Against Heresies* 4.20 is a crucial text for Balthasar, Irenaeus suggests that apocalyptic vision is not only momentary but also that what is seen overflows into multiple images and figures that suggest lack of cognitive adequacy. For Irenaeus, however, Revelation is centrally the text of the Lamb who overcomes death (5.13, 5.31), and offers an unsurpassed account of new Jerusalem, the new heaven and earth (5.33-35), which involves the transfiguration of the earthly rather than its annihilation. Although it is difficult to separate out from *Against Heresies* what is constructive from what is polemical, polemic in the strict sense arises when the other is named, indeed named demonically. Applying Revelation's discourse of the Anti-Christ (5.24, 5.30), Irenaeus sees the figure – connected with Satan (5.29) and serpent (5.20) – as a figure of the seducer who produces a counterfeit of the true God and thus a counterfeit of true worship. Constitutionally, like the Anti-Christ the Gnostics function in the mode of 'as if.' Thus the conclusion of the text links with the beginning (1.11) in which Irenaeus talks of the operation of *metharmottein*,[44] the operation of narrative disfiguration and refiguration in which the triune divine economy and thus the identity of the divine is distorted.

Schooled in Irenaean apocalyptic, tutored in the reading of Revelation that understands it always to demand application, for Balthasar, as for Staudenmaier, Hegelianism is by far the most powerful of the 'counterfeit doubles' of Christianity in the modern period. Unlike other doubles, there appears to be a genuine effort to comprehend Christianity, to honor the Christian narrative, and to place the cross at the center of religious thought. At the same time, Hegelianism presents Christianity in a more concertedly aesthetic and dramatic key than that essayed by many theologians of more orthodox persuasion. The attraction of Hegelianism then is explicable: it answers a need. Yet, the ancient ancestry of Hegelianism needs to be exposed in order to galvanize resistance especially towards contemporary theological manifestations of Hegelianism even as they themselves are involved in attempts at overcoming the Hegelian legacy. At the same time, Balthasar advises that contemporary theology avoid being exclusively determined by what it rejects as a simulacrum, in this instance a Gnostic or Valentinian simulacrum. Although Balthasar has nothing to say on the matter, his precursor Staudenmaier may very well have fallen into the trap of reaction formation. Certainly, his dogmatic theology gives some evidence of retreat to manual theology that the Tübingen School had surpassed as well as, perhaps, sowing the seeds for a return to a mode of theology marked by the maximum of certitude and the minimum of cultural intervention.[45] But then perhaps the thought of Irenaeus too was determined by the Gnosticism he resisted with the result that his view of tradition is too restrictive, too homogenous for the Logos which is best thought of as a grammar than a fixed deposit from which theology draws and regulates its speech.[46]

While it is not exactly poetic license to redescribe Irenaeus' view of the theological tradition in this grammatical way, clearly it is a supplement of the same order as my grammatical redescription of Valentinianism and more specifically Valentinian narrative. Still evidence of Balthasar's own augmentation of Irenaeus is everywhere throughout the trilogy. Although Balthasar adopts a largely Irenaean frame for his articulation of old and new covenant and their relation in *Glory of the Lord* 6-7,[47] clearly he has a more polyphonic view of the Bible as a whole. While the old covenant achieves its realization in the new, Balthasar more successfully shows how the view of God in the old covenant is adequate in and of itself and not simply by reference to the disclosure of God in the new covenant. He is especially adept in showing that, as a 'stairway of obedience' (*GL6*, 215-81), the prophetic dimension of the old covenant is as valid after the appearance of Christ as before, indeed, that a properly anti-Marcionite reading of the old covenant demands that the prophetic dimension remains as pertinent today as yesterday.[48] The prophetic continues as the providential means of bringing to mind the difference between the law of God and the law of human being, of scouring forgetfulness, of encouraging memory of the God who truly makes free, and discouraging the degeneration of doxology into ritualism and a false transcendentalism that accents only the vertical relationship between the individual and God.

The link forged by Irenaeus between the old and new covenants renders the God of Jesus Christ a God of righteousness for whom justice is a constitutive feature of the kingdom. Continual fidelity to the prophetic is one of the main means in and through which Christianity does not degenerate into an aestheticism that is no less idolatrous than power politics, ideologies that legitimate offensive practices and justify exclusion, and cultural complacency. Balthasar even more unequivocally augments or supplements Irenaeus when he views the Christian tradition as necessarily more plural and diverse, both synchronically and diachronically, than the bishop of Lyons would have it, and by considering the authority of institutional church as inalienable, yet only one authority alongside others just as inalienable from a Catholic point of view. In this respect it is interesting that in the very text that presents the strongest possible case for the viability of the institutional church, that is, *The Office of Peter*, Balthasar not only grounds the church in a more primordial Marian amen that is constitutive, he pluralizes ecclesial style. The office of Peter exemplifies a necessary ecclesial style, but so also do the contemplative style of John and the prophetic style of Paul.

Repetition and the Theo-Logic of Supplementarity

Balthasar's exceeding of Irenaeus in addition to his exceeding of Staudenmaier brings us back to the notion or image of repetition. It is obvious that Balthasar has Staudenmaier as his 19th-century precursor when it comes to resisting Hegelian thought on the substantive theological front. It is equally obvious that Balthasar has Staudenmaier as his precursor when resistance to Hegelian thought, especially in its trinitarian elaboration, is accompanied by the consciousness that if Hegelianism is a form of Valentinianism, it is not in every respect a mere recrudescence, but rather an emergence of a specifically modern form in which the accent falls heavily on process, development, and agon of the divine. When John Milbank raises then the important question of who is the modern Irenaeus?[49] chronology cannot be absolutely decisive. From a chronological point of view, Balthasar is belated. But if Balthasar's resistance to Hegel is just as comprehensive, if his refutation of Hegel is more rhetorically effective than Staudenmaier's because he uses Hegel's own categories of 'epic' and 'drama' against him, if he understands better Valentinian hermeneutics, if he sees better the potential in the ancient forms of Valentinianism for a rendering of myth in a more dynamic and dramatic key,[50] if his positive articulation of Christian faith is less determined by resistance to Hegelianism as modern Valentinianism, then without postmodern or more specifically Derridian preciousness one could say that in a value sense Balthasar is the original and that Staudenmaier repeats Balthasar rather than Balthasar repeats Staudenmaier.

But one might ask the more probing question, who is the first Irenaeus? and not simply who is the first modern Irenaeus? At the commonsense level, Irenaeus is the first, and indeed, the only Irenaeus, and Balthasar represents at best a very belated – because modern – repetition. In a way that Staudenmaier does not match, Irenaeus has claims of priority that do not exclusively depend on chronology. For Balthasar, Irenaeus is not only a venerable theologian, he is also a theologian of the first order, and as such, offers a prototype which later theologians ought to imitate. Balthasar himself satisfies his own general imperative, and thus would have no compunction about accepting his secondness, and would be more than happy with a verdict that would elevate him to the status of the primary modern Irenaeus. Still, if one takes fully into account the ways in which Balthasar exceeds Irenaeus, fulfills the promise that is Irenaeus, then one could say that Balthasar is the first Irenaeus and not simply the first modern Irenaeus. Balthasar is the first Irenaeus, since he is Irenaeus absolved from limitations that were ingredient in Irenaeus' resistance to second and third century Gnosticism. Balthasar is the first Irenaeus precisely as the postmodern Irenaeus, the future (*post*) of the anterior (*modo*).[51] As the postmodern Irenaeus, Balthasar releases the tradition into the splendor of variety and plurality, enhances the christological optics and focus so that it opens out to all discourses as gifts, and articulates theology in its eschatological horizon which is that of the Trinity. At this point the postmodern Irenaeus includes rather than excludes Augustine, Anselm, Bonaventure and Aquinas, just as it blesses Francis, Catherine of Genoa, Thérèse of Lisieux and Adrienne von Speyr. A postmodern Irenaeus, then, with the gift of diagnosing and resisting misremembering of the mystery, and the misremembering of the tradition of authentic response to the mystery, will encourage as its complementary side the rich remembering that is the tradition of discipleship, liturgical and devotional practices, prayer, and, of course, theological discourse, which is the second-order discourse of the church that depends on the revelation of God in Jesus Christ vouchsafed in scripture. In this Babette's feast of memory, while the historical Irenaeus is an extremely important voice, he is but one voice among others in the symphony or chorale of tradition. Not only that, when the perspective is exclusively that of memory, the preeminence of Irenaeus' voice is challenged by that of Bonaventure and Anselm, perhaps Origen, even Barth. Irenaeus' indispensable contribution to theology is to remind that the art of memory that defines Christian discourse, which is articulated with such finesse in *Glory of the Lord*, at crucial points in history demands the accompaniment of the resistance to comprehensive acts of misremembering that masquerade as the proper memory of the tradition.

It must be admitted that even if one acknowledges Balthasar's excess, and comes to see the manifold ways in which he supplements Irenaeus, and thereby realizes his promise, this does not get to the issue of justification, which in Balthasar is always specifically theological justification. But this is not to say that such justification is not supplied by Balthasar. There are essentially two orders of justification. The foreground justification is christological. As the dead are voiced in Christ, their pastness is not fatal to their being heard and finding response. By the same token, however, as *Glory of the Lord 1* suggests in principle, and *Glory of the Lord 2-5* demonstrate in fact, in Christ voices of later centuries, which respond to the earlier, are not simply echoes of what has gone before. They are expressions of Christ, who makes visible the invisible one. As the fullness of the Father, who has no lack, no expression, or set of expressions, confined or not to a particular period, exhaust Christ. Christ is ontologically the 'more' that will demand 'more' in terms of representation.[52] *Theo-Drama* adds a new dimension to Balthasar's view of tradition in its delineation of *en Christo*. As enfolded in Christ, voices are cured of the agonies of pastness and futureness, of both unripeness and belatedness. In Christ there is a kind of contemporaneity or synchronicity that does not obviate the diachronic, and in particular does not interfere with the recognition of the forward thrust of history as it tends towards the eschaton. Christology serves, however, as the foreground theological justification rather than the only ground or even the ground. At some level, the constitutive implication of Christology with trinitarian thought in Balthasar's work makes it antecedently likely that if there is a christological justification, then a trinitarian justification is not far behind. The most cursory reading of the trilogy provides ample evidence in favor of this presumption. Balthasar makes it clear in *Glory of the Lord 1* that if Christ is the provocation for all Christian expression, the Spirit plays a fundamental role in the exposition. *Theo-Logic 2 & 3* makes the point in more general terms. The Spirit is the expositor of Christ who is the expositor (*Auslegen*) of the Father (*TL2*, 11, 15). In fact, in *Theo-Logic 3* Balthasar even calls upon Irenaeus' rendition of the Son and the Spirit as the 'two hands' of the Father that work together in history in the formation and reading of scripture, and in the constitution and preservation of the church (*TL3*, 155 ff). Irenaeus' figuration points to the necessarily trinitarian horizon of tradition. Perhaps it is *Theo-Drama 4*, which most explicitly brings this into view. As I commented on at some length in the closing pages of chapter 3, for Balthasar, *traditio* is a 'giving up' or 'surrendering' that finds its origin as well as model in the Father's giving up of his Son, while continuing to support the Son in and through the Spirit. Analogously, or more than analogously, since all the voices that speak Christ participate in him, the traditions of the church and the traditions of its reflective theological discourse in particular, are a gift and a surrender that is inscribed in the horizon of horizons articulated in and by the trinitarian persons.

As I elaborated the way in which Balthasar evokes Staudenmaier in his resistance to Hegelian forms of thought, and invokes Irenaeus as providing a pattern of diagnosis and resistance to Valentinianism, the Kierkegaardian quality of 'repetition' comes to the fore, even as I use the term in a more self-consciously theological and postmodern way than that other great 19th-century detector and refuter of Hegelian gnosis, whose way was that of indirection, irony, and punctual probe. As much by association as anything else, I recall the Chinese box image that frames Kierkegaard's *Either-Or 1* (Preface), which has as one of its central concerns the debits as well as credits of Hegelian 'ethical life' (*Sittlichkeit*).[53] The Chinese box is a box within boxes which holds secrets. While Kierkegaard uses it as a conceit wherein he can disguise the identity of the writer who is a critic of the Hegelian system, the image can be deployed as an analytic construct to unlock the nature of Hegelian discourse itself, which is multi-layered in general and multi-layered specifically with respect to narrative discourses. I indicated in chapter 1 that one of the ways in which Balthasar can be supplemented is to force the question of the order of dominance and recessiveness between the various narrative discourses that express themselves in Hegelian discourse, whether Neoplatonism, apocalyptic, or Valentinianism. In Balthasar's case, as in Staudenmaier's, something like a non-systematic prioritization of Valentinianism exists. This means that the innermost box, which holds the secret, is that of Valentinianism rather than the other narrative languages which are relative and perhaps even hide the truth. The theoretical question is how we are to assess the relation.

The Chinese box image is, of course, helpful then only to a limited extent, and not simply for the reason that Hegel would decry the secret as the epitome of the post-Kantian worshipers of the Unknown God such as Jacobi, Fichte, and Schleiermacher, but perhaps also the epitome of Hamann, the 'magus of the North' (*Magus in Norden*) whom Balthasar judges to be an exception to the trajectory of modernity, indeed to the point of providing critical leverage with respect to it and to Hegel's speculative hallowing of it.[54] The limitation of the Chinese box image applies to all topological images, whether the referent is the self (Freud), society (Marx) or discourse (structuralism). For topological images are in the final analysis metaphors of explanation rather than explanations proper. To consider Valentinianism as providing the narrative infrastructure of Hegel's developmental ontology with apocalyptic and Neoplatonism as narrative superstructures still begs the question of how the dominance of the infrastructure expresses itself. Similar difficulties bedevil all topological models, and eventually encourage critical emendation. For example, difficulties in Marx's topological model lead Louis Althusser to suggest as superior the concept of 'overdetermination,' which implies the reciprocal influence of elements in a non-stratified field of society.[55] Similarly, Lacan and also Ricoeur have felt the need to translate Freud's topographical model of id, ego, and superego into a linguistic model in which communication proceeds indirectly or symptomatically as well as directly.[56] Analogously, as I suggested in chapter 1, the notion of Valentinian narrative grammar marks a way beyond the synchronic and diachronic explanatory handicaps of a model of stratigraphically arranged discourses. Hegel's discourse is Valentinian because it is this narrative discourse that is regulative in the last instance,[57] and because his developmental ontotheology expresses a Valentinian narrative grammar albeit in a determinately modern context.[58] Expressing such a grammar is consistent with Hegel's narrative ontology differing in significant respects from the classical forms of Valentinianism. Importantly for present purposes, it is also consistent with the adoption and adaptation of apocalyptic, Neoplatonic, and even Kabbalistic forms of discourse for an overall Valentinian purpose,[59] which is nothing less than the spoilation of the biblical narrative.

If as the consummate orchestrator of the Catholic tradition, Balthasar has mothers and fathers, when it comes to resisting constitutive acts of misremembering, which effectively puts the Christian tradition out of action, he has only fathers. One modern (Staudenmaier), one premodern (Irenaeus) have particular claims to our attention, even if Balthasar is influenced by Barth's reading of Hegel and contemporary takes on Hegel by Catholic philosophers, and to some extent also primed by Przywara's rejection of Hegel in *Analogia Entis*.[60] Prepared critically to engage Hegel for the sake of Christian theology itself weighed down by its own petrifications, ultimately the stance Balthasar adopts is vigorously unaccommodationist to speculative dialectic. It has been my argument that it is necessary to return to the 19th-century discussion of Hegel for a corresponding perception of just how high the stakes are: Hegel's discourse either saves Christian discourse (and by implication practice) from itself, or cannibalizes it. The 19th-century discussion was itself a raging battlefield in which Hegel was assessed for various purposes, obviously not all of them theological. The theological discussion was itself furious in that Hegel had both his right-wing and left-wing defenders, as well as detractors. Outside of the school of Marheineke and Gans,[61] arguably the most successful promotion of Hegel's thought was offered by F. C. Baur, who read Hegelian thought as offering a developmental trinitarianism that represented the necessary extension of Reformation thought and ancient gnosis and the antidote to the mainline or exoteric tradition of Christianity, represented in the main by Catholicism, but also by Protestant orthodoxies to the degree to which they mimed a dispensation that could only be an interregnum. Baur's proposal, articulated in *Die christliche Gnosis*, was not the familiar rationalist one, and could not be countered by the fideistic alternative, which was the common default during Hegel's own time and with Protestant and Catholic theology in his wake. It was Baur's challenge that was taken up by Staudenmaier.

Nothing comparable to Staudenmaier's resistance is to be found in 19th-century Protestant thought, which largely handled Hegel by changing the subject. What was of interest was not metanarrative – here Feuerbach is an exception – but rather the proper interpretation of scripture with due attention paid to social context, historical probability etc., and intellectual probity. The theological future –such as there was of it – as Hans Frei points out,[62] belongs to the likes of Friedrich Strauss. Staudenmaier then functions as the Catholic symbol of resistance to the unexpurgated challenge of Hegel whose narrative is as encompassing as it is self-legitimating. Of course, this is not to say that Catholic theologians in general saw better than their Protestant counterparts. Accommodation to speculative thought was certainly in evidence in Catholic circles in the shape of the mercurial Franz von Baader,[63] and later in Anton Günther whose work represents the most disciplined appropriation of Hegel's thought by a Catholic thinker in the 19th-century.[64] Staudenmaier, then, is with all his limitations a singular 19th-century religious figure, and an equally singular anticipator of the anti-Hegel, anti-Valentinian Balthasar.

Temperamentally Balthasar is the kind of religious thinker comfortable with patrimony in general. His theological world, which is forever wide and sometimes even wild, is a world with many fathers, not all of whom belong to ancient Christianity, indeed most of whom do not. As suggested already, his is a world of mothers too; for as the church is not without Mary, the church is not without its female saints and its female doctors. When it comes to resisting Christian simulacra, Balthasar's world is exclusively a world of fathers, two of special note, one of whom he acknowledges expressly (Irenaeus), the other functioning horizonally as setting out the terms of debate from a specifically theological point of view which, for all its sophistication, 20th-century theological commentary has not improved on and only rarely matched. I have gone to some lengths in my account of Balthasar's repetition to uncover his theological presuppositions, in which voices of the past are hallowed without taking away Balthasar's own. A christological and trinitarian reading of the tradition forbids both an oedipal reading and its opposite. Balthasar knows from Irenaeus that belated Christian thinkers are not obliged to kill their fathers in order to be original. Oedipus is a figure of blindness (*Adv. Haer.* 5.13) and compulsive novelty that removes one from the only source of expressive life as well as truth. For Balthasar, Irenaeus was right: the desire for originality is an aesthetic virtue but a religious vice, given the original, who is Christ, and the originator who is the Father. At the same time a christological and trinitarian reading of tradition removes the sanction of past fathers eclipsing their sons, taking all their glory by arrogating to themselves the right to be the only ones who relatively adequately express divine glory. In the tradition, there is neither the aggressive violence of Oedipus nor the passive violence of Laius who does not will his son to be an original. In Christ and in the space of the Trinity, willing non-identical repetition is possible because actual. Considered theologically, the tradition proleptically participates in the peace eschatologically given in the triune God. Balthasar understands then in the way that C.S. Lewis did that 'Son of . . .' is not simply comfortable in that it suggests a belonging that extends the self beyond the self, but is at once eschatological and sacramental. As *Chronicles of Narnia* so beautifully put it,[65] one is a 'son of Adam' and suffers the vicissitudes of history, but one can also be a 'son of Aslan,' the incarnate sublime, and one becomes especially a son or daughter when one can distinguish false from true, Anti-Christ from Christ, and when one chooses the one who dazzles and walks into and treads lightly in the infinite space of divine conversation that is the triune God.

Virtual Paternities: Bulgakov and Hamann

ON THE FACE OF IT the search for Balthasarian fathers has been as disappointing as it has been surprising. It has been surprising since the best modern candidate for paternity we have uncovered is a theologian who, to a considerable extent, represents the third – and some might say 'idle' – wheel of the Tübingen School.[66] It is disappointing in that Staudenmaier seems to be the *only* credible modern candidate. This, despite the fact that both Barth and Kierkegaard contribute not a little to Balthasar's Hegel-critique, while at the same time Balthasar's critique of Hegel, which is fully expressed already in *Apokalypse*, undergoes refinement in and through his dialogue with the Communio group of philosophers and theologians. But are there really no other candidates for paternity? I have consistently hedged in referring to Staudenmaier as the 'primary' modern father, even as I refused to name any others. And, as I see it, there are no completely unproblematic others. Still what about the credentials of Sergei Bulgakov, who engages German Idealism on a speculative terrain? Certainly, Balthasar expresses concerns about the orthodoxy quotient of Bulgakov's sophiology, which reflects itself in his Christology, anthropology, and trinitarian thought as well as his eschatology. Sophiology is, for Balthasar, a neuralgic point in his Maximus book,[67] as it is in *Glory of the Lord* (*GL7*, 213): it threatens to disturb the ontological difference between the creator and creature, the unsurpassability of Christ, and the very notion of the triune God by insinuating a fourth hypostasis. Nevertheless, throughout the trilogy, Bulgakov is an obvious lexical presence, and is cited on a number of occasions in support of Balthasar's christological-trinitarian articulation the other side of Hegel's speculative distortion of the Christian narrative. I underscored in chapter 3 two different but related kinds of contribution by Bulgakov: (a) his putting into theological play of meta-symbols such as 'ur-kenosis,' 'supertime,' and 'superspace,' calculated at once to depict in a relatively adequate way the triune God of glory and to recharge the theological tradition that may have degenerated into the compromise of a propositionalism and lazy apophasis, and (b) his non-triumphantalist inflection of the soteriological motif of Christ's descent into hell and his solidarity with the dead. Here while I supply a little more textual detail, especially with respect to 'ur-kenosis' and Christ's descent into hell as a crucial aspect of *mysterium paschale*, my interest is in how the broad contours of Bulgakov's trinitarian theology anticipates Balthasar, and whether and how despite – or perhaps because of – its speculative bent, its relation to Hegelian dialectics is resolutely negative.

There are, then, incentives as well as disincentives for pursuing the question whether Bulgakov can be added to Balthasar's paternity list when it comes to resisting Hegel's specific kind of speculative misremembering. And what about Hamann, concerning whom three years before his death Hegel wrote a long and exceptionally positive review in the *Jahrbücher für wissenschaftliche Kritik*?[68] Never citing Hegel's essay, Balthasar thinks that Hamann and Hegel's fate are linked in modernity, or better that the fate of theology is to a considerable extent at stake in their coupling. Of course, this coupling is at the same time a deep uncoupling, since Balthasar's point in his genealogical reflections in *Glory of the Lord 1* and his substantive account of Hamann in *Glory of the Lord 3* is that Hamann and Hegel are theological contraries, especially when it comes to the christological pivot and the trinitarian horizon of theology. The difficulty with respect to the paternity of Hamann has not got to do with the substance of his thought so much as chronology: coming before Hegel, Hamann can be an object of Hegelian analysis and discrimination, while Hegel cannot be an object of Hamann-critique. Nonetheless, performatively – if not in the order of reflective justification – Balthasar does not seem to allow anachronism to have the last word, suggesting that in the end it can be turned to productive and critical account.

Now, while I mark the difference in critical ratio between Staudenmaier and these two thinkers by speaking of the former as a categorical father of Balthasar in his role as an opponent of speculative misremembering and the latter as virtual fathers, I do so with the knowledge (a) that these latter two figures are more prominent in Balthasar's work and (b) that one should not overestimate the distinction between the categorical and the virtual, which in the end is largely pragmatic. I will argue that both should be added to Balthasar's paternity list, and that even as supplements, or rather precisely as supplements, they add muscle, range, and flexibility to a tradition of resistance to forms of thought that dismember and distort the biblical narrative, and revise the fundamental grammar of Christian understanding of Christ and his salvific role and the nature of the triune God and the relation of this God to the world and human being. This argument also involves linking Bulgakov and Hamann to Irenaeus, and allowing them to be caught up in what I have called the 'theologic of supplementarity.' It also involves some reflection on the apocalyptic substance of both thinkers, which exceeds that of Balthasar's more pedestrian father, Franz Anton Staudenmaier. Both of these thinkers join, as Balthasar does, an apocalyptic view of tradition with an apocalyptic view of Christ and the triune God. As the latter represents the alternative to Enlightenment reductions of Christian substance and the Romantic and Idealist rearticulation, the former is a tradition of discernment that unmasks traditions of Christian discourse that under inspection turn out to be dissimulating and 'alien.'

Bulgakov as Anti-Hegelian and Anti-Gnostic Father

In exploring the extent of Balthasar's enlisting of Bulgakov in anti-Hegelian agenda, arguably, there is no better place to begin than with Bulgakov's conjugation of kenosis, for, as with Balthasar, this conjugation maps the extent and even intent of what is displayed in the Idealist tradition. In chapter 3 I cited a long passage from *GL7* (313-14) in which Bulgakov's contribution is lavishly praised. Struck by Bulgakov's refusal to etherize kenosis or turn it into a purely speculative counter (*TD2*, 264; *TD4*, 278), Balthasar is especially attentive to its biblical bases in Bulgakov's theology, and specifically how in Bulgakov's hands 'kenosis' links Philippians 2:5-11 and the Johannine theology of the Lamb. Crucially, of course, it is Bulgakov, who supplies a tolerable – that is non-Hegelian – instance of construing, or better imagining, kenosis as operative at the level of the immanent Trinity (*TD2*, 264; *TD4*, 313). That Balthasar does more than affirm Bulgakov's insight in passing is evinced in his considerably later avowal in *Theo-Drama*:

> *It is possible to say, with Bulgakov, that the Father's self-utterance in the generation of the Son is the initial "kenosis" within the Godhead that underpins all subsequent kenosis. For the Father strips himself, without remainder, of his Godhead and hands it over to the Son; he "imparts" to the Son all that is his. "All that is thine is mine" (Jn 17:10). (TD4, 323)*

It must be granted that Balthasar's reference to 'all subsequent kenosis' is somewhat indeterminate, although the plural suggests that more is involved than the incarnation and cross of Christ. Balthasar removes the necessity of guessing by making it perfectly clear in other passages throughout *Theo-Drama* that creation, as well as incarnation, should be conceived kenotically (*TD2*, 264; *TD4*, 313). As Balthasar praises Bulgakov's imagining of a kenotic chain, he understands that while this chain maps the Hegelian metanarrative, constituted by the iterative operation of 'emptying,' its meaning is otherwise. It is precisely not connected with Hegel's developmental ontology (*GL7*, 314). The ground for disassociation in the *Theo-Drama* passage, as in the passage from *Glory of the Lord*, lies essentially in the hypostatic density of the trinitarian persons. Hypostases being replete,[69] emptying, however much repeated, is noneconomic. It does not yield epistemic, metaphysical, or existential dividends. More specifically, it does not issue in pleromatic being and knowledge; these are givens. The fact that there is no repetition of Hegel's kenotic economy in Bulgakov does not mean that kenosis is, therefore, frivolous. Balthasar senses in Bulgakov that the other to the seriousness and portentousness of the Hegelian negative (*PS* #19) is not frivolity, but gracious self-giving, sacrifice without reserve to which thought can never catch up.

One implication to which Balthasar draws attention as having particular pertinence to the issue of divine passibility is that suffering of Christ is not without remainder a function of Christ's human nature. Or more technically speaking, Christ's suffering is enhypostatic. Importantly, however, it is not licit to infer from the enhypostatic character of suffering in Christ – connected in Bulgakov, as in Balthasar, primarily with the taking on of sin which alienates from the Father (*TD4*, 313-14) – to divine passibility without qualification. For all predication with respect to divine persons must proceed under the assumption that as divine, the hypostasis of the Son differs from all human hypostases, and thus that the mode of predication is analogical. Undoubtedly, however, for the same reason, recognition of the enhypostatic character of suffering would put a block on complacent assertions of divine impassibility, which sometime function within a metaphysical economy in which impassibility is simply the binary opposite of the passibility, the content of which is provided by observation of the world of change. In general terms, it could be said that in the trilogy Balthasar unites what he disjoins in his much earlier text on Maximus. In that text Maximus and Bulgakov were understood to be opposites, at least in terms of general theological sensibility and ethos. In the trilogy, not only is this not so, but Bulgakov is read as perfectly replicating Maximus' neo-Chalcedonianism, which thinks radically of the communication of properties. The evidence for this is patent. In speaking to Bulgakov's enhypostatic view of suffering, Balthasar refers to A. Feuillet's great text on Maximus' Christology, *L'Agonie de Gethsémani* (*TD4*, 314). That it is Maximus who is important, rather than his commentator, and thus the Maximus-Bulgakov connection, is evident from an earlier reflection in *Theo-Drama 4* on Maximus' two-will Christology where Feuillet is understood to promote a Maximan truth (*TD4*, 252; also *TL3*, 69-70).

Of the three meta-symbols for indicating the triune divine, 'ur-kenosis' is probably the most important, and I make no apology for privileging it here. In due course, I will have a few words to say about the other two, 'supertime' and 'superspace' respectively. First, however, I want to say something about Balthasar's affirmation of Bulgakov's mythologem of Christ's descent into hell and his rescue of the dead. Although Balthasar's most explicit reference to Bulgakov's use of the trope comes in *Theo-Drama 3* (313), where he cites Bulgakov's discussion in *L'orthodoxie*,[70] dating from at least *Mysterium Paschale* (1967), it is evident that Balthasar regards Bulgakov as one witness among many. There is, of course, the biblical witness of 1 Peter and Revelation and of the early patristic tradition, and especially of Irenaeus and his elaboration of the *Christus Victor* theme.[71] Balthasar does not contend by any means that Bulgakov is the only thinker who imagines as other than triumphant Christ's solidarity with the dead, or who asks for a fundamental qualification of the *Christus Victor* image. The claims of Speyr, and even Nicholas of Cusa, especially the Cusa of *De docta ignorantia* (Bk. 4) are too imperative.[72] Nonetheless, Balthasar feels comfortable that Bulgakov too envisions a passive obedience that is the extremity of distance from the power of the Father (*TD4*, 313-14). Perhaps even more generally important than this refiguration of a mythologem of how death is overcome, is Bulgakov's insistence on death's overcoming as a crucial aspect of the paschal mystery. In his reflection on this point in *Glory of the Lord 7*, Balthasar thinks of Bulgakov as a fellow traveler (*GL7*, 13-4, 39, 81-2, 89, 231 *inter alia*). It is in line with Bulgakov's reflections – although not necessarily because of him – that Balthasar considers the vision of Revelation regulative:

> *Ruin, death and Hades must be taken up into the act of the covenant; this was possible only if God's Word became flesh, if the eternal life took death (as judgment, ruin, and hell) upon himself as man, and made it past in himself. "I was dead, but behold I am alive for ever more, and I have the keys of death and Hades" (Rev 1:18). (GL7, 39; also GL7, 228)*

For both, however, it is obvious that the overcoming of death is best understood as a trinitarian activity: Christ's overcoming of death cannot be understood outside of the context that Christ is executing the will of the Father, and that the essential condition of such victory is the empowerment that comes from the Holy Spirit.

Apocalyptic form as well as content matter for Balthasar and Bulgakov. Both reject an overcoming of death that is either 'already' or 'not-yet,' and argue that it takes the complex form of 'already-not-yet.' Of course, there is more than one way of satisfying this requirement. Even superficial comparison of Balthasar's reflections on this topic in *Theo-Drama 4* with those of Bulgakov in *The Bride of the Lamb* [73] reveals that in the latter text the hiatus between the overcoming of death on the Cross and its complete overcoming in 'endtime' is more emphatic, as is the role of Spirit in bringing about such overcoming. This not unimportant difference is still, however, a difference within the same, for both put the overcoming of death as an apocalyptic phenomenon, and see it as an event that has a trinitarian horizon. The apocalyptic index of the meta-symbols of 'supertime' and 'superspace' in Bulgakov, and their insertion into the apocalypse driven two closing volumes of *Theo-Drama*, simply reinforce the point. Moreover, that Revelation supplies the biblical subtext for both meta-symbols is no more an embarrassment for Balthasar than for Bulgakov. Whatever the prospects for misinterpretation and misuse, through its symbolic networks Revelation renders a vision of the triune God even less dispensable in modernity than it was in the past. Moreover, for neither thinker is the symbolic explosion of Revelation a phantasmagoria of pride. Admittedly counterintuitive, Bulgakov and Balthasar underscore its incredible humility: for seeing is not without its non-seeing, indeed it is a form of non-seeing; symbols point to and celebrate the awfulness of that to which they refer, but at the same time declare their own inadequacy (*BL*, 345-47). Bulgakov anticipates Balthasar in arguing that Revelation is continuous with the other biblical texts in this regard. Moreover, he shows himself as anxious as Balthasar to play down the direct referential function of the language of Revelation. While some of the images of Revelation, for example, the Beast of 13:4, have an obvious and univocal historical reference, that is, Rome, most of the symbols of Revelation do not. Elasticity marks most of the images (*BL*, 328-29). If they refer at all to historical reality, they do so either equivocally or indeterminately. The classic example – to which I will return shortly – is the image of the Anti-Christ (Rev 17:8) (*BL*, 330).[74] The image sets in motion a play of reference that might be satisfied in any number of ways, for the marks of identification are quite generic. Any number of historical personages could be referred to synchronically and diachronically.

Bulgakov also provides an important precedent for two other prominent features in Balthasar's recurring to apocalyptic as the frame for an adequate theology, which necessarily in his view is an adequate trinitarian theology. The first is the insistence on the inner connection between the Gospel of John and Revelation, focused as both are, on articulating distinct but related dimensions of the paschal mystery. It is Christ as the paschal lamb who provides the fundamental dramatic figure of both texts, and around which circle other figures: in the Gospel of John human beings who say yes and no to Christ who is the truth; in Revelation human beings who remain firm or who are seduced, but also cosmic forces such as the beast, the dragon, and the Anti-Christ. The Lamb is the center of all reality, because the salvation enacted on Golgotha is invested with absolute meaning. Importantly, for Bulgakov, no more than for Balthasar, does this imply – as it does for Berdyaev – an eternal as well as historical Golgotha.[75] For Bulgakov, this would take biblical and specifically Johannine thought in a Hegelian and Gnostic direction that is antithetical to it. Similarly, while Bulgakov is by no means the source of Balthasar's understanding of the relationship between Revelation and canonic and non-canonic apocalyptic literature, Bulgakov certainly anticipates him. Like Balthasar, Bulgakov understands the eidetic apocalypse of Revelation to sum up both New Testament apocalyptic and Old Testament prophecy. More specifically, Bulgakov thinks that Revelation enacts on a much larger scale the apocalyptic set-pieces of Matthew 24-5, Second Peter, First and Second Thessalonians, while harkening back to Old Testament prophetic texts such as Isaiah 13 and Ezekiel 32 (*BL*, 319-20). Understandably, with the example of Soloviev, who flirted with non-canonic sources,[76] before him, Bulgakov is anxious to stick to canonic texts. The only intertestamental apocalyptic text adduced as an influence is, as with Balthasar, Daniel. The silence with respect to the Enochian literature and Ezra is eloquent, and testifies to Bulgakov's determined attempt to put some distance between himself and the religious philosophy of Soloviev and especially that line that leads to the Gnostic-friendly thought of Berdyaev.[77]

However impressive the evidence for a positive and constructive link between Balthasar and Bulgakov, and however interesting it is that Balthasar, the Western theologian, traffics with speculative Russian religious thought when neo-Patristic Russian orthodox theologians such as Florovsky and Lossky outright refuse, it is not clear how any of this helps to advance the case that Bulgakov's thought is intrinsically anti-idealistic, and thus a factor in Balthasar's Irenaean 'detection' of Hegel's gerrymandering the biblical narrative and his offering of an apocalyptic alternative. Balthasar turns his elaboration of apocalyptic to critical account against idealist and Gnostic speculation in a totally overt way that Bulgakov does not. Nor does Bulgakov ever explicitly claim that he did. Ironically, it may be in just that part of the trilogy, which seems to give the death-certificate to Bulgakov's importance, that best supports the view of Bulgakov as being a second – but not necessarily secondary – kind of anti-Hegelian father, and in consequence a second – but not necessarily secondary – kind of anti-Valentinian father. I am referring to Balthasar's essay on Vladimir Soloviev in *Glory of the Lord 3* (279-352). Even granting that Soloviev is just one of a number of apparently surprising choices to illustrate 'lay styles' in which divine glory is remembered in and into the modern period – Péguy and Hopkins are two others – nevertheless, the interpretive hurdles that Balthasar has to clear are enormous, given the near consensus view that Soloviev is the proximate origin of a specifically Russian line of thought of which Nicholas Berdyaev is the most famous member. If this were true, then Soloviev is vitiated, for in *Theo-Drama* (*TD4*, 149), as in *Apokalypse 3* (428-9), Berdyaev is just the wrong kind of apocalyptic thinker, indeed one who belongs to the Idealist regime that Balthasar makes it his business to overcome. The obverse side of this is the possible displacement of Bulgakov by another and presumably superior Russian thinker, for the number of pages devoted to Soloviev dwarfs Balthasar's desultory dealings with Bulgakov throughout the trilogy. It should be remembered, however, that having a portrait hung in the modern gallery in itself no more decides a figure's theological importance than his or her absence. Do Origen's and Maximus' absence count against them? Does Nyssa's or Barth's? The reminder here is less salutary than usual, for it seems clear that in his interpretation Balthasar at once overcomes the asymmetry in extent of recall, and identifies otherwise Soloviev's lineage. Both needs are addressed when Balthasar reads Soloviev essentially from the point of view of Bulgakov as a *terminus ad quem*. Thus, as Soloviev is read backward from the standpoint of what we might call Bulgakov's 'generous orthodoxy,' Bulgakov is read forward from Soloviev's resistance to all those aspects of Russian thought that justify Balthasar's summary dismissal of Berdyaev. While it is the second aspect that engages us here, the first deserves at least brief comment.

Balthasar's openness to Soloviev's experimental religious thought reflects his anxiety about the prospects of a hyper-orthodoxy,[78] and the need for theological reflection to renew itself. His basic conviction is that tradition is always a process, a conversation and argument, that is only eschatologically completed. And indeed, if we are to take at face value Balthasar's views of *traditio*, expressed in *Theo-Drama 4*, tradition is, even eschatologically, ongoing event, ongoing delight in more and deeper knowing. As with all forms of truly valuable religious thought, Soloviev's religious and cultural reflections evince a complex richness or rich complexity. Balthasar shows particular appreciation for its aesthetic (*GL3*, 281) and apocalyptic (*GL3*, 296) strands, as well as what he takes to be their synthesis (*GL3*, 335-51). Possibly appreciating in advance a potential problem in reconciling a theodramatic with a theological aesthetic,[79] Balthasar recognizes the tension – whether possible or actual he does not say – between the aesthetic and apocalyptic tendencies. He judges, however, that Soloviev remains faithfully within the orbit of 'cosmic liturgy' (*GL3*, 287-88), definitively rendered in the christological-trinitarianism of Maximus the Confessor, while generalizing Maximus' dythelite Christology to underwrite the hospitality to anything of value in culture. Looking back from the vantage point of Balthasar's defense of the *analogia entis* in his Barth book, it is possible to see that this defense of culture and its discourses was at least an aspect of Balthasar's agenda in *Cosmic Liturgy*. The linkage between Bulgakov and Soloviev is here transparent, for the ability to protect the integrity of culture by bringing culture within this particular kind of christological – and as it turns out, trinitarian – bracket is ascribed to Bulgakov in *Theo-Drama*. But Balthasar responds with just as much enthusiasm to the apocalyptic figuration of history (*GL3*, 340-41), which Soloviev shares with Dostoyevski (*GL3*, 351). History is a battle-field of religious ideas in general and ideas of salvation and the savior-figure in particular.[80] Such figuration represents a redress to an aesthetic turned complacent, and thus enlistable in a program that is foreign to biblical truth, a phenomenon, which Balthasar is persuaded is also evinced by Romanticism. It is Christ who, as the still-point of history, is also paradoxically responsible for its agonism: Christ is the sign of contradiction who provokes antagonism. The essential figure of such antagonism is the Anti-Christ. In this figure is enfolded all that would deny Christ, say otherwise, and dissimulate.

Balthasar's treatment of Soloviev becomes truly pertinent to the figuration of Bulgakov, when he considers objections to Soloviev's thought that reasonably might be thought to apply also to that of Bulgakov. There are essentially three objections, all of which have to do with intellectual debts that threaten to vitiate Soloviev's possible contribution to theology, and in effect assimilate him to Berdyaev: (a) Soloviev is too indebted to the esoteric traditions, which is the breeding ground for sophiological speculation (*GL3*, 291-92); (b) Soloviev owes too much to the Valentinian tradition (*GL3*, 284-85, 291-93, 305); and finally, (c) Soloviev does not transcend his Idealist heritage and more specifically that of Hegel (*GL3*, 282-83, 287-88, 295, 300-02, 331). Balthasar does not go into any detail as to how these strands might relate and help to construct an anti-Christian entity. He does not feel he needs to, since in his view Soloviev is innocent of all charges.

With respect to Soloviev's borrowings from the esoteric tradition, which includes Boehme, Swedenborg, and the Christian Kabbalah, Balthasar is more than understanding. In a verdict of exoneration that is as apodictic as it is implausible, he suggests that Soloviev's Christianity remains unaffected 'because in reading all of these and many others he fully appropriates them for himself, thus the muddy waters run through him as if through a purifying agent and is distilled in crystal-clear, disinfected waters' (*GL3*, 291-92). Similarly, whatever Soloviev's borrowings from Valentinianism – especially with respect to sophiology – they do not compromise the Christian integrity of his thought. This judgment, however, is asserted in the teeth of Balthasar's recognition of the unfortunate tendency in Soloviev to identify creation with evil (*GL3*, 311). Whether this Christianly objectionable identification is a wobble or systemic infraction depends, for Balthasar, in large part whether this identification serves a theogonic construal of the divine, which palpably it does in the traditions upon which Berdyaev calls, that is, Boehme, Hegel, the late Schelling and, of course, Gnosticism, at least insofar as Gnosticism is subjected to the kind of dynamic developmental interpretation fairly typical of speculative thought from the early nineteenth century on. Without arguing the point,

Balthasar's verdict is that the identification does not play this role (*GL3*, 305-07). Accordingly, here we are dealing with wobble rather than deformation. It is a matter of no little interest that here Balthasar very much assumes Irenaeus' theogonic reading of Valentinianism. Dissociating Soloviev from Idealism is, obviously, for Balthasar, the most urgent hermeneutic task, for in modernity it is Idealism that essentially purloins Christian discourse, and 'doctors' it. Balthasar remarks on Soloviev's rejection of philosophy as a master discourse, on his refusal to embrace monism (*GL3*, 283-85) and the views of necessity, eros, and kenosis that both underwrite and explicate it (*GL3*, 296-97). And finally, he sees Soloviev as supporting a form of trinitarian thought quite different from that of Hegel despite similar dynamic surfaces (*GL3*, 306-07), and plausibly similar ancestors in Boehme and Leibniz (*GL3*, 309-12).

Reading forward to and backward from Bulgakov makes this essay on Soloviev at least as much an essay on Bulgakov as on the generative Russian thinker. In fact, with little exaggeration this essay, which puts Soloviev in such illustrious company, could be regarded as an essay on Bulgakov by proxy. Not only is Soloviev's thought aesthetic and dramatic in a Christianly requisite way, so also is that of Bulgakov. Not only Soloviev's thought non-esoteric, non-Valentinian, and non-Idealist, so also is that of Bulgakov. And, then, given Soloviev's apocalyptic designation of the Anti-Christ as the figure of the lie, one has to entertain the possibility that what is spoken of as a distinction is on the cusp of being a contradiction: it is difficult not to believe that even within the confines of this essay Balthasar thinks that the above mentioned modes of thought represent significant – if not supreme – instances of the lie. If I am right, then, what can be affirmed of Soloviev cannot be denied Bulgakov. Indeed, it is possible to go one step further: since Bulgakov represents the completion or actualization of Soloviev, something like a 'so much the more clause' is effectively in operation, constituting Bulgakov in a quite literal sense as a hyperbole of Soloviev, that is, a movement of amplification beyond the origin of an audaciously experimental, although ultimately orthodox, line of Christian reflection. Nothing except unseemly hesitation postpones the verdict that Bulgakov is constitutively anti-Hegelian and anti-Valentinian, and thus a candidate for paternity. Arguably, the postponement is even more unjustifiable, when one calls to mind once again the full extent and depth of Bulgakov's contribution to Balthasar's thought, and the anti-Hegelian spin to which many of Bulgakov's ideas are subjected within the trilogy. Still, scruple is called for. In the end Bulgakov is considerably less focused in a negative way on Hegel than is Staudenmaier and after him Balthasar. It is as much the extremity of Staudenmaier's focus in which Hegel effectively becomes the lie of lies as the extent of his rebuttal across the entire Christian narrative that makes him a father in the proper sense. And, of course, we cannot ignore Staudenmaier's genealogical or counter-genealogical efforts in which the systematic Hegelian distortion is traced back to ancient sources, of which Gnostic sources are the most prominent. Notwithstanding Bulgakov's commitment to the Anti-Christ figure, and his interpretation of this figure primarily in terms of the lie, the sense, displayed in their different contexts by Staudenmaier and Irenaeus, of what is at stake when Christianity has to sort out originals from simulacra, is not as keen.

Does this mean that in the end after all his promise Bulgakov is simply not a father? But a denial of paternity seems unjustified, given the way Balthasar saves this particular Russian tradition, which neo-patristic orthodox thought would not consider worth saving, and given the critical way Bulgakov is deployed in the second two parts of the trilogy. Perhaps like home runs in baseball, one could put Bulgakov's paternity in asterisks. This, of course, would amount to sheer avoidance if nothing further were said. The asterisks in this context would mean that Bulgakov does not fully satisfy all the criteria of being an anti-Hegelian father, and that in consequence Bulgakov cannot be regarded as an anti-Hegelian father of the same level as Staudenmaier, whose large-frame genealogies of the return of apocalyptic and Gnosticism in modernity and narrower-frame genealogy of the internal relation between Luther and Hegel are not replicated by the Russian thinker. As an anticipation of the linkage in Balthasar between substantive rebuttal of Hegel and genealogical situating of an anamorphosis of Christianity, Staudenmaier has no equal.

Still, as one grapples here with the issue of fatherhood and, obviously, also to some extent with the issue of criteria for ascription, one is reminded of Heidegger's delphic announcement of what subsequently became a hermeneutic axiom: 'higher than actuality is possibility.' The excess of Bulgakov over Staudenmaier as a resister of 'counterfeit doubles' lies in a number of different areas. First, among equals is both the formal and material apocalyptic nature of his thought, which has both positive and negative dimensions. Like Balthasar, Bulgakov thinks that the Johannine corpus is the pinnacle of biblical witness,[81] and as such the realization of the prophetic and the canonic apocalyptic tradition. Accordingly, Revelation is the text of vision that gives witness to the paschal mystery and presents the only horizon that is wide enough for it, that is, the infinite horizon of the triune God of love. Like Balthasar also, Revelation is not only a text that does not license either messianism or speculative gnosis, it competes with them in two ways: its vision is yet faith not knowledge, and central to its visionary apparatus is figuring the Anti-Christ in terms of the lie (*BL*, 329-30). A second way in which Bulgakov exceeds Staudenmaier as a resource is that whatever his deficits with respect to theological correctness, Bulgakov is an aesthetic theologian who grasps that the vision (apocalypse) of glory is central to Christian witness, and that this glory concerns its kenotic obscuration on the cross and the descent into hell (*BL*, 343-44, 389, 392, 405), as well as the promise that the Lamb will be all in all, nothing short of alpha and omega (*BL*, 384-85). Moreover, divine glory is intended to suffuse the cosmos, rather than leaving it behind. Not only is the glory of human body left behind by neither, neither is the prospect of the transfiguration of the cosmos into 'new heaven and earth.' Revelation 21 is crucial to both, as they imaginatively attempt to render an account of the world of glorification, while acknowledging all the while, the essential unthinkability of this world. As with Balthasar, Bulgakov remains within the fold of Maximus' 'cosmic liturgy,' only to add the eschatological emphasis, and amplify the doxological element that marks the separation from speculative thought. If the biblical and aesthetic bases of his critical relation to speculative thought are the two main advantages Bulgakov has over Staudenmaier as a precursor of Balthasar's critique of speculative thought, arguably, there is a third and final advantage to be taken into consideration. This concerns the very nature of a theology which to a significant extent privileges the Fourth Gospel and Revelation. Often denounced as overly speculative, both theologians think that these texts of images keep theology open, because the images constitutionally demand exploration that is interminable. Thus the open-endedness of theology even in the act of resistance to speculative thought. One does not contend with a closed theological system by appeal to another closed theological system, constituted by ineluctables and certitudes. Theology is a probative as well as anamnetic discipline, the one because the other.

If not actually, then virtually Bulgakov is a Balthasarian father. Indeed, as a virtual father, he is significantly superior to Staudenmaier. As a virtual father he is not really a second modern father, but in a real sense the first. Bulgakov and Staudenmaier represent competing firsts, and one favors one over the other depending on whether the register is that of actuality or possibility. Since on the level of pragmatics I favor the first option, I have thought it best to deal with Bulgakov's paternity credentials separately and not try to fold them directly into a taxonomic-genetic account. To allow for paternity of any sort, no matter how qualified, means that the issue of the relation between the modern father of Balthasar and the ancient father of Balthasar comes into view. Now Irenaeus is not an oft quoted source in Bulgakov. Where Irenaeus is mentioned, the contexts seem essentially to be those of the paschal mystery and Irenaeus' view of divinization. In *Theo-Logic 3*, in a rich discussion on the Trinity Balthasar links them more globally, by situating Bulgakov within the context of Irenaeus' theology of the 'two hands' (165 ff). As he suggests this, Balthasar neither can have forgotten that the *oikonomia* is asserted against Valentinianism's denial of a real incarnation and the possibility of a tradition that would not be the tradition of a secret, nor that an economic trinitarianism will always be called on to stand firm against a trinitarianism that deletes mystery from the triune God's acts in history by explaining them as ingredient in the concept of such a God.

Nonetheless, much of what Balthasar writes in *Theo-Logic 3* suggests that Balthasar believes that Bulgakov represents a genuine deepening of what is only inchoate in Irenaeus, thus a genuine supplement. What I have called the 'theo-logic of supplementarity' applies in Bulgakov's case, as it does in the case of Staudenmaier, and undoubtedly also Balthasar.[82] Of course, this also raises the issue of whether and how Balthasar supplements Bulgakov as an anti-Hegelian and anti-Valentinian father. At some level, Balthasar supplements Bulgakov in the same way in which he supplements any other Christian thinker, by adding and subtracting, usually more the former than the latter. Balthasar is systemically a genealogist of speculative misremembering in a way that Bulgakov is not and, accordingly, is much more intensely focused on a modernity that encourages misremembering as well as forgetting. Balthasar also manages to provide an exhaustive description of speculative forms of thought as paradigmatic instances of dissimulation, and finally forges a deeper connection with the aesthetic and apocalyptic dimensions of Christianity. As I also indicated, however, from a formal or logical point of view, Balthasar can also be considered as supplemented by Bulgakov. *Theo-Logic 3* suggests, however, that the issue of who supplements whom may not remain purely formal. Despite or because of the fact that Balthasar agrees with Bulgakov's assessment of the 'trinitarian inversion' (*TL3*, 34; also *TD3*, 183-4), namely that in the economy it is the Spirit who empowers Christ and that in the immanent Trinity the Son is a condition of the procession of the Spirit, Balthasar sees that problems open up on two fronts, that of the *filioque* (*TL3*, 215-17), and how one is to envisage the activity of the Spirit or speak or fail to speak to its relative autonomy. Here not only are the confessional differences between Catholicism and Eastern orthodoxy most in play, but there is real rivalry between trinitarian forms of apocalyptic that redress the Idealist tradition in addressing the contemporary world. At the most general and formal level these differences would not be unwelcome by a Balthasar who spends considerable time in *Theo-Logic 3* advising about the mutual supplementarity of Western and Eastern trinitarian schemes. For it would indicate among other things that there is no definitive theological system, and that the orthodox tradition need not be considered as monolithically uniform. The tradition is a conversation and argument within the brackets provided by Christ as God's definitive gift of self and the wild and dynamic life of the Spirit.

An exceptionally dialogical Bulgakov would not disagree. Agreement would not involve either the flattening of conversation or the excision of argument. Without going down the Photian line, and without mixing shibboleth with genuine theological reservation, it is still possible to find Western trinitarianism too binary, and to call for a correction.[83] The probe made by Bulgakov in *The Comforter* in particular applies to Balthasar's own trinitarian articulation, even as the Swiss theologian professes the essential complementarity of Western and Eastern modes of trinitarian thought. These differences are by no means a function of the need to resist speculative thought; they are different ways of remembering the God who loves us utterly and whose love calls forth practical and discursive responses that cannot be reduced to a programmatic unity.[84] But as John Milbank has indicated,[85] what might be called the 'second difference,' that is, the difference between the Son and the Spirit, can make a difference in resistance, for it takes away from Hegelian modes of thought what might be thought to be its constitutive advantage, its affirmation of and expansive treatment of the Spirit. Of course, this second difference specifies itself also on the plane of the economy. Bulgakov shows that an undeveloped pneumatology is not a requirement in combatting either Joachimite pneumatology or Valentinian pneumatism, and that it can be extrapolated from the Johannine sources that Balthasar privileges. *The Bride of the Lamb* is self-evidently on the other side of Joachimism and Valentinianism. It is crucial for Bulgakov that Christ effects salvation on our behalf and that the salvation effected is definitive (*BL*, 339). Indeed, this remains true even in the glorification when the kenotic form of Christ is removed. It cannot be otherwise: the cross constitutes nothing less than the enhypostatic image of the Trinity (*BL*, 414). Similarly, in his discussion of John 14:17-18 Bulgakov insists that sanctification comes through Christ (*BL*, 404; also 389). Importantly, however, in both the case of glorification and sanctification more generally considered, Bulgakov believes that the Holy Spirit is a crucial actor. With respect to the glorification of the world, Bulgakov proposes:

> *The parousia signifies not only the power of the Incarnation but also of Pentecost, of Christ in glory and glory in Christ, the appearance in Him, with Him, and through Him of the Holy Spirit. (BL, 399)*

If it is no less true in the case of Bulgakov than it is for Balthasar and before him, Irenaeus, that the Spirit cannot be limited to Pentecost, Bulgakov does not wish to cede Pentecost to the pneumatic fringes of the Christian tradition or to Hegelian speculation, either its presuppositions, or the practical and aesthetic discourses that it makes possible. For the Russian theologian regards both the historical materialism of Marx and the apocalyptic poetry of the Russian Symbolist poet Alexander Blok, who in *The Twelve* uses Revelation as a revolutionary subtext,. as having its roots in this kind of speculation.[86] And just in that part of his text in which Bulgakov insists on Christ's role in sanctification, and on the identity of the Spirit as the Spirit of Christ, he also insists that in John and in the Gospels in general the Spirit is regarded from the beginning as active in the life and ministry of Christ, precisely as a condition of the glorification of Christ in the parousia (*BL*, 406). From this, Bulgakov draws the conclusion that the parousia consists of the manifestation of the glory of the Spirit as well as the Son. Here Bulgakov seems to offer a more satisfying instance of the Catholic 'both-and' than Balthasar himself.

Within the overall horizon of apocalyptic theology, there are any number of differences in emphases between Balthasar and Bulgakov when it comes to considering Christ's descent into hell. This is even more true when it comes to presenting eschatological transformation, specifically the identity of the world transformed and sorting out whether sin as well as death is a prominent feature to be overcome. These emphases are not trivial, even if they presuppose a remarkable commonness of vision and theological style. Still, none of these emphases bear on the critical potential to critique the speculative discourses of modernity, of which Hegel is first among equals. Another difference in emphasis does bear on the critical capacity of Christianity to mount a counterattack on speculative thought that would bleed Christian discourse, action, and forms of life of their authority by reinterpreting its symbols and reshaping its narrative, and by encouraging other practices and forms of life. While Balthasar and Bulgakov think of the church as the site of tradition, neither think of the church as its agent. The agency can only be divine and involves in complex ways Christ and the Spirit. In both cases the point is sometimes made quite straightforwardly.

But, as with Balthasar, Bulgakov sometimes suggests a notion of *traditio* that arises from a reflection on the mystery of the *communio sanctorum* that has roots in reflection on Holy Saturday. Interesting, Bulgakov makes an even more forceful case for the importance of this notion than Balthasar, whose notion of Holy Saturday far from making concessions to the Gnostic trope of a suffering and fallen divine or Hegel's speculative Good Friday represents a definitive criticism. While Bulgakov understands that the communion of saints represents a deep mystery, he wishes to say that even prior to the resurrection the dead were granted a measure of agency through Christ (*BL*, 362-71). This conviction has obvious consequences also for the mode of agency considered possible before the general resurrection and final judgment. While Balthasar suggests that *en Christo* the dead have agency and thus are no longer in principle invisible and voiceless, Bulgakov can more easily legitimate the traditions of sainthood, meditation, and theological reflection as voices that resound against the larger backdrop of invisibility and voicelessness. The tradition is a powerless power arrayed against death and against what would allay its seriousness by taking away the catastrophe that is absolutely unique in each of our cases. The tradition is a powerless power arrayed against the insurgency of the lie that would whiteout death and whitewash the glorious, but also gloriously uncoercive, truth.

Johann George Hamann (1730-1788): Anti-Hegelian Father in the Subjunctive Mood

IN HIS REFLECTIONS ON HAMANN throughout *Glory of the Lord*, Balthasar shows a decided preference for Hamann over Kierkegaard, not only when it comes to relative adequacy concerning the relation between the aesthetic and the religious (*GL1*, 80-3; *GL3*, 241-42), but also when it comes to resisting Hegel. In suggesting that Kierkegaard's actual critique of Hegel is neither sufficiently well thought out nor theological enough, Balthasar opens the space for a Hamannian critique of Hegel. This despite the fact that Hamann almost inevitably ends to be paired with Kierkegaard as a 'Christian humorist,' given to pseudonym, outlandish irony, and multi-layered prose;[87] despite the fact that he is generally – and not incorrectly – cast as a critic of the Enlightenment constituted in significant part by the 'forgetting' of Christian symbols and narratives (*GL3*, 239); and, finally, despite the fact that in history it is Hegel, who in one of the longest pieces he ever wrote on an individual thinker,[88] critically evaluates Hamann, who had been dead for forty years. Hamann's critique of Hegel, then, can only be virtual rather than actual. Indeed, its vitality is of an order different from that of Bulgakov who, although in its wake, does manage to distance himself from German Idealism, even if with less vehemence than Staudenmaier and Balthasar himself. Balthasar is not enough of a postmodern sophisticate to justify the anachronism philosophically, and to the degree to which he allows it, he also tames it in fundamental respects. Hegelian dialectic is the natural fall-out of Luther's theology of the cross; Hamann's aesthetic is the road that could have been taken, albeit under the general condition that this form of Lutheranism not separate itself entirely from the larger 'catholic' tradition (*GL1*, 49-50). Both Hamann and Hegel represent two of the more theologically focused attempts to overcome the depletion of Christianity's symbol and narrative, effected by Enlightenment thought, whose neglect of presupposition and ignoring of context and history, were both fed by and led to a truncated view of reason. Nonetheless, as they articulate their response, even as they materially share a christological focus that features Golgotha and the trope of kenosis, and a trinitarian horizon that features the economy, and even as they formally present a vision of reality of absolutely encompassing scope, the bases from which they articulate their vision, the warrants provided for the authority of their discourse and their view of their status differ so utterly as essentially to be parabolic. I will touch on all of these points even as I favor Balthasar's substantive discussion of the figure of Christ.

In his forty page essay on Hamann in *Glory of the Lord 3*, although Balthasar shows familiarity with Hamann's entire oeuvre, including Hamann's very important meta-critical response to the First Critique,[89] it is evident that in order the three most important texts for the Swiss theologian are *Aesthetica in nuce* (1762), *Golgotha und Scheblimini* (1784), and *London Schriften* (1759).[90] To render an adequate theological aesthetic, Hamann must be at the very least both irreducibly and rigorously christocentric. Irreducibility requires that Christian faith, which responds to the event of salvation in Christ as disclosive of the truth of all reality, not be captured in some larger explanatory scheme as is the wont in German Idealism and speculative precursors. In *Glory of the Lord 1*, Balthasar is eloquent about this all-too-real danger:

> *Aesthetics may likewise be removed from theology by means of a "dialectical" system which would conceive God as exteriorizing himself in nothingness and in that which is his opposite, a God who, therefore, contains his own nothingness and his opposite within himself. Jacob Böhme, Schelling, and Hegel elaborated such a view (in a misuse of the mystical tradition). In this way, the Protestant principle gives back to the old Neoplatonic theoria, which, by means of an aesthetic overview of the whole, is able to reconcile in God himself the final contradiction, now intensified to the extremity of heaven and hell as required by the Christian vision. (GL1, 49-50)*

The general contrast between Hamann and Hegel made a little later in the text (*GL1*, 80-3) makes it clear that Hamann is the figure in post-Enlightenment Protestantism who serves as the internal judge of theological illegitimacy. German Idealism fails miserably the aesthetic test by including Christianity in a larger scheme. Of course, not only German Idealism, but German Romanticism also fails the aesthetic test, and consequently acquires, as we showed in chapter 1, the designation of 'aesthetic theology.' And equally, the governing discourse may be described otherwise than 'neo-Platonism,' which is the preferred choice of the above quotation. Throughout we have seen that apocalyptic, Valentinianism, and even Kabbalah are real genealogical contenders. In any event, with *Aesthetica in nuce (GL3*, 241-43) and *Golgotha und Scheblimini* (*GL3*, 246, 251) particularly in mind, Balthasar thinks that Hamann proposes a theology of the cross in which majesty and abasement are truly objective and as such forever remain inreconcilable and mysterious.[91] Insisting on this point, Balthasar underscores how Hamann has essentially undercut any number of modern species of subjectivism. The event of Christ does not depend for its reality on human appropriation, but rather depends upon the witness of the Spirit, which is distinct from any kind of human memory (*GL3*, 245-46). Here, it is difficult not to imagine Hegelian *Erinnerung* being a potential target, even if the proximate targets are more likely to be 18th-century Pietism's emphasis on personal appropriation and rationalism's emphasis on the human subject and specifically on autonomy. The cross is the site of God's remembering of us who in sin risked putting ourselves beyond God's love. It is the cross also that points to God's glorious freedom (*GL3*, 247-48) – necessarily a loving freedom because a free love – and precisely makes impossible a system of explanation. Arguably, it is the cross also that serves to underwrite Hamann's election of the 'fragment' as the instrument of Christian 'truth-telling,' for no comprehensive view of the nature of God is available outside of an interpretation of the biblical text which, if canonic, is also enigmatic.[92]

As Balthasar's much more sustained analysis of Karl Barth shows, irreducibility is a necessary but not sufficient condition of christocentrism. In the case of Hamann, the vision of Christ is the principle of the integration of the movement of reality and the dynamics of all religions and human culture. Balthasar notes with approval that for Hamann, as the grounding Word of all reality, Christ sums up all creation in his redemption, completes pagan wisdom, whether philosophical or literary, Greek or Latin (*GL3*, 274-77), and functions as the magnetic pole of Hebrew scripture (*GL3*, 250-52, 267-72). Despite, or rather because, Hamann has both Alexandrian and Augustinian precedents for the former, and Irenaeus as a precedent for the latter,[93] he is able to grant a relative autonomy to forms of discourse, and also modes of living, that point to Christianity without necessarily representing prolepses of it. It is axiomatic for Balthasar that the incarnation and cross are unanticipatable. Like the church fathers, and like Balthasar himself, Hamann senses a real connection between Christianity and classical forms of glory that has been lost by the Enlightenment. Although he does not spend an extraordinary amount of time on it, Balthasar underscores the particular importance of the figure of Socrates for Hamann as a precursor of Christ (*GL3*, 254, 276). The profession of ignorance in Socrates is anything but disingenuous, and that which draws him daimonically is what precisely cannot be named, the Unknown God that Hegel will later pillory in the *Encyclopedia* and elsewhere.[94] In addition, more conspicuously than any German religious thinker in the latter half of the eighteenth century, Hamann insists on the indefeasible relevance of biblical Judaism for Christianity. However generous Hamann is with respect to Greek and other religions, nothing approaches the intimacy of relationship Christianity enjoys with Judaism as a radically theocentric and prophetic form of religion. In his short essay, Balthasar does not go into details in Hamann's castigation of Mendelssohn's misidentification of his own faith in *Jerusalem* (1783)[95] and Kant's attempt to cut the Gordian Knot between Christianity and Judaism.[96] He does remind, however, of the importance of the biblical text for Hamann, which throughout displays a form of wild unity that bespeaks a divine rather than a human hand. He is mindful also that it is not simply its wildness, but also its simplicity that functions as an objection. The biblical text is a problem for Kant for this reason and, for Balthasar, there is no evidence in the work of German Idealism that it does not continue to be a problem that cannot be sorted out without serious tendencies in an anti-Semitic direction.

For Balthasar, Hamann not only vouchsafes the canon and thus the biblical narrative in its length and breadth, he also justifies a christological or kyriological hermeneutic of scripture, the opposite of the bibliolatry of the Reformation and the rationalistic reduction to historical, philological, or moral sense that came to commonplaces in Hamann's day (*GL3*, 243). Balthasar confines himself to making the general point and does not harp on the ways in which Hamann thinks of scripture as code or cryptogram to be cracked. He does not go into any particular detail about Hamann's polemic against Mendelssohn's and Kant's reduction of Hebrew scripture and the entire Bible respectively to the moral sense.[97] Nor does he speak directly to Hamann's debate with the orientalist, J. D. Michaelis, who introduces a version of historical-critical method into German thought,[98]although we know from both *Glory of the Lord 6 & 7* and *Theo-Drama 2* just how important this particular shift in mode of interpretation is for him.[99] Balthasar can only approve of a hermeneutic sensibility that he sees, with de Lubac, as characteristic of the early church. He can only approve of an interpretive sensibility that both probes and waits on scripture for delivering meaning and truth. The subtitle of *Aesthetica in nuce*, that is, 'A Rhapsody in Kabbalistic Prose,' affirms the hidden dimension of the biblical text that does not give itself immediately. And yet, crucially for Hamann, 'kabbalistic' interpretation is not allegoresis, but the seeking of Christ in the text. It certainly does not involve, as it does with his contemporary Oetinger,[100] a commitment to a form of Christian Kabbalah that essentially unfolds a theogony. More specifically, scripture is anything but Hegel's wax nose;[101] nor is it resolvable into a narrative code that includes the plain sense of the history of salvation as is the case in Hegel's trinitarian articulations from the *Phenomenology* on, and which Hegel variously identifies as Neoplatonic, Kabbalistic, and Gnostic.[102] On Balthasar's grounds, Hamann's exegesis, whether with or without the Kabbalistic qualification, is Origenistic rather than Hegelian,[103] even if both overcome the more egregious Reformation and Enlightenment contractions to the historical sense.

Although, for Balthasar, the Trinity is more horizon than focus in the thought of Hamann, Hamann's theological aesthetics encourages him to be so deeply trinitarian as to make him eccentric to the main Lutheran tradition, as well as to propose an alternative to the Enlightenment substitutes to confessional forms of Protestant thought which constructed the doctrine of the Trinity as obscurantist and reactionary. Unlike Hegel, who often is credited with singlehandedly bringing back the Trinity into modern Christian thought, Hamann in general avoids speaking of the immanent Trinity, and resists conjugating the relation between the trinitarian economy and the triune God *in se* other than to insist that the economy genuinely discloses who God is. The economic Trinity is, then, ontological, and one is not to imagine an absolute separation between the economic and immanent Trinity, as if the economic Trinity were merely the screen upon which an unknowable divine played. Importantly, neither can the economic and immanent Trinity be identified. There has to be enough separation to guarantee the gratuitousness of creation, redemption, and sanctification. Balthasar states explicitly that in this respect Hamann is Hegel's other, whose thought is ruled by the logic of 'ground and appearance' in which appearance is the necessary expression of the ground (*GL3*, 248).[104] Balthasar's validation of Hamann's trinitarian thought goes well beyond what he says in *Glory of the Lord*. In *Theo-Logic 2 & 3*, which throughout contest Hegel's trinitarianism, Balthasar redeploys with more polemical force an observation about Hamann's trinitarianism he seems to make in passing in his essay: the Son is the exegesis of the Father (*GL3*, 247), and the Spirit is the witness. Balthasar explicitly acknowledges the Johannine provenance of such language, and insists that far from such trinitarian language providing a pretext for a speculative takeover, whether Valentinian or Hegelian, it provides the most capable defense against it.

Now whether this Johannine Hamann is finally construed as aesthetic without remainder is an interesting question in light of Balthasar's treatment of Hamann in *Apokalypse*, in which he was cast as a biblical apocalypticist at odds with the Romantic and Idealist flora and fauna that play fast and loose with Christianity.[105] Even if Balthasar does not speak to Hamann's own apocalyptic self-styling as a witness and a judge of his age, Hamann certainly is a prophetic figure out of kilter with his rationalist age, and not inclined towards the Prometheanism of the emerging alternatives. Now whether or not in his depiction of Hamann in *Glory of the Lord* there is an echo of this styling, a dramatic and an apocalyptic Hamann can be got at through an examination of Balthasar's highlighting of the role of kenosis in Hamann's fragmentary oeuvre. In discussing what most scholars would agree is the central trope of Hamann's rendering of Christ (*GL3*, 249-53), without altogether neglecting the *London Writings*, Balthasar tends to favor *Aesthetica in nuce* and the later *Golgotha in Scheblimini*, which Hegel judged to be Hamann's best realized text, although each is infuriatingly obscurantist, a 'balled fist' that could do with unclenching. Although, as one would expect, Philippians 2:5-11 proves pivotal for Hamann, the horizon of Hamann's understanding is broadly Johannine. Golgotha, which is God's first kenosis, already contains within itself *Scheblimini*, 'Sit thou at my right hand' (*GL3*, 250). This gives an essentially eschatological apocalyptic twist to the glory of the cross of the Fourth Gospel, even if the reference is not explicitly to Revelation. Balthasar rightly understands that this text, which had as its proximate target Mendelssohn's ethical reduction of biblical Judaism, and thus by implication the ethical reduction of the Bible as a whole, is apocalyptic. Hamann reinscribes what the rationalist, Mendelssohn, had removed from serious consideration in his reflection on Jerusalem, that is, the eschatological nature of the City of God in which sin and death are overcome through the sacrifice of the Lamb and those who witness to him. For Balthasar, Hamann clearly understands himself as one of these witnesses (*GL3*, 271). By so doing, one can say, that not only does he effect a biblical 'absorption of the world,' but a specifically apocalyptical absorption of the world. For Balthasar, as well as Hamann, the symbolic nature of Revelation suggests that the only true and proper reading of the text is to read oneself, society, indeed, the whole world into it.

Balthasar recognizes that the Cross, as the 'first' kenosis, does not stand alone, but unfolds – and maybe enfolds – a series. Creation can be understood under the auspices of divine self-humiliation,[106] as long as the Christian thinker does not regard divine self-humiliation as other than gratuitous and ingredient in an economic or erotic network. Balthasar also notes the humility of the Spirit, who in the Bible condescends to speak in the idiom of human being, indeed, the idiom of children (*GL3*, 253). Hamann is instructive for Balthasar in that while kenosis proves to be a regulative feature of reality, precisely insofar as it is love, it is non-Hegelian in that it is not an iterative operation calculated to issue in the perfection of an erotic divine. On Balthasar's account, kenosis for Hamann is not only not a pattern of concept-formation coextensive with reality, but in the strict sense not a concept, but a mark of the irradicable contradiction at the center of Christian faith. Hamann offers then with Bulgakov a Christian precedent for employing kenosis as a central figure of Christian faith, and suggesting an alternative to the way the figure gets deployed in Hegel's speculative system. But he is more like Irenaeus than Bulgakov, whom Balthasar expressly links with Irenaeus in *Theo-Logic.* That is, Hamann's opposition *avant la lettre* to Hegelian deployment of kenosis, is focused on the trinitarian economy, and does not concern itself with the immanent Trinity. From Balthasar's point of view, Bulgakov is in excess of Hamann on this point, and although his view of 'ur-kenosis' is risky, it is necessarily so. One cannot contend with Hegel without elaborating a doctrine of God, which while faithful to the tradition is also explorative and probative.

From *Apokalypse* on, Balthasar was persuaded that although Idealism represented the closed system *par excellence*, rhetorically it came off as more imaginative and interrogative than classical theology, which more concertedly avowed the mystery of God and our search for that superabundant reality that we have already found, or better, who has already found us. For Balthasar, this does not mean that the fragment as such is alethic, and that any large-scale story such as narrated by the Bible must necessarily be false. Hamann's avowal of the fragment gives testimony to the perspectival nature of perception,[107] but also that truth is expressed in a part as much as a whole. Balthasar reads Hamann as being convinced that this is as true – if not more true – of the biblical text as it is of pagan texts, while at the same time the biblical text does provide something like an overarching narrative. But with respect to this overarching narrative, we do not have epistemic mastery. We neglect at our peril the truth that the Bible is the condescension of the Spirit to our discursive condition. Neither, however, can the Bible be regarded as a text to satisfy curiosity; it is a text to live by, or even a text to live within. Hamann articulates then, less a postmodern alternative to Hegel – at least of a Derridian kind – than an Irenaean one in which the status of the Bible is not impugned, and any self-certification belongs to the Spirit who moves us and whom we do not master. Which is not to suggest that Hamann cannot be postmodern in some fundamental respects, as Milbank has suggested, and John Betz has recently filled out. A trait of the postmodern is anachronisticity that in the logical scheme of things counts against a discourse having critical purchase. But Hamann, bolstered by Irenaeus and John's Gospel, is against Hegel before the fact, as against Gnosticism after the fact.

Hamann, then, as well as Bulgakov is a virtual father of Balthasar in his resistance to the Hegelian brand of aesthetics and apocalyptic. As I have suggested, they also complement as well as supplement each other. In addition, singly and together they also complement Staudenmaier, an actual Hegelian father, who scores Hegel's trinitarian narrative throughout his career. They also supplement him by operating within a biblical frame of reference, which while it despises nothing in scripture, has essentially a Johannine horizon, focused on the heavenly Lamb as at once the eschatological and historical figure. Hamann and Bulgakov make it clear to Balthasar that the battle against Hegelian apocalypse and the Hegelian purloining of John has to be fought with apocalyptic and by taking John back from those who would gnosticize it. This means that Revelation becomes with the Fourth Gospel the supreme anti-Gnostic text. In these hugely important respects, while neither can be defined as a Hegel-critic as such, Hamann and Bulgakov offer sketches of a critical optic within which Balthasar can articulate a Staudenmaier critique that unites theological objection and genealogical naming. As Hamann and Bulgakov are closer to Balthasar than Staudenmaier on these fronts, they also more nearly recall Irenaeus, whose optic is christological and whose tendency is genealogical. The son of all four fathers, as a kind of orchestration of resistance to misremembering, Balthasar, I have implied, is in some real sense their father. He is a whole that is yet more than the sum of its parts, yet also in some sense less than any of them. Certainly less than the Johannine corpus, which is adequate to the mystery it ciphers.

Chapter 5

Hegelian and Valentinian Paternity of Contemporary Theological Thought

The Anatomy of Misremembering

As the language of the Trinity turns out to be the language of fathers and sons – albeit a language that is revised to suit the immateriality of eternity and its non-gendered nature – the language of father and sons is ineluctably trinitarian: lines of paternity and filiation flow intelligibly but non-necessarily within the brackets of trinitarian *traditio*. Thus far I have excavated Balthasar's paternity with respect to the aspect of this complex theological task that consists of detecting and refuting a rarefied mythological doubling of the Christian narrative as this is presented in scripture, and over the centuries proved regulative for worship and thought in the Christian community. Balthasar by no means presumes that Hegel's 'speculative transcription' of Christianity is the only such mythological doubling in the modern period, or even the only kind of doubling but, from his perspective, it enjoys a theological authority that no other doubling bears, whether that of Boehme, Schelling, or Berdyaev. The obvious question is, why pay so much attention to a figure who belongs to the past and thus in a sense is dead? Or otherwise put, how dead is Hegel? Is he constituted without remainder by the mausoleum of his texts, and immured in the academy with its discursive rituals? Balthasar would in fact welcome a positive answer, since it would essentially remove a significant aspect of the negative side of the theological task. But Hegel has not been mummified, and become spectacle. Hegel is disseminated; he lives on in many philosophical sons. But, for Balthasar, Hegel also has many theological sons. It is just here that one faces into the wind of a paradox. On the one hand, Balthasar is one of the more facile labelers; in passing just about anyone can be called an apocalypticist, a deficient kind of Neoplatonist, and a Gnostic. On the other, Balthasar is a genealogist of extraordinary scruple for whom such ascriptions should not be made lightly. This is the Balthasar, who usually wins out over the more facile Balthasar, for whom it is intolerable that a candidate for a particular taxonomy not be given the benefit of the doubt. This is especially the case when it comes to the ascription of Valentinianism: if there are lies and damn lies, then Valentinianism is a damn lie. To be Hegelian in essential respects means that this verdict follows automatically.

Now, as it is important for Balthasar to suggest that there might be more than one modern product of a Valentinian seed, it is equally important to hypothesize that there is more than one contemporary theological product of the seed of Hegel. Multiplicity in both cases serve as a stimulus and warrant for his entire apotropaic program. Nonetheless, the claim of multiplicity gains a hearing if and only if there is something like a demonstration of sonship in a particular case. A good argument can be made that in *Theo-Drama* and in *Theo-Logic* it is Moltmann who fulfills this role. It is important – if not necessary – that Moltmann not repeat Hegel in all respects; otherwise there would be the illusion that sonship functions like a syllogism. Balthasar is anxious to underscore the differences between Moltmann and Hegel, but asks whether these differences offset the fearful symmetry that can be observed between Moltmann's and Hegel's tampering with the Christian narrative and the manifold changes rung on the traditional conceptions of creation, redemption, and sanctification, and ultimately on the doctrine of God. For Balthasar, Moltmann is a Hegelian theologian with a Christian bad conscience. He recognizes that it would not take much for Moltmann to tip the balance and constitute himself as a Christian theologian with a Hegelian bad conscience. On a bad day, Balthasar might be prepared to provide this description of Bulgakov's thought; on a not so good day Balthasar might be prepared to render this verdict on the thought of Soloviev, who is very much regarded as Bulgakov's father. Only a fine line divides the one category from the other; and Moltmann and the Russians all walk the razor's edge.[1] The razor's edge calls up an apocalyptic horizon. Only a hermeneutic prosecuted within an apocalyptic horizon can make such fine discriminations, can see clearly and judge properly. The questions addressed to a theology are whether speculative forms of theology sufficiently resist Hegelian and Valentinian thought as they engage it, or whether in the final instance they illustrate a Hegelian narrative code?[2]

Reluctant Genealogy: Sifting

WHATEVER BALTHASAR'S TENDENCY TOWARDS censoriousness, even occasional dyspepsia, the reluctance fully to exclude particular theological expressions from the tradition is a typical feature of his thought. This is evinced in his rehabilitative reading of Pseudo-Dionysius in *Glory of the Lord 2*, where his earlier concerns about the radicality of Dionysian apophasis and christological underdetermination disappear as Pseudo-Dionysius is proposed as an exemplar of a Christian theological aesthetics and thus by definition a theologian who is kataphatically oriented and christologically centered.[3] The same reluctance to exclude is manifested in his readings of Meister Eckhart and Cusa in *Glory of the Lord 5*.[4] Both are roundly criticized for their identity-metaphysic predilection. Yet their infractions are judged in the end not to merit dismissal from the horizon of the tradition, which is the horizon of possible interpretation of the mystery of God disclosed in Jesus Christ. This reluctance to condemn in an outright fashion is also at play throughout *Theo-Drama* and *Theo-Logic* in the reserve Balthasar shows in terms of critical evaluation of those thinkers, particularly of a theological stripe, who are read as belonging to the Hegelian tradition. While to be judged as belonging to Hegelian tradition cannot be regarded as anything other than a fundamental criticism, Balthasar's principle of 'catholic' inclusiveness ensures that he will recognize and acknowledge counterweights in the theologian determined to be a good candidate for consideration as an offspring of Hegel. This principle seems to be acutely in operation in Balthasar's brief treatment of Jüngel in *Theo-Drama 5* (225, 229) in which after associating Jüngel with Moltmann, in much the way Milbank does later,[5] and suggesting the appropriateness of listing a Hegelian patrimony, Balthasar seems to back off the claim in fact without ever, however, actually withdrawing it. Backing off the claim is a function of not producing its argumentative and evidentiary warrants. Although Balthasar can incline sometimes to casualness in assertion, the claim that a theologian is in the Hegelian line is too serious to encourage it. But even more importantly, Balthasar's treatment of Jüngel contrasts significantly with his treatment of Moltmann. Hedges and caveats there are a plenty, but it would be impossible to read the Balthasar of *Theo-Drama 4 & 5* and *Theo-Logic 3* as not prosecuting a case against Moltmann.

The avoidance in the case of Jüngel is eloquent, if not necessarily informative. For Balthasar, it is obvious that *God as the Mystery of the World* is a representative text (*TD4*, 223, 225). Yet, while

Balthasar underscores Jüngel's interpretation of Hegel, he neither critically evaluates it, nor reflects on whether and in what way Jüngel could be understood to modify German Idealism. Again, while Balthasar comments in passing on Jüngel's relationship to his putative theological father, Karl Barth (*TD5*, 239), he does not address an issue that would be *de rigueur* for a Barth aficionado. What is the measure of Barth in Jüngel's work in general, and in his trinitarian thought in particular?[6] Do Barth's scriptural and christological principles constrain the embrace of Hegel's 'death of God' theology, such that it admits of genealogical and existential interpretation, but not of the kind of ontological reading Hegel provides? And is Jüngel's insistence on trinitarian event at one with the best impulses of Luther's and Barth's trinitarian thought, or reflective of a desire to follow Hegel in trading in Parmenides for Heraclitus by replacing a metaphysics of Being with a metaphysics of Becoming?[7]All these questions, which are so obviously in Balthasar's range, are avoided. One can only hypothesize why. Ambivalence towards Jüngel's project represents a possible answer. But a more plausible reason is that Balthasar presumes that since there exist in Jüngel's work more traditional theological features that offset in part at least its Hegelian tendencies, the 'Hegelian' case suffers complications. Were these complications gone into at requisite length it would run rhetorical interference on the alarm bell being sounded that Hegel is unfortunately alive and well in contemporary theology. Or rather not so much alive and well as having passed on his seed, which produces theological monsters in that biblical narrative order and individual episodes are put out of joint and become unrecognizable.

As there is the hyperbolic diffidence, which is betrayed in the avoidance of testing whether a contemporary theology admits of being designated as Hegelian, there is Balthasar's general and characteristic diffidence, which expresses itself in delaying or deferring a verdict by rehearsing the broad outline of the case for the opposite. Importantly, however, this kind of diffidence, even if it sometimes leads to take-backs, does allow for conclusion. Laying considerable theological credit at Moltmann's door, Balthasar still concludes decisively that Moltmann's theology belongs to the Hegelian line, that in effect Moltmann is a son of Hegel. For

Balthasar, it follows that notwithstanding Moltmann's commitments to time and history, his theology convicts him of being a 'son of Valentinus.' In what follows, I will essentially outline what I take to be the implied argument as this is articulated especially in *Theo-Drama 4 & 5* and *Theo-Logic 3*. In this argument, hedges and caveats with respect to Moltmann's Hegelianism are registered, but in the end decisively overridden.

Whatever reservations Balthasar entertains regarding Moltmann's position, he approves of Moltmann making scripture central to the theological task. Moreover, the rhetorical style of Moltmann's theology should be held positively to his account, for that theology should among other things be edifying is for Balthasar a truth that got derailed in the modern period with the emphasis on theology as *Wissenschaft*. Then there is the courage of Moltmann in taking on the sedimented tradition of theology, even to the point of encouraging the reading of marginal and heterodox thinkers. For all of Balthasar's respect for the tradition, and his Gadamerian conviction that the tradition should be given the benefit of the doubt, he finds plenty of room in his canon for such experimental religious thinkers as Vladimir Soloviev and Bulgakov as well as Adrienne von Speyr. There is also Moltmann daring to be speculative. Balthasar is persuaded that this is a double good: theology is essentially an act of vision, even as it is an act of listening and hearing; what is most needed to combat the different visions of Romanticism and Idealism is not refined theological method, but a vision that captures a particular facet of the 'immortal diamond' that is Christ who provokes the tradition.[8] Balthasar also approves of Moltmann's ecumenical interests whether the topic of concern is Trinity, Spirit, Church, history, or view of human being. In addition, it is a matter of fundamental conviction that not only on pragmatic, but also normative, grounds that theology cannot afford merely to be confessional. The challenge of dialogue between religious traditions and confessions, which are themselves highly differentiated and diverse, is a necessity if theology aims to be adequate to the mystery of God's relation to the world. Finally, and crucially, there is the importance of Moltmann's questions and the focus of his answers. For Balthasar, Moltmann has asked two central questions: first, what does it mean for *us* that God acts in the modes of creation, redemption, and sanctification? And second, and relatedly, what does it mean for *God* that God acts in the modes of creation, redemption, and sanctification? Moltmann has not only put these questions on the contemporary theological agenda, and suggested ways in which these questions necessarily fold into each other, but as much as any contemporary theologian he has also pointed to the centrality of the cross and to the Trinity as the ulti mate horizon of God's acts and the ultimate truth about God who is defined by love.

While Balthasar's affirmation of Moltmann is far from procedural, his reflections are indeed marked throughout by deep misgivings regarding Moltmann's theological project. A decided ambivalence is evinced in his evaluation of Moltmann's theological method and his articulation of Christian faith. Putting scripture at the very center of theology, Balthasar believes, is a necessary but not a sufficient condition for theology to be authentic. Everything depends on the adequacy of the criteria adduced and the quality of Moltmann's interpretive performance. Taking the second first, Balthasar remains unpersuaded. Moltmann's interpretive performance is marked by considerable ambiguity, if not incoherence. On the one hand, under the intellectual sway of Ernst Bloch, Moltmann's theology of hope seems to valorize a Jewish form of messianism (*TD5*, 168-175). On the other, Moltmann seems to have disconnected the new from the old covenant. Balthasar observes with alarm the eclipse of the Old Testament in *Trinity and the Kingdom* (*TD5*, 299). Effectively, Moltmann exhibits the Marcionite tendency characteristic of modern Liberal Protestant theology from which he would like to distinguish himself. At the same time, Balthasar notes, Moltmann is critical of John's Gospel, seeing in its 'realized eschatology' (*TD5*, 25-6, 33) an idolatrous chauvinism, an underdeveloped pneumatology, and a seriously distorted view of the Triune God. That Moltmann recurs to the Johannine trope of love in *Trinity and the Kingdom* (see 57-60) does not gainsay the general suspicion of John and his sense of the mischief the Gospel of John has played in the theological tradition (*TD5*, 169). For Moltmann 'realized eschatology' cannot be divorced from privileged media of divine presence and presumptive authorities who distinguish between the true and the false. To put the matter even more sharply, 'realized eschatology' is bound up with an authoritative institutional church and functions to legitimate it, and which almost by definition represses the charismatic and the prophetic. Without denying in the slightest that applications of realized eschatology have in fact resulted in these abuses, Balthasar thinks that the mode of 'realized eschatology' in John is dynamic and ecstatic. From Balthasar's point of view, the plurality of the New Testament is compromised in the excision of John. Indeed, given Balthasar's view of the synthetic role played by the Gospel of John in the New Testament canon (*GL7*, 10, 220, 226 ff),[9] the New Testament is in effect reduced to *disjecta membra*. But, as *Glory of the Lord* makes more clear than any other part of Balthasar's trilogy, the marginalization of John means the excision of Christian vision. Without the ability to see the world truly, there is only activism; there is only politics.

For Balthasar, Moltmann is just as problematic from the point of view of theological hermeneutics. Balthasar neither itemizes, nor goes into detail. We know that Moltmann's failure to support historical-critical method is not one of these inadequacies, since, as *Theo-Drama* and *Glory of the Lord 6 & 7* make clear, Balthasar has his own reservations. But Balthasar would prefer a more reflective hermeneutic proposal in which the reasons for rejection of historical-critical method are proffered and at least an outline of an alternative hermeneutic presented, even if much of what is interesting and valuable in an interpretive scheme can be read off from the practice. In addition, on grounds that he adduces in the trilogy as early as the first volume of *Glory of the Lord*, Balthasar can only be concerned with Moltmann's clearly observed practice of viewing experience unequivocally to be a theological source. While Balthasar thinks that experience is illiminable from Christian theological reflection, both on the ground of a proper doctrine of creation and on the ground that a vision of God is always a vision for a particular person or a particular community, nonetheless, he does not give it the status of a source, which potentially might put it in a competitive relation with scripture and tradition. His most explicit criticism, however, concerns Moltmann's commitment to the basic theological frame of Luther's *theologia crucis*. For this commitment serves to license the dismissing of all philosophy as bankrupt exercises in reason alone, thus a 'theology of glory' in the pejorative sense of representing a raid on the finally inarticulate mystery of God disclosed in the cross.[10] Unlike Barth, then, from Balthasar's perspective, Moltmann remains all too faithful to the Reformation legacy of violent exclusion of non-biblical discourse which Balthasar submits to serious critical scrutiny in *Glory of the Lord 1*.[11] Unsurprisingly, Moltmann's stipulation of a purely theological theology proves ineffective. The principled exclusion of philosophy does nothing to protect Moltmann's thought from philosophical and metaphysical infiltration: it serves merely to make him blind to it. Moltmann is an undisciplined and promiscuous borrower. But even more importantly, he is such an uncritical borrower that what he borrows becomes in a sense determinative of his discourse. Moltmann, Balthasar thinks, seems innocent of the Christian consequences of his borrowings from Bloch (*TD5*, 168-9, 180), from Neoplatonism (*TD5*, 229) and, of course, from Hegel (*TD5*, 168, 175, 224-9 *inter alia*).

Relatedly, Balthasar judges Moltmann's view of tradition to be inherently problematic. There are two essential concerns. The first and most obvious is Moltmann's excoriation of mainline patristic and medieval theological traditions. Throughout *The Crucified God* and *Trinity and the Kingdom* in a matter of paragraphs these traditions are dismissed as having fallen into the trap of a metaphysical discourse that compromises biblical vision and substance.[12] From a Balthasarian point of view, this kind of damning of theological traditions is thoughtless in the extreme. It uncritically repeats the view of Liberal Protestant theology, which in this respect represents a mechanical appropriation of the Protestant principle. This damning of tradition is also sterile in that it deprives theology of resources to deal with modernity by depriving it of a vocabulary and syntax of relatively adequate response to christological and trinitarian mystery. And this damning of tradition is spiritually incapacitating insofar as it deprives Christians of patterns of worship and patterns of discipleship that define the Christian way of life. For Balthasar, Moltmann's construction of the Western theological tradition as a reactionary monolith puts him in an invidious situation regarding theological authority. The options remaining to Moltmann are those of the Romantic theologian-poet, and the theological subversive who primarily appeals to the heterodox sources (e.g. Patripassians, Joachim, Boehme) or marginal figures in Western religious thought such as Berdyaev, Unamuno, and Heschel.[13]

In *Theo-Drama 4*, Balthasar comments on the illegitimacy of the construction of Abraham Heschel, whose prophetic monotheism is repressed in favor of the speculative and explanatory discourse of the Kabbalah which Heschel refers to only in passing (*TD4*, 343-4 n. 29).[14] The criticism of the adoption of Heschel is in turn reflective of broader opposition to the idiosyncrasy of the crowd of witnesses paraded at the beginning of *Trinity and the Kingdom* and at play throughout this and many other of Moltmann's texts. When Balthasar comments explicitly on Moltmann's 'crowd of witnesses' in *Theo-Drama 5* (228), he neither speaks to the eccentric and syncretistic nature of the ensemble, nor does he critically analyze the sources. But he has to be puzzled about how 'pathos,' as it functions in an existential philosophy such as Miguel Unamuno's, who resolutely refuses to make truth claims, rhymes with its use in the speculative religious discourses of Boehme and Berdyaev in which it is a requirement of the self-constitution of the divine. There are issues of substance as well as incoherence. Throughout *Theo-Drama* and *Theo-Logic* Balthasar never has good things to say about Boehme and Berdyaev, whom rightly he regards as a pair.[15] Nor does he find anything admirable in Patripassians (*TD2*, 49). Balthasar's general strategic as opposed to critical response is illustrated in the pages in *Theo-Drama 5* (218-20) immediately preceding his comments on Moltmann's invoking his witnesses. In addressing the contributions to the discourse of pathos by Cyril of Alexandria, Hilary of Poitiers, Gregory Thaumaturgus, Gregory of Nyssa, and Maximus, Balthasar underscores that mainline theological reflection is no stranger to the biblically focused enterprise of seeing who God is through reflection on the cross. At the same time, Balthasar can be seen as insisting on the coherence of this group of witness and its ecclesial nature. Finally, of course, what early Christian reflection reveals is that when it comes to God-talk whatever talk of pathos there is with respect to God has to be coordinated with talk about divine impassibility. The opposition between passibility and impassibility is an opposition appropriate to the world; there is insufficient reason to assume that it is appropriate to the triune God.

Balthasar's misgivings regarding Moltmann's hermeneutic of scripture and tradition fold into his misgivings concerning Moltmann's view of the church, which in his case not only proceeds without palpable institutional authority, but also without authoritative beliefs and practices. Balthasar's misgivings concerning the ecumenical comportment of Moltmann's thought specify the ecclesial concern. For as Moltmann's ability to move between particular confessional traditions opens up the space of dialogue between Eastern and Western Christianity, the question remains whether such a space is possible or desirable. Is this space a genuinely ecclesial space? Is such a space any more than a heuristic fiction? Moreover, Balthasar raises questions as to how inclusive this space is. For example, does it find a place for Catholicism as an institution or for its magisterial thinkers (e.g. Augustine, Aquinas)? Does it find a place for mainline Protestantism to the extent to which it is committed to determinate church structures, determinate liturgical practices, and determinate beliefs, for example, the belief in *sola gratia*?

Even more important are Balthasar's deep misgivings on the substantive theological front. The focus of Balthasar's concern is the christological-trinitarian nerve center of Moltmann's theology. With *The Crucified God* and *Trinity and the Kingdom* taken to be the essential texts,[16] Balthasar sees that Moltmann's reading of creation, theological anthropology, and church is generated by and regulated from this center. Balthasar is uncomfortable with Moltmann's insouciant self-ascription as a 'panentheist,' as Moltmann calls variously on the Neoplatonic trope of *bonum diffusivum sui* (*TK*, 106; *TD5*, 227-8) and the Kabbalistic cipher of *tsimsum* to gain critical leverage against any and all versions of *creatio ex nihilo* (*TK*, 109; implied in 59; *TD2*, 262-4; *TD5*, 94) If, for Moltmann, creation from nothing reveals a deficient form of monotheism that stresses divine sovereignty or monarchy, for Balthasar, Moltmann fails properly not only to understand the doctrine of creation from nothing, but also fails to understand the trope of *bonum diffusivum sui*, which in the specifically Christian context, where it interprets and is interpreted by the Johannine theology of love, essentially points to the giftedness of all that is. A theology of gift supposes absolute distance between the gift giver and the gift receiver consistent with the basic intention of the doctrine of creation from nothing. For Balthasar, theologians of the stature of Augustine, Maximus, Bonaventure, and Aquinas emphatically mark this point as basic to Christian faith. Moltmann's theological anthropology also gives Balthasar cause for concern. As Moltmann makes clear from the publication of *Theology of Hope* on, autonomy is the normative characterization of human being. Whether the appeal is to Kant, Hegel, or to Bloch, Balthasar thinks that Moltmann has not submitted this basically Enlightenment assumption to critical scrutiny. Indeed, this assumption functions at once as axiom and reaction-formation to Barth's anti-Enlightenment and anti-modern stress on heteronomy, and sits uneasily with Moltmann's emphasis on community that dismantles the particularism of the autonomous self.

Balthasar's agreement with Barth regarding the irreducibility of heteronomy does not mean that Balthasar accepts all of Barth's material conclusions regarding the insufficiency of human being and religion. Nor does it mean that Balthasar simply opposes to Moltmann his deep-seated Catholic assumptions about holiness, the necessity of prayer, and his vision of human being as *homo adorans*, although, of course, all of this is in play. Crucially Balthasar is challenging the biblical adequacy of Moltmann's theological anthropology. Needless to say, the Gospel of John is critical here. But so also are the prophets. From Balthasar's perspective, Moltmann has de-emphasized the dimension of radical obedience, which is central to both prophetic message and existence (*GL6*, 154-5, 231-4). The demand that human beings listen to God's 'call' and unconditionally accept it – what in *Theo-Drama* Balthasar will call 'mission' – is central to prophecy, and is what makes it ineluctable. The messianic prophecies of Deutero-Isaiah are at least as important for what they say about the nature of the Messiah as they are in their certitude about a future coming – a point that Balthasar would grant to Liberation Theology.[17] Precisely as Messiah, Christ is the paradigm of obedience from which flows authentic responsibility that defines true freedom (*TD3*, 191-201).[18] Although couched in aesthetic rather than in dramatic ethical categories, Balthasar makes essentially the same point in *Glory of the Lord 1* (139-42) when he considers that Christian action necessarily flows from a contemplative (non-theoretical) center, which is defined by responsiveness towards the mystery of God that is focally christological as it is backgroundedly trinitarian. Once again important issues emerge: is radical autonomy compatible with prayer? Does autonomy make doxology, to which Moltmann pledges allegiance (*TK*, 126), a misunderstanding, or worse, a *flatus vocis*? In this context, it is disappointing that on the one occasion in which Balthasar explicitly addresses the doxological drift of Moltmann's thought, he is frustratingly indeterminate. In *Theo-Logic 3* Balthasar cites approvingly a post-*Trinity and the Kingdom* text to the effect that the 'Triune God is worshiped and adored for its own sake' and where the Holy Spirit is an object as well as subject of worship (*TL3*, 28). Yet it is not clear what sense of worship he believes to be in operation here, whether it amounts to more than the bare acknowledgment of transcendence.

From Balthasar's perspective strains manifest themselves across the full extent and breadth of Moltmann's rendering of the biblical narrative. Moltmann's rendering of Christ is no exception. While Moltmann is perfectly traditional in thinking of Christ as the Son, Balthasar is made anxious by what he takes to be Moltmann's lack of differentiation in Christ between divine and human will, as well as the tendency Moltmann exhibits to fold resurrection into the cross. From Maximus, Balthasar has learned an appreciation for the superiority of two-wills over the more traditional two natures approach of the theological tradition.[19] While in an obvious way the two wills approach is consistent with Chalcedon, it is more adequate to scripture in general, allows for greater balance between 'above' and 'below' approaches to Christology by bringing out the full humanity of Jesus, and avoids the metaphysical overdetermination that was an obstacle to Luther, and which encouraged in him the monophysite tendencies that become patent in Hegel and the Moltmann of *The Crucified God*.

Balthasar is at his most eloquent in *Theo-Drama 2*. He opposes to the particular form of agonic monophysitism, current since Luther, the two wills view (*TD2*, 184), which persist in a single hypostasis without confusion (*asynchutos*) and separation (*adiaretos*) (*TD2*, 201-02).[20] Balthasar also fully recognizes that the folding of resurrection into the cross is in itself not unusual in the mainline Christian tradition. It is, for example, the fundamental tendency of the Gospel of John and, arguably, the identifying gesture of Luther's theology. History shows, however, that it can be enlisted in the service of a Hegelian like deipassionism (*TD5*, 226), an enlisting that is enthusiastically welcomed by Moltmann in *The Crucified God*, and qualified rather than fully renounced in *Trinity and the Kingdom*. The latter text certainly rejects strict Patripassianism, while demonstrating considerably more subtlety in thinking of the different modalities of suffering proper to Father, Son, and Spirit, and at points shows some awareness that suffering in God bears only an analogical relation to that of physical creatures. In addition, Moltmann's appeal in *Trinity and the Kingdom* to Joachim (*TD3*, 400; *TD4*, 558) evinces a pneumatological counterpull to the singularity of Jesus Christ. For Balthasar, typically in Moltmann the necessity of appropriating the meaning and message of Christ takes pride of place over Christ's absolute uniqueness: the ascription of 'sonship' to human beings in a Moltmannian text is rarely – if ever – attended by qualifiers such as 'by grace 'or 'by adoption.'

If Barth might have plausibly helped Moltmann here, so also might Irenaeus, and especially his idea of 'recapitulation' (*anakephalaiosis*). In *Theo-Drama 5*, for example, Balthasar credits Irenaeus with a perfectly modulated synthesis of the 'already' and 'not yet' dimensions of the transformation of time that represents its perfection: 'Christ's time recapitulates and comprehends world-time, while it reveals God's supertime' (*TD5*, 30). The Irenaean trope manages to stress the continuity between the image of God, as this image undergoes not only the trials of sin but the trials of history, and Christ as the archetypal image, but does so without absorbing Christ into the created image. Christ sums up rather than himself being summed up. Irenaeus gets it right because his is a specifically Johannine realized eschatology, which is not the contrary to unrealized eschatology, but rather is inclusive of it (*TD5*, 25-6). For Balthasar, the 'theology of hope' fails to understand this, and in doing so – whatever its own self-understanding – fails to distinguish the temporal future from the absolute future that is the triune God (*TD5*, 57-8). Entertaining the criticism that the emphasis falls too heavily on the 'already' in the Gospel of John (*TD5*, 33, 169), Balthasar suggests that this criticism naturally escalates into the charge that the Gospel of John is infected with Gnosticism, as Gnosticism is classically understood to exaggerate the non-temporal dimensions of reality. For Balthasar, not only is John not a Gnostic text, it is profoundly anti-Gnostic. The verticality one finds in John, he avers:

> *. . . is the locus of a dramatic tension in which the action taking place between God and mankind, centered in Jesus Christ, differs fundamentally from any pagan and mythological epic whether that of fallen aeons or ascending divinities. Here the drama of Christ remains the direct fulfillment of Yahweh's covenant drama with Israel, which has been going on throughout the whole of history. (TD5, 32; also TD5, 150-1)*

The defense of John on this charge prepares the way for Balthasar going on the offensive: the exaggeration of the horizontal axis does not automatically give a philosophy or theology a pass with respect to 'Gnostic' ascription. This would be so if and only if Gnosticism did not have the capacity to include such an exaggeration within its essentially metaleptic program. But it is Balthasar's conviction that it does have this capacity.

A final christological deficit in Moltmann's theology is his inadequate articulation of a theology of atonement. In *Theo-Drama 4*, Balthasar praises Moltmann for not taking the Enlightenment low-road that atonement Christology is rationally indefensible in that it compromises the responsibility of the moral agent and ethically indefensible by supposing a God whose importunate demand for satisfaction goes all the way to human sacrifice. Moltmann is still sufficiently a Christian theologian not to welcome blithe dismissal of God's judgment and righteousness, which are absolutely central to any biblical view of redemption wrought through Christ. Indeed, at his best Moltmann repeats precisely the dramatic view that Balthasar himself supports, that is, that taking on human sin Christ represents the sinner in his and her alienation from God (*TD4*, 332-38). Overall, however, in Moltmann's soteriology, there is much more emphasis upon suffering than there is on sin (*TD4*, 321-23).[21] From Balthasar's point of view, Moltmann would have been much better served had he not strayed so far from Barth, and had he allowed Anselm in particular into his theology as something of a theological scour. As Balthasar lays bare in *Theo-Drama 4* (335-36, 364) the genius of Anselm is not logical demonstration, nor is it aesthetic sensibility – although, as he makes clear in his essay in *Glory of the Lord 2* (211-59) this sensibility is much more in play than has been suspected, and demands that 'necessary reason' be interpreted much more nearly like 'narrative verisimilitude.' The genius of Anselm is finally dramatic. The love of God is such that the Son of the Father for our sake enters into the anti-divine condition of sin as well as death. This substitution on our behalf is at once God's representation of himself to us and the representation of human being to God. Whatever the suggestion in *Cur Deus Homo*, substitution cannot be reduced to logic; it is only anachronism that makes us think that Anselm is suggesting that logic is invested with this authority. If we can speak of logic, it is as *Theo-Logic 2* puts it, it is a logic of love, which transcends the legislation by reason.

From Balthasar's perspective, all of Moltmann's theological problems come home to roost in his influential reflections on the Trinity, concerning which he says and unsays that the world and the cross are necessary (*TD5*, 227-8; also *TD5*, 173). It is in the context of his articulation of the Trinity that Moltmann is most inclined to say that the history and suffering of the world is the history and suffering of God (*TK*, 58-9; *TD5*, 228). For Moltmann, while the expression is bold, the insight is biblical and clearly is focused in the cross of Christ. Granting the fertility of Moltmann's insight, Balthasar demurs. The biblical view is more paradoxical: it suggests that the God who can have no history

> *... now becomes involved, right along with men, in accomplishing their spatial and temporal movements within the sphere of their lives, and this not only as an observer who steers things from above, but as one who journeys and experiences with creatures on their level. (GL6, 47)*

Moltmann's impatience with paradox is symptomatic, perhaps suggesting that Moltmann's honesty resolves in the end to a post-Enlightenment commitment to the univocal. The reduction of paradox occurs when the internal divine processions are confused with salvation history (*TD4*, 322), and the cross comes to be regarded not as the locus of the Trinity's 'self-revelation' – as it is for Barth, Anselm, and Bonaventure – but of its 'self-actualization' (*TD4*, 321). Balthasar acknowledges that there are moments when Moltmann seems to reject such confounding (*TD5*, 173; *TL3*, 41). Ultimately, however, Moltmann fails to protect any truly plausible sense of difference (*TD4*, 322; *TD5*, 278). Balthasar thinks that a useful way of grasping what is the issue between Moltmann and himself is to triangulate with Rahner's trinitarian thought as this is summed up in his famous axiom: the immanent Trinity is the economic Trinity and vice versa.[22] Whereas, on his view Moltmann is prepared essentially to read the axiom as a straightforward identity statement in which the immanent Trinity reduces to the economy (this involves an ignoring of the 'vice versa'), Balthasar thinks that the statement is more nearly that of a hyperbole calculated to remind us that the triune God of Christianity is always ecstatically towards us. However, properly to understand the ecstatic dimension involves paying due attention to Rahner's 'vice versa,' which suggests that the immanent Trinity is irreducible to the economic Trinity. For Balthasar this is precisely what one would expect, even demand from a thinker within the Christian Neoplatonic tradition of Augustine, Pseudo-Dionysius, Thomas, and Bonaventure.

Epical Trinitarianism and Hegelian Overdetermination

THE REHEARSAL OF POSITIVES AND NEGATIVES clearly suggests that at best Balthasar's relation to Moltmann is ambivalent. This ambivalence, however, by no means precludes decisiveness in judgment. It is perfectly clear that the intensity of Balthasar's worries and the extent of his methodological and substantive objections vastly outweigh what he admires in Moltmann. Moreover, the ambivalence is eloquent: its correspondent, *pace* van Beeck,[23] is not Balthasar's state of mind, but rather a structural tension in Moltmann's thought. Descriptively, Moltmann's discourse is evangelical in that it is committed to preaching the Word in a contemporary world that presents multiverse challenges to biblical faith. Explanatorily, however, Balthasar believes that Moltmann's theology exhibits structural dependence on Hegelian modes of thought (*TD3*, 390; *TD4*, 323 (n); *TD4*, 343-4 n.; *TD5*, 228-9).

Simply as a matter of interpretation, Balthasar's pointing to Moltmann's dependence on Hegel is not unusual. As I have pointed out already, not only have others done so, but the relation between Moltmann and Hegel has been an issue almost from the beginning. Indeed, one might even say that the influence of Hegel is an issue of Moltmann's own making given his baptizing of Hegel in *The Crucified God* in which Hegel is read as the adequate trinitarian interpreter of Luther. Moreover, Balthasar is not distinguished by his single-mindedness, but rather by his style of criticism. Specifically, he pursues the issue of dependence by availing of Hegel's very own categories of drama and epic, while at the same time gesturing both to the aesthetic spell of Moltmann's discourse and its ultimate lineage. Moltmann's theology illustrates epic figuration in a mythological key: no clear differentiation between the history of God and the history of the world is presented, or appears to be possible (*TD4*, 323-5, 335; *TD5*, 173). In a fundamental way, then, Moltmann reenacts the Hegelian eclipse of biblical and Christian dramatics, which depend upon distinct spheres of incommensurable – although not incompatible – agency. In this eclipse, the historicization of God is married to the apotheosis of the world and human being. Thus, we have at once the exaggeration of the horizontal and vertical poles of the relation between God and the world, which, Balthasar insists, necessarily need to be thought with reference to each other. The epical eclipse of authentic theodramatics is both root and fruit of those specific features of Moltmann's thought from which, as we have seen, Balthasar recoils. The particular epical form to which Moltmann is indebted is Hegelian, and possesses the core dynamic features of Hegelian epic, that is, development, eros, kenosis, and necessity.

I will discuss shortly each of these Hegelian features. But before I do I should comment on a particular claim of Moltmann's that constitutes a plausible disqualifier of Hegelian ascription: Hegel is called on only to the extent to which he represents a legitimate extension of the Reformation (*TD5*, 173, 227). Aside from the obvious question as to how legitimacy is to be determined within a Moltmannian scheme, there is the problem that Luther's theology of the cross is in Hegelian thought taken in a speculative direction that is expressly forbidden by Luther and Lutheran orthodoxy. In neither *The Crucified God* nor *Trinity and the Kingdom* does Moltmann appear to see that there is little or no correspondence between Luther and Hegel regarding hermeneutic principles and exegetical practices. For example, whereas Luther advocates *sola scriptura* and *sola gratia*, Hegel supports neither. For Hegel the Bible is notoriously unreliable from an evidentiary, ethical, and rational point of view. Here Hegel is in line with the Bible's Enlightenment critics. But with due caution, thematic and narrative elements of the Bible can be appropriated provided they are submitted to the conceptual cleansing that it is the duty of Hegelian *Begriff* to provide. One is called then to take sides: Luther or Hegel? Without fully endorsing Luther, Balthasar, nonetheless, takes his side against Hegel. While Balthasar opposes Luther's demand to stick to the literal-historical sense of scripture, he can have no truck with the Hegel for whom scripture is a 'wax nose' and thus infinitely interpretable. And Hegel's exegesis provides plenty of cause for worry in this respect, especially what he takes to be the adequate interpretation of the Johannine statement 'God is love' (1 John 4:6),[24] a statement which is submitted to a remarkably similar reading by Moltmann in *Trinity and the Kingdom* (57-60) in which the emphasis appears to fall on the dialectical-logical aspect of love rather than on the enunciation of its inexplicability.

These methodological deficiencies vis-à-vis Luther are reflected in Hegel's substantive theological departures which are similarly massive. In concert with his rejection of Moltmann's linking of Luther and Hegel on the hermeneutical level, Balthasar feels called on to interrogate the substantive theological links announced by Moltmann. As *Mysterium Paschale* (63) could not make more clear, Balthasar very much sees the point of the genealogical connection Moltmann makes with much bravado in *The Crucified God*: 'If we rest content with the simple *sub contrario*, then we shall be forced to take the path that travels from Luther to Hegel. A purely dialectical Christology becomes transformed into the sheerly "philosophical" dialectic, into a "worldly" discourse.' What he rejects is the view that there is nothing excessive in the *sub contrario*, nothing that fails to get expressed and justified in Hegelian panentheism. Whether recessive or not, features of the *sub contrario* resist Hegelian enlisting. Although the relevant uncoupling in the following passage pertains to Luther and Kierkegaard rather than Luther and Hegel, it is applicable to this pair, and all the more so, given the suggestion that the genuine Luther comes into view when his theology is led back to its genuinely Johannine base:

> *But if it is true that in Luther's sub contrario the "absolute paradox" (of Kierkegaard) comes to expression, there can be, nonetheless, no resting with this static form of expression. The paradoxical formulation has, rather, an inner dynamism which manifests itself in purposiveness . . . This finality kindles a light in the darkness of rational incomprehensibility. This light is the light of love . . . . (MP, 53)*

Furthermore, Balthasar contends, whatever the criticisms leveled in texts like *The Trinity and the Kingdom* against absolute knowledge and the blatant theodicy program of Hegel's system (*TK*, 15, 17, 21, 135; *TD5*, 173), as a matter of fact Moltmann demonstrates extraordinary certainty regarding the nature of God. God, or God's history, unambiguously can be read off the history of the world. If on the one hand, this confidence violates the epistemic reserve of Luther's theology of the cross, on the other, it actualizes the positivism of the theology of the cross which, as it prohibits metaphysical reflection, also excludes reflection on the nature and limits of all language referring to divine mystery. While Balthasar agrees with Luther that apophaticism runs the risk of losing connection to Christ as the center of revelation, he also insists that a properly christological theology cannot but be apophatically aspirated. No such notice of this is provided by Moltmann any more than Hegel who, as we have seen, rigorously excludes apophatic language and excoriates the slightest hint of mystery as redolent of fideism.

It should be pointed out, however, that Balthasar is not simply chiding Moltmann for getting Luther wrong. Balthasar in fact believes that in significant respects Moltmann gets Luther right as he does also Luther's relation to German Idealism. There is a fundamental rightness in the theology of the cross issuing in a speculative program which similarly does an end-run around reason as it is classically understood both in its prosaic deployment as in its ecstasy. As I have already pointed out, Balthasar is by no means original here. Staudenmaier made the point on behalf of Catholic theology in the nineteenth century. But when he made it he had the authority of F. C. Baur, perhaps Hegel's foremost 'religious' interpreter, and ultimately the authority of Hegel's own texts. Still, the fact that the speculative transcription of the theology of the cross makes sense does not make it logically necessary. Balthasar reserves the right to imagine otherwise; to imagine, for example, a Luther who receives his completion in Hamann rather than Hegel, and where Christ's suffering is parsed otherwise than in Hegelian speculation, where it is required to mean nothing less than the suffering of the divine itself. In *Theo-Drama 5* Moltmann is identified as one of the modern thinkers most invested with denying impassibility of God. He is, however, by no means the only one: Balthasar brings forward a list of names that include Jacques Maritain and Jean Galot – and does so without evident disapproval (*TD5*, 239-44). The challenge to the tradition, Balthasar believes, is necessary for the health of the tradition, although all questioning of divine impassibility is obliged to produce the sense of impassibility that is found objectionable. What cannot be countenanced, however, is a predication of suffering to the triune divine that disobeys the analogy of being, and the rule that beyond similarity lies the ever-greater dissimilarity. What cannot be tolerated is that this suffering in God defines an ineluctable condition for God to be God or rather to become God.

Balthasar's final verdict on Moltmann's theology is that to the extent to which it pretends to be a genuinely Christian ark that rises above the sea of the Enlightenment and the dissolution to which it gives rise, it lists badly from the tradition, takes on water, and finally runs aground due to its commitment to a Hegelian-type trinitarian metanarrative inimical to the biblical narrative. In the etymological sense that Blanchot exploits,[25] Moltmann's trinitarian thought represents a 'dis-aster.' The movement away from the tradition involves Moltmann's theology in movements both towards and away from the Enlightenment. At the same time, the movement away from the Enlightenment towards what appears to be an alternative trinitarian metanarrative may very well inscribe so many crucial features of the Enlightenment to make it problematic as to whether the Enlightenment has been overcome. In any event, in this epical trinitarian romance, God becomes or develops into the being of beings. In this sense, God effects the redemption of the world primarily as an aspect or means of self-redemption, which is at the same time self-creation (*TD4*, 322; *TD5*, 228-9). This is codified in the developmental interpretation of the Trinity in which the immanent processions are identified without remainder with the trinitarian missions (*TD4*, 320). Of course, the trinitarian epic is one that gets expressed in a pantragic key. For this God becomes only in and through the trial of suffering and death (*TD4*, 227, 322-23). As I pointed out in the last chapter, Balthasar realizes that this myth of the becoming of God is inflected on a much higher level than that of ancient myth, and thus evinces a much higher level of cognitive reflection. Since this kind of mythological epic supposes the biblical story, in a chronological sense it is 'post-Christian.' This kind of mythological epic is also 'post-Christian' from an evaluative point of view insofar as it is judged structurally to deviate from the biblical story and does so in ways that are motivated.

To the extent to which Moltmann's theology is epical in a Hegelian fashion, it illustrates the key features of Hegelian epicality, dynamic development, eros, kenosis, and necessity. Balthasar concedes that these features may not quite be on the surface in the way they are in Hegel – there is after all a genuine evangelical component. It should not surprise, then, that one finds Moltmann striking some notes of distinction between the history of God and the history of the world (*TD5*, 173), paying some service to the gratuity of divine love rather than its efficacy in constituting God as God (*TD5*, 227-8), affirming a mode of kenosis more in line with the morphological standard, and suggesting that creation is more appropriately considered to be an expression of divine goodness than indicating some lack or need in God to have an other, which functions as the mirror in which the divine comes to self-consciousness. For Balthasar, however, the assertion of differences is not pitched loud enough, nor articulated clearly enough, to prevent the impression that Moltmann has been bewitched by Hegel's speculative dynamics with the consequence that he has succumbed to a developmental monism. It should be admitted that on the face of it the charge of monism seems blatantly absurd. As *Trinity and the Kingdom* makes perfectly clear, Moltmann is decidedly against monism in any shape or form. Thus his criticisms not only of the philosophical, but also the theological tradition, especially with respect to the classical trinitarian tradition's putative favoring of the unity of divine substance over the plurality of persons, what might be called its crypto-Sabellianism (*TK*, 15, 17, 135-7). Balthasar makes clear in *Theo-Logic 3* that he does not accept that the Western trinitarian tradition can be univocally characterized as monism of either a substance or subject stripe. Interestingly, Moltmann's point here translates into a theological register Heidegger's objection against the Western philosophical tradition of always involving the positing of a *hypokeimenon* or *subiectum* to support qualities, whether the register is objectivistic (ancient) or subjectivistic (modern). While Balthasar is willing to grant that the concern with divine unity has inbuilt limitations, this judgement flattens what is going on in the trinitarian thought of Augustine (*TL3*, 37) and Aquinas (*TL3*, 28, 33), ignores the contributions of the Victorine (*TL3*, 37) and Bonaventuran traditions (*TL3*, 28), and does a grave injustice to the trinitarian thought of Barth. All of these forms of trinitarian thought are fully cognizant of their starting point, and attempt to correct for the privileging of unity. If they do so with various degrees of success, the situation is not essentially different in the case of those who favor *perichoresis*, for correction is required here also since God is one as well as a three.

Leaving aside the problem of Moltmann's more or less Manichaean disjunction of Eastern and Western forms of trinitarianism – the preference is always given to the East – Balthasar pays special attention to the function of Moltmann's appeal to *perichoresis* (*TD2*, 257-9, 302; *TL3*, 157-8). He understands that in addition to the trope serving as a proxy for Moltmann's support of the social doctrine of the Trinity, it is intended positively to mark Moltmann's transcendence of the specifically Hegelian form of monism, which offers merely a triadically articulated unitary subject defined by self-consciousness. Balthasar is skeptical as to whether Moltmann succeeds in escaping Hegel's monist pull, and lacks confidence in the success of Moltmann's trinitarian program despite its allegiance to a social view of the Trinity. In the first instance, more is required to escape monism than the assertion of the primacy of persons in relation. Specifically, it is not evident that *perichoresis* is not reinscribed in a monistic frame when these relations, and thus persons, are not only affected by, but effected by the history of the world. There are two aspects of a Balthasarian reply, which remain somewhat implicit in his texts. The first aspect is suggested in the context of his examination of Hegel's view of the family in *Philosophy of Right* (*TL2*, 44). Although on the surface the family is the dialogical entity par excellence, this does not prevent Hegel from folding the We of family into the larger We of the State which in turn represents the self-mediating subject that is absolute Spirit.[26] The second aspect to Balthasarian objection is more logical in nature. What understanding of *perichoresis* is in play when the intra-trinitarian relations are themselves constituted by the relation of the triune divine to the world? For Balthasar, the dependence of trinitarian relations on the world in effect makes unreal any and all relations within the immanent Trinity.

Should Moltmann's deployment of the trope of *perichoresis* signify that Moltmann's trinitarian orbit is other than Western, and by implication, other than Hegelian, then the theological question becomes, at what price? Is a trinitarian view that opposes the trope of *perichoresis* to the Augustinian-Thomistic attempts to vindicate an aboriginal divine unity likely to be successful? In *Theo-Logic 3*, Balthasar makes the important point that deficits attend both these approaches, and that neither of which can be successful on its own. The approaches are necessarily complementary and mutually correcting (*TL3*, 157-8 n.). No more than in the case of the passibility-impassibility issue, however, does Balthasar proceed to articulate a synthesis. As in the former case, he prefers a *protocol.* Taking its point of departure from the excessiveness of the Trinity, which cannot become a function of any explanatory scheme, trinitarian or otherwise, Balthasar suggests that ideally a trinitarian theology would unite both Augustinian and social Trinity perspectives and thus yield a theology that would maximally respect both divine unity and the plurality of divine persons. Such a theology, he recognizes, has a more or less heuristic character and is only eschatologically realizable. To the extent to which theological production is within history and thus *in via*, the most that can be expected is that the church as a whole tends to balance these different emphases with their different strengths. Precisely what it should not do is choose. Balthasar sees then the antinomic situation of Moltmann's emphasis on *perichoresis*: should Moltmann succeed in transcending Hegelian monism together with other varieties, it will fail from the point of view of theological comprehensiveness. Which, of course, leads to the further question: does Moltmann succeed in escaping Hegel's orbit? Does not the violence of the escape strategy suggest that Hegel's trinitarianism sets the agenda?

For sure these questions express and specify the primal Kierkegaardian fear that Hegelian mediation is the nameless force that drags back and digests all that would escape. One regrets that Balthasar does not supply a metaphorics: no black hole, no theogonic spider whose web is as wide as the world and all of its discourse, or no world wide web of intermediation in which all substantive positions are functions of a discourse that justifies nothing except itself. The Hegelian force invites naming, while oddly resisting it. Perhaps performatively it contradicts the Hegelian system by its profound unknowing, its instantiation of apophasis. Balthasar's language remains coolly analytic, even if the questions about the effect of Hegel on discourses that would transcend their debt are anything but rhetorical. We can and should look to Moltmann's texts for clues as to whether the retro pull away from Hegel is matched or surpassed by an equal force going in the other direction; something like the force of inertia? Balthasar concludes that this indeed is the case. A crucial mark of the effect of Hegel on Moltmann lies in the latter's interpretation of divine love. Moltmann articulates an erotic rather than agapaic trinitarianism.[27]

Importantly, as for Hegel, 1 John 4:6 is crucial. Although Moltmann clearly intends to go beyond Hegel in his specifically 'theo-logical' interpretation in *Trinity and the Kingdom*, from Balthasar's point of view 'logic' seems to dominate with the emphasis falling on the dialectical necessity for otherness and its function in the economy of divine self-constitution. The Hegelian shadow that falls between intention and reality is conspicuous in the slippage between the first and second of six propositions that summarize Moltmann's exegesis. Moltmann's interpretation starts out innocently enough by offering a non-objectionable Christian Neoplatonic reading of love as the 'self-communication of the good' (*TK*, 57). Balthasar notices the shift in the second proposition. Reflecting on this passage, he notes that for Moltmann, love 'is the power of self-differentiation and self-identification.' Balthasar is sure that here Augustine, Pseudo-Dionysius, and Bonaventure have been given up for Hegel. In fact, the full proposition is even more obviously Hegelian than Balthasar makes it out to be. Here is the passage:

> *When we say God is love; then we mean that he is in eternity the process of self-differentiation and self-identification; a process which contains the whole pain of the negative in itself. (TK, 58)*

Although Moltmann's express agenda in *Trinity and the Kingdom* is to separate himself from Hegel, with whom his critics had associated him, its language is not especially helpful in this regard. Balthasar points generally to the *Phenomenology*. It is likely that he has the following famous passage from the Preface in mind:

> *Thus the life of God and divine cognition may well be spoken of as a playing of love with itself; but this idea sinks into mere edification, and even insipidity, if it lacks the seriousness (der Ernst), the suffering (der Schmerz), the patience, and the labor of the negative. (#19)*

With Hegelianism having intruded upon an interpretation of the biblical notion of love, it is difficult subsequently to exclude it. That Moltmann attempts to do just that is evident in his introducing in the third proposition the Barthian language of divine 'decision.' Moltmann proves right a very interesting Balthasarian hypothesis that in contemporary trinitarian theology (*TD4*, 323), however incoherently, necessitarianism and voluntarism may tend to go in hand. That necessitarianism will prove dominant is suggested by proposition four in which Hegelianism reasserts itself. The following recalls any number of passages in *Lectures on the Philosophy of Religion*:

> *The love with which God creatively and sufferingly loves the world is no different from the love he himself is in eternity. And conversely,*

> *creative and suffering love has always been a part of his love's nature. (TK, 59)*

In the terms of *Theo-Logic*, following Hegel Moltmann has wagered everything on an *ana-logic* that can only prove theologically mischievous, since it fails to respect the excess of the triune God that troubles all categories and especially those we feel most confident about. A logic that would respect this excess, and its excessive freedom, is a *kata-logic*, a logic of the otherwise that is otherwise. This logic, which is precisely not a logic, is determined by God, not God by it. Balthasar always keeps in mind the limits of language with respect to God's love, and how aesthetic and dramatic ciphers rather than philosophical concepts are primary. Moltmann's logic of love, which is nothing other than the logic of relationality, reveals itself as a Hegelian reaction-formation to the potential nominalism and voluntarism of the theological tradition. Indeed, it is possible to see Moltmann's unsophisticated effort to combine both in his exegesis of 1 John 4:6 as testimony to the overcoming of the voluntary which involves the dreaded notion of 'lordship.' As such Moltmann's logic of love depends on a prior misidentification of the tradition. For Balthasar, one of the enduring gains of the approach of theological aesthetics is that it shows that it is far from true that the theological tradition in its entirety is dominated by nominalism and voluntarism. As Balthasar makes clear throughout the trilogy, but especially in *Glory of the Lord*, Nominalism is an event – a cacophonous event – in Christian discourse. There is no need to go outside the theological tradition for a cure. The cure is very much inside, in the shape of figures such as Irenaeus, Pseudo-Dionysius and Maximus, Thomas and Bonaventure in the broader 'catholic' tradition, and Hamann in the Protestant. To mimic Hegel: within a Balthasarian framework the tradition is the wound that heals itself.[28]

To the degree to which Moltmann evokes kenosis as a trope to account for the relation between God and the world in the cross he is not different from Balthasar (*TK*, 83), who frequently employs it. For Balthasar, however, there is a significant difference between his own rhetorically hyperbolic use of kenosis and Hegel's use, which points to the operation of emptying in God that dialectically turns out to be an operation of filling. Or in a formula, Balthasar's own use of kenosis resists the confounding of plerosis with kenosis operative in Hegel. Recognizing that Moltmann's view of kenosis is influenced significantly by non-Hegelian sources such as the 19th-century kenoticists Frank and Thomasius and by the 20th-century Anglican Rolt (*TD5*, 223), Balthasar is, nonetheless, persuaded that in his essentialist use of the trope Moltmann repeats an operation that marks Hegel's discourse. In fact, it is possible to see this essentialist use right across the Christian narrative, for example, in creation (*TK*, 59, 118), incarnation and the cross (*TK*, 118-19), and the immanent Trinity itself. Moltmann's essentialist kenosis is ironic as well as iterative. The perfection of the immanent divine depends on the 'intervention of cross and incarnation' (*TK*, 115), although in insisting on the prerogatives of the cross Moltmann by no means excludes creation from being an instrument of divine self-constitution. Here two post-Hegelians come together and separate. Against Moltmann, as much as Hegel, Balthasar enlists Bulgakov's 'ur-kenosis.' With 'ur-kenosis' we are dealing with an eternal and gratuitous surrender of trinitarian persons that requires neither creation nor cross for its actualization (*TD4*, 323). No need is satisfied, since the triune God is characterized by plenitude. This point, which is made quite generally in *Theo-Logic* (*TL2*, 22-3), is made with specific reference to the trinitarian persons in *Theo-Drama*. In a distinguished passage, which emphasizes the excess (*koros*) in the free surrender of persons, emptying describes rather than explains the transparency of the hypostases:

> *The divine hypostases proceed from one another and thus are perfectly open to one another – but, for all eternity, they are not interchangeable. As a result, this divine exchange or dialogue always contains two things: the partners are perfectly transparent to each other; and they possess a kind of impenetrable "personal" mystery. (TD2, 258)*

It is worth noting that it is Balthasar, the Catholic, and not Moltmann, the Reformed theologian, who reserves a special place for Luther, when he thinks of the triune God as essentially a conversation or colloquy.[29] Balthasar's dialogical model of the Trinity might also be regarded as a critical counter to the famous remark by the young Hegel that the Word uttered is the Word heard,[30] which could not more eloquently testify to the reduction of trinitarian dialogue to monologue.

For Balthasar, Moltmann's appeal in *Trinity and the Kingdom* to the Kabbalistic symbol of *tsimsum* or divine self-limitation serves to replace and disguise the commitment to the Hegelian view of kenosis (*TK*, 59; *TD2*, 109, 262-64; *TD5*, 94) It helps to disguise it by introducing an esoteric symbol that ambiguously supports both the rhetorics of freedom and necessity. But in the final analysis the symbol of *tsimsum* serves as the conceptual equivalent of the essentialist and teleological form of kenosis that characterizes Hegel's thought. For Balthasar the point is sufficient. He does not feel under obligation to tease out the implications of the intersection of Christian thought and the Kabbalah in the modern period,[31] nor the role the Kabbalah plays in German Idealism. But it could be said that Moltmann's very appeal to the Kabbalah in this context represents the strongest possible indication of his debt to Hegel who baptizes the Kabbalah in *Lectures on the History of Philosophy*,[32] and does so in a context in which traditional forms of Judaism are consistently, even vehemently disparaged.

Balthasar's instincts here are sharper. He senses that, as deployed in Christian or post-Christian contexts, the Kabbalah is a speculative discourse that bears only a critical relation to its original habitat. While scholars of Kabbalah would likely agree that the Kabbalah constitutes a step beyond common interpretation of the God-world relation, they would on the whole be reluctant to judge that the Kabbalah is constitutionally oppositional.[33] Moltmann has no such compunction, however, and the Kabbalah appears to bear a negative relation to everything Jewish except prophecy, especially prophecy as it bears upon the messianic. Moltmann's privileging of the messianic and kabbalistic aspects of Judaism explains in part Balthasar's use of the term 'Jewish,' which comes to represent something other than Judaism defined by its covenantal relation to God and the practices that make for righteousness and holiness. When Balthasar in *Glory of the Lord 6,* following early Christian conventions, plainly sketches Judaism as a preparation for Christianity, he affirms its Halakic center and refuses to identify it with messianism, apocalyptic, or the Kabbalah. Indeed, he obviously worries about the association between the Kabbalah and Gnosticism, sometimes hyphenating them, as we saw in part 1, without explanation. Without explicitly making the case, he worries that the Christian adaptation of the Kabbalah serves as a vehicle not only for a Marcionite program in which the old dispensation is rendered nugatory, but as a vehicle for a Valentinian program in which the Christian story is refigured so that the meaning of the story is radically altered. For example, he is especially concerned about the explanatory use of the 'silence of God' in the Holocaust. Although more nearly a symbol of prophetic discourse – albeit in the mode of complaint – in modern thought the 'silence' of God has been invested with the explanatory potential of the Kabbalah's discourse on evil. Its hypostatization recalls in fact the 'silence' (*Sige*) of Valentinian Gnosticism (*TL2*, 111-12).

The final element of narrative figuration constitutive of the identification of a profound Hegelian presence in Moltmann's trinitarian thought is the commitment – however latent – to necessitarianism. Moltmann divulges this commitment in the unremittingly negative stance he takes against talk of divine will, divine aseity, and correlatively human being as incommensurate to the divine and thus radically dependent. An unsympathetic Balthasar thinks that Moltmann is dangerously one-sided at the very least, and operates in terms of a binary logic that is typically Hegelian. Despite his talk of divine freedom, Moltmann fails sufficiently to defend it as a primary Christian option. Here his failure parallels that of Hegel, who in good conscience also tries to defend a view of freedom as self-determination that is compatible with necessity. Again, as is the case with respect to kenosis, Moltmann introduces a trope that replaces and disguises its real commitments. Confessing his 'panentheism' in *Trinity and the Kingdom* (*TD5*, 228), Moltmann gives support to the Neoplatonic trope of *bonum diffusivum sui* as representing something of a third option between theological voluntarism and ontological necessity (*TK*, 57). Balthasar lodges no official protest against the trope, and in fact uses it liberally himself. But in his own avowal he seems to have grasped Wittgenstein's point that meaning is use. For whether the trope functions mischievously or not depends on the context of its use. For instance, he thinks that the *Enneads* supports a non-necessitarian reading in a way the context of the *Elements of Theology* does not. Thus, Plotinus is hospitable to Christianity in a way that Proclus is not. While Balthasar's judgment here is open to challenge, his real point is that judgment with respect to particulars is required: no interpretative aprioris should be in operation when the theological tradition is submitted to scrutiny. He reads the tradition as if it is antecedently unlikely that the tradition as a whole is either impeachable or unimpeachable. In *Glory of the Lord*, for example, Balthasar worries about the use of the trope in Eckhart, Cusanus, and Bruno, thinkers whose thought, he believes, shows a decided tendency towards monism. Balthasar is persuaded, however, that in the work of Pseudo-Dionysius, Maximus, and Bonaventure the trope genuinely suggests a third option. His question then is to which of these Neoplatonic traditions does Moltmann more nearly belong, the one that is assimilable by Hegelian discourse, or the one that is not. A definite verdict is implied, if not explicitly rendered: Moltmann's deployment of the trope is more Proclean than Plotinian, more Eckhartian than Augustinian, more Brunan than Bonaventuran, and for all these reasons more heterodox than orthodox.

The epical quality of Moltmann's trinitarianism, together with the casualness with which it names what God 'must be,' make it more continuous with the kind of trinitarian theodicy, illustrated by Hegel, than Moltmann would have us believe. The desire for distance from Hegel is marked throughout Moltmann's texts by his appropriation of brands of thinking in critical dialogue with Hegel such as those of Rosenzweig, Benjamin, and Critical Theory. Even in his earliest texts, Moltmann enlists Bloch's 'principle of hope' to get critical leverage on Hegel's commitment to absolute knowledge and Hegel's brand of realized eschatology (*TD5*, 169). But this retreat to thinkers critical of Hegel is effective theologically if and only if it is accompanied by a strong sense of epistemic reserve concerning the triune God and a disposition towards apophasis. Otherwise a would-be heuristic eschatology fades perceptibly into a constitutive theodicy. From Balthasar's point of view, the fading represents an effect of the Hegelian system such that in Moltmann hope is ignorant only of the when of redemption not of the what, or even the basic constituents of the who. Is hope then itself suspect? Or does hope need to be rethought? Perhaps taken definitely out of its eschatological location? In answer, Balthasar refuses to suspect hope, thinks that it should be rethought, but most certainly not thought outside the context of eschatology, albeit one that has the Triune God as its ultimate horizon.

In and through a report on Péguy's *The Portal of Hope*, in *Theo-Drama 5* (181-88) Balthasar offers a trinitarian-eschatological revisioning of hope.[34] That Péguy's poem is intended by Balthasar to be a foil to Moltmann is clear in that it immediately follows the section of the text devoted to an exposition and critique of Moltmann's thought. The two most basic features of this refiguring are that 'hope' now finds its primary location in God, and that all futurist eschatology finds its rightful place in a realized eschatology (*TD5*, 182). 'Hope' in God expresses God's hyperbolic concern for each and every person, God's determined reluctance to give up on anyone, as this is indicated in the parable of the prodigal son. It is by means of the insertion of our lives into God's hope that our lives are given meaning, and that we are provided with a genuine sense of dynamism and newness. The vertical dimension, therefore, is absolutely crucial. Péguy can serve as a foil for Moltmann because he shares Moltmann's genuine concerns about God's relation to the world, without sharing the latter's tendency to over-explain and thereby become trapped in the web of Hegel's master-discourse. On the basis of scripture, liturgical tradition, and basic Christian spirituality *The Portal of Hope* suggests we can be persuaded that God is a God who cares infinitely and concretely for each of us, indeed to the point that God will put Godself at absolute risk. But this God who holds out the promise of an eternal future is the God who is absolutely distinct from us, yet whose distance is the nearest nearness. We have faith in this God to the extent to which we share in his hope and thus participate in his life. But unlike Hegel's, Bloch's, and Moltmann's autonomy, our anticipation of this sharing in eternal life is characterized by heteronomy, specifically by obedience and waiting. We trust as much as know this God, for our language is only relatively adequate to the gift that is given, that imparts nothing less than the giver. Thus the language of poetry – as should be the case with the language of theology – has its ground and term in the silence from which the Word comes and which it traverses as it enacts our salvation by making present the future of eternity.[35]

No less definitely, even if more subtly than in the case of Hegel, in his epical trinitarianism Moltmann reinscribes theodicy. It is the explanatory predilection that affects or infects aspects of Moltmann's reflection that appear genuinely to point a way beyond Hegel. One of the most conspicuous of these aspects is Moltmann's reflection in the *Trinity and the Kingdom* on the doxological (83, 126). Here, harkening back directly to Calvin, and through him to even earlier traditions, Moltmann attempts to speak of the relation between Father and Son as being constitutively defined as 'handing up' (*paradonai*) and 'being handed up' (80-1). As he speaks this language Moltmann seems for once to be not embarrassed by recalling the Lamb of Revelation. As an apocalyptic Christology of the sort favored by Balthasar comes into view, so also does Balthasar's post-classical reflection on the dramatic relation and colloquy between the eternal Father and Son. As these relations figure divine glory, they also intimate something like an analogy of suffering in God. The suffering of 'giving up' and 'been given up' are equally real, and while related are different. Here is a real opening should Moltmann not wish to say too much, to hypothesize rather than assert. But the opening is closed off in insistence on the reality of suffering almost as if we had direct access to it. The reserve that necessarily goes with such predication is lost.

Perhaps this is not an unexpected result from a theologian, who illustrates contempt for the theological tradition and would deride as mere sophistication the history of Christian reflection on the nature and limits of religious language. But it puts him at odds with his avowal of the non-redundancy of biblical language which does not admit of total translation. Moreover, Moltmann does not seem to know the precedent for his specific version of doxological trinitarianism that aims at rendering a dynamic divine open to the world. The precedent is supplied by the Pietist Friedrich Christoph Oetinger, who in the eighteenth century offered an alternative to the views of Protestant Scholasticism, Spinozism and Voluntarism, by presenting an account of the divine that is influenced especially by the Kabbalah.[36] Of course, at one level acknowledging such a precedent would hardly be unwelcome. Oetinger's thought represents just the kind of minority report that Moltmann finds attractive. And, as we have seen, Moltmann does appeal to Kabbalistic symbols as explanations of how and why the divine is constituted in the way it is. Oetinger's fully elaborated Christian Kabbalistic system centered on divine glory or beauty (*Tifereth*) could easily serve, therefore, as a warrant for Moltmann's more opportunistic citation, but also as something of a template for what a more systematic Kabbalistic orientation would look like. But unfortunately for Moltmann – and Balthasar recognizes this – deeper association with the Kabbalah does not in itself describe an alternative to Hegel. With its theogonic and theodicy agenda, the Kabbalah – at least in its Christian form – is a speculative discourse that admits of being inscribed within a Hegelian epical matrix.[37]

If Moltmann's theodicy reflection is problematic because even in its attempt to articulate a trinitarian doxology it insists on speculative knowledge, it is also problematic for two other reasons. The first concerns some ambiguity concerning who is saved. While in some obvious sense human beings are the object of salvation, it is neither clear that human beings are the exclusive object, nor that a constitutive disadvantage does not apply to those who do not have the good fortune to live or die in end-time. After all, if in and through its enactment in the world and history the divine overcomes the imperfection of non-involvement and realizes a perfection that is coincident with divine pathos, it is difficult to repress the analogy between this view and the Gnostic one of the self-redeeming redeemer. In addition, in chapter 6 of *Trinity and the Kingdom* Moltmann commits himself to a utopianism in which salvation in the full and proper sense belongs to those in 'end time,' who render the kind of interconnectedness, freedom, and knowledge that in the Joachimite scheme, to which Moltmann pledges allegiance, mark salvation. Balthasar resolutely resists both as distorting the biblical view articulated in plural ways in the theological tradition.

With respect to the second problem of the restriction of salvation in the full and proper sense to a community in *Endzeit*, Balthasar would worry whether Moltmann observes his own distinction between a properly apocalyptic view of the future and a teleological view more redolent of Hegelianism,[38] which, however speculative, remains in important respects continuous with Enlightenment progressivism. An authentically apocalyptic figuration takes away the disadvantage of those who do not live in the dangerous time of transition by speaking to the raising of the dead effected by divine power. Paradigmatically in the case of Revelation – which is a text that generally embarrasses Moltmann – the ground of resurrection is supplied by the Lamb. Implicitly, then, for Balthasar, all of his talk of the cross and his occasional nods in direction of the Lamb, notwithstanding, Moltmann lacks any real insight into the paschal mystery as the answer to the theodicy question without it being a theodicy answer. For the Lamb, who enfolds all of history and relativizes distinctions between past and future, is the one in whom we have faith, in whom we hope for resurrection, and whom we love, and all of this by way of response to the love that unmakes us and makes us anew. Talk of hope notwithstanding, in Moltmann this Lamb is made hostage to a Hegelian logic of love, which in the end is the Hegelian logic of divine self-recuperation, which in effect ontologically underwrites worldly suffering. Here Moltmann and Heidegger constitute an unlikely pair: both are passionately interested in purging thought of theodicy, yet both reinscribe it, Heidegger following a Nietzschean,[39] Moltmann the Hegelian line. Balthasar believes that Moltmann's failure to understand the agency of Christ in the paschal mystery is of a piece with his failure to understand christological time, about which Balthasar waxes eloquent in *Theo-Drama 5* (19-57). This blindness in turn hinders acceptance that the God, who gives himself in and to suffering, is also a God of justice and judgment. This is something that must be affirmed on grounds of congruence with scripture and by way of protest against history, irreducible, as Job saw, to an ethically justified equation.

Although more abstract, the concern about whether the divine as well as humanity is the object of salvation is equally important. Obviously, to make the divine the object of salvation transgresses a rule of Christian speech which, if first explicitly formulated in the Christian tradition by Irenaeus and Tertullian,[40] represents an extrapolation of basic biblical logic in continuity with earlier Christian and Jewish traditions. Beyond this, however, divine self-saving is coextensive with the Hegelian renarration of the Christian narrative. While, on the one hand, the self-saving of the divine is different than the salvation of human beings in *Endzeit*, on the other, it includes it as an episode in its own articulation. Self-saving is more nearly the master code. What is implied, but not treated directly by Balthasar, is that, like Hegel, Moltmann's discourse is marked not by one but by two modes of degenerative apocalypse discourse, the one Valentinian, the other Joachimite. As Hegel's discourse showed, the tension between these two apocalypse discourses does not necessarily mean that they cannot be integrated, but leaves open the principle of integration. As I suggested in my supplement to Balthasar's genealogy in chapter 1, good reasons can be supplied as to why we might think that it is Valentinian apocalypse that inscribes Joachimite apocalyptic rather than the other way around.

A major way in which the inscription is facilitated in Moltmann is the univocal identification of what both the divine and human beings need to be delivered from, that is, suffering. In the Bible in general, and in the prophetic literature in particular, human beings need to be delivered much more from sin than suffering, although Job importantly strikes an important complementary note. By and large, the Christian tradition followed suit. And it did so not simply because of the too great importance invested in the fall story of Genesis 3, but rather because the biblical narrative as a whole could be read as a chronicle of human rebellion and disobedience. As Hegel erases sin by redescribing it as appropriate thirst for knowledge, Moltmann puts it in brackets (*TK*, 78). Salvation is essentially salvation from suffering. Again, Moltmann is involved in a reaction formation. He thinks he must choose between Job and the rest of scripture, rather than appeal to Job as a forensic tool to modify idolatrous claims made about the causal nexus between sin and suffering.

Ambiguous Identities: Apocalyptic Naming

GRANTED HIS EVANGELIC INTENTION and his occasional avowal of standard theological positions, on Balthasar's reading in the final analysis Moltmann re-enacts Hegel's epical trinitarianism and thus fundamentally changes the grammar of Christian discourse. This remains true despite the exaggeration of the horizontal line and the explicit disavowal of absolute knowledge. Nevertheless, the culling of Hegel by introducing crucial elements of Left-Wing Hegelian critique does not change its basic frame. It is in Balthasar's consideration of the basic identity of this frame that shows his essential difference from de Lubac. For de Lubac, what is wrong with a theology such as that of Moltmann's is that it repeats Joachimism.[41] Balthasar is persuaded that the Joachimite tradition has demonstrated robustness and adaptability in the modern period, and that it would behoove Christian theology to remain alert to its many forms and to distinguish itself from them. Yet, whether opposing Joachim with Augustine, or placing oneself in Bonaventure's critical shoes, is sufficient will depend very much on the inner complexity and constitution of the form of eschatological trinitarianism that is creating anxiety. Balthasar sees that in some forms of post-Hegelian thought Joachimism is linked to, in fact subordinated to, a speculative discourse that speaks confidently of divine becoming and is hospitable only to a Trinity that develops. To acknowledge this other element is to be compelled to introduce the entirely different taxon of Valentinianism. And should this element be perceived to be dominant in an appropriation of Hegel, then the judgment has to be that what is repeated is Valentinianism, albeit in a form that is more history and suffering friendly than the ancient paradigms, but no less an instance of its grammar. Moltmann turns out, for Balthasar, in the end to be a 'son of Valentinus' because such a good 'son of Hegel.'

Balthasar is less concerned about the apparent preposterousness of the ascription of 'Valentinianism' to Moltmann than in insuring its delay. Some forms of theological thought, for Balthasar, admit of easy naming, whether positive or negative, for example, ressourcement theology and Neo-Scholasticism, ecclesially aesthetic forms of modern theology and Romantic forms, Hamann's version of Romanticism and Schiller's version. Balthasar leaves no one in doubt throughout his career, and especially in *Glory of the Lord*, that the first member of each pair should be as enthusiastically embraced as the second member of the pair should be firmly rejected. But some forms of theology do not admit of easy judgement. Some even hang in the balance after sifting, indeed, after a significant measure of sifting. Moltmann's theology is one of these, but so also are the theologies of Jüngel, Bulgakov, and Soloviev. It is interesting that all these speculative specimens are both post-Hegelian and friendly towards eschatological and apocalyptic styles of thought. But why are these forms important at all, and how does discrimination occur? With respect to their importance, some reasons come readily to mind. These are profoundly aesthetic-dramatic forms of theology that exercise an appeal unmatched by many forms of traditional thought and their post-Enlightenment substitutes. If the general question they raise is whether their charms are in the end specifically Christian or otherwise, the specific question they raise is whether they repeat in novel fashion the biblical narrative, that is, operate in terms of its fundamental grammar, or whether they operate outside it in terms of the transformative grammar of Valentinianism? All four are candidates for avowal and disavowal. Balthasar responds differently to each. He not only exonerates Bulgakov and Soloviev from Hegelian and Valentinian infection, but interprets both to be anti-Hegelian and anti-Valentinian. As he does so, it is evident that Soloviev benefits more from his association with Bulgakov than Bulgakov does from his association with Soloviev. Balthasar queries the Jüngel of *God as the Mystery of the World* and worries whether Jüngel has deserted Barth. Yet, he refuses to prosecute a case. The refusal is motivated, for with his truly Barthian focus on divine freedom, his Lutheran sense that ontology at best follows biblical identification of God in Christ but never catches up with it, his openness to other discourses that matches an insistence on the irradicable mystery of Christ and the triune God, and finally his exploration of symbol and metaphor,[42] Jüngel seems as good a candidate for exoneration from Hegelian ascription as Bulgakov and better than Soloviev.

It is not a little interesting that this is his group, and that Balthasar deprives himself of such easy-outs as the 'death-of-God' theology. Balthasar does mention 'death of God' theology in *Theo-Drama 5* (244) but just as one more example of a theology that wishes to revise the traditional view of the impassibility of the divine. Thomas Altizer is mentioned in this context, but there is no analysis of a position, which although atmospherically is Nietzschean, is substantively Hegelian. Altizer's 'death of God' theology can rightly be interpreted as a sustained interpretation of Hegel's discussion in the section on 'Revealed Religion' in the *Phenomenology* in which the pure divine empties itself into the world and more specifically into Christ. The act of kenosis is not simply one act among others, but absolutely unambiguously defines who God is. Altizer's Hegelianism is significantly more consistent than that of Moltmann, his kenoticism much more radical, his trinitarianism much more casual if it exists at all.[43] Kenoticism is its defining feature, around which orbit the erotic and necessitarian nature of its taking up the Hegelian coding of the Christian narrative. The kenoticism is iterative; the kenosis of the transcendent God initiates a kenotic chain that is complete in the human community. For the same reason, its figure is that of irony, since emptying is the means by which the divine-human is actualized. A remarkable feature of Altizer's work is how little it changes over the years, even when the 'death of God' label gets suspended. Although not obviously, the books of the 'death of God' period admit of 'apocalyptic' designation. This is Altizer's self-understanding in such later works as *Genesis and Apocalypse* and *The Apocalypse of God* in which the emptying of the transcendent divine is the obverse of the eros that marks the development of the truly human divine, which is the really real divine.[44] Altizer indulges in a kind of Dionysian celebration of this becoming that is matched by Hegel only at the very end of the *Phenomenology* (#806) when he famously quotes Schiller's sacramental imaging of the kingdom of spirits as a genuine community founded on a generative love. In his own self-understanding, he has moved definitively beyond classical Christianity. A concession, however, appears in his admitting into discourse the Trinity, but the grounds of admittance testify to his continuous loyalty to Hegel. If the Trinity is a symbol of the virtual divine, then this Trinity can only be understood non-hypostatically. Indeed, Altizer has no compunction about thinking of the Trinity as Sabellian in nature (*GG*, 108). Altizer takes it for granted that the Hegelianism that overcomes classical Christianity overcomes Gnosticism, for on his view classical Christianity presents an exoteric version of Gnosticism as Gnosticism offers an esoteric version of classical Christianity. Irenaeus would demur: Gnosticism and classical Christianity contend with each other. Staudenmaier would add: Hegelianism is the exoteric form of Valentinianism, Valentinianism the esoteric form of Hegelianism.

Balthasar, then, in fact attends only to the difficult cases. Crucially, readings of these species of thought demand more than academic 'on the one hand and on the other.' One could say with only the slightest degree of exaggeration that the site of naming is apocalyptic. Apocalyptic naming is naming in extremis, indeed, a naming of apocalyptic forms of theology as to their patrimony, whether this patrimony is that of Irenaeus and Staudenmaier or rather that of Valentinus and Hegel. It occurs on the razor's edge, and avails of a razor to differentiate forms of theology which otherwise – for good or ill – are not easily distinguished. This is one of the main reasons why Revelation is so important: as it outlines the apocalyptic dimensions of decision, it also announces the apocalyptic dimensions of unveiling forms of thought difficult to tell apart. The telling has to and will occur; the stakes are in the post-Enlightenment period too high. Perhaps Revelation declares a general truth: the stakes are always too high not to intervene, not to unveil and tell apart, not to effect a judgment that is in significant part eschatological. After all the sifting and discerning, what is required is vision that burns away accident. In this sense also, Staudenmaier and even Bulgakov are proponents of apocalyptic naming, although here again they repeat (and supplement) Irenaeus, the great namer of declension of the early Church. *Against Heresies* provides for Balthasar the basic pattern of apocalyptic naming as it also produces a constructive dramatic theology in which the world matters so much to the triune God that he wills it eschatologically to participate in his fullness. There exists, then, a tradition of apocalyptic naming, as there exists a tradition of the named, apocalypse discourses called out as discourses in which the finely tuned balance of the horizontal and the vertical is upset and in effect both spiral out of control. One of Balthasar's essential tasks is to write theologians into this particular page of the book dealing with the anatomy of misremembering. There is plenty of room for theologians who remember the God of Christ, saints who perform the triune God's will, and Christians who find this God unforgettable despite their many lapses of memory.

To speak, as I have done throughout, of relations within theological discourse as relations between fathers and sons is to open on a world of metaphor that articulates fidelity and betrayal. In one way or another, to invoke the relation is to conjure worlds as fraught, to insinuate Oedipus, Uranus, and Chronus into analysis. Certainly, I have been suggesting that Balthasar's relation to the major detectors of comprehensive misremembering in the tradition is non-oedipal, even if, or especially if the son constitutes a genuine development of the father. I have gone to some pains to emphasize that the many ways in which Balthasar supplements his Catholic anti-Hegelian father, Franz Anton Staudenmaier, and his ultimate anti-Valentinian father, Irenaeus, while also recognizing the way in which Balthasar is both faithful to and diverges from Bulgakov and Hamann, both of whom I take in different ways to be 'virtual' fathers. I have taken seriously, but not too seriously, Derrida's view about supplementation, namely that supplementation is irreducibly involved in displacement and replacement. The complement to the non-oedipal relation that defines the continuing process of tradition is that the father invites rather than blocks the necessary supplementation of the son. Or in other words, the complement to the avoidance of the oedipal relation is an avoidance of the Laius complex that would dictate that theological fathers allow only replicas, not genuinely individuated repetitions.

The question of who are Balthasar's fathers and what is the nature of their relation compels the question of who are Hegel's sons. Although Balthasar is persuaded that Hegel's sons are many, it is important rhetorically that he actually sustain the case in at least one instance. Jüngel gives considerable cause for concern in this respect. Balthasar raises red flags, but desists from making the case. This is not something Balthasar deprives himself of with respect to Moltmann. As with Feuerbach, Marx, and Bloch, Moltmann denies Hegelian paternity, even as he attests his proximity in terms of basic vision, essential theological task, and the need for a trinitarian articulation that fully accommodates pathos. Acknowledging Moltmann's intentions to pull out of the Hegelian orbit is one thing, the judgment whether Moltmann really escapes the gravitational pull of Hegel's system, which distorts the Christian narrative in a Valentinian way, is another. One way of framing Moltmann's dilemma is whether Moltmann is oedipal enough to achieve his theological and philosophical liberation. On this point Balthasar is skeptical: Moltmann is unable to kill Hegel as father, and thus is unable to dispatch Valentinus. And it is just this incapacity that releases the other metaphors of fathers and sons to pertinence, that is, the Laius image as the converse of the Oedipus image, and the even more terrifying, because more primordial, pair of images, of Chronos castrating Uranus, and of Uranus devouring his children. From a Balthasarian point of view, Moltmann lies frozen and helpless before the gaping mouth of Uranus. Moltmann is no Chronos who castrates Uranus, achieving his own independence and that of Christian theology. But ultimately, the hyperboles of violent relations going in either direction themselves indicate just how far wide of the mark Moltmann strays. For Balthasar the very violence of the escape strategies indicates how hopeless the situation is, and how repetition – indeed of a non-constructive kind – is inevitable. Oepidus is implicitly Laius, Chronos is implicitly Uranus.

The way out for Balthasar lies in what Hegel and Moltmann give up, that is, the tradition. It is this that sets free, that makes for non-violent relations between sons and fathers, in which fathers become sons of their sons and sons fathers of their fathers, and are empowered to do so by their being symbolic expressions of Christ that are elaborated in the Spirit. In the mainline Christian tradition, genuine repetition happens, not repetition compulsion. The site of tradition, as Balthasar speaks so movingly, is ultimately the space defined by the relation between the divine persons. This space is not only the space of peace; it is the space of freedom, freedom from the anxiety of influence not excluded. Moltmann structurally remains then an extension of the conceptually protected trinitarian narrative he would overcome, and thus provides a living witness to the power of this discourse over time. The result is ironical. Perhaps no philosopher of religion spoke so eloquently of the prerogatives of time, was so anxious to displace eternity, and valorize the moment of intellectual production than Hegel. But by the same token, equally no philosopher of religion so clearly overcomes time in his system, and views all of history *sub specie aeternitatis.* This even such a thoroughgoing supporter of Hegel such as Kojève admits.[45] But overcoming time does not consist simply in making the past present, but in domesticating the past in the eternal present of the Hegelian system. Kierkegaard feared this, but feared even more that in the Hegelian system the 'unanticipatable future' also gets 'recollected,' and that Hegel would make epigones of detractors and supporters alike. It is precisely this mastering of time in all its dimensions that Harold Bloom takes to be an indelible feature of the hermeneutic profile of Valentinianism, and which can be recommended above anything the Jewish or Christian traditions have offered.[46] Arguably, it is the discernment that Moltmann indicates the return of Valentinianism that represents the final codicil to his rejection. In his epical trinitarianism Moltmann is a victim of Hegel's amortizing discourse. To this extent he allows a place for the Valentinian ghost. For according to the genealogist, Balthasar, Hegel's discourse is haunted. Its rejection of much of the artistic, religious, and philosophical tradition does not make for a brave new world, but serves as the condition for it being the site of return of marginal and excluded discourses. Hegel's discourse is a house of ghosts, the first among equals of which is Valentinianism, which presides precisely as the *Doppelgänger* of the ecstatic discourse of the mainline theological tradition.

PART 4

EIDETIC APOCALYPTIC AND ITS CONTEMPORARY RIVALS

Eidetic Apocalyptic

It would seem to follow from Balthasar's searing critique of the Joachimite and Valentinian modes of apocalypse, both of which are structuring principles of Hegel's putative Christian discourse, that he would recommend that theology head resolutely in a non-apocalyptic direction. At the same time, this recommendation logically would be enacted in his own trilogy which, thus, would constitute itself as an exemplary instance of an non-apocalyptic theology. While Balthasar has in fact been interpreted in this way,[1] this would be, for him, precisely the kind of reaction formation he finds problematic and which in different ways finds itself expressed in Liberal Protestant theology and modern Catholic thought. A cure, for theology, he believes, cannot be effected by a sanitized modality of theology that forsakes symbol and story for ethical core or even kerygma. Symbol and story are irreducible: both are necessary if Christianity is to render adequately the paradoxical lordship of Christ as *agnus dei*. Nor can a cure be effected by turning aside the critiques of reason as wrong-headed and restoring *ratio* to the place it once enjoyed before its status in the modern period became so questionable following quickly on its exaggerated elevation. An important part of the problem is the understanding of *ratio* itself, the range of its intentions and applications, and whether it is or is not understood to be situated in a dynamic of knowing that surpasses its reasoning and its conclusions. Even if, as *Glory of the Lord* and *Theo-Logic* clearly show, Balthasar is not fully persuaded that premodern *ratio* requires Kantian critique and post-Kantian metaphysical refiguration,[2] he is as concerned as any transcendental Thomist about the tendency in premodern articulations of *ratio* towards a reductive objectivism.[3] Symbol and story, then, are the necessities of renovation, of the restoration of the actuality and possibility of the future of Christian discourse, theological discourse in particular. As *Glory of the Lord 6-7* make transparent, symbol and story are constitutive features of the biblical canon in general, and Balthasar is not shy about attributing these features especially to biblical apocalyptic, and suggesting thereby that it constitutes the real contrary of Hegel's pseudo-dramatic pyrotechnics. As a true other, the apocalyptic discourse of the New Testament, and the visionary-dramatic theology it encourages, constitute an authentic memory of the future rather than a misremembering that deprives discourse about God of a future, and thus prevents the future of God, or God as future,[4] from appearing. Balthasar's openness to apocalyptic, indeed, the apocalyptic inclination of Balthasar's thought, has been indicated throughout, even when the Bible has not been our explicit theme. This is especially true of Part 3, where it is relatively transparent that all four theological figures enlisted to combat the outbreak of speculative takeover of Christianity are not only biblical, but are even more specifically apocalyptic theologians – albeit ones who display very different styles as they work from quite specific contexts – for whom the Trinity is the encompassing construct.

For Balthasar, the articulation of an adequate apocalyptic theology cannot avoid dealing with the book of Revelation. Aware that Revelation has been a sign of contradiction in the Christian tradition, aware of its sectarian and chiliastic reading, aware also of its appropriation by, and pneumatological inflection in, the Joachimite tradition that finds expression in German Idealism, Balthasar is not prepared to reject or even marginalize this text. For Balthasar Revelation is neither a theological embarrassment, nor a text whose hyperboles and general excess justify the courtesy of silence. Revelation is a text of Christian vision communicated almost exclusively on the level of symbol. It makes a distinct contribution to biblical aesthetics and dramatics in its focus on the suffering of the Lamb and his glorification within an essentially trinitarian horizon. Given its visionary and symbolic surplus, Revelation is the 'eidetic' text par excellence of scripture (*TD4*, 16). While in his use of the word 'eidetic' Balthasar recalls Plato and even more proximally Husserl,[5] the meaning is relatively non-technical in that it indicates that Christian perception or seeing is correlative to the meaning or form that is its object, rather than meaning or form being the objective correlative of perception or vision. Thought one way, the eidetic quality of Revelation disqualifies it both religiously and theologically: it simply says too much about Christ as the object of faith, is too knowing about the structure and dynamic of history, and renders thematic a transcendence that can only be horizonal. Balthasar insists, however, that it is precisely Revelation's christological and trinitarian eidetics that should claim our religious and theological attention. The text could not make it more clear that vision is always a seeing of what exceeds the prospects of vision and that the symbols deployed are inadequate to what they aim to disclose. For Balthasar, the lesson of Revelation is that the eidetic and the apophatic necessarily go together. The point is crucial, for it contrasts with a movement in modern and postmodern thought which, in the wake of Hegel, tends to conceive of apocalyptic in terms of function rather than content, indeed essentially to consider apocalyptic as a form of apophatic discourse, however different in style from the more hieratic Neoplatonic forms in the Christian tradition.[6]

Read properly, Balthasar believes, Revelation can be seen to articulate an apocalyptic or apocalypse form that functions critically to diagnose theological deformation and to represent an alternative to messianism and other forms of apocalyptic that are unable to transcend the inbuilt religious and ethical limits of the apocalyptic genre in the biblical field broadly understood.[7] The critical capability of Revelation is a function, however, of its close relation to the Gospel of John. Balthasar is convinced that as mutually interpreting texts the Gospel of John and Revelation provide the theologian with a narrative frame and a Christian vocabulary and syntax that both expose and offer an alternative to repetitions in Hegelian and post-Hegelian discourse of Valentinianism with its simulacrum of the biblical narrative and its insistence on revelation as a form of knowledge with exhaustive explanatory potential. In short, Balthasar thinks that from Revelation in concert with the Fourth Gospel a theologian can extract or develop an eidetic apocalyptic theology, which is christological in its basic focus, trinitarian in scope, and that has substantial critical force.

The analysis of Balthasar's elaboration of an eidetic apocalyptic theology as a theology that is beyond Hegelian misremembering is the main task of chapter 6. *Theo-Drama* provides the central textual focus. *Glory of the Lord 6 & 7* serve the role of complements and are specifically called on when the link between aesthetic and apocalyptic figuration is under consideration. *Theo-Logic 2 & 3* are deployed as supplements to the extent to which these texts elucidate the logic of divine love that resists not only the logic of the schools, but also Hegel's dialectical logic and its various manifestations in modern theology of a kenotic and apocalyptic bent. In line with part 3, I also attend to the way in which Balthasar leads back his theology with its essentially Irenaean architecture,[8] and its self-consciously Irenaean mode of resistance to theological forms of thought perceived to be extra-ecclesial, to the eidetics of Revelation in its union with and qualification by the Gospel of John which construes history as the battle-ground between truth and the lie. An important feature of the chapter is to show how in addition to the historical Irenaeus, the major figures whom Balthasar calls on to take the fight to Hegel, supplement him here also. This is especially true of Bulgakov, for whom Revelation is not simply an important text as it is with the historical Irenaeus, and also Staudenmaier and Hamann, but the text that is regulative for a theology that would move beyond the impasse of modernity that makes certain styles of theology anachronistic. It is important to underscore also that this regression from Irenaeus to Revelation and John releases Balthasar from the obligation to decide absolutely between Irenaeus and other major traditional theological figures for whom he has special affinity, for example, Augustine, Anselm, and Pascal. Here I will pay some attention to Augustine, for Augustine too is a kind of apocalyptic theologian who also engages in the exposé of speculative and eschatological excesses. I do so here with the understanding that the Augustinian line of reflection, which is appropriately economic and trinitarian, complements rather than displaces the Irenaeanism of Balthasar's apocalyptic diagnosis and rebuttal of speculative deformation. At the same time this is not to say that in Balthasar Augustine is constitutively in second place when it comes to apocalyptic diagnosis and rebuttal. The succeeding volume will show that Augustine or Augustinianism is the main theological constellation called on in diagnosing and rebutting non-speculative forms of apocalyptic of which Heidegger supplies a supreme instance.

Laying bare the hermeneutic decisions Balthasar makes regarding the status of Revelation as an apocalyptic text, and its relation to other textual examples of biblical apocalyptic, is in service of extracting the doxological and liturgical trinitarianism, which Balthasar thinks is the answer to Hegelianism. A further task of this chapter is to show how in and through a hermeneutic of Revelation Balthasar affirms divine justice and limits it at once, with this limitation taking the form of a critical distantiation not only from popular forms of eschatology that cannot eschew vindictiveness, but also a number of theological forms in the mainline Christian tradition that cannot avoid giving succor to those who deploy Nietzsche's notion of *ressentiment.* At the same time, Revelation's central symbol of the *agnus dei* inevitably raises the issue of whether in a different manner than Hegel it inscribes violence into the very fabric of Christianity and its theological elucidation. Although Balthasar does not address the issue straight-on, his interesting discussion of Girard in *Theo-Drama 4* (298-313) and his support of Anselm's atonement theory (*TD4*, 255-66) evince at least an oblique dealing with the difficult issue of divine violence in the 'handing over' of the Son by the Father.

A second line of investigation, already hinted at, is the theme of the final two chapters. Balthasar essentially chooses to fight Hegelian apocalyptic, and thus Valentinian apocalypse and Joachimite apocalyptic, on an eidetic level that matches their own. This is, however, neither the only, nor standard, way of apocalyptically resisting Hegelianism in the twentieth century. Leaving in parenthesis for the purpose of this volume the kind of resistance enacted by Heidegger and Derrida which, it could be argued, has an apocalyptic horizon,[9] the self-consciously apocalyptic Christian theology of Johann Baptist Metz, and the messianic thought of Walter Benjamin, which Metz enlists along with Bloch, have a particular claim to our attention. In chapter 7 I will lay out Metz's apocalyptic answer to a modernity characterized by forgetting and speculative forms of thought, while bringing attention both to the different dominance-recessive ratio of these concerns, as well as how forgetting is differently understood because it has a different object. Yet the Metzian genre of apocalyptic, while not without content, is considerably more epistemically reserved than that of Balthasar as well as his Hegelian opposition, and while invested in scripture to the extent of drawing out the biblical narrative, is avoidant with respect to Revelation and the Gospel of John. Conversely, Metzian apocalyptic is more obviously ethically valenced, and is Christianly concerned with injustice and especially the injustice that creates the victims of history. The chapter addresses the systematic differences between these apocalyptic schemes as well as systemic tensions against the backdrop of some of the same priorities, especially Christ's solidarity with the 'lost.' Although it does not attempt a final adjudication with respect to adequacy, it suggests that Balthasar has to surrender much less of Christian substance than Metz, while allowing for the development of at the very least what we have been calling the 'ethical' side of Balthasar's theology.

Treating the relationship between the apocalyptic forms of Metz and Balthasar necessarily raises the question of the relation between Balthasar and the apocalyptic types that Metz presupposes and attempts to synthesize, that is, those of Bloch and Benjamin.[10] Balthasar mentions Bloch quite often,[11] and has little good to say about a thinker whom, as we have seen already, he tends to fold without remainder into either Hegel or Moltmann. Here, however, with both the differences between Balthasar and Metz and the contribution of Bloch to Metz's thought in mind, I will attempt to bring out more differences between Balthasar and Bloch that cannot be so easily assimilated to Hegelianism. Balthasar does not mention Benjamin as often,[12] and when he does so, it is with a certain ambivalence as if Benjamin's 'lightning flashes' play a positive deflationary role with respect to speculative discourses, while, nonetheless, being implicated in that which they interrupt. Beginning with Balthasar's scattered remarks, chapter 8 explores in some detail the possibility of there being a deeper relation between Balthasar's apocalyptic discourse and that of Benjamin. Furthermore, this relationship raises important issues about the relation between biblical apocalyptic discourses and the apocalyptic function of literature and art in general, which are essentially repressed in the apocalyptic discourse of Metz. I will argue that a battle for and of apocalyptic occurs on the least obvious and most slender of domains, that is, how properly to interpret Baroque drama. Balthasar's anointing of the Spanish Baroque playwrights, Calderón and Lope de Vega, I will suggest, not only represents a different preference to that exercised by Benjamin in the *Trauerspiel*,[13] but touches on deep issues regarding nature and grace, the orders of creation and redemption, and the nature of reason and language. In addition, however, it raises the question as to what is responsible discourse in a modern world, characterized by linguistic debasement and ideological deformation. If both Balthasar and Benjamin declare in the end for the fragment, a crucial issue concerns how the fragment is to be understood. Not surprisingly, it is Benjamin who has a more radical view of the fragment, and who not only rules against encyclopaedism, but against any discourse that would indulge itself in large-scale thematic development. As much through Metz as in himself, Benjamin's view of the fragment and apocalyptic as mutually reinforcing constitutes a real challenge to the kind of apocalyptic theology articulated by Balthasar.

Chapter 6

Maximally Eidetic Apocalyptic and Its Critical Function

Maximally Eidetic Apocalyptic

Theo-Drama 4 and *Theo-Drama 5* represent the high-water mark of Balthasar's affirmation of an apocalyptic mode of theology. By the same token they also represent the most searing critique of the apocalypse dimensions of Hegel's thought and that of his predecessors and successors. The effectiveness of the critique is in significant part a function of the elucidation of a self-consciously apocalyptic theology. Balthasar does not follow the standard critical line and oppose to the realized eschatology of Hegelian thought the 'not-yet' of biblical apocalyptic. In the shape of 19th-century Left-Wing Hegelianism, and in the form given to it by Bloch and Moltmann, this correction can be construed, he believes, to be internal to Hegelianism. Nor does Balthasar oppose to the parousiac thought of Hegel the kind of urgent expectation characteristic of First Thessalonians, found so appealing by the early Heidegger as he struggled to find leverage against the mésalliance of the philosophical and theological traditions.[1] Rather, Balthasar adopts the thoroughly high risk strategy of making hermeneutically pivotal a text, whose canonic status is not only contested throughout the Christian tradition, but which is consistently hijacked by sectarians, whose hyperboles inflame imagination, and whose prognostications are frequently put to chiliastic and millenarium use. Mindful of the manifold dangers, nevertheless, on balance Balthasar thinks that Revelation is a text of extraordinary opportunity. As *Theo-Drama 4* in particular makes clear (15-51), Revelation is a text of panoramic vision that provides a view of the whole of history from creation to eschaton that manages to be both retrospective and anticipatory at once; it is the New Testament text that addresses the question of the cosmic significance of the redemption effected by Christ on the Cross; and it is the great text of the meaning of travail of the church in history.

Crucially Revelation offers to the church nothing less than the theodramatic blueprint of God's loving and sacrificial relation to the world and human being. Nonetheless, it is interesting that Balthasar refuses to give blanket approval to apocalyptic as a literary genre. He makes it clear that while Revelation is continuous with New Testament apocalyptic as instanced in First and Second Thessalonians and 1 Corinthians 15 (*TD 4*, 45), it is not continuous in essential respects with intertestamental forms of apocalyptic in general (*TD4*, 45; *TD5*, 50). It is important to note, however, that in making his assessment of the relation between Revelation and prior texts, especially those of apocalyptic genre, Balthasar is making judgments that are at once historical and evaluative. For instance, in *Glory of the Lord 6* Balthasar engages in a concerted critique of the messianism and apocalypticism of the intertestamental period, which he takes to indicate a 'long twilight' between the testaments (*GL6*, 321-42). However fair Balthasar's overall judgment of the period, it is evident that he sees more discontinuity than continuity between the messianism and apocalypticism of the intertestamental period and the discourses of prophecy and law. Taking these last two essentially to identify the old covenant, messianism and apocalyptic are seen as deviant forms of religion and deformed forms of discourse. Messianism is read as a perversion of prophecy in that it absolutizes the dimension of imminent expectation (*GL6*, 312-13) at the expense of the explicitly ethical component that enjoins obligation to the poor and the critique of idolatry (*GL6*, 316-7).[2] Similarly, intertestamental apocalypses such as Enoch and Second Ezra evince an unseemly curiosity respecting the heavenly world (*GL6*, 324; also *TD4*, 16 n. 3; also 220) and an extraordinary knowingness regarding God's plans for election (*GL6*, 339). For Balthasar, an eschatological dualism of the saved and the unsaved with its truly repellent feature of representing the joys of the blessed against the backdrop of the sufferings of the damned is joined in intertestamental apocalypse to an existential dualism expressed in the seer's escape from the exigencies of the world and history by means of vision (*GL6*, 342-43).[3]

In contrast, for Balthasar, Revelation has roots in the discourses of the old covenant, the defining discourses of prophecy in particular (*GL6*, 324, 339). These roots prevent flights into the fantastical. If prophetic discourse encourages crisis as well as points to it, it also encourages radical obedience that exceeds rather than bypasses the law. The close relation between Revelation and the Gospel of John, in which radical obedience is figured as constitutive of the identity of Christ, guarantees that Revelation does not lose prophetic ballast.[4] In making the contrast between the eidetic apocalypse of Revelation and those of the intertestamental apocalyptic, Balthasar does not adopt the untenable position that Revelation bears no relation to the latter, which has come to be defining from a *Religionsgeschichte* perspective.[5] He recognizes that from a literary point of view there is significant continuity. In terms of cosmic backdrop, basic narrative structuration, and selection and deployment of images, Revelation obviously fits well the genre, whose basic contours are provided by texts such as Enoch and Ezra, and even those of Qumran (*GL7*, 285-86). Balthasar sees no need to deny that Revelation provides an exemplary instance of a visionary thought-form, whose spatial dimensions are as wide as heaven and earth, whose temporal expanse extends from beginning to end of the world, and whose focus is the crisis in which basic decisions for and against the divine are made. Neither has Balthasar any problem accepting that Revelation superbly satisfies the apocalyptic genre in its images of 'seer,' 'vision,' 'revelation,' in its images of the numinous divine and terrifying counter-divine, in its images of secrecy, 'seal,' 'scroll,' in its images of election and trial, and its images of catastrophe, which involve the abrupt transformation of the form of the cosmos as well as society and history (*TD4*, 18-9). Balthasar wants, first, to make the negative point that Revelation is not reducible without remainder to intertestamental apocalyptic whose limits are, he believes, defined by Enoch and Ezra (*GL6*, 324). And he adds the rider that in this respect Revelation continues the stretching of the apocalyptic genre that already is under way in Daniel. The following passage points to the satisfying of two related criteria of overcoming curiosity and possessing prophetic ballast that mark a stretching, indeed a transcending, of the apocalyptic genre:

> *In the biblical seers – Daniel, Paul, John – the mystical element remains strictly related to the commission of revelation and is measured through this commission; the situation is part of the mission; and the seers have their existential share – although this is the share of an instrument - in the context that they must proclaim. If this criterion and the pure relatedness to the matter in question is missing, then there is no way of avoiding the fall into the ambiguities of the occult, of inquisitive gnosis, and of the process whereby the human person makes himself the theme of revelation . . . . (GL6, 324)*

For Balthasar, Revelation is the text of vision that completes the old (*TD4*, 18-9) as well as the new covenant (*TD4*, 19, 45). But, precisely as a text of vision or *apokalypsis*, it neither validates messianism nor speculative narratives that are other to the Christian world of assumption. Together with the Gospel of John, which itself functions in *Theo-Drama 5* as a diagnostic tool for apocalyptic and Valentinian narratives in modern and contemporary forms of thought, Revelation articulates the theodramatic conspectus of existence (*TD4*, 45) that is the opposite of the epical figurations of messianic apocalyptic and Valentinian apocalypse. Balthasar agrees with Adrienne von Speyr that Revelation is through and through a Johannine text (*TD4*, 15, 18), one that relies on the paschal mystery articulated in the Gospel of John, and reflects on its archeological as well as eschatological significance.[6] He agrees with Claudel that Revelation is through and through an iconic text (*TD4*, 181). Insisting that the images in Revelation are taken from the lexicon of Old Testament images, Balthasar argues that these images are refigured or 'reborn' in Revelation (*TD4*, 16, 47). And Balthasar implies – although he does not explicitly state – that the same holds true of those images whose original context is intertestamental apocalyptic (*GL7*, 39). In an important discussion Balthasar proceeds negatively through a series of denials to determine the nature and function of the images of Revelation: the images of Revelation are not reducible to their original meaning in Hebrew scripture; nor are they reducible to the original contexts that gave them meaning; nor are they reducible directly or indirectly to determinate historical correlatives or referents; nor finally are the images, precisely as images, systematically privative and thus primed for sublation in and by a conceptual or explanatory framework (*TD4*, 20, 27). Of course, what holds with respect to the symbols of Revelation holds also with respect to the symbols of the Gospel of John which, if they draw less attention to themselves, possess, arguably, an even greater power to evoke and enact. Fundamentally exceeding discourse, the symbols of Revelation are 'mystical' precisely in their iconic form (*GL7*, 269; also 278-79).[7] This is true of the symbol of the Lamb (*GL7*, 269; also 318), as it is of the image of the heavenly Jerusalem, the dragon and Anti-Christ, and the entire network of secondary symbols. Balthasar captures beautifully the intrinsic connection between the symbolism of the new and old covenant and the inherent apophasis of the symbolism of Revelation in the following eloquent passage:

> *. . . these reborn images remain images: they remind believers that the prophetic content of the evangelical words and deeds of Jesus and the apostles open up dimensions that Christian faith can never change into complacent possession. These dimensions are truly open, for, after all, what we are dealing with is apo–kalypsis, yet they remain only significant hieroglyphs that, however legible, conceal their ultimate mystery in the mystery of God. (TD4, 47; see also TD4, 51-2)*

For Balthasar the iconicity of Revelation is commensurate with apophasis and vice versa. Balthasar points to Revelation 4:3 and 20:11 where the one who sits on the throne is beyond description, and reads it as continuous with Exodus 33 (arguably, the most significant apophatic passage in Hebrew scripture), but also with Isaiah 6:5, where the prophet as a 'man of unclean lips' cannot master the holy as the totally other given in experience (*TD4*, 51-2).[8] At the same time, Balthasar thinks that there are distinctly Johannine precedents, and cites John 1:18 and 1 John 4:12. (*TD4*, 51-2; also 47). The mutual implication of iconicity and apophasis is, of course, a crucial point in the elaboration of the theological aesthetics. As articulated in considerable detail in *Glory of the Lord 1*, as the norm of all appearance, Christ is the icon of icons. Yet precisely as icon Christ reveals a depth of love to which no finite intellect can pretend to be adequate. What is intimated in *Glory of the Lord 1* is explicitly stated in *Glory of the Lord 7*, where not only does the iconicity of Christ not impede recognition of the essential ungraspability of God, but rather specifies its condition (*GL7*, 15-6, 109, 287).[9] Here Revelation is no less forceful on this point than the Gospel of John (*GL7*, 265-66; *TD4*, 47). Moreover, the iconicity of Christ is not one important point among others; for Balthasar, it is the centripetal and centrifugal force of both texts (*TD4*, 51; *TD5*, 50).

Together with the Gospel of John, Balthasar understands Revelation to provide more than a plenary example of theological aesthetics by contrast with an aesthetic theology, where among other things iconicity and apophaticism fall apart with a corresponding reduction to rationalism or naturalism, on the one hand, and a febrile agnosticism or henological metaphysics, on the other. Indeed, Revelation is the biblical text that effects the link between aesthetics and dramatics that all subsequent theology aspires to (*TD4*, 54). It offers as stage heaven and earth (*TD4*, 22-6, 48), time in its vastest extension and intensivity as parenthesis within eternity (*TD4*, 49), the disclosure of the Lamb who, as nothing less than the pivot upon which the world turns (*TD4*, 62-3), is its alpha and omega (*TD4*, 44), and who if he evokes adoration, also provokes rebellion.

Crucially for Balthasar, the dramatic in Revelation is not compromised by the lack of uncertainty with respect to outcome that some critics insist is a necessary feature of drama,[10] and whose absence, they deem, fatally undercuts its possibility. At a limit certainty with respect to outcome transforms theodrama into the epical figuration of the relation between God and the world that Balthasar affects to disdain.[11] For Balthasar, what is truly dramatic is not uncertainty of the denouement (*peripeteia*), but rather the unfolding of the mechanisms or operations in and through which this victory of love is effected against the backdrop of apparent defeat. Of particular dramatic import is the unfolding of the hyperbolic escalation of resistance to the victory of the Lamb evident in the movement of the text. In fact the latter may well supply a key to Balthasar's interpretation of history not only throughout *Theo-Drama* or even the trilogy as a whole, but throughout his entire oeuvre: history is constituted in a fundamental way by the *Auseinandersetzung* between perceptions of reality that are for or against Christ. The following passage, while far from untypical, is especially eloquent:

> *In the Book of Revelation "the law of heightened resistance" is validated in the context of the Lamb's established victory. Here, world history is not a demonstration of progressive integration – Augustine was right – but is characterized by an increasing polarization;*

> *moreover it becomes harder and harder to tell the poles apart, because of the counterfeiting activity of the anti-Trinity and the anti-Lamb (Rev 13:11). In this way we can grasp something of the paradox of the Book of Revelation: the Lamb can appear as the ultimate Victor and the Lord of all history, while at the same time he is depicted as riding out to do battle and to do slaughter (19.11 ff). (TD4, 21; see also TD4, 18, 51)*[12]

Aside from 'polarization' the most important word in this passage is 'counterfeiting.' It is this phenomenon that effects the most direct link between Revelation and the Irenaean theological tradition whose theological business it is in addition to speaking boldly about the Lamb, to detect and refute all counterfeits, and especially those of a speculative kind. But the phenomenon of counterfeiting, whose *raison d'être* is obviously that it is much more destructive of Christian witness than outright rejection, also covers turning the Christ event into the intra-historical construction of the kingdom of God. Although Balthasar does not make the point in his exegesis of Revelation in *Theo-Drama*, the point is implied given the importance of his resistance to Hegel and Marx, the fabulators of progressive history who are their predecessors as well, of course, as their epigones. But this also means that there is an associative relation at least between the 'law of polarization' and the temptation scenes of Luke and Matthew which were of such profound importance for Dostoyevski and Soloviev, and which also are of considerable importance to Claudel. The link is provided by the phenomenon of counterfeiting that is common to both.[13]

Revelation keys the Christian theologian, and indeed the Christian believer in general, into a number of features of God's relation to the world that are also dramatic. No less dramatic than the previously mentioned elements is the coincidence in the Lamb of unsurpassable mercy and judgment (*TD4*, 54-5). The element of judgment in the Lamb is unerasable, for this element manifests the unbreakable link between Revelation and the Old Testament, and thereby subverts beforehand the constitutive modern tendency towards a Marcionite reading of the biblical text (*TD4*, 27, 47-8). Even more importantly, it displays the truly 'dialectical' relation between judgment and the cross. As Balthasar understands it, in Revelation, as in the discourses of the Old Testament,

> *wrath is the sign of God's involvement, to that extent, he [the Lamb] does "suffer" at the world's hand, as we see from the Lamb who was delivered up (traditus) to be slain. God's wrath and the Son's Cross are two sides of a simple reality. (TD4, 55)*

The association with wrath strengthens rather than weakens the constitutive liturgical tendency of the text. Balthasar professes: 'The simultaneity of liturgy and judgment is perhaps the most all-pervading leitmotifs of the Book of Revelation' (*TD4*, 36). Moreover, the liturgical element, which is the rendering present of the one slain on behalf of the world, is intrinsically tied to the doxological motivation of the text. Doxological motifs are everywhere. Balthasar points in particular to Revelation 5:9b-5:10 (*TD4*, 30), but there are numerous other places in Revelation in which the doxological is accented. Adapting the phenomenological language of Rudolph Otto only to relativize it,[14] Balthasar writes: 'The God of the Bible is neither a *tremendum*, nor a *fascinosum*, but first of all an *adorandum*' (*GL7*, 268). Perhaps even more important is the list of citations that he proceeds to add: Rev 3:9; 4:10; 5:14; 7:11; 11:16; 14:7; 15:4; 19:4; (also 15:10; 22:6-9).

For Balthasar, to deny doxological motivation to the text would represent a colossal failure to understand the purpose of revelation which is nothing less than to celebrate the Lord of history and wait patiently for the issuing of judgment. But, from Balthasar's point of view, Revelation is doxologically overdetermined: it suggests not only that the human beings *in via* bear an adorative relationship to God who reveals himself as triune, but also that the dynamism of eternal life as such is characterized by praise (*GL7*, 265).[15] Equally from Balthasar's point of view, the cosmos itself constitutes itself as a liturgy of praise – thus a Johannine thinker such as Maximus can be considered as an apocalyptic thinker [16] – a praise that reaches towards the glorification of each member of the Trinity by the other in whom in any event all praise is founded.[17] If Revelation shows that the Trinity is doxological in character, by contrast with a theologian such as Moltmann, it discloses that doxology is the archeological and not simply teleological mode of relation of the trinitarian persons.[18]

The paradox of wrath and mercy indicates that Revelation is a dangerous as well as necessary text. The paradox is irresolvable: any pulling apart of these dimensions incurs crippling theological loss. To ignore the dimension of judgment in Revelation is theologically to fail to be challenged by the text and by the one who is sacrificed on our behalf. [19] This has been the typical posture of Liberal Protestantism against which Barth inveighed, but a posture increasingly taken up by Catholicism. For Balthasar, as well as for Barth, the exclusion of judgment reflects a profound neglect of the witness of the old covenant while also representing a flight from the true mystery of salvation. Although the salvation of all cannot be precluded, this can only be a matter of hope rather than knowledge.[20] As far as Balthasar is concerned, no interpretation of the Gospels or Revelation in particular should license a unilateral victory of Origen over Augustine.[21] Judgment indicates the possibility of refusal, which takes either the form of being seduced, or of a titanic no. In a series of extraordinary comments in *Glory of the Lord 7* and *Theo-Drama 4 and 5* Balthasar insists that the 'all in all' of Christ does not exclude the prospect of waste, of elements of reality that are not reconciled to God's will.[22] If Balthasar has von Speyr as well as Barth as his proximate precursors here,[23] the insistence on the (im)pertinence of waste recalls Kierkegaard's resistance to Hegelian mediation (*Vermittlung*) whose basic function is to transform the brute and sometime brutal particularity of history into meaning by the cleansing action of the concept.[24]

On the other side, to privilege the wrathful dimension of the depiction of the divine also simplifies and flattens out the text and provides a legitimation for the horrors of history (*TD2*, 33 ff). Revelation then becomes in principle vicious, justice merely retributive, and history just what Hegel called it, that is, a 'slaughter bench.'[25] The valorization of the wrathful dimension of the divine and the Lamb in particular has been commonplace throughout history with Revelation playing a key role. The very possibility of such a reading of Revelation makes intelligible debates about its inclusion in the canon, as well as makes sense of how this text made Christianity so vulnerable to the genealogical critique.[26] It is important for Balthasar that the valorization of wrath has not been simply the perennial sectarian, chiliastic, and millenarian temptation. This would be to build around the possibility of such interpretation a *cordon sanitaire.* Balthasar is aware that even magisterial figures are capable of dark readings of Revelation, indeed that only the most scrupulous reading will prevent it. A splendidly orthodox thinker such as Dante shows in the *Inferno* how such a dark reading can function as a default (*GL3*, 341). For Balthasar, as *Glory of the Lord 3* makes clear (9-104), the *Divine Comedy* is an essential Christian and not simply cultural text. Calling upon all the resources of the Christian tradition, on scripture, on the ascetic and mystical traditions, on Augustine, Aquinas, and Bonaventure, in a poem that is brazenly 'experimental' in the sense of being both probative and experiential, Dante dares to bring into view the 'end things,' to unfold the doxological state of heaven, and the noises and silences of hell that speak to it as execration. The text is 'apocalyptic' in the historical as well as literal sense (*GL3*, 99). It recalls in particular the throne, as the throne had come to admit an apocalyptic interpretation in the Western tradition,[27] and the centrality of praise and adoration as expressive of finite existence. At the same time, Balthasar wishes to dissociate himself from what he considers the conventional vindictiveness of Dante's eschatology, in which the saved gloat over the unhappiness of the unsaved. Balthasar clearly has in mind Nietzsche's criticism, and is prepared to criticize Dante as being out of step with what is best in the Christian tradition which would never relish the pain of eternal exile, nor make certainties out of our best attempts at representing the unrepresentable. Dante's failure is a function of his failure to allow Revelation properly to inform his thought, and to have permitted his thought to regress to 'apocryphal Jewish apocalypse which grew in an inauthentic position between the old covenant and the Gospel of Christ' (*GL6*, 341). This regression in turn reflects the undersaturation christologically of the *divina commedia*, which if it effects Dante's construal of paradise (*GL3*, 101), closes off entirely hell from any influence of the mercy and compassion of God (*GL3*, 82-101; esp. 87, 90, 93).[28]

Balthasar's relative silence on Augustine on this point is especially eloquent, given that the eschatology of *The City of God* provides the basic frame for the *Divine Comedy*, and that in turn Revelation provides the basic frame for it (*GL3*, 89-90).[29] Balthasar sees the last point clearly, and in *Theo-Logic 3* comments favorably on the relation between *The City of God* and Revelation, which is made fully explicit in Bks. 20-22.[30] By the third part of the trilogy, Augustine is not only an irradicable aesthetic resource, but also an ineluctable apocalyptic resource that does not sanction the kind of pneumatological hijacking perpetrated by Joachim, one of the more influential interpreters of Revelation in the history of Christian thought.[31] Arguably, however, there are moments in the apocalyptic theology of *The City of God* when Augustine professes to know too much about God in general and more specifically to have privileged insight into the logic of divine justice.[32] As Origen's view of *apocatastasis* should be regarded as questionable precisely in its positing the purity of mercy without constraint of justice,[33] so too any argument supporting the adamantine necessity of damnation should be taken as not fully capturing the complexity and dialectic of Revelation, which having as its absolute pivot the Lamb, cannot finally be perceived as striking a balance between two equally powerful divine forces. Balthasar does not accuse the historical Augustine of being either vindictive or overdetermined with respect to a divine justice. Supporting fully the later Augustine's anti-Pelagian stance (*TD4*, 377-80), he makes it clear, however, that he has no truck with theologies of double predestination, either Catholic (e.g. Jansenist) or Protestant (e.g. Calvin), that claim Augustine as their main theological source (*TD2*, 415). Of course, in his Barth book, as throughout *Theo-Drama*,[34] Balthasar shows that he is perfectly comfortable with the doctrine of election, although in the latter it is the Ignatian view of 'call' rather than predestination in the full and proper sense that dominates.

In any event, the fact of such dark readings of Revelation, and the identification of this dark reading with magisterial figures in the Christian tradition, underscore its perennial possibility. Balthasar does not explicitly pose the question whether anything in Revelation provokes this dark reading. On the basis of his analysis, which admits the dependence of Revelation on intertestamental apocalyptic as a genre, even if not in terms of substance, an answer is readily available. This possibility may very well lie in the mixed nature of a text whose message of paschal mystery is in tension with, and possibly retarded by, the conventions of intertestamental apocalyptic that provide the means of expression. These conventions work against, but ultimately cannot resist, the mystery of sacrifice that enfolds all of history, so that what is to come has already in some way arrived. There is waiting, which is not simply for the 'not yet,' but for the pleromatic exposition of God's actions that transforms heaven and earth, which provides the stage of God's action. And this exposition is not a possibility of time itself; it is event or advent of the absolute future, or God as the absolute future.

'Irenaean' Apocalyptic

NOW WHILE *GLORY OF THE LORD 6* distinguishes the historical and eschatological urgency of messianism from speculative apocalyptic's prying into the transcendent, in important respects Revelation is thought to resist them both and also *avant la lettre* their union which becomes fairly standard in the Christian or better 'post-Christian' future of apocalyptic. For Balthasar, counter-intuitively, Revelation refuses to valorize in an unilateral way the 'not yet' over the 'already' (*TD4*, 48-51). Rather it supports their synergy and tension. While Revelation sums up the Synoptic apocalypses and apocalypses of Pauline extraction, especially 1 & 2 Thessalonians and 1 Corinthians 15 which emphasize the 'hour' that is imminent (*TD4*, 19), Revelation also validates the Gospel of John in which the 'not yet' is included in the 'already' and makes it dynamic and futural (*TD5*, 25-6). In tandem with the Gospel of John Revelation does nothing less than render 'obsolete' Jewish apocalyptic, defined by its commitment to the 'not yet' (*TD5*, 50). Together Revelation and the Gospel of John can perform this function, since they christologically specify the time between resurrection and eschaton. Chronos – the time of the *saeculum* – is replaced by *kairos* as this anticipates its fulfillment (*pleroma*) (*GL7*, 162 ff, esp. 175, 181). [35]

Read together the Gospel of John and Revelation also delegitimate in advance Kant's unrealized eschatology of the kingdom of ends (*TD5*, 148), Bloch's principle of hope (*TD5*, 142-4, 181), and Moltmann's theology of hope and trinitarian eschatology (*TD5*, 168-9, 181). A central figure delegitimated is Joachim, whose trinitarian eschatology is generated precisely through an interpretation of Revelation.[36] Although Balthasar does not delve into the different ways in which Revelation functions as a critical diagnostic tool, it is evident, for instance, that Revelation's delegitimation of Kant rests on the messianic tenor of Kant's kingdom of ends.[37] In contrast, in the other cases Revelation functions to critique the eidetic elements of the apocalypse discourse and not simply the messianic impulse. This critique applies as much to Bloch's apocalyptic imagination and Moltmann's sense of the rupture of the present as it does to Hegelian *Begriff* itself. I have dealt with Moltmann in part 3, and propose to deal with Bloch somewhat *in extenso* in chapter 8. Joachim is the crucial figure, because seminal. In tracing the Hegelian line back to Joachim, Balthasar implies that Joachim is not only the source of an eschatological view of both history and the Trinity, but also of the kind of certainty of the complete disclosure of truth that is enacted in Hegelian philosophy. Arguably, however, Joachim's actual discourse, as well as his actual interpretation of Revelation is somewhat more complex than Balthasar here allows, who reads Joachim almost exclusively from the point of view of the history of his effects.[38] In particular, it could be argued that in his commitment to symbolism Joachim points – in a way Hegel and his progeny do not – to the essential inadequation between discourse and the divine characteristic of Revelation.[39] Were this to be allowed as even a possible interpretation, then Joachim would occupy a more ambiguous position as a courier of 'Jewish' form of apocalyptic and as precursor of Hegelianism: although he could continue to be regarded as a privileged premodern site of pneumatological torque, he could also be read as contesting precisely the kind of sublation of symbol into concept effected in and by the Hegelian system.[40] The charity exercised with respect to Joachimite apocalyptic does not amount to a retraction. Rather the fact that Joachim's faults stop precisely at the speculative border confirms the point I made in chapter 5, to the effect that the main discursive distorter in Hegelian lines of discourse is Valentinus rather than Joachim. In any event, while both Joachimite and Valentinian apocalypses are capable of inflicting significant theological harm, there is a perceived difference in the degree of potential harm to be inflicted that might well rise to a difference in kind. This is true even when, or especially when, both are found in the same discourse, as is the case in Hegel's own discourse and in the discourse of a theological successor such as Moltmann.

For Balthasar, the Gospel of John, of which Revelation is an annotation, represents the decisive and pivotal text of the New Testament and the crescendo of biblical witness. Given Balthasar's view of the polyphony of genres and theological styles in the biblical text,[41] the Gospel of John does not and cannot reduce other New Testament texts simply to being facets of itself (*GL7*, 10, 220; also 103-04). Still the Gospel of John provides the focus for the New Testament. At the center of this Gospel is the cross which represents the glory of complete divine self-giving. The sacrifice of Christ on the cross, precisely as a happening in a very definite moment, is an event in history. Yet it is the 'once only' (*ephapax*) (*GL6*, 413) that takes up and refigures time christologically and cruciformly. Here Balthasar is at his most Pascalian: Christ will be suffering even to the end of the world. Because of the cross' transhistorical actuality, it is precipitous to cede authority to the Spirit, especially when the Spirit is viewed as a redress to the absence of Christ and a sign of Christ's ineffectiveness, as has been the view of much of theology since Hegel.[42] As Balthasar argues in *Theo-Drama 5*, for Christians the 'not yet' participates in the 'already' of Christ. In a formula, the eschatological future resides in Christ (*en Christo*). One might make the point in another way: the 'not yet' is a distention of the *kairos* whose full realization is the cross (*TD5*, 50-1). The cross is the full expression of divine love, not a promissory note that comes due and gets paid in full eschatologically. It is because of the cross' continuing presence in history that history is liturgical, or at least quasi-liturgical, that it represents not so much a limit to our understanding – although this too – but a mystery of sacrifice that constitutes the real text of history and whose act in itself and the repetition of this act are taken up into the triune life of God.

If anything it is even more illegitimate to justify the shift in authority to the Spirit, as Hegel does, on the basis of the Farewell discourses of the Gospel of John (14-17) (*TD5*, 31).[43] This depreciates the church as an historical and sacramental reality, while constituting the true church as a group of cognoscenti, who are defined otherwise than by discipleship and patient waiting. As it expresses the relations between the *dramatis personae* of Father, Son, and Spirit, the Gospel of John – as annotated by Revelation – is the trinitarian text in which the vertical dimension encompasses the horizontal and historical rather than being reduced to it. To recur to a passage we have already cited:

> *The real "last thing" is the triune life of God disclosed in Jesus Christ. Naturally this Omega also implies an Alpha; it is what is present, first and last, in every "now." And what is this but Being itself? For apart from Being there is "only nothing," while within it there is that mysterious vitality disclosed through christological revelation, so that everything that comes from absolute being must bear its seal, with revelation giving us access to the font of God's life. Theo-drama, in its final act, in its final aspect, can only be trinitarian.* (*TD5, 57; see also 55-56*)[44]

Focally, this trinitarianism is economic. The Lamb is both the expression of the invisible God (*TD4*, 47; also *TL2*, 67-8), and the offer on behalf of a world that has become alienated from God through sin and has brought death upon itself. The Lamb is the one who both substitutes for and represents us in the realm of the most extreme unlikeness, and the Spirit is the one who communicates the gift to the church. In his exegesis in *Theo-Drama 5*, Balthasar speaks of the *diastasis* or distance constituted by sin that is subtended and enveloped by the even greater distance of the love between the Father and the Son, a separation that is spanned by the Spirit (*TD5*, 245, 262; also *TL3*, 66; *GL7*, 240; *LA*, 115). This means that the economy is enfolded in the divine life, the economic in the immanent Trinity. Thinking that they are authentically Johannine, neither Hegel nor Moltmann take the lesson of the relation between death and life depicted in Revelation and the Gospel of John truly seriously. For these texts make it perfectly clear that life and death are defined by infinite opposition that does not admit of reconciliation, logical or otherwise. The relation between life and death is precisely a non-relation. They can be brought together only by the infinite power of love that falls outside all logic, that in effect defies and redefines reason. The opposition to

Moltmann on this point is no less total than it is with respect to Hegel. Expressed in the terms of that text: the fundamental mistake of Moltmann – and arguably of 'death of God' theology – is that he succumbs to an *ana-logic* in which love is speculatively reproduced and thus made intelligible. Johannine love belongs, however, to another logic, what Balthasar calls in *Theo-Logic 2*, a *kata-logic*, that is, a logic from above, that respects the event or act of love that cannot be anticipated and which reason cannot catch up with,[45] even as the surprise functions as a lure that does not destroy reason, but rather makes it ecstatic.

For Balthasar, then, Revelation, properly understood, resists the radically eschatological form of apocalyptic characteristic of Left-Wing Hegelianism (e.g. Bruno Bauer, Feuerbach, Marx). It also represents a critique of, and an alternative to, Valentinian apocalypse, whose most influential instantiation in the modern world is presented by the texts of Hegel, but which perhaps also is exhibited by Schelling (*GL5*, 577-72; *Apok 1*, 204-51), to whom Christian theologians, particularly of the German-speaking variety,[46] have often turned in the hope of a cure from the perceived theological white-out enacted in and by the Hegelian system. Admitting that the vertical dimension is as much to the fore in Revelation as it is in Valentinianism, there is nothing, Balthasar insists, Gnostic about the Lamb sacrificed at the foundation of the world (*TD5*, 150-1). Balthasar sides with Bulgakov in thinking that the image of the Lamb there focuses the once-and-for-allness of the divine sacrifice and its eternal meaning (*GL4*, 413). Here is the real symbol of love. Here is the unsurpassable expression of love of the gift that is not other than a divine person, a gift which, if it beckons mimesis, can never be returned. A genuine apocalyptic theology, which is at the same time a genuine theology, represents then a reproach to theologies that develop exclusively the vertical as well as horizontal axis (*TD5*, 51-2). Balthasar draws the distinction between adequate and inadequate verticality very carefully. In John verticality:

> *is the locus of a dramatic tension in which the action taking place between God and mankind, centered in Jesus Christ, differs fundamentally from any pagan or mythological epic, whether that of the fallen*

> *aeons or ascending divinities. Here the drama of Christ remains the direct fulfillment of Yahweh's covenant drama with Israel, which has been going on throughout the whole of history. (TD5, 32)*

This passage is obviously redolent of Irenaeus, who is a major textual presence throughout *Theo-Drama* and whose genealogical pertinence for Balthasar's thought was treated in some detail in chapter 4. In the name of John it critiques a Marcionite hermeneutic in which the relation between the New Testament and Old Testament is severed. Equally in the name of John it critiques Valentinian mythology. Not only then is a Gnostic or Valentinian reading of John not legitimate,[47] but the Gospel of John and Revelation are pitted against Gnosticism, indeed its very possibility. Specifically, divine judgment and mercy cannot be pulled apart into two ontologically and narratively distinct aspects of the divine. One can consider the classical Valentinian separation of the orders of creation and redemption to reflect precisely such a rending.

Besides the obvious differential of epistemic reserve in John concerning the unelicited and inexplicable sacrifice of the divine on our behalf, Balthasar hints in *Theo-Drama 5* at the representational difference between the Johannine corpus and Gnosticism. In the Johannine writings the story of God's acts takes time to develop, God does not. By implication, Gnostic apocalypse confounds the reality of the divine referent with the time of narration.[48] On this point, Balthasar does not distinguish between Hegel and the historical Valentinus. For while it is true, as we saw in Part 2, that the becoming of the divine in its erotic, kenotic, and necessitarian aspects is more marked in Hegel and his successors than in Valentinianism of the second and third centuries of the common era, Balthasar agrees with Irenaeus that a static ontology may be no more than a surface feature of classical Valentinianism (*GL2*, 39), one that is belied at the narrative depth. In addition, Balthasar sees that the image of the Lamb discourages rather than encourages a deipassionist reading of the divine, which Irenaeus thought was a real – if counterintuitive – result of Valentinian rendition of the biblical narrative, and which religious thinkers from Hegel to Moltmann and Altizer argue represents authentic as opposed to merely conventional Christianity. Contrary to Blake's exploration of this numinous image, and Altizer's appropriation,[49] the image of the Lamb functions as a block to deipassionism precisely because it is an image. As such, it is in excess of thought and categorical positing. It represents the mystery of suffering as expiation which compels us to turn towards a God of excessive love. This love will not be mastered by logic, especially not Hegel's logic of love as the necessity of contradiction and its overcoming. By the same token neither will this love be mastered by the logic of 'immutability' and 'impassibility,' which similarly abolishes paradox and the necessarily symbolic nature of language regarding the divine, and fails to follow the red thread of divine involvement with the world that is something like a passion.

Of the two logics of mastery, it is the former, that is, the logic of contradiction, which in Balthasar's view currently displays more intellectual and spiritual vitality, and which consequently requires more immediate resistance. If Hegel's logic is extra-biblical, at least it appears to engage basic elements of the biblical narrative, and to highlight facets of Christianity such as eschatology that have tended to get neglected in the mainline tradition. Of course, between the appearance and the reality falls the shadow: the strain of Joachimite apocalyptic fatally compromises Christianity's christological center and suggests the necessity of temporalizing the Trinity, just as the strain of Valentinian apocalypse distorts the entire narrative and issues in a trinitarian modalism of a peculiar modern stripe. As I indicated in chapter 5, the logic of deipassionist mastery occluded in and by Hegel's system is even more successfully disguised in Moltmann's apocalyptic theology. *Trinity and the Kingdom* gives every evidence of the sincerity of Moltmann's intention to move beyond Hegel. This is indicated in his insistence on divine persons in relation, in his periodization of the reigns of Father, Son, and Spirit, which underscores personal agency, and in his articulation of the doxological nature of the Trinity. But as I also indicated in the last chapter, questions arise as to how stable the model of persons in relation truly is. Specifically, Moltmann shows himself to be as anxious as Hegel to dissolve the individual terms of Father, Son, and Spirit into relations. In addition, given the loop between the economic and ontological Trinity, the Joachimite assigning of the Father, Son, and Spirit to specific ages with specific existential and noetic configurations in the final analysis contributes to the historicization of the Trinity. And finally, the mutual self-glorification of the persons of the Trinity seems to require salvation history in order to be more than notional. In Moltmann the doxological Trinity gives every appearance of being an effect of creation and redemption, rather than an archeological given which, Balthasar believes, Revelation at least hints at and which the theological tradition, in its non-apocalyptic as well as apocalyptic registers, confirms.

Balthasar's apocalyptic theology plays an Irenaean role vis-à-vis modern forms of theology of speculative disposition. It helps to put into relief these forms of theology as being apocalyptic only in a privative sense. Ultimately, these forms of theology can be read as either regressing to 'Jewish' or intertestamental apocalyptic, on the one hand, or Valentinian apocalypse, on the other. It is worth reminding that in Balthasar's apocalyptic theology there are in addition a host of material Irenaean commitments, such as the elaboration of an economic trinitarianism, Christ as the figure of recapitulation, and even Irenaeus' emphasis that given the drama of freedom there is the possibility of waste, that something or someone will fall outside God's salvific plan (*GL6*, 233-34). When Balthasar recalls the descent into hell motif, he is fully aware that the motif found a forceful expression in Irenaeus. As he acknowledges that the motif is specifically Irenaean, he refuses, however, to adopt Gustaf Aulén's strategy of opposing Irenaeus and Anselm on soteriology.[50] He judges that appearances to the contrary Anselm's soteriology does not obey a demonstrative logic, but ultimately the katalogic of divine gift (*TL2*, 84).[51] Not only does he not oppose Irenaeus and Anselm, he also does not leave Irenaeus unemended. Balthasar refigures in a radical way the *descensus ad infernos*: the emphasis falls not on the activity of Christ, but on his identification with and entry into the state of pure passivity of the dead.[52] Attention is focused on the obedience of Christ in taking on the task of substitution and representation, and shifted away from the omnipotence of Christ disclosed – although previously hidden from sight – that leads to the rout of death and hell. This point is made on a number of occasions throughout the trilogy. The following passage from *Glory of the Lord 7*, which cites Revelation as an exclamation point, is especially eloquent:

> *the complete disarming of the principalities and powers (Col 2:14 ff), the finally effective breaking into the house of the strong man, in order to bind him in chains (Mk 3:24 ff), the robbing of the gates of hell of their power (Mt 16:18) – all this can take place only from within, in participation in the absolute passivity of the dead; it is only thus that the one who is exalted could attain possession of the "keys of death and the underworld" (Rev 1:18). (230)*[53]

The broader issue here is not that Irenaeus is only of limited importance when it comes to interpreting Christ's descent into hell, and that other resources must be called on (e.g. Cusa and von Speyr), but rather that Irenaeus must necessarily be led back to scriptural witness and the witness of the Johannine corpus in particular. A number of consequences follow from this. Although it is impossible to escape the circle of interpretation, Balthasar thinks that the Johannine emphasis on obedience (e.g. John 6:38) becomes pivotal for interpreting the *Christus Victor* theme. But the reduction of Irenaeus to biblical witness has itself important implications. One such implication is that the Irenaean figuration of the battle between orthodoxy and Gnosticism can be inscribed within or 'absorbed by' the biblical text.[54] In particular it can be absorbed by the Johannine figuration of the opposition of truth and falsehood, and by the figure of the Anti-Christ, who in Balthasar's reserved treatment is more a figure of and for ideology than a figure of torment or atrocity. Although Irenaeus shows in *Adversus Haereses* that he is concerned with persecution that demands witness to Christian faith (thus martyrdom) (4:11; 4:33), what is implicit from the opening detection of error becomes apparent in Book 5 in which the emphasis in the apocalyptic figuration of the Anti-Christ falls on that of seducer rather than oppressor (*Adv. Haer.*, 5.20, 5.24).[55] Both the upshot and support is that the devil is the father of lies (*Adv. Haer*, 5.29). Balthasar is Irenaean in all these respects, even to the point of stressing that seduction plays on acceptance of prior biblical truths as these are coded in symbols and narrative. The Gnostics after all are in a fundamental sense 'post-Christian,' with 'post' necessarily being a temporal construct in a way not required in the contemporary thought according to philosophical stipulation.[56] The equivalent in Book 5 of *Adversus Haereses* is Irenaeus' stunning reference to Oedipus. In refusing to bind themselves to the rules of faith, which alone yield as reliable interpretation of scripture – and which are presumed to be a patrimony – the Gnostics blind themselves like Oedipus (5.13.2). Of course, to invoke Oedipus is not only to suggest something like willed ignorance (which in any event is capable of being cured through suffering), but also to suggest a patricide, a killing of the father, the father/mother that is the church and also the true Father, the unconditioned divine who is creator, legislator, and crucially involved in the redemption of the world through his only Son. Needless to say, the regression to Revelation and the Gospel of John, licensed by Irenaeus, enlarges the frame of reference: the lie would not only consist in mythic stories that represent a disfiguration-refiguration of the biblical narrative, but in any world view that implicitly or explicitly denies Christ. Extrapolated into modernity this means that speculative forms of thought – those that constitute misremembering – are not the only thought-forms that require refutation. Numerous discourses in modernity constitute a forgetting of Christ and specifically the paschal mystery. Revelation also endorses their contestation and refutation. The regression to scripture then opens up the entire domain of rhetoric that gets focused but also contracted in Irenaeus' polemic against the perceived gnosticization of Christianity.

Much could be said about the enlargement of the eminent domain of contestation, and especially about the form the rhetoric would take when the forces of denial do not behave metaleptically towards Christianity. Arguably, the mode of rhetoric would not take a polemical form, but would consist rather in the most persuasive rendering in word and deed of the Christian mystery. Such has been the common behavior and disposition of Christianity in the past towards not only its others, but its cultured despisers. A good case could be made that this is the principle that informs Balthasar's vast rehearsal of the tradition not only in his trilogy, but throughout his career. This is a vast topic worthy of separate treatment. Here I limit myself to mentioning two important corollaries of the regression of Irenaeus to scripture: (a) as a theologian Irenaeus has exemplary but not constitutive status in the specific field of thinkers Balthasar evokes or invokes with a view to contesting speculative forms of theology that have the ability of constructing a simulacrum of the Christian narrative; (b) Irenaean 'apocalyptic' – its close relation to scripture earns it this designation – has no principled privileges over other forms of apocalyptic theology in the tradition, for example, that of Augustine, although Balthasar can perfectly consistently prefer Irenaeus over Augustine on certain points.[57] Within very narrow parameters, I will develop each of these points in turn.

(a) I begin with the first point, which involves a somewhat more concrete reflection on how the theological figures in the 'Irenaean' line, whom Balthasar calls or deploys, are, like him, designatable as apocalyptic theologians. I declared such to be the case in the introduction to Part 4, and did so on the basis of my presentation of these figures in chapter 4 and in the case of Irenaeus earlier chapters as well in which I did not hesitate to draw attention to the consistent recurring to Revelation both as a site for the ultimate positive Christian symbol of *agnus dei* and the ultimate negative Christian symbol of the Anti-Christ. Without going back over material already covered under somewhat different auspices, and in particular without repeating what I have said about the Trinity and about kenosis, I would like to speak very generally about the use to which Revelation is put in this tradition, and then discuss in more detail the theological figure whose mature work, one could say with only a small measure of exaggeration, renders itself as a reflection on Revelation, that is, Sergei Bulgakov.

In *Against Heresies*, Revelation is an important biblical text, especially in Book 5 in which Irenaeus links Christ's recapitulation of all things with the realization of the heavenly Jerusalem. Balthasar could very well be talking about Irenaeus' appropriation of Revelation when he writes somewhat generically and prescriptively of a proper theological aesthetics in *Glory of the Lord 1*:

> *The glory of God is nowhere, not for a single instant, separated from the Lamb, nor is the light of the Trinity divorced from the light of Christ, the Incarnate Son, in whom alone the cosmos is recapitulated and elevated to the rank of the bridal city. (GL1, 438)*

This is not to imply that in Irenaeus Revelation functions solo in Irenaeus' combating of Gnosticism, which includes for him Marcionism as well as Valentinianism. What it does not have the power and authority to do on its own, however, it may have in tandem with the Gospel of John which, despite or perhaps because it is the site of battle between the Valentinians and the orthodox, is regarded as theologically central, but in such a way as not to involve the eclipse of the Synoptics or Paul. Something very similar could be said of Hamann who, as I indicated in Part 3, acquired the mantle in some theological quarters of being a 'modern Irenaeus.'[58] Here I will not attempt to adjudicate its warrants, and limit myself to saying that whether by happenstance or not, when it comes to selection of biblical texts and the role that Revelation plays, Hamann operates very much within Irenaean parameters. From a content point of view, from the *London Writings* (1756-58) through *Konxopax* (1780), to *Golgotha und Scheblimini* (1784), the Lamb crucified at the foundation of the world is the fundamental motif. Revelation is an important text in setting the symbolic terms for the brazen and unimaginable 'humility' (*Knechtgestalt*) of God in Christ on the cross, but is constitutive only in its close relation to the articulation of Christ as divine love in the Fourth Gospel and in its association with the kenosis reflection of Philippians (2:6-11) and the discourse of 'condescension' of Paul's letters to the Corinthians. Of course, this textual concentration is no more exclusive in Hamann than in Irenaeus, and opens out onto all of the biblical text, performing as well as stating that all of it is central, because every dot and tittle of it discloses God's providential romance with his creation. In this respect, it is important for both to cite Hebrew scriptures abundantly. If Revelation functions explicitly as first-order disclosure of the really real, it also functions reflectively to speak to its own status and the need and the how of its application to communities and individuals forced to decide between competing incentives and competing truths. Hamann realizes, no less than Irenaeus, that Revelation is exercised by martyrdom as well as truth, but his main interest in his texts is the witness to truth in circumstances in which happily – although one may say also accidentally – this witness does not require the pledge of the body.

Hamann is fully aware that the heavenly Jerusalem founded on the humility of God in Christ will have any number of 'secular' contenders, which run the gamut from the completely exoteric to the esoteric. He accepts, accordingly, that his enlisting of Revelation, or rather his allowing of himself to be enlisted by Revelation, is in the strict sense an intervention intended to force a choice. Since decision requires in the first instance that the crisis be recognized, such recognition is an accepted part of the task. His self-consciousness of invention, and his consciousness of the likelihood of rejection of a symbolically coded message and narrative irreducible to concept or method is such, however, that Hamann encourages styling himself as an apocalypticist whose message by the nature of the case is going to be obscure. The subtitle of *Konxopax*, 'Fragments of an Apocryphal Sibyl on Apocalyptic Mysteries,' provides, perhaps, the clearest example of a general tendency. This 'later' text, written against a form of Freemasonry,[59] which finally is in the service of dilution of the substance of Christianity as well as undermining its authority by imagining a *prisca theologia* as its condition of possibility, is like much in Hamann indicative of 'Christian humor.' The title, which brings together the two syllables *konx* and *opax*, supposedly sacred sounds in esoteric cults, is both a nonsense and a title deflating as nonsense an esoteric form of thought that would displace traditional Christianity as this has been redeemed in modernity by Luther. Balthasar, whose respect for Hamann is enormous, does not follow him down this road of willed obscurity, and opts for more conventional tactics.

I come now to Bulgakov, the figure in the 'Irenaean' line for whom Revelation is constitutive for his theological elaboration in which Christ is the icon disclosing the triune God. Although it is *Bride of the Lamb* that is the most Revelation-focused work of his great trilogy, Revelation figures prominently in *The Lamb* – a text that is extraordinarily important to Balthasar – and *The Comforter*. Without Bulgakov being the reason for Balthasar's insistence on the unity of the Johannine corpus and his resistance to metaleptic discourses, Bulgakov's performance of their intimate relation provides a precedent. Like Balthasar, Bulgakov welcomes the visionary nature of Revelation with its vast conspectus and dramatic pitch, while judging that Revelation is neither eccentric with respect to the New Testament in general, nor involved in a competitive relation with New Testament apocalyptic, for example, the apocalyptic set-pieces of Matthew 24-25, Second Peter, and First and Second Thessalonians (*BL*, 319-20). And again like Balthasar, Bulgakov scrupulously avoids linking Revelation to any Intertestamental apocalyptic text other than Daniel. The silence with respect to the Enoch and Ezra material is especially eloquent, when one considers the use to which this material was put by Soloviev,[60] and which goes uncensured by Balthasar when he discusses Soloviev in *Glory of the Lord 3*. And finally, in assessing the intertextual or intratextual affinities of Revelation, Bulgakov also anticipates Balthasar by linking Revelation up with prophetic material at the same time that he uncouples it from the more speculative apocalypses of the Second Temple period (*BL*, 319-20).[61]

As even more a Revelation aficionado than Balthasar,[62] Bulgakov understands that the text is the most eidetic in the entire biblical canon, but that it is so because it is the most symbolically saturated. The symbols of Revelation disclose transcendent reality (*BL*, 345-47) without these symbols being reducible to determinate signifieds. The images of Revelation, says Bulgakov, are 'elastic' (*BL*, 328-29): to the extent to which they refer to historical reality, they do so either equivocally or indeterminately. Although the terms are not Bulgakov's, or for that matter Balthasar's, the symbols of Revelation involve a 'surplus of meaning,' to use the well-known Ricoeurian phrase. An area in which Bulgakov exceeds Balthasar is in connecting the language of radical transformation in Revelation with the boiler-plate of the 'hour' and the 'now' that characterize the other apocalyptic texts of the New Testament (*BL*, 347, 376, 384). Of course, this 'hour' or 'now' is an element of a grand narrative and not synonymous with the moment of vision itself, which has become one of the favorite ways to interpret and appropriate New Testament apocalyptic in modern and contemporary forms of apocalyptic.

What applies to symbols in general applies with particular force to the symbol of the Anti-Christ (Rev 17:8) (*BL*, 330), which, in Bulgakov's view is as privative as its polar. While Daniel and Second Thessalonians (2:2-10) speak of a single and definite entity, in line with most of the New Testament, Revelation does not, and tends to figure the Anti-Christ in the plural (*BL*, 329-30). Bulgakov grasps well that what might be called the historical underdetermination of the figure is itself a function of its symbolic overdetermination. His specification of the characteristic behavior of the Anti-Christ as consisting in the 'lie' or false teaching (*BL*, 330) provides an even closer link with Balthasar. The Anti-Christ dissimulates rather than persecutes. This is not to say that Bulgakov writes victimization out of Revelation. Bulgakov has a particular interest in how the 'lie' or ideology underlies and underwrites violence. The connection is underscored in fact by the bloody October Revolution, which is the fruit of an ideology of humanism, and in the literary sphere by Dostoyevski and Soloviev, who are also sources for Balthasar's construction of the Anti-Christ figure.[63] The Grand Inquisitor offers a vision of the world against the background or even foreground of an *auto-da-fé*. But it is not only a political system that can be decried as the work of the Anti-Christ, but an entire culture. As far as I am aware, Bulgakov nowhere writes about Alexander Blok's hallucinatory apocalyptic poem, *The Twelve*,[64] which celebrates the making of a new Russian identity out of the blood-bath of Revolution, but this would be the kind of simulacrum of the 'coming' of Christ typical of cultures of apostasy. What makes this greatest of poems of the Russian symbolist movement, which sums up the cultural throes of a Russia, forecast by Dostoyevski in the *Devils*, the double that it is, is that it assumes Revelation as a subtext, only to use it for incendiary purposes. This kind of entity is the simulacrum *par excellence* in that it purloins the very text that Bulgakov and Balthasar suggest is the text that makes imperative the unveiling of the lie and the liar.

Seeing just how structurally similar Balthasar's reading of Revelation is to that of Bulgakov encourages one to think that Balthasar is not disinterested in persecution and oppression, but like Bulgakov is asking for their ground. Of course, lie and sin are intervolved, not only in that lying is a sin, but sin is a form of lying with respect to God and one's own good. Bulgakov is unprepared to give ground on the importance of sin, and that it is a reality that is to be overcome. But he, like Balthasar, insists that the Lamb is victorious not only over sin, but also over death, the greatest violation of all. In this victory lies hope that those who have been, and who thus are permanently in solitude and in a situation of voicelessness, will in Christ acquire a measure of agency and presentness. As the sacrifice of the Lamb grounds the dialogical nature of the communion of saints, it is the enacted *memoria dei* (subjective genitive) that renders unnecessary the heroism of human memory, forever subject to dissipation and betrayal of the dead. Needless to say, the concern with the dead is, from a logical point of view, consistent with a lack of serious focus on circumstances (violent or otherwise) of death, or its instruments. The intent in the case of Bulgakov, no less in the case of Balthasar, is otherwise: God is not only a God of justice but of absolute love, who cares fathomlessly about everything that a human being does and suffers. Suffering and oppression matter enormously to the triune God, but the splendor of Revelation is that it espies the ideational or ideological root of what gives history the appearance of catastrophe.

It should be reminded that I have availed of Bulgakov as the representative of the 'Irenaean' tradition of apocalyptic of which Balthasar is a member. The choice of Bulgakov was based not so much on how this form of apocalyptic theology is focused on the cross and is trinitarian through and through – for these are shared features of 'Irenaean' forms of apocalyptic – but rather because of the way he argues for Revelation being central to the formulation of a theology that on its constructive side is paschal and ecstatically trinitarian and on its polemical side has as its target speculative forms of thought that disfigure Christianity. If the focus does not make Bulgakov excessive with respect to the tradition he represents, it certainly makes him with Balthasar exemplary. Revelation is in play in Irenaeus, as it is in Hamann and even Staudenmaier, but not to this extent, and also not with the same level of reflection on its status.

(b) I turn now to my second qualification, which concerns not so much the capacity of figures in the Irenaean field enjoying functional priority over the historical Irenaeus, but rather that Balthasar can, and indeed does, access other kinds of apocalyptic tradition as he takes aim at Hegelian discourse and its blighted lineage. It is worth mentioning that Balthasar's insight concerning the connection between Augustinian theology and apocalyptic finds a much more ample context in Balthasar's anthologization of *The City of God* than in the trilogy.[65] In the Introduction Balthasar comments on Augustine's portrayal of a world in crisis (9-10) and how crisis demands the resources of apocalyptic (22-3). Importantly, neither the crisis situation, nor imminent expectation of the end, leads to a prediction as to when. Augustine is understood to be faithful to New Testament apocalyptic for which the 'hour' is unknown. Balthasar does not further specify the point in the Introduction, and essentially leaves it to his selection of passages from *The City of God* (Bks. 20-22) to add the missing detail. Book 21.17 is especially important, since not only is Revelation invoked, but it is invoked in such a way as to endorse the little apocalypses (Mk 11, Mt 24), Acts 1:7 and, of course, First and Second Thessalonians. Balthasar does, however, go on to sum up Augustine's view of the 'kingdom of God' as a kingdom without a history (*das Reiche Gottes selbst hat keine Geschichte*) (16). Balthasar's more nearly Irenaean approach to history as a school of learning prevents him from endorsing such a view. Yet Balthasar is not entirely negative as many political theologians have tended to be, both first and third world. Since the time of *Apokalypse* Balthasar has had no truck with discourses whose focus is inner world dynamics. Like Karl Löwith, but also like de Lubac and Ratzinger,[66] for certain purposes Balthasar divides views of history into those that are Augustinian and those that are Joachimite (*Exp 1*, 48). He does so, however, with the caveat that the statics of Augustine's view be replaced by a dynamics that is christologically and trinitarianly controlled. Of course, in a real sense this control is supplied by the adoption of an Irenaean pedagogy and a trinitarian aesthetics that bears Bonaventure's signature. In the final volume of the trilogy, Balthasar in effect suggests a synthesis that marries Augustine's structural opposition of the city of God and the city of Man to the dynamics of history in which the Spirit is economically implicated with the Word incarnate.[67]

In any event, Augustine's fidelity with respect to biblical apocalyptic is such as to immunize him from the charge of 'aesthetic theodicy' that Balthasar leveled against speculative thinkers such as

Hegel. Curiously, Balthasar is more positive about Augustine's eschatology now that he is interpreting this dark later text of Augustine, which features the devastating passage from Matthew 25:41: 'Depart from me, your cursed, into everlasting flame prepared for the devil and his angels.' Without denying regressive features, Balthasar underscores the christological dimension of Augustine's theology, even as his lengthy selection from *The City of God* on divine justice shows how it is constrained. Balthasar also quite self-consciously counters a common objection to Augustine. This objection, which goes under a number of forms, is less concerned with the issue of whether hell is populated or not than with Augustine's certitude concerning this fact and its explanatory status. Because of his insistence on the perfect number of the elect and his traducionist view of original sin, Balthasar fears that Augustine runs the risk of ontologizing the distinction between the saved and the damned and thus in the end associating with forms of Platonism and Gnosticism his thought as a whole overcomes (29-30). Ultimately, however, Augustine does not cross the line; the 'unsaved' are not a necessary feature of the divine economy. Rather, advising that all ontologically freighted eschatological forms of discourse be put in brackets, the true other to the Augustinian ontological style would be the discourse of Julian of Norwich and the discourse of Adrienne von Speyr in which universal salvation is a matter of hope inspired by the love of God revealed by Christ on the cross and his descent into hell.

Yet any and all commentary on the lineage of Balthasar's apocalyptic theology, and especially the sorting out of its Irenaean and Augustinian ratios, risks being an evasion if the contribution of von Speyr is not taken into account. Von Speyr is referred to on a number of occasions in Balthasar's treatment of Revelation in *Theo-Drama 4* (15, 18). But what makes imperative discussion of von Speyr's influence on Balthasar is *Theo-Drama 5*. There, in an elaboration of eschatological trinitarianism that represents an alternative to the Hegelian, Balthasar cites von Speyr so often that his voice blends with hers. What engages him specifically is von Speyr's reading of the Gospel of John and Revelation which focuses on the paschal mystery, and more specifically, on what it suggests about the extremity of a love that goes beyond reason and the human condition of sin, God forsakenness, and death. Balthasar takes von Speyr's insight that in the paschal mystery all of time is enfolded, and develops it in conversation with the theological tradition, and especially with Irenaeus, Anselm, and Pascal, with whose discourses he is much more familiar than is von Speyr. What he is able to extract from her reflection on the Johannine corpus is also a powerful sense of the liturgical character of history as well as the doxological character of existence that calls for further reflection regarding the trinitarian depth of reality.

Perhaps nowhere else in an oeuvre that exhibits so much self-effacement in granting voice to others do we find quite so extensive a measure of ceding place. As a reader of scripture, who is captured and enthralled precisely by the revelation that constitutes it, von Speyr is being accorded the same respect given to Irenaeus, Anselm, and Pascal. Indeed, she represents a true supplement to their perspectives on the mystery of Christ. It now seems that Balthasar's own supplementarity, of which we spoke in chapter 4, is tied directly to that of von Speyr. She supplements Balthasar even as she supplies the prompt for theological elucidation. This relation, which is existential and takes place in real time, is different in kind to the other relations we have addressed. At the same time, however, von Speyr belongs to the tradition of apocalyptic resisters, to the line of those who would rout Christian forgetting by remembering well, which in the end is to allow oneself to be remembered in and through the cross of Christ. She supplements the 'Irenaean' line of apocalypse which earlier we put in play without explicitly naming it. And she can be said to supplement Bulgakov in a particularly intense way, since she like he is an interpreter of the book of Revelation. No more than Bulgakov in his trilogy does von Speyr find the symbolic language an obstacle to truth. Nor does she believe that Revelation is eccentric to the New Testament, and especially the Gospel of John as the Gospel of love. With even greater focus than he, but without his theological range or gifts for theological speculation – which brings him sometimes close to what theologically he cannot abide – she plumbs the depths of a text that has at its center the shocking divine love enacted in and by the paschal lamb.

Apocalyptic Liturgy and the Question of Violence

WE HAVE SEEN ALREADY HOW BALTHASAR is made anxious by the prospect of the apocalyptic genre as a whole mandating righteous violence, and by the fact that Revelation has been so interpreted throughout the Christian tradition. Together with his relative lack of emphasis on Revelation exposing violence, this raises the serious question about whether the theology of sacrifice that Balthasar reads off Revelation and John is not itself a mask for violence, and thus whether his apocalyptic theology in general, and his apocalyptic soteriology in particular, will in the end prove a match for Hegel's ontology of violence which, as David Bentley Hart rightly suggests, is redolent of Heraclitus' view of the logos as the harmonizing of rending opposites.[68] It would be a mistake to think, however, that Balthasar gives no consideration to violence. This is evinced especially in his critical but respectful discussion of the early work of Girard in *Theo-Drama 4* (298-313),[69] the same volume in which we get not only his long reflection on Revelation, but the most in-depth presentation of his soteriology. In this discussion Balthasar displays concern not only about Girard's vision of the relation between the God of Hebrew scriptures and the God of Jesus Christ (*TD4*, 305), but also about his confounding of the concept of violence with those of wrath or justice (*TD4*, 312), the proscription of any notion of sacrifice, and the facile dismissal of theories of atonement, Anselm's theory of satisfaction in particular (*TD4*, 307).[70] I will deal with all of these points in due course, but I begin with an exploration of a section of *Theo-Drama 2* entitled 'Liturgy and Slaughter' (*TD2*, 33-6), which bears an extraordinarily close relation to Balthasar's reflection on the paschal sacrifice in his divagations on Revelation in *Theo-Drama 4*.

Balthasar's heading is both enigmatic and provocative. It is enigmatic in that it is not clear what meaning of 'liturgy' is being deployed. Liturgy or *leiturgeia* can function generically to denote any action that mediates between different planes of existence, whether figured in terms of space (earth and heaven) or time (empty time or full time, old or new aeon). Or liturgy can refer more concretely and specifically to the enactment of sacrifice involving in an intimate way the divine and the human. Just as important, 'slaughter' is itself a challenging word from an ethical and more specifically theodicy point of view, and seems to associate more easily with Hegel's view of history as a 'slaughterbench,' and of reality in general being characterized as agonistic, than with anything defensible on Christian grounds. For Balthasar, if there is a problem with 'slaughter,' it is not simply one of metaphysics. Rather it is a problem with the whole or part of the biblical text, its reading throughout history and the practices that devolved from it. It is a problem in a particular way with Revelation, which displays the same copiousness as Hegelian apocalyptic, but opens up a space to unmask Hegel's speculative system as a *Doppelgänger*. For Balthasar, the Johannine figuration of the Lamb grounds the meaning of 'slaughter' and/or 'sacrifice,' specifies and concretizes *leiturgeia*, and properly frames provocation. The paschal sacrifice is both the point of intersection and dispersal, the centrifugal and centripetal force of the world and human existence, and is so precisely because it is the full self-disclosure of the triune God. In *Glory of the Lord*, despite the insistence on the cruciform configuration of Christ as the *sacramentum*, and a theological aesthetics in which glory represents a superform in which formlessness is integrated with form, ugliness with beauty, the paschal mystery sometimes fades into the background. One of the more urgent tasks of *Theo-Drama* is to correct for the possible imbalance brought about by theological reflection in the aesthetic key.[71] To effect real balance, however, by no means involves de-emphasizing the Johannine corpus in which the central category is glory. Rather the dramatic shape of divine glory needs to be brought out more clearly. For this the accent falls more heavily on pathos and on the inner connection between love and sacrifice.

The endorsement of Revelation as liturgical is, therefore, both intra-textual and quite general. Balthasar does not enlist the standard instruments of historical critical method to assess whether the text can bear such a reading. Although few commentators have proffered a liturgical reading of Revelation as a whole, many have recognized that it is a superbly writerly text which recapitulates a wide variety of symbols and groups of symbols from both biblical and extra-biblical literature.[72] More pertinently, a number of commentators have observed that the text is replete with ritual actions, for example, the opening of the seals (Rev 5:9-10), putting on the vestments of those slain on behalf of the Lamb (Rev 9), as well as the interpretation of ritual actions such as the use of incense as indicating the prayers of the saints (Rev 5:8), and the seven eyes understood to be the seven spirits of God. Of course, the overall liturgical ratio can be seen to be even higher if these ritual actions and their interpretations are seen in connection with the doxologies that saturate the text, from the opening acclamation (Rev 1:5-6), through the exclamation of the trisagion by the four living creatures (Rev 4:8) and the song of the elders (Rev 4:11), to the 'come Lord Jesus' (*amen, erchou kurie Jesou*), which concludes the text. Such an analysis facilitates – although it does not make necessary – a principled connection between apocalyptic and liturgy, despite the scant evidence for the liturgical deployment of Revelation throughout history. Certainly, together with the more general reading of the meaning of liturgy and the Paschal Lamb motif, an analytic reading of Revelation points to its negative capability to illuminate anamnesis, and to understand more clearly its wherefrom and whereto. In Balthasar's circles it is Daniélou who most clearly sees that the day of the Lord represents the inbreaking of the new aeon.[73] Supplied with momentum by the Spirit, in liturgy memory is directed outwards in the hope for the transformation of the whole world. Apocalyptic liturgy, while visionary, is not in the slightest aesthetic in the pejorative sense or senses of the term. It is not decorative, a pleasing spectacle, nor more importantly does it return the subject to *illo tempore* of complacent wholeness. Warping and wrinkling time, it directs the Christian community and by extension the entire world towards the inbreaking of the future that is the triune God.

The provocation of the bringing together of 'liturgy' and 'sacrifice' in *Theo-Drama 2* also gets concretized in Revelation, whose cinematic exposure of the end has left many commentators disinclined to issue this text a clean bill of health when it comes to violence, and quite a few to despair of a text that seems to hark back to the most violent displays of divine power in Hebrew scriptures. Exercising his Nietzschean prerogatives, D. H. Lawrence pronounced the text to be the most 'bloodthirsty' text in the entire Bible.[74] With Claudel, Balthasar refuses this characterization, while insisting that the difficult sayings of the text not be washed out of

Christian scripture. On Balthasar's reading, this is precisely the result of Girard's rendering of the Bible's 'unveiling' of violence, and his understanding of the figure of Christ as breaking the circuit of violence. In *Violence and the Sacred* and *Things Hidden from the Foundation of the World* Girard does, indeed, give Revelation a pass, but does so by dissociating it from Hebrew scripture, which ambiguously offers support for the scapegoat mechanism that it unveils, but from which it does not successfully disimplicate the God of Abraham, Isaac, and Jacob (*TD4*, 305-06). For Balthasar, the theological price is inordinately high: at the very least Girard evinces a decidedly Marcionite tendency, in which the unity between Hebrew scriptures and New Testament texts is severely compromised (*TD4*, 305). The upshot of this sundering is that one denies any agency to God the Father in the paschal mystery, and dismisses all language of 'handing up' as mythological, and by implication 'barbaric.'

As *Theo-Drama 4* makes perfectly clear, articulating an adequate soteriology is a complex business, and one that requires finesse in reading scripture and a critical vetting of a very plural theological tradition, from Irenaeus to Bulgakov, and from Tertullian and Anselm to Barth. The theological task is made all the more urgent by the attractiveness of Hegel's soteriological proposal, which offers a more dramatic – and thus more biblical seeming – rendition of the saving significance of Jesus than many of its more orthodox competitors, while being able to articulate a rationale that answers some of the more pressing objections leveled by Christianity's 'cultured despisers.' But Balthasar is not persuaded at least on the evidence of the texts with which he is familiar that Girard is either faithful to Christian witness and tradition,[75] or a match for the sophistication of Hegel's thought which, although it admits of an anthropological reading, does not announce it. The problems on the constructive front are legion and go well beyond breaking the indissoluble connection between the two covenants for which Ignatius of Antioch, Justin Martyr, and Irenaeus argued so successfully. Girard altogether too blithely dismisses the atonement tradition in which God is very much an actor in what happens on the cross, even if the violence of the cross as such is neither willed, nor perpetrated by him. And Girard's theory of the scapegoat, as elaborated in these early texts, is not designed to favor theology, since it involves a commitment to a sociological method, which at the very least is a-theological. Balthasar complains: 'the phenomenon of sacrifice explains divinity, not divinity the phenomenon of sacrifice' (*TD4*, 303). The more serious objection to Girard, however, is not so much that he deploys a sociological method, but rather the exorbitant claims made on behalf of this method. The sociological theory of the scapegoat is 'scientific' and explains all cultural forms which in one way or another demands a sacrifice for the stability of the system. In terms of form at least, Balthasar sees no difference between the theoretical constructs of Girard and Hegel. The attribution of 'closed system,' which justly applies to Hegel's system, applies to Girard (*TD4*, 308). Girard's theory of the scapegoat (*pharmakos*) represents the *ne plus ultra* of immanentization, and the making impossible of liturgy, which in Balthasar's view makes no sense without Father, Son, and Spirit playing roles that are at once agential and passional.

Balthasar merely mentions in passing Girard's particular hostility with respect to Anselm's theory of satisfaction, which he reads as God exacting an enormous price from a sinful humanity in and through the blood-sacrifice of his only Son (*TD4*, 307). Anselm, however, is an important figure in Balthasar's constructive elaboration of soteriology in *Theo-Drama 4*, and an equally important resource in redressing Hegel's dialectical logic of atonement. In the context of *Theo-Drama 4*, Balthasar readily admits that Anselm's atonement theory is not without its problems (*TD4*, 310-11). But he insists (a) that while a theology of satisfaction does not supply the only or even the best soteriological option, its legitimacy is founded in scripture (*TD4*, 240-44; esp. 241-42); (b) that read aright, Anselm's view is less narrow than it might at first appear. With respect to (a), Balthasar points out that 'satisfaction' is one of a number of symbols that the New Testament deploys, none of which are replaceable, and which theology is under obligation to take into account on pain of being partial (*TD4*, 240-44; 261). With respect to (b), Balthasar has laid the groundwork for a rehabilitation of Anselm in his essay on the medieval figure in *Glory of the Lord 2*, in which he rebuts the stereotype of *Cur Deus Homo* as articulating a juridical model of atonement in a logical key. While the critical force of the essay is in the main levied against the 'logical' attribution that would make Anselm a rationalist like Hegel, the correction, which involves seeing that even 'necessary reasons' are embedded in an 'aesthetic' context that bespeak a reliable God not given to caprice, also has a distinct effect on the juridical ratio in atonement. At the very least, it softens it, and brings Anselm and Tertullian more in line with Irenaeus' dramatic and apocalyptic soteriology (*TD4*, 244-48) which, while it does not dismiss the symbol of satisfaction, is considerably more expansive and celebratory.

As we have already suggested, Balthasar allows for quite different developments of Irenaeus' compact atonement view, which keeps a wide variety of biblical symbols of salvation in play. But again, Irenaeus provides the belated theologian a kind of yardstick with respect to how to conjugate an adequate soteriology, while obviously not being able to supply a recipe. The reversion to Irenaeus naturally leads back to Revelation and the role it plays or can play with respect to the overcoming of violence that Balthasar, no less than Girard, would consider 'devoutly to be wished.' Given his concern with the bodies that witness to truth (*Adv. Haer.*, Bk. 5), Irenaeus and those in his line have the capability of speaking to the Paschal Lamb as involving the overcoming of violence. Intellectual honesty demands, however, that at best this overcoming is an implication in the Irenaean line of which we are speaking – although we want to insist that it is at least this. Here is once again where another line of apocalyptic theology, which articulates itself very much as an interpretation of Revelation, comes into play. I indicated already that especially with respect to Hegelian speculation, the Augustinian line of apocalyptic plays a noticeable, even if secondary, role. When the issue is quite specifically the capacity of Christian apocalyptic or better apocalyptic Christianity to resist the totalitarian Hegelian system, which Balthasar accepts is violent without the postmodern permission provided by Levinas and Derrida,[76] *The City of God* comes into play. Peace is not only the goal of the restless individual and communities that can hope only for a respite from being beset, but peace characterizes the triune God, and is grounded in the eucharistic offer of Christ.

It is interesting that Balthasar notes without comment Girard's framing of the choice individuals and communities have to make: either the Logos of Heraclitus or the Logos of John. On the pragmatic level, Balthasar essentially accepts the terms of the choice, but not their specifically Girardian meaning. Hegelianism and Marxism, and their precursor and successor discourses, do not simply instantiate the Heraclitean maxim that 'all is war,' but either philosophically or theologically justify it. Balthasar is keyed into the structure of validation. And on the other side, the Johannine Logos represents an answer to Heraclitean agonistics only under the condition that it is connected with the texts, history, and inspiration of the old covenant. Still, the generic nature of this opposition should be underscored. In the final analysis, Balthasar is much more interested in what might be called an 'ontotheology of violence' in that agonistics are not simply tied to the 'really real,' but to the really real identified with a divine reality, and more specifically the triune God of Christian faith. While 'ontotheologies of violence' can be elaborated outside of express relation to the biblical text, from Balthasar's point of view typically they adopt a revisionist posture vis-à-vis the biblical text, indeed, often calling on the Johannine material, which Balthasar believes refuses speculative takeover. Certainly, this is as true of classical Valentianism as it is of German Idealism.

Concluding Remarks

I HAVE ARGUED THAT FAR FROM CONSTITUTIVE RESISTANCE to Hegelian-style apocalyptic ruling out apocalyptic inflection in Balthasar's thought, it effectively demands it. At the same time Balthasar's particular form of apocalyptic theology bears little resemblance to the standard apocalyptic profiles of Left-Wing Hegelianism, defined, on the one hand, by the repealing of the parousia and by the emptying of time of the meaning that would transcend it and, on the other, by providing apocalyptic with a socio-political rather than contemplative content. For Balthasar, Feuerbach and Marx provide pretty good examples of this socio-political tack which, he believes, continues by other means the Hegelian project. Arguably, the Left-Wing Hegelian, Bruno Bauer (1808-1882), known now only through Marx's pastiche of him as a 'theologian,'[77] provides just another example – and a not particularly splendid one – of the postmortem career of Hegelian thought. Nevertheless, perhaps more than any other text in Hegel's wake, Bauer's *The Trumpet of the Last Judgment* (1841) brings together,[78] in a way that Balthasar does, Hegelian apocalyptic and the book of Revelation. As one might expect, the relation is antithetical. The fundamental thesis of this unsparing 'unveiling' of Hegelian thought as anti-Christian is given in the Preface:

> *. . . we firmly believe that the Book of Revelation, when it speaks of the Beast, has Hegel the Antichrist in mind, and – when Christian knowledge becomes mature – properties in Hegel will stand revealed that accord themselves to the ten horns of the apocalyptic Beast. (64)*

Throughout the text, but especially in the long Preface, Bauer enlists the symbols, point of view, and tone of Revelation and other supporting apocalyptic texts such as 2 Thessalonians in order to expose the immanent historical and social meaning of Hegelian dialectic. The use to which biblical apocalyptic, and Revelation in particular, is put is, however, purely rhetorical, and involves no commitment to the meaning and truth of its individual symbols, not to mention the atonement Christology expressed in and by the symbol of the Lamb (63). This remains true when Bauer adduces *The City of God*, which presciently he takes to be the supreme apocalyptic text in the theological tradition, and uses it as a baseline to interpret the extent of Hegel's deviance from Christian commitments in his view of the church and state and their relation (84-6).

If Bauer provides a precedent for Balthasar's opposing of two apocalyptic types, the contrast between them could not be greater. Bauer deploys apocalyptic language in order to reveal the non-transcendent trajectory of Hegelian thought and its truly inimical relation to Christianity. The real, as opposed to the supposed, mode of the relation of Hegelian philosophy to Christian thought is that of allegory. This established, Hegelianism is a viable form of thought, indeed, arguably, the only viable form of philosophical thought. If only in the end, Bauer clearly has come to praise Hegel rather than bury him, or perhaps come to unbury him by removing the Christianity that weighs him down. By contrast, in Balthasar's critique of

Hegelianism the appeal to Revelation is thoroughly unironic and yields a vision of reality in which a drama, replete with transcendent meaning, gets played out in history between divine and human actors who, as *Theo-Drama 2* especially makes clear, operate on very different levels. The axis upon which the meaning of history, which is the history of salvation, turns is the sacrifice the Son undergoes on behalf of an errant and willful humanity. The unironic reading of Revelation yields an eidetic counterweight to Hegelian eidetics not found in Bauer who uses the language of biblical apocalyptic in the service of extracting a secular humanism from Hegelian philosophy. As a text, which should be considered to interpret and be interpreted by the Gospel of John, Revelation's ability to redress Hegel's speculative take-over of Christian symbols, narrative, and practice is invested negatively in its ability to discern a counterfeit and positively in its figuring of the paschal sacrifice within a horizon that is ineluctably trinitarian.

In line with our demonstration in Part 3, Balthasar's opposing of Hegelian apocalyptic by means of an appeal to and an articulation of a biblical apocalyptic, whose roots are Johannine, also involves opposing its apocalypse presuppositions (Valentinianism, Joachimism), and its theological and philosophical offshoots. Just as importantly, however, Balthasar's particular apocalyptic form gains purchase when it is seen how Balthasar's position is reinforced by his 'Irenaean' company, in which in every case one or more speculative forms of apocalypse are opposed by a visionary Christian form, which is centered on the cross and not shy about speaking of the role of the trinitarian persons. This chapter develops a point I made in chapter 4 by arguing that in each of the four figures we mentioned (Irenaeus, Staudenmaier, Hamann, and Bulgakov) Revelation is an important text, and in the case of Bulgakov, the absolutely crucial text. As these figures complement each other, they also add to and supplement Balthasar's own articulation of an apocalyptic theology the other side of speculation and its generation of simulacra. I also took some time to expand on the suggestion I made in chapter 4 that even when we restrict our focus to what traditional forms of theology Balthasar deploys against highly speculative forms of apocalyptic, more than the 'Irenaean' line is involved. One cannot afford even here to ignore the Augustinian line, which in any event plays the leading role in the diagnosis and correcting of specifically Heideggerian forms of apocalypse.

Finally, we broached, albeit probatively, the issue of whether an apocalyptic theology based on Revelation was apt for contesting Hegelian apocalyptic, which, arguably, supplies the supreme modern example of what I have referred to as the 'ontotheology of violence.' Acknowledging that the issue of violence is not as focal in the trilogy as it might be, especially considering how much Balthasar opposes Hegelian theodicy, I suggested that there are Irenaean and especially Augustinian resources available to Balthasar that are not sufficiently tapped, and which would highlight more than Balthasar does history as the history of suffering.

Chapter 7

Range and Adequacy of Apocalyptic Refutation of Hegelianism

The Anatomy of Misremembering

I have already made clear not only that Balthasar represents an apocalyptic refutation of Hegelian style apocalyptic as the most powerful form of modern misremembering, but that his apocalyptic refutation is effected on the same maximally eidetic level with a similar commitment to the Christian narrative and to the Trinity as the synoptic symbol that gives itself to thought. In carrying out this purpose, Balthasar can lean on the Irenaean and Augustinian traditions of apocalyptic as these diagnose and contest speculative thought. In suggesting, however, that the maximally eidetic apocalyptic form of apocalyptic presented by Balthasar is neither the only, nor the most common style apocalyptic refutation of Hegelian apocalyptic, effectively I raised a number of questions that require immediate attention. These questions include basic description of these other apocalyptic styles, nomination of their representatives, some account of the way or ways in which their more eidetically reserved style of apocalyptic is understood to be essential both in the process of remembering well that outbids the forgetting characteristic of modernity and that outmaneuvers the misremembering that is Hegelian *Erinnerung*. In the Introduction to Part 4, I mentioned a number of non-maximally eidetic apocalyptic forms that should be engaged against the background of a larger group of such apocalyptic forms that could be engaged. I isolated two as belonging to the former groups, the first, the apocalyptic of Johann Baptiste Metz, the second, the messianic reflection of Walter Benjamin, upon whom Metz depends in a significant way. They merit separate treatment, however, since not only does the Catholic Metz differ from the secular Jew Benjamin in terms of 'theological' commitment, but the eidetic ratio of their apocalyptic forms also differs, with Metz's apocalyptic having a determinate content lacking in the apocalyptic degree-zero of Benjamin. I reserve this chapter for a discussion of the relation-difference between Balthasar and Metz on the nature of apocalyptic, and its relative aptitude with respect to resisting speculative forms of eschatological thought as well, of course, as its capacity to cure the forgetting that is the provocation for all forms of remembering and misremembering.

Admittedly, there are many reasons to bring Balthasar and Metz into dialogue: both can be considered major theological forces in contemporary Catholic thought; while neither addresses the work of the other *in extenso*, on the few occasions when they do,[1] they do so fairly approvingly; a conversation between theologians with very different methods and very different orientations helps to illuminate both; and light can be cast on both differences and commonalities to the extent that both can be thought to articulate the *Exercises* of Ignatius of Loyola in equally dramatic,[2] but decidedly different keys. All of these reasons are important and under other circumstances provide sufficient motivation for dialogue. My reasons here for bringing Balthasar and Metz together, however, are both different and more focused. Given my interest in providing determination to, and exploring the limits of, Balthasar's eidetic apocalyptic, a number of quite specific considerations suggest that conversation between two figurations of apocalyptic theology is not only timely but necessary for the identification of both. (i) It could be argued that Metz supplies a specifically Catholic form of apocalyptic thought which, if it overlaps with that of Balthasar, nonetheless, constitutes an alternative. (ii) Metz's apocalyptic theology is governed by the double agenda that we have seen in Balthasar. On the one hand, it attempts to secure the identity of Christianity by naming what is essential to Christian belief and practice, on the other, it calls on this identity critically to resist the amnesia rampant in modernity, but also – and crucially – to resist forms of eschatological and utopian thought such as those of Hegel and Marx that sanctify the processes and outcomes of history. A crucial question here is whether Metz prioritizes misremembering in the way that Balthasar does, or whether he is more concerned with forgetting. (iii) Although Metz's insistence on *memoria passionis, mortis et resurrectionis Jesu Christi* supplies his apocalyptic form with a content,[3] and thus makes it eidetic in a general sense, much is to be gained by asking the question whether his apocalyptic figuration of Christianity is eidetic in the same way and to the same extent as that of Balthasar, and correlatively whether it is apophatic in the same way and to the same extent. My prompts here are Metz's disinterest in the book of Revelation, his reserve towards the Gospel of John, and his general allergy with respect to trinitarian discourse. (iv) Given their common enunciation of the importance of the doxological, it is also worthwhile to raise the question of their respective understandings of the relation of prayer and liturgy to apocalyptic, and whether important differences are discernible concerning the effectiveness of Christ's passion, death, and resurrection, its range, and its referent (e.g. the dead, sinners). The above considerations constitute a tight and determinate set of issues to which a fifth relates, but admits of being marked off. A further incentive for investigation is Balthasar's and Metz's different, perhaps competing, estimations of the apocalyptic thought of Ernst Bloch and, more broadly, distinct evaluations of the conceptually underdetermined concept of 'Jewish' apocalyptic. On the surface the approval that Metz gives Bloch and Jewish apocalyptic is as unreserved as Balthasar's is reserved.

Well-Tempered Eidetic Apocalyptic

METZ'S THEOLOGY IS A FORM OF well-tempered apocalyptic which, while it relates positively to Balthasar's paschal apocalyptic, also significantly contrasts with it. Thus, even though a proper description of Metz's apocalyptic theology is a desideratum, here it is not pursued for its own sake, but for comparative purposes in the context of an investigation that has an evaluative drive. The evaluative register, however, will be more *ad hoc* than systematic. Metz will be questioned with respect to consistency at various points, and at other points his particular theological judgment will be subject to query. Question and query proceed on the antecedent assumption that Balthasar-style eidetic apocalyptic presents a relatively adequate articulation of Christian faith and displays significant capacity to critique modernity and its spurious overcoming in Hegelian apocalypse and post-Hegelian eschatology. But Metz's apocalyptic option is not refuted, either as a matter of fact or as a matter of principle. It remains logically possible to prefer Metz's less extensive eidetic apocalyptic over Balthasar's maximally eidetic type. More important for my purposes, Metz's apocalyptic remains possible, or even necessary, as either a complement or supplement to Balthasar's trinitarian apocalyptic; a complement in that in line with Balthasar's own view of the multi-perspectival nature of theology, Metz's theology underscores with an emphasis and finesse not found in Balthasar the interruptive and apophatic features of apocalyptic; a supplement in that Metz's apocalyptic teases out with considerably more deliberation and detail the prophetic-critical dimension that Balthasar's apocalyptic allows for, even demands, but fails to explore with sufficient tenacity. In line with the four specific considerations I listed in the introduction as grounds for conversation, I begin with Metz's self-understanding as an apocalyptic theologian (apocalyptic indexing), proceed with a reflection on Metz's apocalyptic theology as defined by resistance and intervention in a field of modern discourse (apocalyptic as intervention), continue by considering the level of eidetics (apocalyptic calibration), and conclude with a reflection on the intersection of apocalyptic with doxology and liturgy (doxological apocalyptic).

Apocalyptic Indexing of Theology

While the apocalyptic indexing of his apologetic fundamental theology was not there from the beginning, and succeeded rather than preceded Metz's social-political turn, Metz's avowal of the centrality of apocalyptic could not be clearer. Apocalyptic, he writes, 'is to a certain extent the hem of my theological approach, although I have not yet learned to speak convincingly about it.'[4] *Faith in History and Society* represents the definitive expression of the centrality of apocalyptic to the theological task as this task bears on the themes of redemption and hope (chs.7, 10) and utilizes the categories of meaning and narrative (chs. 11, 12). Without reproducing Metz's richly complex and open-ended analysis, the following at least is clear: apocalyptic discourse is a discourse of expectation for a fundamental change in the order of history, which is an order of catastrophic injustice, where this change comes through the act of God who vindicates Godself by siding with those whom history devastates, makes voiceless and invisible, and condemns to the second death of being forgotten. Metz admits that the language of apocalyptic appears to be anachronistic, even archaic. But for him herein lies its advantage: such language is par excellence the critical language of non-contemporaneity.[5] After Bloch,[6] Metz thinks of the Western tradition as having given birth to a number of apocalyptic counter-discourses that refuse to be discourses of ratification, that is, discourses that either uncritically express contemporary assumptions (ideology) or self-consciously support the status quo. These include, for example, the apocalyptic discourses of Joachim, Savonarola, and the Left-Wing of the Reformation, and especially the discourse of the visionary Anabaptist reformer, Thomas Müntzer. Every authentic apocalyptic discourse gives witness to the endangered subject of history, reduced to poverty and silence, and subjected to oppression and futility. It also evinces the need and danger of decision for-or-against the status quo, and looks forward to a new order in which impossibly justice will reign. In the final analysis, however, all of the apocalyptic discourses of the Western tradition, which together weave something like a counter-narrative, owe much of their evocative and persuasive power to biblical apocalyptic. Considering the capacity of apocalyptic discourse to evoke what is not, what precisely the world cannot allow to be, Metz responds with deep regret to the excision of the apocalyptic dimension in modern society in general, but also its white-out in theology which has succeeded beyond imagining in reaching an accommodation with the modern world.[7] This is reflected at once in the individualism of an eschatological perspective – should such a perspective continue to persist – and in the assumption of the prerogative of an empty time that shows just enough teleology to avoid entropy. While Metz's analysis of an non-apocalyptic modernity is more focused than Balthasar's, both believe that this accommodation cuts Christianity off from its historical and biblical roots in which apocalyptic plays a significant role and thereby facilitates the loss of identity.

For Metz, apocalyptic is just that discourse, which if it explicitly invites demythologization, ultimately defies it,[8] since the intention that drives the language exceeds the coordinates of immanent and verifiable reality. Metz does not argue for the irreducibility of apocalyptic discourse to concept and ethical precept with either the same degree of attention to specific biblical texts or the same intense hermeneutic reflection on the nature of symbol, as Balthasar does in the trilogy, and especially in *Theo-Drama 4 & 5*. Nevertheless, he readily grasps that apocalyptic discourse cannot be reduced to concept, argument, historical fact, or parenaetic discourse. Granted that in his linking of apocalyptic discourse with narrative in *Faith in History and Society*, Metz does not clarify fully whether the two terms are substitutable, or whether apocalyptic is a specific kind of narrative discourse,[9] nevertheless, he is declarative that narrative discourse resists translation into the more propositional discourses of history, ethics, and metaphysics (ch. 12).[10] More generally, with regard to the excessiveness of apocalyptic discourse, the emphasis in Metz's works falls on content rather than on the form. Apocalyptic discourse is excessive because it speaks of a radical transformation, the irruption of the radically new, that is, the 'new' that cannot be extrapolated from present or past conditions.[11] Tellingly, the new is defined largely in negative and functional terms; negative in the sense that the new gains much of its content by contrast with the regime of the world, characterized by viciousness, injustice, and apathy; functional in the sense that while God and the new are in some sense interdefinable, Metz's practical fundamental theology forbids him to explore, as Balthasar's does, the meaning of God as the new within a theological prospectus that reflects theocentrically on the glory of God and the glory of the Trinity in particular.[12] The objection to Moltmann's thought in the following passage specifies a more general prohibition of trinitarian apocalyptic and/or apocalyptic trinitarianism:

> *His book,* The Crucified God, *was in many respects quite splendid, but since its publication Moltmann has used the concept of praxis increasingly to describe a theology in which the history of the suffering of the Son and the world is rooted in the Trinity. Praxis, which can only prevent the danger of speculative gnosis in such an approach, is no longer an intelligible principle in Moltmann's theology. (FHS, 55)*[13]

Metz makes it perfectly clear that while Balthasar may very well be the pick of post-Hegelian theologians who speak of the Trinitarian framing of historical suffering, he is not excepted from the general concern raised by such forms of theology. The following passage is worth quoting in full:

> *. . . the non-identity of human suffering cannot be cancelled out in theological dialectics of Trinitarian soteriology and still keep its historical character. For the painful experience of the non-identity of*

> *suffering cannot be identified with that negativity found in the dialectical understanding of the historical process, even that of a Trinitarian history of God. (FHS, 132)*

Metz shows himself unwilling to distinguish between Moltmann's *The Crucified God* and Balthasar's *Mysterium Paschale*, which he indicates that he has read (*FHS*, 135, n. 28), and interprets both as offering kenotic forms of Trinitarianism that logicize Luther's *sub contrario*.[14] Again, Metz does not fail to use the adjective 'gnostic' to describe such a position (*FHS*, 132), thereby establishing a general pattern.[15]

At the very least then, in Metz's theology, biblical apocalyptic enjoys a priority over other modes of apocalyptic in the Western tradition to which appeal can and should be made. Both the priority of biblical apocalyptic and its relation to other modes of apocalyptic achieve expression in the form of theses, which echo Benjamin's famous theses on history,[16] which in turn echo Marx's famous theses on Feuerbach.[17] Citationality is a major ingredient in the rhetorical power of the theses, especially theses 14-16, 23-27, which displace argument by insight that cannot and should not prove itself. Obviously, the priority accorded the biblical is somewhat different than that accorded it by Balthasar for whom the priority of biblical apocalyptic is normative rather than functional. If part of the reason for the merely functional priority of biblical apocalyptic in Metz lies in the continuing influence of Bloch and especially Benjamin for whom dislocative function is crucial,[18] a contributing factor is the choice of theological method. The essentially apologetic nature of Metz's theology obliges him at all times to keep the broadest range of analogues to biblical apocalyptic in mind. Thesis 23 refers positively to apocalyptic as an object of the history of religions (*FHS*, 175). This reference is vague, and logically it could include a wide variety of forms of apocalyptic thought, from the apocalypses of indigenous peoples through apocalyptic-eschatological thought of ancient non-biblical religions such as Zoroastrianism to the full panoply of Jewish and Christian apocalypses which clearly have the status of prime referent. In referring to the Jewish idea of the Messiah, thesis 24 not only refers to a biblical apocalyptic motif that might moderate the triumphalism of Christianity, but also any and all varieties of realized eschatology. At the same time it also points to Bloch and Benjamin as proponents of Jewish apocalyptic, and implies that the texts of these thinkers are worthy of attention. Thesis 21 broadens out the apocalyptic program even further by citing Celan's aphorism, 'It is time for it, to be time: it is time (*Es ist Zeit, dass es Zeit wird; Es ist Zeit*).'

Allowing this aphorism to stand on its own, Metz obviously feels that it requires no commentary, that it speaks to the interruption that is the subject of thesis 2. At the same time, the invoking of Celan suggests that in modernity religion is no longer the only discourse of interruption, or even the prime one. Metz does not identify the citation as the last two lines of *Corona* from Celan's first volume of poetry, nor does he stress that the immediately following poem is, arguably, Celan's most realized Shoah poem, that is, 'Todesfuge.'[19] Celan believes that poetry can be a form of witness, indeed given the Holocaust, only poetry can be witness, since only poetry can negotiate its freedom from the conventions of language that made Auschwitz possible. For Metz, at the very least in the post-Holocaust era, biblical apocalyptic shares space then with other actual or possible forms of apocalyptic that foster community identity,[20] invite hope against hope for a future of inclusion and justice, offer critical leverage against discourses and practices that either automatically replicate themselves or justify the status quo, and remember the dead or confess the guilt in not remembering well-enough. While this pragmatic equivalence of apocalyptic forms by no means involves the denial of the generative status of biblical apocalyptic, or in any way commits Metz to deny the incommensurability of biblical apocalyptic, such issues become secondary in Metz's fundamental practical theology in a way that they do not in Balthasar's aesthetic-dramatic thought.

Even when Metz accords biblical apocalyptic a certain privilege, there are differences between him and Balthasar with respect to where apocalyptic is to be found in the biblical text and in what it essentially consists. Conspicuously, Metz relates to apocalyptic as being a more amorphous or polymorphous feature of biblical discourse than does Balthasar: just about any biblical text, in any particular genre, can serve the role of hope and memory and contribute to solidarity with the invisible living and the even more invisible dead. As we have seen, despite his ambitious theological agenda, Balthasar's rendition of biblical apocalyptic bears more than a family resemblance to the *Religionsgeschichte* school in proposing criteria for identification of biblical apocalyptic, and criteria of distinction between biblical apocalyptic and other forms of apocalyptic. Balthasar also shows significant familiarity with New Testament scholarship not only on Revelation, but also on those aspects of Paul and the Synoptic Gospels identified by scholars as articulating apocalyptic.[21] Despite occasional appeals to biblical scholarship, Metz never attempts, as Balthasar does in *Theo-Drama 4 & 5*, to make his case on exegetical grounds. Balthasar would likely understand the motivation behind the appeal to Käsemann's view of the constitutive apocalyptic nature of the New Testament in *Faith in History and Society* (175-76),[22] but would equally find the position to be underdeveloped in that the differences between it and realized and even unrealized eschatology are more nearly asserted than demonstrated. Balthasar, we noted in chapter 6, believes that Revelation has to be given pride of place in any theology that purports to be genuinely apocalyptic,[23] and he underscores the special relation between Revelation and the Gospel of John, as they articulate different but complementary aspects of the paschal mystery. While the promise of a new heaven and new earth is regulative for Metz also, it is this promise, as it is coded in a discourse (or practice), rather than a specific set of expressions that is pivotal. Metz is nervous about the promise having too determinate a content, for such determinacy suggests that the proper stance towards the end of history, and arguably the means towards the end, is knowledge. It is precisely this lack of knowing or unknowing that helps distinguish apocalyptic in the strict sense from mere utopianism (thesis 22). In denying determinacy of content – in insisting on surprise and advent – Metz eschews anything resembling a set of genre criteria for identifying biblical apocalyptic and distinguishing it from other forms of apocalyptic discourse. Nor does Metz distinguish, as Balthasar does, between canonic and non-canonic apocalyptic. Indeed, Metz's consistent avowal of 'Jewish apocalyptic' suggests that Metz either has no interest in the latter distinction, or that he is taking issue with it.

Although Metz is prepared to concede that the promise is more to the fore in some biblical texts than others, for example, in the Gospel of Mark and in certain parts of Paul (e.g., 1 Cor 15:51 ff),[24] the promise can be found throughout the Bible, and as much in Hebrew scripture as in the New Testament. And it is not only Daniel, but Isaiah and Ezekiel that inscribe the promise. Whereas Balthasar showed himself anxious to point to the relation between apocalyptic and prophetic discourse, while underscoring the differences, Metz has no compunction about linking apocalyptic discourse not only to prophetic discourse, but to the Psalms, especially the Psalms of Lament, and even to the Book of Job.[25] He does so because together these discourses figure a non-theoretical theodicy that challenges the bourgeois supposition that history is in no need of justification, and also the reflective theodicies and anthropodicies, ancient and modern, ecclesial and non-ecclesial,[26] that justify the ways of God to men or justify the ways of men to men. The best statement of Metz's point of view comes not from *Faith in History and Society*, but rather from an essay in *Hope against Hope*:

> *. . . a theology which is no longer permitted or expected to present its explanation of the world and its interpretation of human existence in closed, a-situational systems. It knows of no final explanations [Letztbegründungen], but – if you will permit me this word-play – only explanations that finally come at the end [Zuletztbegründungen]. The temporal factor is unavoidably in play; its message has a temporal core. This logic is not really the logic of identity, but of non-identity. This makes it more vulnerable than classical metaphysics, than any way of thinking guided by ideas. (HH, 12)*[27]

Needless to say, Metz by no means shows less interest in the prophetic as such than Balthasar. It is simply that whereas Balthasar is among other things interested in prophetic literature as a genre, just as he is interested in apocalyptic as a genre, Metz is interested in prophetic function. Balthasar, of course, is no more a pure morphologist of the genre of prophecy than he is of apocalyptic. As is clear from *Glory of the Lord 6*, Balthasar understands prophecy to be a discourse of critique in which the judgment of the transcendent God of history is lodged against current social arrangements and practices that are religiously sanctioned. Prophecy ferrets out any and all forms of 'idolatry' that engender and encourage apathy towards the poor (*anawim*) who are the special concern of Yahweh (*GL6*, 318). Moreover, it is ingredient in the very logic of the relation between the old and new covenant articulated in *Glory of the Lord 6 & 7* that Christianity does not abolish the prophetic, but realizes it: realizes it first in Jesus Christ who holds the office of prophet as well as priest and king, and secondarily in the Christian community called to imitate him. One of the clearest statements of the importance of the prophetic as a specifically Christian call to, and enactment of, transformation is to be found in Balthasar's important essay, 'The Claim to Catholicity':

> *Thus faith appears as a world-transforming deed. The transformation of these social structures that directly prevent the message of Christ from being understood by the poor, oppressed and exploited is an essential element of Christian mission. (Exp 4, 84)*

Still it is not an exaggeration to say in Metz faith is assessed from this point of view, which is the point of view of praxis or prophetic action. Any and all content to apocalyptic can and should be led back to the prophetic injunction to transform the condition of the 'poor' of history, which, for Metz, centrally include the 'dead.'

Differences between Metz and Balthasar with respect to *where* apocalyptic can be found in the biblical text bear also on the *what*. For Metz, whatever the case in principle, as a matter of fact, it is the Gospel of Mark that is regulative for his apocalyptic theology. As has been pointed out by Metz scholars,[28] this puts Metz at odds with Rahner whose overall theological orientation is provided by Luke. But it also puts Metz, for whom the paschal mystery is so central, at odds with Balthasar. Here the difference is internal to apocalyptic theology rather than a difference between an apocalyptic form of theology and a non-apocalyptic form. Granted his commitment to the resurrection as well as the death of Jesus, Metz takes the abyssal cry of Mark 15:34, 'My God, my God, why has thou abandoned me,' to be central. Metz's preference is a considered one; he is anxious to avoid an exclusive emphasis on resurrection. Even allowing for Metz's own assessment of the polemical nature of his theology that seeks redress, the interpreter might feel secure in drawing the conclusion that Metz understands his apocalyptic theology to be unproblematically a Good-Friday rather than an Easter theology. Interestingly, Metz does not fully endorse this description. Taking into account those on whose behalf Christ suffered abandonment, at crucial points Metz, like Balthasar, valorizes a theology of Holy Saturday:

> *If I can put it this way, in Christology we have lost the way between Good Friday and Easter Sunday. We have too much Easter Sunday Christology. I feel that the atmosphere of Holy Saturday has to be narrated within Christology itself. For a long time now not everybody has experienced Easter Sunday as the third day after Good Friday. (HH, 45)*

Moreover, Metz stipulates what Balthasar performs, that is, that the theology of Holy Saturday be culled of its notes of victory, and focus on Christ's solidarity with the lost and the dead (*HH*, 46).[29] His suspicion of Balthasar's relation to von Speyr (*HH*, 20), his concern regarding Balthasar's Johannine orientation with its insufficiently jagged dramatics, as well as his preference for general description of the dead as innocent sufferers rather than sinners, divide him from the Swiss theologian. Although Metz himself from time to time cites John,[30] he finds that the ontological style discourse of John encourages a kind of discussion on kenosis and love that is speculative and in the end aesthetic in the pejorative sense.[31] Metz's resistance is both epistemological and ethical. It is epistemological in that however far he moves self-consciously beyond Rahner's transcendental option in *Faith in History and Society*,[32] Metz remains faithful to Rahner's principle of epistemic reserve with respect to talk of God *in se*. This is seen with particular force in his essay, 'Theology as Theodicy.'[33] It is ethical insofar as Metz wonders whether the translation of the rupture of the cross into a trinitarian milieu, predicated on alienation and distance, functions to ameliorate the horror of Christ's abandonment, and removes the solidarity between Christ and those whom history ploughs under.[34] Of course, Balthasar is by no means the only object of critique here – recall the criticism of Moltmann's trinitarian theology – but together with Speyr he is the proponent of a theology of Holy Saturday, and the contemporary Catholic theologian who puts the theology of the cross in a trinitarian perspective.

Intervention of Apocalyptic

I TURN NOW TO THE SECOND REASON for bringing the apocalyptic theologies of Balthasar and Metz into conversation with each other. In his mature thought Metz supports apocalyptic forms of discourse and articulates an apocalyptic form of theology for essentially two reasons. He does so, first, because memory and hope, which animate apocalyptic discourse, constitute the very identity of the *Christian* subject. We remember and hope on our own behalf and on behalf of those who are invisible and without voice in our world, especially those dead who would show our inhuman face and make us face our guilt. We do so, calling to mind the passion, death, and resurrection of Jesus Christ.[35] For Metz *Christian* identity is not formed, as it is in Balthasar, by a retrieval of the Christian tradition, and by deep immersion into the depth and variety of perspectives over time on the mystery of the triune God revealed in Christ. Rather Christian identity is focused in a return to the event that constitutes scripture and is the basis of all relatively adequate theological thought, that is, the passion, death, and resurrection of Christ.[36] Second, by contrast with Balthasar, as Chapter 4 of *Faith in History and Society* makes abundantly clear (*FHS*, 60-70), securing specifically *Christian* identity for Metz takes second place to securing the identity of the Christian *subject* against the social and ideological forces that would make it impossible. This preference both reflects and underpins the option for a fundamental as opposed to a dogmatic theology that would be favored by Balthasar. Metz continues Rahner's programmatic by other means, and by so doing, takes a side in what has been the essential methodological debate within as well as without Catholicism in the modern period.

As Metz understands it, apocalyptic theology represents both a diagnosis of, and a preliminary attempt to overcome, the forgetfulness of the subject characteristic of modernity. As is clear from

Faith in History and Society, mindful of the lessons of both Heidegger and Critical Theory,[37] Metz is fully aware that bourgeois modernity is defined by the turn to the individual subject, considered as the ground of the world and society. His point is that the modern definition of the subject is anomalous both from a historical and normative point of view. In response Metz historicizes the modern subject, making it a function of a particular period, dominated by determinate social and ideological processes. This subject, cut off from other subjects, and relating to the world as a field of incentives and opportunities for self-making and aggrandizement, breaks from a world of assumption in which identity is garnered only in and through relations with other people, and where the world is experienced as an enveloping sphere rather than a set of discrete objects defined by use.[38] The individual 'bourgeois' self is equally judged bankrupt from a normative point of view. Evaluated in light of particular goods that are constitutive of identity, the modern subject fails miserably, indeed, fails to be a subject in the full and proper sense. Introduced into being by a break with the past, the modern subject lacks the incentive to remember the past. Wrapped up in itself, indeed incurved on itself,[39] the modern subject is a machine of rationalization. For example, it justifies its constitutional apathy on the grounds that history is progress and all that happens contributes to the world as the world actually is rather than the world that can be, which is the world of maybe in the pejorative sense. Here one can see Metz's inversion of Kant:[40] whereas in the latter ought implies can, now can implies ought. Neither seeing that the justification is an act of blind faith, nor grasping the contradiction between the subject's activism and its posture of resignation before a world governed by immutable laws, the bourgeois subject is cut off from the suffering and death of those who have fallen in history, connection with whom might give density and extension to a being of unbearable lightness and thinness.[41] The imperatives of mourning, of complaint, and the responsibility to rectify what is broken by recognizing and naming injustice, which is at the core of human and moral identity, is not taken on. The same bourgeois subject, who evades the potential discomfort of the disruption of the complacency of the self by refusing to allow the past to challenge, deepens his or her existential, even ontological, plight by turning his or her eyes away from a future that is not a function of the present and the past. For the authentic subject the future is not an extrapolatable – Balthasar would say an 'anticipatable' – reality; it is rather a reality of genuine surprise. For Metz, the modern subject without memory and hope, without a weighty imperative past and an interruptive future is a subject that is a pure present, indeed a vanishing present, and thus a vanishing subject.

The indicting of the modern subject as amnesiac and the correlative promotion of the anamnestic nature of the Christian subject are the defining attributes of Metz's apocalyptic theology in a way that they are not for Balthasar. This is not to say that Balthasar does not take the amnesia of modernity seriously, or fail to refer to its manifestations in practices and forms of life, as well as manifestations in our speech and our thought. Arguably, the burden of diagnosis is as least as much carried by Balthasar's literary criticism and works such as *Man in History* and *The God Question and Modern Man* as the trilogy which, if it charts the egological and egophanic foundation of modernity,[42] does not offer anything like a 'thick description.' An especially prominent place has to be accorded to Balthasar's magisterial work on Bernanos, whose novels show the collision between Christian forms of thought and life and a modernity that finds them incomprehensible and excessive.[43] Manifestly, however, Balthasar does not foreground amnesia either in the same way or to the same extent. Not in the same way, since Balthasar is concerned with specifically *Christian* forms of thought and practice in a way that Metz is not, who is as much – if not more concerned – with the human ability to empathize and show signs of moral imagination. Not to the same extent, since in Balthasar's texts the features of forgetting are both highly generic and marked only in episodic fashion. For example, the triune God is not a reality in the lives of the secular person defined by self-determination. Even in cases where this God is a possible object of discourse, God is not an object of direct address or praise. To be the latter would require a recognition that a relation between God and the self cannot be founded by the self, and to acknowledge that a condition of addressing God is that one has already been addressed by him. Cumulatively, of course, Balthasar prosecutes a case against the amnesia of modernity, but unlike Metz, the amnesia is as often assumed as it is demonstrated.

Nevertheless, there are dimensions to this amnesia that Balthasar reflects on that are ignored by Metz. Although Heidegger plays a somewhat constructive role in the thinking of both apocalyptic theologians, it is only Balthasar who takes seriously Heidegger's reflections on *Seinsvergessenheit.* Although he is instructed by the historicity of truth articulated in *Being and Time*,[44] Metz does not dally with metaphysical eclipse or the eclipse of metaphysics or explore the properties of truth as *aletheia.* And, as I have insisted on throughout, in a way that echoes Newman's genealogical reflections,[45] Balthasar is concerned with the erosion of what might be called a Christian sensibility, which has as an essential part of its vocabulary awe and a sense of mystery funded by practices that encourage this sense. With the caveat then that Balthasar is often ploughing a very different terrain – although they overlap at some points (e.g. the difficulty of prayer) – one can grant to Metz a definite advantage with respect to the anatomy and genealogy of modernity, however derivative he is, and however dependent in particular on Critical Theory.

Neither distance from, nor relative advantage over, Balthasar seem appropriate to characterize Metz's diagnosis of and resistance to another form of forgetting, which recalls in the closest possible way a distinction made by Balthasar between unreflective and reflective forgetting. Metz opposes to the historical remembering or remembrance (*geschichtliches Eingedenken*) (*PG*, 26, 64), which he recommends, not one but two forms of forgetting, 'not only that which wipes away every trace, so that finally nothing more can be recalled, but also that sort of forgetfulness that we think of as successfully remembering . . .' (*PG*, 62) For Metz the second of the two structural forms of this forgetting, which corresponds to what throughout we have been calling 'misremembering,' is represented by the discourses of Hegel and Marx and their various epigones. Metz contends that Hegel's *Geist* and Marx's proletariat are metahistorical fabrications that disguise and justify the erasure of the suffering subject of history by rendering the subject as the merely incidental means in the self-justifying dialectic of history (*PG*, 52). Metz acknowledges that both these forms of thought represent efforts to overcome the Enlightenment and correct for the bourgeois self, and are in some sense generative with respect to the discourses of Bloch and the Frankfurt school both of which are truly productive for theology. Nevertheless, Hegel and Marx fail to gain an open relationship to a past that challenges and upsets the present, and fail to put themselves in line to experience a future that is not the teleological extension of the now. To recall Marx's famous statement in 'The Eighteenth Brumaire of Louis Bonaparte,'[46] namely that the 'tradition of the dead generations weighs like a nightmare on the brain of the living,' but to invert its meaning, one can read Metz as saying that neither Hegel nor Marx are sufficiently oppressed by the ghosts of the past that would be made visible and that would be heard. These discourses would be rid of ghosts. And they are successful enough at such ridding that there is need for the kind of redress provided by Metz's prophetic-apocalyptic intervention that recalls the past that is erased through ideal or real dialectic and in memory calls the dead into community and reinvigorates their hope (*HH*, 21).[47]

In an important essay, 'Theology as Theodicy' (*PG*, 54-71), however, Metz seems to suggest that Idealist discourse in general, and that of Hegel in particular, has not successfully washed off and rinsed out all ghosts. Interestingly, the spectral nature of Hegel's discourse is not the result of an unsuccessful repression of the voices of the dead, their consigning to a sempiternity of amnesia – Hegel's dialectical program is totally successful on this score. Rather the spectrality of Hegel's discourse lies in the fact that Hegel's discourse repeats the gnosis of the early centuries (*PG*, 42, 69). Metz makes sure that however *ad hoc* the ascription, the point has some genealogical gravity by recalling Irenaeus' resistance to speculative discourses of the first centuries (*PG*, 59).[48] Here Metz is wholly Balthasarian in his isolating of Hegel's contemplative and aesthetic point of view on history that subjects Christ and human beings to an autonomous movement of becoming and development that legitimates the forgetting of both. Metz does not inquire more deeply into the warrants for the linkage between Hegel and early Gnosticism. Still, without becoming a genealogical theologian like Balthasar, and with no more than a basic sense that what unites Hegel to historical Gnosticism is a metanarrative in which the biblical God is enlisted in something like a theogony, it is interesting that Metz qualifies Hegelian misremembering in a way similar to

Balthasar and by doing so figures himself as something of an Irenaeus *redivivus*. Needless to say, this figuration is at a much lower level of clarity, self-consciousness, and exigency than that which we find in Balthasar. Still, Metz makes a real contribution in emphasizing that Gnostic idealization bypasses the individual whose infinite value is inscribed in the fragile and vulnerable body, which in consequence makes resurrection, not immortality, the appropriate redress.[49]

In any event, the post-Enlightenment discourses of Marx and Hegel also unriddle the genuine, that is, non-immanent future, in which the impossible reversal of fortune occurs and God wipes away all tears and justifies Godself. This future act of God is the act of God as the future. In *Faith in History and Society*, thinking of less focused teleological construals of history than those provided by Hegel and Marx, Metz observes: 'Utopias would prove to be the final cunning of evolution, if there were only utopias and not God' (175).[50] Nevertheless, these utopias appear to be mapped onto a Hegelian template. The 'cunning of evolution' (*List der Evolution*) obviously evokes Hegel's 'cunning of reason' (*List der Vernunft*), and intimates the laws of dialectical necessity that ensure that there is no court of appeal outside the internal dynamics of, and judgments within, history.[51] Critical for Metz then is his taking a stand against the spectacle of theodicy, or theodicy as spectacle. But this is not to say, any more than Balthasar, that Metz is taking a stand against theodicy *simpliciter*. Metz's apocalyptic theology is self-consciously directed against theodicy in its implicit and explicit Enlightenment and post-Enlightenment forms, for example, against the socially widespread assumption of progress, against Leibniz's 'best of possible worlds,' derided by Voltaire and deconstructed by Dostoyevski,[52]and finally against narrative and/or historical theodicies or anthropodicies (substitute human being for God) that reflexively justify violence and extermination as a necessary sacrifice to the Moloch of history as reality in its mode of actualization or self-actualization. As articulated within the framework of his apocalyptic theology, for Metz, theodicy will not only have to be heuristic as in Kant; it will have to be Joban. That is, it will have to license complaint and accusation, the rhetoric of appeal to and prayer to the one who can make things right despite the judgment of history, despite the apparent withdrawal of the last court of appeal. For Metz, it is more proper to say that God is the last judgment than to say that to him belongs the prerogative of the last judgment, for in line with Rahner,[53] Metz believes that eschatological statements say more about our hopes than provide real knowledge of states of affairs.[54]

Metz's critique of modern theodicies and anthropodicies does not sanction the kind of theodicy that Christian apocalyptic thought has commonly appealed to throughout the centuries. An apocalyptic form that underpinned much of Christian eschatology was that supplied by Augustine in *The City of God.* In his debate with Ratzinger, as well as elsewhere,[55] Metz makes perfectly clear that he will have no truck with what he takes to be a spuriously apocalyptic specimen of Christian thought. Metz is convinced that Augustine's eschatology is ruled by an anxiety to justify God at all costs. This leads Augustine to place the entire burden of responsibility for the catastrophe of history on human sin, and in turn to interpret salvation exclusively in terms of the next life, which has the different ontological status of eternity.[56] These objections and others such as the objection to Augustine appealing to aesthetic considerations to justify that everything is better in every way, Metz shares with numerous critics of Hegel, including Bloch and Liberation theology. Still, from the point of view of a Ratzinger or a Balthasar, however necessary it may be to modify Augustinian theology in some of its details, and especially to reconceive the nature of God, it is simply not possible to exclude personal sin from consideration, to pass over in silence individual judgment, and to turn a blind eye to the hope that the kingdom is not simply a human kingdom in the future, but the kingdom of God in which not only the ills of history are transcended, but also the frailty of desire and the fragility of human beings marked by physical and psychological vulnerability and mutability.

As I already indicated in chapter 6, Balthasar shares some of the concerns about Augustine raised by Metz. In *Glory of the Lord 2*, Balthasar expresses concern for the purely 'aesthetic' quality of early Augustinian theodicy (*GL2*, 128 ff), and in *Theo-Drama* he shows himself unhappy with Augustine's view of predestination and what he takes to be his unexamined assumption of the power of sin in the light of the message of the New Testament, especially that granted in the Johannine corpus centered around the Paschal Lamb (*TD4*, 316-321). Importantly, Balthasar's reservations do not eschew a theocentric horizon, even if access to this horizon is granted only through Jesus Christ. Balthasar's argument with Augustine is not that God should not be the object of theological discourse, but that Augustine gets it wrong. But in an interesting contrast with Metz with regard to how Augustine gets it wrong, Balthasar believes that at crucial points Augustine avails of intra-worldly forms of aesthetic thought (appropriateness and order, existential gravity) to make his case, and thus fails to be led by the phenomenon of Jesus Christ on the cross. The problem then is not the theocentric, and ultimately trinitarian, horizon of theology, but the lack of scruple in its application. To substitute a more anthropocentric horizon for the theocentric one is precisely the wrong lesson to be learned; and in this case it matters little whether the anthropological horizon more nearly favors the community than the individual. A critical issue for Balthasar is whether the Christian is expected to adopt a Kantian or Augustinian view of hope in the resurrection. However much Metz defines his project as taking leave of Rahner's transcendentalism, on this issue he is regulated by it. Metz does, however, in and through the influence of Benjamin and Critical Theory filter out the metaphysical realism embedded in Rahner's avowal of the transcendental turn.[57] The result is a purified Kantianism which stipulates that the symbols and narratives of resurrection do not provide us with knowledge in the strict sense, that is, knowledge that can be warranted. By contrast, for Balthasar the symbols and narratives of resurrection obviously more nearly belong to the order of faith than knowledge; yet faith is, on the one hand, inchoate knowledge and, on the other, the symbols are real in that they participate in the reality to which they refer.[58] Balthasar shares this view with the other representatives of the Irenaean and Augustinian form of apocalyptic. If the kataphatic thrust of symbols is honored, this thrust is tempered by the inherent ungraspability of the realities which the symbols invoke and evoke. For Balthasar in particular, the symbols of the biblical text represent the prime analogate of the balance between the kataphatic and the apophatic that any good theology strives to achieve. This balance is difficult, and tilts in the kataphatic or apophatic direction are equally injurious. While Balthasar, as with Staudenmaier, Bulgakov, and Hamann, spends considerably more time critiquing forms of theology that exaggerate the competence of the finite subject to know, an apophaticism without reserve also has to be combated. Throughout his long career, Balthasar calls for vigilance with respect to the border in negative theology where participatory 'unknowing' changes into agnosticism.[59]

Calibration of Eidetic Apocalyptic

METZ CAN BE UNDERSTOOD TO ARTICULATE an eidetic apocalyptic theology to the extent to which such a theology has as its content the passion, death, and resurrection of Christ. As *Faith in History and Society* put it, it is our memory of this narratively coded message, thus *memoria passionis et resurrectionis Christi*, that provides us with a perspective other than that of the victors of history (*FHS*, 109-15). Indeed, it is this memory that offers us the perspective of divine judgment on history that vindicates the lost and – although very much secondarily – justifies God in the process (*FHS*, 115-19). The movement of *Faith in History and Society* from the 'dangerous memory' of the passion and death of Christ in chapter 5, through clarification in chapters 6 and 7, to a discussion of the nature of church in chapter 8, testify to the fact that Metz's apocalyptic eidetics are ecclesiological as well as christological. Although Metz's eidetics do not, as in the case of Revelation, and in Balthasar's repetition, feature the church in travail, his vision is ecclesiocentric in the sense that real appropriation through 'dangerous' memory of the narrative of the life and death of Christ is in a sense constitutive of the church as church. This is explicitly stated in chapter 5, and the subsequent movement of the text explicates a thesis stated at the outset. The church is a community of memory, whose vocation is to speak for those who can no longer speak for themselves. The church re-presents the dead by bringing them to mind and to speech, and by so doing releasing the dead from the Sheol of the unremembered – the dead who otherwise would suffer the 'second death' of being forgotten. Yet there are unaddressed problems.

First, while the dangerous memory of the passion, death, and resurrection of Christ has priority over other 'dangerous memories,' the extent of this priority is not clarified. Second, although dangerous memory obviates the 'second death' of memory; it is not evident how it addresses the first death which is the original catastrophe. Third, the extent of would-be redemption is unclear. Dependent on community memory, the 'dead' are liable to the tragedy exposed by Plato in the *Symposium*: immortality of name is different than the repetition of the human subject, and offering the former instead of the latter is an expression of futility, for the latter is subject to the amnesia of individuals and societies. Fourth, by focusing on the specialness of 'dangerous memory,' the question arises whether despite his general aversion to Augustinian eschatology Metz does not functionally repeat the Augustinian view of the election, dramatically figured in plucking selected individuals from the formless pile or *massa* of the lost, which he rejects on epistemological and ethical grounds.

Important points of contrast between Metz and Balthasar remain then, even if one treats Metz's apocalyptic *as if* it were eidetic without remainder, rather than, as I shall argue shortly, a mixed kind of apocalyptic discourse with a significant non-eidetic component. To begin with, given Metz's commitment to fundamental theology,[60] the eidetic component of his apocalyptic theology is less first-order and less direct than that of Balthasar's, but also less alethic. As we have already seen, for Balthasar, as regulative of Christian vision, eidetic apocalyptic is regulative for any theology that would be faithful to biblical witness. Moreover, apocalyptic symbols and tropes disclose the triune God's relation to the world and the vicissitudes of history, while unveiling who God is. The opposition between Metz and Balthasar on this score is irreducible, even if one takes into account the changes Metz rings on Rahner's fundamental theology by calibrating it in a more social-political key. For if in one sense Metz could be read to lessen the Rahnerian gap between fundamental and doctrinal theology by including within fundamental theology the trope of the passion, death, and resurrection of Christ, in another sense, it could be thought to open up the gap even more by emptying out altogether what is of value in doctrinal theology and leaving only the 'dead remains.'

A closely related difference concerns the range of content in the respective eidetic apocalyptic theologies of Metz and Balthasar. For reasons of method, but undoubtedly also of sensibility, Metz's eidetic focus is compact by comparison with that of Balthasar who, although concerned to cull apocalyptic of rhetorical overkill and to restrain its totalizing tendencies, nevertheless, believes not only that a comprehensive apocalyptic theology is possible, but absolutely necessary. Metz's reduction of apocalyptic eidetics to the passion, death, and resurrection of Christ not only puts the focus narrowly on the 'saving' function of Christ rather than on his person, but effectively excludes such important elements of apocalyptic discourse as God's judgment of the sinner, avoids presenting the apocalyptic figures of the devil and the Anti-Christ, and prohibits even mention of the cosmic dimensions of apocalyptic, emphasized with different degrees of intensity in Balthasar, Moltmann, and Bulgakov. Metz rules out, however, not only theological exploration of the person of Christ, but also of the God of Jesus Christ, revealed in a definitive way on the cross. The last point is the crucial one. We have seen how in Balthasar's apocalyptic theology apophasis functions critically to remind the believer of the symbolic nature of apocalyptic discourse. What is true of apocalyptic discourse as a genre is true also, as *Glory of the Lord* in particular makes clear, of all discourse that would name God. Thus, whatever the differences between theological aesthetics and theological dramatics, and however we envisage the correction and/or refiguration of vision initiated by the move towards a dramatic scopus, and its analytic commentary in *Theo-Logic*, the trilogy speaks with one voice concerning both the necessity of apophasis and its secondariness. Mindful in general that the discourse of apocalyptic is a discourse of symbols – thus of signs that present the reality they represent – and mindful in particular that the governing symbol of apocalyptic, that is, the Lamb slain before the foundation of the world, is incorrigibly kataphatic, Balthasar sets limits to apophasis. He does so, however, while remaining convinced that his own work illustrates just the kind of commitment to the apophatic modeled in Pseudo-Dionysius, Maximus, and Bonaventure, sufficient to resist Hegelian *Begriff*, whose vocation is to internalize and neutralize that which would exceed language and the concept.[61]

Metz is self-consciously apophatic. Throughout his work Metz uses the concept of 'negative theology' to distinguish his theology from that of speculative theologians such as Balthasar and Moltmann: these theologians say 'too much' (*PG*, 69) where saying 'too much' means pronouncing on phenomena for which one has no epistemic warrant. Influenced by Rahner's transcendental thought, arguably, Metz regresses behind Rahner's synthesis of Aquinas and Kant (with assists from Heidegger and German Idealism) to a Kant of the *First Critique* who denies that our concepts can have anything more than a regulative or hypothetical deployment with respect to God. This methodological regression to Kant is confirmed rather than disproved in Metz's socio-political trespass of the transcendental. While multiple influences are braided together in Metz's avocation, the fact is that it is Kant who in the *Critique of Practical Reason* and *Religion within the Bounds of Reason Alone* classically argued for the necessity of the supplemental discourses of ethics and religion precisely on the grounds of the incompetence of conceptual or cognitive language to justify its referring to God.[62] In retreating behind Rahner to Kant, Metz opens up a structural gap between his thought and that of Rahner whose own negative theology of mystery is funded by the mysticism of participation that achieves definitive expression in the Christian Neoplatonic tradition.[63] Being out of sync with Rahner, who is very much in sync with the broader catholic tradition, suggests if not a compromise with the Enlightenment on epistemology, at least negative capability on this score. At the same time, the reduction compromises the capacity of eidetic apocalyptic to be a deep critic of the Hegelian system. Indeed, the reduction exposes Metz to the kind of Hegelian critique of Kant and fideists such as Jacobi whom Hegel sought to exclude from the precincts of philosophy and Christianity on the grounds that they worship 'the Unknown God.'[64]

Metz reinforces his particular brand of negative theology by insisting that his apocalyptic theology is open to divine absence in the way that manifestly kataphatic theologies from Scholasticism to theological revisionists such as Balthasar and Moltmann are not. This putative advantage is a double-edge sword, however, and is so in a number of different respects. On the philosophical level, it encourages Metz to throw in his lot – however provisionally – with

Nietzsche's avowal of 'godlessness' (*HH*, 23). But this raises the question whether Metz's apocalyptic theology has the resources to overcome the nihilism that is posited as Nietzsche's starting point. In particular, it raises the question whether the largely rhetorical gestures of positing hope against hope, positing hope despite the absence of God, is in itself sufficient to move beyond it. Within the very different ordinances of radical orthodoxy and deconstruction this dealing with nihilism would seem ineffective in the extreme, and not rule out its own reinscription in a world representing the transvaluation of all values. Of course, it would not be impossible on Metz's own terms to replace Nietzsche with Job, and perhaps even desirable. For on the level of practice rather than theory, Job is dealing with the perceived absence of a God who promises to be 'with' the righteous.[65] As a matter of fact, Metz self-consciously follows Elie Wiesel in thinking of Job as the exemplary figure (*HH*, 23) or at least the Job of protest not the Job of capitulation, the one who 'repents in dust and ashes.' Although the transfer of theological authority to Job does not necessarily bring Metz outside the Kantian horizon,[66] it does reduce the gap between Metz and Balthasar. For if Balthasar refuses to validate Nietzschean 'godlessness' because of its constitutive claims, he can and does validate Job's protest, even if, or especially if, this protest is a moment that qualifies rather than disqualifies faith (*GL6*, 281-90). In fact it would not be going too far to see that Balthasar's concluding sentences, framed in the interrogative, seal his interpretation:

> *And had God himself, in all seriousness, led Job into this darkness, to which he alone has the key and for which he alone is answerable, with all the lamentations and the apparent blasphemies which are uttered in this darkness? And would this mean that the building blocks have been gathered together for the final synthesis which a fortiori only God can achieve: the unity of the glory of God and uttermost abandonment by God, Heaven and Hell? (GL6, 290)*

On the specifically theological level Metz supports the negative theology of divine absence not by appeal to a Christian mystic such as Meister Eckhart (*HH*, 28-30), but to the cry of dereliction of

Mark 15 in which Jesus experiences his abandonment by God. This cry provides the template, if not the frame, for the general experience of God's absence, and for classic experiences of divine absence such as Auschwitz.[67] Although it is difficult to sustain the view that the cry of dereliction is in any sense the ground of our hope unless, despite appearances, God is in some significant respect present, Metz is obviously determined to combat by any and all rhetorical means the realized eschatology of John's Gospel, which Balthasar attempts to show in *Theo-Drama 4 & 5* is consistent with the specific kind of unrealized eschatology proposed by Revelation. The deep difference concerning divine presence is at the root of the different interpretation in Metz and Balthasar of pre-eschatological time. Whereas Balthasar thinks of time before the eschaton as already transformed by Christ and thus kairotic, Metz thinks of pre-eschatological time as bearing the promise of the *pleroma*, but not as in itself kairotic. As chapter 10 of *Faith in History and Society* shows with great economy, while the view that time is homogenous (thus pure *Chronos*) is an illusion, and that it is interrupted by the lightning-flashes of insight, these do not transform time as such: interruption is fragmentary and leaves a breach rather than effecting a transformation. For the same reason in Metz that the intersection of the timeless with time is not kairotic, it is not sacramental. Metz makes it perfectly explicit that his view of time is heavily dependent on Benjamin's reflections. Yet there is a sense in which on the theological level he has inscribed actualist elements of Barth's dialectical program with which Balthasar took issue early on in his career.[68] As a theologian, who believes like Kierkegaard that we will be forever answering Hegel's speculative apocalyptic, and his construal of John in particular, it is necessary to think of the incarnation as kairotic, but also to think through what this implies. For Balthasar, *kairos* is identified with Christ and does not become a property of history as such. History is changed in that it admits of being incorporated into Christ, but that process is disguised to human beings and essentially not in their control. And history most certainly is not already on the way to a kind of pleromatic fulfillment indistinguishable from divine self-fulfillment. As a Christian thinker who intervenes in a dead and flattened modernity, Balthasar cannot think other than T.S. Eliot in *Four Quartets* that the only hope, the hope that is beyond hope, has to be in this intersection that is also the intersection of the cross.[69] The cross gives the rose, or at least the promise of the rose,[70] the presence with the triune God of unsurpassable beauty who excites endless love.

Apocalyptic, Liturgy, and Doxology

METZ'S DISDAIN FOR POSTMODERN DISCOURSE is too well known for him to be mistaken as a critic of the metaphysics of presence. There are real constraints on risking all on such a critique besides personal allergy. First, there is the ecclesial constraint. Metz after all is a faithful member of a Christian confession and community that gives a prominent place to liturgy and remembrance, and espouses the real presence of Christ in the eucharist. In this respect, it is important to note that in Metz memory is less a faculty or discrete cognitive operation than a disposition transferred from the domain of liturgy and generalized as a normative disposition towards the world.[71] Of course, the transfer and generalization is called for in the mass in that *missio* follows on *anamnesis*, so that the move can be considered internal rather than external to the liturgy itself. Still, in its transfer and generalization the ontological implication of memory may be undermined or reinforced. Balthasar insists that in the movement out from the mass, which demands nothing less than the transformation of the world, one can continue to talk of Christ's presence as the presence of divine love. Although there are any number of passages to be found in the trilogy where this point is made (e.g. *TD3*, 384; *TD4*, 405-6), the clearest statement is to be found in *Love Alone*:

> *The celebration of the Eucharist is itself anamnesis, which means that it is contemplation in love and the communion of love with love; and it is only from such celebration that a Christian mission goes out into the world. Ite missa – missio est. (109-110)*[72]

By contrast, in Metz while the memory of the passion, death, and resurrection of Christ does not intend a void, it is not evident that one can talk of real presence, or even presence in an unqualified way. This raises the thorny question of whether the radically eschatological disposition of Metz's thought has the same effect on the notion of sacrament that Marion, operating with Balthasarian optics, exposes in Hegel's pneumatological dislocation in which eschatological community more nearly than Christ is constitutive of divine presence.[73] Balthasar wagers on the eschatological being prehended, or being proleptically present in the paschal event, and in its liturgical celebration:

> *In the ever-present Anamnesis ("Do this in memory of me", 1 Cor 11:25) of the self-sacrifice of God's love (unde et memores), the living and resurrected Christ becomes present (Mt 18:20)—but present "until he comes again" (1 Cor 11:26), and therefore not looking backward, but with eyes set forward, into the future and full of hope (LA, 89).*

It is tempting to construe the difference between Metz and Balthasar to be a function of the definitive commitments to either unrealized or realized eschatology. More specifically, a binary opposition might be constructed on the following lines: Balthasar's view of memory in general is that it renders the divine present in a way similar to and overlapping with the way the church renders Christ present in liturgy; by contrast, Metz, nervous of this pleromatic saturation of presence, understands that in the liturgy anamnesis or *Eingedenken* is intrinsically tied to the kingdom that is to come, and that the generalization of anamnesis beyond the liturgical sphere proper is an attempt to uncover the eschatological tendency of Christianity that is in danger of being covered over (*PG*, 26, 64). The intended contrast, however, breaks down. In the tradition of Daniélou and Scheeben, Balthasar has a genuine grasp of the apocalyptic horizon of liturgy in both its proper and expanded form. He understands well that anamnesis proceeds under the auspices of *maranatha*, the coming of the one whose presence has been vouchsafed, but not in such a way as to saturate and remove the ambiguities of history. What is true in liturgy narrowly considered is true also in history, whose actions and passions, Balthasar, like Metz, allows to be interpreted as carriers of ultimate meaning. This is why Balthasar in *Theo-Drama 2* connects his discussion of biblical apocalyptic with liturgy, and more specifically liturgy and the drama of history. As Balthasar and Metz, therefore, cover the same terrain, the structural contrast that emerges is not that between realized and unrealized eschatology, but rather how the realized and unrealized facets of eschatology go together. Throughout *Theo-Drama* in general and in *Theo-Drama 5* in particular, Balthasar considers realized eschatology to be regulative, and this not despite but because of Revelation, for what is unrealized is marked by the Lamb as the dramatic lynchpin of the story of history that moves essentially within trinitarian brackets. On a Balthasarian view, even an eschatological scheme such as Metz's, which is formally similar, risks confounding the what and obscuring the referent of the one addressed, imperatively, in 'come.'

Prayer both further specifies Metz's negative theology and the difference between the respective eidetic apocalyptic theologies of Metz and Balthasar. For Metz prayer is a non-propositional discourse of memory and hope which, if it takes the form of thankfulness, also takes the form of complaint and remonstration. Of course, prayer is a discourse of address, in this case an address to the personal Other in whose hands lie my personal fate, but more importantly, who is invested with the power to redress the injustice of history (*FHS*, 72).[74] Prayer is not an optional, but rather a truly necessary discourse. It is a discourse that postulates rather than posits God – thereby avoiding metaphysical conundra – and by so doing invests in God our only hope that history is neither blind nor the history of the victors. And it postulates this God in the face of the overwhelming experience of God's absence. Balthasar also thinks of prayer as non-propositional and more basic than discourse about God, therefore as more basic than theology which will display some measure of second-order features. Indeed, it can be said that for Balthasar it is its embeddedness in the matrix of prayer that makes theology authentic, but perhaps even more radically – and here Balthasar is one with Eastern orthodox thought – prayer is authentic theology. Every bit as emphatically as Metz, Balthasar thinks of prayer as a mode of address to the totally Other who remains ungraspable in his self-designation. For Balthasar, however, the undesignatability of God is itself the other side of the God who comes towards us as glory, modulated as justice and compassion. God's incomprehensibility and glory, or his incomprehensible glory, and glory's internal complexity, are compacted in the revelation of Christ as the Lamb of God. Thus prayer is an address to a God of supereminent, if oftentimes paradoxical, presence. This synoptic view of prayer, which I have extracted from Balthasar's scattered remarks in the trilogy, clearly represents a development of Balthasar's earlier reflections in *Prayer* (1957). At the same time it does not depart from it in significant ways. Prayer finds its objective ground in Christ, its subjective ground in the Spirit, its exemplary manifestation in Mary. For all of these reasons, prayer is essentially an ecclesial act which defines itself against the speculative hubris and activist titanism of modernity. Balthasar's use of 'hearers of the Word' language at the beginning of *Prayer* shows that he is in conversation with Metz's mentor, Rahner. He agrees with Rahner that prayer is 'a communication in which God's word has the initiative, and we, at first, are simply listeners' (*P*, 12). He is, however, much more emphatic than Rahner on ecclesial and biblical mediation, and insists that 'it is only in God's language that we can commune with him' (*P*, 12). The difference between Balthasar and Metz follows the same lines of division in the Balthasar-Rahner contrast, with the exception that in the case of Metz transcendental openness has become eschatological openness which finds a ready-at-hand expression in the Lord's Prayer.

Now, for Balthasar, it must be granted that this God does not appear always to be an effective presence in our individual lives or to be manifest in what James Joyce refers to in *Finnegans Wake* as 'the nightmare of history.' From his point of view, the absence of verification of a presence, demanded by the logic of biblical faith, exacerbates rather than takes away the sting of the theodicy question. For just as the denial of the experience of absence represents a palliative, so also does a theology of God's absence which compensates by God's belated appearance on the scene. For Balthasar, hope lies in the cross, in God's presence in Christ on Holy Saturday in which Christ identifies with the dead. This presence is real if mysterious: it accompanies and grounds us in our journey towards the eschaton. Moreover, Christ's representation and solidarity with the dead means that *in Christo*, the dead are mysteriously in community with us even prior to the eschaton which, for Balthasar, as for Irenaeus blazes with the hope of resurrection. If the non-Christian poet Rilke points in the *Duino Elegies* to the mysterious communion,[75] which can be glimpsed only at an angle, it is G. M. Hopkins who in *The Wreck of the Deutschland* captures 'death as resurrection' and 'resurrection as death':

> *Foundering in God – that is the high point of the poem – man finds nothing to cling to, not even his longing, nor reward, nor heaven, nor any of God's attributes, for beyond all that there is nothing but him alone: on the other side of all that is only him: 'Ipse, the only one' – the self beyond any nature. (GL3, 399)*

Moreover, even as the poem makes present the apocalypse of resurrection indicated in the cry 'come,' uttered by the tall nun, it suggests that resurrection is already in some sense granted prior to the end, given the apocalypse of the resurrection in and from death of Christ who is the object and subject of all acts of self-offering.

Accepting that the experience of God's absence is irradicable, Balthasar refuses to make it regulative. His familiarity with, and boundless affection for, the mystical tradition makes him aware that the 'dark night of the soul' is a possibility for all.[76] As a reader of Revelation, Balthasar realizes well that the experience of the absence of God can be more than individual – even if, unlike Metz, he does not comment on what would count as a privileged occasion. With the eyes of faith one can see that God is with us, and with the dead in particular. Hope then cannot be separated from faith. But neither can it be separated from love, love of God and love of others, both of which are made possible by God. In the end then, a major difference between Balthasar and Metz is the former's presumption that before one speaks to God, one has already been spoken to. Prayer is a form of 'wounded speech' – to use the language of Jean-Louis Chrétien[77] – in that God is its condition and the supplement to both its finitude and its opacity. Balthasar goes even further in thinking that the condition for prayer is not only provided *by* God, but in a real sense lies *within* God who is characterized by self giving and surrender. For Balthasar, then, Revelation shows that a properly apocalyptic theology is doxological in a truly theological sense. Apocalyptic theology is not doxological solely because prayer and liturgy play important roles in defining Christian life, but because the self-giving and self-surrender of the triune God provide the grammar of prayer that sounds endlessly in heaven as on earth.

This brings me to the final and, arguably, decisive division between Balthasar's and Metz's form of eidetic apocalyptic, that is, the functioning and status of the Trinity. As I have already presented at length in Part 2, and more synoptically in chapter 6, Balthasar's theology is trinitarian through and through, with the three parts of the trilogy elaborating the trinitarian horizon according to the different transcendentals of 'beauty,' 'goodness,' and 'truth.' Whatever the range, depth, and character of Balthasar's disagreement with Hegel, the regulative status of the Trinity is not one of them. As Balthasar prosecutes his critique of Hegel, it is precisely Hegel's understanding and elaboration of the Trinity that is called into question. *Glory of the Lord* and *Theo-Logic* frame a sustained critique in which *Theo-Drama* plays the pivotal role. In this context, Balthasar's appeal to Revelation in *Theo-Drama 4* is critical in combating not only Hegel's view of drama, but also his non-personal, non-doxological view of the Trinity. Balthasar then is not only unabashedly trinitarian, but unembarrassedly capacious in his description of its reality – a feature that is characteristic of both the Irenaean and Augustinian apocalyptic traditions. Clearly Metz's theology belongs to an entirely different ordinance. While such trinitarianism may be too rich for his taste, Metz's reserve finds its explanation in methodological preferences governed significantly by the principle of epistemic humility. One form Metz's resistance to trinitarianism in general, and the rich trinitarianism of Balthasar in particular, takes is more performative than argumentative, although undoubtedly arguments could be produced by way of support. Given that God is mystery, procedurally, it is better to avoid God-talk altogether. Although Metz does not explicitly draw the inference, it does not take much to see that he would consider illegitimate the kind of trinitarian account of prayer that Balthasar offers in the trilogy and which is sketched in some detail in *Prayer*.

In the end, it is the limitation of theology to fundamental theology that justifies treating the Trinity very much as an adiaphoron. It is instructive to see Metz replicate a strategy common to Kant and Schleiermacher, but also to 18th-century Protestant thought in both its rationalistic and pietistic modes.[78] In this respect, Metz departs from as well as repeats Rahner. He continues to rehearse Rahner's objections to accounts of the Trinity *in se*, but in general fails to replicate Rahner's enthusiasm for economic forms of trinitarianism, to reproduce Rahner's version focused on the triune God's self-communication in history, or to present the kind of eschatologically-oriented version that would rhyme with his fundamental and practical commitments.

Still, not all of Metz's dealing with the symbol of the Trinity proceeds by methodologically justified evasion. There are occasions in which he feels called on to take sides with respect to basic trinitarian orientation, specifically to decide between Rahner's 'economic' and Balthasar's 'ontological' orientation. When these situations arise – and they do not appear to arise often – Metz trumps unilaterally for Rahner over Balthasar. He does so, however, without inquiring into the ontological dimension of Rahner's trinitarianism, which is illustrated clearly in the 'vice versa' of the trinitarian axiom, 'the immanent Trinity is the economic Trinity and vice versa,'[79] and supported by the vision of the self-communication of God, which has Christian Neoplatonism as its conceptual backdrop.[80] Nor does Metz comment on the capacious economic foreground of Balthasar's elaboration of the immanent or ontological Trinity. While this foreground gets outlined in the first and third parts of the trilogy, in *Theo-Drama* it is painted in vivid colors. For Balthasar, any consideration of the ontological Trinity must proceed through an analysis of salvation history which has its pivot in the cross, death, and resurrection of Jesus of Nazareth. It is through considerations of the mission of Jesus and his relation to God as Father and the Spirit that theology proceeds to reflect on his person, and only on this basis to consider the Trinity as a divine community.[81] What is true in general with respect to the Trinity is true also with respect to prayer: worship of the triune God becomes a possibility only to the extent that the Spirit places us within the brackets of Christ's response to the Father's giving of mission to which he is pledged without reserve.

Basic to Metz's prejudice against trinitarian discourse is his conviction that Rahner follows Kant in ruling out the possibility of human beings having knowledge in the proper sense of God as the unconditioned. The application of this epistemic principle, as I have indicated previously, shows that a theologian such as Balthasar professes to know 'too much' – perhaps one might emend this to read 'much too much,' since on Metz's grounds even Rahner said too much. Superadded, however, are a number of telling genealogical observations: (i) Balthasar's theological scheme evinces too much Hegel. As it etherizes the trauma of history, it reduces suffering to the concept. As with Hegel's view, then, Balthasar is guilty of a secret aestheticization (*PG*, 69-70; *HH*, 48). Ironically, here Metz's objection to Balthasar repeats Balthasar's objection to Moltmann. (ii) Turning another accusation made by Balthasar against Moltmann against the accuser, Metz judges that Balthasar's theology is regulated by a reconciliation that occurs outside of history. Although Metz does not state explicitly that this reconciliation seems to serve the purpose of the self-uniting of God, he does suggest it in speaking of it as 'Gnostic' (*PG*, 54-5, 69).[82] (iii) The third objection to Balthasar cuts even deeper, since the ground of Balthasar's Hegelian and Gnostic proclivities is thought to lie in an excessive commitment to Johannine discourse. Here Metz would link what Balthasar definitively separates, for, on Balthasar's account, no other group of biblical texts has quite the same ability to show the way beyond speculation.

While all of these criticisms are important, here I submit the third to a somewhat more extended treatment than the first two. In large part I have already either succeeded or failed to show that Balthasar is defined by his opposition to, rather than by his repetition of, theological apocalyptic schemes of Hegelian vintage. I also have already succeeded or failed to show that although Balthasar thinks of theology under the rubric of aesthetics, he is careful to dissociate his kind of theological aesthetics from the performance of aesthetic theology. As *Glory of the Lord 1* makes especially clear, in aesthetic theology the emphasis falls so heavily on harmony and identity that it compromises the ontological gap between God and the world and God and human being, and facilitates the removal of the ugliness that runs counter to the beauty of the divine and erases sin that is offensive to his holiness. Balthasar believes aesthetic theology bespeaks mystification and idolatry. And this diagnostic category picks out forms of Christian thought besides the Romantic and Idealist modalities that are Balthasar's preferred targets. While appreciative, for example, of Augustine's aesthetic contribution, in *Glory of the Lord 2* Balthasar displays some concern with the propensity in Augustine to posit a reconciling unity of an aesthetic kind in order to vindicate God. For Balthasar, this is deformation: the biblical God, ultimately a God of love who spends himself exorbitantly on the cross, is not a God who is complimented in the insistence that light requires darkness as a background, beauty, ugliness, and mercy, wrath.

It is likely – but by no means certain – that part of the content of Metz's ascription of 'Gnostic' to Balthasar's elaboration of the Trinity is its presumed commitment to something like such an aesthetic theodicy. Overall, however, as deployed by Metz the range of 'Gnostic' is indeterminate. Metz does not clearly state whether the essential criterion for ascription is provided by the actual shape of the metanarrative that renders reconciliation, or whether the criterion is simply that a reconciliation is metaphysically imputed for which no evidence can be found in history. In either case, Metz's labeling suggests a move beyond Rahner's epistemological objection, even as Metz's criticism of Balthasar continues to be informed by Rahner's criticism of Balthasar's lack of epistemic humility. This move is conditioned and facilitated by the new found status of the category of 'narrative' in fundamental theology. Still, with the precedent of Balthasar's own rather equivocal conjugation of 'epic' in mind,[83] in which highly abstract and metaphysical construals of the relation of a self-subsistent divine and the universe of which it is the ground are included with first and second-level narrative accounts of divine becoming in and through the drama and tragedy of the world, the most devoted Balthasarian is not entitled to dismiss summarily Metz on grounds of conceptual confusion or ambiguity, even if Metz's accusation fails to be truly challenging.

As I have already indicated, it is Metz's third objection that cuts deepest. Recognizing that in contemporary trinitarian theology, which is in dialogue with Hegel, that the ontological discourse of love is used to support the ascription of passibility to God, Metz essentially calls for a moratorium. He regrets the regulative function of 'God is love' of 1 John 4:6, whose ontological language wreaks havoc in Hegel's system and after him in Moltmann and Balthasar. Whereas Balthasar, and following him Marion, believe that such theological mischief is possible if and only if love is interpreted in a dominantly erotic rather than agapeic sense, Metz judges that John is theologically problematic to the extent to which his ontology of love excites any trinitarian discourse that is ontologically inflected and refracted in divine pathos. Ironically, Metz is hermeneutically one with Derrida in his searing critique of John's ontology of love.[84] Metz does not go all the way down the Derridean road and essentially demand that it be excised. Rather he has ready at hand a therapy whereby John is ontologically scoured, and thus theologically normalized. The therapy stipulates what can be said responsibly about God given our finite point of view, and offers a set of procedures of translation whereby ontological language is led back to existential and/or prophetic language. The language of suffering with respect to God is normalized by stipulating that suffering not be understood as suffering *in* God so much as suffering *onto* God (*Leiden an Gott*) (*HH*, 48).[85] The connection between suffering and God can be Christianly affirmed only by translating the secondary ontological language into a more primary prophetic and existential key in which the subject of suffering is the human subject and not God. Similarly, the ontological character of John's discourse on God as love can and should be translated into an eschatological key that makes even this language apocalyptic: 'one must hear the Johannine statement that "God is love" as a statement having the character of a promise. God will prove Godself to us as love' (*PG*, 70-1). Once again, John's language undergoes something like a demythologization in which the ontological language is dismissed not so much as untrue, so much as being a husk which has a more functional kernel that bespeaks the Christian believer rather than the object of belief.

If for Metz love is at once too much and too little, the latter because the former, for Balthasar, hope without any grasp of its object – and of being grasped by its object – is unequivocally too little. However christologically contextualized, from a Balthasarian perspective, Metz's practical fundamental theology is involved in a post-Kantian operation of demythologization that insists that all eschatological statements be read against their literal sense. Balthasar is not overly concerned that this orientation justifies an abbreviation of the classic eschatological sequence of death-judgment-heaven-hell, since the impulse to abbreviate also comes from a thoroughly christocentric theology such as his own. What does present cause for concern is the elimination from the picture of a divine judger. When Metz follows Benjamin down this line, he inserts himself in a radicalized Kantian framework. But he also repeats Plato, even as he superficially departs from him. Recall that at the end of both the *Gorgias* and the *Republic*, Plato paints scenes of eternal judgment in which there are actual judges of worth, Er in the latter case, a trio of judges in the former. But it is also clear that the myths of judgment are self-conscious devices to compensate for the limitations of knowledge when it comes to the validation of justice. Thus, to a large extent the myths are demythologized in advance by belonging to the category of 'true lies' (*pseudos alethes*). What matters for Plato, and similarly for Kant and Metz, is that judgment and rectification occur, not that there is a personal judge. From a Balthasarian point of view, this is to give up too much. For our hope lies precisely in a person, and in the end in persons in relation that constitute the triune God. One way of lifting up the difference is to pick out the very different accents in the declarative 'God is the Last Judgment.' Balthasar understands the radicality of this formula to say more than that God effects judgment. For him, the formula means that judgment is nothing less than an effect of the very being of God as love.[86] For Metz by contrast, the statement 'God is the last judgment' represents an echo of Benjamin's reduction of God to the imperative of justice – however impossible this is to conceive. For Balthasar, this is illegitimate, since it scours Christian belief of all realism. In doing so, ironically it perpetuates an allegiance to the Hegelian form of thinking that Metz would dearly like to surpass. Specifically, the Metzian reading of the proposition takes the form of Hegel's speculative proposition.[87] As the proposition 'God is Spirit' empties the grammatical subject into the predicate, so also does the proposition 'God is the last judgment.' It seems as if Metz has fallen into the trap laid by Hegel for thought that would exceed the system.[88]

From Balthasar's point of view, the general lesson to be drawn is that apocalyptic schemes of the Metzian kind are not sufficient to resist Hegelian forms of apocalypse. They are at once fated to reinscribe Hegel at crucial moments, which Metz does when he hard-pedals the unrealized element of eschatology and stresses the power of memory beyond its eucharistic locus, when he accents the functional over the ontological aspects of eschatological statements, and concentrates on the impersonal 'that,' or maybe 'how,' over the personal 'who.' For Balthasar, there is no way beyond Hegel except through him, and this will require the kind of patient, perhaps even literally 'suffering' engagement that his trilogy enacts. This requires decisions on the methodological, genealogical, and substantive theological issues. With respect to the last, what is important for Balthasar is that the paschal mystery, which both he and Metz interpret, be the point of departure for a theology that concedes nothing to Hegel concerning the real decisiveness of Christ's saving act in history (while nonetheless keeping history open), and that considers the church to render Christ's presence while awaiting in hope his coming. For Balthasar, a theology that has the paschal mystery at its center will be an apocalyptic theology that ciphers a triune God going from glory to glory.

Degrees of Separation

Because of significant overlaps in their respective theological projects, Balthasar and Metz were brought into conversation. They belong together in their diagnosis of modernity as constitutionally forgetful, in their resistance to teleological forms of eschatology exhibited in Hegel and Marx and their successors, and in their articulation of an apocalyptic alternative with deep roots in the biblical traditions. In addition, both forms of apocalyptic theology are eidetic. Although differences were observed regarding the relative attention given by both to modernity as an environing culture that disables Christianity, in their anatomy of forgetting, in their rejection of the spurious eschatological antidotes, and in the kind of diagnostic tools employed – more social-scientific in the case of Metz, more literary in the case of Balthasar – the truly fundamental differences were unearthed. As these differences were unveiled, it became evident that the 'belonging together' of Metz and Balthasar is relative, and that in the final analysis they do not occupy the same space of apocalyptic. If the shorthand for the gap is the contrast between a maximalist eidetic apocalyptic and a more minimalist kind of eidetic apocalyptic embarrassed by too much knowing, this contrast is a function of differences in the articulation of apocalyptic content as this content is supported by methodological and epistemological commitments. Although Metz's apocalyptic is paschal, its general tendency is more functional than that of Balthasar and other apocalypticists with whom Balthasar shares space, who feel comfortable in moving from soteriological function to consideration of the person of Christ. Moreover, there are differences even on the soteriological level. Metz does not indulge in a polemic against the doctrine of atonement, but his emphasis much more nearly falls on God's power in Christ being stronger than death. Although Metz articulates a theology of Holy Saturday, solidarity is with the dead and not with the sinner, and *Faith in History and Society* favors speaking of the rescue (*Rettung*) of the dead from the 'second death' of being forgotten than speaking of actual resurrection that is a content of Christian hope.

These differences in turn relate to and are reinforced by other differences in apocalyptic content. Metz refuses to follow Balthasar in providing a trinitarian frame for a paschal theology. He does not provide a rich analysis of Christ's referring his life without reserve to the Father, nor does he discuss the role played by the Holy Spirit in Christ's public ministry or subsequently in the church. The lack of development of the economic horizon is more than matched by the exclusion from consideration of the immanent Trinity. While the latter can be traced back to Rahner, the de-emphasis of the former is a fruit of the development of fundamental theology at the expense of theology's categorial frame. The trinitarian and non-trinitarian specification of apocalyptic theology represents a key discrimen between modes of apocalyptic. Relatedly, however, there are differences in the understanding of the nature and role of liturgy and prayer. Metz fully understands the liturgical context of *anamnesis*, but by comparison with Balthasar is almost exclusively interested in its application beyond the liturgical context. He is not concerned, as Balthasar and Marion are, with liturgy as the site of engagement between the self-giving of the God of Jesus Christ and the self-giving of a community in praise and celebration. Nor does he reflect on the eucharist as an event of presence of the one who gave himself up for us and for our sins. And when it comes to prayer, the emphasis in Metz falls on its counter-cultural aspect, the break in the illusion of autonomy, and its articulation of the hope of redress; it does not fall on the unanticipatable presence of the triune God who makes prayer possible. Importantly, the contrast between Balthasar and Metz on these points does not harden into outright opposition. We have seen Balthasar speak much more to '*missio*' than Metz speaks to 'real presence.' Although preference for one or other apocalyptic type cannot be based solely on the greater capacity for resistance, it does suggest a relevant asymmetry. Still, this would mean neither, that Metz's form of apocalyptic is not a necessary challenge to the undeveloped social justice component of Balthasar's apocalyptic theology, nor that Metz fails to represent a genuine supplement.

The above major content-differences between Balthasar and Metz are conditioned by different choices in methodology and epistemology. Metz's practical fundamental theology represents a significant contraction of theology even by Rahnerian standards. Operating basically in terms of Rahner's double frame of fundamental and doctrinal theology, Metz shows himself prepared to expand the range of fundamental theology by borrowing from theological elements that Rahner thinks more properly belong to the realm of the categorical or Christian specific assertion. But this expansion of fundamental theology is the other side of categorial devastation or emptying. There is a significant loss of theological substance relative to Rahner's framework, notwithstanding the justice of Metz's criticism of Rahner's transcendental method carried out in part 1 of *Faith in History and Society*.[89] By Balthasar's standard Metz's method can only be understood to be intrinsically reductionistic. Indeed, the reduction bears the stamp of the Enlightenment's critique of positivity, and the Romantic move of creating a safe space for a non-positive residual – both quintessential forms of forgetting, according to Balthasar. Of course, a major methodological difference is what counts as forgetting and who the forgetting affects. The kind of forgetting that worries Balthasar, the forgetting of the Christian tradition by the modern subject who becomes assimilated to an aggressively secular culture, does not concern Metz. Metz's interest is in diagnosing and combating the apathy that rules out, or rules against, the obligation to treat as human the dead and the living. Metz's concern is with the subject of history; Balthasar's is primarily with the specifically Christian subject.

A deep difference then is the way in which the relation between prophecy and apocalyptic is conjugated. In Balthasar prophecy is the leaven that prevents apocalyptic from becoming too speculative; prophecy and apocalyptic are, however, not absolutely identical. Vision is a fundamental reality in apocalyptic's economy, and the visionary a fundamental figure. By contrast, in Metz apocalyptic is governed by the prophetic impulse and seeing regulated by hearing. Now, this difference relates in turn to differences in the apophatic register of each of these forms of apocalyptic theology, while not being a function of it. If it is true that the relatively underdeveloped social and prophetic side of Balthasar's discourse gives credibility to the criticism that in the last instance apocalyptic vision is speculative and/or aesthetic, it is also the case that in Metz the tendency towards identity compromises what Christianity stands for and fails to specify adequately who is addressed in prayer and spoken about in theology. Here there are offsetting strengths and weaknesses, in which both species of apocalyptic can tutor each other. As intimated in chapter 6, the exposé of systemic violence, persecution, and their denial, is a structural feature of all apocalyptic, and is every bit as much to the fore in Revelation as the disclosing of the lie. Balthasar seems to have had an opportunity that he does not take, while Metz denies himself the opportunity by avoiding a text he takes to be benighted. Similarly, although Balthasar does no more than argue that the apophatic is always a function of the kataphatic that opens up the horizon of address, he could be accused of being too diffident with respect to the hyperboles of apophasis, and not sufficiently open to the experience of that kind of pointed absence of God which provokes not only lamentation but complaint. But on the other side, Metz seems to so eagerly embrace the most radical forms of apophasis without any reckoning of theological danger, and seems to be on automatic when it comes to the kind of Job-like protestation offered by Elie Wiesel in *Night* and in his other equally harrowing works on the Holocaust.[90]

The contrast is equally stark on the level of epistemology. In line with the methodological reduction evinced by Metz, there is a critique of reason that inscribes a purer form of Kantianism than anything found in Rahner's articulation of transcendental Thomism. Despite Balthasar's often extraordinarily generous estimate of Kant, he would have little time for the Kant adopted by Metz, arguably the real Kant who, subsequent to the critique of ontotheology in the *Critique of Pure Reason*, constructed a purely moral Christianity in which, however, God as rewarder and judger becomes a postulate of practical reason and in which the biblical narrative comes to serve a role in tracing the real individual and communal subjects of history. As the real Kant finds his way into Metz's apocalyptic, God is postulated to redress the injustice of history; and the biblical narrative of the passion and resurrection of Christ represents a necessary supplement in order to make persuasive the hope that defines or ought to define human being. Balthasar recognizes the role of Kantian epistemology in humbling the speculative claims of Hegelian forms of apocalypse. At the same time, Kant is not the only Christian thinker who understands the limits of human knowledge. This recognition marks the entire Christian tradition, and is exhibited splendidly in the entire Neoplatonic tradition and in Aquinas. More, this recognition is internal to the genre of apocalyptic itself; the symbols themselves suggest the unattainability of their object, as they continually 'give rise to thought.'[91]

Epistemically, there is more than one way to be non-Hegelian. What might be called the 'postulatory fideism' of Kant is just one of the ways,[92] and not necessarily the best way, although surely, if a thinker remains interested in God as referent and origin of our language, practices, and forms of life, it is better than the nihilism of Nietzsche or the ludic semiosis of deconstruction. But from Balthasar's point of view, Kantianism in general and Kantianly inflected apocalyptic in particular is in and of itself a form of 'dazzling darkness' in which the 'dazzle' is the infinitely receding star whose death was long ago. Metz's Kantianism is happily, from a religious view-point, far from pure: his narrative commitment functions as an offset and provides a measure of content. But he is pulled in this more apophatic, and dare one say more agnostic, direction, by Benjamin, whose Kantianism is as purified as his apocalyptic – content-wise – moves towards degree zero.

Chapter 8

Between Eidetic and Non-Eidetic Apocalyptic

All results with respect to a Balthasar-Metz comparison in terms of apocalyptic type have been provisional, since we noted merely how Metz's is less eidetic than Balthasar's and how it contrasts on crucial points with his Johannine form. To understand Metz's form of apocalyptic on its own terms, and its essential peculiarity, it is useful – if not necessary – to supplement the taxonomic discussion of the last chapter with a genetic analysis. By 'genetic analysis' I do not mean a causal analysis in the strict sense, which makes the extraordinary over-claim that it provides the actual conditions responsible for why a discourse is what it is and not otherwise. I mean rather an analysis that regresses to Metz's publically confessed philosophical and theological (re) sources as providing a clue as to how he conjugates his particular form of apocalyptic theology. But even with the caveat regarding the nature of 'genetic' analysis, such a procedure has inbuilt complications, not the least of which are the number and variety of such (re)sources that Metz calls on. It would be unwieldy to consider all of these (re)sources, but I take it that Critical Theory in general, and Walter Benjamin in particular, are crucial with respect to encouraging Metz's conviction that, properly understood, apocalyptic discourse represents a criticism of the present in the name of unanticipatable future. Ernst Bloch's philosophy of hope represents another important line of influence that expresses itself in Metz's apocalyptic figuration of Christianity.[1] Even if Metz's apocalyptic is more than the sum of these influences, an illuminating way of reading his work is that of a field of tension between the eidetic apocalyptic strain of Bloch and the non-eidetic strain of Benjamin, which moves towards the condition of 'pure interruption.' Thus considered, we can see more clearly the difference between the apocalyptic spaces of Metz and Balthasar.

But 'genetic reduction' also provides opportunities for further clarification of apocalyptic, since the two forms of apocalyptic, which Metz conjugates, are not without remainder differentials of Metz's apocalyptic. They possess their own integrity, and it is worthwhile comparing both serially with Balthasar's maximally eidetic apocalyptic. While conceptual clarification is sufficient to justify comparison, the fact is that Balthasar is familiar with Benjamin and Bloch and has commented on both species of apocalyptic.

In the first section, both as an apocalyptic entity in himself, as well as providing a form of apocalyptic that Metz conjugates with other types, I will consider what I call the 'soft eidetic apocalyptic' of Bloch, and develop the Balthasarian objections beyond what we have seen already in Balthasar's linking of Bloch with Hegelian style apocalyptic, particularly as this is instantiated in the theology of Moltmann. In the second and by far the more substantial section I will treat the non-eidetic apocalyptic of Benjamin, which exercises even greater influence on Metz both on substantive and rhetorical levels. I will also detail much more than I have in the two previous chapters how Benjamin excites a more complex response from Balthasar than does Bloch, who is rarely given his own voice, but cited as a proponent of 'Jewish apocalyptic' when he is not folded into either Hegel or Moltmann. On the one hand, against the backdrop of an appreciative estimate of the Frankfurt School's critique of Hegel, Balthasar validates Benjamin's 'lightning bolts' as inherently anti-speculative:

> *Walter Benjamin breaks through the aesthetic world of the European tragedy in order to let the lightning bolts on the volcanoes of a mysterious present messianic kingdom break out (or break in).* (Exp 4, 97)[2]

On the other hand, Balthasar finds them extraordinarily problematic from both a philosophical and theological point of view. Balthasar's caveat with respect to Benjamin's critique of Hegel's view of the kingdom is respectful but, nonetheless, telling:

> *Of course, this still leaves the disquieting question of whether this Kingdom can really lie "ahead." Perhaps it is everywhere, but everywhere like a bolt of lightning is; perhaps it looms up suddenly like a ghost or a specter and then sinks back once more just as suddenly: non-temporal in the midst of time, but also, then, ungraspable, or perhaps nowhere.* (Exp 4, 99)

At the most obvious textual level, the quality and volume of response sets Balthasar's analysis of Benjamin apart. Although this excess is not obvious, I will make the case that throughout the prolegomenon to *Theo-Drama*, and most especially in his treatment of Baroque Drama, Balthasar is arguing with Benjamin's *The Origin of German Drama* (*Trauerspiel*) (*TD1*, 163-77).[3] Moreover, the argument is not simply about the superiority of Spanish (Balthasar) or German (Benjamin) Baroque, but about whether discourse, in the first instance literary discourse, but by implication all discourse, functions symbolically (Balthasar) or merely allegorically (Benjamin). The concern for both is the issue of truth, and more specifically whether meaning or its interruption is the more basic requirement. It is especially interesting that in *The Origin of German Drama* just about all examples of German Baroque are apocalyptic in that the present world – living under the auspices of the 'old aeon' – undergoes a transformation that has the form of catastrophe. The battleground between eidetic and non-eidetic apocalyptic is, then, in a quite extraordinary way played out on the arcane field of Baroque drama. What Benjamin says about German Baroque corresponds to what he says about the messianic, just as what Balthasar says about the Baroque drama corresponds to what he says about the repetition of Spanish Baroque in *The Satin Slipper* (*Le Soulier du Satin*) by an author who non-incidentally is one of Balthasar's favorite writers on Revelation, that is, Paul Claudel.

In addition to unfolding Benjamin's messianism and Balthasar's oblique refutation in *Theo-Drama*, in this final chapter, I will both bring together and separate Balthasar and Benjamin on the apocalyptic nature and/or function of discourses other than the biblical text. In line with issues brought to the surface, but not thematized, in the previous chapter on Metz's apocalyptic, I will ask the question whether in the case of Benjamin, literature or art in general, as much as – if not more than – philosophy or Hebrew scripture or the Christian Bible, have the capacity to clear away the fog of apathy regarding the victims of history, and contend with Hegelian speculation that only remembers (*Erinnerung*) the sacrifice, as it argues on behalf of a history that cannot make mistakes. Balthasar's engagement with Benjamin here is also an engagement with Adorno, and to a limited extent with Metz also, who echoes the opinions of both without necessarily working out a consistent and coherent position. Finally, I would like to draw attention to the issue of style raised by different forms of apocalyptic; the leaning of non-eidetic apocalyptic towards hallowing the notion of the 'fragment,' and correlatively the leaning of an eidetic form of apocalyptic towards a non-systematic copiousness.

Bloch and 'Soft' Eidetic Apocalyptic

METZ OPENLY ADMITS THAT Bloch's articulation of the 'new' cured him of his commitment to metaphysics, which, in one way or another, made unthinkable the irruption of a future that was not an extrapolation of the present and the past. The performative correlative of this confession, expressed in an article on Bloch,[4] finds its most adequate illustration in the last chapter of *Faith in History and Society*, which treats at length the difference between a teleological and non-teleological eschatology. Perhaps somewhat surprisingly, given his deeper grounding in the Western philosophical tradition, Metz's assimilation of the ontology of the 'new' (*novum*) is considerably more restrained than that of Moltmann. Specifically, while Bloch's famous contrast between *Zukunft* and *Futurum*, that is, between a future that comes unexpectedly from outside the temporal continuum and a future that is germinated from the present and the past, plays a structurally similar role in both discourses, it is obvious that the distinction functions much less explicitly in *Faith in History and Society* than it does, for example, in *The Theology of Hope*.[5] One can succinctly sum up the difference by saying that whereas Moltmann explores to some degree the semantic potential of the contrast, Metz operates according to the principle that meaning is use. Metz also leaves unexplored whether a relationship exists between his adoption of Bloch and his earlier allegiance to Heidegger,[6] who in *Being and Time* not only focused on temporality and historicity, as Metz rightly underscores, but insisted on the primacy of the future and the possible. Specifically, he does not address the issue of whether Heidegger's future-oriented discourse plays a preparatory role for his adoption of and theological adaptation of Bloch's ontology of the 'not-yet' (*Nicht-Noch*), or whether the reading of Bloch dispatches Heidegger to the history of metaphysics from which he would escape, since it is still not clear whether the future of which Heidegger speaks is teleologically rather than eschatologically inclined.[7]

Arguably, more important than Bloch's philosophy of the *novum* for Metz's articulation of apocalyptic theology is Bloch's comprehensive survey of trans-rational utopian and apocalyptic discourses of the Western intellectual tradition conducted, not incidentally, by philosophy. Utopian and apocalyptic expression erupts in dreams, prophecies, and imaginings of worlds and modes of relation radically different than the emotional, cognitive, social, and political worlds we inhabit. The forms of its cultural articulation can, as Bloch's three volume *The Principle of Hope* makes clear, be equally various, for example, linguistic but also non-linguistic modes of art (especially music),[8] the discourses of religion, both low and high, the discourses of revolution, and finally the discourses of philosophy. Bloch, however, offers more to Metz than a simple catalogue of types and genres, he also supplies a genealogy of such discourses by treating in some detail specific historical instances of apocalyptic discourse. Although he is more interested in the religious and philosophical examples, the plurality of apocalyptic figuration is not unimportant to Metz, even as he self-consciously corrects for Bloch's humanistic bias and immanentist principle of interpretation by insisting that only God can be the agent of the future (*HH*, 21-2), and by laying down the passion, death, and resurrection of Christ as providing the basic coordinates of Christian vision.

I will have more to say momentarily about the relation in Metz's discourse of the acceptance of the plurality of apocalyptic types and genres and his stipulation of a particular vision as norm, for this bears crucially on the characterization of the inflection of Metz's apocalyptic eidetics. But before I get to that a word needs to be said about the attractiveness of Bloch's thought as offering an alternative to the dominant Augustinian construal of history, to which Metz refuses apocalyptic ascription (*HH*, 36-7), and as transcending the eschatological schemes of Marx and Hegel. Dealing with these points in order, it is not hard to see that Metz adopts a contrast already operative in Bloch between Augustine's dialectical view of the *civitas dei* and the *civitas terrena* and the focus on history which validates a temporal rather than eternal perspective concerned with the realization of the kingdom of God in time (*PH2*, 502-09). Although Metz seems to adopt a unilateral distinction made between a one-world and a two-world perspective, he also appeals to a trans-historical reality, thereby relativizing the contrast. Thus in the final analysis the contrast between his view and that of Augustine is not absolute in the way the contrast between Augustine and Hegel and Augustine and Marx clearly is. Moreover, as indicated in chapter 6, the absoluteness of the distinction can undergo further relativization from the side of Augustine, should *The City of God* be read to hold out the promise for the 'New Jerusalem' despite the atrocities of history. Read from the point of view of the overcoming of injustice and the institution of peace, Metz continues to be Augustinian. But, of course, the continuity is purchased at the price of putting fundamental elements of Augustine's apocalyptic construal in brackets. For example, while in Augustine the eschaton involves the transcendence of injustice, it also critically involves the overcoming of the frailty of the self inclined to distraction and the vulnerability of the body. It also involves a deepened seeing and loving of God, and the coming to transparency of God's glory as love and justice. Moreover, in calling on Revelation as providing the interpretive key for human hope, Augustine does not hesitate to think of our hope as truly a form of knowledge, however inchoate this knowledge may be. As Augustine's hermeneutic of eschatological statements forbid a Kantian distinction between hope and knowledge, it also discourages treating hope outside of the context of the divine – ultimately paschal – reality that grounds it, and insinuates similarly with respect to memory that it is truly effective when it is not so much we who find God, but God who finds us. Not one of these elements is reproduced in Metz's inspiring and fragmentary opus. Contrariwise with Balthasar. As we suggested in chapter 6, while Balthasar's apocalyptic strain is in the final analysis more nearly Irenaean than Augustinian, he exercises the Augustinian option on all the points that are in dispute between Metz and Augustine.

One effect or expression of the structural contrast is that genealogically presented with the binary pair of Joachim and Augustine, about which Bloch has much to say in *The Principle of Hope 2*

(502-17),[9] Metz clearly plumps for Joachim. Moreover, the reasons Metz provides for his preference recall those of Bloch, for example, the this-worldliness of Joachim by contrast with the dualism and otherworldliness of Augustine, and the democratization of sanctity of Joachim by contrast with Augustine's view of the church as the means of salvation.[10] Other important details of Bloch's critique of Augustine are also recalled, for example, the view that the failure of Augustine's eschatology as a mode of apocalyptic thought – and by implication the entire Augustinian apocalyptic tradition – rests ultimately on the explanatory primacy of the archeological, what Bloch calls the *primum* (*PH1*, 202-03). While this fault is constitutive of the mainline religious and philosophical traditions, the specific form it takes in the case of Augustine is the doctrine of election. For Bloch, Augustinian eschatology only puts the seal on outcomes that cannot be frustrated (*PH2*, 509; also *PH1*, 202; *PH3*, 855). Metz's preference here is clearly at odds with Balthasar who thinks with de Lubac and Ratzinger among others that Joachim and his lineage are deeply problematic from a Christian point of view. Nothing in the trilogy suggests that Balthasar makes a similar judgment of Augustine, even as he reserves the right to quibble with important details of Augustine's eschatology. What a defense of a Balthasarian preference for Augustine over Joachim would look like can be gleaned from Ratzinger's self-conscious elaboration of an essentially Augustinian eschatology, his determined preference for Augustinian over Joachimite apocalyptic in his reflections on Bonaventure's theology of history, and from his published conversations with Metz.[11] In Ratzinger's view, only an Augustinian scoping of history is calculated to prevent the temporalization and secularization of transcendence that the Joachimite model implies. Again, while the Augustinian model admits of the kind of christological and sacramental inflection evinced in Bonaventure, the irreducibility of the kingdom to history is a condition of a viable eschatology. Moreover, as Balthasar understands it – and here he is very much a student of the de Lubac of *Surnaturel* (1946)[12] – in this context a doctrine of election neither needs to be problematically restrictive, nor invidious with respect to human freedom. Rather election provides the unity of a narrative in which the meaning is inscribed in the vicissitudes of history, and especially in the paschal mystery, but only fully recoverable from an eschatological standpoint.[13]

In any event, as in Bloch, for Metz, a figure such as Joachim is but an example of 'Jewish apocalyptic' that has been repressed and excluded by the mainline Christian tradition which focuses on either the here and now or on eternity. Metz, after Bloch, presumes that the tradition 'sins against time.'[14] If anything, Metz goes even further than Bloch in thinking that the sin against time, which more specifically is a sin against the future, illustrates that Christianity never successfully overcame Gnosticism, indeed continues it by other means.[15] It seems to be just this understanding of 'Jewish apocalyptic' that Balthasar challenges in *Theo-Drama* when he dismisses modern eschatological forms of thought such as Bloch's as examples of 'Jewish apocalyptic.'[16] Ironically, it is just such discourses, he believes, that show significant negative capability for Gnostic modes of expression and thought (*TD2*, 186). As I have already indicated, Balthasar wants more than a merely typological view of 'Jewish apocalyptic' garnished with a few genealogical sprinkles. As he projects Joachim forward to the philosophical and religious discourses of the modern period, at the same time he excavates the textual origins of 'Jewish apocalyptic.' Not surprisingly, he finds them in intertestamental messianism and apocalyptic. As we saw in the last chapter, in *Glory of the Lord 6* and elsewhere, Balthasar renders the judgment that these discourses are cut off from the discourses of prophecy and law that are constitutive for Hebrew scripture. This judgment, however, is coincident with their de-legitimation, since these texts are considered to be extra-canonic. By contrast, specifically Christian apocalyptic has its roots in the prophets and Daniel, and finds its complete expression in the New Testament. But the New Testament does not exclusively focus on the future, but on the future as already in some way prehended in the passion, death, and resurrection of Christ. Balthasar then refuses to make equivalent 'apocalyptic' and 'Jewish apocalyptic.' 'Christian apocalyptic' does not simply repeat 'Jewish apocalyptic': it displaces, refigures, and controls it. Put in postmodern jargon, Balthasar's view is that 'Christian apocalyptic' represents a non-identical repetition of 'Jewish apocalyptic.'

The full force of Balthasar's argument can be felt if Metz's position is plotted against the more copious position presented by Bloch in the third volume of *The Principle of Hope*. It is somewhat ironic that it is Bloch, a self-confessed atheist, committed to historical materialism,[17] who provides the much more fleshed-out genealogical account of biblical apocalyptic. In fact Bloch engages in a reflection similar to that undertaken by Balthasar in *Glory of the Lord 6* and *Theo-Drama 4*, and offers a similar set of judgments on individual texts of the canonic and non-canonic apocalyptic tradition, while endorsing quite different evaluations. As with Balthasar, Bloch valorizes Daniel (*PH3*, 1125). As Bloch's view that Daniel expresses the prophetic tradition links him with Balthasar, his claim that Daniel's interest in the afterlife is an expression of the thirst for justice clearly marks the former off from the latter.[18] Bloch obviously provides the precedent for Metz's reading of Daniel, but even more the linking of the texts of Hebrew scripture across different genres. In addition, albeit in a somewhat less contrastive key than Balthasar, Bloch thinks that the speculative nature of the Enochian literature evinces something of a diminution of the genuine prophetic-apocalyptic spirit, although Bloch decidedly is against confining this spirit to the biblical text (*PH3*, 1126-27). Bloch does not merely qualify Balthasar, but departs from him entirely, however, in his reading of Revelation. While he recognizes that Revelation is a germinal text of the apocalyptic tradition, and that its images and symbols 'refunction' throughout history, that is, that they are deployed with different valences under different conditions, he is sufficiently conscious of both the inner structure of the text and the uses to which the text has been put in history to worry whether this text is what its detractors claim it to be, that is, a text of ressentiment and revenge (*PH3*, 1132). Bloch's negative reading of Revelation hardly helps its case with Metz, although it should be noted that Metz has in addition to ethical objections, epistemological objections, which suggests another and different kind of apocalyptic, one more nearly Kantian in its suspicion of claims to know a would-be transcendent reality.

Other departures from what we find in Balthasar, arguably, cut even deeper. In Bloch's view prophetic-apocalyptic discourse provides the key to interpreting the biblical God. The *eh'je asher eh'je* of Exodus 3:14 is best translated as 'I will be who I will be' (*PH3*, 1235-35). Balthasar thinks that this reading is admissible, and by no means authorizes a Gilsonian reading as the only possible one.[19] Still he would resist reversing ontological discrimination against the present and eternity by insisting with von Rad and other biblical scholars that futurity is a function of God's covenantal promise, while pointing to the relative adequacy of the language of being that renders the ontophanic nature of God as overwhelming power and presence.[20] More importantly, should Exodus 3:14 require refiguring in another interpretive key – which after Barth he thinks can only be supplied by scripture – then the prime candidate has to be John's articulation of agape, which self-consciously translates the idiom of 'I am' into the idiom of a scandalously unencompassable love.[21] Not surprisingly, as a self-confessed atheist, Bloch is not keen to give John or Paul special prerogatives. Neither can, for example, he be read as having supplied definitive answers to the Markan question: 'Who do you say that I am?' Bloch takes it for granted that Christ is a healer and prophet preaching and enacting the kingdom. He thinks that the Pauline view of Christ as the atoner for our sins represents a theological interpretation (*PH3*, 1262), and thus, at best, is secondary, and at worst represents a distortion in which God is made problematic from an ethical point of view. The gospels do not render a God, who sacrifices his Son to make satisfaction for the transgressions of human beings – a view which Balthasar accepts, even if with the caveats we presented in chapter 6. Nor is Jesus, he says, the Messiah *because* he died on the cross, but rather he is the Messiah *although* he died on the cross (*PH3*, 1262). And unlike Balthasar, Bloch thinks that the ontological discourse of John represents a dangerous misinterpretation of the message of Jesus (*PH3*, 1261). One invidious aspect of the discourse of John, with its liturgical bias, and the readiness with which it authorizes the primacy of the present and eternity, is that it anticipates and justifies the quelling of prophecy that will mark Christianity throughout the centuries. At the same time ironically, or perhaps strategically, it is John 16:7 – a favorite passage of Hegel's – where Jesus speaks of going away and sending the Paraclete, that most aptly points to the space for non-identical imitation that renders the meaning of Jesus' messiahship (*PH3*, 1272). Here Bloch seems to have accepted a position Hegel sketches in 'The Spirit of Christianity and its Fate' (1799) and lays down in his christological reflections in the section on Revealed Religion in the *Phenomenology* (1807), namely that focus on the figure of Jesus is a fetishization from which the Christian community has to be relieved.[22] In addition, he follows Hegel in recommending that we concentrate on discipleship, indeed focus exclusively on discipleship.

Needless to say, Metz himself does not subscribe to each and every detail of Bloch's analysis, but he does subscribe to many of them. He refuses the kind of metaphysical analysis of Exodus 3:14, introduced, as Gilson argues, by Augustine, which casts God in terms of eternity and the present; he refuses to offer anything that even approaches an ontological analysis of Christ and is shy about person language; when considering the cross, he refuses to admit the discourse of atonement and sacrifice; although Christ's solidarity with the sufferers in history is exhibited on the cross, he ascetically avoids speaking the language of love, as if the term suggests that God becomes conceptually available to thought, and thus an idol. This complex and comprehensive recapitulation of Bloch divides him from a Balthasar who, if he goes decisively beyond a Gilsonian reading of Exodus in thinking that the God of Jesus Christ is more adequately described as love, is persuaded that no reading of the function of Christ can ignore either his person or its sacrificial aspect, nor ultimately the ground of the gift of Christ in the trinitarian persons.

The dispute between Metz and Balthasar about the value and nature of 'Jewish apocalyptic' amounts to different perceptions of the relation between Christianity and Judaism. While both theologians are committed to ending what they believe to be the Marcionite dispensation in Christian culture and thought, characterized by the effective dispatch of Hebrew scriptures and the operative assumption that Christianity has extracted from Judaism anything that is of perennial value, they have very different views as to where the problem is to be found and in what the solution consists. Whereas Metz thinks that the mainline Christian tradition and culture are systemically Marcionite in their refusal to adopt the Jewish apocalyptic orientation towards history and the future (*PG*, 59-60; also 55; *HH*, 13, 16) and in their related lack of emphasis on the political (*PG*, 36-8), as we have seen, Balthasar suggests that it is precisely the mainline tradition that preserves the biblical orientation, and that it does so by refiguring Jewish apocalyptic in light of the central message of the Gospel. This refiguration, however, supposes a more than one-dimensional view of Judaism as determined exclusively by apocalyptic, as this expresses prophecy in a particularly replete form. Not only has prophecy to be adequately understood, but the dimensions of wisdom, law, and liturgy must all be given their rightful place. Although Balthasar does not expressly pronounce on the point, in an apocalyptic scheme such as his, a position like Bloch's represents the fallacy of misplaced concreteness by focusing narrowly on apocalyptic as defining Judaism, while being insensitive to the prospect of a refiguration that preserves the complexity and integrity of Judaism as well as its fundamental otherness. This refiguring of Judaism does not make mainline Christianity Gnostic, but, as Irenaeus saw, is precisely the refutation of Gnosticism. By contrast, 'Jewish apocalyptic,' precisely because it shortchanges other facets of Judaism, and expressly that of law, either represents a double of Gnosticism, or is already primed for cooperation with and assimilation by philosophical and theological programs that are more nearly Valentinian.

Something needs to be said about Metz's appropriation of Bloch's reading of Hegel and Marx as precursors and provocateurs, especially since Balthasar in the main tends to treat Bloch as a tag-end of the Hegel-Marx complex. Metz appears to grant the double-sidedness of Bloch's estimation of Marx and Hegel: first, the discourses of Marx and Hegel express, in ways that the standard religious and philosophical traditions do not, an embracing of history and the reality of human making of culture and society; second, their discourses evince virtual and real defects that throw them out of an authentically apocalyptic orbit. In the case of Marx, these defects – variously virtual and actual in Bloch and Metz respectively[23] – include his ideological determination of all religious expression, his materialist orientation in which in the final analysis human self-creation is determined by laws of economic production and correlatively by social relations that transcend human creativity, and by a view of the end of history that is both too knowing about the shape of existence and yet leaves out too much. If the eschatologically-laced discourse of Hegel has, for Metz, after Bloch, the advantage of avoiding a materialist reduction, from an apocalyptic point of view its major disadvantages are its abstraction from the real subject of history and the fact that it legitimates the present configuration of social reality. In other words, the Hegelian system represents in philosophically coded language the supreme instance of a realized eschatology. In the end, for both Bloch and Metz, whether contingently or necessarily, the discourses of Hegel and Marx articulate a teleological history such that the future now is simply the result of nows earlier in the series, and yet as result, the future now crystallizes into the non-temporal now of meaning and truth. In both cases, memory or *anamnesis* can prove invidious, for in the case of Bloch anticipation ceases (*PH3*, 863-64) or fails to remember dangerously, to remember in a way not sanctioned by the laws of history, which are the laws of the victor rather than the victim.

In this teleological eclipsing of the future lies the essential criterion of the disqualification of the discourses of Marx and Hegel from 'apocalyptic' ascription. For in apocalyptic thought, the future is not an eruption – however conceived – of the present and the past, but the irruption of a reality irreducible to the seriality of time and the chronology of history. Correlatively, the teleological view of history depotentiates the past and makes it hopeless. What cannot be raised to the level of the concept and rational justification, or in Hegel's memorable lines, whatever does not answer to the philosophical justification of history as the identity of rationality and actuality,[24] is sheer surd and waste. Metz's distinctive negative judgments on Marx and Hegel in *Faith in History and Society* should be viewed against the background of his assimilation of these Blochian judgments on the philosophy of history of Marx and Hegel. In the context of Metz's post-Holocaust discourse,[25] these judgments get recharged and exacerbated in a discourse aimed at exposing and defeating the ever-present temptation of theodicy. Bloch's implied concern with the past becomes in Metz an explicit concern with the dead and whether they can have community with us. This concern is central to Balthasar for traditional as well as Metzian reasons, although his prospectus on *communio sanctorum* has broader scope than Metz's, since Balthasar wishes to include the sinners with the innocent sufferers of history. Still, the theodicy issue reaches in Metz a level of urgency that is not matched in Balthasar and for that matter in any contemporary theologian with the possible exception of Moltmann. Here, however, as we shall see shortly, the contribution of Benjamin proves decisive for Metz.

This sketch of the substantive influence of Bloch on Metz's formulation and enactment of apocalyptic style theology brings me back to my determinative question: what effect, if any, does the apocalyptic of Bloch have on the calibration of Metz's apocalyptic? Here I am especially interested in the question of whether borrowing from Bloch contributes to the evident pull in Metz's apocalyptic towards the functional and away from the content-rich or eidetic mode of apocalyptic that one finds in Balthasar and the Irenaean and Augustinian apocalyptic traditions into which Balthasar taps. I have promoted enough already the content-orientation of Metz's apocalyptic, and thus its eidetic nature, to remove the objection that I consider Metz to be interested only in the general effect of the religious and philosophical apocalyptic discourses to unsay the sedimented Western tradition of discourse and action. Moreover, I have insisted that Metz does not simply repeat Bloch, but theologically modifies him in important ways. Still, Bloch's eidetic apocalyptic is not especially alethic, does not give any preferential option to biblical material, especially canonic biblical material, correlatively takes a negative attitude towards Revelation, resists robust forms of God-talk, and has a significant functionalist bent which makes equivalent different kinds of imagining of the 'not yet.' This is my major reason for calling its palpable content commitment 'soft' in contrast with what we find in Balthasar and the two traditions from which he asymmetrically draws when it comes to resisting the Hegelian tradition.

Now in Metz, there is a symbiosis between the option for a fundamental theology and the principle or practice of making apocalyptic schemes equivalent because of their power to evoke a totally different disposition towards the world, others, and the Other as such than the ones prevalent both inside as well as outside the church, both of which are characterized by amnesia. An important consequence of this is that this horizon exercises a counter-pull against the eidetics of the passion, death, and resurrection of Christ that seems to identify the specifically Christian optic. For it is not clear that the latter is more than a regional instance of a general apocalyptic for which we have either no warrants or none that would not be supplied by ethics. Given this, it is not difficult to see how the functional effect of apocalyptic gets reinforced in Metz in his adaptation of the messianic discourse of Benjamin and the 'negative dialectics' of Adorno. There is then something like an overdetermination of influences on Metz's apocalyptic that stress the more functional or non-eidetic elements of apocalyptic. These other influences in turn temper the visionary facet of apocalyptic that is still very much to the fore in Bloch. More importantly, these influences help to figure a mixed apocalyptic type, which is neither purely eidetic, nor non-eidetic, but rather both at once. Yet by the same token, and in a manner that reminds of Rahner, it is logically possible to read Metz as making the Christian narrative so central to a practical fundamental theology that even as, or precisely as a fundamental theology, it exercises a colonizing function that is not present in styles of theology such as that of Balthasar which denies as fictitious the claim to a neutral space. To echo – but also to modify – a famous Heideggerian phrase:[26] higher than logical possibility is real possibility, in this case the leverage a non-Christian form of apocalyptic has on shaping a self-consciously Christian form of apocalyptic.

Benjamin: On the Way to Non-Eidetic Apocalyptic

IN THE SECOND MAJOR SECTION of this chapter I deal with Benjamin's 'Jewish apocalyptic' as a crucial influence on Metz's thought, which sets its sights on overcoming amnesia and overcoming speculative systems of thought that effectively legitimate amnesia precisely in their claim to memory. I do so with a view not so much to explain Metz, however, as to bring forward forms of apocalyptic that share Balthasar's two-fold agenda, while, nonetheless, being differently calibrated than his. It should be said, however, that Balthasar's dealings with Benjamin are not a function of Balthasar's dealings with Metz, but rather the other way around. Sketching an account of Benjamin's form of apocalyptic, which has very little in it by way of content, is in effect to outline a radical alternative to that of Balthasar, one to which he specifically objects. I will cover both the explicit and implicit sides of Balthasar's objection. If the explicit side can be stated quite succinctly, the implicit objection, which is coded in a discussion about the nature and value of Baroque drama, is by far the more important and interesting aspect of Balthasar's dialogue with Benjamin, who seems to evince more respect as a religious thinker than Bloch manages. The dialogue with Benjamin also manages to focus an issue very much implied in Metz and Bloch, that is, the issue of the status of non-biblical forms of apocalyptic vis-à-vis biblical apocalyptic. It turns out not only that Benjamin's non-eidetic form of apocalyptic is the contrary of Balthasar's eidetic form of apocalyptic as it is the other of that of Hegel, but that a certain kind of philosophy or non-philosophy and certain examples of art – Adorno fills out Benjamin's intuitions on this score while shelving his religious interests – possess a level of interruptive power superior rather than inferior to that of biblical apocalyptic.

Describing Benjamin's Non-Eidetic Apocalyptic

WITHOUT DOWNPLAYING THE INFLUENCE OF Critical Theory on the thought of Metz, and specifically without downplaying the influence of its ideology-critique and its humanist brand of historical materialism that attends to the social and material circumstances of groups and power inequities between them, when it comes to the articulation of apocalyptic Metz owes more to Benjamin than to any single member of the Frankfurt School or even their sum. One obvious reason for the asymmetry is that Benjamin's discourse is theologically aspirated in the way that the discourses of Horkheimer and Adorno are not. If this is particularly the case in the 'Theses on the Concept of History' (*Geschichtsphilosophische Thesen*) and the theoretical section of the *Arcades Project* (*Das Passagen-Werk*),[27] most of Benjamin's texts possess a religious dimension with deep roots in the Kabbalistic tradition as this tradition is messianically inflected.[28] In the *Arcades Project* Benjamin is totally explicit: 'My thinking relates to theology the way a blotter does to ink. It is soaked through with it.'[29] Of course, a religious or theological aspiration of a discourse – here critical discourse – may or may not amount to religious or theological specification. It is possible, for example, to take Adorno's view that Benjamin's discourse is basically secular and that the religious flavor adds rhetorical power and effect. While both interpretations remain possible, it is a fact that Benjamin's work offers a religious inflection not found in either Adorno or Horkheimer. If this is one reason for the greater vitality of Benjamin for Metz, another is that for Benjamin the openness or closure of the past is as imperative as the openness and closure of the future that gains most of Adorno's and Horkheimer's attention.[30] Moreover, in the case of Benjamin this issue is not an abstract one: an appeal against the judgment of history – thus a theodicy or anthropodicy – depends on our remembering the victims of history, on our guaranteeing that they do not suffer the second death of being forgotten by later generations. Now if Benjamin's reflection on memory supplies Metz with both one of his basic terms (*Eingedenkens*) and the determinate meaning of bringing to presence out of absence, his contribution is hardly restricted to this important borrowing. In Metz's texts Benjamin's messianism reinforces important elements of Bloch's apocalyptic, which supply some of the substance and a significant measure of the calibration of his Christian apocalyptic. Blochian contributions that get reinforced include the perception of the importance of Kant's philosophy, the relative superiority of image over concept, a negative judgment on the philosophy of history of Hegelianism and doctrinaire Marxism, and the functional view of the Messiah. I will treat each of these elements in turn, although I do so with the caveat that Benjamin not only reinforces these points in Bloch, but also deepens and integrates them, and in so doing pushes Metz's apocalyptic in a more non-eidetic direction.

It is no accident that Benjamin planned to write a work on Kant. It is clear that throughout his career Benjamin availed of Kant as a leaven to humble the claims of both the Enlightenment and the thought of doctrinaire Marxism and Hegelianism, which purport to have comprehended fully the laws of historical development.[31] For Benjamin, this view of history is that of Pangloss. Looked at with the eyes of the angel,[32] that is, with the open eyes of someone who steps outside the controlled perception of the period or the group, history more nearly reveals itself as a scene of transgression and ruin.[33] The full passage reads:

> *A Klee painting named "Angelus Novus" shows an angel looking as though he is about to move away from something he is fixedly contemplating. His eyes are staring, his mouth is open, his wings are spread. This is how one pictures the angel of history. His face is turned towards the past. Where we perceive a chain of events, he sees one single catastrophe which keeps piling wreckage upon wreckage and hurls it in front of his feet. The angel would like to stay, awaken the dead, and make whole what has been smashed. But a storm is blowing from Paradise: it has got caught in his wings with such violence that the angel can no longer close them. The storm irresistibly propels him into the future to which his back is turned, while the pile of debris before him grows skyward. (IL, 257-58)*

The reply to idealistic construction is here as much empiricist as it is Kantian, for in addition to Kantian restrictions on what is knowable, Benjamin thinks that it is possible to posit counterfactuals. The Kantian element becomes less formal and considerably more explicit, however, in the implied recommendation as to how to read disaster. Reading history as a disaster leads to despair, if one fails to see that history is open and provides some promise for a renovation of the individual and social state of human beings. However mechanically history grinds down the beautiful, the good, and the innocent, history does not and cannot excise the promise of an alternative regime of being and relation. Thus, as with Kant, the 'kingdom of God' is the object of hope rather than knowledge. Importantly, hope is a risk; things may continue as they are, or even get worse. Transformation is just a possibility, and not, as in Hegel and Marx, a logically necessary outcome of the dialectic of history. Moreover, the task of the angel-critic is monumental: how to brush against the grain of history, to repeal its last word, to say the word that will stop the pile-up, to raise the dead, if only figuratively.

For Benjamin, Hegel is just one of the many totalizers who are critiqued for their illicit epistemological assumptions about the knowability of reality and the end of history. As is well known, in

Adorno Hegel assumes the status of the quintessential hubristic thinker who infallibly charts historical development.[34] Sharing features of both, Metz remains undecided between them. If Hegel is not quite the *bête noire* he is for Adorno, he is more than one example among others of titanic epistemic ambition (Benjamin). Despite the considerably greater influence of Benjamin, Metz is at least partially dependent on Adorno's keener sense of the specific dangers to discourse presented by Hegelian thought. Thus, Metz's appeal is to 'negative dialectics,' where negative dialectics recalls only to rebut Hegelian dialectics, marked by the overcoming of difference and the closure of history, which is an object of knowledge and in turn the condition of the totality of knowledge. In promoting 'non-identity' (e.g. *HH*, 12-3), Metz declares his affinity with Adorno's project at its most general level, while at the same time insinuating substantive agreements about particular episodes in history such as the Holocaust that figure radical non-identity.[35]

Although Benjamin's view of the image is different than Bloch's insofar as it does not hark back to Romantic and Idealist prioritizations of 'productive imagination' as the faculty or energy of synthesis,[36] he certainly reinforces the priority of the non-conceptual against modern thought's romance with the concept and the metanarrative of reason coming to itself. For Benjamin, an image is any linguistic or non-linguistic sign whose non-redundancy interrupts the flow and development of time. As Benjamin says in the *Arcades Project*, the image brings 'dialectic to a standstill' (*Dialektik im Stillstand*),[37] and in so doing not only transcends transition, but more importantly, issues a promise of something more than the catastrophe that is the real face of history. An image then is an illumination that is finite, a 'lightning flash' Benjamin says repeatedly,[38] that cognizes by (re)cognizing particulars in danger of being forgotten. It is the image that announces the awakening from the stupor of the given, and gestures to an elsewhere. As such the image represents a 'caesura' in time.[39] While the image does not demand to be interpreted theologically – as the example of Adorno testifies – Benjamin cannot resist giving it a theological interpretation. The language of 'glimpse' and 'lightning flash,' which Benjamin uses, is one that he shares with the post-*Kehre*-Heidegger, who similarly wishes to deconstruct the Western tradition of thought of which Hegel is a supreme and, arguably, final example. Although the mystical tradition can provide an important context for this language, as is the case in Heidegger, in Benjamin the context is the prophetic or apocalyptic gaze that looks not above history, but into it, and renders a verdict other than the one pronounced by history, indeed, other to it. The prophetic-apocalyptic gaze constitutes itself as a last judgment in excess of history's supposedly final verdict.[40]

Benjamin's Kantianism and his emphasis on episodic illumination provide the contours of the category of the 'messianic,' which is so central to Metz's apocalyptic theology. It is with the 'messianic' that one sees most clearly the non-eidetic tendency of Benjamin's apocalyptic, whose presence in Metz's complex apocalyptic effects a significant counter-pull to the eidetic tendency in Metz's complex apocalyptic type, promoted by Bloch. As Benjamin puts it, the messianic kingdom represents the end of history rather than its goal.[41] It represents a leap beyond history or an incursion of the beyond, yet neither a leap into the beyond nor an actualization of the here. The messianic kingdom does not admit of conceptualization, although it admits of symbolization, which in turn provokes thought. In line with Dostoyevski's delineation in the Grand Inquisitor section of *The Brothers Karamazov*, Benjamin accepts that the messianic kingdom is not of this world. Thus an innerworldly Messiah is a contradiction in terms. Benjamin's discomfort with a real historical Messiah, whether of the future, present, or past, is indicated by the preference in 'Theses on the Concept of History' for an adjectival rather than nominal use: 'Messianic' rather than 'Messiah' is by far the more frequently recurring locution.[42] But when Benjamin has recourse to nominal use (e.g. Thesis 6), the Messiah is not the name for a unique agent who effects the redemption of human beings, but a figure for what interrupts and opens up history to a different kind of completion. Nothing can be invested in the Messiah as a real historical figure, since such a figure would represent the abrogation of the autonomy that Benjamin after Kant thinks ineluctable. Indeed, in all likelihood such a real historical Messiah would concretely realize Dostoyevski's fear of the Messiah as totalitarian Anti-Christ.[43] Benjamin, then, exercises an even heavier functionalist torque on the figure of the Messiah than Bloch. The functionalist reduction of the Messiah means that messianism is defined by an image and perception that escapes the general order of time and history and intimates – without constituting – an alternative reality. Whatever else it is, the messianic cannot be identified with the eschaton, defined as the future continuous with time present and past. The same prohibition, of course, applies to the past. The messianic cannot find a place in metanarrative, whether the axis of the metanarrative is supplied by future, present, or past. The messianic is the now-time (*Jetztzeit*) that interrupts the homogenous time (*Das Immergleiche*) of history. As such the messianic cuts against the grain of history and its order of perception.[44]

As at once a mode of knowledge (*Erkenntnis*) and prophetic gaze, in Benjamin the messianic offers both less and more to Metz's apocalyptic theology than Bloch, or paradoxically more because less. After Benjamin, in Metz the messianic subsists without the kind of ontological guarantee of transcendence inscribed in Bloch's anticipatory images. In addition, while the dimension of hope can no more be excised from Benjamin than Bloch, hope in Benjamin finds its measure in the possibility of undoing the past. Hope, then, blends almost imperceptibly with memory. This memory (*Eingedenkens*), which some commentators believe recalls Jewish ritual practices[45] – and thus establishes the liturgical site for Metz's own Christian adaptation – is at once an attempt to complete the incompleteness of lives that came to an abrupt end, and an effort to render incomplete or non-final the judgment of history. Replying to Horkheimer's challenge that the proper orientation of a thinker who would be a historical materialist is the future, since the past cannot be undone, Benjamin writes:

> *The corrective to this line of thought lies in the reflection that history is not just a science but also a form of memoration (eine Form des Eingedenkens). What science has "established," memoration can modify. Memoration can make the incomplete (happiness) into something complete, and the complete (suffering) into something incomplete. That is theology: but in memoration we discover the experience (Erfahrung) that forbids us to conceive of history as thoroughly a-theological, even though we barely dare not attempt to write it according to literally theological concepts.*[46]

Whether this task is a bearable one is the subject of the Ninth Thesis on the Concept of History in which the angel, who would like to awaken the dead, appears impotent. The task then seems to be at once imperative and hopeless, since one can call on neither God nor a real messiah. When Metz adopts Benjamin's focus on memory, he also inherits the aporia with respect to whether redemption is an infinite task, which forever remains in the mode of promise, or a promise that can be delivered on, even if the relation between promise and fulfillment is anything but teleological. Certainly, Metz equivocates with respect to the power of human memory, while not making clear whether we should interpret *memoria dei* as exclusively an objective genitive or whether the subjective genitive is also called for. That is, while we can stem the tide of forgetfulness to a certain extent, it remains undecided whether even in our most heroic posture we can do so more than episodically. Nor is it clear that such memory in and of itself constitutes redemption for the past victims of history who demand a mode of posthumous existence radically in excess of their mere prolongation in our consciousness. Interestingly, in his articulation of memory, Benjamin calls on the early 20th-century dramatist, Grillparzer. Grillparzer's problematization of the strength and purity of memory is crucial for Benjamin, but he thinks that the critic-prophet is obliged to correct for Grillparzer's optimism with respect to the possibilities of human memory.[47] Balthasar, for whom Grillparzer is an important dramatist, who rows against the current of subjectivism and objectivism, would enjoin an even more serious correction. Balthasar has a truly Augustinian sense of the fallibility and redundancy of human memory in both its individual and cultural and social forms. Memory is useless unless prehended by Christ in the Spirit.

It is in answering Horkheimer's challenge about the irrevocability of the past, that Benjamin advocates 'remembrance' as a function of reanimation of the possible in the past. In his answer, of course, Benjamin neither wishes to provide a rational justification for this belief, nor thinks it possible; it belongs essentially to the level of hope that has religious and theological dimensions and is embedded in the messianic and kabbalistic traditions.[48] In an important sense, the answer to Horkheimer articulates the possibility of an anthropodicy or theodicy. While its enunciation would be impossible without religious sources, the claim has broadly a Kantian horizon in that this anthropodicy or theodicy is different in type than the anthropodicy and theodicy of the Enlightenment, of doctrinaire Marxism, and of Hegel, and offers the essential instrument of critique. In *Negative Dialectics*, as we have intimated already, Adorno follows Benjamin in making the case against the constitutive anthropodicy/theodicy of Hegel, while valorizing the moments of action, perception, and expression in which the immanent dynamics of history are put out of action. In *Faith in History and Society* although Metz relies mainly on Benjamin's general prophetic-apocalyptic critique of history as anthropodicy/theodicy, he can also avail of Adorno's concerted critique of Hegel to make the case that reality eludes the dialectic of knowledge and issues in a non-knowledge that anticipates a truth beyond the totality of history and the totalizing discourses that justify it.

Apocalyptomachia Minora and Baroque Drama[49]

WHILE BALTHASAR INSINUATES RESERVATIONS about Benjamin's 'lightning flashes' in *Theo-Drama* and elsewhere by suggesting that, in the last instance, Benjamin belongs in the benighted league of 'Jewish eschatology,' absent is a direct engagement between one apocalyptic type and another. Throughout *Theo-Drama* the main apocalyptic battlefield is defined by Balthasar's resistance to Hegelian-style apocalyptic, which is as eidetic, Johannine, and trinitarian as his own, and his marshaling of the Irenaean and Augustinian traditions of apocalyptic discourse not only against Hegel's form of speculative apocalyptic, but also the particular apocalyptic traditions that are embedded in Hegelian speculation and to which Hegelian apocalyptic gives birth. This does not mean, however, that there is not a deep engagement of an oblique kind conducted throughout the trilogy between Balthasar and Benjamin's non-eidetic apocalyptic option. A good case could be made that what appears to be nothing more than an arcane literary argument between Balthasar and Benjamin about the nature and value of Baroque drama in *Theo-Drama 1* (163-177, 250-67, 356-69) illuminates what is at stake between the eidetic and non-eidetic types of apocalyptic.

At first blush Balthasar's discussion of Baroque drama in *Theo-Drama 1* seems peculiar even by the standards of German encyclopedism. As we suggested in chapter 1, however, the attention is motivated. Certainly, one factor to keep in mind is the obligation Balthasar feels to take on Hegel's aesthetics not only in terms of principles, but in terms of its history of art and its particular judgments. The Baroque does not make an appearance in Hegel's account of drama; thus overcoming Hegel's forgetting here, as this is linked to the larger forgetting of the integration of religion and art in the Christian dispensation, is an important goal of *Theo-Drama 1*. Here Benjamin and Balthasar overlap, for one way of looking at Benjamin's habilitation on Baroque drama is that whatever its more local targets, it too is levied against Hegelian aesthetics, which not only ignored Baroque drama as a genre, but failed to see the synergy in drama between the aesthetic and the religious. Balthasar's description of Baroque drama suggests that he is in conversation with Benjamin's *Origin of German Tragic Drama* or *Trauerspiel*,[50] which plays at the very least a supporting role to Benjamin's own reflection on apocalyptic and messianism, and may in some fundamental respects be generative.[51] I will provide a brief description of *Trauerspiel* or 'play of mourning' momentarily. First, however, I will describe Balthasar's own selection of what he takes to be representative of Baroque drama, and briefly present the contours of his preferred type with some attention to literary affiliations, basic themes, and implied theological commitments.

In *Theo-Drama 1* Balthasar discusses Baroque drama under the auspices of the rubric 'Theater of the World' or 'World Stage,' which if an established coin in literary history, still non-incidentally points to the biblical analogue which, it turns out, is Revelation. This line of connection rhymes with Claudel's insight, and affirms the connection Claudel makes between his own dramaturgy and his exegesis of Revelation. To discuss or not to discuss Baroque drama seems at first to be the crucial issue, since when it comes to describing Baroque drama Balthasar's description moves towards the conventional in a number of different ways. First, it confidently accepts the Spanish Baroque of Calderón and Lope de Vega as exemplary. The Spanish Baroque is not simply Catholic as a matter of historical fact, it is suffused by the Catholic spirit. Second, while Balthasar does not argue for the position, the choice is obviously not hindered by the fact that Spanish Baroque drama has roots in classical drama dominated by plot (*TD1*, 191-92), that it is regulated by the Stoic ideology of exemplarity (*TD1*, 173-76; also 252-54), that it has a distinguished history of effects, influencing as it does Shakespeare (*TD1*, 161-62) and the best of German Romantic drama, and that it achieves a definitive seal of approval in the literary judgment of Goethe who, as *Glory of the Lord 1*[52] just as much as *Glory of the Lord 5* shows, is a canonic figure for Balthasar. Third, thematically, in the 'Theater of the World' all action depends on pregiven natural and historical contexts, in which choice is discerning not only what is called for, but who one is. Both the act of discerning and the form of life embraced usually involve a self-emptying acceptance of a particular mission in life. Although in principle – and this is one of the reasons why Balthasar so admires Calderón – the self-emptying choosing of mission can proceed without reference to title and station,[53] in dramatic representation the exemplary figure is at the center of the political and social universe (*TD1*, 169). Consequently Spanish Baroque focuses on the choices made by, and the conduct and motivations of kings, princes, and councilors, and the religious and moral dilemmas presented by the use of power (*TD1*, 171-72). Importantly, for Balthasar, grace, which provides the horizon of choice and mission, supervenes or completes the nature of stressed selves attempting to discern the good in situations marked by ambiguity and existential ambivalence (*TD1*, 175-76). Fourth, and lastly, the 'Theater of the World' has theological implications that go well beyond the fact that the relation between secular and religious power is a theme, and that potentates have religious as well as other issues. For Balthasar, Spanish Baroque drama provides a marvelous analogue of theo-drama, which the Bible as a whole represents, but, arguably, Revelation in the most complete way. Without making the connection fully explicit then, Balthasar insinuates a correlation between the 'Theater of the World' and authentic Christian apocalyptic. Correlation is fully sufficient for his purposes, since, although he has an interest in bringing to contemporary attention the belonging-together of art and Christianity, he has no interest in confounding them. Literature is not scripture and vice versa; even less so is it theology. The fact that certain forms of drama provide analogues of dramatic structures, rendered in the biblical text in which God is actor as well as horizon, does not disturb the axiom of the incommensurability of scripture. If in his analysis of exemplarity in the 'Theater of the World' Balthasar draws attention to the operation on a substantive level of a positive relation of nature and grace, even if grace remains unanticipated, here the very fact that a genre of drama, which can be perfectly justified on literary grounds, provides an analogue of theo-drama attests formally to the same relation of nature and grace.

I want to argue that in terms of selection of genre, literary presuppositions and effects, basic themes, and finally and crucially theological commitment, Balthasar adopts a posture contrary to Benjamin's *Trauerspiel*, which he clearly shows that he has read (*TD1*, 170, 172). First, in terms of selection of material, Benjamin self-consciously puts aside the 'classical' Baroque of Calderón and Lope de Vega in favor of the later German Baroque, whose major figures such as Gryphius and Lohenstein are minor names in conventional histories of drama.[54] Benjamin does not so much question the consensus regarding the literary and dramatic superiority of the Spanish over the German Baroque (*O*, 49; also 58, 76, 81-4), as raise the larger question of whether such value-judgments are truly pertinent, whether in fact they blind us to an irreplaceable insight that occurred at a particular moment in history (*O*, 38). As he puts it in his famous 'Epistemo-Critical Prologue,' the essential issue is to decide between a view that regards art as an event and an ahistorical mode of evaluative judgment in which 'history is seen as no more than the colored border in their crystalline simultaneity' (*O*, 38). Second, again Benjamin neither essentially disagrees with the conventional reading of the Spanish Baroque as taking up both classical and Renaissance forms of drama, nor with the assessment that this tradition continues in modified fashion in Shakespeare (*O*, 129) and German Romanticism (*O*, 122, 129), nor even that its value is sealed in Goethe's assessment (*O*, 129). His accent being precisely on the novelty of *Trauerspiel*, he insists, however, on its break from classical and Renaissance forms (*O*, 59-62; also 50, 121).

Benjamin shows himself a little more reluctant to acknowledge that only Calderón and company influenced the later greats. He avers that the German Baroque has also played a role in Shakespeare (*O*, 127, 158; also 228-29), in German Romanticism in general (*O*, 229-33), more specifically in Schiller (*O*, 122), in Jean Paul (*O*, 187-88), in Hölderlin,[55] and even in Goethe himself (*O*, 122, 230). These are details; what is at stake is made perfectly clear in the second section of Benjamin's hugely influential book, which reflects on the relation between plays of mourning and classical tragedy. The 'break' with the classical means that no trace of immanent satisfaction can be found, nor even the ambiguous kind of assurance that a play such as Calderón's *La vida es sueño* provides (*O*, 81). Believing it useless to pry apart eschatology from teleology, given their connection in the history of classical drama, but also presumably within a Hegelian manifold of interpretation, which he recalls early on in his text (*O*, 28-34), Benjamin insists on the lack of eschatology in 'plays of mourning.' As one of the more memorable passages in *Origin* puts it:

> *The Baroque knows no eschatology, and for that reason it possesses no mechanism to which all earthly things are gathered in together and exalted before being consigned to their end. (O, 66; also 81)*

To say that the plays of mourning lack eschatology is to say that they are radically apocalyptic, and to anticipate Benjamin's more explicit and general avowal of messianism in his 'Theses on History,' which Metz and other contemporary 'religious' thinkers have found so important.[56]

The third feature of Balthasar's adoption of the more conventional reading of the Baroque, that is, the centrality of exemplarity, is also submitted to scrutiny, and the repressed apocalyptic dimension of the Baroque elaborated in some detail. Benjamin does not deny that the 'Theater of the World' is characterized by exemplarity (*O*, 60-2), but wishes to suggest that in the case of *Trauerspiel* exemplarity is both exacerbated (*O*, 60-2), and finds a different representation. Exemplarity is even more narrowly restricted to potentates, and is much more focused on the lust for power, the intrigues that go with it (*O*, 97-9), and on physical pain and death (*O*, 217-19; 232). There is nothing contemplative about any of the characters, no realization of, or even aim for, tranquility (*sosiego*) typical of the Spanish Baroque (*O*, 97-8); the good go down with the evil, or even go down alone. In an invocation, which can hardly be without influence on his own later reflections on time and history, Benjamin recalls Panofsky and Saxl on Time in their *Dürers 'Melencolia I'*: Chronos creates and devours countless children (*O*, 149-50).[57] Moreover, there is nothing abstract about death. The world and stage are full of corpses (*O*, 217-18). Death rather than life is the more imperative. Benjamin quotes a line from Lohenstein, which he finds important enough to repeat later:

> *Yes, when the Highest comes to bring the harvest from the graveyard, so will I, and death's head, become an angel's countenance. (O, 215; again 232)*

The language is through and through apocalyptic. The view of the world is at the furthest remove from the pastoral idyll, which has a place in Spanish Baroque, because nature has a place (*O*, 92-3).[58] The small word that sums up how it goes with the world is 'ruin.' *Trauerspiel* presents reality

> *. . . in the form of the ruin. In the ruin history has physically merged into the setting. And in this guise history does not assume the form of the process of an eternal life so much as that of irresistible decay. (O, 177-78; also 176, 235)*

Benjamin's pattern of agreement-disagreement with the conventional reading of Baroque drama, which Balthasar adopts, continues when it comes to the crucial question of the relation between Baroque drama and Christianity. Benjamin acknowledges the Catholic, and more specifically counter-Reformation, nature of the Spanish Baroque (*O*, 97-8, 130, 138), even as his emphasis is very much on the Protestant and specifically Lutheran backdrop of *Trauerspiel* (*O*, 138-40). One should expect Christian themes then in both the Spanish and German forms of the Baroque. In fact, by contrast with the Spanish Baroque, the only notions operative in *Trauerspiel* are Christian (*O*, 130). Although in his cryptic book, Benjamin does not elucidate in detail the contrast with the 'Theater of the World,' it is evident that the latter's roots in the classical and the Renaissance provide it with a wider dramatic vocabulary, but correspondingly less intense theological focus. Nothing in Benjamin's analysis thus far moves beyond scholarly consensus. The tone as well as the substance of what is perhaps Benjamin's clearest statements on the Protestant context of *Trauerspiel* help to show what is at stake between the preference for one or other of the two forms of Baroque drama:

> *The great German dramatists of the baroque era were Lutherans. Whereas in the decades of the Counter-Reformation Catholicism had penetrated secular life with the power of discipline, the relationship of Lutheranism had always been antinomic. (O, 138)*

In contrast to the Spanish Baroque, in *Trauerspiel* one witnesses the absolute separation of the orders of nature and grace; nature and history are absolutely fallen (*O*, 180), perhaps even to the point that fallenness is ingredient in nature itself. Benjamin's admission that considered from a formal point of view Spanish Baroque is the more adequate of the two forms of Baroque drama is thoroughly relativized when it comes to substance: for Benjamin *Trauerspiel* gets history and, given the suspension of nature, reality right. This in turn explains the passion for retrieving the German Baroque from the abyss of forgetting to which it has been subject. Benjamin's distrust of history is a match for Hegel's trust: both move towards a condition of the infinite. Long before 'Theses on the Concept of History' Benjamin provides an apocalyptic counterpoint to Hegel's *Philosophy of History*, although obviously one remarkably different from that of Balthasar.

The kind of apocalyptic illustrated by *Trauerspiel* involves no panoptic vision; the German Baroque encourages the insight that all of historical reality is summed up in the sight of catastrophe and ruin, with grace and salvation being precisely that which cannot appear. In terms of apocalyptic the *Trauerspiel* anticipates exactly Benjamin's articulation of messianism, which has migrated into Christian theology under the auspices of 'Jewish eschatology.' Metz accepts this designation, as does Balthasar, only with very different evaluations, Metz being positive, and Balthasar being negative. Of course, either or both could admit that in the hands of Benjamin, Jewish apocalyptic has undergone some measure of secularization. Yet the exposition of *Trauerspiel* we have provided forces us to pause with respect to both of these conclusions, even if pragmatically they tend to be sufficient for Balthasar. A few things should be kept in mind. First, when in *Apokalypse* Balthasar exposes the modern 'eschatological' or 'apocalyptic' consciousness of German high culture in particular, he has in mind precisely the kind of *Blick* that is promoted by Benjamin. Yet, in that text, as opposed to the trilogy, such seeing is not necessarily attributed to Judaism, but rather something like a secularization of Christianity in modern western cultural productions, especially in literature and philosophy. Second, the question that naturally emerges, is what form of Christianity? Bringing together Benjamin and Balthasar on the nature and form of the Baroque provides an answer. It is a Protestant form of Christianity that is dialectical through and through, and is focused on nature as obliterated, or nature as obliteration.

How faithful or anomalous this view is with respect to mainline Lutheranism is an interesting question, but it is clear in *Theo-Drama 1* that Balthasar thinks that the view is that of Luther's *theologia crucis*, which Hegel found so easy to exploit. In a very interesting reflection just before he gets to discussing classical Baroque drama, which involves a side-glance to Gryphius as the major representative of German Baroque, Balthasar points to Luther's penchant for paradox, which goes hand in hand with a view of grace without relation to nature, indeed, its appearance as wrath (*TD1*, 160-61). Diagnostically, then, there is not an essential difference here between Balthasar and Benjamin in terms of description, although there is a decided difference in evaluation. Benjamin favors the Protestant dialectical, Balthasar the Catholic analogical world-views, as these theological mind-sets get expressed in the two genres of Baroque plays. While it is true that Benjamin does not prefer the Lutheran dialectical view for intra-theological reasons, nor does his deeply-seated Kantianism permit him to support the real existence of Luther's hidden and wrathful God, nonetheless, Benjamin's choice here has consequences with respect to how we should judge the so-called 'Jewishness' of his view of the messianic. From the very beginning, the great scholar of Kabbalah, Gershom Scholem, raised the question whether Benjamin's messianism could be considered 'Jewish,' notwithstanding the fact that he borrowed significantly from the Kabbalah. At the very least, Balthasar, who is not a fan of the Kabbalah,[59] but who admires mainline Judaism, is implying here that the apocalyptic attitude recommended by Benjamin has as much a home in the Reformation as it does in ancient Judaism, although he would likely agree that in the last instance religion functions as a subtext – although an absolutely necessary one – for a position that could very well be held on non-religious grounds, as evidenced, for example, in Adorno.

Third, as the Reformation backdrop helps to reframe the issue between the eidetic apocalyptic of Balthasar and the relatively non-eidetic form of Benjamin, it also brings into clear view Balthasar's general argument about the negative capability for Lutheran dialectical to morph into Idealist dialectic in which paradox is overcome and everything is explained. As we saw in Parts 2 & 3, this is Balthasar's considered view of the relation between Luther and Hegel, one that he shares with Staudenmaier, who proved extraordinarily prescient in this matter. Rough characterizations of these forms of thought, governed by polarity, as theopanism and pantheism respectively, were provided by Przywara and are recurred to throughout the trilogy. Significantly, they are recalled in the brief reflection on Luther that immediately precedes Balthasar's reflections on Baroque drama (*TD1*, 159). What Balthasar adds to Przywara is a genealogy, in which theopanism can be enlisted in the service of its pantheistic or panentheistic opposite. Despite looking to be more distant from Idealism than Balthasar's maximally eidetic apocalyptic, the radical dialectic or apocalyptic, which Benjamin recommends in *Trauerspiel* and subsequently practices under the auspices of 'Jewish apocalyptic,' can be folded more easily into Hegelian apocalyptic. Balthasar understands the counterintuitive nature of his proposal, but he thinks that history bears him out. Moreover, Balthasar does not think that either a drama or piece of theological literature that rests on the Catholic conjugation of nature and grace disqualifies itself as apocalyptic. Benjamin clearly thinks this is the case with respect to Calderón and Spanish Baroque drama in general (*O*, 80). In linking the exemplary drama of the Spanish Baroque with exemplary theo-drama illustrated by Revelation, Balthasar suggests that the verticality of biblical apocalyptic permits a measure of integrity to the horizontal that the non-eidetic apocalyptic of Benjamin does not allow.

In the case of both Benjamin and Balthasar the argument about apocalyptic is also an argument about aesthetics and its relation to apocalyptic. Given its specific theological underpinning, for Balthasar, the Spanish Baroque does more than point to the relation between drama and theodrama. It points more broadly to the relation between aesthetics (theological and otherwise) and theodrama, which is summed up as a Johannine form of apocalyptic. As Benjamin makes clear in part 3 of *Trauerspiel*, this is true also for him. Different apocalyptic commitments imply different aesthetic commitments and vice versa. In 'Allegory and *Trauerspiel*' Benjamin launches an assault on the notion of symbol as disclosive and participatory. In doing so, he suggests his fundamental disagreement with what are the twin sources of Balthasar's aesthetics of symbol, German Romanticism as it is summed up in Goethe's theory and practice (*O*, 159-62) and the medieval aesthetics of radiance (*O*, 180), and suggests allegory as its alternative.[60] For Benjamin, the symbol is (a) almost invariably corrupted with notes of consolation, even if the consolation is communicated by the beauty of the language rather than its meaning, and (b) integrated or integratable in larger narratives or totalities of meaning. With respect to the first, the contrast could not be drawn more sharply:

> *Whereas in the symbol destruction is idealized and the tranfigured face of nature is fleetingly revealed in the light of redemption, in allegory the observer is confronted with the facies hippocratica of history as a petrified, primordial landscape. Everything about history that, from the very beginning, has been untimely, sorrowful, unsuccessful, is expressed in a face – or rather in a death's head. (O, 166)*[61]

As allied with ruin, allegory fundamentally lacks eloquence. It lays bare the unspeakable, the unnamable (*O*, 224). In forums as different as aesthetics (Adorno) and fundamental theology (Metz), this point, replayed often in Benjamin's later work, has a significant life. With regard to the second point, Benjamin indicates his opposition to totality from the opening bell, when he criticizes Hegel's system of self-presentation (*O*, 28-34). Benjamin does not say whether Hegel's system is narrative or not, but he clearly regards the commitment of the Spanish Baroque to plot and narrative closure as invidious (*O*, 191-92). If allegory substantively favors ruin, formally it favors the fragment (*O*, 176, 235). It is only Benjamin's insistence that is new here, not the concept of the fragment or its deployment against forms of discourse that tend towards comprehensiveness and conclusiveness. One of the reasons why a Romantic such as Schlegel is important is his valorization of the fragment in addition to irony, although the two are intrinsically connected. Here the disagreement with Balthasar is as real as it is subtle. It is subtle because in an important way Balthasar agrees with Benjamin on this point. Balthasar too appeals to the notion of fragment to oppose the illicit claim to truth of Hegelian speculation and/or apocalypse. Nonetheless, the locution, which Balthasar avails of in order to declare the truth value of the fragment, that is, 'the whole in the fragment' (*Das Ganze im Fragment*),[62] could not declare the difference more eloquently. For Balthasar wholeness, even if it can only be intimated, is essential in order for the fragment to make a claim to truth. In contrast, in Benjamin's scheme of things any reference to wholeness makes a truth claim impossible. From Benjamin's point of view, a locution like Balthasar's suggests the hegemony of the symbol, a validating of its ontophanic potential, and a measure of reliability in knowing. Balthasar would not disagree.

A brief nod to the history of the concept of the fragment is revealing. When Balthasar coins his catchword phrase, he can reasonably be thought to echo Friedrich Schlegel's reflection on the fragment. Schlegel certainly used the notion of fragment as a critique of the encyclopedic and as a prophylactic against system building in the future.[63] It is important to remember, however, that by fragment Schlegel neither meant that a work of art was a shard nor a hieroglyph, but rather that a work of art would dare, in the famous phrase of Goethe, to be finite. Truth, in principle a whole, was graspable only from a particular perspective, and found in representations that are necessarily singular.[64] Balthasar's position on the notion of the fragment is that of Schlegel, and, arguably, self-consciously so. At the same time acknowledging this does not mean gainsaying the role Hamann plays who not only emphasized the fragmentary nature of our knowledge, but provided the specifically biblical warrant for such a view.[65] Schlegel does not play a truly important role on the explicitly theological level in filling out the meaning and import of fragment. In any event, it is quite clear in *Trauerspiel* that Benjamin is going in a completely opposite direction to Schlegel. Schlegel is quite pointedly assigned to the school of symbol rather than allegory, and thus in the last instance to the school of wholeness (*O*, 214).

Like Ricoeur,[66] but for different reasons, Balthasar would deny the conclusion, if not its bases. He would likely go on to raise serious questions about the value of a non-ontophanic view of the fragment, which decides beforehand that all is ruin and that redemption is unnamable because impossible. If Benjamin is worried that symbol colludes with power by means of the radiance of its disclosure, Balthasar would worry that allegory connives with chaos through mimicking it. Relatedly, Balthasar would worry about the notion of the sublime that Benjamin puts in play as exemplifying allegory and which is connected with both ruin and fragment. Benjamin's notion of the sublime has connections with the discourses of both Kant and Burke, the former because of a disturbance in the order of representation,[67] the latter because reality is radically cacophonous and ultimately terrible in the way the French Revolution was for Burke.[68] In Benjamin's hands the sublime is not simply different than the aesthetic, it invalidates it. For the same reason, considered from a specifically religious point of view, the sublime does not simply find Catholicism wanting, essentially it forecloses it. Much more can and should be said about the battle fought between Benjamin and Balthasar. But what matters here is the front that is apocalyptic, and how the contrast between two types of apocalyptic allows for very different views of the sublime. Since the *Trauerspiel* should be regarded as a vehicle of the sublime in the modern period, the Lutheran dialectic, suitably rinsed of theological reference and refracted through a post-Kantian epistemic lens, also has to be considered as providing a template of the sublime. The form of apocalyptic is non-eidetic: it disrupts reason and offers the dazzling darkness of ruin. The eidetic Balthasarian form of apocalyptic allows for form – although form can be inflected by formlessness. In Christian apocalyptic at least there is a tensional union between the aesthetic and the sublime that is not allowed by Benjamin.

Competing Apocalyptic Discourses and Competing Apocalyptic Styles

NOT ONLY IS BENJAMIN NOT SO SUMMARILY DISMISSED by Balthasar as Bloch, but the conversation/argument about the nature and range of apocalyptic cuts deeper, even if to show this we have to extrapolate well beyond the *ipsissima verbi* of Balthasar himself. Balthasar's own privileging in fact finds its echo in Metz. While Bloch as well as Benjamin provides some crucial ingredients to Metz's complex conjugation of apocalyptic, very few commentators and critics would deny that Benjamin is by far the more important influence. At the very least then, Balthasar's conversation with Benjamin, as this is reinforced in and through his conversation with Bloch, throws more light than any direct conversation with Metz on the following set of questions: (i) What is the status of the biblical text in general, and biblical apocalyptic in particular? (ii) What are the apocalyptic credentials of non-biblical discourses and especially art? (iii) What constitutes adequate discursive style, given an apocalyptic perception of reality? Each of these questions will be attended to in turn.

I begin with the question of the status of the biblical text and of biblical apocalyptic, which happily admits of fairly brief reply. Balthasar lies at one end of a spectrum of possible answers. In both his elucidation and deployment of apocalyptic, the Bible is understood to be without equivocation the normative text. To the degree to which apocalyptic holds productive theological interest, Balthasar judges not only that canonic apocalyptic has pride of place and connects better with the prophetic tradition, but he dismisses non-canonic apocalypse as tending either towards Gnosticism, because of speculation into the trans-historical domain, or towards an intra-historical activism whose central aim is transformation of the world. Descriptively, canonic apocalyptic is visionary, has an agonistic christological core, and just as importantly a trinitarian backdrop, construes history dramatically, determines the production of saints as its goal, vouchsafes a liturgical understanding of reality, and endorses doxology both on the plane of historical becoming and eschatological realization. It is important, for Balthasar, for this authentic biblical apocalyptic, evinced in Revelation, to have a 'half-life' in the Christian tradition. Indeed, it does so along two axes, the Irenaean axis which is primary for Balthasar and in which he can be plotted with his modern 'visionary company' of Hamann, Staudenmaier, and Bulgakov, and the Augustinian line in which can be plotted Balthasar's teacher, Przywara, and his talented follower, Marion.[69] In contrast, neither Bloch nor Benjamin grant the Bible normative status, nor when it comes to apocalyptic form give pride of place to biblical apocalyptic. For example, in the case of Bloch biblical apocalyptic is not given preference over the apocalyptic of Joachim, and in the case of Benjamin, the Kabbalah seems to have more standing than Hebrew scripture or the Talmud. When it comes to preferences within the biblical field, Bloch, as we saw, prefers non-canonic modalities of apocalyptic, and is negative about Revelation. Its eidetic index, its Johannine horizon, as well as the christological and trinitarian content, determine that Revelation is not a text that can have genuine apocalyptic status for Benjamin, given his understanding of apocalyptic as radically interruptive, the non-personal and purely heuristic nature of messiahship, and the impossibility of saying anything beyond the bounds set by time, history, and finitude. Of course, the situation is marked by a little irony, since Benjamin recognizes well that the text that governs the *Trauerspiel* is in fact Revelation.[70]

The contretemps between Balthasar and Benjamin makes clear the deep divide that separates the two species of apocalyptic. Benjamin's avowal within his non-eidetic apocalyptic scheme that the Messiah – whether in the form of the Suffering Servant or the Lamb of God – has not come and will not come,[71] and in effect cannot come, represents only one of the more startling differences with the actuality guaranteed in Balthasar's form of apocalyptic. At a structural level, the differences can legitimately be parsed as involving varying perceptions about the relation between creation and redemption, and nature and grace. If it is true that in Balthasar redemption is no more conflated with creation than grace is with nature, nevertheless, in his prioritization of Revelation, he refuses the tendency in Bloch and the explicit recommendation in Benjamin to make discontinuity count for everything. Redemption is redemption of a creation made for redemption; grace is the transformation of a creation that is completed in this operation. Structurally and formally, the apocalyptic commitments of Bloch, the post-Christian, and Benjamin, the post-confessional Jew, tend towards an exacerbated form of Protestant apocalyptic.

The second question concerns the apocalyptic credentials of non-religious discourses in Balthasar's theology and the thought of his two apocalyptic rivals. Although this question is intrinsically interesting, it is welcome here for the potential light that it throws on preferences latent in Metz's form of apocalyptic. As Balthasar acknowledges the existence of philosophical and literary forms of apocalyptic, he insists on their secondariness and the need to refer them positively or negatively to biblical apocalyptic. In *Apokalypse* the treatment of modern philosophical and literary discourses with an apocalyptic flavor is almost exclusively negative, with many – if not most – discourses interpreted as deformations of authentic Christian apocalyptic. Despite a greater irenicism, this attitude is not totally repented of in the trilogy, and Balthasar continues to judge similarly some of his major targets. No less than in *Apokalypse* Hegel and Heidegger are regarded as plying apocalyptic wares that distort 'originary' Christian apocalyptic, as does also a significant portion of Romantic and post-Romantic literature. One notable advance, however, lies in the underscoring of the positive instances of apocalyptic, especially in those examples of literature which, in Balthasar's view, reinforce rather than displace the authority of biblical apocalyptic.

Two features account for the change. The first feature is simply the fruit of reading and rereading. Balthasar sees more clearly how Dostoyevski's disclosure of false forms of apocalyptic is itself a form of apocalyptic, and he sees in the dramatic work of Claudel a successful retrieval of Baroque drama as a form of apocalyptic. Moreover, while his elevation of Hopkins can be justified solely on the basis of Hopkins being a splendid incarnational poet, in *Glory of the Lord 3* Balthasar does not fail to read him as apocalyptic poet, in fact a poet of Revelation. And there is re-reading too. Balthasar understands as well as the very best contemporary students of German Romanticism and Idealism the common problematic of Hegel and Hölderlin,[72] and the similarity of their apocalyptic expectations, but he also wishes to show their irreducibility, which is predicated every bit as much on Hölderlin's Johannine commitments as his non-titanic philhellenism. The second of the two features is more theoretical and argumentative. Balthasar contests Hegel's 'death of art' thesis, which is based on a 'winner takes all' philosophy. The thesis is antecedently unpersuasive, and can only be borne out by denying the actual history of art in general and literature in particular; and when not denying, then gerrymandering the evidence. In the trilogy while Balthasar supports two fundamental Hegelian convictions, that is, drama is the highest of the linguistic arts and the linguistic arts are the highest of all arts, he sees no reason to discount the reality of the category of 'religious drama' throughout Western history. Like Benjamin, who seems to accept many of Hegel's premises only to contest his conclusion, Balthasar suggests that among many other forms of drama Baroque drama in particular represents a counterfactual.

Arguably, however, Benjamin is somewhat more critical of Hegel's genre distinctions. In terms of Balthasar's trilogy as a whole, only the facile would conclude that the playwrights Calderón and Shakespeare are unequivocally preferred over the poets Hölderlin and Hopkins, on the one hand, or over the novelists Cervantes and Dostoyevski, on the other. Balthasar's readings of literary figures and texts amount cumulatively to a demurral; he does not, however, contest Hegel's hierarchy of genres in an explicitly theoretical way. Benjamin adopts the radical strategy, that will be further developed in Adorno, of deconstructing literary genres, as well as narrowing the difference between literature and philosophy. Despite his affinities to Baroque drama, it is from Benjamin's point of view impossible to privilege drama. It is possible that the novel can illustrate just as well as the *Trauerspiel* – if more subtly – the apocalyptic dimension that is the condition of the possibility of truth which goes hand in hand with resistance to theodicy. This is certainly the case when the novelist in question is Kafka,[73] who seems to be spurned by Balthasar. Unsurprisingly – and here Benjamin finds himself on the same ground as Balthasar – the privileging of drama runs aground on the authority of Hölderlin's poetry. The reasons for refusing to accept a diminished alethic role for poetry, and the poetry of Hölderlin in particular, once again point to fundamentally different decisions regarding the nature of poetry: in the case of Balthasar, the option for an ontophanic view of poetry which bears an analogy to biblical disclosure; in the case of Benjamin, a high estimation of Hölderlin's poetry based upon his linguistic innovation,[74] which has done away with all conventions, and especially the conventions of Christian belief, symbol, and narrative. These differences in hermeneutic can be coded in terms of apocalyptic. Benjamin views the poetry of Hölderlin as being essentially a poetry of disaster after the manner of *Trauerspiel*. Hölderlin's poetry is a poetry of crisis and interruption, a poetry that is not so much timeless, as a poetry of a time which is not. By contrast, although it is Przywara rather than Balthasar who characterizes Hölderlin's poetry in terms of apocalyptic, certainly Balthasar's heavily Johannine interpretation of Hölderlin in *Glory of the Lord 5* does not preclude it. As one can see in both Marion as well as Przywara, however, the Johannine matrix guarantees a maximally eidetic apocalyptic just the opposite of Benjamin's apocalyptic form, which in terms of eidetics moves towards degree zero.

The collapse of genres is linked in Benjamin to a general valorization of allegory and irony. One could in fact say it leads to a generalization of the values that Benjamin supports in his preferred kind of Baroque drama. Not only does Balthasar not fully abrogate all genre distinctions within the linguistic arena (the exclusive arena for Benjamin) – although there is on the level of performance some subtle questioning of Hegel's hierarchy – but he makes clear, as we indicated in Part 1, that he shares Hegel's concerns about the deficient alethic potential of self-referential forms of literature. Adorno expands Benjamin's anti-Hegelian approach, which finds no value in Hegelian aesthetics, by dealing with a larger array of modern examples and penetrating more deeply into some of the examples that Benjamin provides.[75] In excess of much of the literary canon, for example, the avant-garde minimalism of Beckett has alethic potential, which has got everything to do with consciousness being raised with respect to what impedes human well-being and expression.[76] Although Balthasar does not speak to the self-conscious – and decidedly apocalyptic – hells of Beckett, he does say enough about related 20th-century experimentalists to make it clear that he is profoundly suspicious of the literary avant-garde.[77] Moreover, it is not a little interesting that in similarly emending Hegel's prognostication of the literature of modernity, they both speak to a commitment to objectivity in literature that is the violent other to the subjective. The example they have in common is Brecht. Once again, however, they offer competing estimations of Brecht. Balthasar thinks of Brecht's work as being objectivistic in the pejorative sense (*TD1*, 83-6, 238-39 *inter alia*),[78] and worries about its totalitarian implications. By contrast, Adorno praises the 'historical materialism' of Brecht, and insists that its commitment to clear perception represents the subversion of the totalitarianism that is the insidious underpinning of the very kinds of Romantic art which a critic like Balthasar would undoubtedly prefer.[79] Hölderlin too is a shared object of sustained reflection. With regard to his interpretation, Adorno moves even further down the line of Benjamin in emphasizing formal innovation and providing an inventory of syntactic rupture or parataxis that characterizes the fragments of the late Hölderlin, which he takes to be emblematic.[80] We have said enough about Balthasar's ontophanic view of Hölderlin already to realize that here once again Adorno and Balthasar are not of like mind with regard to one of the truly great poets in the modern period.

Adorno, then, makes explicit what is merely implicit in Benjamin: the rejection of Hegelian aesthetics and its hierarchies is intrinsically connected with the rejection of Hegelian metaphysics, which is founded on truth being a function of a reconciling totality that makes memory at once possible and impossible. *Negative Dialectics* rejects Hegelian metaphysics and the spurious consolations provided by its closure, pointing, as Benjamin had done, to the unappeased victims of history.[81] This expansion opens up an even wider gap between different kinds of anti-Hegelian thinkers, specifically those who deal in a concentrated way with Hegel's aesthetic reflections. But Adorno not only expands Benjamin's aesthetics, he radicalizes it, and digs even deeper trenches between a post-Hegelianism of a Balthasarian kind and a post-Hegelianism whose foundational texts are Benjamin's *Arcades Project* and *Trauerspiel.* Adorno does so in three different ways: (i) he refuses to sanction Hegel's preference for linguistic forms of art over other forms of art, especially music, which is through and through non-representational. (ii) He contributes to the process of blurring the boundary between criticism and the art work, and by implication the boundary between philosophy and art itself, which marks late 20th-century thought. (iii) Effectively, Adorno cuts religion out of the equation when it comes to puzzling over the relation between high-culture discourses and the issue of cultural authority.

In the context of the present work the most important of these points is the third. Nevertheless, a few words need to be said about points (i) and (ii). To begin with the first issue, the different level of questioning of Hegelian genre theory in effect in the work of Benjamin and Balthasar is limited to the linguistic arts. There does not seem to be a fundamental questioning of the Hegelian hierarchy between the linguistic and non-linguistic arts. In contrast, Adorno makes the case in his *Philosophy of Modern Music* that music has more truth potential precisely because it is non-representational.[82] This is a challenge puzzlingly avoided by Balthasar, the superior musician and music critic,[83] yet hardly out of bounds for a Balthasarian, who might have to think through the actual status of Mozart, given the laudatory comments that sprinkle Balthasar's texts,[84] and who might ask the question what would an apocalyptic piece of music look like. Would the eschatological speculation of Messiaen provide an example?[85] With regard to the relation between criticism and art, and the relation between philosophy and art, Balthasar believes that the integrity of both is respected only in their separation. Balthasar believes that the classical tradition supported a separation, and that only in forms of Romanticism can one see signs of unraveling. High Romanticism, however, in Balthasar's view, productively exaggerates as well as diminishes the contrast, and does so in a way that casts favor on art as the irreplaceable realm of symbol, indicative of human embeddedness in the sensuous, that philosophy as much as theology has shown an inclination to forget. From a Balthasarian point of view, Adorno seems to legislate that art be much more self-conscious, deliberative, and conceptual than is healthy for its integrity and helpful to those other discourses with which it is in relation.

As I have said the crucial issue here is how religion fares in Adorno's aesthetics. There is no good news to share. Adorno assumes rather than argues Nietzsche's 'death of God.' Nothing in Christianity is savable; there is nothing that is not intellectually obsolescent and ethically decrepit. In a sense then, the Hegelian triad of art, religion (especially Christianity), and philosophy is trimmed to a dyad. Adorno goes further than Benjamin here, for Benjamin in a certain respect supplied an intermediating religious *Ersatz* in his appeal to the Kabbalah. The purely secular Adorno does house-cleaning by arguing that this is pious mystification. And as for positing an actual linkage between art and religion in the history of art, and specifically in the history of literature, which hits at a crucial axiom of Hegelian aesthetics, Adorno is much less inclined than either Balthasar or Benjamin to think of the alliance as being productive. Indeed, in his case there ceases to be an 'originary' for the modernist irony and allegory. While avant-garde art is not autochthonous, its proximate origins reach no further back than Romanticism, which both Benjamin and Balthasar think is influenced by the Baroque. As a period, the Baroque is eclipsed every bit as much in Adorno as it is in Hegel. Importantly, this affects the German Baroque, as much as the Spanish Baroque. The fidelity to contingency, violence, and ruin are now the prerogatives of art (and philosophy). Interruption is still key, but now set free from a religious apocalyptic context. In the contemporary world art and philosophy do not share the burden with religion of raising the question of the meaning of our atrocities, and reminding us of our blood-letting and tendencies towards violence, they bear this burden alone and are hindered rather than helped when religion of any kind is involved. In this respect, Adorno is the contrary of Balthasar, even as the questions have to be asked whether in his adaptation of Benjamin he formalizes and immanentizes an essentially Protestant form of apocalyptic in which the hiddenness of God always outbids revealedness, and whether at the core of a nominalist view of the art object there lies recessed a form of theological nominalism that is never admitted. Adorno certainly does not share Benjamin's openness in asking whether the poet or the saint is exemplary, regarding the question of who transcends history and social expectation. When Benjamin answers the saint, he does not become baptized, but he does come into the horizon of Balthasar, who thinks of human being as constituted by a response to a call. Benjamin's emblematic human may be Jewish or Kantian, but a kind of saint, nonetheless, and that is sufficient to initiate and sustain a conversation with Balthasar. The conversation only deepens in the case of Metz, who would be very leery of what looks very much like a Romantic substitution in Adorno.

To support Balthasar on the issues of the general prerogative of Christianity, and his general view of relations against Bloch and Benjamin, is not to say that their questions have been fully answered when it comes to issues of genre, and that their recommendation of the avant-garde have been absolutely foreclosed. To concede this is not, however, to flounder when faced with the aesthetics establishment. It is rather to leave open the question whether the sublime can play a greater role in Balthasar's aesthetics precisely because it plays a significant role in theological aesthetics. It is true that Balthasar can no more offer unilateral support to the sublime in literature and in the other arts than he can offer such support when it comes to handling the passion and death of Christ. Yet there is a nervousness with respect to the jaggedness and opacity of modern works of art in excess of the theological desiderata. Benjamin, and after him Adorno, raise the general issue: what is the proper form of discourse that would remember rather than forget, or perhaps also remember rather than misremember? It would be inaccurate as well as idle to suggest that this is not an issue for theology. And in fact, the issue has deeply penetrated into Balthasar's problematization of the fragment and the refusal of theology as system. It could be that in its scope and commitment to transparence, the trilogy represents something like a performative contradiction of the discourses that would hallow avant-garde minimalism as well as its first-order expressions. It also could be the case that Balthasar has a very different view of fragment than Benjamin, who exercises such an influence on Metz. For Balthasar, a fragment is a particular, irreplaceable seeing of a whole. Nothing suggests that this seeing cannot be sustained, and that it must be an *Augenblick*. For Benjamin, and even more Adorno, there is no whole to see,[86] and the Kantian commitments suggest that our seeing cannot see all the way through to reality. While not wholly siding with Benjamin, Metz is chary of any claim to see wholeness both on ethical and intra-theological grounds. Still, Metz seems to be on Balthasar's side when it comes to style at least in the following respect. However much Metz affirms the jagged and the fragmentary, he neither validates nor performs the difficulty and opacity that both Benjamin and Adorno thought necessary to any truth bearing discourse. Perhaps this marks not only that he cannot go all the way down what might be called the road of sublimity; but he cannot go all the way down the road of a non-eidetic apocalyptic in which discourse also participates fully in the ruin and incomprehension that it would illustrate.

Summary Remarks

In this chapter the apocalyptic forms of Bloch and Benjamin function as more than differentials of the complex apocalyptic type of Metz, which in a quite different way to Balthasar represents within contemporary theology an alternative to Hegelian and post-Hegelian style eidetic apocalyptic. The 'soft-eidetic' and 'non-eidetic' types of apocalyptic, represented by Bloch and Benjamin respectively, have sufficient integrity of their own to be put in direct conversation/argument with the maximalist eidetic type of Balthasar with regard to their adequacy in refuting the Hegelian form of apocalyptic. Although Balthasar sees the merits of non-maximalist forms of apocalyptic in this respect, in the end he refuses to go down this road. He is persuaded that a successful refutation of Hegelianism requires a form of apocalyptic formally similar to that of Hegel in that it is maximally eidetic and includes the entire span of the Christian narrative with the triune God as the parenthesis, but substantively more Johannine, more dramatic, and more doxological. Although Balthasar tends to assimilate Bloch's apocalyptic to that of Hegel, avoiding this misprisoning launches a conversation that proves instructive. Blochian apocalyptic presents a set of challenges to Balthasarian apocalyptic repeated in Metz's theology, for example, a lack of interest in canonic apocalypses and an actual disavowal of Revelation, a democratization of apocalyptic forms across history, an assessment of such forms primarily in terms of efficacy with respect to overturning institutional, political, and cultural hierarchies, a negative view of strong contrasts – often identified with Augustine – between history and that which transcends it, and a view of a future in which the subject of the future is the new state without the courtesy of reference to a divine power. Without actually thematizing these challenges, Balthasar does not fail to engage all of them, and thereby set down a set of benchmarks in and through which one can assess the relationship of his apocalyptic theology to the apocalyptic theology of Metz, which was the topic of chapter 7. To the extent to which Metz's figuration of apocalyptic repeats these fundamental Blochian decisions, despite a number of non-trivial theological correspondences, the apocalyptic forms of Balthasar and Metz remain irreconcilable.

Nonetheless, however far-ranging Balthasar's engagement is with Bloch – albeit implicitly – the engagement with Benjamin goes deeper, and the ultimate opposition is more radical. This has almost nothing got to do with the fact that Balthasar explicitly rather than implicitly engages Benjamin, and everything got to do with how Balthasar reveals what is at stake in their disagreement. In any event, other than some references to the 'lightning flashes' of Benjamin, which provoke worry, Balthasar's engagement with Benjamin is more or less oblique. As I discussed at some length it is coded in what seems at first blush an esoteric dispute about the proper interpretation of Baroque drama. The difference of interpretation here, however, insinuates profound differences about the nature of apocalyptic, the nature of knowledge and symbol, the assessment of the culpabilities and frailties of modernity, the nature of the self and community, and the hazards of forgetting, memory, and misremembering. In a way that Bloch, at least Bloch as uncoupled from Hegel, is not, Benjamin is Balthasar's apocalyptic other. Adorno lessens as well as exacerbates this otherness as he secularizes Benjamin's messianism and brings out more explicitly its anti-Hegelianism. Benjamin's messianism has just the opposite set of problems to that of Hegelian apocalyptic: all immediacy of seeing, no symbolic or conceptual mediation; all alterity, no prospect for registering non-historical otherness; all heterology, no means of articulating commonalities; all sublime, no aesthetics of form and resolution.

In his analysis of Baroque drama Balthasar demonstrates that he has good reasons for suspecting that Benjamin's degree-zero style apocalyptic is just the kind of contrary regulated by Hegelianism insofar as it functions as a bald antithesis. Although the content of apocalyptic is either actually attenuated (later), or indicates the capacity to be attenuated (earlier), the form and shape of this apocalyptic, arguably, has more in common with voluntarist Christian apocalyptic of the seventeenth century than with the apocalypses of the Kabbalah, which do admit of mediation and some measure of explanation.[87] To the extent to which this is the case, however, Benjamin could be viewed as tapping into both the apocalyptic tradition of the 'now' and the 'hour,' which indicates radical discontinuity between this aeon and the unimaginable aeon to come, and the apocalyptic tradition of catastrophe, which is still very much present in Revelation. From a Balthasarian point of view, Benjamin's form of apocalyptic forbids a non-worldly power intersecting with the world, and remits the prospect of transformation. Benjamin's apocalyptic messianism is ultimately that of 'grace alone' which represents something like a double transformation of the formula 'only a God will save us.' The shifts are easy to mark: from 'only a God will save us' to 'only a God can save us,' or perhaps the even weaker form of 'only a God could save us,' to the final form of 'only a God can or could save us if a God would have anything to do with this world with which he has nothing in common.'[88] As we detailed in this chapter, Benjamin's epistemology is Kantian, even as he proceeds entirely to scuttle the hope that Kant allowed. Despite Balthasar's labeling of Benjamin's messianism as 'Jewish,' it is not clear that he does not prove that Benjamin's thought is a Christian product, albeit a highly processed and secular one. In fact, Benjamin seems to have moved beyond Kant through Nietzsche to a kind of Sisyphus-like hopelessness. Of salvation, devoutly to be wished, but only blasphemously asserted, one can have no confidence. He admits the heroism of insight into historical reality, or better reality as historical, but such knowledge is without issue. The thinker who remembers is literally on the side of the angels, but as heralds the angels can only announce ruin, play the role of helpless bystanders, indeed, function as mourners rather than prophets, or if prophets, prophets under erasure, since there is no power whom we can rely on to rectify history and recall the dead. If from a formal point of view there is an anticipation that is correlative to memory, the angel grasps or prehends nothing. As German Baroque drama and the modern avant garde show in different ways, no story of the world is possible, because all narratives in any genre of art provide the illusion of development and resolution and thus an inauthentic consolation. Nor is any drama possible; the heterogeneous world is strangely univocal after all; the good inevitably go down, and drama as a dialogue between infinite and finite freedom is the greatest illusion of all.

One way of reading *Theo-Drama* is to see that it obviates all of this: there is salvation, hope, and the angel as a witness of hope, and there is a story to be told, indeed the story of stories, which only God can tell properly, and there most certainly is drama, because not only are there crises that admit of catharsis and a measure of resolution, but there is a vertical dimension in which God as origin, support, and end of all action is in dialogue with a fragile human freedom. Allowing *Theo-Drama* to set the terms for the engagement, it becomes clearer how Balthasar's aesthetics and logic are also involved. If the aesthetics at the core of Balthasar's theological aesthetics precludes affirmation of works in which difference, non-concordance, and rupture are not given their due, at the same time, neither are these elements, which figure the sublime as such, given so much authority that they function as criteria of artistic excellence. In *Glory of the Lord* the connection with a medieval aesthetic is not proscribed, as it is implicitly with Adorno, who is Benjamin's follower in this respect, and after him explicitly by Eco.[89] Similarly, although the logic embraced by Balthasar is not a logic in which sameness dominates (analogic), neither is it a heterologic, a logic of absolute equivocity. It is rather a katalogic, which is a logic marked by unaccountable features, but features that indicate a semantic and alethic surplus rather than suggest that meaning has become attenuated and truth evaporated. The modernist art promoted by Benjamin, and even more vigorously by Adorno, are decked out with precisely such impotencies.

Nonetheless, sustaining Balthasar's general objections to this minimalist form of apocalyptic does not mean that Balthasar has been sufficiently measured. For with respect to Christian adequacy, the embracing of a Johannine optics should not be so determinative as to exclude altogether other forms of biblical apocalyptic, or overwhelm difference and irresolution. There is something to be said with respect to a more radical dimension of apophasis than that articulated by Balthasar, even if it is true that from a theological point of view the dangers of more radical apophasis, especially those whose interest is in history and injustice, or the history of injustice, often offset the advantages. Nevertheless, the kind of vigilance with respect to violence demanded by Benjamin, and after him, Metz, is a genuine component of biblical apocalyptic which is underdeveloped in Balthasar's eidetic apocalyptic. And Balthasar cannot push the oversight back onto canonic apocalypses or Revelation in particular, since divine judgment on violence is at the heart of Revelation. Nor on the aesthetic front does Balthasar's commitment to a medieval and Goethean aesthetic preclude greater hospitality to the avant garde than he actually shows. For if a general aesthetic illuminates a theological aesthetic, this theological aesthetic, in which the cross as interruption and thus the sublime, in some inalienable respect determines the direction of correspondence, thereby suggesting in principle an openness to a measure of discordance and dissonance in excess of what Balthasar actually tolerates. Balthasar's evasion of the avant garde is not justified on his basic principles. Of course, there would be limits to this openness, since given its logic of salvation, Christianity cannot support all the way down interruption, difference, and irresolution. But from an historical point of view, these strains between concordance and discordance, commonality and difference, and resolution and irresolution are all aspects of a tradition of thought that can be seen as continual mutual adjustment or equilibration. One could say of Metz, for example, that despite his borrowings from Benjamin and Adorno, he in fact constrains interruption and irresolutions; although unlike Balthasar he demonstrates both the tendency to make Christian hope one example among others, and to take the exigency out of truth claims in drawing such a severe contrast between narrative and proposition such that only the latter is the bearer of real ontological commitment.

In Part 4 Metz was examined as supplying the form of Christian apocalyptic, whose agenda of overcoming amnesia and misremembering most nearly corresponds to that of Balthasar. The direction of our analysis throughout has been from Balthasar to Metz, although it should be pointed out that assessment actually comes from the other direction, and that in fact Metz does not distinguish Balthasar from Moltmann and considers both to belong to the Hegelian tradition. Needless to say, with Metz this is as much assumption as conclusion, but he is clearly disturbed by among other things Balthasar's Johannine commitments, his view of Christ's soteriological activity, his facility in talking ontologically about Christ and the Trinity, and his view of the church as constituted by Christ's gift rather than by human justice. And Balthasar has from Metz's perspective unreconstructed views of the liturgical, of doxology, and of prayer. Balthasar would be unrepentant with respect to all of these points and more, and would likely retort against Metz that being in sync with the theological tradition is hardly an objection. Moreover, at the very least the philosophical company that Metz keeps is dangerous, just how dangerous we have shown in this, the final chapter. Metz's apocalyptic thought shows the need to move beyond Hegel, but on Balthasarian principles cannot show us the way. To have looked carefully at Metz's constitutive philosophical resources is to be shown why.

Part 4 has also brought out explicitly what gradually was becoming apparent throughout Parts 2 and 3, that the battle between Balthasar and Hegel is nothing less than an apocalypticomachia. In this battle Balthasar draws heavily on the canonic apocalypses excluded by the Hegelian line of apocalyptic, precursors as well as successors. But he also draws heavily on a line of apocalyptic which we have listed as 'Irenaean,' and which, obviously, includes a number of thinkers across the centuries. I dealt with the more important recent ones, Hamann, who precedes Hegel and whom Hegel engages, and two figures who succeed him, Staudenmaier, who with Kierkegaard is his most ferocious 19th-century critic, and Bulgakov, who less overtly but just as decisively takes his distance. The agon between Balthasarian and Hegelian apocalyptic is within the same maximalist eidetic type. It is precisely the similarity of Hegelian apocalypse to the genuine biblical form that makes Hegel a dangerous thinker for Christianity. Hegel does not forget, he misremembers. The misremembering is structural and displays itself in the way in which the biblical narrative is subjected to torque in which the meaning of each and every episode of the drama of love, creation, incarnation, redemption, sanctification, and eschaton are changed, and other practices and forms of life substituted for determinately Christian ones. Hegel generates a *Doppelgänger* that recalls only to distort what the common tradition has felt to be the community reading and reception of scripture. There are two fundamental aspects of any legitimate form of Christian apocalyptic, which in Balthasar's view will be eidetic in fundamental respects. The first is its diagnostic power, its vigilance with respect to seeing the truth in the shadows of the productive lie; the second is to lay bare the truth of Christianity with respect to which it inevitably falls short. For this purpose, it is neither sufficient to avail of John (Hegel does that) or Revelation (sectarians do that), but of both simultaneously, which is what the 'Irenaean' tradition has achieved. But, of course, this obtains not only with the 'Irenaean' tradition. Within the theological milieu the other apocalyptic strand in the Christian tradition is that of Augustine. I have suggested that even if the Irenaean apocalyptic tradition is the one most called on by Balthasar in refuting Hegel's specific kind of misremembering, the Augustinian tradition plays at the very least a supplementary role. This by no means suggests that the relation of order between both of these forms of eidetic apocalyptic is steady-state in Balthasar. Indeed, when it comes to diagnosing and refuting the Heideggerian form of apocalyptic, we see a fascinating reversal in the order of superordination-subordination.

AFTERWORD / FOREWORD

Afterword / Foreword

There are many reasons for writing at length about the relation between Balthasar and Hegel. The main one, of course, is that this particular engagement – at once constructive and critical – serves a crucial role in identifying Balthasarian discourse, as this discourse interlocks with and justifies particular Christian practices and forms of life. From a textual point of view the evidence of such an engagement, which is at once deep and ramified, is compelling. Balthasar constantly recurs to Hegel throughout his work. Balthasar recognizes that he has common cause with Hegelian thought to the extent to which, in his view, it represents a reconstructive enterprise whose task is to move beyond the amnesia that is a structural feature of the Enlightenment. Understanding the value of tradition, Hegel does much to garner and recommend premodern discourses, and not simply those of philosophy. Balthasar also does not fail to appreciate Hegel's attempt to make Christianity in general, and Christian symbol, narrative, and concept in particular, essential elements of the way beyond the endemic forgetting of the modern era. In addition, Balthasar is aware that there are few modern religious thinkers who have so resolutely held to the commitment that religious discourse aims at an absolute truth, and understood that the full grasp of truth involves moving beyond the ordinance of one discourse to a complex conjugation in which each of the discourses of art, philosophy, and religion are fundamentally enriched. When it comes to the levels of practice and institution, Balthasar once again sees the possibility of a constructive partnership. Balthasar recognizes in Hegel a thinker who is convinced that truth has a practical dimension, that truth consists at least in part in 'making true.' And Balthasar finds in Hegel a formidable ally when it comes to validating against both the Enlightenment and Romanticism the value of institutions which, if they stand over the individual subject, set the conditions not only for genuine community, but also for individual selves that are deeply substantial as well as substantially deep.

Again, Balthasar sees that few modern religious thinkers have been so relentlessly and so appropriately 'aesthetic' in their fundamental orientation. For Balthasar, the aesthetic in Hegel's works operates both on a general and 'regional' plane. On the general plane the aesthetic is inscribed into Hegel's thought commitment to the whole and to resolution and synthesis; on the more 'regional' plane, Balthasar judges Hegel's aesthetic reflections to be, arguably, the most profound the modern world has produced. Imitation being the most obvious form of flattery, Balthasar borrows, for example, the categories of 'lyric,' 'drama,' and 'epic' from Hegel's *Aesthetics*, and extends their reach to the religious and even philosophical domains. Finally, it is impossible to understand the basic structure of the trilogy of theological aesthetics, theodramatics, and theologic without sketching its critical relation to Hegel's aesthetics, logic, and philosophy of religion.

While most scholars of Balthasar have not made addressing Balthasar's relation to Hegel a pressing concern, nonetheless, the relation has hardly lacked recognition. As I have indicated throughout in the main text and more especially in the notes, the connection has been explored to varying degrees by scholars writing in different languages (French, Italian, German, and English) and with different interests. Moreover, commentators have tended to differ with respect to their *relative* emphasis on continuity or discontinuity and also with respect to critical evaluation. The perception of a significant measure of continuity is a *sine qua non* of any parsing of the relation, whatever the emphasis. For without such a perception the assertion of discontinuity lacks point. Furthermore, critical evaluation of the relation between Balthasar and Hegel is logically independent of the decision regarding relative continuity or discontinuity. Commentators who emphasize the continuity do not necessarily agree on evaluation: Balthasar's association with Hegel can damn him, but sometimes it can function as a means to make him relevant. There is a closer correlation between critical evaluation of Hegel and the emphasis on discontinuity between Hegel and Balthasar. If anything should be clear by now it is that this work situates itself very much on the side of discontinuity, indeed, to the point of understanding itself to elaborate a version of the discontinuity thesis greater than which none can be thought.

I have argued that despite, or rather because of, the ambition of Hegelian thought to overcome the amnesia of the Enlightenment by constituting itself as a total recall of the artistic, philosophical, and especially the Christian tradition of symbol, narrative, and construct, from Balthasar's point of view Hegelian memory (*Erinnerung*) constitutes the most blatant form of the misfiring of memory or misremembering in the post-Enlightenment era. From *Apokalypse* to the great trilogy, Balthasar is convinced this form of misremembering of Christianity, and also of the neighborly discourses of art and philosophy, makes Christianity even less available to contemporary thought. Moreover, it is not simply past; rather it lives on in many forms of modern and contemporary theology, even in or especially in those theological discourses which attempt to restrict its influence. Diagnosing and resisting the specifically Hegelian form of misremembering, for Balthasar, represents a theological obligation in a situation in which Hegelian thought plays the role of 'specter,' troubling theological discourses anxious to remember but all too aware of the inadequacies of much of premodern theological discourse. In mutually supportive ways parts 1 and 2 show the structural deficits of the form of Hegelian memory and the actual way in which it constructs a *Dopplegänger* of the Christian narrative and presents at best highly modified forms of traditional Christian practices and forms of life.

Part 1 unfolds Balthasar's dissatisfaction with Hegel's teleological pattern of memory in which all of Western culture and discourse, and most especially Christian discourse and its practical and life-form correlatives, become summed up in the self-certainty of speculative thought. From Balthasar's point of view, this is the height of hubris. Just as seriously, however, Hegelian memory is irreducibly schematic: despite Hegel's encyclopaedism, there are huge gaps in his accounts of the history of the discourses of art, philosophy and religion. Moreover, very few discourses and their supporting practices are offered the kind of thick description that would allow them to stand out as singularities. This is even more the case with the discourse or discourses of Christianity than it is with art and philosophy. Balthasar aspires then to a retrieval of premodern discourses that is fuller extensively and intensively, and that has the capacity to challenge not only the discourses of the Enlightenment, but also post-Enlightenment discourses. Balthasar, however, is not simply interpretively reactive, he is also active. He asks whether the form and content of Hegelian memory, especially when it comes to Christianity, is anticipated by previous discourses. Balthasar does not overlook the influence of Kant and especially of German Romanticism on Hegel's discourse. What he is specifically after is whether any premodern religious discourse serves as a template for Hegel's kind of memory in general, and memory of Christianity in particular, which, Balthasar is convinced, distorts Christian tradition and Christian substance in some significant way. The three candidates proposed are Neoplatonism (especially in the form illustrated by Proclus), apocalyptic (especially in the form illustrated by Joachim), and Gnosticism (especially in the form illustrated by Valentinus). I note that Balthasar operates more nearly at the level of rhetoric than theory: each of the three candidates helps to place Hegel's discourse in a line of succession that reveals particular dangers. Yet, even at this level, it is possible, I argue, to discern that Balthasar is suggesting – but not justifying – that Gnosticism may very well enjoy the status of first among equals.

Part 2 explores the reasons as to why Gnosticism is the most adequate analogue for a deficiency in memory which is best catalogued not as forgetting but as a comprehensive misremembering in which the actual symbolic, narrative, and conceptual content of Christian discourse is subtly but definitely altered, and in which determinate Christian practices and forms of life are either eliminated or redescribed. Moreover, assisting the generation in Hegelian speculation of what Balthasar thinks of as nothing less than a *Doppelgänger* is an epistemology that neither recognizes the finite limits of human knowledge nor the excess of the infinite divine. Critical here is the way Balthasar deploys Hegel's aesthetic categories of 'epic' and 'drama' against him when it comes to comprehending Christianity and its relationship to philosophy. Balthasar argues that Hegel's rendition of Christianity, both in itself and as it is sublated into Hegel's conceptual frame, is epical in point of view and in its metanarrative construction which renders a divine who develops in and through the world marked indelibly by finitude and suffering. To make the same point from a different angle: despite the best attempts of Hegel's supporters, Balthasar judges that neither Hegel's philosophy nor his schematization of Christianity admits of being called dramatic since they lack the essential conditions that make drama possible: dialogue between two personal centers of freedom (divine and human). Balthasar's attack on Hegel's metaleptic narrative by means of categories minted within 'speculative' ordinance is, arguably, his most important contribution towards introducing a significant degree of separation between Christian theology and Hegelian speculation. In the trilogy, however, Balthasar can be seen to complement and deepen the account of global narrative deformation by focusing more specifically on what is wrong with Hegelian Christology and trinitarian thought. With regard to the latter Balthasar understands well that Hegelian distortions of the Trinity are not simply local, since the relation between the immanent and economic Trinity is in effect coextensive with the Hegelian metanarrative. Balthasar suggests that Hegel articulates a dynamic narrative form of Sabellianism that excludes the tri-personal notion of the divine, while understanding that the economy completes the divine who at the immanent level is not so much constituted by ontological fullness as by lack.

Now commentators on Balthasar have not been wrong when they have focused on Christology as the area in which Balthasar and Hegel seem to come within the greatest proximity. On the reading I offer in part 2, however, this proximity simply serves as the backdrop of a pointed and extended critique of Hegelian Christology in which it is found guilty of monophysitism, of exemplarism, and ultimately of pneumatic displacement. Of course, the various problems in Christology and trinitarian thought are mutually reinforcing, since the Trinity provides the encompassing frame for the passion, death, and resurrection of Christ, and Christology reflects on the axis on which the drama of redemption – and in the case of Hegel the drama of divine self-redemption – turns. Balthasar is convinced also that the systemic problems at the level of Christology and the Trinity and, of course, at the level of narrative, lead Hegel to a kind of univocal affirmation of divine suffering which is not sustainable by reference to scripture and tradition. While Balthasar believes that Hegel is not wrong in withdrawing unilateral support from the thesis of divine impassibility, he does not believe that the thesis functions quite so axiomatically in the premodern traditions as Hegel suggests, nor is he convinced that an equally unilateral affirmation of the opposite is the answer. Here a promise of overcoming forgetting has been changed into a misremembering.

Parts 1 and 2, which present respectively the more formal and substantive aspects of Balthasar's critique of Hegelian speculation, complement each other. Together they suggest that Hegel effectively constructs a 'double' of Christianity – especially at the level of discourse – and that in the last instance this double is just that kind of double spoken of by Irenaeus in *Against Heresies*. From an explanatory point of view, Balthasar needs to give an account, on the one hand, of how this squares with his view of the Neoplatonic and apocalyptic dimensions of Hegelian discourse and, on the other, how Gnosticism can be ascribed to a form of thought that is not only quintessentially modern, but is defined by the affirmation of the world and history usually considered to be antithetical to Gnostic thought. Admitting that he does neither, as a supplement I provide tokens of the kind of theoretical model I offered in *Gnostic Return in Modernity*. In the first case, I propose that it is consistent with Balthasar's position to think of all three discourses as being present in Hegelian speculation, but that Gnosticism is the regulating narrative discourse. In the case of the second, I propose that thinking of Gnosticism as constituted by a narrative grammar rather than an invariant narrative enables one to conceive of forms of Gnosticism that demonstrate a greater hospitality to the world, suffering, and history than typically extended by Gnostic texts of the first centuries of the common era.

Given the spectral nature of Hegel's misremembering, and the memorial style of Balthasar's theology which insists on putting the tradition into play in the outing of misremembering, it seemed apposite to excavate further the first in the interest of pertinence and the second in the interest of seeing the tradition as an act of criticism. These are the two tasks of part 3. With respect to the issue of pertinence I underscored Balthasar's scruple with respect to drawing a line in principle between the historical Hegel and those contemporary theologians influenced by him, while at the same time showing how on the level of fact he is always ready to expose just how much Hegelian misremembering has infiltrated contemporary theology especially of German vintage. For Balthasar, the theology of Moltmann and his school is the test case for contemporary theology's haunting by Hegelian modes of thought, which reflect themselves at the level of discourse and their recommended practices and forms of life. In the case of theological discourse, one can expect that the Hegelian features will show up especially in the articulations of the Trinity and of Christ, but also at the level of the infrastructural narrative. Balthasar by no means thinks that Moltmann is unique in being unable to resist the Hegelian construction of a 'double,' but shows himself more reluctant than David Bentley Hart, for example, to insist on extending the negative verdict to other modern and contemporary theologians. Instead, he appears to provide a criteriology whereby the extension can be made. When it comes to Balthasar's ancestry with respect to diagnosing and challenging metaleptic schemes of thought I select four figures as being particularly relevant. They consist of two pairs. The first and primary pair is made up of the Tübingen theologian, Franz Anton Staudenmaier, who offers the most concerted Catholic critique of Hegel in the nineteenth century, and Irenaeus, who supplies the prototypical critique of forms of Christianity in the mode of the simulacrum. The second pair consists of Hamann and Bulgakov, the former functioning as the memorial of the aesthetic-dramatic theological road not taken by Hegel and by implication a critic of Hegel *avant la lettre*, the latter ultimately anti-Hegelian and truly effectively so precisely because of his deep immersion in and negotiation with the Idealist tradition.

As parts 1 and 2 form a pair, so also do parts 3 and 4. This is especially so with regard to part 4 and the second of the two chapters of part 3 which elucidates Balthasar's anti-metaleptic ancestry. It would seem to follow naturally from Balthasar's diagnosis and critique of Hegelian speculation being doubly invested in apocalyptic, first in the kind of second-level apocalyptic illustrated by Joachim of Fiore and second in a form of Valentinian vision which sees through and beyond exoteric Christian symbol, narrative, practice, and form of life, that Balthasar should be cast as a resolutely non-apocalyptic theologian. Balthasar surprises our expectation: not only is he himself declaratively an apocalyptic theologian but, as *Theo-Drama* in particular illustrates, demonstratively so. Moreover, all four religious thinkers who play a role in his diagnosis and critique of Hegelian construction of a *Doppelgänger* are apocalyptically inflected. If this is most obvious in the case of Bulgakov and Hamann, it is also true of Irenaeus and Staudenmaier. When Balthasar has recourse to biblical apocalyptic in his challenging of the metaleptic form of Hegelian apocalyptic, he refuses to put the book of Revelation in brackets. Indeed, he puts it at the center of both a program of memory and a diagnosis of dissimulation. Joachimite thought, Valentinian thought, and Hegelian thought are discourses of simulacrum.

In order to appreciate fully Balthasar's apocalyptic refutation of Hegel, Balthasar is put into conversation with Johann Baptiste Metz who offers his own apocalyptic refutation of Hegelianism while suggesting that apocalyptically inflected theology is the answer to the rampant forgetting that marks modernity. The constructed conversation between Balthasar and Metz on apocalyptic cannot avoid raising the question of adequacy both in terms of the articulation of an apocalyptic theology and the power to refute Hegelian misremembering. Since one of Metz's major sources for an apocalyptic theology is Walter Benjamin, the question of adequacy is further pursued in detailed discussion of the relation-difference between Balthasar's and Benjamin's apocalyptic programs both in their register of memory and in their power to overcome Hegelian misremembering. It probably comes as no surprise that on balance it is decided that Balthasar is the more generally theologically valuable and shows the much greater power for critique. This is not to gainsay, however, that both Metz and Benjamin draw attention to some of the weaker features of Balthasarian apocalyptic, for example, a point of view that is not quite a point of view, a sometime tendency towards a kind of holism that performatively denies Balthasar's explicit commitment to the fragment, aesthetic commitments that allow more a note of resolution into an apocalyptic form of theology that would counteract Hegel, and less emphasis than permitted by apocalyptic to consider suffering as well as sin as appropriate subjects of an apocalyptic theology. As already suggested the apocalyptic characterization of Balthasar's theology ties parts 3 and 4 together. At the same time, however, it links up with parts 1 and 2 in that it reveals that the anatomy of misremembering – and also memory – is not the work of the theologian as mere critic, but a theologian who operates from and within a vision that is the gift of the church, which in turn is the gift of the Spirit.

This ends the recapitulation of my detailed interpretation of Balthasar's texts and my tracing of implication. Nonetheless, this text by no means offers a fully comprehensive account of Balthasar's anatomy of misremembering, and it barely touches on the other aspect of Balthasar's theological program, the orchestration of memory or memories of the church. Hegelian misremembering is only one of the two forms of misremembering challenged by Balthasar in the trilogy. The other form is provided by Heidegger, which like that of Hegel exercises considerable influence in theology, determining for instance that should theology remain in business it can only do so under pain of being 'post-metaphysical.' This form of misremembering is quite different from the Hegelian form in its overall complexion: Heideggerian thought, which is focally concerned with forgetting and memory, avoids Christianity more than Hegel does, while paradoxically retrieving more of Christian discourse, practice, and forms of life, all the time permitting itself to mime Christian discourse, practice, and forms of life when necessary. As Balthasar constructs it, Heideggerian misremembering is not metaleptic in the strict sense, but, nonetheless, infiltrates theological understanding and self-understanding in ways that hardly respect the fullness and coherence of Christianity. This form of misremembering is harder to diagnose and, arguably, harder also to get rid of. This is the story that will be told in volume 2 of *The Anatomy of Misremembering*. Yet, however, different the form of misremembering, the structure of analysis of what might be called Balthasar's 'unwelcoming' of Heidegger will be similar to what we presented here: bringing the two figures together on the level of discourse, recommended practices, and forms of life in order to differentiate them; charting both Heidegger's genealogy and the history of effects of Heidegger's poetic philosophy in theology, Catholic theology in particular; correspondingly charting Balthasar's countergenealogy; and finally coming to grips with the battle between Balthasar's apocalyptic theology and a non-theological form of thought which in addition to biblical resonances, suggests a chthonic form of apocalyptic intimated by the Greeks and by Nietzsche, but belonging properly to neither. Logically speaking

The Anatomy of Misremembering

The Anatomy of Misremembering could begin with the Balthasar-Heidegger conversation, trace the reservations that devolve into *Auseinandersetzung*, and proceed from there to Balthasar's more direct and systematic diagnosis and resistance to the specter of Hegel. Still it has to be said that the Hegelian form of misremembering, which, in Balthasar's eloquent phrase, represents 'the curse of misused love' (*Apok 1*, 616), sets the bar. We understand the resistance to Heideggerian misremembering in a way we might not have when we have dealt with the form that is paradigmatic. And Balthasar's dealing with Hegel needs no introduction: it is a comprehensive and passionate unveiling.

Endnotes

PREFACE

[1]. G. W. F. Hegel, *Phenomenology of Spirit*, tr. A. V. Miller (Oxford: Oxford University Press, 1977), 331

[2]. For the connection between Hegel and Hermetic symbols see Glenn Alexander Magee's fine *Hegel and the Hermetic Tradition* (Ithaca: Cornell University Press, 2001). For the mediation of Cusanus, see 26-8.

[3]. Hans Blumenberg, *The Legitimacy of the Modern Age*, tr. Robert M. Wallace (Cambridge, MA: MIT Press, 1983).

[4]. The notion of survivals and remainders is more to the fore in another of Blumenberg's massive texts than in *The Legitimacy of the Modern Age*. The text I have particularly in mind is *Work on Myth*, tr. Robert M. Wallace (Cambridge, MA: MIT Press, 1985). In the case of Foucault, the text that comes to mind is *Les Mots et les choses: Une Archéologie des sciences humaines* (Paris: Gallimard, 1966). See the translation by Alan Sheridan, *The Order of Things: An Archeology of the Human Sciences* (London: Routledge, 1991). In this text Foucault establishes that there is a monumental divide between the premodern and the modern in terms of basic presuppositions and associated practices. While, for example, the premodern world was a world where the basic logic was associative, the logic that is operative in modernity is scientific, calculative, and pragmatic. For all that, however, elements of the former logic make their way into the modern world, even if they can only operate on its margins.

[5]. Alasdair MacIntyre, *After Virtue: A Study in Moral Theory* (Notre Dame: University of Notre Dame Press, 1981); *Whose Justice? Which Rationality?* (Notre Dame: University of Notre Dame Press, 1988); *Three Rival Versions of Moral Inquiry: Encyclopaedia, Genealogy, and Tradition* (Gifford Lectures of 1988) (Notre Dame: University of Notre Dame Press, 1990). See also Peter McMylor's very useful *Alasdair MacIntyre: Critic of Modernity* (London and New York: Routledge, 1994); Richard Rorty, *Philosophy and the Mirror of Nature* (Princeton, NJ: Princeton University Press, 1980); also Alan R. Malachowski, Jo Burrows, and Richard Rorty, *Reading Rorty: Critical Response to Philosophy and the Mirror of Nature (And Beyond)* (Oxford: Blackwell, 1990); Hans Frei, *The Eclipse of Biblical Narrative* (New Haven: Yale University Press, 1974); Michael J. Buckley, *The Origins of Modern Atheism* (New Haven: Yale University Press, 1987); William C. Placher, *The Domestication of Transcendence* (Louisville, KY: Westminister John Knox Press, 1996); Jeffrey Stout, *The Flight from Authority: Religion, Morality, and the Quest for Autonomy* (Notre Dame: University of Notre Dame Press, 1981) (Distributed by Harper & Row); *Ethics after Babel: The Language of Morals and their Discontents* (Boston: Beacon Press, 1988); John Milbank, *Theology and Social Theory* (Oxford: Blackwell, 2006). This second edition of Milbank's best-know text has a new introduction in which Milbank announces his basic allegiance to the secularization position advanced in the first edition in 1993 even as he points to some developments.

[6]. Here I am referring to Habermas' reconstructive program in which, while diagnosing the Enlightenment as an 'unfinished project,' he wishes to put such basic Enlightenment ideas as autonomy, respect for other persons, and the value of dialogue and argument on a more secure footing. Habermas' bibliography is huge and the commentary and criticism on his work mountainous. The following, however, might be regarded as representative: *Knowledge and Human Interests*, tr. Jeremy J. Shapiro (Boston: Beacon Press, 1971); *Theory of Communicative Action* (Boston: Beacon Press, 1984); *The Philosophical Discourse of Modernity*, tr. Frederick G. Lawrence (Cambridge, MA: MIT Press, 1990).

[7]. The genealogy of Foucault has as one of its aims the radical questioning of the subject as agent and specifically moral agent. Although for the most part, Foucault avails of post-structuralist tools to dismantle the subject, he can also rely on Nietzsche's epochal analysis of the death of God as a transcendent substantial reality to raise the question of whether a necessary implication of this death is also the death of the self as a discrete and determinable substance.

[8]. I provide a sketch of this aspect of Balthasar's thought in 'Balthasar: Between Tübingen and Postmodernity,' in *Modern Theology*, 14.3 Summer (1998), 325-53.

[9]. See *The Office of Peter and the Structure of the Church*, tr. Andrée Emery (San Francisco: Ignatius Press, 1986).

[10]. Needless to say, this is by no means an exhaustive list of Balthasar's patristic repertoire. Augustine and Gregory of Nyssa would also figure prominently. I will postpone discussion of the intricacies of Balthasar's relations to these individual thinkers until the main body of the text. At the appropriate time I will give the necessary bibliographical information.

[11]. For an explicit musical characterization of the Christian tradition, see *Truth Is Symphonic: Aspects of Christian Pluralism*, tr. Graham Harrison (San Francisco: Ignatius Press, 1989).

[12]. For the purposes of the Preface, it is not important to delve into the specifics of Balthasar's criticisms, evaluate his exegesis, or judge the quality of his arguments. More important is the fact that for him 'deformation' throughout the Christian tradition is both plural and varied. Despite overlaps with Radical Orthodoxy concerning Scotus and Nominalism, this makes Balthasar a quite different kind of genealogist.

[13]. For Balthasar's criticism of François-René de Chateaubriand's deficient view of tradition, see *Glory of the Lord: A Theological Aesthetics. Vol. 1: Seeing the Form*, ed. Joseph Fessio, S.J. and John Riches, tr. Erasmo Leiva-Merikakis (San Francisco: Ignatius Press, 1982), 90-4.

[14]. *Phenomenology of Spirit* #546. Here I avail of Miller's translation (332).

[15]. For Péguy, see *Glory of the Lord: A Theological Aesthetics. Vol. 3. Studies in Theological Styles: Lay Styles*, tr. Andrew Louth, Brian McNeil, C.R.V., John Saward, Rowan Williams and Oliver Davies (San Francisco: Ignatius Press, 1989), 400-517; *Bernanos: An Ecclesial Existence*, tr. Erasmo Leiva-Merikakis (San Francisco: Ignatius Press, 1996).

[16]. Here I am availing of the title of one of the better-known novels of the Czech writer Milan Kundera. See *The Unbearable Lightness of Being*, tr. Michael Henry Heim (New York: Harper & Row, 1984). In this novel Kundera associates forgetting and

lightness of being. Acknowledging that there is a loss, he refuses to be nostalgic. The situation has to be accepted; the alternative is purely idealistic and punitive. Moreover, in his view the twentieth century has shown the political dangers of yoking together memory (which can be manipulated) and presumptive depth. Fascism as well as Soviet-style communism represents for him the two emblematic cases.

17. In *The Unbearable Lightness of Being* Kundera shows himself to be somewhat ironical in framing the deracinated state of the 'lightness of being' as 'unbearable,' since it turns out to be very 'bearable' indeed. There is a difference, however, between the self-conscious embracing of 'the lightness of being' as a state, and its unconscious exemplification. The former is healthy in a way the latter is not. Interestingly, Balthasar is more in Nietzsche's camp than Kundera when it comes to assessing the cost of the Enlightenment. Edward T. Oakes has rightly called attention to the importance of Nietzsche for Balthasar's thought. See *Pattern of Redemption: The Theology of Hans Urs von Batlhasar* (New York: Continuum, 1994).

18. Since the voluminous literature on the topic will be attended to in the second volume of *The Anatomy of Misremembering*, here I will confine myself to a few examples: John D. Caputo, *Demythologizing Heidegger* (Bloomington: Indiana University Press, 1993); Jacques Derrida, *Of Spirit: Heidegger and the Question*, tr. Geoffrey Bennington and Rachel Bowlby (Chicago: University of Chicago Press, 1989); Rüdiger Safranski, *Martin Heidegger: Between Good and Evil*, tr. Ewald Osers (Cambridge, MA: Harvard University Press, 1999); Richard Wolin, *The Politics of Being* (New York: Columbia University Press, 1990); Michael E. Zimmerman, *Heidegger's Confrontation with Modernity: Technology, Politics, Art* (Bloomington: Indiana University Press, 1990). One might also add Richard Rorty to the above list. See, for example, his 'Heidegger, Contingency, Pragmatism,' in *Essays on Heidegger and Others: Philosophical Papers Volume 2* (Cambridge: Cambridge University Press, 1991), 27-49.

19. The explorations of Theodore Kisiel and John van Buren. See Kisiel, *The Genesis of Heidegger's Being and Time* (Berkeley: University of California Press, 1995), 69-115, 149-219; van Buren, *The Young Heidegger: Rumor of the Hidden King* (Bloomington: Indiana University Press, 1994), 113-29, 157-202. Heidegger's lecture courses on Christianity (1920-1921), which primarily dealt with Paul, have now been translated. See *The Phenomenology of Religious Life*, tr. Matthias Fritsch and Jennifer Anna Gosetti-Ferencei (Bloomington: Indiana University Press, 2004), 47-111.

20. A particularly vivid account of nihilism as the limit of the modern is provided by Balthasar in part 2 of *The God Question and Modern Man*, tr. Hilda Graef (New York: Seabury Press, 1967), 91-155; esp. 119-41.

21. *Apokalypse der deutschen Seele: Studien zu einer Lehre von letzten Haltungen*, 3 volumes (Salzburg, Austria: Pustet, 1937-39).

22. The characterization of 'Christian philosophy' as an oxymoron is one of Heidegger's more trenchant pieces of rhetoric aimed at segregating philosophy and Christianity to the mutual benefit of both. See *An Introduction to Metaphysics*, tr. Ralph Mannheim (New Haven: Yale University Press, 1959), 7.

23. I speak to this point in 'Balthasar and the Unwelcoming of Heidegger,' in *The Grandeur of Reason: Religion, Tradition, and Universalism*, ed. Peter Chandler and Conor Cunningham (Oxford: SPC, 2010), 264-98.

[24]. David Bentley Hart, *The Beauty of the Infinite: The Aesthetics of Christian Truth* (Grand Rapids, MI: Eerdmans, 2003). Hart tends to think of Hegel and Heidegger as inimical to Christian truth, despite their apparent attractiveness. He is convinced that they have had an enormously damaging effect on Christian theology. The attraction quite literally rests in the fact that both Hegel and Heidegger offer fundamentally aesthetic constructions of reality, which can only be countered by a Christian aesthetic. I will recur to this text throughout both volumes. For Hegel, see esp. 139-40, 157-64, 256-57, 387-88. For Heidegger, see esp. 72-3, 129-33, 213-33.

[25]. *The Heterodox Hegel* (Albany, NY: SUNY Press, 1994).

[26]. For discussion of *metalepsis*, see my *Gnostic Return in Modernity* (Albany, NY: SUNY Press, 2001), 58-60, 148-59. I borrow this literary trope from Harold Bloom, which he self-consciously associates with the kind of transgressive hermeneutic represented by Gnosticism, and I proceed to further specify it by linking it with Irenaeus' diagnosis that what is constitutive of Valentinianism is the way in which it disfigures and refigures the biblical narrative.

INTRODUCTION

[1] For Hans Blumenberg, see especially *The Legitimacy of the Modern Age*, tr. Robert M. Wallace (Cambridge, MA.: MIT Press), 1983. I discuss Blumenberg's view critically in *Gnostic Return in Modernity* (New York: SUNY Press, 2001), 50-65.

[2] For Taylor, see especially his two magisterial studies, *Sources of the Self: The Making of Modern Identity* (Cambridge, MA: Harvard University Press, 1989) and *A Secular Age* (Cambridge, MA: Harvard University Press, 2007); for Dupré, see *Passage to Modernity: An Essay in the Hermeneutics of Nature and Culture* (New Haven: Yale University Press, 1993); *The Enlightenment and the Intellectual Foundation of Modern Culture* (New Haven: Yale University Press, 2004). The scope of Taylor's work is different in a number of important respects: (i) Both of Taylor's books focus on the modern period and only on its antecedents in the premodern period on a per need basis, whereas by contrast *Passage to Modernity* is devoted entirely to its antecedents, both ultimate (nominalism) and proximate (Renaissance and Reformation), against the backdrop of a synthesis between revelation and philosophy that held for a millennium; (ii) The 1400 pages or so of Taylor's two books allow for greater detail than is possible in Dupré's volume on the Enlightenment, which represents, nonetheless, a superb synopsis on the model of Ernst Cassirer's famous volume on the Enlightenment. See *The Philosophy of the Enlightenment*, tr. Fritz C. A. Koelln and James P. Pettegrove (Princeton: Princeton University Press, 1951); (iii) While Taylor's work by and large mines high cultural discourses, it pays more attention to popular culture both in principle (talk of the 'social imaginary') and in fact than Dupré's work, which operates more nearly in terms of the standard model of the history of ideas. Both Taylor's and Dupré's accounts of modernity bear interesting relations to that of Blumenberg. In *Passage to Modernity* Dupré attempts to reconcile Balthasar's substantialist account of modernity in which a significant measure of deviance is at the fore with Blumenberg's

anti-substantialist account in which modernity is an event, a *novum*. Taylor articulates a different 'between.' While Taylor takes Blumenberg's side in arguing that constructing modern thought and ethos as deviant is a theoretical dead-end, he also suggests that accounts which refuse to think that premodern forms of thought and ethos live on are partial.

[3] This is obviously true to the extent to which modernity and the Enlightenment are closely allied. For Balthasar, however, a broader view of modernity necessarily includes also the array of responses to modernity that (a) are ultimately not grounded in the Christian tradition, and (b) do not represent a successful overcoming of the Enlightenment. This complex view of modernity is one that Balthasar arrived at early on in his career. It is evident in his three volume *Apokalypse der deutschen Seele: Studien zu einer Lehre von letzten Haltungen* (Salzburg, Austria: Pustet, 1937-39) that while Balthasar thinks that German Idealism (vol.1), Nietzsche (vol. 2), and existentialist modalities of thought (vol. 3) represent advances on the Enlightenment, he is not convinced that they represent adequate responses.

[4] If outside the trilogy *Apokalypse* is the crucial work, other works that make an important contribution to Balthasar's understanding of modernity as representing a fundamental challenge to Christian belief, practice, and form of life include *A Theology of History* (New York: Sheed & Ward, 1963); *The God Question and Modern Man*, tr. Hilda Graef (New York Seabury Press, 1967); *The Moment of Christian Witness*, tr. William Beckley (San Francisco: Ignatius Press, 1994). Originally published as *Cordula oder der Ernstfall* (Einsiedeln, Switzerland: Johannes Verlag, 1966); *Bernanos: An Ecclesial Existence*, tr. Erasmo Leiva-Merikakis (San Francisco: Ignatius Press, 1996). The German version appeared in 1971 from Balthasar's publishing house, *Johannes Verlag*, as *Gelebte Kirche Bernanos*.

[5] Hans Urs von Balthasar, *The Glory of the Lord: A Theological Aesthetics. Vol. 1: Seeing the Form*, ed. Joseph Fessio, S.J. and John Riches, tr. Erasmo Leiva-Merikakis (San Francisco: Ignatius Press, 1982); *The Glory of the Lord: A Theological Aesthetics. Vol. 5: The Realm of Metaphysics in the Modern Age*, ed. John Riches; tr. Oliver Davies *et al.* (San Francisco: Ignatius Press, 1991); *Theo-Logic. Theological Logical Theory. Vol.1: Truth of the World*, tr. Adrian J. Walker (San Francisco: Ignatius Press, 2000). This represents the translation of *Theologik: Erster Band: Wahrheit der Welt* (Einsiedeln, Switzerland: Johannes Verlag, 1985). The only difference between this volume and *Wahreit: Ein Versuch* (Einsiedeln: Verlagsanstalt Benziger, 1947) is the addition of a second introduction. See also *Theo-Drama: Theological Dramatic Theory. Vol. 1. Prolegomena*, tr. Graham Harrison (San Francisco: Ignatius Press, 1988).

[6] For method and procedural rationality, see *TL1*, 71, 84, 103-04, 171-72. The issue of breaking the bond of the relation between theology and philosophy is a much larger issue, indeed, something of a meta-issue, which if it is implied throughout the text, is rendered thematic in the second introduction that first appeared in the 1985 German edition.

[7] As we will see substantively throughout this and the following volume, Erich Przywara is a major influence on Balthasar's thought. In this respect, we find nothing exaggerated in Balthasar's laudation with respect to his dependence on Przywara's work to which Thomas O'Meara so vigorously objects. But just as important to Balthasar is the form of Przywara's theology which is essentially that of

cultural engagement. See Thomas F. O'Meara, *Erich Przywara, S.J.: His Theology and his World* (Notre Dame: University of Notre Dame, 2002), 133-39. See also O'Meara's fine notes (226-30). A similar point can be made about the influence of Guardini, even if there can be no doubt that for Balthasar Przywara remains the decisive influence as well as being in his view the theological giant. Again, one can see numerous content influences, especially in the areas of Christology and theological anthropology (with Guardini's view of prayer as especially important). See *Romano Guardini: Reform from the Source*, tr. Albert K.Wimmer (San Francisco: Ignatius Press, 2010).

[8] This topic will be treated in detail in the second volume of *An Anatomy of Misremembering*, so I will not say much here. I have given a provisional account of Balthasar's agreement and disagreement with Heidegger's genealogy of modernity in my 'Von Balthasar: Valorization and Critique of Heidegger's Genealogy of Modernity,' in Peter J. Casarella and George P. Schner (ed.), *Christian Spirituality and the Culture of Modernity: The Thought of Louis Dupré* (Grand Rapids, MI: Eerdmans, 1998), 123-58. The crucial texts in the trilogy for understanding the relation between Balthasar and Heidegger are *GL1*, *GL5*, and *TL1*. See also my essay 'Balthasar and the Unwelcoming of Heidegger,' in *The Grandeur of Reason: Religion, Tradition, and Universalism*, ed. Peter Chandler and Conor Cunningham (Oxford: SPC, 2010), 264-98.

[9] Relevant works of Hans-Georg Gadamer: *Truth and Method*, tr. Garett Barden and John Cumming (New York: Seabury Press, 1976); *Philosophical Hermeneutics*, tr. David E. Linge (Berkeley, Los Angeles: University of California Press, 1976). Despite this commitment to Heidegger's finitist view of truth, Gadamer still owes much to Hegel's sense of the historical shape of truth as conveyed in symbols, narratives, and institutions.

[10] Here Balthasar's reflections on the Spirit in *GL1* and *TL3* are especially important, even if Balthasar refuses to make the process of tradition a zero-sum game between Christ and the Spirit: the Spirit is always the Spirit of Christ and Christ is from the beginning empowered by the Spirit. Outside the trilogy Balthasar's main reflections are gathered into two volumes. See *Explorations in Theology. Vol. 3. Creator Spirit*, tr. Brian McNeil, C.R.V. (San Francisco: Ignatius Press, 1993). Originally published as *Skizzen zur Theologie: Bd. 3. Spiritus Creator* (Einsiedeln, Switzerland: Johannes Verlag, 1967); also *Explorations in Theology. Vol. 4. Spirit and Institution*, tr. Edward T. Oakes, S. J. (San Francisco: Ignatius Press, 1995). Originally published as *Pneuma und Institution* (Einsiedeln, Switzerland: Johannes Verlag, 1974).

[11] See *Truth is Symphonic: Aspects of Christian Pluralism*, tr. Graham Harrison (San Francisco: Ignatius Press, 1989). Originally published as *Die Wahrheit is Symphonisch: Aspekte des christlichen Pluralismus* (Einsiedeln, Switzerland: Johannes Verlag, 1972). I have treated Balthasar's theological, and more specifically christological and pneumatological form of pluralism in my 'Between Tübingen and Postmodernity,' in *Modern Theology* 14.3 Summer (1998), 325-53.

[12] G. W. F. Hegel, *Phenomenology of Spirit*, tr. A. V. Miller (Oxford: Oxford University Press, 1977); *Lectures on the Philosophy of Religion*, 3 volumes, ed. Peter C. Hodgson, tr. R.F. Brown, Peter C. Hodgson, and J.M. Steward (Berkeley: University of California Press, 1984-87). One might also consider *Philosophy of Right*, tr. T.

M. Knox (Oxford: Oxford University Press, 1967) (First Published in 1952 by Clarendon Press). There are a number of texts that cover Hegel's relation to the Enlightenment. These include: Laurence Dickey, *Hegel: Religion, Economics, and the Politics of Spirit, 1770-1807* (Cambridge: Cambridge University Press, 1987); Robert Gascoigne, *Religion, Rationality, and Community: Sacred and Secular in the Thought of Hegel and his Critics* (The Hague: Martinus Nijhoff, 1985), 1-65; Judith Shklar, *Freedom and Independence: A Study of the Political Ideas of Hegel's Phenomenology of Mind* (Cambridge: Harvard University Press, 1975); Charles Taylor, *Hegel* (Cambridge: Cambridge University Press, 1975). The work of Frederick C. Beiser is also of considerable value. See his *Enlightenment, Revolution, and Romanticism: The Genesis of Modern German Political Thought, 1790-1800* (Cambridge, MA: Harvard University Press, 1992); *German Idealism: The Struggle Against Subjectivism, 1781-1801* (Cambridge, MA: Harvard University Press, 2002).

[13] In his treatment of the Enlightenment in the *Phenomenology* Hegel is especially sensitive to this contraction. See *PS*#558-61. In making this diagnosis, Hegel proves to be a fundamental inspiration of the sociology of religion and especially of the critical theory of Adorno and Horkheimer, for whom a critique of instrumental reason is pivotal.

[14] Much of the more genetically-oriented literature on Hegel has made this point. Such is the case with the very different works of Stephen Crites, H. S. Harris, and Terry Pinkard. See Crites, *Dialectic and Gospel in the Development of Hegel's Thought* (University Park: Pennsylvania State University Press, 1998); H. S. Harris, *Hegel's Development. Vol. 1. Towards the Sunlight, 1770-1801* (Oxford: Clarendon Press, 1972); *Hegel's Development. Vol. 2: Night Thoughts (Jena 1801-1806)* (Oxford: Clarendon Press, 1983); Pinkard, *Hegel's Phenomenology: The Sociality of Reason* (Cambridge: Cambridge University Press, 1994).

[15] The notion of 'Recollection' or *Erinnerung* is everywhere in Hegel and has a number of different uses. Arguably, the most typical use is to be found in the *Phenomenology* when Hegel speaks explicitly of 'recollection' as being a property of Spirit itself. It is not incidental that he does this in the very last paragraph of the *Phenomenology* (#808).

[16] Here I intend a contrast between Augustine and Hegel, and gesture that Balthasar belongs in the Augustinian tradition.

[17] Here I borrow language I use elsewhere with respect to another commentator on Hegel to characterize Balthasar's understanding of the relation between Christianity and Hegelian philosophy, or more formally stated, between representation (*Vorstellung*) and thought (*Begriff*). The *Aufhebung* of Christian representation represents first a softening up of its dogmatic claims, so that the symbols and narratives of Christianity may intend one thing but mean another, and subsequent to the softening, a justification of philosophical or dialectical discourse as the only adequate discourse for religion, since it is only within philosophy that religion can be rationally justified. See my article, 'The Impossibility of a Christian Reading of the *Phenomenology of Spirit*: H. S. Harris on Hegel's Liquidation of Christianity,' *The Owl of Minerva*, vol. 33, no. 1 (Fall/Winter) 2001-02, 45-95. The texts under discussion were H. S. Harris' two volume commentary on the *Phenomenology*, *Hegel's Ladder 1: The Pilgrimage of Reason* (Indianapolis: Hackett

Publishing Co., 1997); *Hegel's Ladder 2: The Odyssey of Spirit* (Indianapolis: Hackett Publishing Co., 1997).

[18] See Karl Barth, *Protestant Theology in the Nineteenth Century*, tr. B. Couzens and J. Bowden (London: SCM Press, 1972). Part of this was previously published as *From Rousseau to Ritschl* (London: SCM Press, 1959). Barth objected to much of what nineteenth century critics of Hegel objected to, especially his rationalism and necessitarianism, but he does not develop their arguments, nor is there anything remotely like Kierkegaard's intensity.

[19] The *Glaubenslehre* is published in 1821. The 1824 Lectures available in *LPR1* represent a concerted attack against this text in terms of theological method. Hegel had, however, indirectly – but with greater panache – attacked this text in 1822 in his 'Foreword to H. F. W. Hinrich's *Die Religion im inneren Verhältnis zur Wissenschaft*,' tr. A. V. Miller, in *Beyond Epistemology*, ed. Frederick G. Weiss (The Hague: Martinus Nijhoff, 1974), 227-44. For a new translation of this text, with critical commentary and a comprehensive study of its importance, see Eric von der Luft, *Hegel, Hinrichs, and Schleiermacher on Feeling and Reason in Religion: The Texts of their 1821-22 Debate*. Studies in German Thought and History, Vol. 3 (Lewiston & Queenstown: Edwin Mellen Press, 1987).

[20] The acceptance of Balthasar as precursor is both much more pronounced and much more self-conscious in the case of Marion and French Communio thinkers such as Lacoste and Chrétien. Analyzing this trajectory will be part of the agenda of the second volume of this work.

[21] Here I am availing of the language of Jean-Louis Chrétien. See his essay on 'The Unforgettable,' in *The Unforgettable and the Unhoped For*, tr. Jeffrey Bloechl (New York: Fordham University Press, 2002), 78-98. Actually all of the various essays collected in this volume cohere around the idea of 'forgetting' as the correlative of the divine transcendence as the 'unforgettable.'

[22] The two crucial texts of Moltmann remain *The Crucified God* and *Trinity and the Kingdom*. See *The Crucified God: The Cross of Christ as the Foundation and Criticism of Christian Theology*, tr. R. A. Wilson and Robert Bowden (London: SCM Press, 1974); *Trinity and the Kingdom: The Doctrine of God*, tr. Margaret Kohl (New York: Harper & Row, 1981). For Jüngel, see *God as the Mystery of the World: On the Foundations of the Theology of the Crucified in the Dispute between Theism and Atheism*, tr. Darell L. Guden (Grand Rapids, MI: Eerdmans, 1983).

[23] The 'irrevocable past' is not the past as such. The issue here has to do with the validity of non-philosophical absolute forms of discourse, practices, and forms of life as well as non-absolute forms of discourse, practices, and forms of life. Art and religion, and more specifically Christian discourse, practices, and forms of life, continue to exist, so one is not speaking about temporal pastness. The Preface to the *Phenomenology* is especially apt in adopting the retrospective point of view in which historical and contemporary forms (*Gestalten*) of discourses, practices, and forms of life constitute a 'museum,' which paradoxically makes the contemporary manifestations of Spirit alive.

[24] This is the language sometime recurred to by Catherine Pickstock in *After Writing: On the Liturgical Consummation of Philosophy* (Oxford: Blackwell, 1998). Of course, this mode of location is not unique to Pickstock and has been made

popular by Dorothee Soelle. Interestingly, perhaps here Derrida, who is abjured by Pickstock, helps to make sense of the specific charge with respect to Hegel.

[25] There exists significant agreement among Balthasar scholars that Holy Saturday is a pivotal theme of Balthasar's theology. While Balthasar gives expression to this theme both inside and outside the trilogy, arguably his best-known treatment remains that presented in *Mysterium Paschale*, tr. Aidan Nichols, O.P. (Edinburgh: T & T Clark, 1999). A good early treatment of the theme in Balthasar is provided by John Saward. See his *The Mysteries of March: Hans Urs von Balthasar on the Incarnation and Easter* (London: SPCK, 1990). A much more thorough, if unbalanced, treatment, which covers all of Balthasar's expressions on this topic, is to be found in the controversial book by Alyssa Lyra Pitstick, *Light in Darkness: Hans Urs von Balthasar and the Catholic Doctrine of Christ's Descent into Hell* (Grand Rapids, MI: Eerdmans, 2007). Neither Saward nor Pitstick think of Holy Saturday as suggesting among other things a theology of tradition. I will suggest – if not necessarily demonstrate – in the body of the text how Balthasar's view of Holy Saturday could bear this kind of reading.

[26] See *Theologik*, Band II, *Wahrheit Gottes* (Einsiedeln, Switzerland: Johannes Verlag, 1985); *Theologik*, Band III, *Der Geist der Wahrheit* (Einsiedeln, Switzerland: Johannes Verlag, 1987).

[27] For a convenient discussion of these forms of negative theology, which include Kant, Jacobi, and Schleiermacher, see my *The Heterodox Hegel*, 31-44.

[28] See *Vorlesungen* über *die* Ästhetik, ed. E. Moldenhauer and K. Michel, Vols. 13-15, *Sämtliche Werke* (Frankfurt: Suhrkamp, 1970). For a convenient English translation, see *Aesthetics: Lectures on the Fine Arts*, tr. T. M. Knox, 2 Vols. (Oxford: Clarendon Press, 1995).

[29] Here we work backward from Adrienne von Speyr. Of course, Balthasar was a spiritual mentor for Adrienne from the 1940's and clearly exercised enormous influence over her. On his own account, however, it was very much a two-way street, to the point that he suggested on a few occasions that it would be difficult to separate out their work. See especially, *First Glance at Adrienne von Speyr*, tr. Antje Lawry and Sr. Sergia Englund, O.C.D. (San Francisco: Ignatius Press, 1981); *My Work in Retrospect* (San Francisco: Ignatius Press, 1992), *Our Task: A Report and a Plan*, tr. John Saward (San Francisco: Ignatius Press, 1994). For a good synoptic accounts of the relation of Balthasar to Adrianne von Speyr, see Aidan Nichols, *Divine Fruitfulness: A Guide Through Balthasar's Theology Beyond the Trilogy* (Washington, DC: Catholic University of America Press, 2007), 109-23; see also Danielle Nussberger, 'Saint as Wellspring: A Critical Appraisal of Hans Urs von Balthasar' (PhD dissertation, University of Notre Dame, 2007), ch. 5. For Thérèse of Liseux, see *Thérèse of Liseux: The Story of a Mission* (New York: Sheed and Ward, 1954). For Catherine of Genoa, see Balthasar's treatment of 'The Metaphysics of the Saints' (*GL5*, 48-140, esp. 99-102). Julian of Norwich is not mentioned often explicitly by Balthasar (exception is *GL5*, 85-8), but Balthasar's probative view of 'universal salvation' articulated above all in *Dare We Hope* gives some evidence of influence. Frederick Bauerschmidt's book on Julian, with its red thread of universal salvation, provides further evidence. See *Julian of Norwich and the Mystical Body Politic of Christ* (Notre Dame: University of Notre Dame Press, 1999).

[30] For Balthasar's use of the musical metaphor as applied to tradition, see *Truth is Symphonic: Aspects of Christian Pluralism*, tr. Graham Harrison (San Francisco: Ignatius Press, 1987). Originally published as *Die Wahrheit ist symphonisch: Aspekte der Christlichen Pluralismus* (Einsiedeln, Switzerland: Johannes Verlag, 1972). See my essay on Balthasar's view of tradition, 'Balthasar: Between Tübingen and Postmodernity,' in *Modern Theology*, 14.3 Summer (1998), 325-53.

[31] In the second volume of *The Anatomy of Misremembering*, I make the case that Augustine is more important in Balthasar's resistance of Heidegger than Irenaeus, although no more than in the case of Hegel is one talking about a zero-sum game. Outside of reflection on Balthasar I have broached the Augustine-Heidegger relation in a number of different venues. See 'Mystery of Iniquity: Augustine versus Heidegger,' in *Martin Heidegger's Interpretation of Saint Augustine*, in *Collectanea Augustiniana*, ed. Frederick von Fleteren (Lewiston, NY: Edwin Mellen Press, 2005), 383-440; 'Answering Back: Augustine's Critique of Heidegger,' in *Human Destinies: Philosophical Essays in Memory of Gerald Hanratty*, ed. Fran O'Rourke (Notre Dame: University of Notre Dame Press, 2011).

[32] I made this case with some vigor in my 'Balthasar: Between Tübingen and Postmodernity,' esp. 334-41.

[33] For Balthasar's appreciative reflection on Matthias Joseph Scheeben, see *GL1*, 104-17. Aidan Nichols speaks briefly and usefully on Balthasar's appreciation of Scheeben in his commentary on *The Glory of the Lord*. See *The Word Has Been Abroad: A Guide Through Balthasar's Aesthetics* (Edinburgh: T & T Clark, 1998), 19-21.

[34] See my *Theology and the Spaces of Apocalyptic* (Milwaukee: Marquette University Press, 2009), 45-55 (Balthasar), 77-83 (Metz).

[35] Louis Althusser, *The Spectre of Hegel* (London: Verso, 1990).

[36] Jacques Derrida, *Specters of Marx: The State of Debt, The Work of Mourning, and the New International*, tr. Peggy Kamuf (New York: Routledge, 1994). What can be said with respect to the 'undead' element of Marx can also be said with respect to the 'undead' element of Hegel, who, however one differentiates him from Marx, nonetheless functions as a necessary presupposition.

[37] From the very beginning Derrida is fully accepting of the importance of Hegel as a philosopher in French philosophy, and insists that engagement with Hegel is all but a requirement of philosophy. His 1974 classic *Glas* represents however not only an attack against Hegelian philosophy, but an attack against Hegelian philosophy to the extent to which it claims to sum up and redescribe Christian discourse. See *Glas*, tr. Richard Rand and John Leavey, Jr. (Lincoln: University of Nebraska Press, 1986). That Derrida does not depart too much from this view can be seen in the long preface to Catherine Malabou's *The Future of Hegel: Plasticity, Temporality, and Dialectic*, tr. Lizabeth During (New York: Routledge, 2005). For the kind of assistance Derrida gives to a theological – indeed specifically Balthasarian – critique of Hegel, see my 'Hegel, Theodicy, and the Invisibility of Waste,' in *The Providence of God*, ed. Francesca Aran Murphy and Philip Ziegler (Edinburgh: T & T Clark, 2009), 75-104.

[38] Hegel's work is replete with references to death in both non-religious and religious registers. For the former, see esp. the *Encyclopedia* #349, 367 zu; also

#221-22, #251, where death signifies the erasure of the concrete particular. The *Encyclopedia* also connects death more specifically with the death of Jesus (*Enc* #381), but the religious connection is much more to the fore in the *Phenomenology* (Preface, and Section 7 on Revealed Religion) and the *Lectures on the Philosophy of Religion*. While on some occasions, Hegel seems to underscore the paradoxical coincidence of death and life (*PS* #19), for the most part there is the suggestion that death is the condition of the possibility of life, but that there is a gap between death and the arrival of life. This interval is at once the hiatus between the implicit arrival of life and the non-cessation of death. In this sense, it is at once the interval of parousia and the specter.

[39] The evocation of Irenaeus is deliberate here. Irenaeus speaks in the preface of Bk 2 of *Against Heresies* of the 'detection' (*detectionis* in Latin, *elenchos* in Greek) and 'overthrow' (*eversionis* in Latin, *anatrope* in Greek).

PART 1

[1] Of course, whether in fact there is a 'pre-Christian' gnosis has greatly exercised 20th century interpretation of Gnosticism, even if in the more recent historiography this question is no longer regarded as truly exigent. Needless to say, when the answer was affirmative, there was more than one conjugation of what it was. Answers ran the gamut from Iranian dualism, a kind of melange of esoteric discourses of a dualistic sort, and a mutation within Judaism.

[2] In addition to the *Phenomenology*, both the *Lectures on the Philosophy of History* and *Philosophy of Right* are important. See *Lectures on the Philosophy of History*, tr. J. Sibree (New York: Dover, 1956).

Chapter 1

[1]. See my article, 'Von Balthasar: Valorization and Critique of Heidegger's Genealogy of Modernity,' 123-26.

[2]. See Hegel, *The Science of Logic*, tr. A. V. Miller (New York: Humanities Press, 1969), 39-49, where the subject of 'beginning' opens Hegel's reflection on the first division of the Logic, that is, that of Being.

[3]. See *The Theology of Karl Barth*, tr. Edward T. Oakes (San Francisco: Ignatius Press, 1992). There is no reason to discount the conventional view that Balthasar's 1952 book represents one of the most serious Catholic engagements with the thought of Karl Barth. Although Balthasar refuses to paint Barth with a sectarian brush and acknowledges that as a matter of fact Barth does engage cultural discourse, he worries why this remains merely on the level of fact. For two different accounts of the relation between Balthasar and Barth, see Rodney A. Howsare, *Hans Urs von Balthasar and Protestantism: The Ecumenical Implications of his Theological Style* (London: T & T Clark, 2005), 77-99; also John Webster's essay on Barth and Balthasar in *The Cambridge Companion to Hans Urs von Balthasar*, ed. Edward T. Oakes and David Moss (Cambridge: Cambridge University Press, 2004), 241-55.

[4]. If all of Claudel's work is important to Balthasar, this is especially so with respect to this play, which serves a guiding role in *Theo-Drama*. Operating as it does under the banner of an homage to the Baroque dramatist Lope de Vega, it shows the capacity to make contact with a much earlier Christian (and Stoic) form of drama under modern conditions. Merely ironic, or self-reflexive drama, is not, therefore, a historical necessity.

[5]. This is precisely what Hegel is denying in claiming in the Introduction to his *Lectures on Aesthetics* that his treatment is 'scientific.'

[6]. See Hegel's discussion of Shakespeare in the first and second volumes of the Äs*thetik*, although Shakespeare is also very much a presence in Hegel's discussion of modern drama based on character rather than collision in action in the third volume. See Ästhetik, Vol. 13, 300-03; Vol. 14, 219-22.

[7]. For Hegel's championing of *Antigone*, see especially *Phenomenology* #437, #471-76, #736. Hegel's view of tragedy is often recurred to in the secondary literature on Hegel with the aim not simply of clarifying his aesthetic preferences, but of providing a template of dialectic (e.g. Robert Williams). Needless to say, this is not an entirely plausible view insofar as Hegel's view of dialectic necessarily involves a moment of reconciliation. By contrast, *Antigone* suggests something like an aporia between the demands of the State and the family. Even if Hegel's fuller treatment of the movement from Greek tragedy to comedy in his section on 'the spiritual work of art' in the *Phenomenology* (#736-747) indicates his view that relatively speaking Greek comedy represents a fall, it is still the case that the pattern of dialectic is overall comic in its commitment to resolution.

[8]. In the *Phenomenology* the comedies of Aristophanes are not a bolt from the blue but rather are the result of a subjectification within tragedy itself. Since the work of Sophocles is summed up by *Antigone*, the implication is that this subjectification in which the heavens are emptied and fate rules over all is illustrated in and by the drama of Euripides. See Hegel's discussion of the dissolution of drama in *Phenomenology* #736-39. See also Ästhetik, Vol. 15, 546-49.

[9]. See Ästhetik, Vol. 15, 520-33.

[10]. For Nietzsche, see *The Birth of Tragedy and the Case of Wagner*, tr. Walter Kaufman (New York: Random House, 1967), 15-144.

[11]. Here it is best to remind oneself that Balthasar is making these literary judgments not simply as a theologian, but also as a Germanist. To the extent to which Balthasar does function as a Germanist, he is involved in discussions regarding Euripides that exercised the period of Goethe (*Goethezeit*). Although Goethe did not see Euripides as a Romantic author *avant la lettre*, he did think that the dramas of Euripides exhibited a distancing from the ethos of the Greeks not found in Sophocles, and in this respect set the stage for the breakdown of the Greek ethos in the comedy of Aristophanes. Goethe also did not think that Euripides provided a dramatic model to be followed in the modern period. Schiller, who was more open to Shakespeare, was also more open to Euripides, and felt that the move beyond Greek ethos can and should be sustained without disintegration into irony. For a comprehensive discussion of the reception of Euripides, see Uwe Petersen, *Goethe und Euripides: Untersuchungen zur Euripides-Rezeption in der Goethezeit* (Heidelberg: Carl Winter Universitätsverlag, 1974). Balthasar finds himself more

nearly on Schiller's than Goethe's side, but is unwilling to accept that the gap opened up is a gap to be filled by subjectivity rather than transcendence.

[12]. See Simone Weil, *Intimations of Christianity among the Ancient Greeks*, tr. E. C. Geissbuhler (London: Routledge & Kegan Paul, 1972), 9, 13, 22-3. See also my article 'Countermimesis and Simone Weil's Christian Neoplatonism,' in *The Christian Neoplatonism of Simone Weil*, ed. E. Jane Doering and Eric O. Springsted (Notre Dame: University of Notre Dame Press, 2004), 181-208, esp. 184. While overall Weil seems to favor Aeschylus and Sophocles over Euripides, the last named and especially his *Hippolytus*, on some occasions at least seems to get equal billing. See *Intimations of Christianity*, 79, 100.

[13]. This has been a major point in Hegel commentary. Often this point is made in a complimentary way with a view to (a) maintaining continuity between dramatic discourse and that of philosophy, and to (b) suggesting that there is an openendedness implied in dialectic which cannot be reduced entirely to resolution. The work of Robert R.Williams is exemplary in this respect. See among other works, *Recognition: Fichte and Hegel on the Other* (Albany, NY: SUNY Press, 1992); *Hegel's Ethics of Recognition* (Berkeley and Los Angeles: University of California Press, 1997).

[14]. D. C. Schindler is particularly adept at tracking the Thomistic dimension of Balthasar's metaphysics, and especially the way in which this form of Thomism is inflected by Heidegger. For him the two most important influences with regard to this aspect of Balthasar's program are Gustav Siewerth and Ferdinand Ulrich. Schindler does not attempt to adjudicate between the relative influence of these figures and Przywara, although it could be said that with respect to *Wahrheit* at least Przywara's *Analogia Entis* essentially sets the basic metaphysical terms. See his *Hans Urs von Balthasar and the Dramatic Structure of Truth: A Philosophical Investigation* (New York: Fordham University Press, 2004).

[15]. *Apok 3*, 193-315. While Heidegger is not an explicit object of analysis in *Wahrheit*, he is everywhere in the text. See *TL1*, 25-6, 36-7, 71, 82, 87, 99, 180, 189, 197, 206-07 *inter alia*.

[16]. For a discussion of the relation between Balthasar and Heidegger on the role of Descartes, see my 'Von Balthasar's Critique of Heidegger's Genealogy of Modernity,' 134-39. In a way similar to Cornelio Fabro, who engages Heidegger from the vantage point of a retrieval of Aquinas which involves a reflection on the meaning of *esse*, Balthasar thinks that Descartes represents a turn to the self-legislating subject that plays out in modernity. See Fabro's famous 'enucleation' thesis in *God in Exile: Modern Atheism: A Study in the Internal Dynamic of Modern Atheism from its Roots in the Cartesian Cogito to the Present Day* (Westminister, MD: Newman Press, 1968).

[17]. I will speak to Balthasar's attitude to Heidegger's trope of the 'play' (*Spiel*) in the next volume. With respect to *List der Vernunft*, which is the trope that Hegel appeals to in the Introduction to the *Lectures on the Philosophy of History* to suggest a teleological pattern of meaning in history that occurs behind the backs of the actors, the assertion of the 'cunning of reason' is in the Introduction associated with Hegel's appreciation of Anaxogoras' *Nous* and the Neoplatonic *Logos*.

[18]. Hegel makes this point often enough throughout his work, but especially in *Lectures on the Philosophy of History*; *Lectures on the History of Modern Philosophy 3*, and

Lectures on the Philosophy of Right for his readers to be in any doubt with respect to this point. This is a point underscored by any number of Hegel commentators, not excluding Charles Taylor in his *Hegel* (Cambridge: Cambridge University Press, 1975); and his *Hegel and Modern Society* (Cambridge: Cambridge University Press, 1979). A good recent expression of this consensus is provided by Thomas A. Lewis. See his *Freedom and Tradition in Hegel: Reconsidering Anthropology, Ethics, and Religion* (Notre Dame: University of Notre Dame Press, 2005).

[19]. *LHP3*, 220-52, esp. 221.

[20]. The most famous expression of this vocation is to be found in the Preface of the *Phenomenology*, where referring to the conventional interpretation of philosophy (*philosophia*) as love of wisdom, Hegel argues that the love should and can attain its object and become knowledge or wisdom itself (*sophia*). In addition, the last paragraphs of the *Phenomenology* represent a kind of celebration of arrival.

[21]. Eric Voegelin wrote a number of provocative pieces on Hegel. Some of the more important include: 'On Hegel: A Study in Sorcery,' in *The Collective Works of Eric Voegelin*, Volume 12, *Published Essays, 1966-1987*, ed. introd. Ellis Sandoz (Baton Rouge: Louisiana State University Press, 1990), 213-55; 'Wisdom and the Magic of the Extreme: A Meditation,' in *The Collected Works*, Volume 12, 315-75; 'The Eclipse of Reality,' in *The Collected Works of Eric Voegelin*, Volume 28, *'What is History?' And other Unpublished Essays*, ed. Thomas A. Hollweck and Paul Caringella (Baton Rouge: Louisiana State University Press, 1990), 11-162; *From Enlightenment to Revolution* (Durham: Duke University Press, 1975), 240-302. See my essay, 'Voegelin and the Troubled Greatness of Hegel,' in *Eric Voegelin and the Continental Tradition: Explorations in Modern Political Thought*, ed. Lee Trepanier and Steven McQuire (Missouri: Missouri University Press, 2010). The philosopher William Desmond has engaged Hegel throughout his career in his constructive work as well as commentary. Included under the latter are *Hegel's God: A Counterfeit Double?* (Aldershot: Ashgate, 2002), in addition to the already cited *Art and the Absolute.* See my review of Desmond's Hegel book in *Clio* 33.4 Summer (2004), 251-57. The same is true of John Milbank. His most recent expression of engagement with Hegel is also his most concerted. See *The Montrosity of Christ: Paradox or Dialectic*, ed. Creston Davis (Cambridge, MA: MIT Press, 2009). See my review of this book in *Modern Theology* 26:2, April (2010), 278-86.

[22]. See *TL1*, 40-1, 47, 80, 190 for the notion of transcendence. For the notion of mystery, which is its correlative, see *TL1*, 102, 131, 204. Mystery here is defined positively rather than negatively, or more specifically as ontologically excessive rather than epistemically unavailable. For a clarification of the distinction between positive and negative mystery, see O'Regan, 'Newman and von Balthasar: The Christological Contexting of the Numinous,' in Église et théologie, vol. 26, no. 2 Spring (1995), 165-202, esp. 184-202.

[23]. For good English translation of these works, see Theodor W. Adorno, *Negative Dialectics*, tr. E. B. Ashton (New York: Seabury Press, 1973); Emmanuel Levinas, *Totality and Infinity: An Essay on Exteriority*, tr. Alphonso Lingis (Pittsburgh: Duquesne University Press, 1969); Jean-François Lyotard, *The Postmodern Condition: A Report on Knowledge*, tr. Geoff Bennington and Brian Massumi, foreword by Frederick Jameson (Minneapolis: University of Minnesota Press, 1993); Jacques

Derrida, *Glas*, tr. John P. Leavey, Jr. and Richard Rand (Lincoln and London: University of Nebraska Press, 1986).

[24]. Adorno, 'Parataxis: On Hölderlin's Later Poetry,' in *Notes to Literature*, Vol. 2, ed. Rolf Tiedermann, tr. Shierry Weber Nicholson (New York: Columbia University Press, 1992), 109-49.

[25]. For Adorno on Beckett, see *Notes to Literature*, Vol. 1, ed. Rolf Tiedemann, tr. Shierry Weber Nicholson (New York: Columbia University Press, 1991), 241-75. For Adorno on Schoenberg's atonal music, see *The Philosophy of Modern Music*, tr. A. C. Mitchell and W. V. Blomster (New York: Seabury, 1973), esp. 136-47.

[26]. For Lyotard, modernist painting is his privileged illustration of the sublime, which he interprets after Kant in a noetic rather than ontological fashion. For his major reflections on modernist painting, see *Que peindre? Adamai, Arakawa, Buren* (Paris: Éditions de la Différence, 1987). Lyotard's major statement on the sublime is conducted by means of an interpretation of Kant. See *Lessons on the Analytic of the Sublime: Kant's Critique of Judgment* (Stanford, CA: Stanford University Press, 1994). Although Derrida's view of painting and that of Lyotard match up no better than their respective philosophies, one could argue that there is a similar commitment to the sublime. Truly helpful in making the connection is J. M. Bernstein's *The Fate of Art: Aesthetic Alienation from Kant to Derrida and Adorno* (University Park, PA:The Pennsylvania State University Press, 1992). See especially Chapter 3, "The Deconstructive Sublime: Derrida's *The Truth in Painting*,' 136-87.

[27]. For accessible examples of Derrida's reflections on Mallarmé and Joyce, see *Acts of Literature*, ed. Derek Attridge (New York and London: Routledge, 1992), 110-26 and 253-309, respectively.

[28]. For Balthasar's treatment of *Die Zauberflöte*, see his essay, 'The Farewell Trio,' in *Explorations in Theology, Volume 3*, 523-33. A collection of Balthasar's writings on Mozart were published in 1988. See *Bekenntnis zu Mozart* (Einsiedeln, Switzerland: Johannes Verlag, 1988). Nothing that Balthasar says about music in his mature writings suggests that he has fundamentally changed his commitment to harmony and melody which more avant-garde composers such as Schoenberg and Berg decried. Interesting in this respect is his very early work *Die Entfaltung der musikalischen Idee. Versuch einer Synthese der Musik* (Braunschweig, 1925). Nichols provides a very good account of what is one of Balthasar's very earliest publications. See *Scattering the Seed: A Guide through Balthasar's Early Writings on Philosophy and the Arts* (Washingon: CUA Press, 2006), 1-8.

[29]. *Theo-Drama 1* exhibits Balthasar's incredibly high view of Shakespeare, which has its origins in German Romanticism. See *TD1*, 400-09; 465-78 *inter alia.* Interestingly, in terms of the rich and variegated anthropology illustrated by Shakespeare, Balthasar does not prioritize the tragedies. There is much more commentary on the comedies and the history plays than there is on the four great tragedies of *Macbeth*, *Othello*, *Hamlet*, and *Lear.*

[30]. Interpretively Balthasar is fairly even-handed, and does not especially single out these two poems, important as they are. In a short span he manages to touch on a significant part of Hölderlin's oeuvre.

[31]. This is the view that Adorno tends to espouse not only influentially in *Negative Dialectics* but throughout his entire oeuvre.

[32]. Adorno, *The Jargon of Authenticity*, tr. Knut Tarnowski and Frederick Will (Evanston: Northwestern University Press, 1973).

[33]. Mark C. Taylor, *Erring: A Postmodern A/Theology* (Chicago: Chicago University Press, 1984).

[34]. This is famously indicated by Levinas' treatment of Descartes' understanding of the idea of the infinite in *Totality and Infinity*, 49-50.

[35]. The figures of Gregory of Nyssa, Pseudo-Dionysius, Maximus the Confessor, and Bonaventure are important throughout Marion's work, and especially his early work. Bonaventure and his notion of 'good' beyond being is especially important in *God without Being*, tr. Thomas A. Carlson (Chicago: University of Chicago Press, 1991), 74-5. Marion reflects in concentrated fashion on Pseudo-Dionysius in an extended essay in *The Idol and Distance: Five Studies*, tr. Thomas A. Carlson (New York: Fordham University Press, 2001), 139-95.

[36]. Caputo's most sustained attack against the ultimacy of Neoplatonic-style negative theology and his favoring of deconstruction is to be found in *The Prayers and Tears of Jacques Derrida: Religion without Religion* (Bloomington and Indianapolis: Indiana University Press, 1997). Of course, earlier in his career, in his studies of Aquinas and Eckhart, Caputo tended towards a position that he later disavows. Neoplatonic negative theology is insufficiently radical in what is 'beyond being' (*hyperousia*); for it is still a reality that grounds and is accessible, if not necessarily through cognition proper.

[37]. Necessarily included in the promotion of Neoplatonism as a carrier of a metaphysics of excess are the following: 'Can a Gift be Given? Prolegomena to a Future Trinitarian Metaphysic,' in *Modern Theology* 11.1, January (1995), 119-58; 'The Soul of Reciprocity, Part 1: Reciprocity Refused,' in *Modern Theology* 17.4, October (2001), 335-91. Among Milbank's most recent writings which demonstrate his ongoing fidelity to Neoplatonic comitments, see for example his dialogue with Slavoj Žižek in *The Monstrosity of Christ*, in which Milbank offers a spirited defense of Eckhart as the quintessential Christian Neoplatonist (129-33). On the basis of the suspicions that Balthasar expresses about Eckhart at the beginning of *Glory of the Lord 5*, it is fairly safe to conclude that Balthasar and Milbank fundamentally disagree. See my 'Balthasar and Eckhart: Theological Principles and Catholicity,' in *The Thomist* 60.2, April (1996), 1-37.

[38]. See 'Intensities,' in *Modern Theology* 15.5, Fall (1999), 445-97.

[39]. For the most part, both in *Apokalypse 1* (347 ff) and in *GL 5*, 513-46 *inter alia*, Balthasar's dominant concern is whether the overall drift in Schiller's plays and poems moves towards or away from Christianity. Even if Balthasar's interpretation of Schiller's work lacks detail, there can be no doubt that Balthasar thinks that it is these works rather than his more theoretical speculations that decide the issue. Balthasar does broach the latter outside the main body of his reflections on Schiller in *Apokalypse 1* (125-28) and speaks to the Über die ästhetische Erziehung des Menschen in terms of its overall aim to recast the Enlightenment and Kant in particular. Still, even here he points out that effectively Schiller succeeds in creating an 'aesthetic religion' that is hardly coextensive with traditional Christianity. As always Nichols is reliable. For Schiller in *Apokalypse*, see *Scattering the Seed*, 54-7, 90-8; for *Glory of the Lord 5*, see *The Word Has Been Abroad*, 176-78.

[40]. See *System of Transcendental Idealism*, tr. Peter Heath (Charlottesville: University Press of Virginia, 1978). Balthasar does not seem to focus on the *The System of Transcendental Idealism* either in *Apok 1* or *GL5*. Arguably, in both cases the accent tends to fall on the works of Schelling's middle period, exemplified by a text such as *Die Weltalter* (1815), which presents something like a theogony. Perhaps the closest Balthasar comes to focusing on the relative advantage of art over philosophy, as outlined in the *System of Transcendental Idealism*, is in *Apokalypse 1* (211).
[41]. As is clear from his defense of the *analogia entis* in his Barth book, Balthasar is anxious in a way that Barth is not, to insist on the relative autonomy of the created order.
[42]. At least 'high Romanticism.' There are certain features of Romanticism such as the emphasis on the fragment that are antithetical to Hegelianism. This will become important in Part 1 where we treat *in extenso* the relation between Balthasar and Benjamin. H. S. Harris and Charles Taylor are but two of a multitude of commentators on Hegel who foreground the connection. Of the two, Harris provides by far the greater amount of detail in his four huge archeological volumes on Hegel to which we have already referred.
[43]. Here Balthasar's view bears comparison with the views of both Louis Dupré and Hans Blumenberg. Louis Dupré is a reader of Balthasar and especially of his theological aesthetics. See his fine 'The Glory of the Lord: Hans Urs von Balthasar's Theological Aesthetic,' in *Communio* 16 (1989), 384-412. There is no evidence, however, that Dupré's view of the role of Renaissance thinkers is dependent on Balthasar's genealogy. In *Passage to Modernity* it seems clear that Dupré's influences tend to be intellectual historians such as Paul Oskar Kristeller.
[44]. See *GL5*, 29-47. I have dealt in some detail with Balthasar's anxiety concerning Eckhart's swerve from the theological tradition in 'Balthasar and Eckhart: Theological Principles and Catholicity,' in *The Thomist* 60.2, April (1996), 203-39.
[45]. On this point comparison with Hans Blumenberg is apt. For Blumenberg as well as Balthasar, the Italian Neoplatonist, burnt at the stake in 1600 for his heterodox views, is an important transitional figure from pre-modernity to modernity. However, whereas Blumenberg's reading is overwhelmingly positive, Balthasar's is negative. For Blumenberg's treatment, see *The Legitimacy of the Modern Age*, 549-96.
[46]. Marion is not concerned so much with the politics of elitism and exclusion as with the coherence of a position in which a special apparatus for knowing is suggested. In *Idol and Distance* apophaticism seems to be regulated by the appearance of Christ. This is especially evident in Marion's essays on Pseudo-Dionysius and Hölderlin. By contrast in *Sauf le nom* Derrida shifts attention from the religious epistemology issue, indeed even from the phenomenological issue of appearance to the politics of initiation with its promise of a particular kind of seeing. See *On the Name*, ed. Thomas Dutoit, tr. David Wood, John P. Leavey, JR., and Ian McLeod (Stanford: Stanford University Press, 1995), 34-85. For Marion's reply, which insists that Derrida has misunderstood him and negative theology, see 'In the Name: How to Avoid Speaking about It,' in *In Excess: Studies of Saturated Phenomena*, tr. Robyn Horner (New York: Fordham University Press, 2002), 128-62.
[47]. One could see Balthasar's reflections in *GL5* on the trajectory of mystical thought in the Rhineland School and beyond as providing historical examples

of the perfect match between contemplation and action. It would be rewarding to trace the relation between Balthasar and Thomas Merton, an early reader and active correspondent with Balthasar, on this point. Fed from the same sources, Merton is less anxious about a mystical thinker such as John of the Cross than Balthasar appears to be in his essay in *GL3*, even if the portrait is far from negative.

48. See especially *Two Sisters in the Spirit.* While Balthasar is understanding with respect to idiosyncracy, it is important that specialness not be confused with sainthood. He argues that idiosyncracy introduces an element of opacity when the real issue is to be transparent with respect to Christ. The presence of idiosyncracy and specialness, which are features of the biography of Thérèse, are put by Balthasar on the negative side of the ledger, and provide a reason for his relative preference of Elizabeth of Dijon.

49. For Franz von Baader's appropriation of the German mystical tradition, which includes Jacob Boehme (1575-1624) as well as Meister Eckhart, see *Sämtliche Werke*, ed. Franz Hoffman *et al* (Leibzig: Bethmann, 1851-1860), 16 vols. See especially Volumes 2, 3, and 13. Another somewhat known 19th-century religious figure who underscored the connection between Hegel and both German mystics – but especially Meister Eckhart – was Hans L. Martensen (1808-1884), against whom Kierkegaard inveighed. In 1840 Martensen wrote in Danish a text on Eckhart now translated as *Meister Eckhart: A Study in Speculative Theology*. See *Between Hegel and Kierkegaard: Hans L. Martensen's Philosophy of Religion*, tr. Curtis L. Thompson and David J. Kangas (Atlanta, GA: Scholar's Press, 1997), 148-241. In this text, Hegel is regarded as the continuation of Eckhart by post-Reformation means.

50. Much of my own work on Hegel has taken this interpretive line. In addition to *The Heterodox Hegel*, see 'Hegel's Philosophy of Religion and Eckhartian Mysticism,' in *New Perspectives in Hegel's Philosophy of Religion*, ed. David Kolb (Albany, NY.: SUNY Press, 1992), 109-29; 'Hegel and Anti-Judaism: Narrative and the Inner Circulation of the Kabbalah,' in *Owl of Minerva* 28.2, Spring (1997), 141-82; 'Hegel's Retrieval of Philo and the Constitution of a Christian Heretic,' in *Studia Philonika Annual*, vol. 20 (2008), 33-59. See also Glenn Alexander Magee, *Hegel and the Hermetic Tradition* (Ithaca, NY: Cornell University Press, 2001). In his archeological investigations of Hegel H. S. Harris does not ignore Hegel's mystical sources; nor does the important Italian commentator on Hegel, Piero Coda. See his *Il negativo e la trinita: ipotesi su Hegel* (Rome: Città Nouva Editrice, 1987), 70-81.

51. *Lectures on the History of Philosophy*, 3 volumes, tr. E. S. Haldane and Frances H. Simson (Lincoln and London: University of Nebraska Press, 1995) (Originally published by Kegan Paul, Trench, Trübner & Co Ltd., London, 1896). See *LHP3*, 119-37.

52. Schelling offers an even more impressive example of German Idealism's interest in Neoplatonism, and Renaissance Neoplatonism in particular. In fact, Schelling devotes an entire book to Bruno. See his *Bruno: Or On the Natural and the Divine Principle of Things (1802)*, ed & tr. Michael G. Vater (Albany, NY: SUNY Press, 1984).

53. For Hegel's appreciative treatment of Neoplatonism in general see *LHP2*, 374-453. For Plotinus and Proclus, see *LHP3*, 404-31, 432-53. The figure who

christened Hegel as *Proclus redivivus* was Friedrich Creuzer, who also produced an edition of Proclus' works in 1820. The doyen of modern scholarship on the relation between Neoplatonism and German Idealism in general and the relation between Proclus and Hegel in particular is undoubtedly Werner Beierwaltes. See especially his *Platonismus und Idealismus* (Frankfurt am Main: Klostermanm, 1967).

[54]. I have spoken in a very general way to Balthasar's reprise of Möhler's concept of tradition in my essay 'Balthasar: Between Tübingen and Postmodernity.' There I did not touch on the genealogical side of Möhler's discourse. Without reference to Balthasar, I did discuss this aspect of Möhler's thought in *Gnostic Return in Modernity* where I pointed to the importance of genealogical drift as the complement to the operation of retrieval of patristic sources. One can see the genealogical and retrieval features side-by-side, for example, in *Die Einheit in der Kirche* (1825). Unlike Staudenmaier, and unlike Baur's *Die christliche Gnosis* (1835), the paradigm of analysis is psychological or existential rather than narrative: Gnosticism represents a spiritual pathology. For my discussion of this and related points, see *Gnostic Return in Modernity*, 41, 46, 55, and esp. 246-47 n. 10. For specific passages on Gnosticism in *Die Einheit*, see *Unity in the Church or the Principle of Catholicism: Presented in the Spirit of the Church Fathers of the First Three Centuries*, ed. intro. tr. Peter Erb (Washington, DC: Catholic University of America Press, 1996), 161, 164, 288.

[55]. The most important text by Staudenmaier is *Zum religiösen Frieden der Zukunft mit Rücksicht auf die religiös-politische Aufgabe der Gegenwart*, Vol. 3 (Tübingen: Minerva, 1851), 109-79. I discuss this aspect of Staudenmaier's work in *Gnostic Return in Modernity*, 27, 31, 36, 249. n. 20.

[56]. See *TD2*, 144. In addition, track Balthasar's long discussion of 'theological persons' in part three of *TD3*.

[57]. For Ferdinand Christian Baur, see *Die christliche Gnosis: Oder Die christliche Religions-Philosophie in ihrer geschictlichen Entwicklung* (Tübingen: Osiander, 1835). For an analysis of this text, see my *Gnostic Return in Modernity*, 23-47.

[58]. For Voegelin's attribution of 'Gnosticism' to Hegel, see *Science, Politics, and Gnosticism: Two Essays* (Chicago: Regnery, 1968), 40-4, 67, 79-80; *New Science of Politics: An Introduction* (Baton Rouge: Louisiana State University Press, 1982), 112-13, 124, 136; 'Wisdom and the Magic of the Extreme,' in *The Collected Works of Eric Voegelin. Volume 12. Published Essays*, 315-75, esp. 333-34; also 'A Response to Professor Altizer' in *Published Essays*, 292-303, esp. 296-98; 'The Eclipse of Reality,' in *The Collected Works of Eric Voegelin. Volume 28. 'What is History?' and Other Unpublished Essays*, 11-162, esp. 143-44.

[59]. For a representative sample of Voegelin's pathological analysis, see 'The Eclipse of Reality,' 137-38, 158-62.

[60]. See Hans Jonas, 'Delimitation of the Gnostic Phenomenon – Typological and Historical,' in *The Origins of Gnosticism*, ed. U. Bianchi (Leiden: Brill, 1967), 90-108.

[61]. See *LHP2*, 396-99 where Hegel gives a very positive account of Gnosticism in association with a positive account of Neoplatonism and the Kabbalah. In *Lectures on the Philosophy of Religion*, Hegel refers positively – if somewhat anachronistically – to a Valentinian rendition of the Trinity (*LPR3*, 85, 196-97, 287-88, 364) and creation (*LPR3*, 89). See my discussion of the latter aspect of Hegel's thought in *The Heterodox Hegel*, 180-87.

[62]. See my discussion of Blumenberg's thesis in *Gnostic Return in Modernity*, 50-65.
[63]. I have in mind here especially what I have called elsewhere the 'theologically aspirated' phenomenology illustrated in *Idol and Distance* and *God without Being.* I choose this somewhat periphrastic way of speaking to avoid committing to the judgment of Dominique Janicaud that because of theological content Marion has thereby violated the would-be presuppositionlessness of Phenomenology. See my essay 'Jean-Luc Marion: Crossing Hegel,' in *Counter-Experiences: Reading Jean-Luc Marion*, ed. Kevin Hart (Notre Dame: University of Notre Dame Press, 2007), 95-150, esp. 99-114.
[64]. For Balthasar, see *GL6*, 73 where Gal 4:9; 1 Cor 8:3, 13:12; 2 Cor 5:11, Phil 3:12 are cited. In *GL7*, all the above passages are cited numerous times and with point. In the hugely important section on image (273-95), in addition to the Gospel of John, 1 Corinthians (5-7) and 2 Corinthians are the pivotal texts.
[65]. See Henri de Lubac, *La postérité spirituelle de Joachim de Flore: Volume 1. de Joachim à Schelling* (Paris: Lethielleux, 1979).
[66]. For Balthasar's positive appraisal of de Lubac on this point, see *TD4*, 458, and especially *The Theology of Henri de Lubac: An Overview* (San Francisco: Ignatius Press, 1991), 124-26, where Balthasar lauds this text as de Lubac's greatest achievement. Balthasar does not explicitly endorse de Lubac's view that Protestantism is the main carrier of Joachimism in the modern period. My own *Gnostic Apocalypse: Jacob Boehme's Haunted Narrative* (Albany, NY: SUNY Press, 2002), 161-76 does, however, explicitly support de Lubac's thesis.
[67]. See *The Office of Peter and the Structure of the Church*, tr. Andrée Emery (San Francisco: Ignatius Press, 1986), 9, 24, 84-6.

[68]. For a brief treatment of both Aquinas' and Bonaventure's critical relation to Joachim, see Bernard McGinn, *The Calabrian Abbot: Joachim de Fiore in the History of Western Thought* (New York: MacMillan, 1985), 209-24. See also Joseph Ratzinger (now Benedict XVI), *Theology of History in St. Bonaventure* (Chicago, IL: Franciscan Herald Press, 1991).
[69]. Staudenmaier, *Zum religiösen Frieden der Zukunft*, Vol. 3, 116 ff.
[70]. Critical vetting does not automatically mean negative judgment. See, for example, Balthasar's vindication of Valentin Tomberg (1900-1973) whose book on the Tarot he judges to be an act of Christianizing of the esoteric rather than esoteric purloining of Christianity. In the French edition of the text originally published eight years earlier in German, Balthasar writes an important foreword. See *Méditations sur les 22 arcanes majeurs du Tarot* (Paris: Aubier Montaigne, 1980. See the English translation of this text by Robert A. Powell, *Meditations on the Tarot: A Journey into Christian Hermeticism* (New York: Tarcher/Putnam, 2002). See also Kevin Mongrain, 'Rule-Governed Christian Gnosis: Hans Urs von Balthasar on Valentin Tomberg's *Meditation on the Tarot*,' in *Modern Theology* 25.2, Spring (2009), 285-314.
[71]. For Bloom, see 'Lying Against Time: Gnosis, Poetry, and Criticism,' in *The Rediscovery of Gnosticism* Volume 1. *The School of Valentinus*, ed. Bentley Layton (Leiden: Brill, 1980), 57-72. See also Bloom's own Valentinian retelling of the biblical narrative in *The Flight to Lucifer: A Gnostic Fantasy* (New York: Farrar, Straus, and Girard, 1979).

[72]. I am especially thinking of an early Taylor work such as *Erring: A Postmodern A/theology* (Chicago: University of Chicago Press, 1984).

[73]. Although Balthasar does not make this point explicit, it is evident that he has grasped it. Kevin Mongrain makes explicit what is implicit in Balthasar in his fine *Balthasar's Systematic Thought: An Irenaean Retrieval* (New York: Crossroad, 2001).

[74]. How Christianity relates to Platonism is an issue for Balthasar as early as 1939. See 'Patristik, Scholastik und Wir,' in *Die Theologie der Zeit* (Vienna), 65-104. See translation of Edward T. Oakes S. J. in *Communio* 24 (1997), 347-96. See also *Kosmische Liturgie: Das Weltbilt Maximus' des Bekenners* (1941), tr. Brian Daley, S.J., *Cosmic Liturgy: The Universe According to Maximus the Confessor* (San Francisco: Ignatius Press, 2003). In his text on Maximus, Balthasar contrasts him favorably with Pseudo-Dionysius with regard to the Trinity, Christ, theological anthropology, and issues of religious language. The best essay on the relation of Balthasar to the patristics is that of Brian Daley. See his 'Balthasar's Reading of the Church Fathers,' in *The Cambridge Companion to Hans Urs von Balthasar*,' 187-206.

[75]. See *Origen: Geist und Feuer. Ein Aufbau aus seiner Schriften* (Salzburg: Otto Mühler Verlag, 1938), tr. Robert J. Daly, S.J., *Origen: Spirit and Fire: A Thematic Anthology of his Writings* (Washington: Catholic University of America Press, 1984).

[76]. This is a refrain in *Présence et pensée: Essai sur la philosophie religieuse de Grégoire de Nysse* (Paris, 1942). See the English translation by Marc Sebanc *Presence and Thought* (San Francisco: Ignatius Press,1995).

[77]. Balthasar's reading of Pseudo-Dionysius in *GL3* is quite different from the reading he provides in his book on Maximus (1941) where Ps.-Dionysius constitutes a foil to Maximus. See my article, 'Von Balthasar and Thick Retrieval: Post-Chalcedonian Symphonic Theology,' in *Gregorianum* 77.2, Spring (1996), 227-60. It also can be shown that while Balthasar submits Meister Eckhart to severe criticism in *GL5* and elsewhere, he never pushes hard on his heterodoxy. For discussion of this relation, see my 'Von Balthasar and Eckhart: Theological Principles and Catholicity,' in *The Thomist* 60.2, April (1996), 1-37.

[78]. Without specific attention to Balthasar, in *Gnostic Return in Modernity* I focus on the particular figure of *metharmottein* (changing shape or form) in *Against Heresies* (1.8, 1.11, 12.0). See *Gnostic Return in Modernity*, 108, 116, 118, 125, 135-36, 148-49.

[79]. See *Gnostic Return in Modernity*, 137-207. For a treatment of Irenaeus, see 143-66.

[80]. See *Gnostic Return in Modernity*, 99-136 for a detailed treatment of these three Valentinian texts, two from Nag Hammadi, one a description of a Valentinian scheme provided by Irenaeus in *Against Heresies.*

[81]. As a criterion for ascription of 'Gnosticism' dualism has increasingly undergone scrutiny. Apart from the fact that dualism does not help to discriminate between Gnosticism and many other forms of Hellenistic thought including Neoplatonism, Neopythagoreanism, etc, it is actually refuted by a close reading of the *Gospel of Truth.* Benoit Strandaert and William R. Schoedel are just two of the scholars who have brought attention to the monistic strain of this text. For Standaert, see 'L'Évangile de vérité: Critique et lecture,' in *New Testament Studies* 22 (1975), 243-75. For Schoedel, see 'Gnostic Monism and the *Gospel of Truth*,' in *The Rediscovery of Gnosticism*, Vol. 1, 379-90; also 'Typological Theology and Some

Monistic Tendencies in Gnosticism,' in *Essays on the Nag Hammadi Texts in Honor Alexander Böhlig*, ed. Martin Krause (Leiden: Brill, 1972), 88-108.

[82]. Here the criticisms of such archeoteleological economies by Georges Bataille and Jacques Derrida can safely be enlisted for theological purposes. See Georges Bataille, *Theory of Religion*, tr. Robert Hurley (New York: Verso Books, 1989), 46-61; *Inner Experience*, tr. intro. Leslie Anne Boldt (Albany, NY: SUNY Press, 1988), 51-61. For Derrida, see his essay on Bataille, 'A Hegelianism without Reserve,' in *Writing and Difference*, tr. intro. Alan Bass (Chicago: University of Chicago Press, 1978), 251-77. Bataille is also a major presence in Derrida's critique of Hegel in *Glas*. See *Glas*, 1, 43, 53, 60, 70-1, 105-06, 115, 226-27.

[83]. The movement away from a tripersonal view of the Trinity to a model of triadically structured self-consciousness is fundamental to my analysis of Hegel in *The Heterodox Hegel*. See especially chs. 1 and 7. Others who have underscored this point include Dale M. Schlitt and William Desmond. For Schlitt, see *Hegel's Trinitarian Claim: A Critical Reflection* (Leiden: Brill, 1984). I will speak in Part 2, ch. 3 of Hegel's construction of a new form of Sabellianism.

[84]. One speaks of distention relative to the classical versions of Valentinianism spoken of by Irenaeus and illustrated by the *Gospel of Truth* and the *Tripartite Tractate* in the Nag Hammadi Library. See my discussion of this point in *Gnostic Return in Modernity*, 196-207.

[85]. This avenue, which is not explored by Balthasar, but is intimated by de Lubac, is the subject of my book, *Gnostic Apocalypse: Jacob Boehme's Haunted Narrative*.

[86]. This is an important emphasis for Kevin Mongrain. See his *The Systematic Thought of Hans Urs von Balthasar* (New York: Crossroad, 2002), 27-50.

[87]. See *Work on Myth*, tr. Robert M. Wallace (Cambridge, MA: MIT Press, 1985), 554 ff.

PART 2

[1]. I borrow this locution from Hans Frei who in *The Eclipse of Biblical Narrative* (New Haven: Yale University Press, 1974) articulated the 'plain sense' of scripture as the community sense. This sense is deformed as easily by recurring to the so-called historical reference as indulging in allegorizing interpretation. Although both can be found throughout history, both also mark modernity. Frei rightly judges Hegel to belong to the stream of allegoresis (233-37, 287-91).

[2]. The consensus view is that throughout his work, Kierkegaard is involved in a polemical relationship with Hegelianism as it makes inroads into the construction of Christianity from the 1830's on. The point that is disputed, however, is how much Hegel's actual texts are a target as well as the texts of a Hegel epigone such as Hans Martensen. For the more standard account in which Hegel's texts are significantly targeted, see Nils Thulstrup's still very useful *Kierkegaard's Relation to Hegel*, tr. George L. Strengen (Princeton, NJ: Princeton University Press, 1980), 133-50. For a more revisionist account in which Kierkegaard's critique has as its object a group of Danish rationalists, who are altogether faithful disciples

of Hegel, see Jon Stewart, *Kierkegaard's Relation to Hegel Reconsidered* (Cambridge: Cambridge University Press, 2003).

[3]. See Claude Bruaire, *Logique et religion chrétienne dans la philosophie de Hegel* (Paris: Seuil, 1964). This very expository text is interested in Hegel's conceptualization of Christian representation (*Vorstellung*) of the Trinity and the extent to which Hegel's syllogistic adaptation of it allows for the integrity and coherence of philosophy. Questions of fidelity to the Christian tradition are put in brackets. They get fore grounded, however, in a companion work *L'Affirmation de Dieu: Essai sur la logique de l'existence* (Paris: Seuil, 1964). Other texts are more critical of Hegel, even if Hegel is presumed to have earned the status of being the philosopher that modern theology must engage. See Bruaire, *Schelling ou la quête du secret de l'être* (Paris: Seghers, 1970) and especially *L'être et l'esprit* (Paris: PUF, 1983). Not only does Balthasar know Bruaire's work but is, arguably, influenced by it especially in *TL2* and *TL3*, where essentially he tends to favor Bruaire's more metaphysical approach to gift over the phenomenological approach of Marion. A commentator on Bruaire who has a particularly good sense of the relationship between Balthasar and Bruaire is Antonio López, F.S.C.B. See his *Spirit in Gift: The Metaphysical Insight of Claude Bruaire* (Washingon, DC: Catholic University of America Press, 2006), 9, 150. For Brito, see *La christologie de Hegel: Verbum Crucis* (Paris: Beauchesne, 1983); also *Hegel et la tâche actuelle de la christologie* (Paris: Lethielleux, 1978). In both of these volumes Brito shows explicitly that his sympathies lie with Balthasar when it comes to differences between Hegel and Balthasar. Balthasar is a major presence throughout *La tâche actuelle.* Brito cites Balthasar's works copiously; especially prominent are *Glory of the Lord 1-3*, *Theo-Drama 1-3*, but *Mysterium Paschale*, *Cosmic Liturgy*, and *Apokalypse 1* are also cited. Although best known for his work on Hegel's logic, which limits itself to exposition, André Léonard shows a more critical side in his *La foie chez Hegel* (Paris: Desclée, 1970). The great historian of German Idealism, Xavier Tillette, also gets involved in a subtle critique of Hegel that shows some sign of indebtedness to Balthasar. See his *L'absolu et la philosophie* (Paris: PUF, 1987); also *Schelling: une philosophie en devenir* (Paris: Vrin, 1970). Tillette's indebtedness to Balthasar is even more pronounced in 'L'exinanition du Christ: Théologies de la kénose,' in *Les quartres fleuves*, *Cahier* 4: *Le Christ visage de Dieu*, 48-60; also 'Le Christ des philosophes et le problème d'une christologie philosophique,' in *Savoir, faire, espérer: les limites de la raison*, Tome 1.1 (Bruxelles, 1976), 249-63.

Chapter 2

[1]. The text that is clearest on this point is *Wahrheit.* See *TL1*, 65, 88, 131, 148, 217-19.

[2]. In *Wahrheit* Hegel's system, which thinks of the ground of experience as a conceptual datum, is regarded as problematic from a classical as well as a Heideggerian perspective. For Balthasar, reality is not viewable *sub specie aeternitatis* and is not reducible to a self-comprehending whole. See *TL1*, 50-1 (against the Hegelian whole); 67-8 (against German Idealism and its dynamism of self-constitution);

126 (the connection between the desire for the whole and Prometheanism); 185-87 (against Hegel's non-perspectivalism). Perhaps the best expression of the perspectival alternative to Hegelianism is to be found in *TL1*, 155: 'The perspectival character of truth is not simply a temporary condition that can be sublated and synthesized into a total standpoint by an intensive information, by a sort of reconaissance of the land of truth (as Hegel, for example, attempted in his *Phenomenology of Spirit*).'

[3]. If Balthasar's accounts of Heidegger in *Apok 3* (193-229) and *GL5* (429-50) respectively represent Balthasar's most explicit reflections on Heidegger, it could be argued that *Wahrheit* represents his most intensive and constructive encounter, especially when this comes to Heideggerian critique of Hegelian essentialism and infinitism. This is understandable, given that Balthasar is likely under the influence of Przywara's *Analogia Entis* in which Heideggerian critique of Hegel is accepted. There are palpable Heideggerian traces in Balthasar's support of mystery over Hegel's recommendation of its excision (*TL1*, 9, 37, 138, 146, 206): in Balthasar's insistence on the finitude of the self (*TL1*, 51, 68, 70), his rendition of the finite subject as servant rather than master (*TL1*, 64, 68) and as seeker rather than securer (*TL1*, 22-3, 49, 208), and in his considered judgment that the horizon of reality takes the form of futurity (203).

[4]. This is the view of the mature Hegel. It is articulated in texts such as the *Phenomenology*, *Lectures on the Philosophy of Religion*, and the *Encyclopedia*. For particularly clear expressions of the identity of content, see *PS* (#788, 802); *LPR1* 1824 E 333, G 235; *LPR1* E 396-97, G 292; *Enc* #573. For a critical evaluation of Hegel's claim with an analysis of all the relevant primary texts as well as engagement with the secondary material, see my *The Heterodox Hegel*, 327-70.

[5]. See Heidegger's famous essay, 'The Onto-Theological Nature of Metaphysics,' tr. Kurt F. Leidecker (New York: Philosophical Library Inc., 1960), 35-67; also *Hegel's Phenomenology of Spirit*, tr. Parvis Emad and Kenneth Maly (Bloomington and Indianapolis: Indiana University Press, 1988), 98-100, 124-26.

[6]. Hegel most assuredly identifies *to on* with *to theion* when from the very opening of the *Encyclopedia* (#1) he identifies metaphysics and theology, since both have truth as their object. When Hegel does this, on Heideggerian grounds he continues to make the fatal mistake of identifying Being with the highest being, a category mistake that is there from the beginning of the philosophical tradition and which receives exemplary expression in the works of Aristotle, and especially within the *Metaphysics*. If Hegel's remarks on Aristotle in *LHP1* are anything to go by, then the opening paragraph of the *Encyclopedia* directly recalls Aristotle's *Metaphysics*, where 'first philosophy' moves easily from defining metaphysics as the science of being as being (*to on he on*), the science of being as unitary (henology), the science of substances (ousiology), and, lastly and crucially, the science of the highest being (theology, or better, theiology). The engagement with Aristotle throughout the *Encyclopedia* is deep. If the text opens with a nod to Aristotle, it ends with an invocation of the 'self-thinking thought' (*noesis noeseos noesis*) of Book 10 of the *Nicomachean Ethics* (*Enc* #574). It is important to understand that the linkage between metaphysics and theology here – or ontotheology in the strict sense – is logically distinct from the issue of the relation between philosophy

and religion and certainly from the issue of the relation between philosophy and Christianity. This particular relation can also be defined as ontotheological, but the parameters are here provided by the Kant of the *First Critique* rather than Heidegger. When the renegade Heideggerian Karl Löwith speaks of Hegel, he operates in terms of Kant's definition. This represents in him a refusal to Heidegger's refusal to take seriously the actual relation between philosophy and Christianity throughout history. See Löwith, 'Hegel and the Christian Religion,' in *Nature, History, and Existentialism*, ed. A. Levinson (Evanston, IL: Northwestern University Press, 1966), 162-203, 163.

[7]. See John Milbank, 'Only Theology Overcomes Metaphysics,' in *The Word Made Strange: Theology, Language, and Culture* (Oxford: Blackwell, 1997), 36-52, esp. 41, 44. Of course, everything depends on the meaning of 'evacuation,' whether it is rhetorical or conceptual.

[8]. See Rodolphe Gasche, *The Tain of the Mirror: Derrida and the Philosophy of Reflection* (Cambridge, MA: Harvard University Press, 1986), 38-54, esp. 43-5. See also Gasche's essay 'Yes Absolutely,' in *Inventions of Difference: On Jacques Derrida* (Cambridge, MA: Harvard University Press, 1995), 199-226. This essay is on Hegel's 'logic of essence' in the speculative, precisely as a separating and a mirroring occurs.

[9]. Throughout *GL5*, and especially in his long reflection on Cusanus in *GL5*, 205-46, Balthasar worries about the tendency towards an Identity-Metaphysics that is the tendency of the Neoplatonic tradition, especially in its Eckhartian inflection. See especially *GL5*, 213-14, 220-21, 228. Nonetheless, he insists in the last instance that the *analogia entis* is sufficiently in operation to protect Cusansus from this particular declension (*GL5*, 230-38). Balthasar comes nearest to treating Cusanus' perspectivalism in *GL5*, 238-46, but is concerned only with the epistemological rather than theological ruminations of Cusanus. Balthasar has to be aware of the christologically generated perspectivalism of *De visione dei* in which Christ is the inexhaustible icon that demands an infinity of points of view. Although Cusanus is hardly the only figure in the background when in *Glory of the Lord* (*GL1*, 212 provides just one example) Balthasar determines that Christ is the determinant in the plurality of perspectives – on the authority of de Lubac's *Catholicism* he can regard this as a part of a patristic consensus – Cusanus likely plays at least a supporting role in a different (more epistemological) key.

[10]. 'Releasing' is the translation of the technical term '*Entlassung*' which Hegel uses to characterize the movement from the virtual or logical plane of reality to the world of nature and finite spirit. See especially *Enc* # 246 zu. The term has Neoplatonic precedents, and one of the reasons why Hegel feels comfortable with it is that one can qualify it by the adjective '*frei*.' This is important for Hegel since he wants to distinguish his view from that of Spinoza. The fact that Hegel uses this more formal philosophical language does not mean that he absolutely abjures the language of 'creation.' In a number of his major texts Hegel does not fail to speak positively of the symbol of creation, even as he makes a concerted effort to refute views of creation based upon divine will or efficient causation. *Lectures on the Philosophy of Religion* and the *Phenomenology* are particularly apropos. In most of his texts, he shows little interest in or patience for the doctrine of *creatio ex nihilo.*

[11]. Interestingly, Balthasar arrived at this view long before the trilogy; indeed his sense of the importance of Hegel for the Trinity is to the fore already in *Apokalypse 1* (see 608). Samuel L. Powell provides a very useful synopsis of this familiar story in his *The Trinity in German Thought* (Cambridge: CUP, 2001), 104-41.
[12]. *Glory of the Lord* spends considerable time charting the pre-modern and pre-Reformation conditions of the collapse of the persuasive authority of Christian vision. This is especially true of the early part of *GL5* in which in different ways Scotus and Nominalism, but also Eckhart and *devotio moderna* damage the revelation center and trinitarian matrix of theology. But the notion of 'lay style' itself marks a break. If great theology gets produced from the fourteenth century on, it will have to do so in an environment in which there is a diminishment in terms of basic presupposition and an escalation of the questionable.
[13]. Even as Balthasar fails to indict either Leibniz or Kant of rationalism in *GL5*, he does not gainsay what he has already intimated concerning modernity in *Apokalypse* in which rationalism sets the stage for the wild speculative and vitalist intellectual experimentation of nineteenth and early twentieth centuries. In *Apok 3*, for example, it is evident that he takes for granted Husserl's reservations about the contraction of reason in the modern age, and to a significant extent Heidegger's view of modernity as representing an extreme form of 'desacralization'. Traces of the anti-rationalist view are also evident in *Wahrheit* in which Balthasar inveighs against the hegemony of method in philosophy. In addition, in his reading of Heidegger near the end of *GL5* (429-50), which essentially updates his earlier account of Heidegger in *Apok 3* (largely focused on *Sein und Zeit* and the *Kantbuch*), Balthasar gives no indication that he fundamentally disagrees with Heidegger's diagnosis of modernity, even if he is unwilling to ontologize its deficits.

[14]. See *Vorlesungen* über *die* Ästhetik, ed. E. Moldenhauer and K. Michel, vols. 13-15, *Sämtliche Werke* (Frankfurt: Suhrkamp, 1970). For a convenient English translation, see *Aesthetics: Lectures on the Fine Arts*, tr. T. M. Knox, 2 vols. (Oxford: Clarendon Press, 1995). For good general accounts of Hegel's aesthetics, see Stephen Bungay, *Beauty and Truth: A Study of Hegel's Aesthetics* (Oxford: Oxford University Press, 1984); William Desmond, *Art and the Absolute: A Study of Hegel's Aesthetics* (Albany, NY: SUNY Press, 1986).
[15]. For example, Graham Ward takes the former track, Ben Quash the latter. For Ward, see 'Kenosis, Death, Discourse, and Resurrection,' in *Balthasar at the End of Modernity*, ed. Lucy Gardner, David Moss, Ben Quash, and Graham Ward (Edinburgh: T & T Clark, 1999), 15-68. For Quash, 'Between the Brutely Given and the Brutally, Banally Free: von Balthasar's Theology of Drama in Dialogue with Hegel,' in *Modern Theology* 13.3, July (1997), 293-318; also 'Drama at the Ends of Modernity,' in *Balthasar and the End of Modernity*, 139-71. In fact, Quash goes even further in a recent book by suggesting that there is more negative capability in Hegel than Balthasar towards escaping the epical and thus a totalizing philosophy. This involves prioritizing in Hegel's work objective Spirit, or more specifically ethical Spirit (*Sittlichkeit*), over absolute Spirit. See *Theology and the Drama of History* (Cambridge: Cambridge University Press, 2005), 87-118; also 137-56, 187-96. For criticism of *Theology and the Drama of History*, see my review in *Modern Theology* 23.2, April (2007), 293-96. For criticism of Ward, see my review of *Balthasar*

at the End of Modernity in *Modern Theology* 16.4, October (2000), 566-69. Quash's view is congruent with that of Rowan Williams, whose reading of Hegel depends significantly on the English philosopher, Gillian Rose. In a text such as *Hegel Contra Sociology* (Cambridge: Cambridge University Press, 1981) Rose rejects a speculative interpretation of Hegel, and argues that Hegel provides the best modern example of a philosophy sensitive to history without being reductively historicist, practical but irreducible to doctrinaire Marxism, religious but not apolitical. For Williams, see 'Logic and Spirit in Hegel,' in Phillip Blond (ed), *Post-Secular Philosophy: Between Philosophy and Theology* (London: Routledge, 1998), 116-30; 'Hegel and the Gods of Postmodernity,' in Philippa Berry and Andrew Wernick (eds), *Shadow of Spirit: Postmodernism and Religion* (London: Routledge, 1992), 72-80; also 'Between Politics and Metaphysics: Reflections in the Wake of Gillian Rose,' in *Modern Theology* 11.1, January (1995), 3-22.

[16]. In *GL4* Balthasar shows himself anxious to avoid a rationalistic interpretation of Plato (166-215) and Plotinus (280-313). Truth is not a deliverance of discursive thought but an insight into the 'really real' that discloses itself. For reference to the 'sudden' (*exaiphnes*), see *GL4*, 305. This presentation of Platonism is consistent with Balthasar's presentation of the true nature of classical philosophy in *TL1*.

[17]. See Hans Urs von Balthasar, *Das Ganze im Fragment* (Einsiedeln: Johannes Verlag, 1963).

[18]. See also *TL1*, 51, 107, 131, 206, 219-23. Similar asseverations are made in *Glory of the Lord*, even as Balthasar warns against unrestricted apophasis. See also *GL1*, 148, *GL2*, 51-2 (Irenaeus); *GL6*, 12.

[19]. See my discussion of this aspect of Hegel's thought in *The Heterodox Hegel*, 31-43.

[20]. Balthasar is on Hegel's side to the extent to which he rejects the specifically modern versions of the privatively mysterious God of Deism, that are exacerbated forms of theism in which God functions to get the world system going and then essentially falls out of the picture; and with Hegel, he also rejects Kant's agnosticism, and the various species of post-Reformation and post-Kantian fideism that speckle modernity. Balthasar is also on Hegel's side in thinking that Western philosophical and religious systems go awry to the extent to which there is an overemphasis on the incomprehensibility and unknowability of God. Both would cite forms of classical and Christian Neoplatonism as having this tendency. Hegel gives more than an intimation of this particularly in his discussions of Plotinus and Proclus in *Lectures on the History of Philosophy*. For Balthasar, however, diagnosis is not itself the solution. Apophasis is irremediable even when, or especially when, it is tied to disclosure. This is the central thrust of Balthasar's interpretation of biblical religion in *GL6* and *GL7*.

[21]. Raymond Gawronski is helpful on this point. See his *Word and Silence: Hans Urs von Balthasar and the Spiritual Encounter between East and West* (Grand Rapids, MI: Eerdmans, 1995). Gawronski concentrates in particular on those forms of apophasis in the Christian tradition that threaten to upset the delicate balance between kataphasis and apophasis that characterizes the best of the tradition. A number of figures are discussed about whom Balthasar expresses reservations

concerning the lack of christological regulation of apophasis. These include Evagrius (48-51), Gregory of Palamas (56-9), Eckhart (63-7), and John of the Cross (67-73).

[22]. Heidegger offers an interesting etymological analysis of the 'skepticism' that drives the dialectical movement of the *Phenomenology*. He suggests that the regulative *skepsis* of which Hegel speaks (rather than any specific historical version) is defined less by a withholding of commitment to particular content than an anticipation of a fully adequate content which makes both denial and movement possible. See Heidegger, *Hegel's Concept of Experience* (New York: Harper & Row, 1970), 65-70, esp. 65-6. *Skepsis*, Heidegger writes, in the following illustrative passage, means 'seeing, watching, scrutinizing, to see what and how beings are as beings. Skepticism in this sense pursues the Being of beings with its gaze. . . Its watching has caught sight of something, before it ever looked at the thing itself, and it is from this perspective that it scrutinizes it' (65).

[23]. Theodor W. Adorno, *Negative Dialectics*, tr. E. B. Ashton (New York: Seabury Press, 1993); Jacques Derrida, *Glas*, tr. John P. Leavey, Jr. and Richard Rand (Lincoln and London: University of Nebraska Press, 1986); also 'From Restricted to General Economy,' in *Writing and Difference*, tr. Alan Bass (Chicago: University of Chicago Press, 1978), 251-78.

[24]. See *Cosmic Liturgy*, 162-63, where Balthasar contrasts Hegel's essentially idealistic view of multiplicity unfavorably with the realism of Maximus. Still, as will become his wont, Balthasar's relation to Hegel is complex. He recommends as well as criticizes him. An interesting example of such recommendation is his recognition that, for both, knowing is viewed as a kind of 'eating' of intelligible content. Balthasar does not see what Derrida in *Glas* sees, that is, the inherent violence of the metaphor – especially if it is to be regulative. Nor does he discern that in Hegel 'eating' is linked to a form of restless pursuit of knowledge that will only come to term in absolute knowledge. The other side of the argument, however, is Derrida's hostility to the very idea of sacrament which is playing a role in Maximus' account of knowledge that Balthasar affirms. For a good synoptic account of how Maximus functions in a critique of Hegel with a particular emphasis on the christological and trinitarian dimensions, see Georges de Schrijver, *Le merveilleux accord de l'homme et de Dieu:* Étude *de l'analogie de l'être chez Hans Urs von Balthasar* (Louvain: Belgium: Leuven University Press, 1983), Chapter 12 (217-254).

[25]. The basic argument of *Cosmic Liturgy* is that in the figure of Maximus the Confessor one finds a theologian who is throughly christocentric while allowing the orders of creation, reason, and culture a real – if relative – autonomy. Maximus represents a theological anticipation of Przywara's *analogia entis* and a bulwark against the kind of attack on Catholic thought conducted by Barth.

[26]. To develop is not necessarily to surpass. As is obvious, Balthasar's estimation of Bonaventure is extraordinarily high. In *Glory of the Lord* Bonaventure's importance is less plausibly indicated by the fact that he has an essay, than by the use to which Bonaventure's christocentric theology is put in the construction of the outline of theological aesthetics in *GL1*. In this lies his advantage over Aquinas who in *GL4* (393-412) is constructed more nearly as a philosopher whose main intellectual contribution is his articulation of a general ontology (395). Balthasar

corrects for this limiting of Aquinas in *TL2 & 3.* He is now prepared to accept that Aquinas is a christological-trinitarian theologian.

[27]. See *TL2-3*, wherein trinitarian difference is the ground of all other differences (*TL2*, 27-34, 173-8, 196-9; *TL3*, 17-24, 117-30, 441-8). As Balthasar points out in his Barth book, this position is also that of Barth in both *Church Dogmatics* and his book on Anselm. See *The Theology of Karl Barth*, 157, 164.

[28]. One of the major thrusts of *Glas* is that Hegel's antisemitism is not confined to such early essays as 'The Positivity of Christianity' and 'The Spirit of Christianity and its Fate' (1799), but that it is built into Hegel's speculative system and is amply illustrated in later texts such as the *Phenomenology* and the *Encyclopedia* as well as *Lectures on the Philosophy of Religion.* Antisemitism is not an accusation that Rosenzweig makes explicitly against Hegelian thought with which it is involved in a profound negotiation. Rosenzweig's two-volume *Hegel und der Staat* (1920) involves no substantial critique of either Hegel's political thought or its logical and metaphysical presuppositions. Rosenzweig's 'new thought' (*das neue Denken*), which finds expression in *The Star of Redemption (Der Stern der Erlösung*), involves a serious critique of both the totalizing and explanatory pretensions of German Idealism and a refiguration of the notion of God, world, and human being, and their relations. Rosenzweig's general call in *The Star of Redemption* for alterity and his insistence on the relative independence of these spheres is illustrated especially in his reinstatement of the mystery of God and the mystery of the divine in the world and their relation to humanity. The contrast between 'revelation' and 'manifestation' (*Offenbarung*) is especially important. It recalls a fundamental 19th-century objection to Hegel, wherein the former was incapable of logical adoption and the latter was 'logical' from the beginning – but also looks forward to a contrast that is implied in Levinas' adoption and adaptation of theological categories such as 'creation,' 'incarnation,''inspiration,' and 'witness' as central to his revision of phenomenology. See *Otherwise than Being or Beyond Essence*, tr. Alphonso Lingis (The Hague: Martinus Nijhoff, 1981).

[29]. See especially Walter Kasper, *Das Absolute in der Geschichte: Philosophie und Theologie der Geschichte in der Spätphilosophie Schellings* (Mainz: Matthias-Grünewald, 1965); Wolfhart Pannenberg, *Offenbarung als Geschichte* (Göttingen: Vandenhoeck & Ruprecht, 1963).

[30]. For a good account of Catholic thinkers who quite early on signed onto Hegel's speculative program, see John Edward Toews, *Hegelianism: The Path Toward Dialectical Humanism, 1805-1841* (Cambridge: Cambridge University Press, 1985), 78-82.

[31]. On this point, see Thomas O'Meara, *Romantic Idealism and Roman Catholicism: Schelling and the Theologians* (Notre Dame: University of Notre Dame Press, 1982), esp. 77-89.

[32]. For an account of Balthasar's indebtedness to Adam Möhler, founder of the Tübingen School, especially with respect to the christocentric view of the Church and tradition, see my 'Between Tübingen and Postmodernity,' in *Modern Theology* 14.3, Summer (1998), 325-53.

[33]. Among the Communio group Brito is, perhaps, first among equals in recalling Staudenmaier's critique of Hegel. See especially the constructive section that ends

the largely descriptive *La christologie de Hegel* in which there are eleven references to Staudenmaier.

[34]. For a convenient account of Barth's reading of Hegel, see *Protestant Thought from Rousseau to Ritchl* (Partial translation of *Die Protestantische Theologie im 19 Jahrhundert*) (New York: Simon and Schuster, 1959), 268-305. For positive statements regarding the nature of the relation between philosophy and theology, see 280, 293, 295. For critical assessments of Hegel's rendering of this relation, see 286, 295, 304.

[35]. In the 1820's Franz von Baader's (1765-1841) enthusiasm for Hegel waned. He gradually became persuaded that, his borrowings from the Christian tradition notwithstanding (especially Eckhart and Boehme), Hegel's thought was fundamentally pantheistic or panentheistic. Accordingly, he concluded that the prospects of a fruitful dialogue between Christian thought and the philosophy of Schelling were considerably better, since Schelling's thought displayed less inclination to go in the exaggerated pantheistic direction of Hegel where the unity of God and the world and God and human being were 'logically' justified. For Baader's dissatisfaction on this point, see especially Eugène Susini, *Franz von Baader et le romantisme mystique*, vol. 2 (Paris: Vrin, 1942), 466-71. See also Emmanuel Tourpe, 'Manifestation et Médiation: Franz von Baader lectuer de Jacob Boehme,' in *Archives de Philosophie* 69 (2006), 2117-41. Although the focus of Tourpe's article is on Baader's retrieval of the Lutheran mystic, Jacob Boehme (1575-1624), Baader's search for an alternative to German Idealism is very much to the fore.

[36]. This position of Ricoeur achieves definitive form in *The Symbolism of Evil*, tr. Emerson Buchanan (Boston: Beacon Press, 1969). For specific reference to Hegel, see 'The Status of *Vorstellung* in Hegel's Philosophy of Religion,' in *Meaning, Truth, and God*, ed. Leroy S. Rouner (Notre Dame: University of Notre Dame Press, 1982), 70-82.

[37]. This is, of course, the case in *Glas* as it is also in Derrida's famous 'White Mythology.' See *Margins of Philosophy*, tr. Alan Bass (Chicago: University of Chicago Press, 1987), 207-71, esp. 210-11, 225-26, 268-71. See also 'From Restricted to General Economy: A Hegelianism without Reserve,' in *Writing and Difference*, 251-77.

[38].This position is of long-standing in Hegel. It comes to the surface as early as *Glauben und Wissen* (1802) in Hegel's critique of Jacobi. See *Faith and Knowledge*, tr. W. Cerf and H. S. Harris (Albany, NY: SUNY Press, 1977), 118. A number of scholars recognize the importance of this connection in Hegel's philosophy of religion, including Claude Bruaire. For a good general account of the interconnection of philosophy and worship, see William Desmond, *Hegel's God: A Counterfeit Double?* (Aldershot, England: Ashgate, 2003), 56-62.

[39]. In Hegel's thought there are reasons for making the connection internal to thought (and its history) and reasons that have to do with the relationship between Christianity and philosophy. In the case of the former, it is not only that the connection between thought and worship is of long-standing, and that its pedigree can be traced back to Stoicism – Hegel in fact mentions Epictetus – but that this connection is essentially made also by Spinoza in Bk. 5 of the *Ethics* in which he discusses the *amor intellectus dei.* One can consider the closing paragraphs of the *Encyclopedia* (# 564-73) to represent Hegel's rearticulation of this idea. In

the case of the latter, one is taking into consideration the fact that Hegel thinks that Christianity is defined by cultic practices as much by thought, and that philosophy essentially saves this aspect of Christianity as it does its fundamental symbols and narrative articulation.

[40]. See *Prayer* (San Francisco: Ignatius Press, 1986). Raymond Gawronski analyzes in depth Balthasar's view of prayer in his fine *Word and Silence*, 147-80. While Gawronski begins his analysis with *Das Betrachtende Gebet* (1955), not only does he glean much of its fundamental structures from the trilogy, and especially from *Glory of the Lord*, but also insists that the fundamental theological importance of prayer lies in its being grounded in Christ and enfolded by the relations between the trinitarian persons.

[41]. Jean-Louis Chrétien, *The Ark of Speech*, tr. Andrew Brown (London: Routledge, 2004), 17-38.

[42]. For a similar avowal, see *Enc* 24 zu. It is extremely interesting that Balthasar quotes a very similar passage from John of the Cross (*GL2*, 127): 'The very same cautery that touches the wound also heals it, but it heals it only by penetrating deeper.' Balthasar's quoting of this passage should be read against the backdrop of him associating John of the Cross with Hegel in terms of their description of the momentum of experience that can only be satisfied in the absolute (*GL2*, 109).

[43]. See Heidegger, *Hegel's Concept of Experience*, With a selection from Hegel's *Phenomenology of Spirit* (New York: Harper & Row, Publishers, Inc., 1970), 37-41.

[44]. It is not a little interesting, however, that Cardinal Angelo Scola, who is a major Balthasar scholar, is at the very least a contributor to *Fides et Ratio* (1998). For a good example of Scola's work, see *Hans Urs von Balthasar: A Theological Style* (Grand Rapids, MI: Eerdmans, 1995).

[45]. See also *TD5*, 489; *TL2*, 101; *Exp 3*, 305, 325.

[46]. For a more detailed exploration of this point, see *The Heterodox Hegel*, 44-63.

[47]. See also *GL1*, 195-6, where Eriugena and Cusanus are cited as theologians who suggest that there is a divinity beyond the Trinity. Although Balthasar worries whether apophasis is sufficiently christologically regulated and constrained by a commitment to the mystery of the Trinity, he suggests that there are kataphatic offsets in all three cases.

[48]. Balthasar thinks Gal 4:9, 1 Cor 8:3 and 13:12, 2 Cor 5:11, and Phil 3:12 are especially worth mentioning.

[49]. For some of the more explicit challenges to Hegel in these two thinkers, who both invoke the negative theology tradition, see Georges Bataille, *L'Expérience intérieure* (Paris: Gallimard, 1954). For a convenient translation, see *Inner Experience*, tr. Leslie Anne Boldt (Albany, NY: SUNY Press, 1988), 52-60, 80-1, 101-03. For Maurice Blanchot, see *L'entretien infini* (Paris: Gallimard, 1969), 1-3, 94.

[50]. See *PS* #207 ff; also #752.

[51]. For Marion's articulation of the icon, see *Idol and Distance: Five Studies*, tr. intro. Thomas A. Carlson (New York: Fordham University Press, 2001), 198-53; also *God without Being*, tr. Thomas A. Carlson with a foreword by David Tracy (Chicago: University of Chicago Press, 1991), 7-24. Elsewhere I have made the case that these texts, which are influenced by the French Communio group in general and Balthasar in particular, are more concertedly anti-Hegelian than they first

appear. It is not only Heidegger who is convicted of conceptual idolatry, but also Hegel. See especially the study of Pseudo-Dionysius in *Idol and Distance*, 139-195. In this study Marion develops the iconic and christological reading of Pseudo-Dionysius Balthasar elaborated in *GL2*, and on a number of occasions turns this form of apophasis against Hegel (140, 150, 160, 174). See also *God without Being*, 163-69. For a discussion of the relation between Jean-Luc Marion and Hegel, see my 'Jean-Luc Marion: Crossing Hegel,' in *Counter-Experiences: Reading Jean-Luc Marion*, ed. Kevin Hart (Notre Dame, IN: University of Notre Dame Press, 2007), 95-150, esp. 99-114.

52. Here Graham Ward contrasts with John Milbank, on the one hand, and Conor Cunningham on the other. For Milbank, see *Theology and Social Theory: Beyond Secular Reason* (Oxford: Blackwell, 1990), 147-76; also 'The Second Difference,' in *The Word Made Strange: Theology, Language, and Culture* (Oxford: Blackwell, 1997), 171-93, esp. 180-83. For Milbank also, see his recent *The Monstrosity of Christ: Paradox or Dialectic*, ed. Creston Davis (Boston: MIT Press, 2009), 110-223. This book is essentially a 'conversation' between Milbank and Slavoj Žižek, with the latter defending Hegel's own interpretation of his philosophy as essentially justifying all that can be justified of Christianity, and the former questioning whether any philosophy is vested with this power of justification, and drawing attention not only to the palpable failure of speculation to justify Christianity, but the way in which it appears to justify alternatives. For Cunningham, see *Genealogy of Nihilism*, 100-30.

53. In 1942 at the height of his patristic period Balthasar wrote a monograph on Gregory of Nyssa. See *Presence and Thought: Essay on the Religious Philosophy of Gregory of Nyssa*, tr. Marc Sebanc (San Francisco: Ignatius Press, 1995). This text shows a compendious knowledge of Nyssa, and especially of his theological anthropology which is so intimately tied to Nyssa's doctrine of God. For particularly explicit passages on *epektasis*, see *The Life of Moses*, 162-63, 225-26.

54. This is not a dividing line between theologians who belong to Concilium and those who belong to Communio. See Rahner's reflection on the constitutive incomprehensibility of God in *The Trinity*, 46, 47, 50-1. In his book *The God of Jesus Christ*, tr. Matthew J. O'Connell (Nww York: Crossroad, 1986), Walter Kasper follows Rahner at something of a safe distance, suggesting divine incomprehensibility is (a) absolute (88 n. 10) and (b) admits of being linked to notion of God as absolute future (96-7). With respect to his making the connection, Kasper has the 'later' Schelling as an influence here. Unlike Rahner, Kasper avoids intimating anything about the beatific vision.

55. For an echoing of John of the Cross similar to that of Balthasar, see Part 3 of Eliot's 'East Coker,' especially the following lines: 'I said to my soul, be still, and wait without hope/For hope would be hope for the wrong thing; wait without/love/For love would be love of the wrong thing; there is yet faith/But the faith and the love and the hope are all in the waiting' (lines 125-28) in *Four Quartets* (New York: Harvest, 1971), 28.

56. The accidental nature of the echo contrasts with the, arguably, more deliberate recall of Schelling's emphasis on the futurity of God in Kasper's *The God of Jesus Christ*.

[57]. See David Bentley Hart, *The Beauty of the Infinite: The Aesthetics of Christian Truth* (Grand Rapids, MI: Eerdmans, 2003), 231-60, 402-11.
[58]. Both Edward Oakes and David Schindler, Jr. are right about the general influence of Goethe on Balthasar's theology. That Goethe is a major influence in Balthasar's construction of a theological aesthetics does not relativize the medieval contribution and especially that of Bonaventure.
[59]. See *Apok 1*, 157-208. Aidan Nichols offers a very good account of Balthasar's reading of Fichte in *Apokalypse* in *Scattering the Seed*, 59-67. Without attribution, in *Wahrheit* Balthasar critiques modes of philosophy that point to Act (*Tat*) as the ground of action (*TL1*, 67-8). Balthasar's essay on Fichte in *GL5*, 546-57, confirms Balthasar's earlier assessments of Fichte as a representative of the Promethean movement in modern thought, although arguably the emphasis on unrealized eschatology is more muted. A possible reason for this is Balthasar's knowledge of the entire oeuvre of Fichte in which one can find outside of the various editions of the *Wissenschaftslehre* texts which articulated an eschatological perspective that is both more genuinely Johannine and realized that what is offered in *The Science of Knowledge.* Balthasar refers in particular to *Die Anweisung zum seligen Leben* (1806) (*GL5*, 554-56). Balthasar had, however, drawn attention to this text already in *Apok 1*, 201-04. Nichols takes due note of this. See *Scattering the Seed*, 67.
[60]. It is interesting that Balthasar emphasizes the point about 'infinite progress' rather than the more famous one of the aporia between accidental truths of history and necessary truths of reason. This is not to say, of course, that the latter is incidental to him, and that he does not see that this is one of the constitutive problems of theology, especially as this theology would justify itself in a secular environment. What Balthasar writes about Lessing here is basically consistent with what he writes in his short section on Lessing in *Apok 1.* Although Lessing fails to get a section devoted to him in *GL5*, his name, even if only in passing, is associated with the view of infinite progress that is asymptotic (*GL5*, 482).
[61]. See *Work on Myth*, 278-82 where Blumenberg gives an interesting twist to a point already made by Balthasar in *Apokalypse*, namely, that Lessing is betwixt and between two different eschatologies – static completion and infinite progress (*Apok 1*, 51). Blumenberg views *The Education of the Human Race* as Lessing's definitive statement on behalf of the Enlightenment view of 'infinite progress.' Interestingly, he does not note the Joachimite element that a scholar such as de Lubac is aware of in *La postérité spirituelle de Joachim de Flore*. Noting that Lessing also wrote a play on the Faust theme (but lost the manuscript), Blumenberg suggests that there is evidence that in the play Lessing experimented with the alternative to the ideology of 'infinite progress' by having Faust fully satisfy his insatiable intellectual and spiritual appetite.
[62]. I mention these three French thinkers here, since all three are seriously engaged with Hegel. This is, more obviously true of Bataille and Derrida than it is of Foucault. Derrida declares: 'We have never finished with a reading or rereading of Hegel, and, in a certain way, I do nothing other than attempt to explain myself on that point.' See *Positions*, tr. Alan Bass (Chicago: University of Chicago Press, 1981), 77. Foucault is equally insistent on the importance of Hegel whose thought insidiously almost always gets reincribed. See *The Archeology of Knowledge*

(New York: Pantheon, 1972), 235. He is interesting in 'deranging' it. For a very interesting discussion of Hegel's view of madness in light 20th-century understandings, including the cultural understanding elaborated by Foucault, see Daniel Berthold-Bond, *Hegel's Theory of Madness* (Albany, NY: SUNY Press, 1995).

[63]. See Michel Foucault, *Madness and Civilization: A History of Insanity in the Age of Reason*, tr. Richard Howard (New York: Random House, 1965).

[64]. However implausible this notion, it is represented in the secondary literature on Hegel. Alan Olson is a good case in point. See his treatment of the Hegel-Hölderlin relation in *Hegel and the Spirit* (Princeton: Princeton University Press, 1992).

[65]. See, for example, *Thérese of Lisieux. Story of a Mission* (London, 1953); *Elizabeth of Dijon: An Interpretation of a Spiritual Mission* (London, 1956). One cannot ignore Balthasar's relation to Adrienne von Speyr and the way he tends to treat her not only as a saint but also as a doctor of the church. See his little book *First Glance at Adrienne von Speyr* (San Francisco: Ignatius, 1981). For a wonderfully subtle and supple dissertation on Balthasar's reflection on sanctity and the saints as exemplars, see Danielle Nussberger, 'Saint as Wellspring: A Critical Appraisal of Hans Urs von Balthasar,' Ph. D dissertation (University of Notre Dame, 2007).

[66]. For Balthasar, there are different kinds of difficulty in classical and Christian Neoplatonism. The first concerns whether there is an ethical component and its relation to the contemplative. The second concerns whether contemplation is all the way through a work of the self. Balthasar can think of problems on both fronts. Obviously classical Neoplatonism in general shows more tendency than Christian Neoplatonism to assert the latter. In this respect, Balthasar shares an Augustinian concern with classical Neoplatonism illustrating a tendency towards pride (even if at its very best classical Neoplatonism has resources to resist this trend). The case of Meister Eckhart, and to a lesser degree Johannes Scotus Eriugena, shows that Christian forms of Neoplatonism are not exempt from this temptation. With respect to the first, in classical Neoplatonism the status of purification is not always clear. Does it serve a purely instrumental or intrinsic role with respect to participation in the divine? This is a problem, which in Balthasar's view, is not absent from Christian Neoplatonism. As he indicates in his work on Nyssa and Maximus in the early forties, it bedevils Origenism and finds an acute expression in Evagrius.

[67]. Having argued in *Ästhetik 3*, 146-320, the superiority of linguistic over the non-linguistic arts of painting, sculpture, architecture, and music, Hegel goes on to present his theory of genres (*Ästhetik 3*, 321 ff) which focuses on 'lyric,' 'drama,' and 'epic.' While the distinctions between the genres are in concrete cases fairly fluid, Hegel thinks he can offer criteria of distinction. As he does so, he seems to have quite different criteria in mind: (i) the level of the expressivity of the individual self: here there is a descending line from lyric through drama to epic; (ii) the level of communal incorporation – here the order is just the reverse of the first; (iii) the determination of freedom – here drama is superior to lyric in which there is insufficient objectivity and epic in which there is too much of it; (iv) ultimate seriousness, which concerns how death is faced. Once again Hegel determines that drama is in the ascendency; (v) level

of discursivity, for which the advantage once again goes to drama in that for its discursivity it is neither solipsistically reductive (lyric) or disinterested (epic). For a good treatment of the complexity of Hegel's reflections on genres, see Stephen Bungay, *Beauty and Truth: A Study of Hegel's Aesthetics* (Oxford: Oxford University Press, 1989), 142-87.

[68]. If David Burrell is right about the non-contrastive construal of the relation between God and the creature (each defined by freedom) in Aquinas, then, however important Hegel is as an interlocutor, Balthasar operates within a very traditional protocol. For a representative expression of a view that is central to Burrell's work as a whole, see *God and Action*, 2nd ed. (Scranton, PA: University of Scranton Press, 2008).

[69]. In *TD1*, 34-7, 626-43, Balthasar underscores the importance of a dialogical philosophy for an adequate theology. It is no accident that this occurs in the very same volume in which he announces the necessity of overcoming Hegel both on the methodological and substantive levels. In *TD1* Martin Buber, Ferdinand Ebner, and Franz Rosenzweig are the three main examples of the dialogical principle. Balthasar is especially aware of how Rosenzweig's work, and especially *The Star of Redemption*, articulates a philosophical alternative to German Idealism that is at once more friendly to Judaism and Christianity (636-39). For support of Rosenzweig's anti-Idealism, see also *GL7*, 440.

[70]. #62-5 in the Preface of the *Phenomenology* make this point in a highly condensed way. The idea that the virtuality of the divine is sufficient to establish that it is the grammatical subject but not the real subject of discourse has numerous registers in Hegel's work. *LPR* provides one register, in which the intra-trinitarian divine posited at the beginning is said to require nature and finite spirit in order to become a divine that is fully actual. The *Encyclopedia* provides another. At the level of 'logic' the divine subject is not sufficiently substantial. This requires the generation and opposition of the world of nature and finite spirit that is spoken to in *The Philosophy of Nature* and the *Philosophy of Mind*, the two other parts of the *Encyclopedia*.

[71]. Passages in Hegel's work that come out definitively against a tri-personal view of the Trinity include *PS* #771, *LPR3* 1821 MS E 82, G 20; 1824 E 194, G 127-28; 1827 E 283, G 208-09; *Enc* #99-103. The passage from *PS* sets the terms for both the later passages and Hegel's self-conscious departure from the theological tradition. Hegel judges that the picture of a relation between three separate subjects or substances is invalid from a philosophical point of view. The putting out of action of the tri-personal view necessarily demolishes any and all view of the Trinity as inherently social, notwithstanding Hegel's insistence on the 'we' of community. For when Hegel talks of we, he is talking of the unification that happens between individual finite spirits due to a force (Spirit) both within and beyond them. Balthasar is not happy about Hegel's departure from the tradition. But neither is Wolfhart Pannenberg. See his 'Die Subjektivität Gottes und die Trinitätslehre. Ein Beitrag zur Beziehung zwischen Karl Barth und der Philosophie Hegels,' in *Kerygma und Dogma* 23 (1977), 25-40.

[72]. I am here obviously referring to Jack Miles' well-known book, *God: A Biography?* (New York: Random House, 1995).

[73]. If Irenaeus is a good example, Tertullian, whose tradition of discourse is more juridical than philosophical, is even better. His *Against Praxeas*, especially books 1-4, represent a classic defense of the divine immutability.
[74]. In his extraordinarily useful exposition of the first volume of *Apokalypse 1*, Aidan Nichols underscores this aspect of Balthasar's diagnosis more than any other. See *Scattering the Seeds*, 37, 63-4, 69, 72-4, 85-6, 102-03.
[75]. Iljin fled Communist Russia in the 1920's to Germany. He is the translator of the Russian text published by Franke in Bern.
[76]. Iljin, *Die Philosophie Hegels*, 2-3-30; esp. 2-3-14. Iljin thinks of the movement in Hegelian thought from *Sein* to *Begriff* or *Sein* to *Idee* as articulating a 'theogenetic process' (*theogenetische Prozess*).
[77]. There can be no denying that Iljin did, indeed, hold such convictions, although he insisted that his work on Hegel was without remainder analytic-interpretive rather than evaluative. Whether such separation of method and immunization against theological convictions played a role in interpretation is an open question. In this respect, it would be interesting to explore whether the remaining chapters that deal with Hegel's non-logical reflections show more evidence of theological convictions of an evaluative sort. See Ivan A. Iljin, *The Philosophy of Hegel as a Doctrine of the Concreteness of God and Humanity*, Volume One: The Doctrine of God and Volume Two: The Doctrine of Humanity, ed. tr. Philip T. Grier, (Evanston, IL: Northwestern University Press, 2011).
[78]. In *Work on Myth* Romanticism and Idealism represent the two main forms of the recrudescence of myth on this side of modernity. Blumenberg notes the process character of both Romantic and Idealist forms of metanarrative (269, 290-91). He insists that this feature distinguishes them from Gnostic myth with which they might appear to have so much in common, given their obsession with evil and its overcoming. Other than chronology, Blumenberg presents no criteria for the distinction. Indeed, he seems to undermine it when he makes the point that the constructive work of Hans Jonas, the foremost scholar of Gnosticism of the first half of the twentieth century, which is best characterized as a kind of post-Idealist theogony, represents a modified form of Gnosticism (290-91). For Blumenberg, although it admits a 'mythological' ascription, Gnosticism differs from a myth such as the myth of Prometheus in that it is more self-conscious and constructed. In line with Balthasar in *Apokalypse 1*, the two great loci for myth of a second-order type are Romanticism (208, 213) and Idealism. The implication in both cases is that Romanticism and Idealism connect with Gnosticism as a prime example of myth whose creation and reception is quite different from the way myth usually functions.
[79]. In *Work on Myth* Blumenberg makes a distinction between an organic myth – a myth such as the myth of Prometheus which has great staying powers within and across cultures – and an artificial myth, which is self-consciously produced in a situation in which myth has supposedly been overcome (209, 266-69, 291), and thus came the reaction of Romanticism and Idealism to the Enlightenment break with myth. A somewhat similar distinction – albeit expressed in somewhat different language – is operative in the 'early' Ricoeur. In *The Symbolism of Evil* (327) Ricoeur makes the interesting suggestion that German Idealism

reproduces the tragic myth of the Babylonian creation hymn albeit in a form that differs radically from the 4,000 year old original. The precise nature of the reproduction can be gleaned from two essays which are more or less contemporaneous with this text. In speaking about Augustine's relation to the biblical view of fall Ricoeur talks about the 'logicization of myth.' More, Ricoeur points to Gnosticism as the exemplar of such logiciziation. Relevant to the first point is 'Original Sin: A Study in Meaning,' and to the second, 'The Hermeneutics of Symbols and Philosophical Reflection: 1,' in *The Conflict of Interpretations*, ed. Don Idhe (Evanston, IL: Northwestern University Press, 1974), 269-86, 287-314. For the first point, see esp. 273, for the second, 312.

[80]. While the extent to which German Idealism and Hegel in particular are objects of unique critical concern in *The Star of Redemption* still remain somewhat controversial, the fact that Rosenzweig's dissertation, *Hegel's Theory of the State*, is expository rather than critical does not count against it. For a good account of the importance of Rosenzweig's relation to Hegel, see Peter Eli Gordon, *Rosenzweig and Heidegger: Between Judaism and German Philosophy* (Berkeley, Los Angeles, and London: University of California Press, 2003), 82-118.

[81]. See especially chapter 6 of *Otherwise than Being or Beyond Essence*, tr. Alphonso Lingis (The Hague: Martinus Nijhoff, 1981).

[82]. In his earliest work Rosenzweig's examination of Hegel's view of the State in itself and in its relation to civil society does not seem to exclude dialogue, since it touches on recognition and self-recognition which are ingredients in both. This is not the case, however, in *The Star of Redemption.* From the opening page this text challenges modern forms of Idealism by suggesting that they represent forms of Parmenideanism in which it is insisted that being is correlative to thought (*to gar auto noein estin te kai einai*).

[83]. There are any number of contemporary readings which emphasize the non-speculative aspects of Hegel's thought centered in a community in which institutions not only provide social coherence and identity but also genuine liberation. See Paul Lakeland, *The Politics of Salvation: The Hegelian Idea of the State* (Albany, NY: SUNY Press, 1984); Andrew Shanks, *Hegel's Political Theology* (Cambridge: Cambridge University Press, 1991); Walter Jaeschke, *Reason in Religion: The Foundation of Hegel's Philosophy of Religion*, tr. Peter Hodgson and Michael Steward (Berkeley and Los Angeles: University of California Press, 1990); Robert R. Williams, *Hegel's Ethics of Recognition* (Berkeley and Los Angeles: University of California Press, 1997).

[84]. In *Glas* Derrida ties together Hegelian reflection on the family, which is the lowest level of objective Spirit (*Sittlichkeit*), with the doctrine of the Trinity, which offers the most adequate symbol of the absolute at the level of Christian representation (*Vorstellung*). This doctrine or symbol is primed for sublation by speculative philosophy which renders self-positing Spirit in a fully adequate way. For Derrida, the analogy between the family and the Trinity suggests that the doctrine of the Trinity enacts the same politics of exclusion that the family does. Derrida's reading is tendentious. He insists that the analogy between family and the doctrine is deep and holds within the Christian tradition itself and is not simply a function of Hegel's discourse. Balthasar makes sure to avoid the Hegelian danger. The family

offers an analogy of the Trinity, no more. They do not belong on the same explanatory plane.

[85]. It is integral to the distinction between God and finite creatures that the Aristotelian structure of potency and act that characterizes material and temporal beings not be applied to God. By contrast with finite creatures God is pure act (*ST* 1, Q2, art 3; Q3, art 1).

[86]. See Gustaf Aulén, *Christus Victor: A Historical Study of the Three Main Types of the Idea of Atonement*, tr. A. G. Herbert (New York: Macmillan, 1969).

[87]. See Anders Nygren, *Agape and Eros*, tr. Philip S. Watson (London: SPCK, 1982). Gawronski offers helpful comments on Balthasar's prioritization of agape over eros and yet refusal of an either-or. See *Word and Silence*, 132-36.

[88]. See *Protestant Theology in the Nineteenth Century*, 304. Whatever the level of Barth's lexical dependence on German Idealism in his first articulation of the Trinity in *Church Dogmatics*, he opposes any figuration of the triune God as necessarily expressive. Barth's guiding construct is that of 'God who loves in freedom' (*CD2/1*, 128), and it is this construct that interprets all other trinitarian forays, including Barth's return to the Trinity in *Church Dogmatics 4*. The more or less absolute distance between Barth and Hegel on this issue has not prevented theologians such as Peter Hodgson from thinking that Barth and Hegel can be reconciled on this point. See his *God in History: Shapes of Freedom* (Nashville: Abingdon Press, 1989), 97-9, 109-10. See also *Winds of the Spirit: A Contribution to Christian Theology* (Louisville, KY: Westminister Press John Knox, 1994), 153-55. For evidence of Balthasar's concern with Barth's view of divine sovereignty, see Balthasar's *The Theology of Karl Barth*, 99-100, 105, 192, 198. The label for the concern is 'actualism,' a pure form of sovereignty that is beyond appeal to ethics, reason or aesthetics.

[89]. A commentator on Balthasar who emphasizes the biblical warrant for versimilitude is Christopher Steck, S. J. See his *The Ethical Thought of Hans Urs von Balthasar* (New York: Crossroad, 2001), 26, where he underscores the *dei* of Luke 9:22 and the *rectitudo* of Anselm.

[90]. Francesca Murphy, who combines literary appreciation and more than usual knowledge of the Bible, grasps this point well in her *Christ and the Form of Beauty: A Study in Theology and Literature* (Edinburgh: T&T Clark, 1995). In this text Murphy reads Balthasar's theological aesthetics (131-94) as both throwing light on the dynamic forms of literature and in turn being illuminated by them.

[91]. Hegel surprisingly defends Anselmian views at a number of crucial junctures throughout *Lectures on the Philosophy of Religion*. He defends, for example, Anselm's view of the ontological argument against Kantian critique, arguing that if his concept of God is interpreted rightly, then Anselm offers a totally defensible view that shows only the weakness of Kant's epistemological constructs, which remain purely subjective and static (*LPR3* 1831 E 352-57, G 271-75). Hegel confirms his support of Anselm over Kant on the ontological argument in his *Lectures on the Proof of the Existence of God*, tr. ed. Peter C. Hodgson (Oxford: Clarendon Press, 2007), 188-90. Useful studies of Hegel that highlight his preference for Anselm over Kant include: Patricia Marie Calton, *Hegel's Metaphysics of God: The Ontological Proof as a Development of a Trinitarian Divine Ontology* (Aldershot: Ashgate, 2001);

Louis Girard, *L'Argument ontologique chez Saint Anselm et chez Hegel* (Amsterdam: Rodopi, 1995); Bernard Lakebrink, *Studien zur Metaphysik Hegels* (Freiburg: Rombuch, 1969), 182-201. Surprisingly, Hegel also finds some use for Anselm's soteriology. Hegel recalls Anselm's theory of satisfaction without any obvious sense of embarrassment in *LPR3* 1824 E 219, G 150. In Hegel's hands, however, the meaning of 'satisfaction' undergoes radical change. If the bringing together of humanity and God is the agreed on result of the life and death of Christ, everything else is different. Fulfilling the demands of justice has nothing to do with it. Moreover, the reuniting of the divine and the human not only integrates human being but also God, a view that would make no sense to Anselm, and which Irenaeus would recognize as Valentinian.

92. In *GL2* Balthasar argues that Anselm's soteriology (a) does not proceed by logical necessity, and (b) that it is not determined exclusively by concerns of justice. In *TD4* (255-61) Balthasar continues to support Anselm's soteriology in general and thinks that 'satisfaction' is an expugnable element of Christian soteriology. At the same time, Anselm's view suffers from a certain one-sidedness. This also limits its ability to be the other to Hegel. Comparatively speaking Irenaeus' less precise – but more ample – soteriology is in a better position. See *TD2*, 261. Other anti-necessity passages include *TD2*, 256; *TD4*, 322-23; *TD5*, 227-28.

93. See Przywara, *Hölderlin: Eine Studie* (Nuremberg, 1949). This book greatly influences Marion's interpretation of Hölderlin in *The Idol and Distance*, 81-138, esp. 105.

94. An especially good discussion of this norm is to be found in Balthasar's essay 'Kenosis of the Church' in *Exp 4*, 125-38, esp. 126

95. See also *TD5*, 223-24. If G. Thomasius is the most important of these thinkers, F. H. R. Frank and G. Gess are also major representatives.

96. For a similar statement – but without reference to Bulgakov – see *Exp 4*, 410-11. For a similar statement with a reference to Bulgakov, as the Russian theologian is enlisted against Moltmann, see *TD4*, 323.

97. Altizer could not make the point more clearly in his *Genesis and Apocalypse: A Theological Voyage to Authentic Christianity* (Louisville, KY: Westminister/John Knox Press, 1990) when he identifies the operation of kenosis with the realization of a pleroma that is in excess of what is given in the beginning (88; also 100).

98. I have given information on most of the Communio circle that write in French in note 3, Introduction to Part 2. Giovanni Marchesi represents the Italian group of Communio and is the author of a still important book on Balthasar's Christology in which a major theme is the contrast between the Christologies of Balthasar and Hegel. See *La Cristologia di Hans Urs von Balthasar: La figura di Gesù Cristo expressione visibile di dio* (Rome: Gregoriana Ed., 1977).

99. For information on the stances taken by the various members of the Radical Orthodoxy movement, see note 52 in Chapter 2.

100. This is as much the language of the *Encyclopedia* as it is of the *Phenomenology*.

101. This is the language that Hegel adopts to describe the movement from the logical sphere to the real sphere of nature. On his own terms – especially given his interdefining of freedom and necessity – Hegel is entitled to use this term. At the same time, it would be naive not to recall Hegel's interest in avoiding

another pantheism controversy and his concern that a Schellingian critique of his position made under the auspices of the concept of 'freedom' would not gain traction.

[102]. If the general importance of Schiller's aesthetics for Hegel's formulation of the concept has not always been appreciated, recent scholarship has left us in no doubt about its importance. Two of the more important commentators are Jacques Taminiaux and H. S. Harris. For Taminiaux, see *La nostalgie de la Grèce à l'aube de l'idéalisme allemand, Kant et les grecs dans l'itinéraire de Schiller, de Hölderlin et de Hegel* (The Hague: Martinus Nijhoff, 1967). For Harris, see *Hegel's Development 2: Night Thoughts (Jena 1801-1806)* (Oxford: Clarendon Press, 1983), 16, 404, 561, esp. 534; *Hegel's Ladder 1: The Pilgrimage of Reason* (Indianapolis: Hackett Publishing Co., 1997), 3-4, 55, 563, esp. 551, 553; *Hegel's Ladder 2: The Odyssey of Spirit* (Indianapolis: Hackett Publishing Co., 1997), 368.

[103]. Balthasar sees the dangers for the confounding of agape with eros both in the premodern and modern periods. As Balthasar makes especially clear in *GL4 & 5* it is precisely because of the possibility of confusion, that theology has to be extremely vigilant with regard to its borrowing from Neoplatonism. And much of the Renaissance and almost all of Romanticism and Idealism show symptoms of this substitution of eros for agape. In making the latter judgment in *GL5*, where he is thinking of the Neoplatonic erotics of Giordano Bruno being completed in German Idealism, Balthasar essentially confirms the judgment he made in *Apok 1*. At the same time, however, he judges that the preference for agape over eros should not be absolute. That is, Balthasar goes to some pains to indicate that agape includes rather than excludes eros. It does so in two different ways. First, and most obviously, it includes it in the sense that eros is the human response to divine agape. Second, while indeed God does not gain in and through the creation of the world and engagement with it, divine love is erotic in that God is supremely interested in and concerned with the world. Eros speaks to a passion that is without need or without the prospect of in any way diminishing God in an existential or ontological way. Balthasar thinks that this 'interested' God is faithful to biblical witness and the best of Christian Neoplatonism. In their general resistance to Hegel there is a remarkable correspondence between Balthasar and the work of the Irish philosopher, William Desmond. Desmond has used the distinction of agape and eros to great critical effect from the very beginning of his oeuvre, and argued that Hegel is exemplary with the respect to the figuration of the erotic God who is actualized in and through a process of self-mediation. See *Beyond Hegel and Dialectic: Speculation, Cult, and Comedy* (Albany, NY: SUNY Press, 1992), 181-82; *Being and the Between* (Albany, NY: SUNY Press, 1995), 165-66, 169, 242-51, 252-65. The overlap with Balthasar is specific, not generic. Desmond points that the motor of eros in Hegel is lack (248-49); that at its best Neoplatonic construal of an origin excessive with respect to that which derives from it is the contrary to the Hegelian dialectical view (259); that the eros of human being has its ground and warrant in the agapeic origin (260); and finally the agapeic origin does not require an other to (dialectically) complete it. Desmond writes: 'For the agapeic origin does not become itself in a dialectical detour through finitude rendered as its self-other. There is no absorption of finite creation as part within

an engulfing whole. Put in more theological language: God does not create himself in creating the world' (261). Desmond's most sustained critique of Hegel's God as erotic is to be found in *Hegel's God: A Counterfeit Double?* (Albany, NY: SUNY Press, 2003), 103-20.

[104]. In *Gnostic Return in Modernity* I underscore these important differences while arguing that these changes do not alter the observable continuity in narrative grammar. 'Valentinian narrative grammar,' as I point out, is a transformation grammar in the sense that its *raison d'être* is the alternation of the biblical narrative, at least as that narrative is regulated by the rule of faith, and the construction of a narrative that amounts to knowledge as such. See 99-136.

[105]. Both the gift of tradition and phenomenological givenness are important to Balthasar and essentially refer to and support each other.

[106]. See especially Balthasar's discussion of the *kalokagathon* (*GL1*, 25, 59; *GL5*, 201-04). For an appreciation of the integration of the beautiful and the good in Plato – with the integration of the true with the good more or less taken for granted – see *GL4*, 179-80.

[107]. Alexandre Kojève, *Introduction to the Reading of Hegel*, tr. J. H. Nichols, ed. Allen Bloom (New York: Basic Books, 1969), 112.

[108]. There is an intimate relation between Balthasar's hagiographical work and his more systematic articulation in the trilogy of the saint as the norm of Christian life. Although key concepts such as 'mission' are not in play until *Theo-Drama*, it is obvious from Balthasar's discussion of 'holy fools' and his charting of figures such as Ruusbroec and Catherine of Genoa in *GL5* that the notion of 'saint' as translating Christ's archetypal response to the salvific demand of the Father is hugely important.

[109]. Balthasar's criterion of sainthood is decidedly non-juridical. He is solely interested in the match between life and reflection and their relative transparence with respect to Christ.

[110]. Balthasar's *A Theology of History* (San Francisco: Ignatius Press, 1994) can be taken in its totality as containing a revision of the Hegelian understanding of history, which he deems 'the most grandiose attempt to master the realm of fact and history through reason' (11). See 10-14.

[111]. The famous 'owl of Minerva' image is used by Hegel in the Preface to *The Philosophy of Right* to indicate that the philosophical task is descriptive rather than prescriptive, recollective rather than prophetic.

[112]. See the important section on the prophets in *Glory of the Lord 6* titled 'Staircase of Obedience' (*GL6*, 225-98).

[113]. It would be interesting to compare and contrast Balthasar's reflections on Homer with Weil's powerful, similar-length, essay 'The Iliad as a Poem of Might.' See *Simone Weil: An Anthology*, ed. Sian Miles (New York: Weidenfeld & Nicholson, 1986), 162-85. The point made by Weil is that the *Iliad* represents nothing less than a deconstruction of martial ideology and an opening beyond to another kind of glory ultimately realized in Christ. Although Balthasar does not have Weil's panache when it comes to illustrating how the martial ideology of the *Iliad* deconstructs itself, he does hold to revelation of glory that is other to glory as validating the group.

114. Jean-Yves Lacoste, *Experience and the Absolute: Disputed Questions on the Humanity of Man*, tr. Mark Raferty-Skehan (New York: Fordham University Press, 2004), 122-24, 131, 136, 181-2, 185-6.

115. The general theme of the difficulty of distinguishing between glory that has real weight and its counterfeit is an important one for Weil. See *Gravity and Grace*, tr. Emma Craufurd (London: Routledge & Kegan Paul, 1972), 62-5, 119, 144-46; *Intimations of Christianity among the Greeks*, tr. E. F. Geissbuhler (London: Routledge & Kegan Paul, 1957, 1976), 93-100, 169-76.

116. In the *Phenomenology* Hegel thinks that Sophocles is the exemplary figure of Greek tragedy with *Antigone* essentially being the unsurpassable example of the genre of Greek tragedy because of the conflict between the demands of the family and the State. The *Aesthetics* confirm this verdict, and summarily dismiss Euripides as being a tragedian of a lower order, one given to ironic distance that favors self-expression. For more information, see n. 7 & 8 of Chapter 1.

117. For especially clear expressions of Hegel's opposition to the non-philosophical view of eternity as never-completed duration, see especially *LPR1* 1821 E 195, G 105; *LPR3* 1831 E 386 G 305; also *LPR3* 1827 E 314 G 227-28. The identification of true knowing with eternity is the result of the itinerary of Spirit that is communicated by the *Phenomenology*, presupposed in *The Science of Logic*, and articulated across the *Encyclopedia* from the *Logic* to the *Philosophy of Mind.* It should be pointed out that while Spinoza's notion of *scientia intuitiva* provides the warrant for Hegel's view, at the very least the mysticism of Meister Eckhart serves to reinforce it. See my discussion of this point in *The Heterodox Hegel*, 250-63, esp. 256-58. See also 289-90.

118. Recall here Hegel's view of scripture as a 'wax nose.' See *LPR1* 1824 E 123, G 39-40.

119. William T. Dickens has done a real service in *Hans Urs von Balthasar's Theological Aesthetics: A Model for Post-Critical Biblical Interpretation* (Notre Dame: University of Notre Dame Press, 2003) in dealing with Balthasar's critique but also critical appropriation of historical-critical method. Rightly, he spends considerable time analyzing *GL6 & 7*, and touches on the biblical exegesis of *Theo-Drama* only to a limited extent. This work remains to be done.

Chapter 3

1. Desmond's reading of Hegel in *Hegel's God: A Counterfeit Double?* is very close to the reading prosecuted in *The Heterodox Hegel*, with the difference that its overall register is philosophical, while the register of *The Heterodox Hegel* is theological. That Desmond is in principle hospitable to my analysis is shown by his willingness to acknowledge the relation between his notion of 'counterfeit double' and what I have been calling *metalepsis.* See *God and the Between* (Albany, NY: SUNY Press, 2008), 212.

2. *Theo-Drama 2* refers back to *The Theology of Karl Barth*, 233-34, where Balthasar opposes Barth's view of the 'concrete universal' to that of Hegel.

[3]. By contrast in the *Encyclopedia* the incarnation and passion narrative belong to the third rather than the second trinitarian moment. Accordingly, they are assigned to the moment of the 'Spirit.' Each of the schematizations has problems built into them, the latter (with its Joachimite emphasis) as much as the former. Arguably, some knowledge of the first contraction is shown in *TL2*, 22-3.

[4]. That the Christologies of exemplary theologians are not identical in every respect is not a difficulty for Balthasar. Christ exceeds all Christologies, indeed, their sum. It would be invidious to choose between the five examples, even if over the course of his career, arguably, Balthasar gave more attention to the Christologies of Maximus and Bonaventure than the others. The focus of Balthasar's book on Maximus in 1942 is christological. In addition, Maximus remains an important figure in the background of the christocentric reading of Pseudo-Dionysius in *GL2*, and is increasingly cited throughout *Theo-Drama*, with *TD4* perhaps as a high-point. The Christocentrism of Bonvaventure is not simply to the fore in the portrait of Bonaventure in *GL2*, but is a constitutive element in the elaboration of theological aesthetics in *GL1*. Against the backdrop of the drama of Irenaeus making a fundamental decision that affects the subsequent history of Christianity, it is a point with Balthasar to paint Irenaeus as a deeply christological thinker. The dramatic nature of this Christology, or more precisely Irenaeus' soteriology is, arguably, more to the fore in *Theo-Drama*. The immense importance of Irenaeus in *Theo-Drama* may well reside in the fact that an apocalyptic figuration of Christ is intrinsically connected with the agon between truth and the lie, between the Catholic tradition and Gnostic refigurations of the biblical narrative which undo Christ's centrality. Balthasar's rehabilitation of Anselm in *GL2*, and especially his argument that Anselm's rationale of incarnation is fundamentally aesthetic rather than logical in the strict sense, prepares for the rehabilitation of the notion of satisfaction conducted in *TD4*. And, finally, whatever the problems with Origen as a speculative thinker, and especially his articulation of theological anthropology that is overly influenced by Neoplatonism – these concerns get expressed in the book on Maximus – the anthology of Origen's writings Balthasar presents in 1938 has as its fundamental premise that for Origen Christ is the referent of all of scripture. For a convenient translation of *Origenes: Geist und Feuer*, see *Origen: Spirit and Fire*, tr. Robert J. Daly, S.J. (Washington, DC: Catholic University of America Press, 1984).

[5]. Pannenberg provides an important bench-mark, since his theology presupposes a deep knowledge of Hegel's thought, and patiently engages it from the very beginning of his career. His refusal in *Systematic Theology* to eclipse the resurrection as Hegel had done is a piece of a broader debate with Hegel about the conditions of the possibility of eschatology. Even to a greater extent than Balthasar, Pannenberg argues that resurrection is a prolepsis of the eschaton. As with Balthasar all reflection on the relation of resurrection and eschaton is done within the horizon of the knowledge and acknowledgment of the trinitarian God of history. See *Systematic Theology*, vol. 1, tr. Geoff Bromily (Grand Rapids: Eerdmans, 1991), 63-464; *Systematic Theology*, vol. 2, tr. Geoff Bromily (Grand Rapids: Eerdmans, 1993), 1-174. Pannenberg's position on the resurrection is clearly stated in his

much earlier *Jesus – God and Man*, tr. Lewis Wilkins and Duane Priebe, 2nd ed. (Philadelphia: Westminister Press, 1997), 1-209.

[6]. From the *Phenomenology*, for especially explicit passages see #19, 32. Also relevant are #77-78, #724, #759, and #808. For particularly apropos passages in *Lectures on the Philosophy of Religion*, see *LPR3* 1821 MS E 124-25, G 59-60 and 1827 E 325-26, G 249-50. Hegel is fully aware that the exposure to death and in general the non-divine is constitutive of the definition of love. Note that the Hegelian language of 'death,' 'otherness', and 'fragility' is recalled in Balthasar's essay on 'Descent into Hell' in *Exp 4*, 402-14, esp. 410-11.

[7]. Hegel's pledge of fealty notwithstanding, not too many theologians have been persuaded that Hegel remained faithful to Luther in fundamental respects. For a full account of the fundamental substantive and hermeneutic departures, see Ulrich Asendorf, *Luther und Hegel. Untersuchungen zur Grundlegung einer neuen systematischen Theologie* (Weisbaden: Steiner, 1982). For a more focused account of the departure at the level of Christology with specific reference to divine judgment and wrath, see Annegrit Brunkhorst-Hasenclever, *Die Transformierung der theologischen Deutung des Todes bei G. W. F. Hegel. Ein Beitrag zur Formbestimmung von Paradox und Synthese* (Bern & Frankfurt: Herbert and Peter Lang, 1970), esp. 228-42.

[8]. As that author of *Apokalypse* knows well, not all forms of Romanticism elaborate aggressive forms of autonomy – that is, those that would admit of being labeled 'Promethean.' For instance, an assertion of Dionysian openness to reality would be equally consistent with finding objectionable the effective agency of another.

[9]. In *GL5* (298-338) Hölderlin's status is ambiguous: he both exceeds Romanticism and remains captive to its fundamental axioms. This is why Hölderlin can have critical leverage on Hegel as well as anticipate him. *GL5* does not differ radically from Balthasar's account of Hölderlin in *Apok 1*. Hölderlin is not obviously a Promethean thinker in the way that the German Idealists are, but *Hyperion* (*Apok 1*, 312-14), and *The Death of Empedokles* (*Apok 1*, 324), on the other, are essentially Romantic texts. Balthasar attempts a determination of Hölderlin from the entire body of his works, and does not favor as do Przywara and Marion, his great odes and hymns which bring Hölderlin beyond the Romantic orbit.

[10]. Here I echo Matthew Arnold's bleak conclusion to 'Dover Beach,' which suggests that the battle between religion and non-religion is essentially over, and that contemporary battles are merely posthumous. Arnold, of course, thinks that disbelief and skepticism have won out.

[11]. *Cosmic Liturgy* understands itself to be an intervention into the field of theology in general, and Christology in particular, and precisely for this reason opposes Hegel. The best account of Balthasar's use of Maximus in opposition to Hegelian views on Christ and the Trinity is still de Schrijver, *Le merveilleux accord de l'homme et de Dieu*, 217-51; also James Naduvilekut, *Christus der Heilsweg: Soteria als Theodrama im Werk Hans Urs von Balthasars* (St Ottilien: EOS Verlag, 1987), 150-60. Aidan Nichols has as usual a grasp of the opposition, see *The Word Has Been Abroad*, 115.

[12]. Balthasar agrees with Maximus that Dythelitism represents a development of Chalcedon precisely to the extent that it represents a biblical regression. Although the point is not uncontroversial, and it may, for example, stand behind some of

the disagreements between Rahner and Balthasar on how one should or should not talk about suffering and God. For a detailed discussion of this point as focused in *Cosmic Liturgy*, see my 'Von Balthasar and Thick Retrieval: Post-Chalcedonian Symphonic Theology,' in *Gregorianum* 77.2, Spring (1986), esp. 238-53.

[13]. This is the view of André Léonard in 'Le primat du négative et l'interpretation speculative de la religion. Un example: la reprise hégelienne du dogme christologique de chalcédoine,' in *Hegels Logik der Philosophie*, ed. Dieter Henrich and Rolf Peter Horstmann (Stuttgart: Klett-Cottal, 1984), 160-71. This is also my own conclusion in *The Heterodox Hegel* (210-31) where I argue that Hegel develops the monophysite line of Luther's Christology.

[14]. Balthasar also has the proximate example of Sergei Bulgakov before him. We will be examining this relation in some detail in part 3.

[15]. Nichols emphasizes the Hamann-Irenaeus connection. See *The Word Has Been Abroad*, 112-14.

[16]. This statement is from Balthasar's very important essay, 'The Claim to Catholicity,' in *Exp 4*, 65-121.

[17]. I have spoken to the Heideggerian and Derridian charges already. Karl Löwith's classic statement of Hegelianism as a realized eschatology is to be found in *From Hegel to Nietzsche: The Revolution in Nineteenth Century Thought*, tr. D. E. Green (New York: Doubleday, 1967).

[18]. 'The Claim to Catholicity' and *TD5* are but two of the texts in which Balthasar validates at a fundamental level 20th-century philosophical and theological critique of 'realized eschatology' of the kind represented by Hegel's system.

[19]. Balthasar's reflections on Pascal's thoughts on the love of Christ displayed on the cross (*GL3*, 218-33) contrast sharply with similar reflections in Hegel: whereas in Hegel, the note of manifestation is struck, in Pascal the note is that of hiddenness; whereas in Hegel the emphasis falls on the confidence of our knowledge of salvation in Christ, in Pascal the emphasis is on its uncertainty; whereas Hegel plots a developmental scheme in which elevation gradually replaces the suffering that is figured by Christ, in Pascal the suffering of Christ is our suffering even to the end of the world; whereas for Hegel the cross even further marginalizes sin by uploading even more anthropological potential, in Pascal the cross reveals the recalcitrance and depth of sin.

[20]. The language of 'parenthesis' is anticipated by Przywara and especially Romano Guardini. See Balthasar, *The Theology of Karl Barth*, 329-30.

[21]. See Balthasar, *The Theology of Henri de Lubac: An Overview* (San Francisco: Ignatius Press, 1991) in which *La postérité spirituelle de Joachim de Flore. 2 vols* (Paris Lethielleux, 1979) is praised (119-24).

[22]. See also *TL2*, 205-09; *TL3*, 416-18; *SI*, 4-5; *Exp, 4*, 105-06.

[23]. One of the most intelligent of such critiques is that of Steffen Lösel. See his 'Unapocalyptic Theology: History and Eschatology in Balthasar's Theodrama,' in *Modern Theology* 17.2, April (2001), 201-25.

[24]. The assertion that the Aquinas in play is heavily Neoplatonic does not imply a judgment with respect to probity. Balthasar need not be construed as reinventing the medieval Scholastic whom, he believes, with Rahner, transcends the logical and the propositional. In stressing the Neoplatonism of *Wahrheit*, I should not be

thought to deny the influence of Heidegger. This influence will be an object of analysis in volume 2 of *The Anatomy of Misremembering.*

25. See Marion, 'Saint Thomas d'Aquin et l'onto-théo-logie,' in *Revue Thomiste* 95.1 (1995), 31-66.

26. See, for example, *LPR3* 1824 E 233-36, G 164-67; 1827 E 333-9, G 256-62.

27. This point is rightly underscored by Walter Jaeschke in *Reason in Religion: The Formation of Hegel's Philosophy of Religion*, tr. J. Michael Steward and Peter Hodgson (Berkeley, CA: University of California Press, 1990), 325-58. Jaeschke believes, however, that in switching the line of emphasis to the community, Hegel does much more than affirm a Protestant sacramental theology. Given the fact that self-affirmation of divine presence in the community extends beyond the bounds of the cult into social institutions of the family and civil society, Hegel's various reflections on the cult functions as nothing less than a legitimation of the modern world.

28. Increasingly throughout the trilogy Balthasar reflects on manifestation of the Spirit as a form of non-manifestation, at once an appearance in the mode of the incognito and a kind of deferral in which personality but not personhood disappears. Bulgakov also understands the unusual character of the Spirit. In the 20th-century Catholic tradition, this is not an insight that escapes Congar, who shows an encyclopedic knowledge of the pneumatological traditions of both East and West. In terms of tackling the systematic issue of how the different behavior effects or does not the notion of the person of the Spirit, the major thinker for Balthasar as for all Catholic systematics is Heribert Mühlen. See especially *Der Heilige Geist als Person in der Trinität bei der Inkarnation und im Gnadenbund. Ich-Du-Wir* (Münster: Aschendorff, 1963).

29. Bellarmine (1542-1621), the great Counter-Reformation controversialist, throughout a career offered a veritable compendium of refutation of Reformation positions in which he linked their positions on God, Christ, and the church to ancient heresies. In the final volume of the four volume *Disputationes de controversiis Christianae fidei adversus huius temporis haereticos*, he attacks the spiritualism of the Reformation position which puts in question the embodied nature of selves and ultimately the resurrection. The Reformation, therefore, repeats just that kind of position that church fathers such as Irenaeus and Tertullian tried to combat.

30. Balthasar's preference for Revelation will come in for discussion in Part 4.

31. Although Balthasar suggests these points from the opening bell in *Theo-Drama*, they are made with particular force in *Theo-Logic*. For his inversion of the priority of structure over event, see *TL1*, 37, 41, 50-1, 62, 71, 84; *TL2*, 22-4, 42. For the inversion of the priority of manifestation over revelation, see *TL1*, 57, 65, 88.

32. See Patrick Kavanagh, *Lough Derg* (Ireland: Goldsmith Press, 1978), 16 line 8.

33. Michel Foucault, *The Archeology of Knowledge* (New York: Pantheon, 1993), 235. 'Anti-Hegelianism is,' Foucault writes, 'possibly one of his [Hegel's] tricks directed against us, at the end of which he stands, motionless, waiting for us.'

34. *Apok 1*, 205, 238 for Schelling; *Apok 1*, 618 for Hegel. In *Apok 1* in addressing the more metaphysical tendencies of Fichte in a later text such as *Die Anweisung zum seligen Leben* (1806), Balthasar draws attention to its Neoplatonic rather than Johannine flavor (176-77). Balthasar's account of Fichte in *GL5* (546-57) does

not essentially move beyond what he wrote in *Apokalypse*, and again *Anweisung*, which presents a metaphysics of love, is to the fore (*GL5*, 554, 556). There is one exception, however. Balthasar not only acknowledges the presence of the Johannine writings in Fichte's work (this is true in particular of *Anweisung*), but of German Idealism as a whole. He writes: 'The Old Testament, which is the site of glory, is rejected in favor of the Johannine final form of the New Testament, dissociated from Paul and the Synoptics, in order to be able to reinterpret agape directly and freely in the direction of *gnosis*' (*GL5*, 548).

[35]. Here Balthasar agrees with such an exemplary commentator on Hegel as Albert Chapelle about the dynamic nature of the Trinity, although he does not agree that it attenuates the case against Hegel. See Chapelle, *Hegel et la religion*, vol. 2, n. 228. For supporting analysis, see 86-8. Other readers of Hegel make a more generic accusation of modalism, without trying to connect Hegel's particular form with that evident in the second and third centuries of the common era. In an important essay on Hegel's trintitarian thought Pannenberg speaks of the *Dreimomentigkeit* of subjectivity. See 'Die Subjektivität Gottes und die Trinitätslehre. Ein Beitrag zur Beziehung zwischen Karl Barth und die Philosophie Hegels,' in *Kerygma und Dogma* 23 (1977), 25-40. See also Ludger Oeing-Hanhoff, 'Hegels Trinitätslehre. Zur Aufgabe ihrer Kritik und Reception,' in *Theologie und Philosophie* 52 (1977), 379-407. See esp. 402-04.

[36]. See *PS* #771 (übergehende Momente); *LPR3* 1821 E 82, G 20; 1824 E 194, G 127-28; 1827 E 283, G 208-09. Balthasar is a little less forgiving than a number of Communio Catholics on this point. In addition to Chapelle, see also Bruaire, who in *Logique et religion* (65, 91) notes the stress Hegel's trinitarian dynamism puts on the distinction between economic and immanent spheres of the Trinity, but does not bring in a verdict. See *TL3*, 40-41 where Balthasar leaves no doubt that in his view the distinctive mark of Hegelianism is that it overcomes the immanent-economic Trinity distinction. A crucial element of the disintegration of the economic-immanent Trinity distinction is that the subjectivity which underpins the entire movement is result rather than origin, although without some anticipation of resultant subjectivity, without which the entire movement would be impossible. Although Hegel effectively avoids the entire mainline discourse on the Trinity, when he does compare and contrast his view of the Trinity with the somewhat odd assortment of positions he takes to be trinitarian, for example, Neoplatonism, Gnosticism, and Indian Trimurti (Brahma, Vishnu, Siva), he distinguishes his version from these by emphasizing the perfection of the third moment. See esp. *LPR3* 1821 MS E 86, G 23-24, where Hegel thinks that the only problem with Gnosticism is its lack of grasp of the importance of return into itself (*Rückkehr in sich*).

[37]. See Milbank, 'The Second Difference,' in *The Word Made Strange: Theology, Language, and Culture* (Oxford: Blackwell, 1997), 180-83; Hart, *The Beauty of the Infinite*, 155-67, where Hart critiques Hegelianism on this point by showing its invidious influence on the trinitarian theology of Robert Jenson. Although in no sense a writer 'after' Balthasar, William Desmond is also useful here. See his reflection on Hegel's trinitarian thought in *Hegel's God*, 121-42, esp. his contrast between an erotic and agapeic Trinity (132) and his insistence on a form of transcendence

that 'exceeds the economy of the interplay of finite beings in the finite between' (139).

[38]. This is the main story-line of *The Legitimacy of the Modern Age*. Medieval voluntarism represents the unsuccessful overcoming of Gnosticism; modernity, as illustrated in its discourses, represents the second overcoming by overcoming what is harmful in the failed first overcoming.

[39]. Blumenberg's self-styling as a disinterested proponent of the history of ideas does not survive close scutiny. Idealism is not simply a discursive phenomenon that as a mere matter of fact succeeds voluntarism; it should succeed it. For a more detailed analysis and criticisms of Blumenberg, see *Gnostic Return in Modernity*, 50-65.

[40]. The principle of reciprocal dependence is a touchstone of Idealist thought. It receives its foundation in Fichte's *Wissenschaftslehre* (1794) and thereafter plays a regulative role in the trajectory of Idealism. Stated abstractly the principle is simple: the ground depends on what it grounds in order to be ground. Hegel makes this principle a matter of logic (Essence). The consequences for theology are revolutionary: if the world depends on God to be world, God depends on world to be God. Before Process Theology Hegel breaks with the classical view summed up by Aquinas in *ST1,* Q13, art 7, which insisted that the relation of dependence is essentially one-way. In the self-actualizing divine, which it is the program of the *Phenomenology* and *Lectures on the Philosophy of Religion* to illustrate and the *Encyclopedia* to demonstrate, the dependence of the divine and world is reciprocal. Hegel shows – or thinks he shows – that God without a world would not be God.

[41]. *B*, 95, 275. Given Balthasar's view that nominalism represents the insertion of an unconstrained voluntarism that destabilizes not only the God-world relation but also the proper understanding of God, Barth (along with the Reformation) is being accused essentially of reinscribing this moment. There is the suggestion of a fatal round: Hegelianism as the overcoming of theological voluntarism, theological voluntarism as the overcoming of German Idealism.

[42]. While Balthasar acknowledges that Barth's theology matures greatly as he takes his distance from his dialectical stance of the early twenties, nonetheless, his actualism is systemic, and characterizes all of the *Church Dogmatics* in some significant respect. Even if this is a matter of more or less, any statement about the triune God (which by necessity is led by an understanding of God's relation to the world), is liable to an actualist or voluntarist accent. An exception cannot be made for Barth's famous description of the triune God as the 'One who loves in freedom' in *CD2/1*.

[43]. Hegel does not typically associate the so-called 'immanent Trinity' with the good. Throughout the major work, however, it is implied, since the world is often characterized as 'evil' as the antithesis of this divine that exists on the plane of virtuality. Sometimes, however, the attribution of 'goodness' or 'holiness' is direct. See, for example, *LPR3* 1824 E 194, G 127; also *The Science of Logic* (818-26; *Glockner 4*, 320-7) in which Hegel speaks of the noetic sphere of the divine as 'the infinite good' (*die unendliche Gute*). With respect to goodness, but also with respect to the related attribute of perfection, Hegel always underscores the non-optional nature of the dynamic of self-manifestation. Brito has been particularly anxious

to distinguish Hegel's thought here from that of the mainline theological and philosophical traditions in which goodness is replete and is not a process. See *La christologie de Hegel*, 551-52; *Hegel et la tâche actuelle de christologie*, 10.

[44]. In terms of basic orientation this implies a preference for the Greek East over the Latin West. Yet there is a subversion of the cliché that finds Augustine and Aquinas as culpable, insofar as neither of them is being criticized.

[45]. See my discussion of Hegel's view of the interrelation of creation and evil in *The Heterodox Hegel*, 151-68. For the eschatological inflection of human being's equality with the divine, which essentially amounts to a displacement, see especially 157-68.

[46]. On Hegelian grounds, the crucial difference between art, religion, and philosophy and the structures of 'Ethical Life' is that the former are transparent of the absolute content in a way the structures of 'Ethical Life' are not.

[47]. Rejecting Hegel's ambitions for a fully comprehensive reason that can transcend culture and its symbols, Ricoeur by no means rejects all elements of Hegel's philosophy. For example, he looks generally favorably on Hegel's view that the self becomes in and through the 'detour' of culture. This is a view that is articulated in his book on Freud, and which remains in *Time and Narrative* as this view is submitted to Augustinian, Heideggerian and postmodern pressures. See *Freud and Philosophy: An Essay in Interpretation* (New Haven: Yale University Press, 1970).

[48]. One of the tactics deployed by Derrida throughout *Glas* is to deny Christianity any room from separation from its Hegelian elevation in speculative philosophy. Hegel simply justifies commitments that are implied in Christianity. At the very least at an implicit level Christianity identifies itself with a totalizing metanarrative that Hegel brings up to philosophical code. It goes without saying that the refusal to uncouple Christianity and Hegelianism even to the smallest extent bespeaks a thoroughly negative understanding of Christianity. In particular, it speaks to Derrida's negative view of Christian articulations of the Trinity. As the dogma of Christian dogmas, its power to exclude is in Derrida's view without compare. Derrida, however, provides no clue as to how we might go about testing this truth, which seems much more like a declaration than a hypothesis.

[49]. The case of Mary is exceptional in that the level of openness to the divine represents a prototype with respect to other human beings. A fundamental asymmetry exists: our openness can be interpreted in terms of the Marian amen, but Mary cannot be interpreted through us. This is not to say (a) that there is no analogy between Mary and us; and (b) that the gap between us and Mary is the same as the gap between Christ and us. There is a definite analogy between Mary and us, which does not obtain between Christ and us. Balthasar sometimes marks the difference lexically by talking about Mary as 'prototype' and Christ as 'archetype,' but unfortunately does not explicate the distinction with any great rigor. Given a general tendency towards openness that is broadly phenomenological – *TL1* and *GL1* are exemplary in this respect – one might have thought that he would be able to mark the difference in this way. Instead, he sometimes gives the impression that the dogmatic claim with respect to the person of Christ, i.e. that Christ is divine as well as human, plays the major role in making the discrimination.

[50]. Here Balthasar could be regarded as retrieving the Boethian notion of 'incommunicability' that played such an important role in medieval trinitarian theology, as much in Bonaventure as in Aquinas. Although for these theologians incommunicability may have been a limit-concept and totally consistent with an emphasis on defining persons through relation, it is not consistent with what we might call a pure logic of relation in which 'incommunicability' ceases to play any role.

[51]. In *Apokalypse* Hegel is regarded as the exemplar of the Promethean stance in which the subject elevates himself to divine status largely through an exaggeration in the power of reason. By contrast, Nietzsche, as one would surmise, is the representative of the Dionysian posture. Here the divine is displaced not by a storming of heaven, but by a burrowing deep into what Christianity has denied, the primeval energies that are worldly and enfleshing.

[52]. In *The Beauty of the Infinite* Hart makes the contrast between Hegel and Nietzsche in terms of Being and Becoming. These are categories that are internal to the metaphyical tradition (they are used by Hegel) and are even in play in Heidegger's own historiography.

[53]. The Hegel commentator who most sharply makes this point is Walter Jaeschke. See his *Reason in Religion: The Formation of Hegel's Philosophy of Religion*, tr. J. Michael Steward and Peter Hodgson (Berkeley, CA: University of California Press, 1990), 325-58.

[54]. Of course, this judgment is part of a very complex judgment in which Catholicism is reproved of being a cunning, self-reproducing worldly power. Hegel does not understand these very different descriptions to contradict each other. He sees them as two sides – in his sense dialectically mediated sides – of the phenomenon of Catholicism whose less than adult 'unworldliness' is compensated for by a less than adult 'worldliness.'

[55]. In making this judgment Balthasar cannot be thought to include the Tübingen School, which in any event he may be construing as belonging to the Romantic period.

[56]. See *God without Being*, 142-43, 188.

[57]. The relation between Son and Father is at the basis of Marion's interpretation of Hölderlin's poetry in *Idol and Distance*, 81-136. See especially 81-2, 89 (reference to Balthasar), 112, 125-26, 129-36.

[58]. As is well-known in his soteriological reflections Balthasar goes further. *Mysterium Paschale* and *TD4* are only two of the many places in which he recurs to the Pauline hyperbole of Christ being made sin for us.

[59]. On this point there is an essential agreement with Francis Fiorenza. See his *Foundational Theology: Jessu and the Church* (New York: Crossroad, 1984).

[60]. Grabmann, Chenu, and Gilson are only some of the more familiar names that advise a return to Aquinas himself rather than a reliance on his intepreters and their interpreters. Undoubtedly, a proximate influence on Balthasar in this respect is Przywara. Radical Orthodoxy is the latest in a long-line of movements interested in making a distinction between Aquinas and Suarez.

[61]. Umberto Eco is correct in thinking of support for the transcendental of beauty being fairly general in the medieval period. Bonaventure and Aquinas are preceded by other thinkers in this respect. Robert Grosseteste and Albertus Magnus

are only two of the major contributors, although the ultimate source is, of course, Pseudo-Dionysius, and especially his *Divine Names* 4.7.10. See Eco, *The Aesthetics of Thomas Aquinas*, tr. Hugh Bredin (Cambridge, MA: Harvard University Press, 1988), esp. 21-38. Eco notes a development in Aquinas on two fronts: (i) with respect to beauty becoming a transcendental. (It is not present in the list of transcendentals given in his *Commentary on the Sentences*, but it is in a similar listing in the *Summa* 1, Q5, art 4); (ii) with respect to beauty making it into sacred doctrine. In the *Summa* 1 Q 27, which opens reflection on the Trinity, beauty and goodness are said to have the same divine referent. The crucial passage is Question 39 where beauty is associated with the Word or the Son. The major difference with Bonaventure is that the association of Beauty with the Son and thus the trinitarian ordinance is consistent throughout his work. It is evident in the *Breviloquium* and in the *Itinerarium*. Moreover, in the case of Bonaventure, the connection between the beauty of the Son as the second person of the Trinity is directly tied to Christ on the cross. For a still pertinent account, see E. J. Spargo, *The Category of the Aesthetic in the Philosophy of St. Bonaventure* (New York: Fordham University Press, 1953).

[62]. See Gilles Emery, *The Trinitarian Thought of Saint Thomas Aquinas*, tr. Francesca Murphy (Oxford: Oxford University Press, 2007). Very different thinkers who would think that a proper understanding of *esse* at the very least provides a necessary explanatory backdrop of Aquinas' understanding of a dynamic Trinity include Cornelio Fabro, Gustav Siewerth, Thomas Weinandy, and Jean-Luc Marion. For Fabro, see 'Actualité et originalité de l'esse thomiste,' in *Revue Thomiste* 56 (1956), 240-70, 280-507; *Participation et causalité selon saint Thomas d'Aquin* (Louvain, Belgium: Publications univeritaires de Louvain, 1961); Siewerth, *Das Schicksal der Metaphysik zu Heidegger* (Einsiedeln, Switzerland: Johannes Verlag, 1959); also *Die Abstraktion und das Sein nach der Lehre des Thomas von Aquin*, in *Gesammelte Werke*. vol. 1: *Sein und Wahrheit* (Düsseldorf: Patmos Verlag, 1975); Thomas Weinandy, *Does God Suffer?* (Notre Dame: University of Notre Dame Press, 2000); Marion, 'Saint Thomas d'Aquin et l'onto-théo-logie,' in *Revue Thomiste* 95.1 (1995), 31-66.

[63]. See, for example, Weinandy who understands that Balthasar is unlike Moltmann in that he is unprepared to depart with the notion of divine impassibility. He also lauds him for not taking the easy-out of defining 'impassibility' ethically, specifically that its content is God's unwavering fidelity to human beings. He does judge, however, that Balthasar gives far too many concessions to modern supporters of divine passibility and does not do enough to articulate and defend the impassibility tradition. See *Does God Suffer?* (Edinburgh: T & T Clark, 2000), 13, 63, 163. In this respect Balthasar is very much like Jean Galot, whom Balthasar explicates in *TD5*, who does not enter Balthasar's caveats with respect to divine passibility. The title of Weinandy's book in fact reprises Galot's *Dieu, Souffre-t-il?* (Paris: Lethielleux, 1976). The most balanced as well as thorough treatment of Balthasar's attempt to steer a middle course between metaphysical views of divine impassibility and mythological views is still G. F. O'Hanlon, *The Immutability of God in the Theology of Hans Urs von Balthasar* (Cambridge: Cambridge University Press, 1990).

[64]. This is the basic question of Thomas G. Dalzell's article, 'The Enrichment of God in Balthasar's Trinitarian Eschatology,' in *Irish Theological Quarterly* 66 (2001), 3-18.

[65]. For Jasper's notion of both ciphers and the 'Encompassing' (*das Umgreifende*), see texts such as *Vernunft und Existenz* (München: R. Piper & Co Verlag, 1960) and *Die Philosophie Glaube* (Zürich: Artemis Verlag, 1950). Ciphers, which are trans-categorial symbols that transcend the subject-object dichotomy, participate in the Encompassing which they intend. Ciphers operate at different levels of reflection. Although there are relatively reflective ciphers, there are also philosophical ciphers in which transcendence of language is intimated in the very use of language. In his analysis of the great philosophers, Jaspers gives a certain primacy to the Neoplatonic tradition.

[66]. For Hegel, see *LPR3* 1821 MS E 82; 1827 E 287. For a good account of the incoherence of this position from a theological point of view, see W. Pannenberg's 'Die Subjektivität Gottes und die Trinitätslehre. Ein Beitrag zur Beziehung zwischen Karl Barth und die Philosophie Hegels,' in *Kerygma und Dogma 23* (1977), 25-40, and L. Oeing-Hanhoff 'Hegels Trinitätslehre: Zur Aufgabe ihren ihrer Kritik und Rezeption,' in *Theologie und Philosophie* (52) (1977), 387-407.

[67]. I consider this exception in some detail in *The Heterodox Hegel.* See especially 56, 70, 78, 93-4 118-19, 131, 138-39, 278-88.

[68]. See *Being and Time*, 485 (G 434). While Heidegger does a brief review of many of the more important passages by Hegel on time and the concept, the passage which most clearly links time and the concept (time is the *Dasein* of the concept) is the very last paragraphs of the *Phenomenology* (#808). Largely on the authority of Heidegger, this passage was foundational for Kojève's interpretation of Hegel which proved constitutive in France in the middle of the twentieth century.

[69]. As is well-known, the treatment of the Trinity marks Nyssa's entire oeuvre. It is especially to the fore in *The Life of Moses* and *Against Eunomius.* Although the latter is by far the more developed in terms of trinitarian doctrine, perhaps it is the former that gives a more dynamic account of the triune God whose inexhaustibility stretches out the self in longing. In *On the Making of Man* (Bk 1) Nyssa thinks of time as expenditure without real development and growth. For a deep account of Nyssa, see Michel René Barnes, *Power of God: Dynamis in Gregory of Nyssa* (Washington, DC: Catholic University of America Press, 2001). As I have previously indicated, however, Nyssa is not assumed to be the contrary of Augustine, who is Przywara's preferred theologian to make the point. .

[70]. David Bentley Hart, *The Beauty of the Infinite*, 233-60.

[71]. Sticking solely to *Theo-Drama 5*, see *TD5*, 77-8, 130, 137, 397, 401-02, 408, 482.

[72]. Balthasar uses this term as a *terminus technicus.* See *TD5*, 425.

[73]. Walter Kasper, *Das Absolute in der Geschichte. Philosophie und Theologie der Geschichte in der Spätphilosophie Schellings* (Mainz, 1965); W. Pannenberg, *The Idea of God and Human Freedom* (Louisville: Westminister/ John Knox Press, 1973). Nichols provides a very good account of Balthasar's treatment of Schelling in *Apokalypse 1.* See *Scattering the Seed*, 69-78.

[74]. Balthasar oscillates between temporal and spatial metaphors to speak to the trinitarian divine. 'Moment' is the preferred temporal term and, arguably, given Hegel's view of time's higher level of synthetic unity, the more adequate descriptor. Throughout *Lectures on the Philosophy of Religion*, however, following Kant as much as Lessing, Hegel uses spatial metaphors.

[75]. The above quoted passage from *Idol and Distance* is from Marion's essay on Pseudo-Dionysius. This essay continues a reflection on distance that is crucial in Marion's essay on Hölderlin in which Marion releases Hölderlin from Heidegger's non-Christian or anti-Christian interpretation. Distance is more rather than less than the ontological difference which is more than Hegelian difference. For Marion's going beyond Heidegger who goes beyond Hegel, see my 'Jean-Luc Marion: Crossing Hegel,' in *Counter-Experiences: Reading Jean-Luc Marion*, ed. Kevin Hart (Notre Dame, Indiana: University of Notre Dame Press, 2007), 95-150, esp. 100-02.

[76]. This is especially true in the case of such a late work by Bruaire as *L'être et l'esprit* (Paris: PUF, 1983), although even in his earliest work which featured Hegel's syllogistic translation of Christian representation, Bruaire was convinced that Hegel would help Christian theology to think through divine freedom rather than make it impossible. For a wonderful account of Bruaire's thought in general and his relation to Hegel's trinitarian thought in particular, see Antonio López, F.S.C.B., *Spirit's Gift: The Metaphysical Insight of Claude Bruaire* (Washington, DC: The Catholic University of America Press, 2006), esp. 184-223.

[77]. None of the Cappadocians makes the point as insistently as Gregory Nazianzen. See his *Theological Orations* 2.5, 2.13. At the same time this is a general Cappadocian point. Gregory of Nyssa is also emphatic on the point in *Against Eunomius* 1.2.

[78]. In *The Beauty of the Infinite* Hart greatly expands and develops this point.

[79]. See *The Theology of Karl Barth*, 26-9. See also Balthasar's essay, 'The Farewell Trio,' which is on *The Magic Flute* in *Explorations in Theology: 3. Creator Spiritus*, tr. Brian McNeil, C.R.V (San Francisco: Ignatius Press, 1993), 523-34.

[80]. Aquinas' description of God as *actus purus* is intended to reinforce the distinction between God and all else that is. God is the reality who does not require anything in order to be perfect. The explicit ruling out of change and development is made throughout his work. See especially *De Potentia* 7.2 and *ST 1, Q4, art 1*. For a good discussion of this, see Weinandy, *Does God Suffer?*, 120-27; also *Does God Change?: The Word's Becoming in the Incarnation* (Still River, MA: St Bede's Publications, 1985), 74-82. See also Michael Dodds, *The Unchanging God of Love* (Fribourg: Editions Universitaires Fribourg Suisse, 1985), esp. 227-80.

[81]. This notion has been made popular by the work of David Burrell and Kathryn Tanner. For the latter, see *God and Creation in Christian Theology: Tyranny or Empowerment* (Oxford: Blackwell, 1988).

[82]. Although any good Thomist would say as much, here I am thinking especially of Matthew Levering. See his *Scripture and Metaphysics: Aquinas and the Renewal of Trinitarian Theology* (Oxford: Blackwell, 2004).

[83]. Neither the Jewish writer Wiesel nor the Catholic Gutiérrez speaks directly against theodicy as such. In novels such as *Night* Wiesel figures a rebellious Job who no longer experiences the divine presence. Gutiérrez's reflections on Job are in the form of a meditation on hope in the marginalized. For appeals to Job, where the interest is in dismantling the category of theodicy, see Kant, 'On the Miscarriage of all Philosophical Trials in Theodicy' (1791) in *Religion within the Boundaries of Mere Reason and Other Writings*, ed. tr. Allen Wood and George

di Giovanni (Cambridge: Cambridge University Press, 1998), 17-30; esp. 25-7; Ricoeur, 'Evil, a Challenge to Philosophy and Theology,' in *JAAR* 1985, vol. 53, no. 4, 631-48; esp. 638-39, 647; 'The Hermeneutics of Symbols 1,' in *The Conflict of Interpretations*, ed. Don Ihde (Evanston: Northwestern University Press, 1974), 287-314, esp. 313-14, where Joban hope in spite of the evidence of meaninglessness is contrasted with Hegel's dialectical justification of evil; Burrell, *Deconstructing Theodicy: Why Job has Nothing to Say to the Puzzle of Suffering* (Notre Dame, IN: University of Notre Dame Press, 2008).

[84]. As is clear especially from *Lectures on the Philosophy of Religion 3*, although Hegel cannot think of sin as offense and rebellion, he can think of self-love or self-will involving an alienating contraction. In this he comes close to Augustine. Even here, however, Hegel brings this idea in a completely different direction. Such contraction is necessary if human being is to be actualized as the image of God. Especially revealing passages include *LPR3* 1821 MS E 205-06, G 137-38; 1824 205-06, G 137-38 1827 E 296-99, G 22-23.

[85]. Hegel uses this alchemical term in the Lesser Logic (*Enc* #42) to refer to what 'remains' of God after knowledge has reached its prescribed noumenal limit. One way of thinking of Derrida's *Glas* is that not only does he side with Kant on the epistemological issue, but he brings out the entire philosophical and social ramifications of a conceptual apparatus which is both anxious that there are realities that resist being worked over by the concept, and denies that there is any production of waste.

[86]. Hegel is very much in the tradition of Spinoza who inveighed against the representation of postmortem existence on the model of everlastingness. For the most part in his philosophical articulation the critique of representation is more or less implicit. As the *Logic* and the *Encyclopedia* (#564-73) have it, thought has not durational features. For this point, see also *The Heterodox Hegel*, 339-63. In *Lectures on the Philosophy of Religion*, however, Hegel is more explicit. See especially *LPR1* 1821 MS E 195, G 105; *LPR3* Fragments E 386, G 305).

[87]. See *Gnostic Return in Modernity*, 58-9, 92-4, where I define metalepsis as transgressive disfiguration-refiguration of the biblical narrative.

[88]. In his account of Gnosticism as well as Neoplatonism in *Lectures on the History of Philosophy,* one of Hegel's most interesting interpretive moves is to suggest that both forms of ancient thought are characterized by a movement towards a state of being that is in excess of what is given aboriginally. The importance of this interpretation is magnified when it becomes central in F. C. Baur's *Die christliche Gnosis.*

[89]. Hegel's famous comment about *Identitätsphilosophie* is to be found in the Preface to the *Phenomenology* (#16) in which the target is usually thought to be Schelling. While Schelling is a target, he may not be the only target. Nor for that matter is Hegel's quip totally original. It has its origin in critical remarks on Schelling by Friedrich Schlegel. See H. S. Harris, *Hegel's Ladder 1*, 51-3.

[90]. See *Glas*, 28-32, 56-8, 64-5, 75-80. I deal with the relation between Balthasar and Derrida on this point somewhat more extensively in my essay 'Hegel, Theodicy, and the Invisibility of Waste,' *The Providence of God*, ed. Francesca Aran Murphy and Philip G. Ziegler (Edinburgh: T & T Clark, 2009), 75-108.

[91]. See *The Beauty of the Infinite*, 85-7. Although not favorably disposed to Levinas, Hart supports Levinas' critique of Hegel's philosophy of history as violent.
[92]. See Benedetto Croce, *What is Living and What is Dead of the Philosophy of Hegel*, tr. Douglas Ainslie (New York: Russell & Russell, 1915).
[93]. See also *TD5*, 50, 207, 271; also *TD3*, 37-8.
[94]. Paul Claudel, *Interroge L'Apocalypse* (Paris: Gallimard, 1952). Although Claudel does concern himself with violence and persecution as the book of Revelation does, the emphasis seems to be somewhat more on the ideological deformation that makes it possible. There are both Enlightenment figures such as Voltaire who leads to the revolutionary terror perpetrated by Robespierre (301-02) and Danton (109), and figures such as Marx and Lenin (109). These are figures of the Anti-Christ in the mode of the lie.
[95]. Although Hegel does contrast 'reflection' and 'speculation,' insisting that the former is a mode of analysis that breaks down, whereas the latter does not, speculation is in fact another kind of mirroring, one in which not only is something given to the self but the self itself. To insert the Christian narrative into this matrix is necessarily to distort it, to deflect it.
[96]. As already indicated Balthasar does not demur from Hegel in a fundamental way and counter by asserting the value of architecture, painting, or music. This may or may not indicate fundamental agreement with Hegel on this point. It may simply be tactical. The categories of 'lyric,' 'drama,' and 'epic' are more ready for application to theology as discourse, and these categories are both illuminative and carry a certain kind of intellectual authority.

PART 3

[1]. Although it would be a mistake to suggest that Balthasar is a 19th-century specialist in the way that much of the French Communio group of thinkers such as Chapelle, Bruaire, Tillette, and Brito are, as his early work on German apocalyptic indicates, Balthasar has far more than a general knowledge of 19th-century thought and of German Idealism in particular. Perhaps of those 19th-century religious thinkers who were critical of Hegel's program, while being open to change in the protocols of religious philosophy, he is closest to Franz von Baader. He would not be sympathetic, however, to Baader's championing of the Lutheran mystic Jacob Boehme, who is regarded throughout as a problematic figure. Nor would Balthasar be quite as enthusiastic as Baader about the prospect of Meister Eckhart leading the way forward beyond rationalism and fideism. He agrees with Baader about the connection between Eckhart and Hegel, which in his eyes is a problem for Eckhart rather than a relief for Hegel (*GL5*, 40, 45, 47). For a good synoptic account of Baader's relation to Hegel, see Peter Koslowski, 'Religiöse Philosophie und spekulative Dogmatik – Franz von Baaders Theorie der Gesamtwirklichkeit,' in *Die Philosophie, Theologie und Gnosis Franz von Baaders. Spekulatives Denken zwisschen Aufkärung, Restauration und Romantik*, ed. Peter Koslowski (Vienna: Passagen Verlag, 1993), 289-325.

[2]. Liberal Protestant theology rather than speculative philosophy was the main target of Barth's dialectical as well as post-dialectical theology throughout his long career. This, together with what appears to be Barth's assumption about the pertinence as well as validity of Kierkegaard's critique, arguably, accounts for the surprising lack of edge in Barth's criticisms of Hegel. For Balthasar's sense of the importance for Barth of Kierkegaard's critique of Hegel, see *The Theology of Karl Barth*, 73, 90-1, 207-08, 233. Besides the general argument against a speculative discourse becoming the master discourse of Christianity, Barth takes Kierkegaard's points about the lack of christological center in Hegel and the abolition of the incommensurability of God and the world and God and human being in and through a necessitarian dialectic. Balthasar is aware both that Barth's point of view is much more thickly biblical and traditional than Kierkegaard's and has a number of non-Kierkegaardian criticisms. The one that Balthasar picks out in *The Theology of Karl Barth* (234) is also one which is highlighted in Barth's essay on Hegel in his book on nineteenth century German theology, that is, Hegel's philosophy of history, which is constructed as theodicy. Balthasar's dealing with Hegel is vastly more expansive and detailed. And Balthasar diverges totally from Barth in thinking that precisely what Barth thinks is Hegel's strongest Christian point, namely, his articulation of the Trinity, is precisely his weakest. For Barth's very favorable estimation of Hegel's trinitarianism, see *Protestant Thought: From Rousseau to Ritchl*, 295.

[3]. Figures who provide good examples of what might be regarded as a Catholic baseline include Immanuel Hermann Fichte, the nephew of the famous Gottlieb Fichte, the philosopher who inaugurates German Idealism in the *Wissenschaftslehre* and who is the provocateur of the *Atheismusstreit*, and Christian Hermann Weisse. Fichte's *Die Idee der Persönlickeit und der individuellen Fortdauer* (Elberfeld, 1834) and Weisse's *Die Idee der Gottheit* (Dresden, 1833) were essentially stipulative. Hegel's religious thought could be embraced as along as it could be interpreted theistically rather than pantheistically - which, of course, was precisely a point at issue – and more specifically as long as it could be read as countenancing personal postmortem existence, which palpably it did not.

[4]. In the case of Dostoyevski I am especially thinking of *The Brothers Karamazov* whose narrative thrust and meditative center is parricide, and Turgenev whose famous book, *Fathers and Sons*, makes the relation a modern question. Of course, the relation between fathers and sons is to some extent coincident with Greek literature and the work of Sophocles in particular.

[5]. See in particular Balthasar's references to Staudenmaier in *GL1*, 73 and *TD2*, 331-33. In the latter he shows that he has both a synoptic grasp of Staudenmaier's oeuvre, and indicates some familiarity with the secondary material on the Catholic thinker. He specifically references a book on Staudenmaier by the great *Tübingen-School* scholar, Peter Hünermann. See *Trinitarische Anthropologie bei Franz Anton Staudenmaier* (Freiburg and München: Karl Albert Verlag, 1962).

[6]. Although the way in which I speak to Balthasar's continuation of Irenaeus recalls what I say about Irenaeus in *Gnostic Return in Modernity* (148-59) in basic form, it will only become more apparent that I have learned much from Kevin Mongrain's *The Systematic Thought of Hans Urs von Balthasar.*

[7]. Aidan Nichols draws attention to the close relation between Balthasar and Bulgakov, and judges that this influence is not simply one among others. The following passage from *Wisdom from Above: A Primer in the Theology of Father Sergei Bulgakov* (Leominster, England: Gracewing, 2005), 310, is worth quoting in full: 'In the body of the text I made a comparison with the work of Hans Urs von Balthasar. Both men believed in the necessity for Christian intellectuality of a confident metaphysic, for which they drew elements not only from Hellenic but also from Germanist thought, tutored in their choice of materials and themes by the biblical revelation. Each was a thoroughgoingly Trinitarian thinker in his approach to modern theology, finding the Trinity most fully displayed in the Cross and Resurrection of Christ. Both writers combined a Chalcedonian Christology with a moderated kenoticism. They were equally concerned to integrate nature and grace, not least in the form of eros and agape. Implicitly, they sought to negotiate a *via media* between tradition and modernity . . . Explicitly, their overall project was comprehensive, and into its service they pressed a large variety of sources from Scripture and patristics, the Liturgy and other poetic texts. Despite their Christian humanism they were remarkably eschatological in outlook. Both leaned heavily on Scripture's last book, the Apocalypse of St. John. Each was tempered in universalism: yet neither found optimistic humanism convincing in the slightest degree' (310).

[8]. From *Apokalypse* on Balthasar evinces a consistently negative attitude towards the thought of Berdyaev and is convinced that it offers a 'theosophy' that amounts to neither a viable philosophy or theology. See *Apok 3*, 424-30.

[9]. The double-effect of this ascription is prevalent in those late eighteenth century (Jacobi, Herder, and Goethe) and early nineteenth-century (Hegel) German thinkers who worried about the nature of Hamann's discourse, while thinking of him as a peculiarly German 'genius.' In contrast, its use in modern historiography has in general been more univocally pejorative. This is certainly true of Isaiah Berlin's highly influential *The Magus of the North: J. G. Hamann and the Origins of Modern Irrationalism*, ed. Henry Hardy (New York: Farrar, Straus, & Giroux, 1993).

[10]. This is the view Newman expresses in various forms throughout his entire oeuvre, but perhaps most conspicuously in the chapter on the indefeasibility of certitude in *A Grammar of Assent* (ch. 9).

[11]. Here I am evoking the concept of 'overdetermination' from the French Marxist thinker who in a series of brilliant texts in the 1960's and 70's articulates a view of Marxist historical causation that was not univocal as it was in Hegelian *Geist* and doctrinaire Marxism's view of the economic infrastructure. See especially *For Marx*, tr. Ben Brewster (London: Penguin Press, 1969), 87-128.

[12]. Although Derrida and Levinas are major targets in Hart's *The Beauty of the Infinite*, a case could be made that Hegel and Heidegger, who are presupposed – even if resisted – are even more so. Hart has interesting critical things to say throughout about Hegelian views of totality and truth, of symbol and concept, of time and eternity. He is even more eloquent about the *Wirkungsgeschichte* of Hegel in theology. For the purposes of proving that this influence is widespread, he chooses as his test-case the North American theologian Robert Jensen who, if critical of certain standard confessional assumptions about the divine (e.g aseity

and impassibility), nonetheless, self-consciously wishes to remain within the precincts of Lutheran orthodoxy (*BI*, 160-66).

13. Balthasar's worry on this score does not amount to an actual thesis of inclusion. On my own behalf, however, I do advance the thesis of inclusion of the Kabbalah in the speculative narrative of Hegel in 'Hegel and Anti-Judaism: Narrative and the Inner Circulation of the Kabbalah,' in *The Owl of Minerva* 28.2, Spring (1997), 141-82.

14. In the case of Milbank I am thinking of his important essay on trinitarian thought, 'The Second Difference,' in *The Word Made Strange*, 171-93. Milbank has particularly trenchant things to say about Moltmann and Jüngel's form of trinitarianism, which in the end, he believes, reduces to that of Hegel (180-83) with the consequences that it deserves to be classed as 'gnostic.' We examined the issue of entitlements in the case of Milbank in part 1.

15. I have in mind especially texts such as *Genesis and Apocalypse: A Theological Voyage Toward Authentic Christianity* (Louisville, KY: Westminister/John Knox, 1990); *The Genesis of God: A Theological Genealogy* (Louisville, KY: Westminister/John Knox Press, 1993). In these writings, while figures such as Boehme, Blake, and Schelling continue to be important in Altizer's recommendation of a refiguration of Christianity that brings it back to itself, Hegel in general and the *Phenomenology* in particular play a central role. By and large Altizer thinks that in general, but particularly in the *Phenomenology*, which is the most vital of all of Hegel's texts, the trope of kenosis does not simply refer to what happens on the cross, but to the entire movement of Spirit within and without the immanent network of the divine; it regulates his specific account of Christianity, philosophy, and their relation. See especially *Genesis and Apocalypse*, 87-8, 100; *Genesis of God*, 100. It is Altizer's conviction that 'apocalyptic' is the best ascriptor of Hegel's thought as it is of the other major thinkers in his genealogy. It is his presumption that apocalyptic and Gnosticism are contraries and that his revival of apocalyptic represents a cure to the latent Gnosticism of orthodox Christianity. I have questioned these presumptions in *Gnostic Return in Modernity*, 65-71 and will do so again in the conclusion to part 2.

Chapter 4

1. See Chapelle, *Hegel et la religion*, 3 vols (Paris: Éditions universitaires, 1964-67); Léonard, *Commentaire littéral; de la logique de Hegel* (Paris: Vrin, 1974); also *La foi chez Hegel*; 'Le primat du négative et l'interpretation de la religion. Un example: la reprise hegélienne du dogme christologique de chalcédoine,' in *Hegels Logik der Philosophie*, ed. Dieter Henrich and Rolf Peter Horstmann (Stuttgart: Klett-Cottall, 1984), 160-71; Tillette, *L'absolu et la philosophie* (Paris: PUF, 1987); Brito, *Hegel et la tâche actuelle de la christologie*; *La christologie de Hegel: Verbum Crucis.* Claude Bruaire cannot be excluded from this list, although more than the others – Chapelle comes closest – he thinks that Hegel still remains a potential resource for theology in general and Catholic theology in particular. Bruaire's most scholarly interpretation remains his penetrating *Logique et la religion chrétienne dans la philosophie de Hegel* (1964). Other texts by Bruaire with a significant reference to Hegel and

involving some measure of appropriation (some of it critical) include a text contemporary with his major work on Hegel, *L'Affirmation de Dieu: Essai sur la logique de l'existence* (1964) and the considerably later *L'Être el l'esprit* (1983).

[2]. Although Balthasar articulates a notion of faith in *Glory of the Lord 1*, he amply illustrates it by historical examples throughout succeeding volumes, and fully secures it in the volumes on scripture. From the very beginning he is conscious of the propensity in Western history to understand 'faith' as something of a remainder concept. He understands that this is especially the case in modernity, although in his view the Reformation and late medieval Nominalism will have played a preparatory role. This confirms the central truth of Hegel who sees that fideism rises in direct proportion to the ascending arc of a narrow rationalism. With respect to diagnosis, then, Balthasar is on the side of Hegel. The issue throughout *Glory of the Lord* concerns the solution which can only be the articulation of a richer account of reason. From Balthasar's perspective this view lacks balance, and arrogates to itself a point of view that can only be divine. *Glory of the Lord* remains consistent in this respect with criticisms lodged against Hegel's view of reason as early as *Wahrheit* (1946).

[3]. Arguably, an exception to the rule of irony is the form that Balthasar finds in Hamann. The irony of Hamann is Christianly requisite for a number of reasons: (i) it is essentially biblical; the Bible is a text that upsets our expectations as it subverts conventional moral and intellectual decorum; (ii) precisely because of its biblical nature irony involves a critical but not subversive attitude towards the theological traditions. In particular, irony is consistent with considerable doctrinal thickness; (iv) finally, and summarily, irony is objective and in fundamental respects 'theological' rather than subjective. It is so because the central figure of irony is Christ who is the object of Christian faith. Without putting an exclamation point on it, Balthasar suggests that in his articulation of irony Kierkegaard may well be too indebted to Romantic models. It is interesting that the difference in the nature of irony supports the general separation of Kierkegaard and Hamann effected by Balthasar in *Glory of the Lord* in which Kierkegaard represents the continuation of what is most theologically problematic about the Reformation – the split between the *fides quae creditur* and the *fides qua creditur* – whereas Hamann represents the Reformation at is rehabilitated best.

[4]. Balthasar cites Staudenmaier's *Johannes Scotus Erigena und die Wissenschaft seiner Zeit. Mit allgemeinen Entwicklungen der Haupwahrheiten auf dem Gebiete der Philosophie und Religion, und Grundzügen zu einer Geschichte der spekulativen Theologie* (Franfurt, 1834).

[5]. Perhaps the most learned of all the Communio writers, Brito, is the most cognizant of the importance of Staudenmaier as a critic of German Idealism. In the evaluative conclusion of *La tâche actuelle* when it comes to criticism of Hegel, Brito cites Staudenmaier a number of times.

[6]. Kierkegaard, *Repetition: An Essay in Experimental Psychology*, tr. Intro. Walter Lowrie (New York: Harper & Row, 1964).

[7]. Hegel's *Lectures on Aesthetics* have been enormously influential, and continue to excite both interpretation and development. On the side of interpretation it is worth mentioning Stephen Bungay, *Beauty and Truth: A Study of Hegel's Aesthetics* (Oxford: Oxford University Press, 1984); William Desmond, *Art and the Absolute:*

A Study of Hegel's Aesthetics (Albany, NY: SUNY Press, 1986); Brian K. Etter, *Between Transcendence and Historicism: The Ethical Nature of the Arts in Hegelian Aesthetics* (Albany, NY: SUNY Press, 2006); Richard Dien Winfield, *Systematic Aesthetics* (Gainesville: University Press of Florida, 1995). On the side of development Hans-Georg Gadamer stands to the fore, even if Gadamer can be said to further historicize Hegel's aesthetics in and through his recall of Heidegger. The Hegelian allegiance is perhaps most evident in *The Relevance of the Beautiful and other Essays*, tr. Nicholas Walker, ed. Robert Bernasconi (Cambridge and New York: Cambridge University Press, 1986).

[8]. The affirmation of religious pluralism is for an important Hegel commentator such as Peter Hodgson one of the most attractive and contemporary features of Hegel's work. See his *Hegel and Christian Theology: A Reading of the Lectures of the Philosophy of Religion* (Oxford: Oxford University Press, 2005), chapter 10 (203-243) and esp. 282-4.

[9]. Although agnosticism is a general stance when it comes to the problem of innocent suffering, this just as often leads accounts that provide at least a minimum amount of intelligibility for some suffering. Camus and Buber provide just two examples. For a lucid presentation of accounts of evil that resist explanation and also nihilism, see Sarah Pinnock, *Beyond Theodicy: Jewish and Continental Thinkers Respond to the Holocaust* (Albany, NY: SUNY Press, 2002).

[10]. See *Darstellung und Kritik des Hegelschen Systems, Aus dem Standpunkte der christlichen Philosophie* (Mainz: Kupferberg, 1844). Reprinted (Frankfurt: Minerva, 1966); *Die Philosophie des Christenthums oder Metaphysik der heiligen Schrift als Lehre von den göttlichen Idee und ihrer Entwicklung in Natur, Geist und Geschichte. Erster Band. Die Lehre von der Idee: in Verbindung mit einer Entwicklungsgeschichte der Ideenlehre und der Lehre von göttlichen Logos* (Giessen, 1840). Reprinted (Frankfurt: Minerva, 1966); *Zum Religiösen Frieden der Zukunft. Mit Rücksicht auf die religiöse-politische Aufgabe der Gegenwart*, 3 vols (Freiburg, 1846-51). Reprinted (Frankfurt: Minerva, 1967). Although English titles will be given, all page references given in parentheses will be from the German editions.

[11]. For example, positive assessment of Hegel is lavish in important essays that date from the early 1830's. See especially 'Andenken an Friedrich von Schlegel' (1832) and 'Die protestantische Dogmatik in ihrer geschichtlichen Entwicklung' (1833). For these essays, see *Franz Anton Staudenmaier: Frühe Aufsätze und Rezensionen (1828-1834)*, intro. Bernhard Casper (Freiburg: Herder, 1974), 199-227, 228-67, respectively.

[12]. A compelling account of the extent and intensity of Staudenmaier's engagement with Hegel is rendered by Albert Franz in his irreplaceable book *Glauben und Denken: Franz Anton Staudenmaiers Hegelkritik als Anfrage and das Selbstvertändnis heutiger Theologie* (Regenburg: Verlag Friedrich Pustet, 1984). Although the book covers both phases of Staudenmaier's response – the largely positive phase of the 30's and the largely negative phase that characterizes the 40's – as the subtitle suggests, the book does not simply intend to be of historical interest, but through a single figure to get at the vocabulary of response to a major philosophical figure who exercises influence on religious thought in general and theological thought in particular. On the descriptive side the bulk of the book is appropriately

allocated to the mature work of the 40's. See *Glauben und Denken*, 46-76, for the early positive phase.
[13]. For a good account of this point, see Franz, *Glauben und Denken*, 135-38; also 100.
[14]. As a critical category, 'pantheism' is in play even in the period of the thirties when Staudenmaier's attitude towards Hegel is not unrelentingly negative. See among other essays, 'Über den unpersönlichen Gott des Pantheismus und den persönlichen Gott des Christentum,' in *Jahrbüchern für Theologie und christliche Philosophie* 2 (1834), 259-339; A. Günther, 'Vorschule zur spekulativen Theologie des positiven Christenthums,' reprinted in *Frühe Aufsätze* (1832), 408-26; Karl Rosenkranz, '*Enzklopädie der theologishen Wissenschafften*,' in *Frühe Aufsätze* (1833), 371-407.
[15]. See *Darstellung und Kritik*, 90, 592. On the second of these two pages, Staudenmaier speaks of the 'free playing-together of divine and human freedom' (*freies Zusammenspiel der göttlichen und der menschlichen Freiheit*) being overcome in Hegel.
[16]. For theogonic ascription see also *Die Philosophie des Christenthums*, bd. 1, 231-32. This makes Staudenmaier not only an anticipator of Balthasar, but an anticipator of the Russian orthodox thinker, Iljin, to whom we referred in Part 2, Chapter 2.
[17]. For similar concerns, see *Die Philosophie des Christenthums*, bd. 1, 803-05. Here, as in *Darstellung und Kritik*, Hegel's *Lectures on the Philosophy of Religion* is the text that is privileged.
[18]. Staudenmaier's support of aseity is consistent throughout his work, even his constructive work. For example, aseity gets defended in the first and second volumes of Staudenmaier's dogmatics. See his *Die christliche Dogmatik*, 4 vols. (Freiburg: Herder, 1840, 1844, 1848, 1852), esp. *Dogmatik*, vol. 2, 228-32.
[19]. See also *Die Philosophie des Christenthums*, 803-04.
[20]. While, as indicated, Staudenmaier has a more positive view of Hegel in the 1830's this does not prevent him from worrying about Hegel's pantheistic tendencies. In this respect, Staudenmaier thinks that Hegel is more discontinuous with Christian Neoplatonism than continuous, and that this is true even if one considers the more speculative strand of Christian Neoplatonism. See *Johannes Scotus Erigena und die Wissenschaft seiner Zeit. Mit allgemeinen Entwicklung der Hauptwahrheiten auf dem Gebiete der Philosophie und Religion, und Grundzügen einer Geschichte der spekulativen Theologie* (Frankfurt: Andreäische Buchhandlung, 1834). By 1840 Staudenamaier has become somewhat more reserved about the contrast between Hegel and Eriugena. In *Die Philosophie des Christenthums* (535-632) Staudenmaier offers a complex description of Erigena in which his visionary system is thought to be the tension between pantheism and atheism. Specifically, this means that there is considerable tension between thinking of creation as the gift of a free God (570) and as a necessary expression of the divine (572). The relative hardening of attitude towards Erigena modeled in Staudenmaier is repeated in Balthasar. As already indicated in his early book on Maximus Balthasar very much sees the point of opposing Erigena and Hegel. Maximus would have been a better contrast, but Erigena is relatively adequate. By the time of the trilogy, and *Glory of the Lord* in particular, Balthasar is persuaded that Neoplatonic ontology is not a skin that can easily be removed. It is harmful to Christian substance, not excluding the redemptive role of Christ and Christ's nature. In their mature periods

then both Staudenmaier and Balthasar see a considerable amount of continuity between Erigena and Hegel. Although quite different in terms of evaluation, the work of Werner Beierwaltes largely concurs with the continuity thesis. For Beierwaltes, see especially *Denken des Einen: Studien zur neuplatonishen Philosophie und ihrer Wirkungsgeschichte* (Frankfurt am Main: Klostermann, 1985).

[21]. When it comes to contemporary reflection on Hegel's theism as this might be either indicated or concentrated in something like a doctrine of creation, there are essentially three strategies. (1) Although Hegel does not officially support a theistic position, he does not fundamentally exclude it. Thus his position admits of a theistic reading. (2) Hegel's position is indeed non-theistic, but pantheistic or rather panentheistic. This is regrettable and undermines Hegelian claims of continuity between specifically Christian discourse and speculative philosophy. (3) Hegel's position is pantheistic or panentheistic, and this is regrettable neither philosophically nor theologically. Christian theology throughout its long history has been crippled by a view of *creatio ex nihilo* that undergirds the view of the incommensurability between God and world and God and human being. For a good example of the first stance, see Quentin Lauer, *Hegel's Concept of God* (Albany, NY: SUNY Press, 1982), 311-12. For good examples of the second position, represented by Staudenmaier and Balthasar, see among others William Desmond: *Hegel: A Counterfeit Double?*; Iljin, *Die Philosophie Hegels als kontemplative Gotteslehre*, 181-202; Walter Kern, 'Schöpfung' bei Hegel,' in *Theologische Quartalschrift* 162 (1984), 131-46. For good examples of the third position, see Raymond Keith Williamson, *Introduction to Hegel's Philosophy of Religion* (Albany, NY: SUNY Press, 1984); Fackenheim, *The Religious Dimension of Hegel's Thought*, 121-33; Peter Hodgson, *Hegel and Christian Theology*.

[22]. *Philosophical Fragments* represents the closest that Kierkegaard gets to doing theology. It offers a christological critique of Hegelianism as well as a critique of Hegel's Christology and that of his epigones.

[23]. Ferdinand Christian Baur, *Die christliche Gnosis: Oder christliche Religions-philosophie in ihrer geschichtlichen Entwicklung* (Tübingen: Osiander, 1835). See also Baur, *Die christliche Lehre von der Dreieinigkeit und Menschwerdung Gottes in ihrer geschichtlichen Entwicklung*, vol. 3, *Die neuere Geschichte des Dogma von der Reformation bis in der neueste Zeit* (Tübingen: Osiander, 1843).

[24]. In part 1 I indicated that Baur essentially speaks to two nodes in and through which this modern trinitarianism comes into being: (i) the modern Protestant node in which Jacob Boehme is a key figure; (ii) an ancient node in which a variety of forms of thought from Valentinianism, Neoplatonism, and Neopythagoreanism are included under the umbrella of 'gnosis.' Baur is neither being totally original in his two-node view, nor in his scheme of inclusion. In the case of the former, he is simply developing points made by Hegel in his *Lectures on the History of Philosophy*. In the case of the latter, he is significantly influenced by the historian of religion, August Neander. I have discussed Baur's contribution in some detail in *Gnostic Return in Modernity*, 21-47. Neander's most influential text was *Genetische Entwicklung der vornehmsten gnostischen Systems* (Berlin: Dümmler, 1818).

[25]. Desmond, Milbank, Marion, and Hart provide different expressions of this.

[26]. Page numbers are from *Die Philosophie des Christenthums.* See especially 798-810, where Staudenmaier examines the trinitarian thought of *Lectures on the Philosophy of Religion.*

[27]. Staudenmaier makes clear, however, that Hegel does not inaugurate this specifically modern species of modalism, but is anticipated in this respect by Jacob Boehme. See *Die Philosophie des Christenthums,* 726-40, esp. 738-39.

[28]. Commentators on Hegel such as Bruaire and Chapelle, affiliated with Communio group, presciently raise the issue of modalism, if only in the end to dispute its application to Hegel. For Bruaire, see *Logique et religion,* 65, 91; Chapelle, *Hegel et la religion,* 86, 88. Chapelle puts forward the unpersuasive argument that since classical modalism or Sabellianism depends upon a static view of substance, and Hegel's construction in contrast focuses on self-developing subjectivity, that in consequence Hegel's view cannot be modalistic. This is a non-sequitur, since there is no reason to rule out a dynamic non-substance version of modalism. See Chapelle, *Hegel et la religion,* 92 n. 228. In comparison, Altizer, who in general tends to view the Trinity as a reactionary theological construct, opines that the only plausible rendition of the Trinity would necessarily have to be modalistic or Sabellian. See *The Genesis of God,* 108. A view similar to Altizer is implied by Blumenberg. In *Work on Myth,* Blumenberg who affirms the absolute narrations of German Romanticism and Idealism argues that a traditional hypostatic view of the Trinity represents a block against narration (260). To the degree to which the Trinity is operative in these discursive regimes, it is warranted only to the extent to which would-be persons are narrative moments in the engendering of the divine-human subjectivity.

[29]. In *Die Philosophie des Christenthums* the determination of the autonomy of the church vis-à-vis the State is a matter of principle, as it is in Möhler's *The Unity of the Church* (1827) upon which it, undoubtedly depends. The rationale for such a distinction is also distinctly Möhlerian: the church has a spiritual ground that is personal (756), whereas the natural tendency of the State is that of the collective. Staudenmaier moves from enunciation to declamation in *Zum Religiösen Frieden der Zukunft.* In a world whose order is breaking down and in which anarchy is the rule, the only critical and transformative power available is the church, founded and modeled on Christ and regulated by the dogmas and precepts of the early church (vol. 3, 317 ff.). The fractiousness and anarchy of the modern world has its ultimate origin in the emergence of Protestantism (vol. 2, 26-39) and its proximate origin in Hegel and his left-wing successors (vol. 3, 45-108, 154-74), who carry forward rather than deny the French Revolution (vol. 2, 271-74; vol. 3, 281 ff). Balthasar's relation to Staudenmaier is strong on both of these points. Throughout the trilogy, the church not only is separate from the State, but truly enjoys a personal status by being founded and modeled on Christ (who is defined by his relation to the Father) and energized by the Holy Spirit. Famously in *Theo-Drama 3* the church is treated as 'person.' With respect to the second point, an analogue can be found in the more interventionist *The Office of Peter,* which sees the post-conciliar church as tending towards a kind of Protestant fractiousness, just at the time when the world requires the church as a symbol of unity. The dependence on Möhler on both points is evident. For a general account of the

relation between Balthasar and Möhler, see my 'Balthasar: Between Tübingen and Postmodernity.'

[30]. For Balthasar's opinions on Marx, see especially *GL5*, 591, 599; *TD4*, 440-41. Mongrain is especially strong on the way in which Balthasar links Hegel and Marx. See his *The Systematic Thought of Hans Urs von Balthasar*, 144-49.

[31]. See especially *Encyclopedia* #564-71, where Hegel discusses both the religious and philosophical syllogisms in order. This is a somewhat rarefied aspect of Hegelian thought that the theologian Balthasar rarely approaches, but which Communio colleagues such as Bruaire, Brito, Chapelle discuss in detail. This has also been an object of much discussion in North American scholarship. See my *The Heterodox Hegel*, 325-71.

[32]. Iwan Iljin, *Die Philosophie Hegels als Kontemplative Gotteslehre*. The general background to a theogonic reading of Hegel is provided by Iljin's use of the language of 'epoch' to speak of the various moments of the self-articulation of the system, even at the logical level. His 'theogonic' understanding of Hegel's work is made explicit when he designates the self-actualization of the Idea as a 'theogenetic process' (*theogenetische Prozess*), 203. In terms of parsing the relation between faith and knowledge, and representation and concept, Iljin's deep knowledge of Hegel's logic gives him the advantage over both Staudenmaier and Balthasar.

[33]. Jean-Francois Lyotard, *The Postmodern Condition: A Report on Knowledge*, tr. Geoff Bennington and Brian Massumi (Minneapolis: University of Minnesota Press, 1984), 6. The attack against discursive justification makes sense then of Milbank's claim that theology is rhetorical. In this field, as between fields, there is going to be a contest of symbols and narrative with no prior agreed on rules of adjudication. For both Staudenmaier and Balthasar the self-justification features of discourse are the prerogative of logic. In *Darstellung und Kritik* Staudenmaier specifies Hegel's form of pantheism as essentially 'logical,' and understands that logic essentially compromises both mystery (450-51) and divine freedom (455, 462). While Balthasar gestures to this in *Theo-Drama*, it is one of the burdens of *Theo-Logic* to argue that Hegel's 'logical' discourse is stipulative rather than explicative. Arguably, of Hegel critics Iljin is in a relatively better position than Staudenmaier and Balthasar to make this kind of point due to his significantly superior understanding of Hegel's logical works and his privileging of Hegel's logical texts.

[34]. For an excellent discussion of Staudenmaier's *Die christliche Dogmatik* with a specific focus on its articulation of the Trinity in volume 2, see Karl Friedrich Reith, *Die Gotteslehre bei Franz Anton Staudenmaiers* (Berne and Frankfurt: Lang and Lang, 1974), 98-140, 162-89. Reith points out a number of interesting corollaries of Staudenmaier's three main presuppositions which anticipate Balthasar: (1) persons are ineluctable – the medievals would say 'incommunicable' – thus in an important sense persons are not reducible without remainder to relations. To the extent to which Richard of Saint Victor does identify persons with relation (*D 11*, 580-82) – and thus facilitates Hegelian conjugation – Staudenmaier resists this highly influential trinitarian thinker. (2) *Perichoresis* of the divine persons supports rather than subverts the Augustinian-Thomistic notion of appropriation since one cannot legitimately conceive of any divine action without the cooperation of all (*D 11*, 584-85). (3) The *Filioque* is supported less on grounds of its probity

on the level of the immanent Trinity than the way it supports a focus on Christ that blocks the pneumatism that is endemic to modernity. Christ is the objective ground of the sending of the Spirit, although Staudenmaier does point out that the Holy Spirit is active in history before Christ, plays a role in the anticipation of Christ, and in the incarnation. Reith underscores a point in Staudenmaier's dogmatics that becomes pivotal for Balthasar (109), that is, that the relation between Father and Son on the level of the immanent Trinity should be gleaned from the economic relation between Son and Father illustrated in the Gospel of John (*D 11*, 544). See also Bradford E. Hinze's excellent article 'Tracing the Trinity in Tradition: The Achievement of Franz Anton Staudenmaier,' in *Zeitschrift für Neuere Theologiegeschichte. Journal for the History of Modern Theology* (Berlin: de Gruyter) 8 (2001), 134-57. In this article *Die christliche Dogmatik* figures prominently.

35. See also *Die Philosophie des Christenthums* in which the concepts of 'pantheism' and 'Neoplatonism' are relatively interchangeable. At the same time Staudenmaier makes clear that the form of pantheism presenting the major contemporary challenge is dynamic, developmental, and theogonic in kind (234, 809).

36. As we saw in chapter 1, Balthasar expresses particular concern with Proclus, and in *Glory of the Lord* he charts a line between Proclus and Hegel. While Staudenmaier does not single out Proclus for special approbium, his concern with certain forms of Neoplatonism is similar to his concern with Spinoza: these are forms of speculative thought that articulate forms of identity-metaphysic in which the analogy between God and the world is obliterated.

37. *Zum Religiösen Frieden der Zukunft*, vol. 3, 116-37. The responses of Irenaeus to Gnosticism, on the one hand, and the response of Ruysbroeck to the heresy of the Free Spirit, on the other, are regarded as emblematic theological responses. They serve as models for Staudenmaier's own response to Hegel's thought and its intellectual and real-life effects.

38. Here one can see a genealogical development in Staudenmaier's position. Already in the 1830's Staudenmaier had come to the conclusion that the only way for theology to survive was to steer a course between fideism and speculation, or in his terms between 'supernaturalism' and 'naturalism.' This point is underscored by Balthasar Schrott. See his *Die Idee in der Geschichte: Zur theologischen Denkform Franz Anton Staudenmaiers* (Essen: Ludgerus Verlag Hubert Wingen, 1976), 37, in which he quotes a passage from Staudenmaier's work on Eriugena that he understands to be paradigmatic: '*Der Supernaturalismus hat die Natur und das Wesen des Glaubens falsch aufgegriffen; der Naturalismus aber die Natur und das Wesen des Wissens missachet.*' The 1840's sees a Staudenmaier with more genealogical capability. See *Die Philosophie des Christenthums*, 624 ff, in which Staudenmaier argues that the Protestant commitment to grace alone, particularly as specified in the doctrine of predestination, replicates and/or sets a condition for pantheism in the full and proper sense by voiding the world's integrity and subsistence. The theme of preparation for pantheism in the very foundation of Protestantism is even more persistently a theme in *Zum Religiösen Frieden der Zukunft*. Protestant thought is typified by an 'acosmic' version of pantheism in which the creature is nothing before God (vol. 1, 263 ff; vol. 2, 137). This acosmic version of pantheism begets, according to Staudenmeier, the cosmic version of pantheism typical

of Romanticism and Idealism in which the finite and infinite mutually condition each other (vol. 1, 262-66; vol. 3, 38, 79). If the former represents a 'loss of world' (*Weltlosigkeit*), the latter represents a loss of God (*Gottlosigkeit*). For the foundational expression of this development, see *Die Philosophie des Christenthums*, 233-35. In line with Baur's *Die christliche Gnosis*, Boehme and Hegel represent the two most important links in the genealogical chain of the emergent cosmic form of pantheism (vol. 3, 362-67). In the post-1848 revolutionary environment Staudenmaier is convinced that pantheism ceases to be a viable alternative between theism and atheism. To claim that without the world God is not God is effectively to claim that only the world is and that God is not (vol. 3, 38). The process in and through which Hegel's thought devolves through Left-Wing Hegelianism reaching something of an apogee in Feuerbach's principle of humanization (*Vermenschlichung*) (vol. 3, 45-58; 72, 78) represents the fated conclusion of Protestantism's break with Catholicism. As we have seen in part 2, Balthasar also sees the connection between the fideistic stance of the Reformation and the full-blown apocalypsis of German Idealism, but does not draw the line either as straight or as powerfully as Staudemaier. Most certainly he underscores more nearly the dialectical nature of the relationship.

[39]. It is not a small matter that in *Theo-Drama* the overall contours of mission and thus election are provided by Ignatius. This provision, which links election more nearly to the creature as created than the creature as sinful, allows the creature and the world – social and cultural as well as natural – which is given to it and which envelops it, a relative autonomy. I will discuss in part 4 how Balthasar sharpens the contrast between Lutheran and Catholic elaboration of theological anthropology by looking at the drama of the Baroque period.

[40]. In *Analogia Entis* it is a point with Przywara to distinguish between 'theopanism' (what corresponds to Staudenmaier's 'acosmism'), which characterizes systems in which the ground of beings is all and the beings nothing, and 'pantheism,' which involves the presence of the ground in the world and the world in the ground. Hegel is the typical pantheist. The influence of this scheme is obvious in Balthasar's book on Barth in which the worry is expressed that the great Reformed theologian continues the voluntarism and actualism of the Reformation and thus in the last instance is a 'theopanist.' However appreciative of Barth he is, Balthasar also insists that Catholicism's favoring of analogy does not confound God and world as Barth claims. Beyond the theopanism-pantheism binary opposition lies the Catholic *tertium quid.* Przywara provides a vocabulary for Balthasar rather than a grammar of genealogical conjugation. Absorbing this Przywarian vocabulary Balthasar puts it into genealogical operation. As it does so, he non-identically repeats a conjugation presented by Staudenmaier in the nineteenth century.

[41]. I referred already to Staudenmaier's recall of Irenaeus as the figure for the combating of any and all forms of gnosis. The analogy of proportion is obvious: Irenaeus vs Gnosticism: Staudenmaier vs Hegel. Of the two main Tübingen theologians, it is obvious that it is Möhler who is more given to such heresiological stylizing. As already indicated in chapter 1, Möhler does not have a great deal of compunction figuring his work as a kind of heresiological intervention in a situation of theological chaos. Staudenmaier differs in a number of important

respects in stylization, which make Irenaeus rather than Möhler his precursor when it comes to resisting speculative forms of thought: (i) although the attenuation and fragmentation of Christian discourse is a problem, speculative Idealism constitutes a particular problem. (ii) As a discourse speculative Idealism is formally and materially similar to Gnosticism of the earliest centuries, which is dangerous because it can look like genuine Christian discourse. (iii) Gnosticism is best thought of not in terms of psychology, but in terms of the narrative of Christianity as disfigured and refigured in and expressed as a narrative ontology.

[42]. In addition to the texts cited already as expressive of the early Staudenmaier's more open – but not uncritical – relation to Hegel, one could also cite a number of essays explicitly dealing with one or other of Hegel's texts. For example, 'G. W. F. Hegel, *Vorlesungen über die Philosophie der Religion*, in *Jahrbüchern für Theologie und Philosophie*, Bd. 1 (1834) 92-158; 'G. W. F. Hegel, *Vorlesungen über die Philosophie der Geschichte*,' in *Zeitschrift für Theologie*, Bd. 1, Heft 1 (1837), 116-204; 'Kritik der Vorlesungen Hegel über die Beweise von Dasein Gottes,' in *Jahrbüchern für Theologie und Philosophie* (1836), 251-359.

[43]. In the pages that follow I am indebted to Scott Moringiello's 'Irenaeus Rhetor' (Ph. D dissertation, University of Notre Dame, 2008).

[44]. See my account and development of this figure in *Gnostic Return in Modernity*, 148-59.

[45]. The Revolution of 1848 in an important sense put Staudenmaier's theology in a bind. On the one hand, Revolution made cultural and social intervention absolutely necessary, on the other, it made it inordinately complicated and even dangerous. Better, therefore, to grasp and disseminate enduring Catholic truths to a hostile age. Already in the late Staudenmaier, one can see traces of return to the sure line -of Saint Thomas that will be validated two decades later in Joseph Kleutgen (1811-1883).

[46]. For this point about reconceiving 'deposit' as more of a grammar than a fixed sum of right beliefs, see *Gnostic Return in Modernity*, 159-67.

[47]. I take it that this point has been successfully demonstrated by Mongrain in his *The Systematic Thought of Hans Urs von Balthasar.*

[48]. Although a Marcionite or disjunctive reading of the relation between Hebrew scripture and the New Testament, as Ireneaeus shows, is a systemic possibility for Christianity, it is a particular problem in modernity. Of course, bringing Hebrew scripture and the New Testament together necessarily raises the specter of supercessionism. With respect to Balthasar this is dealt with in very different ways by Richard Kendall Soulen and Anthony Sciglitano. For Soulen, see *The Blessing of an Other: The Theological Significance of Christian Anti-Judaism and a Way Beyond* (New Haven: Yale University Press, 1992). Soulen interprets Balthasar to be, on the one hand, the heir of the classical model of salvation history (articulated by Irenaeus) which displaces the God of Israel and, on the other, not too far distant from moderns such as Kant and Schleiermacher in which the dissociation gets exacerbated. In his forthcoming book, *Cross and Covenant: An Anti-Marcionite Theology of Religion* (New York: Crossroad, 2013), Anthony Sciglitano offers a much more positive reading of Balthasar. As it operates in Balthasar the canonic narrative does not do the mischief that Soulen suggests it does. This is not to say that his

allegiance to the canonic narrative protects Balthasar from insensitivity vis-à-vis existing Judaism.

[49]. Milbank raises the issue of the identity of the modern and postmodern Irenaeus in the context of his critique of speculative metanarratives in *Theology and Social Theory*, 147-76, 189, 302, 311.

[50]. My technical way of putting this recognition in *Gnostic Return in Modernity* is that while there are modern as well as ancient instances of a Valentinian narrative grammar, modern instances represent 'rule-governed deformations' of ancient paradigms in that they will tend to be non-dualistic rather than dualist, dynamic rather than static, and their circularity will not simply reinstate a perfection that is lost, but introduce a perfection that is more than the perfection lost. See *Gnostic Return in Modernity*, 196-207.

[51]. Here I avail of Lyotard's attempt in *The Postmodern Condition* to give 'postmodern' some degree of independence from temporal sequence (especially its posteriority vis-à-vis modernity).

[52]. I discussed this point in detail in 'Between Tübingen and Postmodernity' in which not only do I comb *Glory of the Lord* for expressions of this, but highlight Balthasar's relation to Möhler on this point, as well as the influence exercised by de Lubac, especially his book *Catholicisme.*

[53]. Kierkegaard, *Either/Or*, vol. 1, tr. David F. Swenson and Lillian Marvin Swenson with revisions and foreword by Howard A. Johnson (Princeton, NJ: Princeton University Press, 1971) (Originally published 1843), Preface, 1-15. The Chinese box conceit of discovery of papers in a secret drawer is presented by Victor Eremita. If once it was unproblematic to claim that this text represents an attack against Hegelian 'ethical nature' especially in its most basic institutional shape of marriage, due to the work of Jon Stewart it has become problematic. Still in the end, whatever the Danish translation and modification of Hegel, Hegel's views are targeted.

[54]. Interestingly, Hegel and Balthasar agree that the ascription of the title 'magus of the North' to Hamann is precisely not to brand him a fideist or irrationalist which is the purpose of Isaiah Berlin in his *Magus of the North: J. G. Hamann and the Origins of Modern Irrationalism*, ed. Henry Hardy (New York: Farrar, Staus, and Giroux, 1993). For Balthasar, Hamann is an aesthetic thinker, but one with a very different complexion than Hegel, one that is properly theological and properly traditional at the same time. The late 18th and early 19th-centuries are moments of fundamental choice. Hamann rather than German Idealism is precisely the road not taken (*GL1*, 80-3; also, 49).

[55]. Central to *For Marx* and *Reading Capital* is the deconstruction of the doctrinaire Marxist model of economic infrastructure and institutional and discursive superstructures, in which the determining element is always the economic base. In Althusser's new model, all elements that influence society and politics and effect change are fundamentally thought to belong to one field. Any of these elements or group of elements can play a decisive role in change even if the economic is almost always part of the equation and often the decisive component.

[56]. Both Ricoeur and Lacan think of the unconscious less as an unreachable or barely reachable depth and more as a language or a force in language. For

Ricoeur, see *Freud and Philosophy: An Essay in Interpretation*, tr. Denis Savage (New Haven: Yale University Press, 1970). For Lacan, see Écrits (Paris: Éditions du Seuil, 1966). For a good account of Lacan's semiotic view of the unconscious, see Roger Grigg, *Lacan, Language, and Philosophy* (Albany, NY: SUNY Press, 2008). For the relation and differences between Ricoeur and Lacan, see Karl Simms, *Ricoeur and Lacan* (London: New York: Continuum, 2007).

[57]. In *The Heterodox Hegel* I went to some trouble to show that both apocalyptic forms of thought (primarily Joachimite) and Neoplatonic forms of thought (primarily Proclean) exercise a significant influence on Hegel's narrative ontotheology in addition to the more Gnostic line that has its major modern representative in the 16th-century Lutheran mystic, Jacob Boehme. In my article 'Hegel and Anti-Judaism: The Inner Circulation of the Kabbalah' I added the Kabbalah. The point that I kept implicit was that the influence of all these discourses on Hegel was not equal. In *Gnostic Apocalypse* I showed in detail how all of these discourses influence Boehme while it is Valentinianism that regulates the deployment of the other narrative forms. The corollary is that such is the case in Hegel also.

[58]. In *Gnostic Return in Modernity* I argued that in articulating a Gnostic or Valentinian genealogy modernity counted in two ways: (i) even if the claims for modernity being in fundamental respects a *novum* necessarily had to be humbled somewhat, nonetheless, however we temporally mark it, modernity is different in decisive respects from periods that precede it; (ii) although it debates with itself at different levels, there is a sense that when it turns speculative modern discourses will tend to have as inalienable features a dynamic and developmental view of reality. I argue that in speculation these features do not disturb a commitment to a Valentinian narrative grammar.

[59]. The general theory of what I call 'Valentinian Enlisting of Non-Valentinian Narrative Discourses' is presented in *Gnostic Return in Modernity*, 207-25.

[60]. In *Analogia Entis* Hegel's philosophy is regarded as the *ne plus ultra* of essentialism in which the mystery of existence is conceptually overcome. See especially *Analogia Entis*, 55-6, 71, 86-95. As already indicated, the terms of Przywara's opposition to Hegel are repeated in *Wahrheit*, 50-1, 67-8, 88, 138, 185-87, 244-45.

[61]. For a lucid account of the split into left-wing and right-wing Heglianism, see John Edward Toews, *Hegelianism: The Path Toward Dialectical Humanism, 1805-1841* (Cambridge: Cambridge University Press, 1985).

[62]. Hans Frei, *The Eclipse of Biblical Narrative: A Study in Eighteenth Century and Nineteenth Century Hermeneutics* (New Haven, CT: Yale University Press, 1974).

[63]. The accommodation cut both ways, however. Baader was, undoubtedly, influenced by the two major figures of German Idealism, Hegel and Schelling. Baader was persuaded of Hegel's monumental philosophical importance, and felt that one should at least delay a verdict as to whether his philosophy was invidious or not with respect to the Christian tradition. Certainly, he corrected crude forms of theism, which ought not to have had purchase in the premodern tradition and necessarily could not have purchase in the modern. Baader was heavily influenced by Schelling's *Naturphilosophie*. See Thomas O'Meara, *Romantic Idealism and Roman Catholicism: Schelling and the Theologians* (Notre Dame: University of Notre Dame Press, 1982). At the same time Baader is responsible for Hegel's knowledge of the

German mystics Meister Eckhart and Jacob Boehme, whom he believed offered a third way between crude theism and pantheism (which was Hegel's own predilection). If Baader was not solely responsible for the shift in Schelling's later thought to an *Existenz-Philosophie*, Schelling's avowal that all philosophy presupposed an existence that could not itself be explained owed something considerable to Baader's ministrations.

[64]. The most consistent and thoroughgoing appropriation of Hegel by a Catholic thinker in the nineteenth century is that of Anton Günther. Balthasar speaks only sparingly of Günther in the trilogy, but when he does so he speaks sympathetically of Günther's career as 'tragic,' but offers no detail with respect to what he means. Possibly Balthasar is thinking of the condemnation in the 1860's of his speculative theology which was viewed as determined by Hegel's view of absolute knowledge. Although it would go too far to say that in terms of Catholic thought Günther represents the anti-type to Staudenmaier, it is certainly the case that his early high – although not uncritical – opinion of his philosophy and his confidence of its Christian ratio is maintained throughout his career in a way it is not in Staudenmaier. Early on in his career, Günther saw as clearly as Staudenmaier many of the problems in Hegel's thought, indeed, significantly influenced Staudenmaier in this respect. An important early text is *Vorschule zur spekulativen Theologie des positiven Christenthums*, 2 vols. (Vienna, 1828-29). Later texts are less critical. A good example is provided by *Lydia, Philosophiches Taschenbuch* (Vienna, 1949-54). For an exceptional diachronic account of Günther's thought with a special emphasis on its relation to Hegelianism, see Christoph Kronabel, *Die Aufhebung der Begriffsphilosophie: Anton Günther und der Pantheismus* (Freiburg and München: Verlag Karl Alber, 1989).

[65]. See especially the second volume of the series, *The Lion, the Witch, and the Wardrobe* (Oxford: C. S. Lewis (Pte) Limited, 1950).

[66]. The two main Catholic theologians of the Tübingen School are Möhler and Drey. Another Tübingen religious thinker is Johannes Evangelist von Kuhn (1806-1887). Kuhn's critical engagement with Hegel is limited to the 1830's and early 1840's. Kuhn agrees with many of Hegel's Catholic critics on the need for theology to be scientific (*wissenschaftslich*), and that with respect to this aim Hegel can be an enormous help. At the same time, Kuhn worries about the apriorist nature of Hegel's epistemology and its ambitions for systematic completeness. The following text in which Jacobi is used to critique Hegelian apriorism is illustrative: 'Über den Begriff und das Wesen der spekulativen Theologie,' in *Theologische Quartalschrift* 14 (1832), 253-304, 411-44. In addition to concerns about philosophical foundations, Kuhn also had explicitly dogmatic and hermeneutical reservations. He is worried about Hegelian Christology and biblical interpretation, particularly as the Hegelian view is given critical shape in the work of David Friedrich Strauss' *Das Leben Jesu* (1835). His response is contained in *Das Leben Jesu wissenschaftlich bearbeitet* (Mainz, 1838). Kuhn's response has been judged the most capable Catholic response of the period. See William Madges, *The Core of Christian Faith: D. F. Strauss and his Catholic Critics* (New York and Berne: Peter Lang, 1987), 44-90. Staudenmaier is usually regarded as the fourth member of the Tübingen School. He is so, however, because of an affinity of thought rather than appointment.

Staudenmaier never taught at Tübingen. There is significant literature on the Tübingen School. See especially Josef Rupert Geiselmann's classic study *Die katholische Tübinger Schule: Ihre Theologische Eigenart* (Freiburg: Herder, 1962).

[67]. See *Cosmic Liturgy: The Universe According to Maximus the Confessor*, 190. In *GL3*, 287, 324, Balthasar joins Soloviev's sophiology to Maximus' view of the cosmic Christ, and thus by implication suggests that Bulgakov's sophiology represents a development of Maximus' thought. In *Cosmic Liturgy* (190) his view of Bulgakov (one can presume also his view of Soloviev) is much more critical: 'The "Sophia" that Bulgakov sees as a remarkable intermediate being, hovering between God and created nature – one face turned toward eternity as everlasting creaturehood, as a superessential yet passive, feminine world of ideas, the other face turned toward the world as its source and root: this "Sophia," to which Böhme, Schelling, Baader, and Soloviev pay their respects, flows down to them, through Byzantium, from ancient Platonic and Gnostic springs.'

[68]. Hegel, 'Hamanns Schriften,' in *Jahrbücher für wissenshaftsliche Kritik* (1828). Reprinted in *Berliner Schriften*, 1818-1831, vol. XI of *Werke*, ed. E. Moldenhauer and K. M. Michel (Franfurt: Suhrkamp, 1986), 275-352. This review is discussed in some detail by Stephen N. Dunning in his *The Tongues of Men: Hegel and Hamann on Religious Language and History* (Missoula, MT: Scholars Press, 1979), 103-33. Hegel is more than persuaded that Hamann's work vastly exceeds in value that of Jacobi, with whom Hamann is sometimes associated. As is well-known, Jacobi is perhaps the philosophical figure most despised by Hegel, and who is the object of sarcastic remarks throughout his entire career, from *Glauben und Wissen* (1801) to the last rendition of the *Encyclopaedia of the Philosophical Sciences* (1831). By contrast with Jacobi, Hamann's work is not typified by the reference to the knowing subject, but to the objectivity of history and language. Hegel's main problem with Hamann is the problem with 'genius,' and more specifically communication. Hamann articulates his position with a 'clenched fist' (the contrast presumably being an 'open hand'). This means that Hamann's eliptical style and prophetic predilection hinder discourse, which from Hegel's point of view moves towards a condition of transparence. Hegel's problem with Hamann mirrors Kant's problem with those thinkers whom Kant accuses in the 1790's of favoring an 'apocalyptic tone' and poetic style over the prose and the labor of reason. In addition, while Hegel does not cavil with Hamann's interpretation of scripture, for Hamann is far from literalistic, points between them include the status of the biblical text and the possibility of its application to modern individual and social existence.

[69]. Even more clearly than in the first two parts of the trilogy, Balthasar insists on the 'fullness' of the Triune God and by implication the triune persons in *Theologic 2 & 3*. See especially *TL2*, 22-3. Bulgakov, who does not have the same Western interest in divine unity that Balthasar has is even more insistent on this point. See *The Comforter*, tr. Boris Jakim (Grand Rapids, MI: Eerdmans, 2004). The original text in Russian dates from 1936. This is the second volume of the trilogy on 'Godmanhood' (*bogochelovechestve*). *The Lamb of God*, published three years earlier (1933) in Russian, and whose French translation of the forties was read by Balthasar, is the first.

[70]. *L'Orthodoxie* (Paris: F. Alcan, 1932).

[71]. The fact that Balthasar is going to imagine otherwise than Irenaeus the modality of Christ's descent into and sojourn in hell does not mean that Irenaeus is not a serious influence. The emphasis on Christ's solidarity with the dead, characterized by impotence, wrings an important change on Irenaeus' sense of Christ as powerful rescuer.

[72]. Peter Casarella has persuasively drawn attention to the precursorship of Cusanus on this point. See his 'The Descent, Divine Self-Enrichment, and the Universality of Salvation.' Adrienne von Speyr is even more important. Among the many texts that exercise an influence on Balthasar's particular approach to the mythologem is her two volume work, *Kreuz und Hölle: Aftragshöllen* (Einsiedeln: Johannes Verlag, 1972). For a good synoptic essay on this topic in Balthasar, which also has a real appreciation for the contribution of von Speyr, see Juan M. Sara, '*Descensus ad inferos*, Dawn of Hope, Aspects of the Theology of Holy Saturday in the Trilogy of Hans Urs von Balthasar,' in *Communio* 32.3, Fall (2005), 541-572.

[73]. See *The Bride of the Lamb*, tr. Boris Jakim (Grand Rapids, MI: Eerdmans, 2002). The original Russian text was published in 1945 and is the third volume of the 'Godmanhood' (*bogochelovechestve*) trilogy.

[74]. Bulgakov thinks of Revelation as summing up other mentionings of the descent into hell in the New Testament and Intertestamental literature: Daniel and 2nd Thessalonians (2:2-10); 2 John 7; 2 Peter 3:3; Jude 1:18; Tim 4:1-3 (*BL*, 329-30). As Aidan Nichols has suggested in *Wisdom from Above* (310), it would be difficult to overestimate the importance of the book of Revelation for Bugakov. In addition to *Bride and the Lamb*, in which Revelation is the pivotal and integrating text, Bulgakov also produced a theological commentary on Revelation. See *Apokalipsis Ioanna: opyt dogmaticheskogo istolkovaniia* [The Revelation of John: A Dogmatic Interpretation] (Paris: YMCA Press, 1948).

[75]. This imaging relation, which has precedents in the Gnosticism of the early centuries of the common era, is a fairly standard move in Berdyaev, who depends for his own expression largely on the 'later Schelling' and the 17th-century speculative mystic, Jacob Boehme. See especially Berdyaev's essay on Boehme called 'Unground and Freedom,' in the English translation of Boehme's *Six Theosophic Points* (Ann Arbor, MI: University of Michigan Press, 1958), V-XXXVII.

[76]. Bulgakov, who shows himself far from anxious to suggest heterodoxy in Soloviev's Sophiology, nonetheless, admits to Soloviev's flirtation and problematic choice of textual and traditional basis. See his *Sophia: Wisdom of God: An Outline of Sophiology* (New York: Lindisfarne Press, 1993), 9-10. This represents a translation from the Russian text of 1937. Even the strongest supporters of Soloviev recognize the heterodox tendencies in his thought. See for example, Paul Valliere, *Modern Russian Theology: Bukharev, Soloviev, Bulgakov: Orthodox Theology in a New Key* (Grand Rapids, MI: Eerdmans, 2000), 109-223. See especially Valliere's admission of heterodox elements drawn especially from Hegel and Schelling (155-57, 166). Valliere also draws attention to Bulgakov's criticism of Soloviev's view of Sophia (292). Other scholars have traced a deeper ancestry in the heterodox tradition. See Judith Deutsch Kornblatt, 'Soloviev's Andrgynous Sophia and the Jewish Kabbalah,' in *Slavic Review* 50 (1991), 487-96; Maria Carlson, 'Gnostic

Elements in the Cosmogony of Vladimir Soloviev,' in *Russian Religious Thought*, ed. Judith Deutsch Kornblatt and Richard E. Gustafson (Madison and London: University of Wisconsin Press, 1996), 49-67.

[77]. As an extra-confessional religious thinker, Berdyaev does not feel the doctrinal weight of the doctrine of the Trinity as he elaborates his Sophiology. He has no compunction, for example, of commending Sophia as a fourth hypostasis, just as he has no compunction about suggesting that the fully realized reality of God depends upon God integrating a dark side. With respect to both views Berdyaev again has Boehme as a proximate source and, arguably, Gnosticism as an ultimate source. For Balthasar's association of Berdyaev with a Gnostic view of an almost symmetrical evil source, see *Apok 3*, 429.

[78].This is the other side of Balthasar's concern with heterodoxy. Balthasar makes it plain in his discussion of Chateaubriand and those like him in *GL1* that tradition is not a museum. Chateaubriand wants perfect recall of all of Christian culture, which in Balthasar's view is as undesirable as it is impossible. In an important way Balthasar agrees with Nietzsche's sense of history and historical tradition, that forgetting is an element in all memory, since to remember is to foreground and thus to make everything else background. More important than Balthasar's continuity with Nietzsche here is his continuity with the Tübingen School, and specifically with Drey who balanced more nearly than Möhler and Staudenmaier the concern for hyperorthodoxy as well as heterodoxy. For a fine account of Drey's concern with hyperorthodoxy, see John E. Thiel, *Imagination and Authority: Theological Authorship in the Modern Tradition* (Minneapolis: Fortress Press, 1991), 63-94. As Thiel points out, Drey elaborates this notion in one of his earliest texts (1819), *Kurze Einleitung in das Studium der Theologie mit Rücksicht den wissenschaftlichen Standpunkt und das katholische System*. For this point see *Imagination and Authority*, 84, 90.

[79]. As Mongrain has pointed out, Balthasar sometimes frames *Theo-Drama* as if it were a redress to the elaboration of a theological aesthetics in *The Glory of the Lord*. See his *The Systematic Thought of Hans Urs von Balthasar*, 66, 193.

[80]. Soloviev's extraordinarily influential piece 'A Brief Tale on the Anti-Christ' (*Kratkaia povest ob antikriste*) is discussed in some detail in Valliere in *Modern Russian Theology*, 213-23. For a convenient translation, consult *War, Progress, and the End of History: Three Conversations. Including a Short Story of the Anti-Christ*, tr. Thomas R. Beyer, Jr. (Hudson, NY: Lindisfarne Press, 1990).

[81]. Balthasar has much less support in his own tradition for his judgement about the central theological importance of Revelation than Bulgakov has in his, at least if one prioritizes the Russian tradition that immediately preceded him. Valliere makes it clear in *Modern Russian Theology* that in this respect Bulgakov is simply continuing a tendency that can be observed in Bukharev (23-5, 78-98) and Soloviev (205-23).

[82]. As I have indicated already, despite Balthasar's retrieval of patristic thought, it would be a mistake to designate him as a 'neo-patristic thinker.' Obviously, given the contretemps between Bulgakov and the likes of Lossky and Florovsky almost no commentator on modern Russian religious thought would be inclined to apply that label to Bulgakov.

[83]. In *The Comforter* Bulgakov has critical things to say about what he takes to be the Western binatarianism rather than trinitarianism for which he thinks Augustine is largely at fault (87-95). But he has also critical things to say about Photius and the Photian line in the East (95-9) which also failed to think through properly the nature and role of the Spirit and its relation to Son and Father.

[84]. Whatever the probity of its historical analysis, here Michael Aksionov Meerson's work on the Trinity proves useful. See *The Trinity of Love in Modern Russian Theology: The Love Paradigm and the Retrieval of Western Medieval Love Mysticism in Modern Russian Trinitarian Thought (from Solovyov to Bulgakov)* (Quincy, IL: Franciscan Press, 1998).

[85]. 'The Second Difference,' in *The Word Made Strange*, 171-93.

[86]. For a good account of Blok and other Russian apocalyptic writers of the modern period, see David M. Bethea, *The Shape of Apocalypse in Modern Russian Fiction* (Princeton, NJ: Princeton University Press, 1989).

[87]. For an articulation of a relationship between Hamann and Kierkegaard that does not reduce Hamann's work to an outline of what is fully realized both in terms of thought and expression, see John R. Betz , 'Hamann and Kierkegaard: A Systematic Theological Oversight,' in *Pro Ecclesia* 16, Summer (2007), 299-333.

[88]. Hegel's 'Hamanns Schriften' is approximately 80 pages long. This is a longer treatment of any thinker in his *Lectures on the History of Philosophy*, with the exception of his treatment of Plato and Aristotle. It is considerably longer than his treatment of any modern thinker not excluding Spinoza and Kant. Indeed, one has to go back to the very beginning of Hegel's philosophical authorship to find any treatment of modern thinkers that remotely rivals it. *Glauben und Wissen* (1801) devotes about sixty pages each to Kant, Jacobi, and Fichte. And the *Differenzschift* (1801-02) has over a hundred pages devoted to a comparison between Fichte and Schelling.

[89]. John Betz does a splendid job in advancing the importance of Hamann's critique of the epistemology of *Critique of Pure Reason* (1781) in *Metakritik über den Purismum der Vernunft* (1784). See *After Enlightenment*, ch. 10 titled 'Hamann's *Metacritique* of Kant: Deconstructing the Transcendental Dream,' 230-57. See also chapter 10 (217-29) in which Jacobi and Hamann are seen as presenting different forms of a metacritique. To a certain extent Betz follows Milbank in thinking of Hamann and Jacobi as presenting a two-stage attack on the so-called presuppositionless articulation of pure reason. See Milbank, 'KNOWLEDGE the theological critique of philosophy in Hamann and Jacobi,' in *Radical Theology: A New Theology*, eds. John Milbank, Catherine Pickstock, Graham Ward (New York: Routledge, 2006). Other essays of Milbank in which Hamann figures prominently include 'The Linguistic Turn as a Theological Turn' and 'Pleonasm, Speech, and Writing' in *The Word Made Strange*, 84-120 and 53-83, respectively. Hamann's metacritical work is now available in an English translation. See Gwen Griffith-Dixon, *Hamann's Relational Metacriticism* (Berlin: de Gruyter, 1995). Nonetheless, in line with Balthasar, in Hamann there is nothing of Jacobi's fideism (*GL3*, 265-66), and correspondingly a much richer articulation of christological and trinitarian dimensions of faith. Betz supplements Balthasar on both fronts; his canvas of the latter is much deeper than that provided in Balthasar's

essay, and he sharpens the issue of what is at stake between Hamann and the Enlightenment by forcing the question whether it is more correct to call Hamann a fideist or an example of a 'radical Enlightenment.' Following the doyen of Hamann studies, Oswald Bayer, he decides in favor of the latter (16). For Bayer, see *Zeitgenosse in Widerspruch: Johann Georg Hamann als radiclaer Aufklärer* (Munich: Piper Verlag, 1988).

[90]. Excellent chapters on all of these texts are to be found in *After Enlightenment*. For *The London Writings* (ch. 2, 38-62), for *Aesthetica in nuce* (ch. 3, 63-87), for *Golgotha and Scheblimini* (ch. 12, 258-90).

[91]. At best these texts are first among equals. In making his case with respect to Hamann's christocentric optic and articulation of an economic trinitarian horizon of a dramatic sort, Balthasar adduces as evidence texts from the entire span of Hamann's career. Balthasar succinctly states his rationale: 'From *Biblical Reflections* (*Biblische Betrachtungen*) to *The Final Page* (*Das Letze Blatt*) Hamann never deviated one iota from this consistent and unbroken Christocentricity . . .' (*GL3*, 246). The emphasis on the christocentrism of Hamann is consistent with Balthasar's brief discussion of Hamann in *Apok 1*, 60-1.

[92]. In his essay Balthasar makes his point about the biblical text without tying the condenscension evident in the biblical text with the notion of fragment (*GL3*, 251-53, 256). This might seem to suggest that when Balthasar appeals to the notion of fragment that he has other sources in mind. In part 4 I suggest that while there are other post-Enlightenment precedents, nonetheless, the influence of Hamann cannot be ruled out.

[93]. Balthasar certainly figures Hamann as a decidedly anti-Gnostic thinker, but makes a little more of Hamann's refusal to derogate the flesh than his biblical hermeneutics, which are equally important. See *GL3*, 257-58, 261-62. Betz comments on Hamann's anti-Gnosticism on a number of occasions. See *After Enlightenment*, 130-32, 240, 250. In the last two citations, 'Gnosticism' is an accusation leveled against Kant's thought. Against the backdrop of Balthasar's essay, and, being undoubtedly aware of Balthasar's famous essay on Irenaeus in *GL2*, Betz has no compunction about labeling Hamann an 'Irenaeus *redivivus*.' See *After Enlightenment*, 132.

[94]. In *Encyclopaedia* #73 Hegel makes a famous disparaging reference to the tendency in modern religious thought to retrieve the 'Unknown God.' Similar passages are not hard to find. See also *Encyclopaedia* #36 zu. Of course, the *Encyclopaedia* expressions merely a long-standing point of view, first expressed against Kant, Fichte, and Jacobi in *Faith and Knowledge* (1801), reiterated in the *Phenomenology* (1807), and given its most voluminous expression in *Lectures on the Philosophy of Religion* (1821, 1824, 1827). For a detailed discussion of the relevant texts in Hegel, see *The Heterodox Hegel*, 31-43.

[95]. The closest Balthasar comes to underscoring Hamann's critique of Mendelssohn on the point of his misinterpretation of Judaism is *GL3*, 267-67. Betz gives a wonderful account of Hamann's defense of Judaism against the Enlightenment that Mendelssohn is illegitimately importing in *After Enlightenment*, 258-91.

[96]. No more here in the Hamann essay than in his reflections on Kant in *GL5* (481-513) does Balthasar show an inclination to bring Kant to tasks for his

anti-Semitism. *Religion within the Bounds of Reason Alone*, in which Kant excoriates Judaism as a purely legal religion, is not a text that comes in for much discussion. He has no such reserve with respect to Hegel.

[97]. Although Balthasar cites with approval Hamann's recommendation of the Bible to Kant precisely because it is a 'text for children' (*GL3*, 243), he neither explores why Kant, the prophet of the Enlightenment, would have much more interest in a philosophical texts for adults, and how or why this would take an ethical form. Hamann's privileging of 'childhood' over 'adulthood' is, obviously, of major interest to Balthasar. 'Childhood' for him is synonymous with being a Christian, and as David Schindler has pointed out, Balthasar is heavily influenced by the theology of childhood of Ferdinand Ulrich. See *Hans Urs von Balthasar and the Dramatic Structure of Truth*, 101-10 *inter alia*. See *Der Mensch als Anfang: Zur philosophischen Anthropologie der Kindheit* (Einsiedeln, Switzerland: Johannes Verlag, 1970).

[98]. See Betz, *After Enlightenment*, 100-02, 114-16.

[99]. Balthasar's sense of the limitations of historical-critical method are critically examined by William Dickens in his *Hans Urs von Balthasar's Theological Aesthetics: A Model for Post-Critical Biblical Interpretation* (Notre Dame, Indiana: University of Notre Dame Press, 2003).

[100]. See Friedrich Christoph Oetinger, *Gegenüberstellung hebräischer und zeitgenössischer Philosoph* in *Die Lehrtafel der Prinzessin Antonia*, ed. Reinhard Breymayer and Friedrich Häussermann, 2 vols. (Berlin: de Gruyter, 1977), vol. 1, 131-44. If Hamann shows no knowledge of Oetinger's use of Kabbalah to establish an alternative metaphysic, he shows some awareness of the work of the Jewish convert J. G. Wachter. At the turn of the 18th century Wachter made available to Christians a history of Jewish mysticism that gave a first-hand account of Jewish textual practices and intellectual systems as well as offered arguments against their ultimate validity.

[101]. This is the formula Hegel uses in *LPR 1* (1824), 123 (G 39-40).

[102]. See *Lectures on the History of Philosophy. Volume 2. Plato and the Platonists*, tr. E. S. Haldane and Francis H. Simson (Bristol England: Thoemmes Press, 1999), 374-387, 394-453.

[103]. In the commentary material, as well as his introduction to his selection of Origen's sermons in the 1940's, Balthasar makes it clear that Origen does not indulge in fanciful allegorizing. Rather respecting the literal sense of scripture, Origen is persuaded that it has a deeper sense. In the final instance it is christological rather than philosophical. Christ is *anagogia*.

[104]. In *Wahrheit* Balthasar essentially postulated that Hegel's model of appearance (*Erscheinung*) had distinct advantages over a more Kantian scheme in which the relation of appearance (*Schein*) to ground is extrinsic. This is not to say, however, that a Hegelian model of manifestation is fully accurate. As we have seen, Balthasar worried about the overcoming of mysteriousness and gratuity in expression. This, of course, is exactly Rosenzweig's worry also in *Die Stern der Erlosung*, which Balthasar indicates in *Theo-Drama* he values highly.

[105]. On this point Aidan Nichols is apt. See *Scattering the Seed*, 46-8.

[106]. Betz brings out the emphasis on divine humility in all its ramifications exceptionally well in *After Enlightenment*, 28, 43-4, 51-2, 58-9, 103, 118 *inter alia*.

[107]. See Betz, *After Enlightenment*, 55-59, in which he brings out Hamann's self-consciousness that the notion of fragment is first theological because biblical and only secondarily literary. In an important passage in *The London Writings*, Hamann glosses 1 Cor 13:12: 'We live here on scraps. Our thoughts are nothing but fragments. Indeed, our knowledge is a patchwork' (*After Enlightenment*, 57).

Chapter 5

[1]. John Milbank would likely disagree. In his important essay 'The Second Difference' Milbank is persuaded that Moltmann's Hegelian pedigree is not a matter of dispute. By contrast, 'Sophiology and Theurgy: The New Theological Horizon' involves a vindication of Soloviev and Bulgakov that surpasses that of Balthasar. See *Encounter Between Eastern Orthodoxy and Radical Orthodoxy*, ed. Adrian Pabst & Christoph Schneider (Burlington, VT: Ashgate Publishing Company), 86-92.
[2]. If the content of this question is my own, it does resonate with similar formulations in Kevin Mongrain's *The Systematic Thought of Hans Urs von Balthasar*, chs. 6 & 7. Commentators who link Moltmann to Hegel include Brian Spence and Randall E. Otto. See Brian Spence, The Hegelian Element in von Balthasar's and Moltmann's understanding of the Suffering of God,' in *Toronto Journal of Theology* 5.14, Spring (1998), 45-60. Although Spence links Moltmann in the closest possible way to Hegel, he is as undisturbed by this fact as Peter Hodgson is with respect to the association of his work with that of Hegel, and he does not seem to recognize at all any major differences between the positions of Moltmann and Balthasar; Randall E. Otto, *The God of Hope: The Trinitarian Vision of Jürgen Moltmann* (Lanham, MD: University Press of America, 1991). Otto underscores the link without, however, trying to explore its extent or tease out its consequences. The Moltmann commentator who seems most anxious to uncouple Hegel and Moltmann is Richard Bauckham. See his *The Theology of Jürgen Moltmann* (Edinburgh: T & T Clark, 1995), 47-69.
[3]. For a more detailed account of this move, see my 'Von Balthasar and Thick Retrieval: Post-Chalcedonian Symphonic Theology,' in *Gregorianum* 77.2 (1996) 227-60, esp. 227-39.
[4]. I have dealt with Balthasar's reluctance to exclude Meister Eckhart in some detail in 'Balthasar and Eckhart: Theological Principles and Catholicity,' in *The Thomist* 60.2, April (1996), 203-39.
[5]. Milbank, 'The Second Difference,' 180-83.
[6]. These are questions asked by Paul de Hart in his fine work on Jüngel. See *Beyond the Necessary God: Trinitarian Faith and Philosophy in the Thought of Eberhard Jüngel* (Oxford: Oxford University Press, 2000).
[7]. This is a line of questioning extrapolated from David Bentley Hart's *The Beauty of the Infinite*, 39, and which subsequently applies to all theologians judged to be in the Hegelian tradition. Hart finds it unproblematic to render this judgment with respect to Jüngel (148-49). Jüngel is linked with Moltmann (157) who, overall throughout *Beauty and the Infinite* does not seem worthy of mention. Presumably the reason is that Moltmann is so obviously Hegelian that it requires no

demonstration. One can presume Hegelian determination of Moltmann's thought and proceed to more difficult cases.

[8]. I am here exploiting Balthasar's reference to Hopkins' famous invocation of Christ as 'immortal diamond' from the poem, 'That Nature is a Heraclitean Fire.' In this poem, while the central motif is the contrast between mutability and immutability, corruptibility and uncorruptibility,one can sense also the inexhaustibility of Christ given the multifaceted nature of the diamond. See *GL3*, 361-62.

[9]. Balthasar's view of the synthetic role of John is stated on the outset of *GL7*: 'Our concern is to make a synthesis: therefore the last theology of the New Testament, the Johannine theology, will always be the vanishing point, the point towards which we are traveling – though all the theologies of the New Testament remain open both forwards (into the mediation of the church, which can never be brought to an end) and upwards to God' (10)

[10]. There are both formal-epistemic and material-theological sides to Luther's *theology of the cross.* The material-theological side of Luther is a Christology that seems to oscillate between a Jesusology and a monophysitism, which in its avoidance of the lessons of Chalcedon make a Hegelian take-over likely – if not inevitable. For a compendious and fair-minded account of the relation between Balthasar and Luther, see Rodney A. Howsare, *Hans Urs von Balthasar: The Ecumenical Implications of his Theological Style* (London and New York: T & T Clark, 2001), ch. 2 titled 'Balthasar and Luther's *Theologia Crucis*,' 42-76. For a good overall view of Luther's Christology with a special emphasis on the tension between the strong monophysite strain and the more traditional Chalcedonian Christology, see Marc Lienhard, *Luther: Witness to Jesus Christ: Stages and Themes of the Reformer's Theology* (Minneapolis: Augsburg, 1986). Very useful also especially with respect to the negative capability of Luther's Christology being transposed into a speculative philosophy where the consequences for monophysite tendencies are radically different and, arguably, radically more consequential, is Annegrit Brunkhorst-Hasenclever, *Die Transformierung des theologischen Deutung des Todes bei G. W. F. Hegel. Ein Beitrag zur Formbestimmung von Paradox und Synthese* (Bern & Frankfurt: Lang, 1970).

[11]. The formal-epistemology side of Luther is evident, for example, in *The Heidelberg Disputations* (1517) and is commonly rehearsed in the standard secondary literature on Luther. Scholars of Luther who have a deeper than usual appreciation of the difference and relation between various aspects of the trope of 'theology of the cross' include Jüngel and Ulrich Asendorf. The representative text for Jüngel is *God as the Mystery of the World*; the representative text for Asendorf is *Hegel und Luther: Untersuchungen zu Grundlegung einer neuen systematischen Theologie* (Weisbaden: Steiner, 1982).

[12]. In Moltmann's theological corpus, this approach is most readily seen performatively in terms of his approach to patristic and medieval traditions, and his particular marshaling of viable theological sources and resources; nonetheless, there are a few places in which, in a matter of paragraphs, he explicitly dismisses these traditions. See, for example, Moltmann, *Trinity and the Kingdom*: *The Doctrine of God,* tr. Margaret Kohl (Minneapolis: Fortress Press, 1993), 16-20, and *The Crucified God*, tr. R. A Wilson & John Bowden (Minneapolis: First Fortress Press,

1993), 239ff; also, it is around this theme that Moltmann structures the two sections 'Theism and the Theology of the Cross' and 'The theology of the Cross and Atheism,' 207-218 and 219-226, respectively.

[13]. Abraham Heschel is the only thinker invoked by Moltmann as witness for the probity of his trinitarian position whom Balthasar would regard as a mainline religious thinker. Of course, Heschel is a mainline Jewish thinker and as such not a trinitarian thinker.

[14]. Throughout the trilogy Balthasar links Hegelianism with the Kabbalah or at least its Christian adoption and adaptation. Moltmann's endorsement provides evidence for the prosecution. The presence of the Kabbalah also provides evidence of Gnosticism. To make the connection Balthasar does not need to suppose that the Kabbalah is intrinsically Gnostic, but simply that in Christian hands it begins to function so. After Oetinger, Hegel suggests that in Christian hands, and especially in Christian trinitarian hands, the Kabbalah could serve a speculative role that it might have served in its original Jewish domain.

[15]. Although Balthasar makes nothing of Berdyaev's avowal of Boehme, the general association of Boehme and Berdyaev is easy to make. There are four main elements: (i) there is a process of divine self-development predicated on an excess of potentiality in the divine over actuality; (ii) the ultimate origin of all that is (whether good or evil) is prior to the immanent as well as the economic Trinity; (iii) the Trinity is not unambiguously tri-personal; (iv) in addition to Father, Son, and Spirit, Sophia functions as a fourth element which mediates between the divine and the non-divine realm.

[16]. *Theology of Hope* comes in for consideration in *TD5*, 167, 171. See also references to *God and Creation* in *TL3*, 424.

[17]. See 'Liberation Theology in Light of Salvation History,' in *Liberation Theology in Latin America*, ed. James V. Schall, S, J. (San Francisco: Ignatius Press, 1982), 131-46.

[18]. As Balthasar's one and only work of what might be called fundamental theology, *Wahrheit* articulated obedience or service as the constitutive feature of authentic freedom that is indistinguishable from responsibility. See *TL1*, 53, 64, 71, 108 for obedience which counterintuitively defines freedom rather than pure spontaneity, which gets criticized (62-3, 83). Already here, freedom is subsumed by the broader categories of truth and love, which also illustrate that obedience and freedom are structures whose issue is action and form of life. Looking prospectively from *Wahrheit* Christ is the archetype of obedience and freedom. Looking back retrospectively from the point of view of *TD3*, it is clear that not only subsequently in *TD4* but previously in *Wahrheit* Balthasar has operative a particular understanding of the *imago dei.*

[19]. Endorsement of the two-will Christology is an important element in Balthasar's expansive treatment of Maximus in *Cosmic Liturgy.* Balthasar never subsequently reneges on its importance both as a key element of any adequate Christology and as diagnostic lens of christological deformation. See my discussion of this point in 'Von Balthasar and Thick Retrieval,' 245-55.

[20]. The language here is Chalcedonian and thus performs the continuity between Maximus' dythelite view and the Chalcedonian view of two natures/one person.

[21]. While Balthasar does not exclude the otherness of 'sin' when speaking about Moltmann in *TD4*, 221-23, Moltmann's connection with Hegel suggests that 'sin' is really a negation coextensive with the order of creation and/or history as an order of suffering.

[22]. Rahner, *The Trinity*, tr. Joseph Donceel, intro. Catherine LaCugna (New York: Herder, 2005), 22.

[23]. Joseph van Beeck's disagreement with Balthasar regarding theological method is rationally defensible. What is not defensible is that this disagreement issues promptly in a pathological diagnosis of Balthasar's motives in expressing his disagreements with Rahner about what constitutes the way forward for the church in the postconciliar period. See his *God Encountered: A Contemporary Catholic Systematic Theology*, vol. 2/1 (Collegeville, MN: Liturgical Press, 1993), 6-7.

[24]. Although early in his career Hegel used the term Love as equivalent to the absolute which functioned to reconcile distinct dimensions of the finite as well as the alienation between the finite and the infinite, by the time of the *Phenomenology* Spirit (*Geist*) is the term for the absolute. Nonetheless, Hegel not infrequently in later texts uses the notion of love to interpret Spirit. This is especially true of the *Phenomenology* (#19) and *LPR3*.

[25]. Maurice Blanchot, *The Writing of the Disaster*, tr. Ann Smith (Lincoln and London: University of Nebraska Press, 1986), 2, where Blanchot defines 'dis-aster' as anything separate from the star (*aster*) that would guide and provide it with meaning. In an obvious sense, 'dis-aster' represents a metaphorization as well as consequent conceptualization of Nietzsche's famous 'death of God' proclamation in *The Gay Science* where the horizon that gave the earth its meaning is wiped out. It does not take Blanchot long into his text to make it clear that Hegel is one of the main targets of subversive discourse, just as Hegelian form of knowledge (we referred to in Part 2) is a target of Blanchot's 'non-knowledge.' He writes: 'I will not say that the disaster is absolute; on the contrary it disorients the absolute' (4).

[26]. Balthasar's objection to Hegel here is surprisingly similar to one made by Derrida in *Glas*. Without rehearsing Hegel's own argument for the relation between the family as the lowest level of Objective Spirit and Absolute Spirit which is relatively adequately presented in the Christian doctrine of the Trinity, Derrida thinks of the family as the mirror of the Hegelian Trinity, which cleansed of representational content is subsumed into the realm of concept or the idea of self-positing Spirit. From Derrida's point of view the relation is a two-way mirror: the family is indemnified in and by the absolute. At the same time, however, the exclusionary dynamics of the family with its insistence on the third, with its reservations about illegitimacy, its injunction against same-sex union leaves much reality outside as waste and detritus.

[27]. Although the language here is borrowed from William Desmond and specifically his *Hegel: A Counterfeit Double?*, its meaning could not be more Balthasarian.

[28]. For this famous passage, see *LPR3*, 206. For a similar expression see also *Enc* #24 zu.

[29]. Luther does not always think of the Trinity in these terms, but often does. For an illuminating account of this, see Christine Helmer, *The Trinity in Martin Luther: A Study on the Relationship between Genre, Language and the Trinity in Luther's Works*

(1523-1546) (Mainz: Verlag Philipp von Zabern, 1999), 176, 185 *inter alia*. As she makes the case for the specificity of genre, she shows that Luther speaks in a different way about the Trinity in his hymns and sermons than in his polemical tracts. Helmer points to his use of prosopographic exegesis, that is, the exegesis of scripture in which the commissioning of the Son by the Father and the obedience of the Son is imagined as an intra-trinitarian dialogue. That there is nothing esoteric about this mode of exegesis and that it belongs to the non-dogmatic figuration of the relation between the Father and Son is immediately obvious from Book 1 of Milton's *Paradise Lost* where there is considerable discussion between the Son and the Father about the creation/salvation of human kind antecedent to creation, fall, and the incarnation of Christ.

[30]. Hegel makes this observation within an important passage in 'The Spirit of Christianity and its Fate' in which he reflects on the Logos doctrine of the Johannine Prologue. See *Early Theological Writings*, tr. T. M. Knox (Philadelphia: University of Pennsylvania Press, 1948; Partial translation of H. Nohl, *Hegels theologische Jugendschriften*), 253-281, esp. 256-9.

[31]. In general, Moltmann is heavily dependent on Gershom Scholem's pioneering 20th-century study of the Kabbalah and has not consulted widely in it. The closest he gets to anything like familiarity with Christianity is a single mention of Oetinger (*TK*, 237 n. 23).

[32]. See *Lectures on the History of Philosophy*, vol. 2, 394-96. Oetinger is by far the most creative Christian/philosophical appropriation of the Kabbalah, since not only is he able to read Hebrew and exposit its various systems, but he also puts the Kabbalah to constructive purpose in the refutation of Spinozism. Moreover, he is aware of the distinction between the various kinds of Kabbalah, and introduces into Christian/philosophical discourse the symbol of *zimstum*, which so captivates Moltmann. Hegel does not recall Oetinger in an explicit way. His proximate sources are the standard compendiums by Protestant rationalists of the eighteenth century such as Jacob Brucker and Johann Gottlieb Buhle, who cannot be thought to be favorably disposed towards Judaism as a world-historical religion based on the Torah.

[33]. While refusal of total disjunction is typical of the historiography of the Kabbalah, there are different emphases with respect to the proximity of the relation. For example, Gershom Scholem is more willing to allow more distinction and tension, for example, than Moshe Idel. For Scholem, see *Major Trends in Jewish Mysticism*, tr. Ralph Mannheim (New York: Schocken Books, 1969). For Idel, see *Kabbalah: New Perspectives* (New Haven: Yale University Press, 1988). Of course, Moltmann's enlisting of the Kabbalah is predicated on exploiting the difference between written and oral Torah suggested by Scholem.

[34]. In *GL3* Balthasar doubly compliments Charles Péguy first by awarding him one of the seven 'lay-style' spots and second by devoting over a hundred pages to him (*GL3*, 400-517). Péguy is extensively and lavishly praised by Balthasar for his diagnosis of the modern condition and the obstacles that its ethos, social structures, and general deracination presents to authentic Christianity. Authentic Christianity is always represented by the saints. Péguy is also praised for his Pascalian figuration of the relation between Judaism and Christianity, which is

constitutively anti-Gnostic (435), as well as his commitment to social justice and change. With respect to the latter, however, Balthasar points to how Péguy is all the time mindful that the temporal is bounded by the eternal. What is carried forward from that analysis is a critique of Hegel and post-Hegelian philosophy contained in section 5, called 'The Heart of God' (493-509), which features *The Portal of Hope.* Against Hegel the intimacy of the divine and the human is interpreted not in terms of metaphysical reciprocity, but rather in terms of the parable of the prodigal son (498), in which God shows just how spendthrift love is. The similarity of Péguy's text to that of the *Showings* of Julian of Norwich is apparent.

[35]. The category of the 'future' is a dominant one for Balthasar as well as Moltmann. This privileging is a function of, on the one hand, phenomenological commitments of the sort that has its grounds in Przywara and gets developed in Marion and his followers and, on the other, a theological commitment to the enduring value of apocalyptic with its non-teleological notion of the future.

[36]. Not only in *Gegenüberstellung hebräischer und zeitgenössischer Philosophie*, but also in *Neue Metaphysisch Erwägungen über das Kabbalistische System, woraus de Ausflüge Gottes begreiflicher Werden*, in *Lehrtafel*, vol. 1, 131-44, 170-81. For a good discussion of this point, see Sigrif Grossmann, *Friedrich Christoph Oetingers Gottesvorstellung: Versuch einer Analyse seiner Theologie* (Göttingen: Vandenhoeck & Ruprecht, 1979), 59-66.

[37]. While it is a matter of dispute among Jewish scholars of the Kabbalah as to the level of tension between the Kabbalah with standard forms of Judaism regarding becoming in the divine, theogony is definitely a feature of its Christian and specifically Christian adaptation. This is true certainly of Oetinger, and after him in Hegel and Schelling – although the Kabbalistic borrowing is considerably slighter than it is in the 18th-century Pietists. Oetinger owes much, of course, to Jacob Boehme. For a synoptic account, see Ernst Benz, *Les sources mystiques de la philosophie romantique allemande* (Paris: Vrin, 1968), 67-8.

[38]. In *Theology of Hope* Moltmann appropriated Bloch's distinction between *futurum*, which is the future considered as an extrapolation from the present and the past, and *Zukunft*, the future as unanticipatable precisely because it cannot be extrapolated from the present and the past. It was not difficult to appropriate Bloch's philosophically articulated distinction, given that when it came to his articulation of *Zukunft*, Bloch depended to a considerable extent on the articulation of the future in the biblical apocalyptic tradition.

[39]. See my 'Mystery of Iniquity: Augustine versus Heidegger,' in *Martin Heidegger's Interpretation of Saint Augustine*, in *Collectanea Augustiana*, ed. Frederick van Fleteren (Lewiston, NY: Edwin Mellen Press, 2005), 383-440. I also address the issue in the sequel to the present volume.

[40]. I have spoken to Tertullian's objections to patripassianism in his *Against Praxeas.* It is important to remember that Tertullian's objection is not motivated by metaphysical anxiety about divine immutability – Tertullian belongs more to the rhetorical than the philosophical tradition – but derive from concerns about whether a God wounded can be a God that saves. Interestingly, here there is a very interesting overlap between Tertullian and a Feminist thinker such as Elizabeth Johnson. See *She Who Is* (New York: Crossroad, 2002), ch. 6.

[41]. See de Lubac, *La postérité spirituelle de Joachim de Flore*, vol. 2 (Paris: Lethielleux, 1979).
[42]. For a good synoptic essay reflective of Jüngel's interest in the intersection of theology and metaphor, see 'Metaphorische Wahrheit. Erwägungen zur theologische Relevanz der Metapher als Beitrag zur Hermeneutik einer narrativen Theologie,' in *Beiträge zur evangelischen Theologie: Theologische Abhandlungen* 88, Munich (1980), 103-51.
[43]. In his early 'death of God' theology Altizer has little time for the doctrine or symbol of the Trinity. Indeed, in a later work such as *The Genesis of God* he continues to think of standard views of the Trinity as reaction (108).
[44]. See *Genesis of God*, 80, 95, 100, 106, 131-32, 161; also *From Genesis to Apocalypse*, 87-8.
[45]. Alexandre Kojève, *Introduction to the Reading of Hegel*, 101, 112. In terms of his analysis of Hegel taking the divine point of view, Kojève is enormously influenced by Heidegger's reflections on Hegel's articulation of the relation of time and Spirit in *Being and Time* (486-88).
[46]. See Harold Bloom, 'Lying Against Time: Gnosis, Poetry, Criticism,' in *The Rediscovery of Gnosticism*, vol. 1, *The School of Valentinus*, ed. Bentley Layton (Leiden, The Netherlands: Brill, 1980), 57-72.

PART 4

[1]. Steffen Lösel is arguably the most influential proponent of the view that Balthasar fails to be an apocalyptic theologian (whereas, for example, Moltmann succeeds). In contrast, on Balthasar's view Moltmann fails to be a genuine apocalyptic theologian. And, obviously, on my view, Balthasar succeeds, as do those in the Irenaean apocalyptic line, of which the most important 20th-century example is Bulgakov. See Lösel's 'Unapocalyptic Theology: History and Eschatology in Balthasar's Theo-Drama,' in *Modern Theology* 17, April (2001), 201-25. See also his somewhat more popular article, 'A Plain Account of Christian Salvation? Balthasar on Sacrifice, Solidarity, and Substitution,' in *Pro Ecclesia* 12.2 (2003), 141-71. In this article essentially the same negative case is prosecuted. Unsurprisingly, the criteria of definition are supplied by political theologies of the likes of Moltmann and Metz.
[2]. In *Theo-Logic 1* Aquinas' *de veritate* provides for Balthasar a relatively adequate model of truth, as well as suggesting the negative capability for understanding its co-extensivity with beauty and goodness (*TL1*, 29, 142, 222-223 *inter alia*). Importantly, Balthasar does not make it a 'zero-sum' game between correspondence and disclosure, since adequation comes in and through a response of the entire self, affective, and embodied as well as intellectual, to the disclosure of reality (*TL1*, 40-4, 53). *Theo-Logic 1* shows itself to be against that notion of philosophy as method, whether Cartesian or Kantian (*TL1*, 71, 76, 131, 138). With Heidegger, Balthasar is persuaded that method involves instrumentalization and the eradication of mystery. From Balthasar's perspective, rightly understood, *de veritate* never leaves behind the original well-spring of philosophy which is wonder (*thaumazein*)

(*TL1*, 208; also 49) and the searching that it excites (*TL1*, 203), and never forgets the horizon of mystery that is constitutive of being as excess (*TL1*, 9, 37, 131, 206). Obviously, Baltahsar is complementing or supplementing Aquinas with a significant draft of Neoplatonism which is, arguably, more typical of Pseudo-Dionysius and Bonaventure, nonetheless, he thinks that being as excess can be interpreted as love or agape. For the latter point – but without the language of complement or supplement – see David C. Schindler, *Hans Urs von Balthasar and the Dramatic Structure of Truth: A Philosophical Investigation* (New York: Fordham University Press, 2004), 101-05, 131-35, 139. Although *TL1* is written approximately twenty years before *GL1*, the two texts structurally correspond: as *TL1* intimates the relation of beauty and goodness to truth, *GL1* intimates, but also to a degree in excess of the earlier text, the relation of truth and goodness to beauty. No less than in the case of *TL1*, in *GL1* Balthasar suggests the need to move beyond the subjectivism of modernity. Descartes and Kant are not major figures in *GL1*, and get treated in the first part of the trilogy only in *GL5*, where it seems Balthasar has moderated his negative construal of both, in the case of Kant by refusing to allow him to be interpreted primarily in and through the *Critique of Pure Reason*. *Love Alone*, which postdates the writing of *Glory of the Lord*, has no such scruple. See *Love Alone is Credible*, tr. D. C. Schindler (San Francisco: Ignatius Press, 2004), 31-6.

[3]. As Schindler points out in *Hans Urs von Balthasar and the Dramatic Structure of Truth* (4-5) it is apposite to put Balthasar in the line of the transcendental Thomism of Blondel, Rousselot, and Maréchal to the extent to which Balthasar wants to open up the dynamic orientation of the self to a transcendence that can never be an object of inspection and verification. While formally similar, however, Balthasar leaves behind the Kantian commitments that bedevil transcendental Thomism. His position on truth has in Schindler's view much in common with that of Gustav Siewerth. There is no denying that Siewerth is one of the more important philosophical influences on Balthasar, just as it is no accident that Siewerth is constantly negotiating the relationship of Aquinas to Heidegger, which Balthasar has obviously engaged in *Wahrheit*. As I will be treating the Catholic engagement with Heidegger *in extenso* in volume 2 of the present work, there is no need to go into great detail here. I will simply mention what is perhaps Siewerth's best-known work, almost certainly the one which involves the deepest working out of the relation between Aquinas and Heidegger: *Das Schicksal der Metaphysik von Thomas von Aquin bis Heidegger* (Einsiedeln, Switzerland: Johannes Verlag, 1959). Although Schindler insists on the importance of Siewerth, he is not anxious to force a decision between Siewerth and Przywara whom he also acknowledges to be important for Balthasar. Certainly, the latter's *Analogia Entis* is a crucial text for *Wahrheit*.

[4]. For the definition of God as the future (*der Zukunft*), see *TL1*, 196-97. These are important pages in which Balthasar speaks of the future as that which 'comes towards' (*zukommt*) the human existence and of 'futurity' (*Zukünftigkeit*) as defining being, indeed being as eternal. Defined thus, Balthasar has no problem throughout the trilogy talking of the coming or appearance of the future of God in the past, indeed, precisely as Christ (*TD5*, 55-6), and making this a criterion whereby

to get critical leverage on forms of eschatological thought which temporalize rather than ontologize the future.

5. 'Eidetic,' defined technically by 'eidetic reduction,' as this functions in Phenomenology, is not of interest to Balthasar. Balthasar shows familiarity with Husserl's thought in general, including his discussions of the various reductions, in *Apokalypse 3* (112-25). Balthasar affirms the instinct to return to the things themselves (*die Sache Selbst*), but worries about the subjectivism (122-23) and essentialism (125) of Husserl's mode of Phenomenology. As *Apokalypse 3* proceeds, it becomes evident that Balthasar embraces the change in overall phenomenological profile represented by Heidegger in *Sein und Zeit* and the *Kantbuch.* Essentialism is also a target of *Wahrheit,* but now the category has general extent and covers not only Husserl's belated species of essentialism, but essentialism throughout the philosophical tradition, not excluding that of Plato. See *TL1,* 105-07, and especially 148-51, where Balthasar discusses the Thomistic principle of conversion to phantasm. As Balthasar's attack on essentialism owes much to Przywara and more specifically his *Analogia Entis,* but with respect to conversion Rahner's *Spirit in the World* at the very least functions as a template.

6. 'Hieratic' forms of Christian Neoplatonism are those in which intensities of being, beauty, and value get marked off from lower intensities. Thus there is a close correlation between the commitment to hier-archy and hieratic form. The classical Christian representation of this form of Neoplatonism is provided by Pseudo-Dionysius. Given the extraordinary influence of Pseudo-Dionysius within Christian Neoplatonism, it would seem counter-intuitive to imagine forms of Christian Neoplatonism that are non-hieratic, although obviously there are non-Neoplatonic forms of Christian piety and mysticism that stress the everyday and are non hierarchical. One could think of Ignatius of Loyola, for example, as expressive of a non-hieratic form of mysticism. But there are in fact forms of Neoplatonism that correct for the hierarchical. Eckhart and Cusanus, for example, could be construed as representing a democratization of access to and participation in the reality that gives being. One aspect at least of Derrida's debate with Marion on this issue in *Sauf le nom* is his relative preference – along with Heidegger – for these more democratic species of Neoplatonism, even if in the last instance the entire metaphysical system, which these democratic forms support, needs to be transcended. See *Sauf le nom* (Post-Scriptum), tr. John P. Leavey Jr., in *On the Name,* ed. Thomas Dutoit (Stanford: Stanford University Press, 1995), 35-85. Balthasar's way of handling the tension is different: essentially he forges a third position. He worries about metaphysical hierarchy as the supporting frame for Christian view of participation in God, while he shows himself to be at least as worried about the democratization which, if not understood properly, secularizes transcendence. For him, in much of Christian Neoplatonism, emblematically in Maximus (but not absolutely ruling out even Pseudo-Dionysius), the insistence on Christ as pivotal maintains a sufficient measure of the hieratic, while dismantling the hierarchy, at least hierarchy comprehended in a topological manner. Whereas Blumenberg avails of a Neoplatonic thinker such as Cusanus (also Bruno) to explode hierarchy, thereby making a secular modernity possible, Balthasar thinks of the dismantling of hierarchy as

ingredient in the liberation of the authentically Christian form of the hieratic. The argument between Balthasar and Blumenberg is not simply about what constitutes a proper interpretation of Cusanus, but the logic of entailment in discourse that undermines topological Neoplatonism. For Blumenberg, see *The Legitimacy of the Modern Age*, Part 4, 487-596.

[7]. As the scholarship on apocalyptic has developed, the socio-cultural construction of the emergence of apocalyptic from marginal spaces in which discourses constitute both a reaction and an imaginary solution to a situation construed as both intolerable and refractory, has gained considerable currency. In this context social location is thought to provide the motivation at least for the images of recompense that involve the destruction of enemies. Often this reading of canonic and non-canonic biblical apocalypses is associated with a genetic view of the corpus of apocalyptic texts which sees the extra-canonic apocalypses as determinative of the canonic and especially of Revelation. As a theologian convinced of the probity of the canon, Balthasar agrees only in part with this view. He refuses to engage in what he takes to be sociological reductionism, and does not think that the anterior explains the posterior – to the degree to which the non-canonic is anterior – but rather sets conditions for it. One of these condition – although not the only one is a propensity towards violent recompense. This is a challenge that canonic forms of apocalyptic have to overcome. Some dissension also exists in the ranks of experts on biblical apocalyptic, especially those not wholly unsympathetic to a theological construal. Two examples of scholars of apocalyptic who wish to give the socio-cultural reading its due but no more than its due are Christopher Rowland and, more recently, Gregory Carey. See Rowland's classic text, *The Open Heaven* (London: SPCK, 1958). For Carey, see *Ultimate Things: An Introduction to Jewish and Christian Apocalyptic Literature* (St. Louis, MO: Chalice Press, 2005); see also his *Elusive Apocalypse: Reading Authority in the Revelation to John* (Macon, GA: Mercer University Press, 1999).

[8]. As I have already indicated, the essentials of Mongrain's thesis in *The Systematic Thought of Hans Urs von Balthasar* can be maintained as long as the interpreter thinks in the main of architectural design without insisting either that all or even the majority of the substantive theological features of Balthasar's asystematic system (oxymoron is necessary) are Irenaean. Even if one were to stick to the patristic tradition, as Brian Daley has suggested, one could not afford to discount either Augustine, Origen, or Maximus. See Brian E. Daley, 'Balthasar's Reading of the Church Fathers,' in *The Cambridge Companion to Hans Urs von Balthasar*, ed. Edward T. Oakes, SJ and David Moss (Cambridge: CUP, 2004), 187-206. For this point, see also Aidan Nichols' *Divine Fruitfulness: A Guide through Balthasar's Theology Beyond the Trilogy* (Washington, DC: CUA Press, 2007), 23-56. See especially 28-31, where he directly engages Mongrain's thesis. At the same time, it would not make a great deal of sense to insist on the primacy of Irenaean design and then to deny that there is any appreciable influence on the level of substance. I touched on some main points of influence in Part 3, and here I will focus on those that have to do with biblical apocalyptic and the centrality of the *descensus ad infernos*, especially as these are intended to counter speculative forms of thought.

[9]. I will be dealing with the relation between Balthasar's mode of apocalyptic and those of Heidegger and Derrida in detail in the second volume of *The Anatomy of Misremembering.*
[10]. Metz's dependence on these two sources will be discussed in Chapter 7. This dependence also conditions my detailed treatment of the relation between Balthasar and each of these apocalyptic thinkers in Chapter 8.
[11]. For a negative judgment of Bloch, see *GL7*, 129, where Bloch is said to provide 'an example of 'Jewish gnosis.' Consider also *TD5*, 141-4, 181; also 50, 56-7, where the kind of horizontal eschatology of Bloch is regarded as being surpassed by a Johannine form of apocalyptic that integrates the vertical and horizontal axes. For a negative judgment of Bloch's eschatology outside of the trilogy, especially with regard to its problematic relation to Jewish messianism and Joachimite apocalyptic in particular, see 'Improvisation on Spirit and Future,' in *Explorations 3*, 135-71, 140-41, also 144, 159; 'The Claim to Catholicity,' in *Explorations 4*, 65-121, esp. 98.
[12]. See *TL2*, 45; see also Balthasar's remarks on Benjamin in 'The Claim to Catholicity' in *Explorations 4*, 97, 99.
[13]. *Trauerspiel* – literally 'plays of mourning' – was Benjamin's Habilitation. It is translated as *The Origin of German Tragic Drama*, tr. John Osborne (London: New Left Books, 1977).

Chapter 6

[1]. It could be argued that even in his anti-Hegel writings in which the German Idealist is criticized as a parousiac thinker, Heidegger himself has not left behind the apocalyptic roots of his own thought which precede production of *Being and Time.* Whether and in what way Heidegger's apocalyptic ethos gets modified along the way, first through *Being and Time*, and subsequently in Heidegger's engagement with the Greeks (especially Heraclitus) and with Hölderlin and Nietzsche, are issues intrinsically worth developing, but they can be postponed until the second volume. Nevertheless, even here it is worth mentioning just how important the apocalyptic texts of Thessalonians are for him. Heidegger gave lectures on Paul in 1920-21 in which eschatology was to the fore. For an excellent account of this, see Theodore Kisiel, *The Genesis of Being and Time*, (London: University of California Press, 1993), 179-91. A convenient translation of Heidegger's reflections can be found in *The Phenomenology of Religious Life*, tr. Matthias Fritsch and Jennifer Anna Gosetti-Ferncei (Bloomington and Indianapolis: Indiana University Press, 2004), 61-82, 91-111.
[2]. These are the hallmarks of the prophetic, which is put in high relief in *Glory of the Lord 6*. Moreover, however, the Old Covenant is supposed to get surpassed as it is realized in the New Covenant, the prophetic aspect of biblical religion is not thought, thereby, to have become expendable. Not only is Christ priest and king, but prophet too. A Balthasarian understanding has all of these found in Christ in a hyperbolic and unsurpassable form.
[3]. The escape from time and history are also features of ancient Gnosticism. Balthasar very much sees the connection, but is sufficiently historical enough

not to blur the lines that separate this speculation that does, indeed, pretend too much knowing, and Gnosticism as a form of thought that is expressly anti-Christian as it is anti-Jewish.

[4]. Two issues here: (a) the way in which Balthasar follows Speyr; (b) the way in which John is indicative of the New Testament as a whole. Balthasar follows von Speyr in reading Revelation in light of the Gospel of John, while availing of Revelation as dramatically heightening the paschal and liturgical aspects of the Gospel. Balthasar makes clear that while he gives priority to the Gospel of John over the Synoptics, the Gospel of John does not make redundant Mark, Matthew, or Luke.

[5]. The work of Adela and John J. Collins has been particularly important in this respect. For Adela Yarbro Collins, see especially *Crisis and Catharsis: The Power of the Apocalypse* (Philadelphia: Westminister Press, 1984); John Collins, see among other texts *Apocalypse: Morphology of a Genre. Semeia 14* (Missoula: Scholars Press, 1979); *The Apocalyptic Imagination: An Introduction to the Jewish Matrix of Christianity* (New York: Crossroad, 1984); *Apocalypticism in the Dead Sea Scrolls* (Ne York: Routledge, 2005).

[6]. Textually this becomes even clearer in *Theo-Drama 5* in which in his articulation of an eschatological trinitarianism Balthasar appeals promiscuously to von Speyr's commentary on the Gospel of John. It is crucial for Balthasar that the trinitarian horizon of the paschal mystery and divine involvement in history is a biblical datum, and it is so in his view in Johannine writings.

[7]. For Balthasar's insistence on the privileges of the symbol with respect to the mystical in *Glory of the Lord 7*, see *GL7*, 324, 325, 329, 366, 382.

[8]. This brings together different kinds of numinosity and makes them qualify each other. Isaiah is important for Balthasar in order to give experiential anchor to an experience of transcendence that could otherwise be both free-floating and self-elevating. The experience of transcendence is a reminder not only of the terrifying otherness of the divine, but the terrible incapacity of the self. Here Balthasar and the early Ricoeur are of one mind. See Ricoeur's use of Isaiah 6 in *The Symbolism of Evil*, tr. Emerson Buchanan (Boston: Beacon Press, 1969), 34, 57.

[9]. See in addition, *GL7*, 284, 324, 366; also *TL2*, 67-8, where there is a reference to *Adv. Haer.* 4. 20. 1. The regulative function of Christ's iconicity is illustrated copiously in the essays on individual figures in *Glory of the Lord 2-3*, perhaps paradigmatically in the essays on Pseudo-Dionysius and Bonaventure. In *Glory of the Lord* Balthasar's considered opinion is that theological aesthetics is christological apophatics. This position is anticipated in Balthasar's great studies in the 1940's on Origen and Maximus, and is already clearly outlined in *Wahrheit*.

[10]. In *TD4*, 51, Balthasar writes: '. . . the dramatic quality of revelation does not lie in any uncertainty as to outcome, for God's victory . . . is achieved. What is dramatic in revelation is to be found in its specific uniqueness: namely, that God is at the same time superior to history and involved in it.'

[11]. See Ben Quash, '"Between the Brutely Given, and the Brutally, Banally Free": Von Balthasar's Theology of Drama in Dialogue with Hegel,' in *Modern Theology* 13.3, July (1997), 293-318; see also Quash's article, 'Drama and the Ends of Modernity,' in *Balthasar at the End of Modernity*, 139-71. In the second article Quash does not renege on the critical judgments of the first with respect to Balthasar's

supposed inability to separate himself from Hegel and the inability of his theology to escape from the epicalism that his so-called 'dramatic theology' claims to overcome. Indeed, in his book in which Balthasar features, Quash goes a step further by suggesting that there are resources in Hegel, not there in Balthasar, for a more dramatic construal of history and thus a more adequate eschatological theology. See *Theology and the Drama of History* (Cambridge: CUP, 2005). See my somewhat critical take on this aspect of Quash's argumentation in my review in *Modern Theology* 23.3, April (2007), 293-96.

[12]. See also *TD5*, 199-202; 285.

[13]. In the trilogy Balthasar's most explicit treatment of the Temptation scene, which can be classed as a form of 'political apocalypse,' is to be found in *Glory of the Lord 7* (72-4). Balthasar is here reprising his analysis of Dostoyevski in *Apok 2*. There Dostoyevski is regarded as a thoroughly apocalyptic thinker, indeed, one whose form of apocalyptic is involved in a resistance to Hegel's form of eschatology. Balthasar even goes so far as to think that the resistance of Hegel is intentional in Dostoyevski's work. Further warrants for making the connection between Balthasar and Dostoyevski include Balthasar's favorable treatment of Soloviev in *GL3* in which the diagnostic contributions of Soloviev and Dostoyevski are affirmed (294-96).

[14]. Balthasar recurs to Otto's *The Idea of the Holy* throughout his readings, but almost always to assimilate it biblically. Together with the language of the 'wholly other' (*das Ganz andere*), Balthasar avails of Otto's formula for the Holy quite regularly throughout his work. The following are but a few of the instances: *GL6*, 10; *GL7*, 268; *Exp 1*, 31, 105-06. The normative status of the biblical numinous relative to other *mysteria* is clearly stated in *GL4*, 14, 246-47. Thus, by the time Balthasar discusses the Sinai theophany (Exodus 33) in *GL6* (12), the only possible interpretation is that as a theophany it is incommensurable with the obvious exception, of course, of the event of the incarnation. For a fuller discussion of the relation between Balthasar's thought and the phenomenology of religion as illustrated by *The Idea of the Holy*, see my 'Newman and von Balthasar: The Christological Contexting of the Numinous,' in Église et Théologie 26 (1995), 165-202. See esp. 184-202.

[15]. An even more important text is *TD5*, 410. Speaking of the Augustinian quadrate of *vacare*, *videre*, *amare*, *laudare*, Balthasar observes that within the space of the immanent Trinity 'these concepts must be filled out, at the very least, with all of the vitality of spontaneous, free, inventive living.' Prayer also is an intra-trinitarian reality. Balthasar makes explicit in *Theo-Drama* what is at best only a tendency in his much earlier book on prayer. See *TD5*, 95-6.

[16]. Whether intended or not, the consistent emphasis on the centrality of liturgy in Revelation evokes Maximus, whose overall position comes under the rubric of 'cosmic liturgy.' This means that in a certain respect Maximus can be included in the Irenaean line of apocalyptic. Certainly, Maximus' cosmic emphasis is consistent with the cosmic dimension brought out most clearly in Bulgakov's interpretation of Revelation. Of course, for the purposes of inclusion, it helps that Maximus' particular form of Christian Neoplatonism is leveled against speculative Platonic and Neoplatonic forms, and that also at the time when Balthasar wrote

the Maximus book, Hegel's philosophical appropriation of Christianity is a target that Balthasar has very much in mind. For a good reflection on the use of Maximus against Hegel, see George de Schrijver, *Le merveilleux accord de l'homme et de Dieu: étude de l'analogie de l'être chez Hans Urs von Balthasar* (Leuven: Leuven University Press and Peeters, 1983), 217-251. Also useful in this respect is James Naduvilekut, *Christus der Heilsweg: Soteria als Theodrama im Werk Hans Urs von Balthasars* (St. Ottilien: EOS Verlag Erzabtei, 1987), 161-64; see more generally 150-60.

[17]. While Balthasar's interpretation of the relation between the economic and immanent Trinity is complex, and there is by no means a one-to-one correspondence, as witnessed by his account of the trinitarian inversion in which in the economy the Spirit is an agent in the sending of the Son whereas in the eternal Trinity the Spirit proceeds from the Son as well as the Father; still, without erasing the distinction, as he believes Hegel does, precisely because of his enormous respect for the economy Balthasar aims for as much continuity as possible: if praise is an act of any of the persons in the economy, the ground for praise is found in the orientation of the divine persons in the immanent Trinity.

[18]. Although in *Trinity and the Kingdom* (ch. 5) Moltmann articulates a Trinity of the mutual glorification of the persons, given his Hegelian logic, mutual glorification requires the happening that is world and history. As we saw in Parts 2 and 3 of this book, this is anathema to Balthasar.

[19]. In addition to Balthasar's discussion of judgment in Revelation in *Theo-Drama 4* and his supporting soteriologically grained discussions of Anselm and Girard, see in particular *GL7*, 205, 297; also *TD5*, 356-59.

[20]. 'Hope' is the crucial term in Balthasar's well-known little book *Dare We Hope*. Any pretense at knowledge makes salvation captive to a human scheme. Needless to say, both in terms of raising the question of universal salvation as well as its basic vocabulary, Balthasar is indebted to Barth. See Balthasar's important discussion of Barth's rendition of *apokatastasis* in his *The Theology of Karl Barth*, 185-86. Here Barth's book on the Creed shares the limelight with the *Church Dogmatics*.

[21]. Particularly good places for Balthasar's explication of the neither-nor of Augustine and Origen are *Dare we Hope*; *TD5*, 300-22; and *TL2*, 345-61. We are here, of course, speaking of Origen's view from the perspective of its history of effects, which centrally involves its reiterated condemnation in the Latin and Greek churches. This is not to get to the issue of the status that Origen intended his view of universal salvation to have, which may well have been more probative than declarative. In significant part Balthasar regards Origen primarily as a biblical theologian. This comes through especially clearly in Balthasar's early anthology (1938) of Origen's writings called *Origenes Geist und Feuer: Ein Aufbau aus seinen Werken* (Salzburg, 1938). This has been translated as *Origen, Spirit and Fire: A Thematic Anthology of His Writings*, tr. Robert J. Daly, S.J. (Washington: CUA Press, 1984). See especially the translator's foreword (xi-xviii) and Balthasar's introduction (1-24). In a certain sense this styling of Origen applies reflexively to Balthasar, who like Origen permits himself some speculative moments.

[22]. This is a point that Balthasar insists on both because of its intrinsic importance and because the failure to assert it renders incoherent all talk of freedom and the more substantial talk about vocation, especially as this is rendered in

TD2. For an especially clear statement, see *TD5*, 233-34. This passage happily mentions *Mysterium Paschale* in which this point is to the fore, but in line with that text it suggests Irenaeus as the template. It refers specifically to *Adv. Haer.* 4.22.1.

[23]. Balthasar is extraordinarily influenced by von Speyr whose particular form of mysticism most nearly recalls that of Julian of Norwich both in its visionary dimension, biblical basis, christological inflection, and eschatological dynamic. Like Julian, von Speyr raises the prospect of universal salvation as an element or at least an implication of vision and the logic of divine love in Christ, but without asserting it and contravening church teaching, and not without leaving open the prospect of an incorrigible decision taken by the creature against God. See especially *TD5*, 300-22, and above all *TL2*, 345-61. In the latter text Balthasar essentially cedes theological authority to von Speyr's two volume *Kreuz und Hölle*, saying in passing that it surpasses his own efforts in *Mysterium Paschale* which he argues was hurried. What he does not say, however, is that von Speyr's and his texts are quite different. Whereas von Speyr gets at the descent into hell in and through a meditation on the biblical material, Balthasar's text more nearly is a critical vetting of the theological tradition.

[24]. The point I am making here is formal. That is, the idea of universal salvation does not play the role of justifying God, thus of theodicy and in this respect lining up with Hegel. See my essay, 'Hegel, Theodicy, and the Invisibility of Waste,' in *Providence of God*, ed. Francesca Murphy and Philip Ziegler (Edinburgh: T & T Clark, 2009), 75-108.

[25]. See the introduction to *Lectures on the Philosophy of History*, 21. For a fuller discussion, see *The Heterodox Hegel*, 310-23.

[26]. I have in mind Nietzsche, especially his genealogical construction of Christianity in which Christianity has its psychic or spiritual origin in resentment of a vitality that is out of the reach of those who are Christian.

[27]. The throne is a central image of Revelation and makes an appearance in the very first chapter. Obviously, it harks back to the famous epiphany in Ezekiel 6. The *Merkabah* of Ezekiel not only continued to have an after-life in Christianity through Revelation, but it proved central to also to a brand of esoteric Judaism that was popular as well as influential between the fifth and ninth centuries of the common era.

[28]. Balthasar suggests that the influence of Augustine, especially the 'later' Augustine, proves mischievous (*GL3*, 87).

[29]. Balthasar is hardly being idiosyncratic here. The importance of Revelation for Dante – whether rightly interpreted or not – while not a commonplace, is well-represented in the critical literature. See among others James C. Nohrnberg, 'The First-Fruit of the Last Judgment: the *Commedia* as a Thirteenth Century Apocalypse,' in *Last Things: Apocalypse, Judgment and Millenium in the Middle Ages* (Sewanee, TN: University of the South Press, 2002), 111-59; Ronald B. Herzman, 'Dante and the Apocalypse,' in *Irenic Apocalypse: Some Uses of Apocalyptic in Dante, Petrarch, and Rabelais*, ed. Dennis Costa (Saratoga, CA: Anma Libri, 1981), 398-413.

[30]. For other passages in the trilogy in which there is an affirmation of Augustine's apocalyptically inspired idea of the two cities, see *TD2*, 88-9, 166-67, 204; *TD4*, 67, 210.

[31]. As Marjorie Reeves and Bernard McGinn among others have pointed out, Joachim's entire oeuvre is inspired by Revelation. At the same time Joachim wrote directly on Revelation. See his *Enchiridion super Apocalypsim*, ed. Edward K. Burger (Toronto: Pontifical Institute of Medieval Studies, 1986).

[32]. *Dare We Hope* (134-42) and *TL3* (345-61) adopt von Speyr's epistemically humble stance with respect to outcomes. The problem with Augustine's eschatology is that the mercy of Christ seems to get limited by the logic of perfect number, on the one hand, and the logic of shared culpability on the other, which rests on a particular interpretation of Romans 12-21 (see *TD4*, 188-89). The limitations of Augustine are also mentioned in *TD5*, 318-21.

[33]. For explicit criticism of Origen, and specific recall of his heterodoxy, see *TD5*, 316-17. While Balthasar is not neuralgic with respect to orthodoxy, and is prepared to grant theologians of the caliber of Origen a very wide scope, he does think that Origen was in tension with the received ecclesial views on a number of important matters. For instance, one ineluctable Maximan contribution is that he corrects for the Origenist view of the relation between soul and body and his account of the fall of the soul.

[34]. See *The Theology of Karl Barth*, 182-83, 236. The Ignatian view of election as 'call' is particularly to the fore as it dovetails into the notion of mission that is crucial in *TD3*. Of course, long before the writing of *Theo-Drama* Balthasar had shown how he favored the Ignatian view. He deploys it in his treatment of Thèrese of Liseux and Elizabeth of the Trinity in the fifties, and makes conformity with Christ constitutive of sainthood. This point has been brought out exceptionally well by Danielle Nussburger in her disseration 'Saints as Wellspring: A Critical Appraisal of Hans Urs von Balthasar' (Notre Dame, 2007).

[35]. In addition, see *TD4*, 36, for other temporal terms.

[36]. Revelation is the pivotal text for Joachim. It is the text that he submits to commentary (*Enchiridion*); from which he extracts 'figures' (*Figura*) and then proceeds to elucidate their meaning; and which provides the unity between the old and the new covenant (*Concordia*).

[37]. In *Theo-Drama* Kant is regarded as an eschatological and borderline apocalyptic thinker. This is despite Kant's official stance of being anti-messianic and in another camp entirely to Bengel, Oetinger, and others who take the 'end of history' seriously. Balthasar, obviously, pays attention to the fact that Bloch includes Kant in the apocalyptic line. We will see in chapter 9 how in a certain way Benjamin also includes him, although Kant requires some emendation. It should be noted that Balthasar's stance in *Theo-Drama* is continuous with what he wrote about Kant in *Apokalypse*. See *Apok 1*, 93-103, in which Balthasar pays considerable attention to the eschatological dimensions of *Religion* and 'The End of All Things' (1794). See Nichols, *Scattering the Seed*, 50-4.

[38]. In this sense Balthasar remains a student of de Lubac whose *La postérité spirituelle de Joachim de Flore* he eulogizes in *The Theology of Henri de Lubac* tr, Joseph Fessio, S.J. and Michael M. Waldstein (San Francisco: Ignatius Press, 1991), 123-27.

[39]. Based on her understanding of the symbolic nature of all of Joachim's works and not simply the *Figura*, this is essentially the interpretation adapted by Marjorie Reeves in her major works on Joachim already cited. See especially, however,

Reeves' very important article on Joachim's *Liber della Figura*, 'The *Arbores* of Joachim of Fiore,' in *Studies in Italian Medieval History Presented to Miss E. M. Jamison*, ed. Philip Grierson and John Ward Perkins (London: British School at Rome, 1956), 57-81. Others who are aware of the importance of the symbolic in Joachim are Bernard McGinn and Henri Mottu. For McGinn see *The Calabrian Abbot: Joachim de Fiore in the History of Western Thought* (New York: Macmillan, 1985), 101-22, esp. 113. Chapter 3 has the illuminating title 'Joachim the Symbolist.' For Mottu, see *La manifestation de l'Esprit selon Joachim de Flore* (Neûchatel and Paris: Delachaux and Niestle, 1977), 173-77.

[40]. For the specific contrast between Joachim and Hegel, even or especially for allowing for the contrast between symbolic openness and plurality of interpretation and the closedness and univocity of the Hegelian concept, see the extraordinarily interesting reflections by Paul S. Miklowitz, *Metaphysics to Metafictions: Hegel, Nietzsche and the End of Philosophy* (Albany, NY: SUNY Press, 1994), 87-104, esp. 100. In these pages Miklowitz critically engages my analysis of Hegel's relation to Joachim in *The Heterodox Hegel*, esp. 263-79.

[41]. The polyphony of genres or types of literature is an important interpretive construct in Balthasar's analysis of the biblical text in *GL6* and *GL7*. So also is a variety of styles within a genre, for example, the styles of non-canonic and canonic apocalyptic, and the narrative styles of the Gospel writings. Needless to say, Balthasar does not think that variety is such as to suggest absolute heterogeneity. In the Bible, as well as the theological tradition, polyphony and symphony go together. If Balthasar throughout his career and especially in the trilogy constructs the tradition as indelibly plural, he does think of it in the last instance as being symphonic. His clearest statement of this is to be found in a text with the declarative title of *Truth is Symphonic*. I have explored this aspect of Balthasar's thought in 'Balthasar: Between Tübingen and Postmodernity,' in *Modern Theology* 14.3, Summer (1998), 325-353.

[42]. Here the measure of effectiveness is the measure of transformation. We have spoken to this issue on a number of occasions already. Arguably, Balthasar's definitive answer to this kind of Joachimite pneumatology is given in *Theo-Logic 3* which records Balthasar's most considered view of the matter. Precisely because Balthasar is more constructive than polemic in this volume, while avoiding giving succor to Hegelians regarding the prospect of unhitching the Spirit from Christ, he gives the Spirit greater autonomy than anywhere else in the trilogy. It is likely that Bulgakov, whose thought, as we have seen, is highly respected by Balthasar, is largely responsible for this broadening of the role of the Spirit.

[43]. Numerous passages throughout the trilogy bespeak to Christ as both condition and object of the witnessing of Spirit. In making the point against Hegel and his epigones I have already provided enough texts from *Theo-Drama*. However, see for example, *GL1*, 134, 166, 188, 196-97, 201, 231, 240-41, 248-50, 295, 355, 409-10, 493-94, 530, 541-56, 601, 605-06; *TL2*, 15, 24, 32 *inter alia*; *TL3*, 17, 27 *inter alia*.

[44]. It is good to keep in mind Balthasar's essential agreement with Hegel in *Apokalypse 1* that the end is not the 'fifth act' (*Apok 1*, 602) both separate from the previous four and towards which they all led with the consequence of their own

redundancy. On the one hand, Balthasar wishes to put conventional Christian eschatology under pressure to the extent to which it tends to abolish the drama. On the other hand, Hegel is not and cannot be right about the fulfillment of history as the fulfillment of its immanent aim.

45. A considerable portion of *TL2* is devoted to articulating the various dimensions of the katalogic (171-362), which in essence articulates 1 John 4:6, 'God is love.'

46. As in the period immediately following the death of Hegel, which welcomed Schelling's 'later' philosophy on the grounds that it was more open to absolute freedom as event that cannot be conceptualized, a number of modern German theologians such as Kasper and Pannenberg have held the view that Schelling is the more useful dialogue partner. As we saw in Part 2, while in *GL5*, in line with a number of prominent French scholars of the Communio group (Bruaire, Brito, Tillette), Balthasar does have positive things to say about the post-Idealist Schelling; it is not clear that Schelling ever gets a clear bill of health, or that the determination made in *Apokalypse 1* that his system or systems are ruled by 'potentiality' and thus by eros is ever fundamentally called into question. *Apokalypse 1* (238 ff), indeed, sets up a very interesting contrast between the kind of apocalypse illustrated by Schelling's later work, especially his *Philosophie der Mythologie* and *Philosophie der Offenbarung*, and Johannine apocalypse which depicts a God who is absolutely sovereign and who does not require to world in order to become God.

47. From a historical perspective, both the letters of Paul and the Gospel of John were particularly susceptible to Gnostic takeover. A classical Valentinian text such as the *Gospel of Truth* deploys John more than any biblical text, and an Alexandrian thinker such as Origen – a representative of legitimate Christian gnosis – had to do battle with Heracleon over the proper interpretation of John. It is not a little interesting that from early on in his career John is a crucial text for Hegel who refuses to see that it is antithetical to the Gnostic systems he recommends in the second volume of his *Lectures on the History of Philosophy*.

48. Hans Blumenberg puts the concept of absolute narration, which is also the narration of the absolute, into play in *Work on Myth* (260) in order to point out the antimony that has to be endured by the doctrine of the Trinity. My amendment is that the classical understanding of the Trinity does not repress the antimony of narrative and logic, but rather distinguishes between the planes of reality appropriate to each. By contrast, thinkers of absolute myth such as Hegel and Schelling confound these dimensions and like the ancient Gnostics narrate all the way down.

49. See Altizer, *The New Apocalypse: The Radical Christian Vision of William Blake* (East Lansing, MI: Michigan State University Press, 1967).

50. See Gustaf Aulén, *Christus Victor: A Historical Study of the Three Main Types of the Idea of Atonement*, tr. A. G. Herbert (New York: McMillan, 1969).

51. Although kata-logic is not the language of *Theo-Drama*, it is implicitly in operation to the extent to which theological truth is to be found outside the purposeful pursuit of the logical as merely *ana*-logical and without a corresponding vertical or *ano* dimension. See *TD4*, 116; *TD4*, 313-14,

52. This emendation of the figuration of *Christus Victor* is obviously influenced by von Speyr. As Balthasar rehearses the theological tradition in *Mysterium Pachale*, it

becomes evident that Nicholas of Cusa is a precursor in this respect, especially Book 4 of *Coincidentia Oppositorum.*

53. For other relevant passages in *Glory of the Lord* that touch on the overcoming of death and sin, see *GL7*, 13-4, 39, 81-2, 86, 89, 237.

54. I am here using a locution coined by the Yale theologian George Lindbeck and made popular by Bruce D. Marshall. For Marshall, see 'Absorbing the World: Christianity and the Universe of Truths,' in *Theology in Dialogue: Essays in Conversation with George Lindbeck*, ed. Bruce D. Marshall (Notre Dame: Notre Dame University Press, 1990), 69-102.

55. Interestingly, Irenaeus does not fail to make the connection between the seducer of the Johannine writings and the tempter of the Synoptics, who gets significant billing in forms of apocalyptic thought that Balthasar finds compelling, for example, those of Dostoyevski and Soloviev.

56. Denials of 'post-modern' as an epochal marker are frequently made by thinkers such as Lyotard and Derrida.

57. That Irenaeus might not have privileges in principle does not mean that he does not enjoy privileges in fact.

58. For Balthasar's own judgment on this matter, see *GL3*, 257, 261. See also Betz, *After Enlightenment*, 190.

59. Betz's discussion of the content, motive, and function of this text in *After Enlightenment*, ch. 9, 189-215, is superior.

60. In his peculiar Russian situation Bulgakov has to deal with a tradition of theological experimentation, especially with respect to sophiology in which extra-canonic apocalypses have the same status as the canonic, and in which Gnostic material is also congenial. If Soloviev, in Bulgakov's view, is not blameworthy in the way that Berdyaev is, at the very least he is guilty at least of over-attachment to the esoteric stream. Valliere notes Bulgakov's tendency in *Lamb of God* to consider Soloviev's view of Sophia as Gnostic. See *Modern Russian Theology*, 161-62, 292. See especially *Sophia: Wisdom of God: An Outline of Sophiology* (New York: Lindisfarne Press, 1993), 9-10. Balthasar in general is concerned about sophiology. For example, in *Apokalypse* he expresses concern with Berdyaev's sophiology (*Apok 2*, 344), and he worries about Bulgakov's sophiology in the slightly later (1942) book on Maximus. Balthasar, however, tends to grow less rather than more concerned. In his essay on Soloviev in *GL3* Balthasar makes note of Soloviev's commitment to Sophia on a number of occasions (*GL3*, 291-92, 308-09, 314-15) without serious criticism. Noting the plethora of esoteric sources Balthasar offers a stunningly positive assessment that Bulgakov himself would not make: 'the muddy stream runs through him as if through a purifying agent and is distilled in crystal-clear, disinfected waters' (*GL3*, 291-92). Paul Valliere, who is a staunch supporter of Soloviev, nonetheless, has no problem accepting that the esoteric streams of thought on which Soloviev depends make him less than orthodox in his sophiology and concept of 'Godmanhood.' See *Modern Russian Theology*, 109-223, esp. 140, 160-62.

61. According to Bulgakov, as Revelation is in continuity with Daniel, it is also in continuity with Isaiah 2 and Ezekiel.

[62]. In addition to Revelation being a crucial text for Bulgakov, Bulgakov wrote a long commentary on Revelation which is yet to be translated. See Valliere, *Modern Russian Theology*, 391 ff.

[63]. In *Apok 2*, 235, Balthasar praises the Grand Inquisitor section of *The Brothers Karamazov* and takes Dostoyevski's side against the revolutionaries displayed in the *Devils* (or the *Possessed*). Balthasar explicitly links Dostoyevski and Soloviev together with respect to their particular (political) interpretation of the Anti-Christ (*GL3*, 294-96). For Balthasar, the figuration of the Anti-Christ is an important item in the even more important agonistic construal of history (*GL3*, 340-41, 351).

[64]. For a good discussion of the dependence of this poem on the book of Revelation, see John Garrard, '*The Twelve*: Blok's Apocalypse,' in *Religion and Literature* 35.1, Spring (2003), 45-72.

[65]. Balthasar's anthologization of Augustine proceeds under the title of *City of God*.

[66]. For Ratzinger (now Pope Benedict XVI), see *The Theology of History of St. Bonaventure* (Chicago: Franciscan Herald Press, 1971); for Löwith, see *Meaning in History: The Theological Implications of the Philosophy of History* (Chicago: University of Chicago Press, 1949).

[67]. One could think of *TL3* as the privileged textual site for the most adequate articulation of the activity of the Spirit, which is not determined by reaction to the excessive pneumatism he discovers in the Western tradition (or as its shadow).

[68]. See *The Beauty of the Infinite*, 37-39. Of course, Hart's real target is not Heraclitus, but the adoption of Heraclitus in modern philosophy, whether by Hegel, Heidegger, or Nietzsche, and their subsequent influence of these philosophies in theological circles. While it is his view that both Heidegger and Nietzsche are straightforwardly more Heraclitean than Hegel, Hegel is the more potent because (a) he gives the appearance of reconciling Heraclitus and Parmenides, thereby satisfying two sets of philosophical interests; and (b) arguably, Hegel has been by far the most influential of these three philosophers in modern theology and certainly contemporary theology.

[69]. Balthasar is dealing with texts from Girard such as *La violence et le sacré* and *Des choses cachées depuis la fondation du monde* which were written in the 1970. Girard has not only published much since then, but most scholars of Girard espy significant development and change. In *TD4* Balthasar also engages the thought of Girard's foremost theological translator, Raymund Schwager (*TD4*, 310-13), who is specifically interested in testing traditional Christian soteriologies.

[70]. Anselm's theory of atonement is discussed in some detail throughout *Theo-Drama 4*. See especially *TD4*, 255-6; *GL4*, 61-6, for an account of the relation between Aquinas' view and that of Anselm. There are numerous other references to Anselm throughout *TD4*. Anselm in fact is referred to as often as Aquinas and less often only than Augustine.

[71]. In his *The Systematic Thought of Hans Urs von Balthasar* Mongrain points out Balthasar's anxiety that despite his best efforts to distinguish between a theological aesthetic and an aesthetic theology, he may very well have produced an overly aestheticized theology.

[72]. See especially David Aune, *Word Biblical Commentary on Revelation*, 3 vols (Nashville: Thomas Nelson Publisher, 1998). For a particularly useful discussion of the liturgical, see volume 3, 1235-38.
[73]. Jean Daniélou made a number of contributions to ressourcement that Balthasar accepts as givens. These include a fascination with Origen, and concomitantly an interest in modes of exegesis and the relation between Christianity and Judaism in the early centuries of the Common Era. But Daniéou is also the retrievalist of early Christian thought most interested in apocalyptic, and who does not accept that patristic thought represents its erasure.
[74]. See D. H. Lawrence, *Apocalyptic and the Writings on Revelation*, ed. Mara Kalnins (Cambridge and New York: Cambridge University Press, 1980).
[75]. It is an open question as to whether the modifications to his position made by Girard with respect to the tearing apart of the New Testament and Hebrew scriptures has been successful. Not a little of the more recent secondary literature on Girard has been engaged with this issue. A common strategy is to suggest a development in which if earlier stages of Hebrew scripture do not successfully avoid linking God and violence, increasingly Hebrew scripture does, indeed, does so to an extent that the unlinking of the divine and violence is not wholly the achievement of the New Testament. James Alison and Mark Heim are just two of the many theologians whose work is influenced by Girard and who make this point. For Alison, *Raising Abel: The Recovery of the Eschatological Imagination* (New York: Crossroad, 1996). For Heim, see *Saved from Sacrifice: A Theology of the Cross* (Grand Rapids, MI: Eerdmans, 2006).
[76]. Levinas' *Totality and Infinity* and Derrida's *Glas* are classic texts that isolate the violence that is concomitant with speculation's aim for totality.
[77]. Marx, for example, lambasts Bauer on *Zur Judenfrage* (1843). Two years later Bauer is the object of a vitriolic attack in 'The Holy Family' – a jointed article by Marx and Engels. For a convenient translation of the first piece, see the *Marx-Engels Reader*, ed. Robert C. Tucker (New York: Norton, 1978), 26-52.
[78]. The full title of this text is *The Trumpet of the Last Judgment Against Hegel the Atheist and Antichrist: An Ultimatum*, tr. Lawrence Stepelevich (New York: Edwin Mellen Press, 1989).

Chapter 7

[1]. The connection between Metz and Balthasar has not received much attention despite some favorable remarks by Metz on the Communio theologian. Mongrain's *The Systematic Thought of Hans Urs von Balthasar* (231 n. 9) is the exception that proves the rule. When speaking of Balthasar Metz does not avail of the canard of Balthasar as being primarily a papal theologian. Rather Balthasar is an original spiritual and aesthetic theologian. See his *Hope against Hope: Johann Baptist Metz and Elie Wiesel Speak out on the Holocaust*, ed. Ekkehard Schuster and Reinhold Boshert-Kimmig, tr. J. Matthew Ashley (Mahwah, NJ: Paulist Press, 1999), 20-1. Although Metz seems to be appreciative of Balthasar's Holy Saturday theology, he never seems to entertain the prospect of Balthasar's theology as being apocalyptic

as well as aesthetic. His work in general treats these forms of theology as if they were mutually exclusive.

[2]. Matthew Ashley makes the interesting point that in Metz's articulation of a self-consciously post-idealist paradigm in theology he is significantly influenced by the *Exercises* of Ignatius Loyola. He argues convincingly, for example, that by contrast with Rahner's spirituality, which seems focused on the Third Week ('Contemplation and Attention'), that of Metz seems centered on the Fourth Week, concerning Jesus' passion. See *Interruptions: Mysticism, Politics, and Theology in the Work of Johann Baptiste Metz* (Notre Dame: University of Notre Dame Press, 1998), pp. 189-92. Although Balthasar's spirituality includes elements of the Third Week, his articulation of theodrama suggests that its basic horizon like that of Metz is that of the Fourth Week. To this symmetry here, one might add that Metz and Balthasar come much closer together when it comes to the interpretation of Ignatius' two standards than does Rahner. The standard of Christ entails judgment of the world as the Anti-Christ, that is, as the refusal of Christ. Selves and communities are literally in a crux, and require decision that has effects in the worldly and not simply in the transcendental sphere.

[3]. See *Faith in History and Society: Toward a Practical Fundamental Theology*, tr. David Smith (New York: Crossroad, 1980). This represents a translation of *Glaube in Geschichte und Gesellschaft* (Mainz: Matthias Grünewald Verlag, 1977), 109-15.

[4]. See Metz, *A Passion for God: The Mystical-Political Dimension of Christianity*, tr. & ed with introduction by J. Matthew Ashley (New York: Paulist Press, 1998), 47.

[5]. In *FHS*, see especially chapter 10 (169-79) in which Metz offers his 'non-contemporaneous' theses on apocalyptic. Although all thirty five theses are intended to suggest the rupture of the 'timelessness' that characterizes our perception of the world in modernity, especially important are theses 6, 11, 20, 21. Thesis 6 is as pithy as it is important: 'The shortest definition of religion: interruption' (171). Ashley allows this thesis as well as Metz's 1981 text *Unterbrechungen* (Gütersloh: Gütersloher Verlaghaus, 1981) to determine the title of his own book. Although Metz frames this chapter as a homage to Bloch, it is obvious that there is also a considerable amount of Benjamin. See especially the recall of Benjamin's notion of the messianic in theses 11, 12, 15, 20. See also *PG*, 52.

[6]. Ashley underscores this point in *Interruptions*, 180. Although very good on the issue of Metz's general dependence on Bloch, Ashley does not make explicit Metz's dependence on Bloch on this point. Consistently Bloch reliefs the apocalyptic counter-history to what he takes to be an essentially non-apocalyptic tradition of Christianity that betrays its biblical roots. This is a leitmotif of his wide-ranging *The Principle of Hope*, 3 volumes, tr. Neville Plaice and Paul Knight (Cambridge, MA: MIT Press, 1995.) Joachim and his tradition function as the alternative to the mainline Christian tradition. See *PH2*, 509-14; *PH3*, 1272-73. Münzer is mentioned in *PH2*, 511-12, 518. Münzer is a major figure in Bloch's canon. In the early twenties Bloch published a monograph, *Thomas Münzer als Theologe der Revolution* (1921), on this most famous figure of the Left-Wing of the Reformation.

[7]. For Metz theology is influenced by the modern *Weltanshauung*, even if its expressions are various. Some theologies are influenced by modernity's blatant

progressivism, others by a speculative (Hegelian) or activist (Marxist) alternative, others again by a deep individualism (Rahner).

8. See *PG*, 48-50.

9. The lack of clarification probably attests to the two main sources from which Metz borrows, Bloch, on the one hand, and Benjamin, on the other. Bloch neither eschews narrative nor symbols; either carry the 'new' that is not a function of the present. In contrast, in Benjamin the emphasis falls upon 'interruption' (*Unterbrechung*), even if apocalyptic still involves something like a point of view, and cannot do without images that are in effect crystallized narratives.

10. With respect to his elaboration of narrative in chapter 12 Metz is highly eclectic. Besides the Bible, Bloch and Benjamin, Metz calls on the German dramatist Berthold Brecht and Gershom Scholem, the preeminent scholar of the Kabbalah in the first part of the twentieth century. The contrast would be the kind of disciplined philosophical justification of narrative provided by Paul Ricoeur in *Time and Narrative*, tr. Kathleen McLaughlin and David Pellauer, 3 vols. (Chicago: University of Chicago Press, 1984-1986).

11. This general definition fits with Metz's aim in this chapter to pay attention as a Christian theologian to Bloch's reflection on hope and the *novum*. One could say that Metz inflects (and corrects) Bloch with Benjamin and thereby changes the stress on non-continuity into the hyperbole of discontinuity.

12. With regard to trinitarian thought, Metz confesses in *Hope against Hope*: 'When it comes to specific content, for example, arguments over the Trinity, I always stood decisively in Rahner's camp' (20). The polemic conducted against post-Idealist thought, which supplies the context of the essay, suggests that Metz is dissociating himself not only from the history of the doctrine which presumptively too much emphasizes the immanent Trinity, but precisely those post-Hegelian revisionist forms of trinitarianism represented by Moltmann and Balthasar. Although Moltmann is the usual stand-in for this group of modern theologians, here the contrast is obviously intra-Catholic, since Metz has just praised Balthasar (20). Metz's dissociation from Balthasar follows exactly Rahner's in *Cordula und Einfeld* (1966). Indeed, it is possible that Metz even repeats the accusations. Throughout *The Passion for God* (42, 58, 69), Metz uses the word 'gnostic' to apply to post-Hegelian trinitarianism. Again, while as we have seen, this ascription is used by Balthasar to describe a number of other post-Hegelian forms of thought, given that Rahner has applied the label to Balthasar, there is no reason to suppose that Metz does not have Balthasar in mind. For a sound reflection on Metz's reservations about trinitarian theologies, see *Interruptions*, 194.

13. Metz returns to this topic in the very important seventh chapter which has 'Emancipation and Redemption' as its theme (*FHS*, 131-32). He speaks respectfully of the group of German theologians who, after Hegel, suggest a trinitarian framework for suffering in history. In addition to Moltmann, he mentions Jüngel, H. Mühlen, and Hans Küng – he is thinking of *Menschwerdung Gottes* (Freiburg, 1970). He singles out Balthasar. He writes: 'To my knowledge, however, the most impressive and forceful considerations are found in Hans Urs von Balthasar's interpretation of the paschal mystery within the framework of the Trinitarian understanding of God's history of self-emptying' (132).

[14]. This, of course, was Moltmann's recommendation in *The Crucified God*, a position which he attempts to modify in *Trinity and the Kingdom.* As indicated in parts 2 and 3 there have been widely different estimates of Moltmann's success here, with Balthasar being definitively on the side of the skeptics in this regard.

[15]. It is interesting to note that neither does Metz refuse to take on the mantle of Irenaeus when it comes to challenging such speculative positions. See *PG*, 59. Mongrain duly attends to Metz's figuration in *The Systematic Thought of Hans Urs von Balthasar* (231 n. 91)

[16]. 'Theses on History' can be found in *Illuminations*, tr. Harry Zohn (New York: Harcourt, Brace & World, 1968), 253-64

[17]. The echoing of *Theses on Feuerbach* (1844) is not purely a literary device. Marx's theses centrally involve a critique of idealism, and a demand to take account of the real and suffering subject of history, that is, the proleteriat. In 'Theses on History' Benjamin embraces Marx's materialist view of history and his view of the exploited who are not acknowledged, while not paying allegiance to Marx's view of the invariant dialectical laws of history, or thinking of the proleteriat as the only suffering subject in history.

[18]. Ashley thinks that this insight of Benjamin is constitutive for Metz's work. Thus, his choice of title, *Interruptions.* In the case of Benjamin, what in the first instance is interrupted is homogenous time or 'ever the same time' (*Immergleiche Zeit*). A good representation of this aspect of Benjamin's thought can be found in the notes for the Preface to the *Arcades Project.* See 'N [Re The Theory of Knowledge, Theory of Progress],' in *Benjamin: Philosophy, Aesthetics, History*, ed. Gary Smith (Chicago: University of Chicago Press, 1989), 43-83, especially 59. This essay – which in essence is a series of fragments – is translated by Leigh Hafrey and Richard Sieburth. The dislocation is suggested most powerfully by the term 'now-time' (*Jetztzeit*) with its insistent punctuality (80). For a confirmation of the importance of this notion, see Richard Wolin, *Walter Benjamin: An Aesthetic of Redemption* (New York: Columbia University Press, 1982), 48. In the Epistemological Preface, 'now time' is associated also with 'lightning flashes' (43, 64) which, as we have seen already, Balthasar directly recalls.

[19]. 'Corona' and 'Todesfuge' are from the 1952 collection of poems called *Mohn und Gedächtnis.* The English translation as well as the German originals can be found in *The Poems of Paul Celan*, tr. & intro. by Michael Hamburger (New York: Persea Books, 1972). For 'Corona,' see 60-1; for 'Todesfuge,' see 62-5.

[20]. This identity can only be complex, maybe even dialectical, since it can no longer can be taken as a reliable given. Community is what is called into being by communication that is purged of conventions implicated in barbarism. One could think of Blanchot as offering in *The Infinite Conversation* something of a generalization of this.

[21]. In the Pauline corpus besides First and Second Thessalonians, 1 Corinthians 15 is important. The apocalyptic dimensions of Mark and Matthew 24-25 are in general to the fore. For Balthasar, this is by no means a full list. For example, in *GL7* he gives an apocalyptic interpretation of Romans, especially Romans 8 (510-20); similarly with 2 Corinthians (520-26). And 2 Peter, which is the *locus classicus* of the descent into hell, is most obviously apocalyptic.

[22]. Thesis 24 specifically mentions Käsemann; theses 25 and 26 could be viewed as more clearly articulating his position. In *GL7* Balthasar productively engages the work of Oscar Cullman on apocalyptic in forging an argument that NT apocalyptic is other in kind to what Bloch and his ilk would make of it. For Culmann, see *GL7*, 422, 470; also 348, 376. For resistance to Bloch, see *GL7*, 510 ff.
[23]. Revelation is a text that is not much cited by Metz presumably on the grounds that it is more utopian than apocalyptic in his sense. Interestingly, in light of Blanchot and Derrida's (ab)use of Revelation 22, Metz reads 'Come, Lord Jesus' not as connected with a doxology, but as prescription of imitation (thesis 26) (*FHS*, 176).
[24]. For the functional priority of Mark over the other Gospels, see *Interruptions*, 159-60; also 193-94.
[25]. The importance of the figure of Job for Metz is confirmed by Ashley in *Interruptions*, 126. Metz is not untypical of Christian theologians who are both influenced by Bloch and exercised by the theodicy question. Here Moltmann and Metz are one. For Bloch, see *PH3*, 1126. Of course, not only Bloch, but also Moltmann and Metz have read Kant's famous 1791 essay 'On the Miscarriage of all Philosophical Trials in Theodicy.' See George di Giovanni's recent English translation of this ground-breaking text in *Immanuel Kant: Religion and Rational Theology*, ed. & tr. Allen Wood and George di Giovanni (Cambridge: Cambridge University Press, 1996), 19-37. For Job references, see 32-3.
[26]. There is plenty of textual evidence to support Ashley's view in *Interruptions* (124-26) of the importance of the theodicy issue for Metz. Christian theology in general (*PG*, 55) and Augustine (*HH*, 49) come in for censure on this point. But Marxism is also criticized for its more immanent form of explanation (*PG*, 38). The attack against Prometheanism in modernity in *A Passion for God* (52) – which closely recalls the early Balthasar – necessarily has to include Marx, who famously invokes Prometheus' cry of 'I hate all gods' as his motto. The brunt of the attack is borne, however, by Hegel and his theological epigones (*PG*, 22, 26, 40-2).
[27]. The invocation to 'non-identity' is an obvious reference to the 'negative dialectics' of Adorno, which is set against the metaphysical monisms of the philosophical tradition and particularly against Hegel's dialectical holism. Adorno is explicitly referenced a little later in the text. See *HH*, 23.
[28]. See especially Ashley, *Interruptions*, 160, 181.
[29]. See *FHS*, 129. This, indeed, is the crux of Pitstick's attack against Balthasar's view of Holy Saturday as being heterodox. She thinks that the tradition unilaterally endorses *Christus Victor.* See Alyssa Lyra Pitstick, *Light in Darkness: Hans Urs von Balthasar and the Catholic Doctrine of the Descent into Hell* (Grand Rapids, MI: Eerdmans, 2007). While 1 Peter 3:18-4:6 is the crucial text, Revelation is also important, especially Revelation 1:17-18. While it is far from clear that Pitstick sustains her case that Balthasar is heterodox, she does succeed in showing that there are highly individual elements to Balthasar's soteriology that put stress on a very important line of emphasis in the tradition, and that this emphasis on 'pathos' ramifies across an entire theology influencing Christology, the doctrine of the Trinity, the notion of eucharist, and the notion of the church.

[30]. See, for example, the reference to John 15:18 about life being at issue (*PG*, 47-8), and the not unapproving reference to 1 John 4:6 (*PG*, 70-1).

[31]. In the *Passion for God*, while Metz suggests that the statement 'God is love' of 1 John 4:6 is permitted as long as it is resolvable into the eschatological statement that God will vindicate the trust we have in him (*PG*, 70-1), he clearly objects to the ontological form of the statement. The grounds are general and specific; general in that he prefers that all descriptions of God be soteriological; and specific, in that this proposition indemnifies the speculative form of Trinitarianism, evinced in Balthasar as well as Moltmann to whom he objects. Metz's relation to the Johannine corpus is similar to that of Bloch. Bloch too has some positive things to say about John. He cites with approval John's reflection on 'life everlasting' (6, 54) (*PH3*, 1129) – a favorite passage of Schelling in his so-called 'positive philosophy' – and he is, as was Joachim and Hegel, taken with John 16:7 where Jesus says he has to go away in order to make room for the Spirit (*PH3*, 1272). But Bloch is totally against what he takes to be John's reification of the person of Christ over his function (*PH3*, 1259-62). Writing in a chastising tone, he says: 'Jesus is not the Messiah *although* he died on the cross, but *because* he died on the cross' (*PH3*, 1262).

[32]. The practical revision/correction of fundamental theology, of which Rahner represents the most influential modern instance, defines the task of part 1 of *Faith in History and Society*. Metz's clearest statement with respect to the necessity of moving beyond Rahner's methodology is to be found on 62-5. See also 13, n. 15.

[33]. *PG*, 54-71.

[34]. See especially *PG*, 56, 69-70.

[35]. See especially *FHS*, chs. 5 and 6.

[36]. Chapter 6 of *FHS* (100-18) is crucial in articulating the centrality of the *memoria passionis, mortis et resurrectionis Jesu Christi*. Metz makes his priorities clear, however, when he suggests that the *memoria passionis* is fundamental. See especially *FHS*, 113-15.

[37]. For the Frankfurt School in general, see *FHS*, 37, 48, 125, 128, 236, also notes on 81-2 *inter alia*. For Adorno, see *FHS*, 69, 81-2. For Critical Theory in general, see also *HH*, 23-5; and for Adorno, see *HH*, 23. Ashley is especially strong on the relationship between Metz and the Frankfurt School. See *Interruptions*, 108-15; also 33, 43. For Horkheimer, 33, 110; for Adorno, 28.

[38]. Metz's critique of 'middle class religion' (*FHS*, ch. 3) depends not only on Critical Theory but also Max Weber, with Heidegger playing a supporting rather than constitutive role. The bourgeois self cannot relate to the world in any other manner than that of 'exchange' (*FHS*, 35) and 'calculation' (*FHS*, 40), 'knowledge as control' (*FHS*, 43), and 'technical knowledge' (*FHS*, 44).

[39]. In echoing Augustine here, needless to say, I am being interpretive. Given his antipathy to what he takes to be the hypertrophy of hamartology in Augustine, Metz does not appeal to the Augustinian formula of *incurvatus in se*. He can plausibly be read, however, as offering a social interpretation of Augustine's formula.

[40]. While the relation between Metz and Kant is complicated, there is sufficient evidence to suggest that the relation is fundamentally positive. This is especially so when practical rather than theoretical reason is under consideration. It is, after